environment u.s.a.

u.s.a.

A GUIDE TO AGENCIES, PEOPLE, AND RESOURCES

Compiled and edited by
THE ONYX GROUP, INC.

Glenn L. Paulson, Ph.D., Advisory Editor

Janet Y. Willen
Robert S. Anderson
Kenneth R. Greenhall
Loretta Paulson
Louis Slesin

R.R. Bowker Company
New York & London, 1974
A Xerox Education Company

XEROX

Library of Congress Cataloging in Publication Data

Onyx Group, Inc.
   Environment U.S.A.; a guide to agencies,
people, and resources.

   Bibliography: p.
   1. Environmental protection—United States—Directories.
   2. Conservation of natural resources—United States—Directories.
I. Paulson, Glenn L., ed. II. Title.
TD171.E58 333.7'2'02573 73-20122
ISBN 0-8352-0671-8

Published by R. R. Bowker Co. (a Xerox Education Company)
1180 Avenue of the Americas, New York, N.Y. 10036
Copyright © 1974 by The Onyx Group, Inc.
All rights reserved.
Printed and bound in the United States of America.

Contents

Foreword		vii
Preface		xi
1	Government Environmental Agencies	
	Federal Government	2
	State Government	43
2	Private Environmental Organizations	
	Citizens' Organizations	75
	Trade and Professional Organizations	129
	Disbanded and Inactive Organizations	136
3	Environmental Consultants (classified by state)	137
4	Environmental Officers of U.S. Corporations, by JANET Y. WILLEN (classified by industry)	185
5	Labor Unions and the Environment, by GLENN PAULSON, Ph.D.	218
6	Environmental Employment, by ODOM FANNING	222
7	Environmental Education Programs (classified by state)	228
8	Environmental Libraries (classified by state)	245
9	Environmental Fund-Raising, by JOSEPH WILLEN	253
10	The Environment and the Law, by ANGUS MACBETH	258
11	Environmental Conferences and Meetings (classified by topic)	275
12	Films (classified by subject)	282
13	Newspapers, Radio, and Television (classified by region)	326
14	Bibliography, by WENDY and MYRON E. MENEWITCH (classified by subject)	340
	Glossary	406
	Classified Index to Federal Agencies	429
	Alphabetical Index	433

Foreword

American society can justifiably boast of the fact that, on several occasions in the past, it has been able to convert with great speed its political decisions or its recognition of a social problem into effective action programs. The evolution of the campaign for environmental improvement during the past few years is the most striking recent example of this rapid change from ignorance or indifference to social concern and then to large-scale practical action.

A decade ago the word environment, if it was used at all by the general public, evoked only a vague awareness that the pollution of air and water was reaching objectionable levels. This awareness culminated in the manifestations of Earth Day in April 1970—manifestations that were highly emotional and visible, but amateurish and rather ineffective. Today in contrast, discussions about the environment immediately bring to mind a multiplicity of institutions and of action programs such as those which are listed in *Environment U.S.A.* To measure the extent of the change which has taken place during the past few years one needs only recall that, not so long ago, it was difficult to prevent tanneries from dumping their wastes into the Croton Aqueduct serving New York City, and that as sophisticated a man as Mayor La Guardia could hardly believe that there was anything wrong in smoke.

It is often stated that the present enthusiasm about environmental improvement is just a fad and will vanish as soon as people begin to experience the cost and the inconveniences that effective control measures will inevitably entail. But I believe that the response of the public to the situation will be far more complex and far more interesting than this fad theory suggests. The new element in the situation is that the public has come to regard the right to a healthy and pleasant environment as one of its natural rights, to be satisfied by society. There will be much political agitation of course about financing and trade-offs of environmental improvement. There will certainly be protests against the measures taken to improve the environment if these measures appear elitist and unfair. The formulation of sound environmental policies will require a kind of social accounting for which our society is not prepared. But while all these difficulties will generate resentment and confusion, they will not make people forget that they are entitled to environmental quality.

History shows in fact that social controversies have been part of the environment movement from its very beginnings. Almost a century ago, John Muir pleaded for the protection of trees and the wilderness purely for the sake of the trees and the wilderness. But Gifford Pinchot, who had been his disciple, broke away from his teachings because he was primarily interested in good management of forests for man's use. Aldo Leopold gained many followers by preaching a land ethic focused on the quality of nature. But George Marsh, who had created the ecological movement, was primarily concerned with the quality of man-made agricultural lands for the sake of man. In our times, the Department of Agriculture and the Department of the Interior each has its own set of different policies for the utilization of the environment. But these policies are often in conflict with the social philosophies of the Sierra Club and the Audubon Society, which themselves do not agree on all issues. Profound differences of attitudes with regard to the environment occur even in educational programs. Some of these programs are entirely focused on theoretical ecology—where man has no place or is at best considered an intruder—whereas others emphasize the purely human aspects of environmental problems.

The very diversity of the points of view from which environmental problems are being considered in our society reflects the fact that environmental considerations now constitute integral components of virtually all major issues in public and private life. Only a few general items can be mentioned here to illustrate how extensive and profound is the penetration of environmental concern into modern American society:

—the increase in number and size of the citizens' organizations dedicated to the preservation of natural and man-made environments;

—the greater scientific and social sophistication with which environmental problems are approached by professional and trade associations;

—the establishment of large units devoted to environmental research and control in practically all large corporations;

—the growth and reorganization of governmental structures at the federal, state and local levels to deal more effectively with environmental problems;

—the development of a new environmental specialty in the legal profession;

—the acceptance, at all levels of the educational system, of environmental studies as a legitimate part of the curriculum, and the creation of new schools entirely focused on these studies.

The institutionalization of environmental concern is thus now widespread in American society. It is creating new demands not only with regard to specialized scientific information, but also to knowledge of the persons and institutions engaged in research and action programs. It is this latter need, especially, that *Environment U.S.A.* has been designed to fill.

As already mentioned, environmental problems impinge on every aspect of social life and must therefore be considered from a multiplicity of different points of view. For this reason, *Environment U.S.A.* includes a much larger variety of topics than is the usual practice in volumes of this sort. In addition to traditional items such as lists of governmental and citizens' organizations, *Environment U.S.A.* deals with many other topics which have acquired practical importance only during very recent years. These include environmental law, how to raise funds for environmental projects, names of officers concerned with the environment in major corporations and unions, a schedule of conferences on environmental matters, and opportunities for education and employment in the environmental fields.

Through its very comprehensiveness, this volume reflects the complexity of environmental problems, and the extent and depth to which they affect the life of all people, irrespective of professional occupation and economic status. It constitutes in my opinion a uniquely useful practical guide for all workers in the environmental field, but it is also much more than a guide.

Our period might come to be known as the Age of Introspection, during which we spent more time examining our navels than trying to change the world. Yet experience shows that environmental improvement has come from pressure groups rather than from the proceedings of academic discussions groups. *Environment U.S.A.* is an essential instrument for those in the environmental field who are more concerned with action than with the history of navel examining. It documents America's prodigious ability to identify, mobilize, and organize an immense variety of skills and talents for studying and attacking the problems of modern societies.

RENÉ DUBOS
The Rockefeller University
New York, New York

Preface

In the late 1960s, as concern for environmental problems spread from a small group of scientists and committed citizens to become a broadly based movement affecting all phases of American life, a need arose for a new type of reference source. Because virtually all fields of science, technology, industry, and government bear in some way on environmental problems, persons seeking information about environmental matters or assistance in dealing with environmental problems had great difficulty in locating even the major sources of information and assistance. For example, a person concerned with a particular environmental issue such as urban air pollution might require access not only to information about a host of scientific and technical aspects of such pollution, but also might need to familiarize himself with the issue's political, economic, and social ramifications. He might need to consult numerous sources and agencies in widely diverse fields, and it was seldom clear where to turn for the necessary facts or assistance.

As in any expanding movement, a more efficient communication network evolved to replace the primarily personal information exchange systems. Many new journals, newsletters, dictionaries, and teach-yourself books appeared to aid the uninitiated. Environmental organizations sprang up and existing organizations created new environmental arms. More information and assistance thus became available to meet the demands posed by the increasingly complicated issues, but the information and assistance remained difficult to find. Too often the maze of available data was so complex and unstructured that only researchers with time for lengthy investigations could be effective. Even then, the final product left many sources of information untapped.

This book was conceived in 1971, when a group of people with varied backgrounds in the environmental and publishing fields joined together to prepare a reference work that would make it easy for professionals and laymen alike to locate the most important sources of environmental information and the most important sources of assistance to people attempting to cope with environmental problems. Among the sources covered in this first edition are federal and state government agencies, private environmental and conservation organizations, professional societies and trade associations, corporations and unions closely involved with environmental problems, as well as annotated listings of books and films. Short but comprehensive chapters on fund raising and environmental law are included to serve as introductions to or reviews of these fields, depending upon the background of the reader. The listings in each subject area are comprehensive and will suit the needs of all but the most detailed investigations. Even then, the references provided will often lead to a large number of useful sources.

By scanning the table of contents the reader can quickly locate the chapter dealing with the type of information in which he is interested. In general, the subject matter of each chapter is self-explanatory, and many of the chapters are preceded by introductions indicating their scope and organization.

A further guide to the numerous entries on federal and state agencies, private orga-

xii Preface

nizations, and consultants is provided by the Alphabetical Index beginning on page 433. The user should consult this index for information on a particular government agency, private organization, or consultant whose name he knows. Because of the complexity of the federal government's bureaucratic structure, a separate Classified Index to Federal Agencies is also provided. The user should consult this index to determine which federal agencies deal with a particular area of environmental quality or conservation, such as fish and wildlife, radiation, or solid waste.

The directory will be updated periodically to keep abreast of new developments in the environmental field. The editors will be grateful for all corrections and suggestions for improvement to be incorporated in the next edition.

Many people contributed to the planning and preparation of this book. The editors wish particularly to thank William B. Barker, Carolyn Wronker, Steven Moll, Joseph H. Sullivan, Valerie J. R. Sonnenthal, and Peter Y. Sonnenthal for their invaluable help in coping with the laborious details of compiling, copy editing, and typing the directory listings. Our thanks are due also to Joseph Willen for his patient counsel during the planning of the directory.

1 Government Environmental Agencies

This chapter, which includes government organizations with important environmental or conservation functions, is divided into federal and state sections. The federal organizations, which are treated first, include both agencies of the executive branch and legislative committees.

Executive agencies are treated in five groups. In the first group, here called "The Environmental Core," are placed four agencies that occupy a central position in the federal government's attack on environmental problems. These are the Citizens Advisory Committee on Environmental Quality, the Council on Environmental Quality, the Federal Energy Office, and the Environmental Protection Agency. The second group includes all federal departments that have important environmental and conservation functions. The third group includes independent agencies other than the Environmental Protection Agency. The fourth group includes various executive committees and councils other than those included in "The Environmental Core," and the fifth group is made up of three quasi-official agencies: the National Academy of Sciences, the National Academy of Engineering, and the National Research Council. Entries in each of these five groups are listed in alphabetical order.

The section on the legislative branch of the federal government includes Senate and House committees and subcommittees whose functions bear importantly on conservation and the environment. The address, phone number, and meeting days of each committee are provided, together with the names of the committee chairman and director (or equivalent). For the subcommittees, which have the same address and phone number as their corresponding committees, the names of the chairman and of the ranking minority member are provided.

To help the reader find his way through the maze of federal agencies with environmental and conservation functions, a classified index to key agencies and officials is provided on page 429.

The state government section of the chapter, like the federal section, includes governmental agencies that have important environmental or conservation functions. The state sections appear in alphabetical order, and governmental agencies are listed alphabetically under each state. Since the entries for any one state take up only a page or two of the directory, it is easy to find the agency responsible for a particular aspect of environmental quality, such as air pollution, by scanning the entries for the state in question.

For each federal and state agency the editors have attempted to provide an address and phone number, together with the names, addresses, and phone numbers of all divisions and officials with important environmental or conservation responsibilities.

FEDERAL GOVERNMENT

EXECUTIVE BRANCH

THE ENVIRONMENTAL CORE

CITIZENS' ADVISORY COMMITTEE ON ENVIRONMENTAL QUALITY
1700 Pennsylvania Ave. N.W., Washington, D.C. 20006
202-223-3040

The fifteen-member committee was established to advise the President and the Council on Environmental Quality on matters affecting environmental quality.
Chairman: Laurance S. Rockefeller

COUNCIL ON ENVIRONMENTAL QUALITY
722 Jackson Pl. N.W., Washington, D.C. 20006
202-382-1415

The Council on Environmental Quality was established in the Executive Office of the President to formulate and recommend national policies to promote the improvement of the quality of the environment. The Office of Environmental Quality, which provides staff for the council, was subsequently established.

The council develops and recommends to the president national policies that promote environmental quality, performs a continuing analysis of changes or trends in the national environment, and assists the President in the preparation of the annual environmental quality report to the Congress.
Chairman: Dr. Russell W. Peterson

FEDERAL ENERGY OFFICE
4001 New Executive Office Building, Washington, D.C. 20461

The Federal Energy Office (FEO) performs all major energy resource management functions of the federal government. FEO (being organized at the time of printing) is composed of divisions transferred from other governmental departments and of newly created divisions.
Administrator: William E. Simon
Deputy Administrator: John C. Sawhill
Executive Officer: Nicholas M. Golubin
Policy Analysis: William A. Johnson
Public Affairs: Robert E. Nipp
General Counsel: James Haynes; Thomas Nelson
Assistant Administrator for Management: Bruce A. Wilburn
Assistant Administrator for Economic and Data Analysis and Strategic Planning: Eric R. Zausner
Assistant Administrator for Policy, Planning and Regulation: John A. Hill
Assistant Administrator for Operations and Compliance: Frank G. Zarb
Assistant Administrator for International Policy and Programs: Steve Wakefield
Assistant Administrator for Energy Conservation and Environment: John H. Gibbons
Assistant Administrator for Energy Resource Development: Robert Shatz

ENVIRONMENTAL PROTECTION AGENCY
401 M St. S.W., Washington, D.C. 20460
202-755-2673

The Environmental Protection Agency (EPA) was established as an independent agency of the executive branch of the federal government effective December 2, 1970.

EPA brings under one organizational roof federal activities in controlling air and water pollution, drinking water quality, solid wastes, pesticides, environmental radiation, and noise. It is an independent regulatory agency that has only one mission: to protect and enhance the environment. In general, the agency is responsible for conducting research and demonstrations, for establishing and enforcing standards, for monitoring pollution in the environment, and, perhaps most importantly, for assisting state and local governments in their own efforts to protect the environment. The purpose is to mount an integrated attack on pollution and, at the same time, to make orderly progress toward understanding the environment as a single system of independent, but interrelated parts. The EPA encourages the fullest possible public disclosure of information to any person or group requesting it. It also encourages public participation in EPA hearings.

The administrator of the EPA is responsible to the President for providing overall supervision to the agency. There are five assistant administrators in program and functional areas, all operating from the Washington headquarters. In addition, there are ten regional administrators, who report directly to the administrator and exercise broad operational responsibility in the field.

EPA, in fulfilling its assigned functions, cooperates closely with the Council on Environmental Quality. The council, created by the National Environmental Policy Act of 1969, operates in the executive office of the President to coordinate and assess federal environmental programs.

Administrator: Russell E. Train   202-755-2700
Deputy Administrator: John R. Quarles, Jr.   755-2711

Office of Federal Activities

This office coordinates and develops policies and procedures related to EPA's review of federal environmental impact statements and preparation of its own impact statements. It coordinates EPA policies and programs to deal with environmental problems arising at federal facilities and federally supported or authorized activities.

Director: Sheldon Meyers   755-0777

Legislation

The Office of Legislation reviews and advises the administrator on all legislation orginating within or affecting EPA. It also performs legislative drafting services, coordinates the preparation of testimony, and reviews transcripts of congressional hearings.

Acting Director: Robert G. Ryan   755-2930

Public Affairs

The Office of Public Affairs represents the administrator in relations with the press, television, radio, and other information media. It also acts as liaison for concerned citizens groups and EPA.

Director: Ann Dore   755-0700
Chief, EPA Information Center: Hilda Borrks   755-0707

Planning and Management

The Office for Planning and Management is responsible for the overall planning activities of the agency. It develops, initiates, and monitors new and redirected agency programs and goals and administers a program-planning-budget system for the agency.

Assistant Administrator for Planning and Management: Alvin L. Alm   755-2900
  Standards and Regulations Evaluation Division: Ellison S. Burton   755-2811
  Policy Planning Division: Glen Kendall   755-0340
  Program Evaluation Division: Victor Kimm   755-2265
  Economic Analysis Division: Roy Gamse   755-0734
Deputy Assistant Administrator for Resources Management: Richard D. Redenius   755-2741
  Program Reporting Division: Dario Monti   755-0550
  Program Analysis Division: Gary Dietrich   755-0688
Deputy Assistant Administrator for Administration: Howard M. Messner   755-2911
  Grants Administration Division: Alexander J. Greene   755-0850
  Management Information and Data Systems Division: Michael L. Springer   755-0984

Enforcement and General Counsel

The Office for Enforcement and General Counsel serves as the principal advisor to the administrator in matters pertaining to the enforcement of standards for environmental quality and is responsible for the conduct of enforcement activities on an agency-wide basis. This office also serves as the principal legal advisor to the administrator.

Assistant Administrator for Enforcement and General Counsel: Alan G. Kirk II   755-2500
Acting Deputy General Counsel: Robert V. Zener   755-2511
  Water Quality Division: G. William Frick (Acting)   755-0753
  Air Quality and Radiation Division: Robert L. Baum   755-0744
  Pesticides and Solid Waste Management Division: Anson M. Keller   755-0763

Acting Deputy Assistant Administrator for Water Enforcement (provides program policy direction to the water enforcement activities of EPA): Richard Johnson 755-0440
Office of Permit Programs: Albert C. Printz, Jr. 755-7470
  Review and Coordination Division: Thaddeus Rajda 755-2783
  Enforcement Proceedings Division: Murray Stein 755-2783
Deputy Assistant Administrator for General Enforcement (provides program policy direction to agency enforcement activities in the air, noise, pesticides, radiation, and solid waste program areas): George V. Allen 755-2530
  Mobile Source Enforcement Division: Norman D. Shutler 755-2870
  Stationary Source Enforcement Division: Richard D. Wilson 755-2877
  Pesticides Enforcement Division: Gus E. Conroy, II 755-0297

Hazardous Materials Control

The Office for Hazardous Materials Control is responsible for the agency's pesticides, radiation, noise, toxic substances, and solid waste management programs. It additionally develops and evaluates policies for pollution source standards and criteria.

Assistant Administrator For Hazardous Materials Control: Vacant 755-2800
Deputy Assistant Administrator for Pesticides Programs: Henry J. Korp 755-8033
  Operations Division: Dr. John V. Osmun 755-5687
  Registration Division: John R. Ritch (Acting) 755-2451
  Criteria and Evaluation Division: Dr. Leonard R. Axelrod 755-2516
Deputy Assistant Administrator for Radiation Programs: Dr. William D. Rowe 755-4894
  Technology Assessment Division: E. David Harward 755-4362
  Criteria and Standards Division: Dr. William A. Mills 755-4871
  Field Operations Division: Charles L. Weaver 755-5482
Deputy Assistant Administrator for Noise Programs: Dr. Alvin F. Meyers 557-7777
  Program Planning and Management Staff: K. Kirke Harper 557-7305
  Standards and Regulatory Development Staff: John Schettino (Acting) 557-7743
  Coordination and Technical Assistance Staff: Rudolph Marrazzo (Acting) 557-7750
Deputy Assistant Administrator for Solid Waste Management Programs: Samuel Hale, Jr. 254-7820
  Technical Information Staff: Thomas F. Williams 254-7496
  Solid Waste Information Retrieval System (SWIBS): John A. Connolly 254-7438
  State and Local Affairs Office: Ralph J. Black 254-6786
  Resource Recovery Division: Arsen J. Darnay 254-7406
  Hazardous Waste Management Division: John T. Talty 254-6837
  Systems Management Division: Robert Colonna (Acting) 254-6833

Air and Water Programs

The Office for Air and Water Programs is responsible for the administration and operation of the agency's air and water programs. This includes program policy evaluation assistance and technology transfer, and selected demonstration projects.

Assistant Administrator for Air and Water Programs: Robert L. Sansom 755-2640
Deputy Assistant Administrator for Air Quality Planning and Standards (Durham, N.C. 27711): Bernard J. Steigerwald 919-688-8146
  Control Programs Development Div.: Jean J. Schueneman 688-8146
  Emission Standards and Engineering Div.: Donald Goodwin 688-8146
  Monitoring and Data Analysis Div.: Robert Neligan 688-8146
  Strategies and Air Standards Div.: Joseph Padgett 688-8146
  Air Pollution Technical Information Center (Research Triangle Park, N.C. 27711): Peter Halpin 919-549-8411
Deputy Assistant Administrator for Mobile Source Air Pollution Control: Eric O. Stork 202-426-2464
  Emission Control Technology Div. (2565 Plymouth Rd., Ann Arbor, Mich.): John DeKany 313-761-5230
  Advanced Automotive Power Systems Development Div. (2565 Plymouth Rd., Ann Arbor, Mich.): John J. Brogan 313-761-5230
Deputy Assistant Administrator for Water Program Operations (Crystal Mall, Bldg. 2, 1921 Jefferson Davis Hwy., Arlington, Va. 20460): John Rhett 703-426-8856

Municipal Waste Water Systems Div.: Harold Cahill 426-8986
Oil and Hazardous Materials Div.: Kenneth E. Biglane 426-3971
Water Quality and Non-Point Source Control Div.: Albert J. Erickson 426-2707
Water Supply Div.: James H. McDermott 426-2467
Deputy Assistant Administrator for Water Planning and Standards: Mrs. Lillian D. Regelson 202-755-0402
Effluent Guidelines Div. (Crystal Mall, Bldg. 2, 1921 Jefferson Davis Hwy., Arlington, Va. 20460): Allen Cywin 703-426-2571
Monitors and Data Support Division: Edmond Notizen 426-7764
Water Planning Division: Mark A. Pisano 202-755-6928

Health Effects Division: Dr. Wesley J. Clayton (Acting) 755-0626
Ecological Processes and Effects Division: Dr. Frank Wilkes (Acting) 522-1826
Deputy Assistant Administrator for Monitoring Systems (responsible for agency research, development, and demonstration activities in the area of measuring and monitoring equipment, techniques, and systems): Willis B. Foster 744-2606
Office of Monitoring Systems: Donald C. Holmes 755-0635
Quality Assurance Division: Guntis Ozolins 755-0646
Equipment and Techniques Division: Dr. Henry F. Enos 755-0646
Data and Information Research Division: H. Matthew Bills 755-0636

Research and Development

The Office for Research and Development is responsible for the development, direction, and conduct of a national research program in pollution sources and effects, the environmental sciences, and pollution control technology.
Assistant Administrator for Research and Development: Dr. Stanley M. Greenfield 755-2600
Deputy Assistant Administrator for Program Integration: Dr. Leland D. Attaway 755-2611
Deputy Assistant Administrator for Environmental Engineering (responsible for agency research, development, and demonstration activities in the area of pollution prevention, control and abatement): Albert C. Trakowski, Jr. 755-2532
Office of Environmental Engineering: Dale E. Oyster 755-0633
Technology Transfer Staff: Robert Crowe 557-7700
Municipal Pollution Control Division: William A. Rosenkranz 522-0773
Industrial Pollution Control Division: William J. Lacy 522-0103
Non-Point Pollution Control Division: Dr. Thomas A. Murphy 522-0440
Air Pollution Control Division: Richard E. Harrington 755-0658
Deputy Assistant Administrator for Environmental Sciences (responsible for agency research, development, and demonstration activities in the areas of criteria development, establishment of environmental quality standards, and location of control activities): Dr. Herbert L. Wiser 755-0655

National Environmental Research Centers and Associated Laboratories

Under the direction of the assistant administrator for research and development, the four NERC's are responsible for the management of the agency's programs in research, development, and monitoring at their respective centers. They supervise and coordinate a number of satellite laboratories, pilot plants, and field stations that conduct more limited and specific research programs. Although each center performs varied research programs, the Cincinnati center gives a particular emphasis to pollution control methods; the North Carolina center to health effects of environmental stresses; the Corvallis center to the ecological effects of environmental pollution and control; and the Las Vegas center to environmental monitoring.

National Environmental Research Center
Research Triangle Park, N.C. 27711
Director: Dr. John F. Finklea 919-549-8411

Chemistry and Physics Laboratory
Director: Dr. Aubrey P. Altshuller 549-8411

Human Studies Laboratory
Director: Dr. John H. Knelson 549-8411

Quality Assurance and Environmental Monitoring Laboratory
Director: Dr. S. David Shearer 549-8411

Meteorology Laboratory
Director: Dr. Robert A. McCormick 549-8411

6 Government Environmental Agencies

Control Systems Laboratory
Director: Dr. John K. Burchard   688-8146

Experimental Biology Laboratory
Director: Dr. R. John Garner   549-8411

Primate and Pesticides Effects Laboratory
Box 490, Perrine, Fla. 33157
Director: Dr. William F. Durham   305-238-6110

Chamblee Toxicology Laboratory
4770 Buford Highway, Chamblee, Ga. 30341
Chief: August Curley   404-633-3311

Wenatchee Research Station
Box 73, Wenatchee, Wash. 98801
Chief: Homer R. Wolfe   509-663-8331

National Environmental Research Center
200 S.W. 35 St., Corvallis, Oreg. 97330
Director: Dr. A. Fritz Bartsch   503-752-4310

  National Marine Water Quality Laboratory
  Box 277, West Kingston, R.I. 02892
  Acting Director: Dr. Eric Schneider   401-789-9751

  Bears Bluff Field Station, National Marine Water Quality Laboratory
  Box 368, Johns Island, S.C. 29455
  Chief: Richard J. Berry   803-559-0371

  National Water Quality Laboratory
  6201 Congdon Blvd., Duluth, Minn. 55804
  Director: Dr. Donald I. Mount   218-727-6692

  Western Fish Toxicology Laboratory
  3080 S.E. Clearwater, Corvallis, Oreg. 97330
  Chief: Gerald R. Bouck   503-752-4211

  Newtown Field Site
  3411 Church St., Cincinnati, Ohio 45244
  Chief: William B. Horning   513-871-1820

  National Ecological Research Laboratory
  200 S.W. 35 St., Corvallis, Oreg. 97330
  Director: Dr. Norman Glass   503-752-4211

  Arctic Environmental Research Laboratory
  College, Alaska 99701
  Director: Richard W. Latimer   907-479-2251

  Pacific Northwest Environmental Research Laboratory
  200 S.W. 35 St., Corvallis, Oreg. 97330
  Director: Dr. Norbert A. Jaworski   503-752-4211

  Ely Field Station, Shagawa Lake Project
  222 W. Conan St., Ely, Minn. 55731
  Chief: Robert M. Brice   218-365-3208

  Grosse Isle Laboratory
  9311 Gron Rd., Grosse Isle, Mich. 48138
  Director: Dr. Tudor T. Davies   313-675-5000

  Robert S. Kerr Environmental Research Laboratory
  Box 1198, Ada, Okla. 74820
  Director: William C. Galegar   405-332-8800

  Gulf Breeze Environmental Research Laboratory
  Sabine Island, Gulf Breeze, Fla. 32561
  Director: Dr. Thomas W. Duke   904-932-5326

  Southeast Environmental Research Laboratory
  College Station Rd., Athens, Ga. 30601
  Director: Dr. David W. Duttweiler   404-546-3134

National Environmental Research Center
Cincinnati, Ohio 45268
Director: Dr. Andrew W. Breidenbach   513-684-8348

  Radio Chemistry and Nuclear Engineering Research Laboratory
  Director: Dr. Berno Kahn   684-3237

  Solid Waste Research Laboratory
  Director: Robert L. Stenburg   684-4320

  Analytical Quality Control Laboratory
  Director: Dwight G. Ballinger   684-2925

  Environmental Toxicology Research Laboratory
  Director: Dr. Jerry Stara   684-7411

  Advanced Waste Treatment Research Laboratory
  Director: John J. Convery   684-8232

  Water Supply Research Laboratory
  Director: Gordon G. Robeck   684-8311

Edison Water Quality Research Laboratory
Edison, N.J. 08817
Director: Dr. Peter Lederman   201-548-3402

Crown Pilot Plant
Box 555, Rivesville, W. Va. 26588
Chief: Robert B. Scott   304-343-6181 (ask for 278-5376)

Lebanon Pilot Plant (Field Site)
Rte. 2, Box 7A, Lebanon, Ohio 45036
Chief: E. Timothy Oppelt   513-932-0931

Pomona Pilot Plant (Field Site)
295 S. Roselawn Ave., Pomona, Calif. 91766
Chief: James E. Haskins   714-623-6721

Blue Plains Pilot Plant
5000 Overlook Ave. S.W., Washington, D.C. 20032
Chief: Dolloff Bishop   202-962-0592

National Environmental Research Center
Box 15027, Las Vegas, Nev. 89114
Director: Dr. Delbert Barth   702-736-2969

Washington Environmental Research Center
401 M St. S.W., Washington, D.C. 20460
Director: Dr. Larry E. Ruff   202-755-0650

REGIONAL OFFICES

The regional offices serve as the agency's principal representative in each region in contacts and relationships with federal, state and local agencies, industry, academic institutions, and other public and private groups. The country is divided into ten regions in which each regional office is responsible for accomplishing national program objectives.

Region I
(Connecticut, Maine, Massachusetts, New Hampshire, Rhode Island, Vermont)
Rm. 2203, John F Kennedy Federal Bldg., Boston, Mass. 02203
Administrator: John A.S. McGlennon   617-223-7210

Region II
(New Jersey, New York, Puerto Rico, Virgin Islands)
Rm. 908, 26 Federal Plaza, New York, N.Y. 10007
Administrator: Gerald M. Hansler   212-264-2525

Region III
(Maryland, Pennsylvania, Virginia, West Virginia)
Curtis Bldg., 6 and Walnut St., Philadelphia, Pa. 19106
Administrator: Daniel J. Snyder, III   215-597-9801

Region IV
(Alabama, Florida, Georgia, Kentucky, Mississippi, North Carolina, South Carolina, Tennessee)
1421 Peachtree St. N.E., Atlanta, Ga. 30309
Administrator: Jack E. Ravan   404-526-5727

Region V
(Illinois, Indiana, Michigan, Minnesota, Ohio, Wisconsin)
1 N. Wacker Dr., Chicago, Ill. 60606
Administrator: Francis T. Mayo   312-353-5250

Region VI
(Arkansas, Louisiana, New Mexico, Oklahoma, Texas)
1600 Patterson St., Suite 1100, Dallas, Tex. 75201
Administrator: Arthur W. Busch   214-749-1962

Region VII
(Iowa, Kansas, Missouri, Nebraska)
1753 Baltimore Ave., Kansas City, Mo. 64108
Administrator: Jerome H. Svore   806-375-5493

Region VIII
(Colorado, Montana, North Dakota, South Dakota, Utah, Wyoming)
1860 Lincoln St., Suite 900, Denver, Colo. 80203
Administrator: John A. Green   303-837-3895

Region IX
(Arizona, California, Guam, Hawaii, Nevada)
100 California St., San Francisco, Calif. 94111
Administrator: Paul Defalco   415-556-6695

Region X
(Alaska, Idaho, Oregon, Washington)
1200 6 Ave., Seattle, Wash. 98101
Administrator: James L. Agee   206-442-1220

FEDERAL EXECUTIVE DEPARTMENTS

DEPARTMENT OF AGRICULTURE
14 St. and Independence Ave. S.W.,
  Washington, D.C. 20250
202-655-4000

OFFICE OF THE SECRETARY

Secretary: Earl L. Butz   202-447-3631
Assistant Secretary for Conservation, Research, and Education: Robert W. Long   447-2796
Assistant Secretary for Marketing and Consumer Services: Richard E. Lyng   447-4623
Director, Science and Education: Ned D. Bayley   447-4581
Director, Agricultural Economics: Don A. Paarlberg   447-5681
Director of Information: Claude W. Gifford   447-5247
Coordinator of Environmental Quality Activities: Dr. Fred Tschirley   447-7803

Agricultural Research Service

The Agricultural Research Service (ARS), which operates under the Office of Science and Education, provides knowledge and technology to help farmers produce efficiently, conserve the environment, and meet food and fiber needs. Research is conducted in cooperation with the states, as well as with other research agencies in the U.S. Department of Agriculture, other federal agencies, industry and private groups, and foundations.

Ecological and pollution concerns of the ARS include protecting crops against diseases, pests, and pollutants; control of destructive insects; promoting the use of beneficial insects in producing crops and animals, and evaluating the use of nonpesticidal methods to prevent residues and to avoid contaminating the environment; developing new, safe, and effective farm uses for electrical energy; effectively utilizing the productive capacity of soil and water resources, with concern for problems of pollution and preservation of these resources; improved livestock feeding and management practices that minimize pollution due to animal wastes; eliminating health-related problems for consumers of farm products; protecting quality of agricultural products in marketing channels and developing objective measurements of quality to aid inspection and grading programs; and determining human needs for foods, nutrients, and diet patterns. Many ARS offices are located at the Agricultural Research Center, West, Beltsville, Maryland 20705.

Administrator: Talcott W. Edminster   202-447-3656
Assistant Administrator for Livestock and Veterinary Sciences: P.D. DeLay   447-5121
Assistant Administrator for Marketing Nutrition and Engineering Sciences: F.R. Senti   447-5134
Staff Scientist, Agricultural Structures and Electrification (Beltsville): L.B. Altman   301-344-2740
Staff Scientist, Food Safety and Health (Beltsville): H.W. Hays   344-3648
Staff Scientist, Human Nutrition and Family Living (Beltsville): W.A. Gortner   344-2743
Assistant Administrator for Plant and Entomological Sciences: H.O. Graumann   202-447-3961
Assistant Administrator for Soil, Water, and Air Sciences: C.W. Carlson   447-7157
Staff Scientist, Environmental Quality (Beltsville): J. Lunin   301-344-3278
Staff Scientist, Soil Fertility and Plant Nutrition (Beltsville): H.L. Barrows   344-3217
Staff Scientist, Soil-Plant-Atmosphere (Beltsville): W.A. Raney   344-3109
Staff Scientist, Waste Management and Microbiology (Beltsville): R.G. Yeck   344-3106
Staff Scientist, Watershed Hydrology (Beltsville): D.I. Brakensiek   344-3107
Staff Scientist, Erosion and Sedimentation: L.M. Glymph   202-447-5211
Staff Scientist, Remote Sensing: R.H. Miller   447-6548
Acting Chairman, Agricultural Environmental Quality Institute (Beltsville): L.L. Danielson   301-344-3030
Acting Chairman, Animal Parasitology Institute (Beltsville): F.D. Enzie   344-3338
Acting Chairman, Animal Physiology and Genetics Institute (Beltsville): J.W. Smith   344-2056
Acting Chairman, Insect Identification and Beneficial Insect Introduction Institute (Beltsville): R.I. Sailer   344-3182
Acting Chairman, Nutrition Institute (Beltsville): W. Mertz   344-2160
Acting Chairman, Plant Genetics and Germ Plasm Institute (Beltsville): J.G. Moseman   344-3235
Acting Chairman, Plant Physiology Institute (Beltsville): H.R. Carns   344-3036

Acting Chairman, Plant Protection Institute (Beltsville): J.P. Meiners 344-3600

Animal and Plant Health Inspection Service

The Animal and Plant Health Inspection Service (APHIS), which operates under the Office of Marketing and Consumer Services, was created to conduct regulatory and control programs to protect the wholesomeness of meat and poultry products for human consumption and to protect and improve animal and plant health. In cooperation with states, the service administers federal laws and regulations pertaining to animal and plant health and quarantine, meat and poultry inspection, and humane treatment of animals, as well as to the control and eradication of pests and diseases.

Administrator: F.J. Mulhern 202-447-3668
Director, Information Division: R. Norton 447-3977
Associate Administrator, Meat and Poultry Inspection: K.M. McEnroe 447-7663
Associate Administrator, Animal and Plant Health: G.H. Wise 447-3861
Deputy Administrator, Scientific and Technical Services: H.C. Mussman 447-3473
Deputy Administrator, Plant Protection and Quarantine: L.G.K. Iverson 447-5601
  Ecological Evaluation: J.O. Lee, Jr. 301-436-8529
  Pest Survey and Technical Support Staff 436-8425

Economic Research Service

GHI Bldg., 500 12 St. N.W. Washington, D.C., 33024

The Economic Research Service (ERS), which operates under the Office of Agricultural Economics, conducts programs of research in agricultural economics and marketing, in both domestic and foreign commerce, and coordinates the department's programs of foreign assistance and training.

Among the various types of research conducted by ERS is land and water research involving studies of economic utilization of land and water resources, the impact of urban and industrial expansion, land-tenure problems, legal-economic aspects of land and water use, and the relationship of resource use and tenure to income and values. River basin and watershed investigations are conducted.

Administrator: Quentin M. West 202-447-8104
Assistant Deputy Administrator, Environmental Quality: Velmar Davis 447-8679
Director, Natural Resources Economics: Melvin Cotner 447-8239
  Environmental Economics: Dr. Velmar Davis 447-8151
  Resource Economics: Orville Krause 447-8081
  Assistant Director, Water Planning Activities: William Green 447-8748
  Assistant Director, Policy and Legislation: vacant 447-8748

Forest Service

The Forest Service operates under the Office of Rural Development and Conservation. It supervises the National Forest System, which includes 155 national forests and 19 national grasslands, comprising 187 million acres in 41 states and Puerto Rico. About 14.5 million acres of forest are set aside as wilderness and primitive areas; the remainder is harvested on a multiple-use, sustained yield basis. The environmental objectives of the Forest Service include the following: promoting a pattern of natural resource use that will best meet the needs of people now and in the future; protecting and improving the quality of air, water, soil, and natural beauty; helping to protect and improve the quality of the open space environment in urban and community areas; generating forestry opportunities to accelerate rural community growth; encouraging the growth and development of forestry-based enterprises that readily respond to consumers' changing needs; seeking optimum forest land-ownership patterns; expanding public understanding of environmental conservation; and developing a scientific base for the advancement of forestry.

The programs and activities of the service include emergency seeding treatment to prevent massive erosion and stream siltation; protecting the land, as much as possible, from wildfire, epidemics of disease and insect pests, erosion, floods, and water and air pollution; building roads and trails where needed for timber harvesting; and timber harvesting methods that protect the land and streams, assure rapid renewal of the forest, provide food and cover for wildlife and fish, and have minimum impact on scenic and recreation values. The Forest Service cooperates with state and local governments, agencies and organizations, forest industries, and private landowners in the protection, reforestation, management, and utilization of forests and associated lands vital for watershed protection.

Forest insect and disease damage is assessed annually in surveys sponsored by 26 states and the Forest Service under the Forest Pest Control Act. Cooperative programs are carried out with state forestry agencies, the Soil Conservation Service, and local water conservation districts to control fires, stabilize gullies, improve forest growth, and prevent floods under the Watershed Protection and Flood Prevention Act of August 4, 1954. The Forest Service also runs the naval stores conservation program and assists in the supervision of forestry work in agricultural conservation programs. The service is also responsible for some basic research. Many of the service's offices are located at Rosslyn Plaza, Bldg. E. Rosslyn, Virginia 22209.

Office of the Chief: John McGuire   202-447-6661
Information and Education Div: Alexander Smith   447-3760
  General Information   447-3957
  Publications   447-6851
  Cooperative Outdoor Environmental Program   447-7013
  Environmental Education   447-6605
Manpower and Youth Conservation Programs Div: Robert M. Lake   447-7783
Forest Insect and Disease Research Div. (Rosslyn): Robert Callaham   703-557-0413
Forest Fire and Atmospheric Sciences Div. (Rosslyn): Craig Chandler   557-9107
Forest Economics and Marketing Research Div.: H. R. Josephson   202-447-2747
  Forest Products Marketing   447-3730
  Forest Survey   447-3734
  Forest Survey Techniques   447-3732
Forest Environment Research Div. (Rosslyn): J. B. Hilmon   703-557-5653
Forest Products and Engineering Research Div.: John Zerbe   202-447-5653
National Forest System: Edward W. Schultz   447-3523
Fire Management Div. (Rosslyn): Henry DeBruin   703-557-1837
Range Management Div. (Rosslyn): Frank J. Smith   557-1460
  Environmental Coordination   557-1460
  Ecosystem Analysis Planning   557-1460
  Ecology   557-1460
Recreation: F. Leroy Bond   202-447-3706
Watershed Management (Rosslyn)   703-557-0544
  Soil and Water (Rosslyn)   557-9013
  Geology   202-557-9013
  Water Resource Management   557-9013
  Environmental Management   557-9013
  Wild Rivers   557-2141
  Impact Surveys   557-2141
Program and Legislation: Philip Thornton   202-447-6663
  Environmental Matters   447-5020
Cooperative Forestry: J. S. McKnight   447-2270
  Forestration and Tree Improvement   447-3003
  Environmental Forestry   447-2986
Flood Prevention and River Basin Programs Div.: Sidney Weitzman   447-7767
Forest Pest Control Division (Rosslyn): Russell K. Smith   703-557-9160
  Insect Survey and Control   557-9160
  Disease Survey and Control   557-9060

National Agricultural Library
Beltsville, Md. 20705
301-344-3780

The National Agricultural Library, which operates under the Office of Science and Education, is the largest agricultural library in the United States, covering the field of agriculture in the broadest sense, including botany, zoology, chemistry, veterinary medicine, forestry, plant pathology, livestock, poultry, entomology, and general agriculture. The library has resources of about 1,300,000 volumes and receives regular publications from more than 120 governments and jurisdictional entities, printed in approximately 50 different languages.

Information contained in the collection is disseminated through loans, photocopies, and reference services. Bibliographic data is stored in the cataloging–indexing system. Outputs from this system include two monthly publications, *Bibliography of Agriculture* and *National Agricultural Library Catalog*, both published by private corporations. These services and information from the collection are available to anyone in the United States and abroad.

Director: Lloyd Davis   301-344-4531
  Reference Desk, Main Reading Room   344-3750
  Reference Division: Charles Bebee   344-3836

Rural Electrification Administration

The Rural Electrification Administration (REA), which operates under the Office of Rural Development and Conservation, makes loans to finance electric and telephone service in

rural areas. REA itself does not own or operate any facilities. The systems it finances are pledged to provide modern, adequate electric and telephone service to rural people under rates and conditions that permit full and productive use of these utility services.
Administrator: David Hamil   202-447-5123
Environmental Engineer: Joseph R. Binder   447-3446

Soil Conservation Service

The Soil Conservation Service (SCS), which operates under the Office of Rural Development and Conservation, is responsible for developing and carrying out a national soil and water conservation program in cooperation with landowners, operators, and other land users and developers, with community planning agencies and regional resource groups, and with other government agencies—federal, state, and local. The SCS also assists in agricultural pollution control, environmental improvement, and rural community development.

The soil and water conservation program is carried on through technical help to locally organized and operated conservation districts; local sponsors of watershed protection projects and resource conservation and development projects; and consultative assistance to other individuals and groups. More than 3,000 SCS conservation districts cover almost 2 billion acres in all the states, Puerto Rico, and the Virgin Islands.

Among its other activities, the SCS gives technical help to landowners and operators who participate in the Rural Environmental Assistance Program, cropland conversion, cropland adjustment, and Water Bank programs of the Department of Agriculture.
Administrator: Kenneth Grant   202-447-4531
Plant Sciences (Auditors Bldg., Washington, D.C. 20250): Victor Barry   447-2587
Deputy Administrator for Watersheds: William Davey   447-4527
Deputy Administrator for Soil Survey: William Johnson   447-3905
Information Division: Hubert Kelley, Jr.   447-4543
Education and Publications: Walter Jeske   447-5063

DEPARTMENT OF COMMERCE
14 St. between Constitution Ave. and E St. N.W., Washington, D.C. 20230
202-783-9200

OFFICE OF THE SECRETARY

Secretary: Frederick B. Dent   202-967-2113
Assistant Secretary for Science and Technology (The Assistant Secretary for Science and Technology is responsible for the research and development activities pertaining to science and technology programs, as well as environmental impact statements of the department): Betsy Ancker-Johnson   202-967-3111
Special Assistant for Technological Information: Mrs. Grace Burns   967-3914
Deputy Assistant Secretary and Director, Office of Product Standards: Vacant   967-3221
Deputy Assistant Secretary for Environmental Affairs: Sidney Galler   967-4335

Economic Development Administration

The primary function of the Environmental Development Administration (EDA) is the long-range economic development of areas with severe unemployment and low family income problems. It aids in the development of public facilities and private enterprise to help create new, permanent jobs. The EDA programs include public works grants and loans; business loans for industrial and commercial facilities; guarantees for private working capital loans; and technical, planning, and research assistance for areas designated as redevelopment areas by the assistant secretary. Environmental projects that have been supported include water pollution control facilities, water and sewer utilities, and industrial park facilities.
Acting Assistant Secretary for Economic Development: William W. Blunt   202-967-5081
Special Assistant for Environmental Affairs: Phillip Reiss   967-4208

The Maritime Administration

The Maritime Administration is engaged in research to eliminate marine pollution resulting from commercial ship operation and to develop port reception facilities for shipboard wastes and oily ballast.
Assistant Secretary for Maritime Affairs: Robert J. Blackwell   202-967-2595
Public Affairs Officer: Walter Oates   967-2746

Government Environmental Agencies

National Bureau of Standards
Gaithersburg, Md. 20850
301-921-1000

The National Bureau of Standards, which operates under the Assistant Secretary for Science and Technology, seeks to promote U.S. science and technology. It conducts research, provides a basis for national measurement systems, and provides various technical services.
Director: Dr. Richard W. Roberts   301-921-2411

INSTITUTE FOR BASIC STANDARDS

The Institute for Basic Standards provides the central basis within the United States of a complete and consistent system of physical measurement, coordinates that system with the measurement systems of other nations, and furnishes essential services leading to accurate and uniform physical measurements throughout the nation's scientific community, industry, and commerce.
Director: Dr. Ernest Ambler   301-921-3301
 Radiation Safety Coordinator: James Wyckoff   921-3307

INSTITUTE FOR MATERIALS RESEARCH

The Institute for Materials Research conducts research leading to improved methods of measurement standards and data on the properties of well-characterized materials; develops, produces, and distributes standard reference materials; relates the physical and chemical properties of materials to their behavior and their interaction with their environments; and provides advisory and research services to other government agencies.
Director: Dr. John Hoffman   301-921-2828
 Manager, Measures for Air Quality: Dr. James McNesby   921-3141
 Technical Information Specialist: Rosemary Maddock   921-2855

INSTITUTE FOR APPLIED TECHNOLOGY

The Institute for Applied Technology services to promote the use of available technology and to facilitate technological innovation in industry and government, cooperates with public and private organizations in the development of technological standards and test methodologies, and provides advisory and research services for governments on all levels.
Director: Dr. Karl Willenbrock   301-921-3434
 Technical Analysis: Dr. Edward Cushen   921-3563
 Building Technology: Dr. James Wright   921-3377

Center for Radiation Research

Director: Dr. James E. Leiss   301-921-2551

National Oceanic and Atmospheric Administration
Washington Science Center, 6010 Executive Blvd., Rockville, Md. 20852
301-496-8910

The environmental activities and functions of the National Oceanic and Atmospheric Administration include management, use, and conservation of animal and mineral resources; monitoring and predicting the characteristics of the physical environment; and warning against impending environmental hazards.

OFFICE OF THE ADMINISTRATOR

Administrator: Dr. Robert White   202-967-3567
 Ecology and Environmental Conservation: Dr. William Aron   967-5181
 Coastal Environment: Robert Knecht   301-496-8491
 Associate Administrator for Environmental Monitoring and Prediction: Dr. Clayton Jensen   496-8646
 Associate Administrator for Marine Resources: David Wallace   496-8251
 Assistant Administrator for Environmental Modification: Donald Moore   496-8721

ENVIRONMENTAL DATA SERVICE

Collects, processes, and analyzes statistical data relating to geodetic, seismological, geomagnetic, meteorological, aeronomic, and oceanographic information.
Director: Thomas Austin   202-343-6226

NATIONAL OCEAN SURVEY
Washington Science Center, 6010 Executive Blvd., Rockville, Md. 20852

Director: Rear Admiral Allen Powell 301-496-8204

NATIONAL ENVIRONMENTAL SATELLITE SERVICE
Federal Office Bldg., Suitland, Md.
Mailing address: Washington, D.C. 20023

The National Environmental Satellite Service (NESS) provides satellite observations of the environment and operates a national environmental satellite system. NESS conducts a program of research and services relating to the earth, its oceans and inland waters, its atmosphere, and its space environment.
Director: David Johnson 301-763-7190

NATIONAL MARINE FISHERIES SERVICE
Page II Bldg., 3300 Whitehaven St. N.W., Washington, D.C. 20235

The National Marine Fisheries Service engages in research on the resources of the sea, does biological research on important species of fish, and seeks answers to other relevant questions concerning marine life.
Director: Philip Roedel 301-495-4993
 Associate Director for Resource Research: Dr. William Royce 202-343-8581

NATIONAL TECHNICAL INFORMATION SERVICE
Sills Bldg., 525 Port Royal Rd., Springfield, Va. 22151
703-321-8500

The National Technical Information Service provides reports on government-sponsored research in the areas of science, business, and engineering to commerce, industry, and the public.
Director: William Knox 202-967-3227
Office of Publications: Reed Ness 703-321-8511

Social and Economic Statistics Administration
Federal Office Bldg. III, Suitland, Md.
Mailing address: Census Bureau, Dept. of Commerce, Washington, D.C. 20233
301-763-7662

Director: Edward Failor 301-763-5461
Associate Director for Demographic Fields: Daniel B. Levine 763-5167
 Current Population Surveys: George Bray 763-2773
 Current Health Statistic Surveys: Richard Dodge 763-5508
 Current Household Surveys: Edward Knowles 763-2802
Chief, Housing Div.: Arthur Young 763-2863
Chief, Population Div.: Meyer Zitter 763-7646
 Fertility Statistics: Wilson Grabill 763-5303
 Marriage and Family Statistics: Robert Grymes 763-5189
 Estimates and Projections: Meyer Zitter 763-7646
 National Population Estimates and Projections: Cambell Gibson 763-5300
 State and Local Population Estimates and Projections: Donald Starsinic 763-5072

DEPARTMENT OF DEFENSE
The Pentagon, Washington, D.C. 20301
202-545-6700

Secretary: James R. Schlesinger 202-695-5261
Assistant Secretary for Health and Environment: Richard S. Wilbur, M.D. 697-2111
Director for Environmental Quality: George W. Milias 695-3010

Army Corps of Engineers
Forrestal Bldg., Washington, D.C. 20314
202-545-6700

The activities of the corps are organized by river basins rather than state boundaries. When local interests feel that a need exists for construction or improvement of a navigation or flood control project, they may petition their representatives in Congress. The congressman then requests the appropriate congressional committee to direct the corps to investigate and furnish a recommendation in the matter under consideration. Comprehensive surveys of suggested projects are made to determine their economic and engineering feasibility and necessity. In making these surveys the corps cooperates fully with all other federal agencies concerned, as well as with state and local authorities.

In the initial stages of investigation the corps holds public hearings at which the desires and opinions of the people concerned are noted for later study and evaluation. In some cases, public hearings are also held during or at the end of the investigation to explain plans being considered and to receive opinions.

In addition to the development of projects designed to meet specific local problems, the corps undertakes planning for long-range coordinated development of the water resources of entire river basins. Such investigations include consideration of navigation, flood control, generation of hydroelectric power, domestic and industrial water supply, water-quality management and improvement, the protection of fish and wildlife, recreation, and other potential uses of water. Other federal and state agencies may contribute their specialized knowledge and skills through active participation in the study.

Considerations that enter into a recommendation to Congress to undertake a project generally include a determination that benefits will exceed costs, that the engineering design of the project is sound, that the project will meet the needs of the people concerned, and that it makes the fullest use possible of the natural resources involved.

The Chief of Engineers set up an environmental advisory board in April 1970 to advise the corps on how to improve its relations with conservation groups and the general public and to help define the corp's environmental responsibilities. In 1972, the corps established a six-member board to make an environmental resources inventory to assist districts in mapping their resources—not only hydrologic and physiographic, but also biotic and cultural. This will assist the corps by providing essential environmental data needed for the evaluation of project proposals to meet local demands for water and related land-resource development.

The Chief of Engineers has directed that an environmental evaluation or assessment be undertaken and an environmental-impact statement be prepared on all proposed major Corps of Engineers' actions that significantly affect the quality of the human environment. An assessment requires a rigorous examination of the effects of the proposed actions with attention to the alternatives. The environmental impact statement is a more formal document, which incorporates and updates the data obtained in the assessment, discusses the environmental implications and trade-offs associated with the proposed action and each of its alternatives, and reflects the views and comments of federal, state and local governmental agencies as well as interested groups and the general public. To comply with the National Environmental Policy Act of 1969, a draft and fully coordinated environmental impact statement must be filed with the Council on Environmental Quality.

Other areas of environmental involvement for the corps include a strip mining pollution study done in 1972, environmental litigation, and waste-water management.

Chief of Engineers: Lt. Gen. F. J. Clarke 202-693-7300
Chief, Public Affairs Office: Col. John V. Foley 693-6326
  Assistant, Conservation Liaison: Francis X. Kelly 693-6329

CIVIL WORKS

Director: Maj. Gen. J. W. Morris 693-7154
Chief, Recreation and Environmental Branch: Dr. C. Grant Ash 693-7290
Chief, Fish and Wildlife Section: Berton M. MacLean 693-7290
General Information 693-6456

FIELD OFFICES
(District Offices, if any, are listed below each division office)

Lower Mississippi Valley Div.: Box 60, Vicksburg, Miss. 39180
  Memphis: Federal Office Bldg., Memphis, Tenn. 38103
  New Orleans: Box 60267, New Orleans, La. 70160
  St. Louis: 210 N. 12 St., St. Louis, Mo. 63101
  Vicksburg: Box 60, Vicksburg, Miss. 39180
Missouri River Div.: Box 103, Downtown Sta., Omaha, Neb. 68101
  Kansas City: Federal Office Bldg., Kansas City, Mo. 64106
  Omaha: U.S. Post Office and Courthouse, Omaha, Neb. 68102
New England Div.: 424 Trapelo Rd., Waltham, Mass. 02154
North Atlantic Div.: 90 Church St., New York, N.Y. 10007
  Baltimore: Box 1715, Baltimore, Md. 21203
  New York City: 26 Federal Plaza, New York, N.Y. 10007
  Norfolk: 803 Front St., Norfolk, Va. 23510
  Philadelphia: U.S. Customs House, Philadelphia, Pa. 19106
North Central Div.: 536 S. Clark St., Chicago, Ill. 60605

Buffalo: 1776 Niagara St., Buffalo, N.Y. 14207

Chicago: 219 S. Dearborn St., Chicago, Ill. 60604

Detroit: P.O. Box 1027, Detroit, Mich. 48231

Rock Island: Clock Tower Bldg., Rock Island, Ill. 61201

St. Paul: U.S. Post Office and Custom House, St. Paul, Minn. 55101

North Pacific Div.: 210 Custom House, Portland, Oreg. 97209

Anchorage: Box 7002, Anchorage, Alaska 99510

Portland: Box 2946, Portland, Oreg. 97208

Seattle: 1519 Alaskan Way South, Seattle, Wash. 98134

Walla Walla: City-County Airport, Walla Walla, Wash. 99362

Ohio River Division: Box 1159, Cincinnati, Ohio 45201

Huntington: Box 2127, Huntington, W. Va. 25721

Louisville: Box 59, Louisville, Ky. 40201

Nashville: Box 1970, Nashville, Tenn. 37202

Pittsburgh: 2032 Federal Bldg., Pittsburgh, Pa. 15222

Pacific Ocean Division: Bldg. 96, Fort Armstrong, Honolulu, Hawaii 96813

Honolulu: Bldg. 96, Fort Armstrong, Honolulu, Hawaii 96813

South Atlantic Division: 510 Title Bldg., Atlanta, Ga. 30303

Charleston: Box 919, Charleston, S.C. 29402

Jacksonville: Box 4970, Jacksonville, Fla. 32201

Mobile: Box 2288, Mobile, Ala. 36628

Savannah: Box 889, Savannah, Ga. 31402

Wilmington: Box 1890, Wilmington, N.C. 28401

South Pacific Division: 630 Sansome St., San Francisco, Calif. 94111

Los Angeles: Box 2711, Los Angeles, Calif. 90053

Sacramento: 650 Capitol Mall, Sacramento, Calif. 95814

San Francisco: 100 McAllister St., San Francisco, Calif. 94102

Southwestern Division: 1114 Commerce St., Dallas, Tex. 75202

Albuquerque: Box 1580, Albuquerque, N.Mex. 87103

Fort Worth: Box 17300, Fort Worth, Tex. 76102

Galveston: Box 1229, Galveston, Tex. 77550

Little Rock: Box 867, Little Rock, Ark. 72203

DEPARTMENT OF HEALTH, EDUCATION, AND WELFARE

330 Independence Ave. S.W., Washington, D.C. 20201
202-245-6296

Secretary: Caspar Weinberger   245-6306

OFFICE OF CONSUMER AFFAIRS

Director: Virginia H. Knauer   202-245-6158

State and Local Programs Division: Betty A. Bay   245-9891

Public Affairs Division: Joseph C. Dawson   245-6875

Federal Programs Division: Frank R. Marvin   245-6270

Health and Environment: Howard N. Seltzer   245-6509

Public Health Service

The Public Health Service embraces the Food and Drug Administration, the Health and Mental Services Administration, and the National Institutes of Health.

Assistant Secretary for Health: Charles C. Edwards   202-245-7694

Deputy Assistant Secretary for Health: Dr. Henry R. Simmons   245-6611

Food and Drug Administration

5600 Fishers La., Rockville, Md. 20852
301-443-4480

Commissioner of Food and Drugs: Alexander M. Schmidt M.D.   443-2410

Deputy Commissioner: Sherwin Gardner   443-2400

Associate Commissioner for Medical Affairs: John Jennings M.D.   443-4124

Associate Commissioner for Compliance: Sam D. Fine   443-1594

Associate Commissioner for Science: Lloyd B. Tepper M.D.   443-3216

Environmental Impact Staff: Kenneth E. Taylor D.V.M.   443-4490

BUREAU OF FOODS

Federal Bldg. 8, 200 C St. S.W., Washington, D.C. 20204

The bureau conducts research and develops standards on the composition, quality, nutrition,

and safety of foods, food additives, colors, and cosmetics; conducts research designed to improve the detection, prevention, and control of contamination that may be responsible for illness or injury conveyed by foods, colors, and cosmetics; coordinates and evaluates Food and Drug Administration (FDA) surveillance and compliance programs relating to foods, colors, and cosmetics; reviews industry petitions and develops regulations for food standards to permit the safe use of color additives and food additives; and collects and interprets data on nutrition, food additives, and environmental factors affecting the total chemical insult posed by food additives.
Director: Virgil Wodicka   202-245-1057
Nutrition Div.: Ogden Johnson   245-1561
Chemistry and Physics Div.: Vacant   245-1036
Toxicology Div.: L. Friedman   245-1372
   Compliance Office: Robert Angelotte   245-1243
Food Technology Div.: A. D. Berneking   245-1164
Chemical Technology Div.: Charles Jelinek   245-1466
   Industrial Chemical Contaminants: George Yip   245-1152
   Color Technology Division: Alfred Weissler   245-1082
   Cosmetics Technology Div.: H. J. Eiermann (Acting)   245-1061

BUREAU OF DRUGS
Parklawn Bldg., 5600 Fishers La., Rockville, Md. 20852

The bureau develops standards and conducts research with respect to the efficacy, reliability, and safety of drugs; evaluates new drug applications and claims for investigational drugs; conducts a program of clinical studies related to the safety and efficacy of drugs; operates an adverse drug reaction reporting system; coordinates and evaluates the FDA's surveillance and compliance programs relating to drugs; develops or coordinates the development of regulations, model codes, and other standards covering drug industry practices; fosters development of good manufacturing practices; and directs the FDA's antibiotic and insulin certification program.
Director: J. Richard Crout M.D.   301-443-2894
Scientific and Medical Information: Howard Slavin M.D.   443-1016

Poison Control: Henry L. Verhulst   301-496-7606
Scientific Evaluation: George F. Leong (Acting)   301-443-4330
Over-the-Counter Drug Products: G. Yingling   443-4960
Product Research and Surveillance: Joseph Belson   443-2263
Clinical Research Div.: Vacant   443-4750
Compliance Office: Theodore Byers   443-3740
Pharmaceutical Research and Testing Office: W. W. Wright   202-245-1135

BUREAU OF RADIOLOGICAL HEALTH
Environmental Control Administration, Twinbrook Bldgs., 12720 Twinbrook Pkwy., Rockville, Md. 20852

The bureau carries out programs designed to reduce the exposure of man to hazardous radiation; develops methodology for controlling radiation exposures; conducts research on the health effects of radiation exposure; and conducts an electronic product radiation control program to control the emission of radiation from electronic products.
Director: John Villforth   301-443-4690
Information Office: John Bailey   443-4434
Biological Effects Div.: Dr. Morris Shore   493-2356
Radioactive Materials and Nuclear Medicine Div.: Dr. William Cole (Acting)   443-2473

Health Services and Mental Health Administration
Parklawn Bldg., 5600 Fishers La., Rockville, Md. 20852

Administrator: Vernon E. Wilson   301-443-2106

National Institute of Occupational Safety and Health

The institute plans, directs, and coordinates the national program effort to develop and establish occupational safety and health standards and to conduct research, training, and related activities to assure safe and healthful working conditions.
Director: Dr. Marcus Key   202-443-1530
Assistant Director for Safety: Alfred Blackman   443-2130

Assistant Director for Research and Standards Development: Dr. Charles Powell 443-3680
　Acting Deputy Director for R&D: Dr. Herbert E. Christensen 443-3680
　Criteria Development: Dr. Keith Jacobson 443-4216
　Toxicity and Research Analysis: Dr. Herbert Christensen 443-3680
　Information Resources Branch: Thomas Luginbyhl 443-3063
Assistant Director for Health Surveillance and Biometrics: Dr. J. Lloyd 443-1418
　Hazard Surveillance: Charles Glennon 443-3227
　Illness and Injury Surveillance: Pierre DeCoufle 443-3227
　Data Processing and Statistical Services: Philip McClain 443-3843
Director, Laboratories and Criteria Development (1014 Broadway, Cincinnati, Ohio 45202): Dr. Elliott S. Harris 513-684-2595
　Deputy Assistant Director: John M. Bryant 684-2595
　Toxicology Branch: Dr. Herbert Stokinger 684-2697
　Physical and Chemical Analysis: John Crable 684-3545
　Behavioral and Motivational Factors: Dr. Alexander Cohen 684-2331
　Engineering: Clark M. Humphries 684-2591
　Physical Agents: Wordie H. Parr 684-3540
Director, Field Studies and Clinical Investigations (1014 Broadway, Cincinnati, Ohio 45202): Dr. Joseph Wagoner 513-684-3255
　Environmental Investigation: Philip J. Bierbaum 684-2186
　Medical Investigation: Dr. William D Parnes 684-2325
Director, Technical Services (1014 Broadway, Cincinnati, Ohio 45202): Vacant 513-684-2141
　Deputy Director, Division of Technical Services: Paul E. Caplan 684-2141
　Accident Prevention Services: James Walters 684-2141
　Technical Information Services: James Oser 684-2691
　Hazard Evaluation Services: Jerome Flesch 684-2176
Director, Division of Occupational Health Programs: A. Walter Hoover 202-443-2102
Director, Appalachian Laboratory for Occupational Respiratory Diseases (Morgantown, W. Va. 26505): Dr. Keith Morgan 304-296-3474
Deputy Director: Earl P. Shoub 296-3474
Medical Research: N. Leroy Lapp 296-3491
Infectious Diseases: Dr. Herbert Eckert 296-3491
Biochemistry Branch: Dr. Harold Resnick 296-3491
Statistics Branch: Robert B. Reger 296-3501

National Institutes of Health
9000 Rockville Pike, Bethesda, Md. 20852

Director: Robert S. Stone 301-496-2433

NATIONAL LIBRARY OF MEDICINE
Director: Dr. Martin M. Cummings 496-6221
Office of Public Information and Publications Management: Robert Mahnert 496-6308
Specialized Information Services: Dr. Henry M. Kissman 496-3147
　Technical Files Implementation: Bruno M. Vasta 496-1131
　Toxicology Information: Frederick W. Clayton 496-1131

DIV. OF RESEARCH SERVICES
Director: Dr. Joe R. Held 301-496-5793
Environmental Services: Vinson Oviatt 496-6034
Information 496-1087

DIV. OF RESEARCH RESOURCES
Director: Dr. Thomas G. Bowery 301-496-5606
Special Assistant for Program Planning and Evaluation: Dr. Francis Kendrick 496-1817

NATIONAL INSTITUTE OF ENVIRONMENTAL HEALTH SCIENCES
National Environmental Health Sciences Research Center, Triangle Park, N.C. 27709
919-549-8110

Director: Dr. David Rall 919-549-3201
Public Information Office 549-3345
Associate Director for Scientific Information: Dr. Douglas Lee 549-3214

Research Services: Lyle Thomas 549-3327
Pathologic Physiology: Dr. Robert Dixon 549-3332
Animal Science and Technology: Dr. John Moore 549-3253
Pharmacology and Toxicology: Dr. James Fouts 549-3378
Mutagenesis: Dr. Frederick de Serres 549-3378

OFFICE OF EDUCATION
400 Maryland Ave. S.W., Washington, D.C. 20202
Director, Office of Environmental Education: Walter Bogan 202-755-7682

DEPARTMENT OF THE INTERIOR
18 and C Sts. N.W., Washington, D.C. 20240
202-343-1100

Secretary: Rogers C. B. Morton
Assistant Secretary for Fish and Wildlife and Parks: Nathaniel P. Reed 202-343-4416
Assistant Secretary for Mineral Resources: Hollis M. Dole 343-2186
  Deputy Assistant Secretary, Energy Programs: Stephen Wakefield 343-4476
  Deputy Assistant Secretary, Mineral Programs: John B. Rigg 343-5871
  Deputy Assistant Secretary, Minerals and Energy Policy: Harry L. Moffett 343-3804
  Director, Ocean Resources: Leigh S. Ratiner 343-8442
Assistant Secretary for Program Policy: John W. Larson 343-6181
  Director, Environmental and Project Review: Bruce Blanchard 343-3891
  Director, Regional Planning: Lance Marston 343-3878
Assistant Secretary for Public Land Management: Harrison Loesch 343-4174
  Education and Social Development: Janice Johnson 343-6971
Assistant Secretary for Water and Power Resources: James R. Smith 343-2191
  Assistant and Power Engineering Advisor: J. Emerson Harper 343-5113
  Staff Assistant, Power Research: Francis Fox Parry 343-8713
  Staff Assistant, Water Planning: Jack C. Jorgensen 343-5466
  Staff Assistant, Legislation: Vern Stephens 343-4266
  Staff Assistant, Water Resources: Edward G. Altouney 343-4001
  Staff Assistant, Economics: James J. Flannery 343-8275

OFFICE OF OIL AND GAS

This office deals with emergencies affecting the nation's supply of oil and gas, and administers restrictions on the importation of crude oil, unfinished petroleum oils, and finished petroleum products, including residual fuel oil to be used as fuel. The Office of Oil and Gas (OOG) develops, evaluates, and coordinates oil and gas information to provide bases for establishment and implementation of government oil and gas policies and programs. It provides information and services to government agencies with respect to physical and economic factors affecting the petroleum and gas industries both in the United States and abroad. It recommends programs and policies to improve the position and capabilities of the oil and gas industries.

OOG conducts a continuing study of the effects of oil and gas production, transportation, manufacturing, and consumption on the environment, and reviews for accuracy and completeness the environmental impact statements that relate to oil and gas.

Director: Gene P. Morrell 202-343-8071
Assistant Director, Oil Importation: Dell V. Perry 343-6951
Assistant Director, Emergency Preparedness and Oil Import Compliance: John Ricca 343-3831

OFFICE OF SALINE WATER

This office conducts research and development of practical means for the economical production, from sea or other saline water, of water suitable for agricultural, industrial, municipal, and other uses and for related studies and research.

Director: J. W. (Pat) O'Meara 202-343-5881
Chief, Thermal Processes: Robert H. Evans 343-5965
Chief, Environmental Services: Walter W. Rinne 343-6888
Assistant Director, Research: W. Sherman Gillam 343-8964

Office of Coal Research

This office seeks to develop new and more efficient methods of mining, preparing, and utilizing coal to insure abundant supplies of clean energy.

All research is performed by contracts with public and private organizations. OCR does not issue grants, maintain its own labs, or perform "in-house" research. It has no field offices. Major expenditures and most research have been directed toward developing methods of converting coal into clean alternative energy forms. This work includes the refining of coal to produce low-sulfur, low-ash solid fuels; both high- and low-b.t.u. synthetic gaseous fuels; and low-sulfur liquid fuels. Other portions of the OCR program include development of improved methods of generating electricity from coal with minimum damage to the environment, such as magneto-hydrodynamic systems, fluidized-bed boilers, fuel cells, and gas turbine systems. A number of small integrated projects support the basic objectives of the program.

Persons wishing to submit unsolicited proposals on coal research should contact the Director of Coal Research, Department of the Interior, Washington, D.C. 20240.

Director: George R. Hill   202-343-5533
Chief, Research and Development: Neal P. Cochran   343-5573

Office of Water Resources Research

The major purposes of the Office of Water Resources Research (OWRR) are to develop new technology and more efficient methods for resolving local, state, and nationwide water resource problems; train water scientists and engineers through on-the-job participation in research work; and facilitate water research coordination and the application of research results by furnishing information about ongoing and complete research. OWRR does not maintain its own labs or perform "in-house" research.

The office operates a water resources scientific information center to furnish information to the nation's water resource community, in project abstract and other summary formats, regarding ongoing water research projects and the completed water resources studies and investigations.

Under Title I of the Water Resources Research Act of 1964, OWRR provides annual fund allotments to support one state university water resources research and training institute in each state and in Puerto Rico. Additional funds are also provided to these institutes for specific research project work on a dollar-for-dollar matching-fund basis. Other universities and colleges may participate in the Title I program work of the designated state institutes. Under Title II of the act, grants and contracts are made with academic, private, public, or other organizations and individuals having water research competence for support of urgently needed water resources research work. Generally contracts and grants are awarded on the basis of unsolicited proposals submitted in response to a listing of priority research areas of interest.

Director: H. Garland Hershey   202-343-5075
Manager, Water Resources Scientific Information Center: Raymond A. Jensen   343-8435

Office of Hearings and Appeals
Ballston Tower No. 3, 4015 Wilson Blvd., Arlington, Va. 22203

The Office of Hearings and Appeals is responsible for departmental quasi-judicial and related functions. Hearing examiners and five formal boards of appeal render decisions in cases pertaining to contract disputes; public and acquired lands and their resources; submerged offshore lands of the Outer Continental Shelf; mine health and safety; oil import quotas; enforcement of the importation and transportation of rare and endangered species; and other matters.

Director: James M. Day   703-557-1500
Chairman, Board of Land Appeals: Newton Frishberg   557-9040
Chairman, Board of Mine Operations Appeals: Christian E. Rogers, Jr.   557-9037
Oil Import Appeals Board: Lewis S. Flagg   557-1427
Chief Administrative Law Judge, Hearings Div.: Ernest F. Hom   557-1407

Office of Communications

Director: Robert A. Kelly   202-343-6416
Current Press Releases: Jim Kendrick   343-9295

OFFICE OF LEGISLATION

Legislative Counsel: Frank A. Bracken 343-6706

OFFICE OF THE SCIENCE ADVISOR

Assistant to the Secretary and Science Advisor: Vacant
Deputy Science Advisor: Martin Prochnik 343-4186

United States Fish and Wildlife Service

BUREAU OF SPORT FISHERIES AND WILDLIFE
Washington, D.C. 20240

The bureau is responsible for programs for research, development, and management of fish resources; federal aid to state fish and wildlife agencies; and technical assistance in preserving and enhancing water and related resources for sport fishing. A system of nearly 100 fish hatcheries is operated, and the stocking of public waters and farm fish ponds is carried out in cooperation with state fish and game departments.

Wildlife programs have the goal of protecting and enhancing the values of the nation's wildlife species, enjoyed through hunting for recreation, bird watching, photography, and related activities. Research is conducted through waterfowl management study, other migratory bird research, upland wildlife work, pesticide-wildlife relationship studies, disease and parasite studies, bird and mammal control methods, and replenishment and protection of endangered wildlife species.

The National Wildlife Refuge System is approximately 30 million acres and includes 329 refuges and game ranges managed for migratory birds, protection of endangered species, public enjoyment of natural resources, and economic benefits from sales of land products and concessions. Wildlife surveys carried out under the Migratory Bird Treaty Act and other acts provide information for the establishment of federal hunting regulations monitored through a nationwide wildlife law enforcement program.

Programs for training in fish and wildlife research and management are available to a wide variety of people at bureau training camps, or in cooperative units functioning under agreements with universities and the fish and game department of the state where the unit is located. Under the Youth Conservation Corps Program the bureau operates 18 camps in the summer months.

Financial assistance programs allow funds annually to state fish and wildlife departments for use in fish and game management programs. The conservation and development of anadromous fish is performed under a state-federal cooperative program.

Environmental impact statements and water-use projects proposed by federal or private agencies are studied for the probable effects of such projects on fish and wildlife resources, and measures are recommended for their conservation and development. Emphasis is placed on conservation of estuaries and development of comprehensive river basin plans that consider future fish and wildlife recreational needs.

Acting Director: Spencer Smith 202-343-4717
Office of Environmental Quality: Raymond E. Johnson 343-6394
Office of Endangered Species: Harry A. Goodwin 343-5687
Office of Conservation Education: Charles Saults 343-5634
Div. of River Basin Studies: Daniel V. Slater 343-4442
Div. of Management and Enforcement: Charles H. Sawrence 343-3191
Div. of Wildlife Refuges: Vacant 343-3922
National Fisheries Center and Aquariums (Matomic Bldg., 1717 H St N.W., Washington, D.C. 20006): Warren J. Wisby 343-3861
Div. of Fishery Services: Vacant 343-4786
Div. of Wildlife Services: Jack H. Berryman 343-8213
Div. of Fish Hatcheries: Harvey Willoughby 343-2197
Div. of Wildlife Research: Thomas Baskett 343-4102
Patuxent Wildlife Research Center (Laurel, Md. 20810): Director: Eugene H. Dustman 301-776-4880
Migratory Bird Population Station (Laurel, Md. 20810): Director: Walter F. Crissey 776-4880
Bird and Mammal Laboratories (National Museum of Natural History, Constitution Ave. between 10 and 13 Sts., Washington, D.C. 20560): Director: Richard C. Banks 202-628-5633

Regional Offices

Region 1
(Arizona, California, Hawaii, Idaho, Nevada, Oregon, Washington)
1500 N.E. Irving St., Portland Oreg. 97208
Director: John D. Findlay   503-234-3361

Region 2
(Arkansas, Louisiana, New Mexico, Oklahoma, Texas)
Federal Bldg., 500 Gold Ave. S.W., Box 1306, Albuquerque, N.Mex. 87103
Director: W. O. Nelson, Jr.   505-843-2321

Region 3
(Illinois, Indiana, Michigan, Minnesota, Ohio, Wisconsin)
Federal Bldg., Fort Snelling, Twin Cities, Minn. 55111
Director: Travis S. Roberts   612-725-3500

Region 4
(Alabama, Florida, Georgia, Kentucky, Mississippi, North Carolina, South Carolina, Tennessee)
Peachtree St., 7th Bldg., Atlanta, Ga. 30323
Director: C. Edward Carlson   404-526-5100

Region 5
(Connecticut, Delaware, Maine, Maryland, Massachusetts, New Hampshire, New Jersey, New York, Pennsylvania, Rhode Island, Vermont, Virginia, West Virginia)
U.S. Post Office and Courthouse, Boston, Mass. 02109
Director: Richard E. Griffith   617-223-2961

Region 6
(Colorado, Iowa, Kansas, Missouri, Montana, Nebraska, North Dakota, South Dakota, Utah, Wyoming)
10597 W. 6 Ave., Denver, Colo. 80215
Director: Merwin A. Marston   303-234-2209

Alaska Area
6917 Seward Hwy., Anchorage, Alaska 99502
Director: Gordon Watson   907-344-2503

National Park Service

The National Park Service administers an extensive system of national parks, monuments, historic sites, and recreation areas for enjoyment and education; to protect the natural environment of the area; and to assist states, local governments, and citizen groups in the development of park areas, the protection of the natural environment, and the preservation of historic properties.

There is a service center in Denver, Colorado, that provides planning, architectural, engineering, and other professional services; and a center for production of interpretive exhibits, audiovisual materials, and publications in Harpers Ferry, West Virginia. There are more than 280 units within the National Park System, in four categories—natural, historic, recreational, and cultural.

The activities of the service are varied. They include developing management plans for, constructing facilities in, and staffing the areas under its administration. Usually lodging, food, and transportation services are provided through concessioners. Information on a wide variety of subjects is provided for visitors. Environmental education programs are presented in cooperation with local school administrations.
Director: George B. Hartzog   202-343-4621
Land Acquisition: Philip O. Stewart   343-2713
Park Operations: Vacant   343-4874
Youth Conservation Programs (1100 L St. N.W., Washington, D.C. 20005): Grover M. Barham   386-6417
Director, Harpers Ferry Center: William Everhart   343-6864
Director, Information Office: Edwin N. Winge   343-6843
  Chief, Information Services: Adele N. Wilson   343-4747
  Chief, Media Services: Gerald A. Waindell   343-4214
Federal Agency Coordination: J. Robert Stottlemyer   343-3919

Geological Survey
General Services Bldg., 18 and F Sts. N.W., Washington, D.C. 20242

The broad objectives of the Geological Survey are to perform surveys, investigations, and research covering topography, geology, and the mineral and water resources of the United States; classify land as to mineral character and water and power resources; enforce departmental regulations applicable to oil, gas, and other mining leases, permits, licenses, development contracts, and gas storage contracts; and publish and disseminate data relative to the foregoing activities.

22 Government Environmental Agencies

The survey reviews environmental impact statements generated by other agencies and develops guidelines for preparing effective impact statements. For information, write the assistant director for research, Room 5236, at the above address.

The activities of the survey are broken down into five main areas.

Conservation. The survey classifies federal lands as to their value for leaseable minerals or for reservoir and waterpower sites; supervises the operations of private industry on mining and oil and gas leases on public domain, acquired, Indian, outer continental shelf, and certain Naval petroleum reserve lands to ensure maximum utilization and prevent waste of the mineral resources, to limit environmental damage and pollution, and to protect public health and safety; assures the public a return for the disposition of its mineral resources; establishes maximum rates of production for producing wells on the outer continental shelf; maintains production accounts and collects royalties; prepares and publishes maps and reports of mineral and water resource investigations on federal lands; and provides certain federal agencies with geologic and engineering advice, evaluations, and inspection services for the management and disposition of public and Indian lands and mineral resources.

Chief, Conservation Div.: Russell G. Wayland 202-343-5953

Chief, Branch of Mineral Evaluation: Emmett A. Finley 343-3787

Chief, Branch of Mining Operations: Vacant 343-3264

Chief, Branch of Oil and Gas Operations: Robert C. Speer 343-4528

Chief, Branch of Waterpower Evaluation: Vacant 343-5508

Water Resources. The survey determines the source, quantity, quality, distribution, movement, and availability of both surface and ground waters. This work includes investigations of floods and shortages of water supply; the evaluation of available waters in river basins and ground-water provinces; the determination of the chemical and physical quality of water resources and its relationship to various parts of the hydrologic cycle; special hydrologic studies of the interrelations between climate, topography, vegetation, soils, and the water supply; research to improve the scientific basis of the investigations and techniques; scientific and technical assistance in hydrologic fields to other federal agencies and to licensees of the Federal Power Commission; and the coordination of federal water data acquisition activities, through a national water data network, and publication of its investigations.

Chief, Water Resources Div.: Ernest L. Hendricks 202-343-9425

Assistant Chief Hydrologist for Scientific Publications and Data Management: George W. Whetstone 343-3792

Chief, Branch of Surface Water: Walter Hofmann 343-5529

Chief, Branch of Quality Water: Ranard J. Pickering 343-5519

Geology. The survey conducts geologic surveys and related paleontological, geophysical, and geochemical studies to develop data and knowledge needed to appraise and use our land resources optimally. This information is published in reports and maps for use in solving problems related to society's impact on the natural environment; evaluating mineral resources and construction materials; identifying natural hazards; and determining the stability of the land in the construction of roads, buildings, dams, and pipelines. The survey administers an exploration program for the discovery of domestic minerals by private industry with federal assistance.

Chief Geologist, Geology Div.: Richard P. Sheldon 202-343-2125

Office of Scientific Publications: George E. Becraft 343-6306

Nontechnical Reports: William L. Newman 343-6306

Technical Reports (1625 I St. N.W., Washington, D.C. 20006): Norman Hatch 343-2784

Marine Geology Office: Henry L. Berryhill, Jr. 343-8501

Mineral Resources Office: Edwin W. Tooker 343-3834

Environmental Geology Office: Robert B. Raup, Jr. 343-5531

Geochemistry and Geophysics Office: Richard Fiske 343-4176

Energy Resources Office (National Bureau of Standards, 4200 Connecticut Ave. N.W., Washington, D.C. 20008): Gordon Wood 655-7251

Topographic Mapping. The survey prepares, publishes and revises maps of the National Topographic Map Series, covering the United States and outlying areas, and it operates the Map Information Office.

Topographic Mapping Div.: Robert H. Lyddan 202-343-3790

Map Information Office: Daniel L. Pinkerton 343-8471

EROS Program: The Earth Resources Observation Systems (EROS) is a departmental

program for acquiring, processing, distributing, and applying remote sensor data collected from aircraft and spacecraft toward the solution of resource and environmental problems. A data center has been established at Sioux Falls, South Dakota, as a focal point for the receipt of spacecraft and aircraft remote sensor data and its dissemination to the users.
Manager: William A. Fischer   202-343-9182

Bureau of Land Management

The bureau classifies, manages, and disposes of the public lands and their related resources according to the principles of multiple-use land management. It also administers mineral resources connected with acquired lands and the submerged lands of the outer continental shelf. The bureau headquarters is in Washington, D.C., and three detached offices having bureau-wide responsibilities are in existence as well as regional offices.
Director: Burton W. Silcock   202-343-3801
Office of Information: John A. Mattoon   343-5717
Environmental and Planning Coordination Div.: Robert A. Jones   343-5682
Chief, Pipeline Coordination Staff: Burke Riley   343-4562
Chief, Lands and Realty Div.: Vacant   343-3811
Branch of Land Resources: Lawrence Montross   343-5537
Chief, Range Div.: Kay W. Wilkes   343-4328
Chief, Forestry Div.: Murl W. Storms   343-3229
Chief, Watershed Div.: Euel L. Davis   343-5994
Chief, Wildlife Div.: Robert J. Smith   343-6188
Chief, Recreation Div.: Eldon F. Holmes   343-4364
Chief, Upland Minerals Div. (1129 20 St. N.W., Washington, D.C. 20036): Robert E. May   343-2718
Chief, Marine Minerals Div. (1129 20 St. N.W., Washington, D.C. 20036): John W. Sprague   343-8537

PRINCIPAL FIELD OFFICES

Alaska
555 Cordova St., Anchorage 99501
Curtis V. McVee   907-277-1561

Arizona
Federal Bldg., Phoenix, Ariz. 85025
Joseph T. Fallini   602-261-3873

California
Federal Office Bldg., 2800 Cottage Way, Sacramento, Calif. 95825
J. Russell Penny   916-481-2676

Eastern States
7981 Eastern Ave., Silver Springs, Md. 20910
Doris A. Koivula   301-495-3200

Idaho
334 Federal Bldg., 550 W. Fort St., Boise, Ida. 83702
William L. Mathews   208-342-2401

Montana
Federal Bldg., 316 N. 26 St., Billings, Mont. 59101
Edwin Zaidlicz   406-245-6463

Nevada
Federal Bldg., 300 Booth St., Reno, Nev. 89502
E. I. Rowland   702-784-5451

New Mexico
Federal Bldg., S. Federal Pl., Santa Fe, N.Mex. 87501
W. J. Anderson   505-981-3217

Oregon and Washington
729 N.E. Oregon St., Portland, Oreg. 97208
Archie D. Craft   503-234-4001

Utah
Federal Bldg., 125 S. State St., Salt Lake City, Utah 84111
Robert D. Nielson   801-524-5311

Wyoming
Federal Bldg., 2120 Capital Ave., Cheyenne, Wyo. 82001
Daniel P. Baker   307-778-2326

Bureau of Mines

The Bureau of Mines conducts research and administers regulatory programs to stimulate the private sector toward the production of national mineral and fuel needs. Concern is directed toward the satisfaction of current and emerging needs, the real cost of such achievements, the assessment of related social-economic factors, minimization of occupational hazards to workers, reduction of wastes, and assurance that mineral raw materials are supplied and mineral-based products are used and disposed of without objectionable social and environmental cost. To accomplish these objectives, the bureau performs research, provides information to the public, conducts inquiries, inspects mines, and administers laws pertinent to the extraction, processing, use, reuse, and disposal of minerals and mineral fuels.

Functions include surveillance and evaluations of the industrial and commercial outlook for minerals and fuel deposits; studies to determine the relationship of mineral supply, demand and technology to the national and world economy; studies and projects concerning the relationship of the mineral industries to environmental problems; collection, evaluation, and publication of mineral industry statistics; and conducting engineering studies regarding effective mining practices. Also included are research programs concerning extraction processing, use, and disposal of minerals and mineral fuels; helium production; and research on mine health and safety.

Programs are conducted to control health hazards and to reduce fatalities and injuries in the mineral industries. This is accomplished through mine inspections, field investigation, approval and testing of mining equipment and protective devices, analysis of accident statistics, safety education, training and motivation, health studies, and devising and enforcing appropriate health and safety standards.

Acting Director: Dr. John D. Morgan   202-343-4815

   Chief Scientist: Earl Hayes   343-5643
   Office of Mineral Information: R. O. Swenarton   343-4964
   Mineral Resources and Environmental Development: T. A. Henrie   343-6336
   Special Assistant, Environmental Activities: L. Norman   343-3941
   Assistant Director, Energy: W. S. Crentz   343-7905
   Chief, Coal Div.: G. A. Mills   343-4665
   Chief, Petroleum and Natural Gas Div.: (Ballston Tower No. 3, 4015 Wilson Blvd., Arlington, Va. 22203): J. A. Watkins   703-557-2247
   Chief, Shale Oil Div.: (Ballston Tower No. 3, 4015 Wilson Blvd., Arlington, Va. 22203): J.E. Phillips   703-557-2062
   Chief, Helium Div.: H. W. Lipper   202-343-4911
   Assistant Director, Metallurgy: Carl Rampacek   343-8311
   Chief, Solid Wastes Div.: C. B. Kenehan   343-4743
   Assistant Director, Mining: J. J. Yancik   343-4318
   Chief, Health and Safety: R. L. Marovelli   343-8243
   Chief, Mining Research-Resources Div.: J. J. Yancik   343-8077
   Chief, Environment Div.: J. A. Corgan   343-3663
   Chief, Fossil Fuels Div.: (Ballston Tower No. 3, 4015 Wilson Blvd., Arlington, Va. 22203): T.R. Scollon   703-557-2193
   Coordinator for Wilderness and River Basins (Ballston Tower No. 3, 4015 Wilson Blvd., Arlington, Va. 22203): Wilbert Dare   703-557-0350
   Director, Health and Safety: D. P. Schlick   202-343-4041
   Assistant Director, Coal Mine Health and Safety: J. W. Crawford   343-4249
   Assistant Director, Metal and Nonmetal Mine Health and Safety: Art Nelson
   Administrator of State Plans (Ballston Tower No. 3, 4015 Wilson Blvd., Arlington, Va. 22203): J. I. Craig   703-557-2197

Bureau of Outdoor Recreation

The bureau has government-wide responsibilities in outdoor recreation and, as the federal focal point in outdoor recreation, is in the mainstream of efforts to enhance and protect the environment.

Under the Land and Water Conservation Act of 1965, the bureau administers a program of financial assistance grants to states for facilitating outdoor recreation planning, acquisition, and developmental activities. The bureau has a wide range of responsibilities for planning, coordination, and establishment of recreation policies, of assessing recreational needs and resources available, and of maintaining a national plan for recreation, among others. Under the National Environmental Policy Act, the bureau reviews projects having an impact on outdoor recreation. Under the Department of Transportation Act, the possible adverse effects of transportation projects and programs on parks, recreation areas, and wildlife and waterfowl refuges are reviewed. The bureau also acts on applications from state and local governments requesting the conveyance of surplus federal real property for public park and recreation purposes.

Director: James W. Watt 202-343-5741
Environmental Affairs Office: Jerome Anderson 343-5711
Federal Programs Div.: Stuart Davey 343-5971
Federal Land Acquisition Div.: Lawrence Mirkes 343-7665
Redwoods Task Force: John G. Tkach 343-5595
Assistant Director for State Programs: A. Heaton Underhill 343-5723

Bureau of Reclamation

The program of the bureau is designed to stabilize and to promote the growth of local and regional economies through optimum development of water and related land resources throughout the seventeen contiguous western states. Reclamation projects provide for some or all of the following concurrent purposes: irrigation water service, municipal and industrial water supply, hydroelectric power generation and transmission, water quality improvement, fish and wildlife enhancement, outdoor recreation, flood control, navigation, river regulation and control, and related uses.

The bureau has responsibility for the sale, interchange, purchase, or transmission of electric power and energy generated at: (1) power plants constructed and operated by the bureau, except surplus electric power from nine hydroelectric plants operated by the bureau in the Pacific Northwest; and (2) six power plants on the Missouri River and one on the Rio Grande that were constructed by other federal agencies.

In cooperation with other agencies, the bureau reviews environmental statements for proposed federal water resource projects, renders technical assistance to foreign countries in water resource development and utilization, and administers youth conservation programs.

Commissioner: Ellis L. Armstrong 202-343-4157
Assistant to the Commissioner, Ecology: Elwood Seaman 343-4991
Assistant to the Commissioner, Scientific Affairs: Thaddeus Mermel 343-4272
Assistant to the Commissioner, Geothermal Resources: Dr. C. M. Wong 343-8278
Chief, Water and Land Div.: Maurice Langley 343-5104
Chief, Power Div.: William Graham 343-5337
Chief, Youth Conservation Program: Charles Butler 343-9366

REGIONAL OFFICES

Region 1
550 W. Fort St., Box 043, Boise, Idaho 80225
Director: Edwin F. Sullivan 208-342-2101
Information Officer 342-2108
Environmental Specialist: John R. Woodworth 342-2109

Region 2
Federal Office Bldg., 2800 Cottage Way, Sacramento, Calif. 95825
Director: Robert J. Pafford 916-481-2571
Information Officer: Jim Hart 481-2647
Environmental Specialist: J. Bruce Kimsey 481-2792

Region 3
Nevada Hwy. and 46 Park St., Box 427, Boulder City, Nev. 89005
Director: E.A. Lundberg 702-293-8411
Information Officer: W.J. Williams 293-8419
Environmental Specialist: F. Phillip Sharpe 293-8560

Region 4
125 S. State St., Box 11568, Salt Lake City, Utah 84111
Director: L.D. Crandall 801-524-5592
Information Officer: W.L. Ruglio 524-5403
Environmental Specialist: Harold N. Sersland 524-5580

Region 5
Herring Plaza, Box H-4377, Amarillo, Tex. 79101
Director: James A. Bradley 806-376-2401
Information Specialist: James D. Terrell 376-2402
Environmental Specialist: Alfred W. Hill 376-2408

Region 6
316 N. 26 St., Box 2553, Billings, Mont. 59103
Director: Harold E. Aldrich 406-245-6214
Information Officer: Curtis O. Ness 245-6218
Environmental Specialist: Elcy P. Denson 245-5558

Region 7
Bldg. 20, Denver Federal Center, Denver, Colo. 80225
Director: James M. Ingles 303-234-4441
Information Officer: C.A. Knell 234-4257
Environmental Specialist: Richard B. Eggen 234-3779

DEPARTMENT OF JUSTICE

Constitution Avenue and 10 St. N.W., Washington, D.C. 20530
Phone: 202-737-8200

Attorney General: William B. Saxbe   739-2001

Land and Natural Resources Division

The Land and Natural Resources Division supervises all suits and matters of a civil nature in the federal district courts, in the state courts, and in the Court of Claims relating to real property, including not only lands but water and other related natural resources and the outer continental shelf and marine resources, and to the protection of the environment. This includes condemnation proceedings for the acquisition of property and actions to recover damages, to determine boundaries, to establish rights in minerals (including mineral leases, in oil reserves and in other natural resources), to establish water rights and protect water resources, to abate water and air pollution, to defend actions for compensation for the claimed taking by the United States of real property or any interest therein, and to defend actions seeking to establish an interest in real property adverse to the United States. The division is also responsible for criminal prosecutions for air and water pollution.

Assistant Attorney General, Land and Natural Resources Div.: D. Kent Frizzell   202-739-2701

DEPARTMENT OF LABOR

14 St. and Constitution Ave. N.W., Washington, D.C. 20210
202-393-2420

Secretary: James D. Hodgson   202-393-2001

Occupational Safety and Health Administration

The Occupational Safety and Health Administration develops and promulgates occupational safety and health standards, develops and issues regulations, conducts investigations and inspections to determine the status of compliance with safety and health standards and regulations, and issues citations for noncompliance with safety and health standards and regulations.

Deputy Assistant Secretary/Administrator: Chain Robbins   202-393-2144
Chief, Policy and Evaluation: Robert Copeland   393-2066
Director, Office of Compliance and Standards: Fred Bishoff   393-2603
Director, Office of Standards: Gerald Scannell   393-2333
Director, Office of Technical Information: George Yatsko   393-3496
Director, Office of Standards Development: John Proctor   393-2340
Director, Office of Training and Education: Earl Heath   393-5194
Director, Office of Information Services: Samuel Sharkey   393-3914
  Division of Publications: Marcia Hovey   393-2069
  Division of Media Services   393-3914

DEPARTMENT OF TRANSPORTATION

400 7 St. S.W., Washington, D.C. 20590
202-426-4000

OFFICE OF THE SECRETARY

Secretary: Claude S. Brinegar   202-426-1111
Director, Planning and Program Review: Robert Prestemon   426-4450
  Highway and Mass Transit: Michael Finkelstein   426-9605
  Maritime Programs: William Cass   426-4465
  Aviation: David Lawhead   426-9603
  Rail and Safety: Richard Bowman   426-4470
  Planning and Evaluation: Clifford Parker   426-4480
Director, Public Affairs: H. David Crother   426-4570
  Assistant Director for Information: Oscar Griffin, Jr.   426-4531
Chairman, Hazardous Materials Regulations Board: William Burns   426-0656

POLICY AND INTERNATIONAL AFFAIRS OFFICE

Functions of this office include the analysis, development, and articulation of new and revised policies, plans, and programs for domestic and international transportation; analysis of the social, environmental, and economic interplay between transport systems operations and established policies, regulations, and laws; and a comprehensive transportation data and information system.

Assistant Secretary: John L. Hazard 426-4544
Director, Systems Analysis and Information: Ira Dye 426-4220
Director, Policy Review: Samuel Eastman 426-4331
Regulatory Div.: Edward Oppler 426-2903
Policy Review Div.: John Flynn 426-4428
Legislative Div.: Bruce Schultheis 426-2912

Environment and Urban Systems Office

This office has responsibility for environmental and overall urban transportation needs, goals, and policies; and innovative approaches to urban transportation and environmental enhancement programs. The assistant secretary serves as catalyst for the translation of these programs into balanced and responsive transportation systems.

Assistant Secretary: John Hirten 426-4563
Director, Environmental Quality: Martin Convisser 426-4357
Director, Urban Transportation Systems: William Goodman 426-4315

Systems Development and Technology Office

Activities conducted by this office include scientific and technological research and development advancing transportation capability as to its safety, effectiveness, economy, and viability; technological input to development of transportation policy; abatement of noise generated by transportation equipment; and telecommunications. The assistant secretary also has responsibility for the Transportation Systems Center in Cambridge, Mass. The center is responsible for enhancing transportation safety and improving the nation's transportation system by performing or arranging for the performance of advanced systems research and technological research and development in all transportation disciplines.

Assistant Secretary: Robert Cannon, Jr. 426-4461
Chief Scientist: Vacant 426-0190
Director, Noise Abatement: Charles Foster 426-4553
Environmental Research Div.: William Close 426-4560
Regulatory Policy and Standards: Robert Paulin 426-4558
Technical Div.: Frank Fulton 426-2082
State Programs Div.: Walter Kurylo 426-2392
Industry Programs: Melvin Judah 426-2082

Transportation Systems Center
Kendall Sq., Cambridge, Mass. 02142
617-494-2000

Director: James Elms 617-494-2222
Director of Transportation Systems Concepts: John Hodge 494-2563
Advanced Program Planning Division: Frank Hassler 494-2563
Director of Transportation Systems Development: Robert Wedan 494-2490
Director of Technology: Louis Roberts 494-2028

Safety and Consumer Affairs Office

This office is responsible for coordinating the department's safety programs; serves as the department's point of contact in relations with public and private organizations and groups directed to consumer interests; performs the functions of the secretary under the Natural Pipeline Safety Act of 1968; develops and coordinates departmental programs for the regulation of the transportation of hazardous materials; and is responsible for the department's program for enhancing the safety and security of passengers and cargo in transit and for the coordination of the program with other government and industry interests.

Assistant Secretary: Benjamin Davis 202-426-4474
Director, Hazardous Materials: William Burns 426-0656
Regulations Div.: Alan Roberts 426-2075
Technology Div.: Charles Smith 426-2311
Director, Pipeline Safety: Joseph Caldwell 426-2392
Program Analyst: David Watson 426-2392
Regulations Div.: Joseph Jeffrey 426-2392

Urban Mass Transportation Administration

The missions of the administration are to assist in the development of improved mass transportation facilities, equipment, techniques, and methods; to encourage the planning and establishment of area-wide urban mass transportation systems; and to provide assistance to state and local governments in financing such systems.

Associate Administrator, Research, Development and Demonstrations: Robert Hemmes 426-4052
New Systems Div.: Charles Broxmeyer 426-4047

National Highway Traffic Safety Administration

This administration was established by the Highway Safety Act of 1970. It carries out programs relating to the safety performance of motor vehicle drivers, under the National Traffic and Motor Vehicle Safety Act of 1966 and the Highway Safety Act of 1966. Under the authority of the Clean Air Amendments of 1970, the administration certifies as to the consistency of Environmental Protection Agency state grants with any highway safety program developed pursuant to section 402 of title 23 of the U.S. Code.

Motor Vehicle Programs

Office of Standards Enforcement: Francis Armstrong 426-2832
Office of Standards for Vehicles-in-Use: Harold Jacklin 426-2852
Office of Defects Investigation: Andrew Detrick 426-2850

Traffic Safety Programs

Office of Standards Development and Implementation: Glenn Carmichael 426-0068
Office of State and Community Comprehensive Programs: Willard Howell 426-1760

Research Institute

Office of Experimental Safety Vehicle Programs: William Scott 426-1458
Office of Vehicle Structures Research: Lynn Bradford 426-4850
Office of Operating Systems Research: Lynn Bradford 426-4850

National Transportation Safety Board
800 Independence Ave. S.W., Washington, D.C. 20591

The board investigates U.S. civil aviation accidents, except those delegated by the board to the Federal Aviation Administration; determines accident cause and reports the facts and circumstances in all aviation accidents; and conducts special studies and makes recommendations on matters pertaining to aviation safety and aviation accident prevention.

The board also covers the fields of railroad, highway, pipeline, and marine safety. The board delegates accident cause determinations of most accidents to the administrations within the Department of Transportation, but reserves the right to investigate, determine cause, and report the facts and circumstances of all surface transportation accidents which it declares to be major. The safety board conducts special studies and makes recommendations on matters pertaining to surface transportation safety promotion and surface transportation accident prevention.

Bureau of Surface Transportation Safety

Highway Safety Div.: Anthony Schmieg 426-8994
Marine Safety Div.: Luigi Colucciello 426-8688
Railroad Safety Div.: Thomas DeW. Styles 426-8981
Pipeline Safety Div.: Barry Sweedler 426-8981

Federal Aviation Administration
800 Independence Ave. S.W., Washington, D.C. 20591

Director, Environmental Quality Office: Richard Skully 426-8406

Chief Environmental Scientist: John Powers 426-8406
Chief Technical Environmental Planner: Cole Morrow 426-8406
Director, Supersonic Transport Office: Frampton Ellis, Jr. 426-8483
Systems Research and Development Service: Aircraft and Noise Abatement Division: George Bates 426-3861
Noise Abatement Branch: James Woodall 426-8442
  Noise Section: William Sperry 426-3314
  Sonic Boom Section: J.K. Power 426-3314

INDEPENDENT AGENCIES

APPALACHIAN REGIONAL COMMISSION
1666 Connecticut Ave. N.., Washington, D.C. 20235
202-967-5728

The commission consists of the governors of the thirteen Appalachian states, or their representatives, and a permanent federal cochairman appointed by the president. Every six months the governors select one of their number as state cochairman.

The purpose of the commission is a joint federal–state partnership concerned with the economic, physical, and social development of the thirteen-state Appalachian region. Yearly development plans are filed by each of the member states. Projects contained in the plans can be funded only if they meet the guidelines of the commission. After a project is approved by the commission and has the state's approval, it is passed on to the federal agency involved in that type of program for evaluation and actual execution.

Some of the programs included in the plan are: construction of a development highway system, construction of access roads, construction and operation of multicounty health projects, application of land treatment and erosion control measures, reclamation of land damaged by past mining practices, support of timber development organizations, research grants, operation of a comprehensive water resources survey, construction of sewage treatment facilities, and the supplementation of a number of existing grant-in-aid programs providing for the acquisition of land and the construction and equipment of public facilities.

Executive Director: Alvin J. Arnett 202-967-5728
Public Information Office 967-3835

ATOMIC ENERGY COMMISSION
Germantown Headquarters Bldg., Germantown, Md.
Mailing Address: Washington, D.C. 20545
301-973-1000

The Atomic Energy Commission has a dual responsibility: to foster, through research and development, the beneficial uses of nuclear and other energy, and to regulate private nuclear activities—particularly nuclear powerplants and associated facilities. The developmental and the regulatory functions of the agency are carried out by separate organizational components, each of which exercises its respective responsibilities for the commission independently of the other. The commission has responsibility to protect the health and safety of the public, and to regulate the control and use or source, byproduct, and special nuclear materials.

The commission is composed of five members appointed by the president by and with the advice and consent of the Senate. One of the members is designated by the president as the chairman.

Chairman: Dr. Dixie Lee Ray 301-973-6111
General Manager: Robert E. Hollingsworth 973-6666
Director, Information Services: John Harris 301-973-4536
Assistant Director for Public Information: Joseph Fouchard 973-4538
Assistant Director for Technical Information: E. E. Stokely 973-3338
  Chief, Science Services Branch: Joseph Gratton 973-5454
Assistant Director for Educational Services: Charles W. Pelzer 973-1210

DIVISION OF REACTOR SAFETY RESEARCH

This division reports directly to the general manager.
Director: Dr. Herbert J. C. Kouts 301-973-3008
Assistant Director for Operations: William H. Layham 973-3548
  Chief, Plant Engineering Branch: John F. Pearson, Jr. 973-5578
  Chief, Project Management Branch: Robert W. Barber 973-4484

Chief, Reactor Engineering Branch: (Acting) R. B. Foulds   973-3548
Assistant Director for Water Reactor Safety Research: Long Sun Tong   973-5465
　Chief, Separate Effects Branch: Jerry D. Griffith   973-4131
　Chief, PBF Programs Branch: William U. Johnston   973-5465
Assistant Director for Fast Breeder Safety: Vacant   973-5465
　Chief, Experimental Fast Breeder Safety Branch: Vacant

Chief, Health Protection: Dr. Donald Ross   973-3331
Chief, Nuclear Explosives Environmental Safety: Tommy McCraw   973-3015
Assistant Director for Facilities Safety: Robert E. Yoder   973-5281
　Chief, Reactor Safety Branch: Mayhue Bell   973-4273
　Chief, Process Facilities Safety: Blake Brown   973-4138
　Chief, Industrial Safety and Fire Protection: David Patterson   973-3161

Biomedical and Environmental Research and Safety Programs

Assistant General Manager: Dr. James Liverman   301-973-3208

DIVISION OF BIOMEDICAL AND ENVIRONMENTAL RESEARCH

Director: Dr. James Liverman   973-3208
Deputy Director: Dr. W. W. Burr, Jr.   973-3153
Assistant Director for Regulatory Liaison: Dr. Jeff Swinebroad   973-4155
Assistant Director for Laboratory and Interagency Liaison: Dr. John Kirby-Smith   973-4486
Assistant Director for Special Programs: Dr. Nathaniel F. Barr   973-4258
Assistant Director for Operations Liaison: Vacant
Assistant Director for Research Development Programs: Dr. Charles W. Edington   973-3785
Assistant Director for Planning Coordination: John C. Witnah   973-5411
Scientific Advisor: Hal Hollister   973-3610
Manager of Environmental Programs: Dr. Charles L. Osterberg   973-4208
Manager of Physical and Technological Programs: Dr. Robert W. Wood   973-5355

DIVISION OF OPERATIONAL SAFETY

Director: Dr. Martin B. Biles   973-3157
Assistant Director for Health Protection: L. Joe Deal   973-4093
　Chief, Environmental Protection: Arthur Schoen   973-4585

DIVISION OF WASTE MANAGEMENT AND TRANSPORTATION

Director: Dr. Frank Pittman   973-4285
Deputy Director: Alex F. Perge   973-4068
　Chief, Engineering Branch: Owen P. Gormley   973-4002
　Chief, Operations Branch: Gerald H. Daly   973-4214
　Chief, Transportation Branch: William A. Brobst   973-4361

Physical Research and Laboratory Coordination

Assistant General Manager: Dr. John Teem   301-973-5565

DIVISION OF CONTROLLED THERMONUCLEAR RESEARCH

Director: Dr. Robert L. Hirsch   973-3347
Special Assistant to Director: William L. R. Rice   973-3350
Assistant Director, Confinement Systems: Dr. Stephen O. Dean   973-4095
Assistant Director, Development and Technology: Dr. Robert W. Bussard   973-5143
Assistant Director, Research: Dr. Alvin W. Trivelpiece   973-4596

DIVISION OF PHYSICAL RESEARCH

Director: Dr. John M. Teem   973-5565
Associate Director: Dr. Spofford English   973-4563
Special Assistant to the Director: Dr. Herbert L. Kinney   973-5125

Assistant Director for Molecular Sciences and Energy Research: Dr. Elliot S. Pierce 973-3167
Assistant Director for Materials Sciences: Dr. Donald K. Stevens 973-3427
Assistant Director for Nuclear Sciences: Dr. George L. Rogusa 973-3613
Assistant Director for Energy Physics: Dr. W. A. Wallenmeyer 973-3624

OFFICE OF LABORATORY COORDINATION

Director: Vacant 973-5565

Production and Management of Nuclear Materials

Assistant General Manager: George Quinn 301-973-3311

DIVISION OF PRODUCTION AND MATERIALS MANAGEMENT

Director: Frank Baranowski 973-4413
Assistant Director for Uranium Enrichment and Combined Operational Planning: Jarvis Schwennesen 973-3516
Assistant Director for Reactor Products and Inventory Management: George Pleat 973-3757
Assistant Director for Raw Materials: Robert Nininger 973-5311

Energy and Development Programs

Assistant General Manager: (Acting) John J. Flaherty 301-973-6927

DIVISION OF REACTOR RESEARCH AND DEVELOPMENT

Director: Thomas A. Nemzek 973-5203
Deputy Director: Edwin E. Kinter 973-5033
Assistant Director for Project Management: John W. Crawford 973-3134
Assistant Director for Reactor Engineering: Vacant
Assistant Director for Army Reactors: Vacant

Assistant Director for Engineering Standards: Melvin A. Rosen 973-4105
Assistant Director for Plant Engineering: Richard E. Kosiba 973-4362
Assistant Director for Nuclear Safety: Andrew J. Pressesky 973-3424
  Chief, Environmental Safety Branch: Vacant 973-3701
  Chief: Fast Reactor Safety Branch: Vacant 973-3431
Assistant Director for Reactor Technology: Edward E. Sinclair 973-3465
Assistant Director for Program Analysis: Merrill J. Whitman 973-4366
  Chief, Environmental Effects Branch: Andrew P. D'Zmura 973-5403

DIVISION OF APPLIED TECHNOLOGY

Director: Dr. Gerald W. Johnson 973-3022
Assistant Director for General Energy Development: James Bresee 973-3184
Assistant Director for Isotopes Development: E. E. Fowler 973-3151
Assistant Director for Peaceful Nuclear Explosives: Edward Fleming 973-4426

National Security

Assistant General Manager: Maj. Gen. Edward Giller 301-973-3091

DIVISION OF NUCLEAR MATERIALS SECURITY

Director: (Acting) Leonard M. Brenner 973-3671
Assistant Director for Policy and Inspection: Leonard Brenner 973-3672
Assistant Director for Research and Development: Samuel McDowell 973-5067
Assistant Director for Administration and Reports: Thomas Haycock 973-4254

DIVISION OF REGULATION

Director: L. Manning Muntzing 973-7511
Directorate of Licensing: John F. O'Leary 973-7563

Directorate of Regulatory Standards: Lester R. Rogers   973-7376
Directorate of Regulatory Operations: Donald F. Knuth   973-7397

DELAWARE RIVER BASIN COMMISSION

Office of the Executive Director: 25 State Police Dr., Box 360, Trenton, N.J. 08603
609-883-9500

The Delaware River Basin Commission was created as a Federal–Interstate Compact organization consisting of the U.S. government and the states of Delaware, New Jersey, New York, and Pennsylvania. The commission is responsible for the development and maintenance of a comprehensive plan and for programing, scheduling, and controlling projects and activities within the Delaware River Basin. The plan will provide for regulation and development of ground and surface water supplies for municipal, industrial, and agricultural uses; abatement of stream pollution; flood damage reduction; promotion of forestry, soil conservation, and watershed projects; propagation of fish and wildlife; development of water-related recreational facilities; and development of hydroelectric power potentialities.

Responsibility for review and processing of environmental statements by and for the commission rests with the secretary of the commission, Box 360, Trenton, N.J. 08603.

U.S. Commissioner (Rm. 5625, Department of the Interior Bldg., Washington, D.C. 20240): Paul Van Wegen   202-343-5761
Executive Director: James Wright   609-883-9500
Public Information Office: Dawes Thompson   609-883-9500

FEDERAL MARITIME COMMISSION

1405 I St. N.W., Washington, D.C. 20573
202-393-3111

The Federal Maritime Commission is composed of five members, appointed by the president. The purpose of the commission is to protect the interests of the public by regulation of waterborne shipping in the foreign and domestic offshore commerce of the United States.

The commission administers a section of the Water Quality Act of 1970 with respect to evidence of financial responsibility by owners and operators of vessels which may be subjected to liability to the United States for the cost of removal of oil from the navigable waters of the United States, adjoining shorelines, or waters of the contiguous zone.

Chairman: Helen Delich Bentley   202-393-3111
Office of Oil Pollution Responsibility: Robert Drew   202-382-8181

FEDERAL POWER COMMISSION

General Accounting Office Bldg., 441 G St. N.W., Washington, D.C. 20426
202-386-4506

The Federal Power Commission (FPC) regulates the interstate aspects of the electric power and natural gas industries. It consists of five commissioners, appointed by the president with the advice and consent of the Senate, serving five-year terms.

The commission issues permits and licenses for nonfederal hydroelectric power projects; regulates the rates and other aspects of interstate wholesale transactions in electric power and natural gas; issues certificates for interstate gas sales and construction and operation of interstate pipeline facilities; and requires protection of the natural environment in the construction of new hydroelectric projects and natural gas transmission lines. It requires development of recreational facilities for the general public at licensed hydroelectric projects.

The FPC has divided the country into regional districts for the voluntary interconnection and coordination of facilities for generation, transmission, and sales of electric energy. It reviews plans for dams proposed by other federal agencies and makes recommendations concerning facilities for the development of hydroelectric power. The FPC can direct pipelines to supply natural gas to local distributors. FPC authorization is required for the abandonment of facilities or the discontinuance of service.

The FPC collects data on the entire electric power industry and on natural gas companies under its jurisdiction. A national gas survey was initiated in 1971 to study factors of demand, supply, and alternate fuel sources, facilities expansion, and interfuel competition. The survey was also to evaluate proved reserves in the United States.

The FPC also regulates the exporting of electric energy and the exporting and importing of natural gas, and issues permits for border facilities for these transactions.

Chairman: John N. Nassikas   202-386-4566

Advisor on Environmental Quality: Richard Hill 386-6084
Chief, Bureau of Natural Gas: Thomas Joyce 386-5237
  Chief, Pipeline and Producer Rates Div.: Lundy Wright 386-3442
  Chief, Pipeline Div.: William Drescher 386-3339
Chief, Bureau of Power (1425 K St. N.W., Washington, D.C. 20005): T. A. Phillips 382-1738
  Chief, River Basins Div.: George Adkins 382-1768
  Chief, Power Surveys and Analyses Div.: Bernard Chew 382-2065
  Chief, Rates and Corporation Regulation Div.: William Lindsay 382-3976
Chief, Economics Office (1425 K St. N.W., Washington, D.C. 20005): Haskell Wald 382-2604
  Chief, Economic Studies Div.: John Wilson 382-2777
Director, Public Information Office: William Webb 382-6102

NATIONAL SCIENCE FOUNDATION
1800 G St. N.W., Washington, D.C. 20550
202-655-4000

The National Science Foundation was created to strengthen research and education in the sciences in the United States. It is composed of twenty-four members, a director, deputy director, and four assistant directors, each appointed by the president with the advice and consent of the Senate.
Director: H. Guyford Stever 202-632-4001
Deputy Director: Raymond L. Bisplinghoff 632-4376

RESEARCH DIVISIONS

The foundation awards grants to universities, nonprofit and other research organizations to support fundamental research, including research on the fundamental processes influencing man's environment and research aimed at improving environmental quality.
Assistant Director: Edward Creutz 202-632-7342
Division Director, Environmental Sciences: A. P. Crary 632-4274
Deputy Assistant Director: Edward P. Todd 632-4240
Head, Atmospheric Sciences Section: Fred White 632-4198
Head, Earth Sciences Section: William Benson 632-4210
Head, Oceanography Section: M. Grant Gross 632-4227
Division Director, Biological and Medical Sciences: Eloise E. Clark 632-4338
Head, Ecology and Systematic Biology Section: Vacant 632-7318
Division Director, Engineering: (Acting) Israel Warshaw 632-5790
  Civil and Environmental Technology Program: C. A. Babendreier 632-5787
  Fluid Mechanics Program: G. K. Lea 632-5787
  Industrial Technology Program: M. S. Ojalvo 632-5867
  Solid Mechanics Program: C. J. Astill 632-5787

RESEARCH APPLICATIONS DIVISIONS

Research aimed at stimulating economic growth and productivity, improving environmental quality, and enhancing capabilities for dealing effectively with social issues is supported.
Assistant Director: Alfred Eggers 202-632-7424
Deputy Assistant Director for Science and Technology: Joel Snow 632-7426
Division Director, Environmental Systems and Resources: Phillip Johnson 632-4345
Division Director, Advanced Technology Applications: Richard J. Green 632-5726

NATIONAL AND INTERNATIONAL PROGRAMS

Major national and international programs are supported. Information relating to scientific resources is developed and disseminated to facilitate decisions to strengthen the scientific effort of the nation. The development and use of computer and other scientific methods and technologies are supported. Programs to improve the information systems and services available to U.S. scientists, foster the interchange of scientific information among scientists of the United States and foreign countries, and provide support for the translation of foreign scientific information are also undertaken.

Support is given, through contracts, to national centers where large facilities are made available for the use of qualified scientists. International programs, including cooperative scientific research activities, are supported through the exchange of American and foreign scientists and engineers, international science education assistance programs, and participation in the International Biological Program of the International Decade of Ocean Exploration.

Head, Polar Programs: Joseph Fletcher 202-632-7300
  Chief Scientist, Polar Science Section: George Llano 632-4162
Head, International Programs: Bodo Bartocha 632-5798
Head, National Centers and Facilities Operations: Daniel Hunt 632-5717
Head, Computing Activities: John Pasta 632-5960
Head, Science Information Service: Lee G. Burchinal 632-5824
  Director, Document Systems Program: Gordon Ward 632-5800
  Director, User Support Program: Joel D. Goldhar 632-5850
  Director, Research Program: Edward Weiss 632-5818
Head, Office for the International Decade of Ocean Exploration: Feenan Jennings 632-7356
  Manager: Environmental Forecasting Program: Curtis Collins 632-4334
  Manager, Seabed Assessment Program: Adward Davin 632-4334
  Manager, Living Resources Program: Deane Holt 632-7356
Head, Office for Oceanographic Facilities and Support: Mary Johrde 632-4102

EDUCATION DIVISIONS
5225 Wisconsin Ave. N.W. Washington, D.C. 20550

This division seeks to improve the capability of the educational system at all levels to produce the trained scientific and technical manpower to meet national needs. Graduate fellowships are awarded on a competitive basis in the various sciences, including history and philosophy of science.

Assistant Director: Vacant 202-282-7920
Division Director, Higher Education in Science: Francis O'Brien 282-7754
  Director, Fellowships and Traineeships: Douglas Chapin 282-7764
  Director, Faculty and Postdoctoral Fellowships Program: Hall Taylor 282-7758
Head, Office of Experimental Projects and Programs: Lyle W. Phillips 282-7930
Division Director, Pre-College Education in Science: Howard Hausman 282-7786
Division Director, Science Resources Studies: Charles E. Falk 282-7704

OCCUPATIONAL SAFETY AND HEALTH REVIEW COMMISSION
1825 K St. N.W., Washington, D.C. 20006
202-382-6214

The Occupational Safety and Health Act of 1970 represents an effort to reduce the incidence of employment-related personal injuries, illnesses, and deaths among working men and women in the United States. The review commission was created to insure just and equitable enforcement of those occupational health and safety standards that are contested by employers, employees, and representatives of employees. The three members of the review commission are appointed by the President with the advice and consent of the Senate for staggered terms of six years each.

The Occupational Safety and Health Act covers virtually every employer in the country. It requires each employer both to furnish employment and a place of employment that are free from recognized hazards that are likely to cause death or serious physical harm to employees and to comply with occupational safety and health standards promulgated under the act.

Chairman: Robert D. Moran 202-382-8765
Executive Director: Richard J. Wise 382-5287
Director of Judicial Administration: Patrick Creamer 382-6657
Director of Management Information Services: Jeffrey A. Miller 382-5077
Director of Information and Publications: Linda P. Dodd 382-5437

SMITHSONIAN INSTITUTION
1000 Jefferson Dr. S.W., Washington, D.C. 20560
202-628-4422

The Smithsonian Institution administers a number of government programs placed under its control by the Congress and funded by federal appropriations. The institution itself is a federally chartered, nonprofit corporation. It receives and administers contracts and grants and accepts gifts and bequests from both private and public sources. These activities are administered in its capacity as a private organization. The Smithsonian's functions are both private and governmental.

The institution performs fundamental research; publishes the results of studies, explorations, and investigations; preserves for study and reference over 60 million items of scientific, cultural, and historical interest; and engages in programs of education and national and international cooperative research and training.
Secretary: S. Dillon Ripley   202-381-5005

NATIONAL MUSEUM OF NATURAL HISTORY

The museum serves as a national and international center for the natural sciences. Its fundamental studies in systematics and biology provide new information required for the solution of major national problems of conservation and pollution, food protection, improvement of medical knowledge; for planning national and international programs leading to predictive ecology and environmental management; and for furnishing basic information to the scientific community and researchers engaged in environmental studies. Among the wide variety of additional programs, the institution participates in joint educational programs with universities by teaching courses, training graduate students, conducting science seminars, and providing leadership in the improvement of museum techniques, and data storage and retrieval.
Director: Daniel J. Boorstin   202-381-5785

NATIONAL ZOOLOGICAL PARK
Adams Mill Rd., Washington, D.C. 20009
202-265-1868

The park covers an area of approximately 168 acres in Rock Creek Valley. Research objectives include investigations in animal behavior, ecology, maintenance of wild populations and long-term captive breeding and care of endangered species.
Director: Theodore H. Reed   202-265-1868
Assistant Director, Zoological Programs: F. M. Garner   265-1868

RADIATION BIOLOGY LABORATORY
12441 Parklawn Dr., Rockville, Md. 20852
301-443-2306

The laboratory is engaged in the study of basic problems of radiation biology at the cellular, subcellular, and molecular levels.
Director: William H. Klein   301-443-2306
Assistant Director: W. Shropshire, Jr.   443-2306

SMITHSONIAN TROPICAL RESEARCH INSTITUTE
Box 2072, Balboa, Canal Zone
BAlboa 2-2485

The institute, a research organization devoted to the study and support of tropical biology, education, and conservation, focuses broadly on the evolution of patterns of behaviors and ecological adaptations. The institute operates a live-in laboratory on Barro Colorado Island and an inland laboratory in Ancon including one of the world's finest tropical biology laboratories. In addition, there are two marine biology laboratories.
Director: Martin Moynihan
Assistant Director: Ira Rubinoff

SMITHSONIAN SCIENCE INFORMATION EXCHANGE
1730 M St. N.W., Washington, D.C. 20036
202-381-5511

The exchange receives, organizes, and disseminates information about research in progress in the life, physical, and social sciences. It informs individual investigators about others currently working on problems in their special fields. It offers, for a fee, subject searches and administrative information searches, periodic dissemination of subject information, historical searches, investigator searches, accession number searches, standard tabulations, and magnetic tape data.
President: David Hersey   202-381-5511

OFFICE OF ENVIRONMENTAL SCIENCES
Rm. 3300, L'Enfant, Smithsonian Institution, Washington, D.C. 20560
202-381-5365

The office supports research and education concerned with ecological problems through its programs in ecology, oceanography, and limnology. Ecological studies are also conducted by its Chesapeake Bay Center for Environmental Studies and Center for Short-Lived Phenomena.

Director: William L. Eilers   381-5365
Director, Ecology Program: Dr. Dale W. Jenkins   381-5945
Director, Center for Natural Areas: Stephen L. Keiley   381-6204
Program Manager, International Environmental Assessment Studies: Peter H. Freeman   381-5947
Director, Oceanography and Limnology Program: Dr. Robert Higgins   381-6571
Deputy Director, Oceanography and Limnology Program: Dr. David Young   381-6571
Acting Director, Oceanographic Sorting Center (Navy Yard Annex Bldg. 159, Smithsonian Institution, Washington, D.C. 20560): Dr. Richard Houbrick   381-5642
Program Manager, Peace Corps Environmental Program: Robert Poole   381-5058

TENNESSEE VALLEY AUTHORITY
Woodward Bldg., 15 and H Sts. N.W., Washington, D.C. 20444
202-343-4537

The purpose of the Tennessee Valley Authority (TVA) is to conduct a unified program of resource conservation, development, and use to speed the economic development of the Tennessee Valley region, and to advance its national defense capabilities.

The TVA has built dams on the Tennessee River and its larger tributaries. It provides flood regulation on the rivers, operates the river control system, and investigates the need for and feasibility of additional river control projects. It gives assistance to state and local governments in reducing local flood problems.

The TVA is a wholesale power supplier for 160 local municipal and cooperative electric systems. It supplies power to several federal installations and industries whose power requirements are large or unusual. Power to meet these demands is supplied from twenty-nine dams and eleven stream plants operated by TVA, seven Corps of Engineers dams in the Cumberland Valley, and twelve Aluminum Company of America dams whose operation is coordinated with the TVA system.

The TVA operates a national laboratory for development of new and improved fertilizers and processes at Muscle Shoals, Ala. Research results are made available to industry. In cooperation with other agencies, TVA conducts research and development programs in forestry, fish and game, watershed protection, health services related to its operation, and economic development of Tennessee Valley tributary areas through citizen associations. In the western part of the valley, TVA is developing Land Between the Lakes as a demonstration project in outdoor recreation and conservation education.
Chairman: Aubrey J. Wagner   202-343-4537
Director, Environment Planning Division (713 Edney Bldg., Chattanooga, Tenn. 37401): F. E. Gartrell   615-755-3011
Director, Forestry, Fisheries, and Wildlife Development Div. (Norris, Tenn. 37828): Thomas H. Ripley   615-755-3011
Director, Information Office (333 New Sprankle Bldg., Knoxville, Tenn. 37902): Paul L. Evans   615-637-0101
Washington Representative: Jacob D. Vreeland   202-343-4537

COMMITTEES, COMMISSIONS, ETC.

MIGRATORY BIRD CONSERVATION COMMISSION
Department of the Interior Bldg., Washington, D.C. 20240
202-343-4676

The commission was created to consider and pass upon any area of land and/or water that may be recommended by the secretary of the interior for purchase or rental for migratory bird refuges.
Secretary: Walter R. McAllester

MISSISSIPPI RIVER COMMISSION
Corps of Engineers, U.S. Army, Box 80, Vicksburg, Miss. 39180
601-636-1311

The commission was created to coordinate planning and engineering for the improvement of the Mississippi River. Subsequent legislation made the commission responsible for the construction of a project to control floods in the alluvial valley of the lower Mississippi River and for improving navigation from Cairo, Illinois, to New Orleans, Louisiana.
Executive Assistant: E.P. Blankenship

NATIONAL FOREST RESERVATION COMMISSION
1621 Kent St., Arlington, Va. 22209
703-557-9170

The commission was established to consider and pass upon lands recommended by the secretary of agriculture for acquisition as national forests by purchase or exchange under the act (36 Stat. 962; 16 U.S.C. 513).
Secretary: Gerald W. Van Gilst

NATIONAL PARK FOUNDATION
Department of the Interior Bldg., Washington, D.C. 20240
202-343-6578

The foundation, a nonprofit, tax-exempt corporation, was established to accept and administer gifts of any nature for the benefit of or in connection with the National Park Service, its activities or its services.
Assistant Secretary: John L. Bryant, Jr.

NATIONAL WATER COMMISSION
800 N. Quincy St., Arlington, Va. 22203
703-557-1960

The commission was established to consider ways of meeting national water requirements in the future, including more efficient use of water, reduction of water pollution, interbasin transfers, and the use of various technological advances such as weather modification and desalinization; to consider economic, social and esthetic consequences of water resources development; and to advise on such specific water resources matters as may be referred by the president and the Water Resources Council, and to submit reports on its studies to the president and the Congress.
Executive Director: Theodore M. Schad

WATER RESOURCES COUNCIL
2120 L St. N.W., Washington, D.C. 20037
202-254-6303

The council was established to maintain a continuing study of the adequacy of supplies of water necessary to meet the requirements in each water resource region in the United States, of the relation of regional or river basin plans and programs to the requirements of larger regions of the nation, and of the adequacy of administrative and statutory means for the coordination of the water and related land resources policies and programs of the several federal agencies. The council also reviews the plans of the river basin commissions and transmits these plans with its recommendations to the president for his review and transmittal by him to Congress. It administers a program of federal financial grants to states to aid them in comprehensive water and related land resource planning.
Director: W. Don Maughan

QUASI-OFFICIAL AGENCIES

NATIONAL ACADEMY OF SCIENCES–NATIONAL ACADEMY OF ENGINEERING–NATIONAL RESEARCH COUNCIL
2101 Constitution Ave. N.W., Washington, D.C. 20418
202-393-8100

The National Academy of Sciences

The National Academy of Sciences (NAS) is an organization of distinguished scientists and engineers dedicated to the furtherance of science and its use for the general welfare. Although not a governmental agency, the academy has long enjoyed close relations with the federal government.
President: Philip Handler 202-961-1231
Executive Officer: John S. Coleman 961-1234

The National Academy of Engineering

The National Academy of Engineering (NAE) shares in the objectives and responsibilities of the NAS by bringing to bear the leadership of the nation's most eminent engineers in sponsoring engineering programs aimed at meeting national needs, encouraging engineering research, and advising the federal government upon request in matters of engineering.
President: Clarence H. Linder 202-961-1868
Executive Officer: J. H. Mulligan, Jr. 961-1658

The National Research Council

The National Research Council (NRC) was organized by the NAS to facilitate the participation of a broader representation of scientists and technologists in carrying out its objectives. The NRC now serves the NAE and the Institute of Medicine in a similar capacity and has become, in effect, the principal operating agency for both academies and the institute. The purpose of the council is to stimulate research in the mathematical, physical, and biological sciences, and in the application of these sciences to engineering, agriculture, medicine, and other useful arts, with the object of increasing knowledge, of strengthening the national defense, and of contributing in other ways to the public welfare.

The council does not maintain laboratories of its own but seeks to stimulate and support the work of individual scientists and engineers and to coordinate investigations dealing with broad problems in research both nationally and internationally.

Chairman: Philip Handler   202-961-1231
Executive Officer: John S. Coleman   961-1234
Chairman, Div. of Biology and Agriculture: Donald Farner   961-1200
Chairman, Div. of Earth Sciences: Allan V. Cox   961-1204
Chairman, Div. of Engineering: Ernst Weber   961-1331
Chairman, Div. of Physical Sciences: Roman Smoluchowski   961-1237
Director, Office of Information: Howard J. Lewis   961-1518
    Public Information Officer: Bradley Byers   961-1511

Boards, Committees, Etc.

Aeronautics and Space Engineering Board. Executive Director: LaRae Teel   961-1356
Agricultural Research Institute. Staff Officer: Harvey Sheppard   961-1437
Arctic Science and Technology, Committee on. Executive Secretary: Maurice Rifkin   961-1744
Atmospheric Pollutants, Committee on Biologic Effects of. Executive Director: T. D. Boaz   961-1805
Atmospheric Sciences, Committee on. Executive Secretary: John Sievers   961-1395
Bureau of Mines, Committee Advisory to the. Executive Secretary: Dana Stewart   961-1502
Climatic Impact Committee. Executive Secretary: William Bartley   961-1479
Effects of Herbicides, Committee on. Executive Secretary: Philip Ross   961-1762
Environmental Engineering, Committee on. Staff Officer: Frances Hightower   961-1438
Environmental Studies Board. Executive Director: Richard A. Carpenter   961-1861
Global Atmospheric Research Program, U.S. Committee for the. Executive Secretary: John Sievers   961-1395
    Executive Scientist: David Rodenhuis   961-1619
Hazardous Materials, Advisory Committee to the U.S. Coast Guard on. Staff Officer: Howard Fawcett   961-1579
Highway Research Board (Joseph Henry Bldg., 2100 Pennsylvania Ave. N.W., Washington, D.C. 20037). Executive Director: W. N. Carey, Jr.   961-1336
Maritime Transportation Research Board (Joseph Henry Bldg.). Executive Director: John Oren   961-1440
Mineral Resources and the Environment, Committee on. Executive Secretary: Joseph Berg, Jr.   961-1204
Motor Vehicle Emissions, Committee on (Joseph Henry Bldg.). Executive Director: John E. Nolan   961-1621
Nuclear Science, Committee on (Joseph Henry Bldg.). Executive Secretary: Charles Reed   961-1581
Ocean Affairs Board (Joseph Henry Bldg.). Executive Secretary: Richard Vetter   961-1394
Polar Research, Committee on (Joseph Henry Bldg.). Executive Secretary: Louis DeGoes   961-1496
Pollution Abatement and Control, Committee on (Joseph Henry Bldg.). Executive Secretary: Robert Crozier   961-1701
Radioactive Waste Management, Committee on (Joseph Henry Bldg.). Staff Officer: Cyrus Klingsberg   961-1727
National Oceanic and Atmospheric Administration (Joseph Henry Bldg.). Executive Secretary: Kent Howard   961-1363
Significance of Community in the Metropolitan Environment, Panel on (Joseph Henry Bldg.). Executive Secretary: Vincent Rock   961-1564
Solar Terrestrial Research, Committee on (Joseph Henry Bldg:). Executive Secretary: William Bartley   961-1479
Space Applications Board (Joseph Henry Bldg.). Executive Secretary: Clotaire Woods   961-1858
Toxicological Information Program, Committee on. Staff Officer: Henry S. Parker   961-1393
Toxicology, Advisory Center on (Joseph Henry Bldg.). Director: Ralph Wands   961-1751

Transportation, Committee on (Joseph Henry Bldg.). Executive Secretary: John Fowler 961-1848

Oceanic Resources, Engineering Committee on (Joseph Henry Bldg.). Acting Director: Jack Boller 961-1602

Pacific Science Association (Joseph Henry Bldg.). Staff Officer: Augustus Nasmith, Jr. 961-1532

LEGISLATIVE BRANCH

STANDING COMMITTEES OF THE SENATE

Aeronautical and Space Sciences
Old Senate Office Bldg., Suite 231, Washington, D.C. 20510
202-255-6477
Meets Tuesdays
Chairman: Frank E. Moss
Staff Director: Robert F. Allnutt

Agriculture and Forestry
Old Senate Office Bldg., Suite 324, Washington, D.C. 20510
202-255-2035
Meets first and third Wednesdays
Chairman: Herman E. Talmadge
Chief Clerk: Cotys M. Mouser

    Environment, Soil Conservation and Forestry Subcommittee
    Chairman: James O. Eastland
    Ranking Minority Member: Jesse A. Helms

    Rural Development Subcommittee
    Chairman: Dick Clark
    Ranking Minority Member: Carl T. Curtis

Appropriations
New Senate Office Bldg., Suite 1235, Washington, D.C. 20510
202-255-3471
Meets upon call of chairman
Chairman: John L. McClellan
Chief Clerk: Thomas J. Scott

    Agriculture, Environmental and Consumer Protection Subcommittee
    Chairman: Gale W. McGee
    Ranking Minority Member: Hiram L. Fong

    Housing and Urban Development, Space, Science, Veterans Subcommittee
    Chairman: William Proxmire
    Ranking Minority Member: Charles McC. Mathias, Jr.

    Interior Subcommittee
    Chairman: Alan Bible
    Ranking Minority Member: Ted Stevens

    Labor; Health, Education, and Welfare Subcommittee
    Chairman: Warren G. Magnuson
    Ranking Minority Member: Norris Cotton

    Public Works, AEC Subcommittee
    Chairman: John C. Stennis
    Ranking Minority Member: Mark O. Hatfield

    Transportation Subcommittee
    Chairman: Robert C. Byrd
    Ranking Minority Member: Clifford P. Case

Armed Services
Old Senate Office Bldg., Suite 212, Washington, D.C. 20510
202-255-3871
Meets Thursday
Chairman: John C. Stennis
Chief Counsel and Staff Director: T. Edward Braswell, Jr.

    Nuclear Test Ban Treaty Safeguards Subcommittee
    Chairman: Henry M. Jackson
    Ranking Minority Member: Vacant

Banking, Housing, and Urban Affairs
New Senate Office Bldg., Suite 5300, Washington, D.C. 20510
202-255-7391
Meets last Tuesday
Chairman: John J. Sparkman
Staff Director and General Counsel: Dudley L. O'Neal

    Housing Subcommittee
    Chairman: John J. Sparkman
    Ranking Minority Member: John G. Tower

Commerce
New Senate Office Bldg., Suite 5202, Washington, D.C. 20510
202-255-5115

Meets first and third Tuesdays
Chairman: Warren G. Magnuson
Staff Director: Frederick J. Lordan

    Aviation Subcommittee
    Chairman: Howard W. Cannon
    Ranking Minority Member: Norris Cotton

    Communications Subcommittee
    Chairman: John O. Pastore
    Ranking Minority Member: Howard H. Baker, Jr.

    Consumer Subcommittee
    Chairman: Frank E. Moss
    Ranking Minority Member: Marlow W. Cook

    Environment Subcommittee
    Chairman: Philip A. Hart
    Ranking Minority Member: Marlow W. Cook

    Merchant Marine Subcommittee
    Chairman: Russell B. Long
    Ranking Minority Member: J. Glenn Beall, Jr.

    Oceans and Atmosphere Subcommittee
    Chairman: Ernest F. Hollings
    Ranking Minority Member: Ted Stevens

    Surface Transportation Subcommittee
    Chairman: Vance Hartke
    Ranking Minority Member: James B. Pearson

Interior and Insular Affairs
New Senate Office Bldg., Suite 3106, Washington, D.C. 20510
202-255-4971
Meets third Wednesday
Chairman: Henry M. Jackson
Staff Director: Jerry T. Verkler

    Minerals, Materials, and Fuels Subcommittee
    Chairman: Lee Metcalf
    Ranking Minority Member: James L. Buckley

    Parks and Recreation Subcommittee
    Chairman: Alan Bible
    Ranking Minority Member: Clifford P. Hansen

    Public Lands Subcommittee
    Chairman: Floyd K. Haskell

    Ranking Minority Member: James A. McClure

    Territories and Insular Affairs Subcommittee
    Chairman: J. Bennett Johnston, Jr.
    Ranking Minority Member: Paul J. Fannin

    Water and Power Resources Subcommittee
    Chairman: Frank Church
    Ranking Minority Member: Mark O. Hatfield

Labor and Public Welfare
New Senate Office Bldg., Suite 4230, Washington, D.C. 20510
202-255-5375
Meets second and fourth Thursdays
Chairman: Harrison A. Williams, Jr.
Staff Director: Stewart E. McClure

    Labor Subcommittee
    Chairman: Harrison A. Williams, Jr.
    Ranking Minority Member: Jacob K. Javits

    Health Subcommittee
    Chairman: Edward M. Kennedy
    Ranking Minority Member: Richard S. Schweiker

    National Science Foundation Subcommittee
    Chairman: Edward M. Kennedy
    Ranking Minority Member: Peter H. Dominick

Public Works
New Senate Office Bldg., Suite 4202, Washington, D.C. 20510
202-255-6176
Meets first and third Thursdays
Chairman: Jennings Randolph
Chief Counsel and Chief Clerk: M. Barry Meyer

    Air and Water Pollution Subcommittee
    Chairman: Edmund S. Muskie
    Ranking Minority Member: James L. Buckley

    Economic Development Subcommittee
    Chairman: Joseph M. Montoya
    Ranking Minority Member: James A. McClure

    Water Resources Subcommittee
    Chairman: Mike Gravel
    Ranking Minority Member: William Lloyd Scott

Roads Subcommittee
Chairman: Lloyd M. Bentsen, Jr.
Ranking Minority Member: Robert T. Stafford

Disaster Relief Subcommittee
Chairman: Quentin N. Burdick
Ranking Minority Member: Pete B. Domenici

STANDING COMMITTEES OF THE HOUSE

Agriculture
Longworth House Office Bldg., Suite 1301, Washington, D.C. 20515
202-255-2171
Meets first Tuesday
Chairman: W. R. Poage
Chief Clerk: Christine S. Gallagher

Forests Subcommittee
Chairman: John R. Rarick
Ranking Minority Member: George A. Goodling

Appropriations
Capitol Bldg., Suite H218, Washington, D.C. 20515
202-255-2771
Meets first Wednesday and upon call of chairman
Chairman: George H. Mahon
Clerk and Staff Director: Keith F. Mainland

Agriculture, Environmental and Consumer Protection Subcommittee
Chairman: Jamie L. Whitten
Ranking Minority Member: Mark Andrews

Housing and Urban Development, Space, Science, Veterans Subcommittee
Chairman: Edward P. Boland
Ranking Minority Member: Burt L. Talcott

Interior Subcommittee
Chairman: Julia Butler Hansen
Ranking Minority Member: Joseph M. McDade

Labor; Health, Education, and Welfare Subcommittee
Chairman: Daniel J. Flood
Ranking Minority Member: Robert H. Michel

Legislative Subcommittee
Chairman: Bob Casey
Ranking Minority Member: Louis C. Wyman

Public Works Subcommittee
Chairman: Joe L. Evins
Ranking Minority Member: John J. Rhodes

Transportation Subcommittee
Chairman: John J. McFall
Ranking Minority Member: Silvio O. Conte

Banking and Currency
Rayburn House Office Bldg., Suite 2129, Washington, D.C. 20515
202-255-4247
Meets first and third Tuesdays
Chairman: Wright Patman
Clerk and Staff Director: Paul Nelson

Housing Subcommittee
Chairman: William A. Barrett
Ranking Minority Member: William B. Widnall

Consumer Affairs Subcommittee
Chairman: Leonor D. (Mrs. John B.) Sullivan
Ranking Minority Member: Chalmers P. Wylie

Urban Mass Transit Subcommittee
Chairman: Joseph G. Minish
Ranking Minority Member: Garry Brown

Interior and Insular Affairs
Longworth House Office Bldg., Suite 1324, Washington, D.C. 20515
202-255-2761
Meets Wednesday
Chairman: James A. Haley
Staff Director and Chief Clerk: Sidney L. McFarland

Environment Subcommittee
Chairman: Morris K. Udall
Ranking Minority Member: Philip E. Ruppe

National Parks and Recreation Subcommittee
Chairman: Roy A. Taylor
Ranking Minority Member: Joe Skubitz

Water and Power Resources Subcommittee
Chairman: Harold T. Johnson
Ranking Minority Member: Craig Hosmer

Territorial and Insular Affairs Subcommittee
Chairman: Phillip Burton
Ranking Minority Member: Don H. Clausen

Mines and Mining Subcommittee
Chairman: Patsy T. Mink
Ranking Minority Member: John N. Happy Camp

Public Lands Subcommittee
Chairman: John Melcher
Ranking Minority Member: Sam Steiger

Interstate and Foreign Commerce
Rayburn House Office Bldg., Suite 2125, Washington, D.C. 20515
202-255-2927
Meets Tuesday and on call of chairman
Chairman: Harley O. Staggers
Clerk: W. E. Williamson

Communications and Power Subcommittee
Chairman: Torbert H. Macdonald
Ranking Minority Member: Clarence J. Brown

Public Health and Environment Subcommittee
Chairman: Paul G. Rogers
Ranking Minority Member: Ancher Nelsen

Transportation and Aeronautics Subcommittee
Chairman: John Jarman
Ranking Minority Member: James Harvey

Merchant Marine and Fisheries
Longworth House Office Bldg., Suite 1334, Washington, D.C. 20515
202-255-4047
Meets first Tuesday
Chairman: Leonor Kretzer (Mrs. John B.) Sullivan
Chief Clerk: Frances P. Still

Merchant Marine Subcommittee
Chairman: Frank M. Clark
Ranking Minority Member: William S. Mailliard

Fisheries and Wildlife Conservation and the Environment Subcommittee
Chairman: John D. Dingell
Ranking Minority Member: George A. Goodling

Coast Guard and Navigation Subcommittee
Chairman: John M. Murphy
Ranking Minority Member: Philip E. Ruppe

Oceanography Subcommittee
Chairman: Thomas N. Downing
Ranking Minority Member: Charles A. Mosher

Public Works
Rayburn House Office Bldg., Suite 2165, Washington, D.C. 20515
202-255-4472
Meets first Tuesday
Chairman: John A. Blatnik
Chief Counsel: Richard J. Sullivan

Water Resources Subcommittee
Chairman: Ray Roberts
Ranking Minority Member: Don H. Clausen

Transportation Subcommittee
Chairman: John C. Kluczynski
Ranking Minority Member: William H. Harsha

Public Buildings and Grounds Subcommittee
Chairman: Kenneth J. Gray
Ranking Minority Member: James R. Gorver, Jr.

Energy Subcommittee
Chairman: James J. Howard
Ranking Minority Member: Gene Snyder

Science and Astronautics
Rayburn House Office Bldg., Suite 2321, Washington, D.C. 20515
202-255-6371
Meets Tuesday
Chairman: Olin E. Teague
Executive Director and Chief Counsel: Charles F. Ducander

Aeronautics and Space Technology Subcommittee
Chairman: Ken Hechler
Ranking Minority Member: John W. Wydler

Science, Research, and Development Subcommittee
Chairman: John W. Davis
Ranking Minority Member: Alphonzo Bell

Space Science and Applications Subcommittee
Chairman: James W. Symington
Ranking Minority Member: Marvin L. Esch

International Cooperation in Science and Space
Chairman: Richard T. Hanna
Ranking Minority Member: Louis Frey, Jr.

Energy Subcommittee
Chairman: Mike McCormack
Ranking Minority Member: Barry M. Goldwater, Jr.

STATE GOVERNMENT

ALABAMA

Dept. of Agriculture and Industry, Agricultural Chemistry Div.
Box 33356, Montgomery, Ala. 36009
205-269-6164
(Pesticides research and regulation)
Director: John J. Kirkpatrick

Dept. of Conservation and Natural Resources
64 N. Union St., Montgomery, Ala. 36104
205-269-7221
Commissioner: Claude D. Kelley

GAME AND FISH DIV.
Director: Charles D. Kelley
269-6701

INFORMATION AND EDUCATION SECTION
Acting Chief: Robert C. Boone
269-6668

LANDS DIV.
Director: Edward H. Reynolds
269-7361

MARINE RESOURCES DIV.
Box 188, Dauphin Island, Ala. 36528
205-861-2882
Director: William F. Anderson

PARKS DIV.
Director: Condee C. Nason
269-7406

Dept. of Public Health, Environmental Health Bureau
State Office Bldg., Montgomery, Ala. 36104
205-269-7632
Director: W. T. Willis

AIR POLLUTION CONTROL DIV.
645 S. McDonough St., Montgomery, Ala. 36104
205-269-7841
Director: James W. Cooper

GENERAL SANITATION DIV.
Director: Robert V. Barnes
269-7622

PUBLIC WATER SUPPLY DIV.
Director: Joseph E. Downey
269-7624

RADIOLOGICAL HEALTH DIV.
Director: Aubrey V. Godwin
269-7634

SOLID WASTE AND VECTOR CONTROL DIV.
Director: Alfred S. Chipley
269-7697

WATER IMPROVEMENT COMMISSION
Director: James Warr
269-7632

Forestry Commission
513 Madison Ave., Montgomery, Ala. 36104
205-269-6634
State Forester: C.W. Moody

ALASKA

Dept. of Environmental Conservation
Pouch O, Juneau, Alaska 99801
907-586-6721
Commissioner: Max C. Brewer

LAND USE AND URBAN DEVELOPMENT DIV.
Director: Dale Wallington

MARINE AND COASTAL ZONE MANAGEMENT DIV.
Director: Y.R. Nayudu

WATER AND AIR QUALITY CONTROL DIV.
Director: James A. Anderegg

Dept. of Fish and Game
Subport Bldg., Juneau, Alaska 99801
907-586-3392
Commissioner: James W. Brooks

Dept. of Health and Social Services, Radiological Health Program, South Central Regional Office
MacKay Bldg., 338 Denali St., Anchorage, Alaska 99501
907-279-6684

Dept. of Natural Resources
Pouch M, Goldstein Bldg., Juneau, Alaska 99801
907-586-6352
Commissioner: Charles F. Herbert

AGRICULTURAL DIV.
Box 800, Palmer, Alaska 99645
907-745-3236
(Pesticides regulation and information)
Director: William G. Lewis

LANDS DIV.
323 E. Fourth Ave., Anchorage, Alaska 99501
907-279-5577
Director: F. J. Keenan

OIL AND GAS DIV.
3001 Porcupine Dr., Anchorage, Alaska 99504
907-279-1433

PARKS DIV.
6323 E. Fourth Ave., Anchorage, Alaska 99501
907-279-5577

ARIZONA

Atomic Energy Commission
1601 W. Jefferson, Phoenix, Ariz. 85007
602-271-4845
(Radiation control)
Executive Director: Donald C. Gilbert

Dept. of Health
1740 W. Adams, Phoenix, Ariz. 85007
602-271-5571
Commissioner: Louis C. Kossuth, M.D.

AIR POLLUTION CONTROL DIV.
Hayden Plaza West, 4019 N. 33 Ave., Phoenix, Ariz. 85017
Director: Arthur Aymar
602-271-5306

ENVIRONMENTAL HEALTH DIV.
Administrator: Edmund Garth
602-271-4655

SANITATION DIV.
Administrator: John H. Beck
602-271-4642

WATER QUALITY CONTROL DIV.
Administrator: Robert Follett
602-271-5453

Game and Fish Dept.
2222 W. Greenway, Phoenix, Ariz. 85023
602-942-3000
Director: Robert A. Jantzen

Natural Resource Conservation Commission, Land Dept.
400 State Office Bldg., Phoenix, Ariz. 85007
601-271-4621
Commissioner: Andrew L. Bettwy

Office of the State Chemist
University of Arizona Experimental Sta., Box 1586, Mesa, Ariz. 85201
602-964-7182
(Pesticides information)
State Chemist: Floyd Roberts

ARKANSAS

Committee on Stream Preservation
Contact: Mrs. Howard Stern, 2404 West 47 St., Pine Bluff, Ark. 71601
501-534-8281

Dept. of Agriculture, Feeds, Fertilizers, and Pesticides Div., State Plant Board
421½ W. Capitol, Little Rock, Ark. 72203
501-371-1021
Director: Henry DeSalvo

Dept. of Health, Radiological Health Program
4815 W. Markham St., Little Rock, Ark. 72201
501-661-2301
Director: Frank E. Wilson

Dept. of Pollution Control and Ecology
8001 National Dr., Little Rock, Ark. 72209
501-371-1701
(Air, water, solid waste disposal)
Director: S. Ladd Davies

Forestry Commission
3821 Roosevelt Rd., Box 4523, Asher Sta., Little Rock, Ark. 72204
501-371-1731
State Forester: B.G. Gresham

Game and Fish Commission
Game and Fish Commission Bldg., Little Rock, Ark. 72201
501-371-1145
Director: Andrew H. Hulsey

CALIFORNIA

Dept. of Food and Agriculture, Agricultural Chemicals and Feed Div.
1220 N St., Sacramento, Calif. 95814
916-445-2741
(Pesticides regulation and information)
Chief: John C. Hillis

Dept. of Education, Conservation Education Service, Health and Safety Unit
721 Capitol Mall, Sacramento, Calif. 95814
916-445-8010
Consultant: Rudolph J.H. Schafer

Dept. of Health
714 P St., Sacramento, Calif. 95814
916-445-1248
Director: J. M. Stubblebine, M.D.

BUREAU OF SANITARY ENGINEERING
(Solid waste disposal)
Chief: Henry J. Ongerth

RADIOLOGICAL HEALTH PROGRAM
Chief: Simon Kinsman, Ph.D.

Resources Agency
1416 9 St., Sacramento, Calif. 95814
916-445-5656
Secretary: N.B. Livermore, Jr.

AIR RESOURCES BOARD
1025 P St., Sacramento, Calif. 95814
916-322-2892
Chairman: Dr. A.J. Haagen-Smit

CONSERVATION DEPT.
Deputy Director: Ed Ehlers
445-3976

FISH AND GAME COMMISSION
Executive Secretary: Leslie F. Edgerton
445-5708

FISH AND GAME DEPT.
Director: G. Ray Arnett
445-3531

PARKS AND RECREATION DEPT.
Director: William Penn Mott, Jr.
445-2358

SAN FRANCISCO BAY CONSERVATION AND DEVELOPMENT COMMISSION
30 Van Ness Ave., San Francisco, Calif. 94102
415-557-3586
Executive Director: Joseph Bodovitz

STATE RECLAMATION BOARD
Chief Engineer and General Manager: Col. Albert E. McCollam
445-9454

STATE WATER RESOURCES CONTROL BOARD
Chairman: Winifred W. Adams
445-1553

WATER RESOURCES DEPT.
Director: William R. Gianelli
445-6582

WILDLIFE CONSERVATION BOARD
Executive Officer: Raymond J. Nesbit
445-8448

State Land Commission
Rm. 3123, 107 S. Broadway, Los Angeles, Calif. 90012
213-620-3010

COLORADO

Office of the Governor
136 State Capitol Bldg., Denver, Colo. 80203
Assistant to the Governor for Environmental Affairs: John R. Bermingham
303-892-2471

Dept. of Agriculture, Div. of Plant Industry, Pesticides Section
State Services Bldg., 1525 Sherman St., Denver, Colo. 80203
303-892-2838
Supervisor: R.I. Sullivan

Dept. of Health
4210 E. 11 Ave., Denver, Colo. 80220
303-388-6111
Executive Director: Roy L. Cleere, M.D.

AIR POLLUTION CONTROL COMMISSION
Chairman: Dr. James P. Lodge

AIR POLLUTION CONTROL DIV.
Director: Dr. Gerald P. Wood

RADIOLOGICAL HEALTH PROGRAM
Director: Robert Siek

SOLID WASTE CONTROL DIV.
Director: Orville J. Stoddard

WATER POLLUTION CONTROL COMMISSION
Chairman: T.W. Ten Eyck

WATER POLLUTION CONTROL DIV.
Director: Frank Rozich

Dept. of Natural Resources
1845 Sherman, Denver, Colo. 80203
303-892-3311
Director: T.W. Ten Eyck

DIV. OF PARKS AND OUTDOOR RECREATION
6060 Broadway, Denver, Colo. 80216
303-825-1192
Director: George T. O'Malley, Jr.

DIV. OF WILDLIFE
6060 Broadway, Denver, Colo. 80216
303-825-1192
Director: Jack R. Grieb

Forest Service
Colorado State University, Fort Collins, Colo. 80521
303-482-8185
State Forester: Thomas B. Borden

Soil Conservation Board
251 Columbine Bldg., 1845 Sherman St., Denver, Colo. 80203
303-892-3351
Director: Kenneth Kirkpatrick

Water Conservation Board
102 Columbine Bldg., 1845 Sherman St., Denver, Colo. 80203
303-892-3441
Director: Felix L. Sparks

CONNECTICUT

Dept. of Agriculture and Natural Resources
State Office Bldg., Hartford, Conn. 06115
203-566-4667
Commissioner: John T. MacDonald
Open Space Coordinator: Carl N. Otte

AQUACULTURE DIV.
Director: John E. Baker

SOIL AND WATER CONSERVATION DIV.
Chief: Joseph A. Ward, Jr.

Dept. of Environmental Protection
State Office Bldg., 165 Capitol Ave., Hartford, Conn. 06115
Commissioner: Dan W. Lufkin
Deputy Commissioner for Preservation and Conservation: Theodore B. Bampton
Deputy Commissioner for Environmental Quality: Douglas M. Costle

AIR COMPLIANCE UNIT
Director: Eckhart C. Beck

FISH AND WATERLIFE UNIT
Chief: Cole W. Wilds

FORESTRY UNIT
State Forester: Edmund Vandermillen

PARKS AND RECREATION UNIT
Chief: William F. Miller

PESTICIDES COMPLIANCE UNIT
Acting Director: Linda Gardiner

RADIATION COMPLIANCE UNIT
Assistant Director: Arthur T. Heubner

SOLID WASTE MANAGEMENT PROGRAMS
Director: Robert L. Schulz

WATER AND RELATED RESOURCES UNIT
(Water supply)
Director: Stephen C. Thompson

WATER COMPLIANCE AND HAZARDOUS SUBSTANCES UNIT
(Water quality)
Director: Robert B. Taylor

DELAWARE

Dept. of Agriculture, Standards and Inspections Div.
Drawer D, Dover, Del. 19901
302-678-4824
(Pesticides regulation and information)
Director: James Kilvington

Dept. of Health and Social Services, Radiological Health Program
State Health Bldg., D and Federal Sts., Dover, Del. 19901
302-678-4734
Director: E. Lee Stein

Dept. of Natural Resources and Environmental Control
Tatnall Bldg., Legislative Ave. and D St., Dover, Del. 19901
302-678-4403
Secretary: John C. Bryson

ENVIRONMENTAL CONTROL DIV.
Director: N. C. Vasuki
678-4761
Air Resources Section Manager: Robert R. French
(Section also includes solid-waste disposal.)
678-4791
Water Resources Section Manager: Lee F. Beetschen
678-4761

FISH AND WILDLIFE DIV.
Director: Darrell Louder
678-4431

PARKS, RECREATION AND FORESTRY DIV.
Director: Peter Geldoff, Jr.
678-4401

SOIL AND WATER CONSERVATION DIV.
Director: William R. Ratledge
678-4411

DISTRICT OF COLUMBIA

Dept. of Environmental Services
1875 Connecticut Ave. N.W., Washington, D.C. 20009
202-629-3415
Director: James P. Alexander

BUREAU OF AIR AND WATER POLLUTION CONTROL
Chief: John V. Brink
629-3748

ENVIRONMENTAL HEALTH ADMINISTRATION
Director: Malcolm C. Hope
629-3105

FLORIDA

Central and Southern Florida Flood Control District
901 Evernia St., Box 1671, West Palm Beach, Fla. 33402
305-655-3411
(Flood control, water conservation, and wildlife conservation)
Secretary and Executive Director: G.E. Dail, Jr.

Dept. of Administration, Bureau of Land Planning
Miles Johnson Bldg., Tallahassee, Fla. 32304
Chief: Robert Rhodes

Dept. of Agriculture and Consumer Services
The Capitol, Tallahassee, Fla. 32304
904-488-3022
Commissioner: Doyle Conner

FORESTRY DIV.
Collins Bldg., Tallahassee, Fla. 32304
904-488-6961
Director: John M. Bethea
Forest Management Chief: R. A. Bonninghausen

CHEMISTRY DIV.
Director: V. E. Stewart
599-7324

Dept. of Health and Rehabilitative Services, Radiological and Occupational Health Section
Box 210, Jacksonville, Fla. 32201
904-354-3961
Administrator: Dr. Chester L. Nayfield

SANITARY ENGINEERING BUREAU
Chief: Sidney A. Berkowitz
Solid Waste Planning Section Supervisor: J. Benton Druse

Dept. of Natural Resources
Larson Bldg., Gaines St. at Monroe, Tallahassee, Fla. 32304
904-224-7141
Executive Director: Randolph Hodges

COASTAL COORDINATING COUNCIL
Coordinator: Bruce Johnson
904-488-8014

GAME AND FRESH WATER FISH DIV.
Bryant Bldg., Tallahasee, Fla. 32304
904-488-2972
Director: O. Earle Frye, Jr.

INTERIOR RESOURCES DIV.
Director: Dr. Robert O. Vernon
904-488-7500

MARINE RESOURCES DIV.
Director: Harmon Shields
904-488-6559

RECREATION AND PARKS DIV.
Director: Ney C. Landrum
904-488-6131

Dept. of Pollution Control
Montgomery Bldg., 2562 Executive Center, Tallahassee, Fla. 32301
904-488-1836
(Air and water pollution; solid-waste management)
Executive Director: Peter Baljet

Soil and Water Conservation Council
Drawer EE, Gainesville, Fla. 32601
904-376-1990
Acting Coordinator: Lyle C. Dickman

Southwest Florida Water Management District
Box 457, Brooksville, Fla. 33512
Director: Donald R. Feaster, P.E.

GEORGIA

Coastal Plain Area Planning and Development Commission
Box 1223, Valdosta, Ga. 31601
912-244-2048
Executive Director: Hal Davis

Dept. of Agriculture, Feed, Fertilizer, and Pesticides Div.
19 Hunter St. S.W., Atlanta, Ga. 30334
404-656-3637
Director: Cecil R. Spooner

Dept. of Natural Resources
270 Washington St. S.W., Atlanta, Ga. 30334
404-656-3500
Commissioner: Joe D. Tanner

EARTH AND WATER DIVISION
State Agriculture Bldg., Atlanta, Ga. 30334
Director: Sam Pickering

ENVIRONMENTAL PROTECTION DIV.
Rm. 609, 47 Trinity Ave. S.W., Atlanta, Ga. 30334
404-656-4713
Director: R. S. Howard

Air Quality Control Section
116 Mitchell St. S.W., Atlanta, Ga. 30303
404-656-4867
Chief: Robert H. Collom, Jr.

Land Reclamation Section
Box 4845, Macon, Ga. 31208
912-743-5886
Chief: Sanford Darby

Solid Waste Management Section
47 Trinity Ave. S.W., Atlanta, Ga. 30334
404-656-4887
Chief: Moses N. McCall

Water Quality Control Section
47 Trinity Ave. S.W., Atlanta, Ga. 30334
404-656-4807
Chief: Leonard Ledbetter

Water Supply Section
47 Trinity Ave. S.W., Atlanta, Ga. 30334
404-656-4807
Chief: Robert H. Byers

GAME AND FISH DIVISION
270 Washington St. S.W., Atlanta, Ga. 30334
404-656-3523
Director: Jack Crockford

PARKS AND RECREATION DIV.
270 Washington St. S.W., Atlanta, Ga. 30334
404-656-2754
Director: Henry D. Struble

PLANNING AND RESEARCH OFFICE
270 Washington St. S.W., Atlanta, Ga. 30334
404-656-5160
Director: Chuck Parrish

Dept. of Public Health, Radiological Health Service, Div. of Environmental Health
535 Milam Ave. S.W., Atlanta, Ga. 30315
404-894-5795
Director: Richard H. Fetz

Forestry Commission
Box 819, Macon, Ga. 31202
912-746-3531
Director: A. Ray Shirley

Institute of Natural Resources
203 Forestry Bldg., University of Georgia, Athens, Ga. 30601
404-542-1555
Director: E. L. Cheatum
Associate Director for Marine Resources: Edward Chin
Associate Director for Water Resources: Ronald M. North
Associate Director for Biological Resources: A. Sydney Johnson

Natural Areas Council, Dept. of Natural Resources
544 Agriculture Bldg., 7 Hunter St. S.W., Atlanta, Ga. 30303
Chief: Jim Wilson

Slash Pine Area Planning and Development Commission
902 Grove Ave., Box 1276, Waycross, Ga. 31501
912-283-3831
Executive Director: Max W. Harral

Soil and Water Conservation Committee
318 Extension Annex Bldg., Athens, Ga. 30601
404-542-3065
Executive Secretary: Frank E. Stancil

HAWAII

Dept. of Agriculture, Marketing and Consumer Services Div., Economic Poisons Section
Box 5425, Pawaa Sta., Honolulu, Hawaii 96814
808-941-3071
(Pesticides regulation and information)
Supervisor: Stanley M. Tanaka

Dept. of Health
Box 3378, Honolulu, Hawaii 96801
Director, Walter B. Quisenberry, M.D.
Deputy Director for Environmental Programs: Dr. Henri Minette
808-548-4139

ENVIRONMENTAL HEALTH DIV.
(Air and water pollution control, solid waste management)
Executive Officer: Shinji Soneda
548-6455

Air Sanitation Branch
Acting Chief: Paul Aki
548-6355

Noise Control Program
Chief: Sadamoto Iwashita
548-3076

Radiologic Health Program
Chief: Sadamoto Iwashita
548-3075

Sanitary Engineering Branch
(Water pollution control and solid waste management)
Acting Chief: Ralph Yukumoto
548-3077

Dept. of Land and Natural Resources
Box 621, Honolulu, Hawaii 96809
808-548-6550
Chairman: Sunao Kido

FISH AND GAME DIV.
1179 Punchbowl St., Honolulu, Hawaii 96813
808-548-4000
Director: Michio Takata

FORESTRY DIV.
1179 Punchbowl St., Honolulu, Hawaii 96813
808-548-5929
State Forester: Tom K. Tagawa

LAND MANAGEMENT DIV.
Box 621, Honolulu, Hawaii 96809
808-548-7517
Administrator: James J. Detor

STATE PARKS OUTDOOR RECREATION AND HISTORICAL SITES DIV.
Box 621, Honolulu, Hawaii 96809
808-548-7455
Director: Joseph M. Souza, Jr.

WATER AND LAND DEVELOPMENT DIV.
Box 373, Honolulu, Hawaii 96809
808-548-7533
Manager: Robert T. Chuck

IDAHO

Dept. of Agriculture, Bureau of Plant Industry
Box 790, Boise, Idaho 83701
208-384-3240

(Pesticides regulation)
Director: Wallace R. Fisher

Dept. of Environment and Community Service
Statehouse, Boise, Idaho 83707
208-384-2390
Administrator: James A. Bax

ENVIRONMENTAL MANAGEMENT DIV.
(Solid waste management)
Director: Vaughn F. Anderson

ENVIRONMENTAL PROTECTION DIV.
(Air and water pollution control)
Assistant Administrator: Alfred J. Eiguren

RADIATION CONTROL PROGRAM
Chief: Michael Christie

Dept. of Parks
Statehouse, Boise, Idaho 83707
208-384-2154
Director: R. P. Peterson

Dept. of Water Administration
Statehouse Annex 2, Boise, Idaho 83707
208-284-2215
(Public water supply sources, protection of streams)
Director: R. Keith Higginson

Fish and Game Dept.
600 S. Walnut, Box 205, Boise, Idaho 83707
208-384-3700
Director: Joseph C. Greenley

State Soil Conservation Commission
Statehouse, Boise, Idaho 83707
208-384-2148
Administrative Officer: Doyle L. Scott

ILLINOIS

Dept. of Agriculture
531 E. Sangamon Ave., Springfield, Ill. 62706
217-525-7655
(Pesticides regulation and information)
Chief Chemist: Stan Jones

Dept. of Conservation
State Office Bldg., Springfield, Ill. 62706
217-525-6302
Director: Anthony Dean

EDUCATION DIV.
Supervisor: Glenn W. Harper
525-7454

FISHERIES DIV.
Supervisor: William J. Harth
525-6424

FORESTRY DIV.
State Forester: H. F. Siemert
525-2361

LONG-RANGE PLANNING
Supervisor: Bruce Rogers
525-3884

PARKS AND MEMORIALS DIV.
Supervisor: Ronald D. Johnson
525-6752

SITE PLANNING
Supervisor: Gene De Turk
525-3715

WILDLIFE RESOURCES
Supervisor: James M. Lockart
525-6384

Department of Health, Radiological Health Program
535 W. Jefferson St., Springfield, Ill. 62706
217-525-3397
Acting Chief: Jack M. Marco

Environmental Protection Agency
2200 Churchill Rd., Springfield, Ill. 62706
217-525-3397
Director: William L. Blaser

AIR POLLUTION CONTROL DIV.
Chief: John Roberts
525-7326

LAND POLLUTION CONTROL DIV.
Chief: C. E. Clark
525-6270

NOISE POLLUTION CONTROL DIV.
Chief: J. S. Moore
525-3334

PUBLIC WATER SUPPLIES DIV.
Chief: John Anderson
525-2027

WATER POLLUTION CONTROL DIV.
Chief: Verne Hudson
525-6171

Natural History Survey Div.
Natural Resources Bldg., Urbana, Ill. 61801
217-333-6880
(Research dealing with plant and wildlife resources)
Chief: George Sprugel, Jr.

Nature Preserves Commission
819 N. Main St., Rockford, Ill. 61103
815-964-6666
Executive Secretary: George B. Fell

INDIANA

Board of Health
1330 W. Michigan St., Indianapolis, Ind. 46206
317-633-4273
Commissioner: William T. Paynter, M.D.
Assistant Commissioner for Environmental Health: Ralph G. Pickard
317-633-4420

AIR POLLUTION CONTROL BOARD
Technical Secretary: Ralph G. Pickard
317-633-4420

AIR POLLUTION CONTROL DIV.
Director: Harry D. Williams
317-633-4273

RADIOLOGICAL HEALTH DIV.
Acting Director: Hal S. Stocks
317-633-6340

STREAM POLLUTION CONTROL BOARD
Technical Secretary: Oral H. Hert
317-633-5467

WATER POLLUTION CONTROL DIV.
Director: Sam Moore
317-633-4941

Dept. of Natural Resources
State Office Bldg., Indianapolis, Ind. 46204
317-633-6344
Director: Joseph Cloud

FISH AND WILDLIFE DIV.
Director: Richard E. Bass
633-5857

FORESTRY DIV.
State Forester: John Datana
633-6517

INFORMATION AND EDUCATION, OUTDOOR INDIANA
Head: Herbert R. Hill
633-4294

NATURE PRESERVES DIV.
Director: William D. Barnes
633-4382

RESERVOIR MANAGEMENT DIV.
Director: G. T. Donceel, Jr.
633-4629

STATE PARK DIV.
Head: David L. Herbst
633-4192

WATER DIV.
Director: Robert F. Jackson
633-5267

LAND, FORESTS, AND WILDLIFE RESOURCES ADVISORY COUNCIL
Chairman: James Lahey

NATURAL RESOURCES COMMISSION
Chairman: John A. Hillenbrand, II

WATER AND MINERALS RESOURCES ADVISORY COUNCIL
Chairman: Daniel P. Morse

IOWA

Conservation Commission
State Office Bldg., 300 4 St., Des Moines, Iowa 50319
515-281-5145
Director: Fred A. Priewert

FISH AND WILDLIFE DIV.
Chief: Harry M. Harrison
281-5154

LANDS AND WATERS DIV.
Chief: John Stokes
281-5207

Dept. of Agriculture, Pesticide Section, State Chemical Laboratory
E. 7 and Court, Des Moines, Iowa 50319
515-281-5861
Director: M. R. Van Cleave

Dept. of Environmental Quality
Lucas State Office Bldg., Des Moines, Iowa 50319
515-281-3045
(Air and water pollution control, solid waste management, radiological and hazardous materials control)
Executive Director: Kenneth M. Karch

Dept. of Soil Conservation
Grimes State Office Bldg., Des Moines, Iowa 50319
515-281-5851
Director: William H. Greiner

Natural Resources Council
Grimes State Office Bldg., Des Moines, Iowa 50319
515-281-5914
(Programs for water and other resources)
Director: Othie R. McMurry

KANSAS

Biological Survey of Kansas
Dyche Hall, University of Kansas, Lawrence, Kans. 66044
913-864-3369
Director: Frank B. Cross

Board of Agriculture, Control Div.
State Office Bldg., Topeka, Kans. 66612
913-296-3786
Director: Robert H. Guntert

Conservation Commission
Mills Bldg., 109 W. 9 St., Topeka, Kans. 66612
913-296-3600
Secretary: C. F. Bredahl

Dept. of Health, Environmental Health Div.
535 Kansas Ave., Topeka, Kans. 66603
913-296-3821
Director: Melville W. Gray

AIR QUALITY CONTROL SECTION
Chief: Howard F. Saiger
296-3895

RADIATION CONTROL SECTION
Chief: Robert C. Will
296-3821

WATER QUALITY CONTROL BOARD
Chief: N. Jack Burris
296-3825

Forestry, Fish and Game Commission
Box 1028, Pratt, Kans. 67124
316-672-6473
Director: Richard Wettersten

Park and Resources Authority
801 Harrison, Topeka, Kans. 66612
913-296-2281
Director: Lynn Burris, Jr.

State and Extension Forestry
Kansas State University, 2610 Clafin Rd., Manhattan, Kans. 66506
913-532-5752
State Forester: Harold Gallaher

Water Resources Board
Rm. 407, Mills Bldg., 109 W. 9 St., Topeka, Kans. 66612
913-296-3185
Executive Director: Keith Krause

KENTUCKY

Dept. of Agriculture, Fertilizer and Pesticides Program
Kentucky Agricultural Experiment Station, Div. of Regulatory Services, Lexington, Ky. 40506
606-258-2827
Director: Dr. H. Massey

Dept. of Fish and Wildlife Resources
State Office Bldg. Annex, Frankfort, Ky. 40601
502-564-3400
Commissioner: Arnold L. Mitchell

Dept. of Health, Radiological Health Program, Division of Occupational Health
275 E. Main St., Frankfort, Ky. 40601
502-564-3700
Director: Charles M. Hardin

Dept. of Natural Resources and Environmental Protection
Capital Plaza Tower, Frankfort, Ky. 40601
502-564-3350
Commissioner: Thomas O. Harris
Deputy Commissioner for Environmental Quality: Herman Regan
502-564-7030
Deputy Commissioner for Land Resources: John Dixon
502-564-3350

OFFICE OF INFORMATION AND EDUCATION
Capitol Plaza Tower, Fifth Floor, Frankfort, Ky. 40601
564-3350
Executive Assistant: John Anderson

OFFICE OF INVESTIGATION
Capitol Plaza Tower, Fifth Floor, Frankfort, Ky. 40601
564-3350
Chief Investigator: Francis Stockdale

OFFICE OF PLANNING AND RESEARCH
Capitol Plaza Tower, Sixth Floor, Frankfort, Ky. 40601
564-7320
Chief Planner: Robert Nickel

AIR POLLUTION DIV.
311 East Main St., Frankfort, Ky. 40601
564-3382
Director: John Smither

CONSERVATION DIV.
564-3080
Director: W. C. Gayle

FORESTRY DIVISION
564-4496
Director: Harry Nadler

RECLAMATION DIV.
564-6940
Director: John Roberts

SOLID WASTE DIV.
564-6717
Director: Sam Johnson

SPECIAL PROGRAMS DIV.
564-7274
Director: E. T. Reed

WATER POLLUTION DIV.
564-3410
Director: Harold Snodgrass

Water Resources Section
564-3980
Executive Assistant: Oscar McCutchen

Dept. of Parks
Capital Plaza, Plaza Bldg., Frankfort, Ky. 40601
502-564-4260
Commissioner: Ewart W. Johnson

LOUISIANA

Board of Nuclear Energy, Div. of Radiation Control
Box 44033, Capitol Sta., Baton Rouge, La. 70804
504-389-5936
Director: Dr. Roy A. Parker

Dept. of Agriculture
Box 16390-A, Baton Rouge, La. 70803
504-389-5575
(Pesticides regulation and information)
Chief Chemist: Ernest A. Epps, Jr.

Dept. of Conservation
Box 44275, Capitol Sta., Baton Rouge, La. 70804
504-389-5161
Commissioner: R. T. Sutton

Forestry Commission
Box 15239, Broadview Sta., Baton Rouge, La. 70815
504-389-7361
State Forester: James E. Mixon

Health, Social, and Rehabilitative Services Administration, Bureau of Environmental Health
Box 60630, New Orleans, La. 70160
504-527-5115
Director: John E. Trygg

AIR CONTROL AND OCCUPATIONAL HEALTH DIV.
Head: Vernon C. Parker

LOUISIANA AIR CONTROL COMMISSION
Chairman: John E. Trygg

PUBLIC HEALTH ENGINEERING DIV.
(Water pollution control)
Director: John E. Trygg

State Parks and Recreation Commission
Drawer 1111, Baton Rouge, La. 70821
504-389-5761
Director: Gilbert C. Lagasse

Wildlife and Fisheries Commission
400 Royal St., New Orleans, La. 70130
504-527-5126
Director: J. Burton Angelle

FISH DIV.
Box 44095, Capitol Station, Baton Rouge, La. 70804

504-389-5351
Chief: Kenneth Smith

GAME DIV.
Box 44095, Capitol Sta., Baton Rouge, La. 70804
504-389-5351
Chief: Joe L. Herring

OYSTER, WATER BOTTOMS, AND SEAFOOD DIV.
Chief: Harry Schafer

REFUGE DIVISION
Chief: Allan Ensminger

WATER POLLUTION CONTROL DIV.
Drawer FC, University Sta., Baton Rouge, La. 70803
504-389-5309
Chief: Robert A. LaFleur

MAINE

Dept. of Agriculture, Div. of Consumer Protection
State Office Bldg., Augusta, Maine 04330
207-289-3841
(Pesticides information and regulation)
Director: C. P. Osgood

Dept. of Environmental Protection
State House, Augusta, Maine 04330
207-289-2811
Commissioner: William R. Adams, Jr.

AIR QUALITY CONTROL BUREAU
Director: Frederick C. Pitman
289-3762

BOARD OF ENVIRONMENTAL PROTECTION
State House, Augusta, Maine 04330
Chairman: William R. Adams, Jr.
289-2811

LAND QUALITY CONTROL BUREAU
Director: Henry E. Warren
289-3762

WATER QUALITY CONTROL BUREAU
Director: George C. Gormley
289-2591

Dept. of Conservation
State House, Augusta, Maine 04330
Commissioner: Donaldson Koons

FORESTRY BUREAU
289-2791

GEOLOGY BUREAU
308 State St., Augusta, Maine 04330
289-2801
Director: Robert G. Doyle

LAND USE REGULATION COMMISSION
35 Capitol St., Augusta, Maine 04330
289-2631
Director: James S. Haskell

PARKS AND RECREATION BUREAU
State Office Bldg., Augusta, Maine 04330
289-3821

Dept. of Health and Welfare, Bureau of Health
State House, Augusta, Maine 04330
Director: Peter J. Leadley, M.D.
289-3826

RADIOLOGICAL HEALTH PROGRAM
Director: Donald C. Hoxie
289-3826

SANITARY ENGINEERING DIV.
(Solid waste management)
Director: Earle W. Tibbetts
289-3826

Dept. of Inland Fisheries and Game
State Office Bldg., Augusta, Maine 04330
207-289-3371
Commissioner: Maynard F. Marsh

Dept. of Marine Resources
State House Annex, Augusta, Maine 04330
207-289-2291
Commissioner: Spencer Apollonio

Soil and Water Conservation Commission
State House, Augusta, Maine 04330
207-289-2666
Chairman: Lionel C. Ferland
Executive Director: Charles L. Boothby

MARYLAND

Dept. of Agriculture, State Inspection Service
University of Maryland, College Park, Md. 20742
301-454-2721
(Pesticides regulation and information)
State Chemist: A. B. Heagy

Dept. of Health and Mental Hygiene, Environmental Health Administration
610 N. Howard St., Baltimore, Md. 21201
301-383-2740
Director: Howard E. Chaney

AIR QUALITY CONTROL ADVISORY BOARD
Chairman: Dr. Joseph M. Marchello
383-2779

AIR QUALITY CONTROL BUREAU
Acting Director: George P. Ferreri
383-2779

RADIOLOGICAL HEALTH PROGRAM
383-2747
Chief: Robert E. Corcoran

Dept. of Natural Resources
Rowe Blvd. and Taylor Ave., Annapolis, Md. 21401
Secretary: James B. Coulter

FISHERIES ADMINISTRATION
Administrator: Robert J. Rubelmann
267-5558

FOREST SERVICE
Director: Adna R. Bond
267-5776

MARYLAND ENVIRONMENTAL SERVICE
Director: Thomas D. McKewen
267-5351

MARYLAND ENVIRONMENTAL TRUST
8 E. Mulberry St., Baltimore, Md. 21202
Director: Paul Allen
383-4264

PARK SERVICE
Director: William A. Parr
267-5761

WATER RESOURCES ADMINISTRATION
Administrator: Herbert M. Sachs
267-5846

WILDLIFE ADMINISTRATION
Administrator: Ralph A. Bitely
267-5195

MASSACHUSETTS

Committee for Soil, Water, and Related Resources, Conservation Services Div., Dept. of Natural Resources
100 Cambridge St., Boston, Mass. 02202
617-727-3171
Director: George R. Sprague

Dept. of Natural Resources
Leverett Saltonstall Bldg., 100 Cambridge St., Boston, Mass. 02202
617-727-3163
Commissioner: Arthur W. Brownell

CONSERVATION SERVICES DIV.
Director: Matthew B. Connolly, Jr.
727-3170

FORESTS AND PARKS DIV.
Director: Bruce S. Gullion
727-3180

MARINE FISHERIES DIV.
Director: Frank Grice
727-3193

WATER POLLUTION CONTROL DIV.
Director: Thomas C. McMahon
727-3855

WATER RESOURCES DIV.
Director: Charles F. Kennedy
727-3267

Dept. of Public Health, Environmental Health Div.
600 Washington St., Boston, Mass. 02111
617-727-5246
Director: John C. Collins

AIR USE MANAGEMENT BUREAU
Director: Gilbert T. Joly

FOOD AND DRUGS DIV.
(Pesticides regulation and information)
Director: George A. Michael
727-2670

RADIOLOGICAL HEALTH PROGRAM
80 Boylston St., Boston, Mass. 01226
617-727-6234
Head: Gerald S. Parker

MICHIGAN

Dept. of Agriculture

LABORATORY DIV.
1615 S. Harrison Rd., East Lansing, Mich. 48823
517-332-0885

(Pesticides research and information)
Chief: C. Colton Carr

SOIL AND WATER CONSERVATION DIV.
Louis Cass Bldg., Lansing, Mich. 48913
517-373-3898
Chief: Donald Schauer

Dept. of Natural Resources
Mason Bldg., Lansing, Mich. 48926
517-355-1220
Director: A. Gene Gazlay

AIR POLLUTION CONTROL DIV.
Chief: Lee E. Jager

ENVIRONMENTAL HEALTH BUREAU
(Solid waste management)
Chief: Fred B. Kellow

FISHERIES DIV.
Chief: Wayne H. Tody
373-1280

FORESTRY DIV.
Chief: T. E. Daw
373-1275

INFORMATION AND EDUCATION DIV.
Chief: William J. Mullendore
373-1214

LANDS DIV.
Chief: Robert G. Wood
373-1246

PARKS DIV.
Chief: O. J. Scherschligt
373-1270

PLANNING SERVICES
Chief: Norman F. Smith
373-1170

WATER DEVELOPMENT SERVICES DIV.
Chief: William D. Marks
373-1950

WATER QUALITY CONTROL DIV.
Chief: Robert Courchaine
373-1947

WILDLIFE DIV.
Chief: Merrill L. Petoskey
373-1263

Dept. of Public Health
3500 N. Logan St., Lansing, Mich. 48914
517-373-1320
Director: Maurice S. Reizen, M.D.

RADIOLOGICAL HEALTH PROGRAM
Chief: Donald E. VanFarowe

Soil Conservation Committee
Rm. 324, Natural Resources Bldg., East Lansing, Mich. 48823
517-355-3346
Executive Secretary: R. G. Hill

Water Resources Commission
Stevens T. Mason Bldg., Lansing, Mich. 48926
517-373-3560
Executive Secretary: Ralph W. Purdy
Chief Environmentalist: C. T. Black

MINNESOTA

Dept. of Agriculture, Division of Agronomy Services
State Office Bldg., St. Paul, Minn. 55101
612-221-6121
(Pesticides regulation and information)
Supervisor: Leo M. Lehn

Dept. of Health, Radiological Health Program
717 Delaware St. S.E., Minneapolis, Minn. 55440
Chief: Alice Dolezal

Dept. of Natural Resources
301 Centennial Bldg., 658 Cedar St., St. Paul, Minn. 55155
612-296-2549
Commissioner: Robert L. Herbst

GAME AND FISH DIV.
Director: Milo Casey
296-2894

INFORMATION AND EDUCATION BUREAU
Administrator: Roger W. Schoenecker
296-3336

LANDS AND FORESTRY DIV.
Director: William Aultfather
296-4484

PARKS AND RECREATION DIV.
Director: Don Davison
296-2531

PLANNING BUREAU
Administrator: Jerome H. Kuehn
296-2941

WATERS, SOILS, AND MINERALS DIV.
Director: Eugene R. Gere
296-2965

Pollution Control Agency
717 Delaware St. S.E., Minneapolis, Minn. 55440
612-378-1320
Executive Director: Grant J. Merritt

AIR QUALITY DIV.
Director: Edward M. Wiik

SOLID WASTES DIV.
Director: Floyd J. Forsberg

WATER QUALITY DIV.
Director: Clarence A. Hohannes

Soil and Water Conservation Commission
318 North Hall, University of Minnesota, St. Paul, Minn. 55101
612-229-3767
Executive Secretary: Marshall W. Qualls

Water Resources Board
Rm. 206, 555 Wabasha St., St. Paul, Minn. 55102
612-296-2840
Administrative Secretary: Erling M. Weiberg

MISSISSIPPI

Air and Water Pollution Control Commission
Robert E. Lee Bldg., Box 827, Jackson, Miss. 39205
601-354-6783
Executive Director: Glen Wood, Jr.

AIR POLLUTION DIV.
Chief: Jerry Stubberfield

WATER POLLUTION DIV.
Chief: John Smith

Board of Health
Underwood State Board of Health Bldg., Box 1700, Jackson, Miss. 39205
601-354-6646
Health Officer: Hugh B. Cottrell, M.D.

RADIOLOGICAL HEALTH UNIT
Supervisor: Eddie S. Fuente
354-6657

SANITARY ENGINEERING DIV.
(Solid waste management)
Director: Joe D. Brown
354-6616

Dept. of Agriculture and Commerce, Div. of Plant Industry
Box 5207, State College, Miss. 30762
601-325-5713
(Pesticides regulation)
Chief Inspector: Jack D. Coley

Forestry Commission
1106 Woolfolk State Office Bldg., Jackson, Miss. 39201
601-355-9361
State Forester: Billy T. Gaddis

Game and Fish Commission
Game and Fish Bldg., 402 High St., Box 451, Jackson, Miss. 39205
601-354-7333
Executive Director: Billy Joe Cross

Soil and Water Conservation Committee
Carthage, Miss. 39041
601-276-9882
Executive Secretary: B. H. Dixon

MISSOURI

Air Conservation Commission
112 High St., Box 1002, Jefferson City, Mo. 65101
314-635-9145
Executive Secretary: Harvey D. Shell

Clean Water Commission, Dept. of Public Health and Welfare
Capitol Bldg., Box 154, Jefferson City, Mo. 65101
314-635-9117
Executive Secretary: Jack K. Smith

Dept. of Agriculture, Plant Industry Div.
Jefferson Bldg., Jefferson City, Mo. 65101
314-636-7166
(Pesticides regulation and information)
Director: Lester H. Barrows

Dept. of Conservation
Box 180, Jefferson City, Mo. 65101
314-751-4115
Director: Carl R. Noren

FISHERIES DIV.
Chief: Charles A. Purkett, Jr.

FORESTRY DIV.
State Forester: Osal B. Capps

GAME DIV.
Chief: Mike Milonski

Dept. of Public Health and Welfare
Broadway State Office Bldg., 221 W. High St., Jefferson City, Mo. 65101
314-635-4111

ENVIRONMENTAL HEALTH SERVICES SECTION
(Solid waste management)
Director: L. F. Garber

RADIOLOGICAL HEALTH PROGRAM
112 W. High St., Box 1002, Jefferson City, Mo. 65101
314-635-4111
Director: E. A. Fullgrabe

MONTANA

Dept. of Fish and Game
Helena, Mont. 59601
406-449-3066
Director: Wesley Woodgerd

ENVIRONMENT AND INFORMATION DIV.
Chief: James A. Posewitz
449-2602

FISHERIES MANAGEMENT
Chief: A. N. Whitney
449-2449

GAME MANAGEMENT
Chief: Wynn Freeman
449-2612

RECREATION AND PARKS
Administrator: Ashley Roberts
449-3066

Dept. of Health and Environmental Sciences
Cogswell Bldg., Helena, Mont. 59601
406-449-2544
Director: John S. Anderson, M.D.

ENVIRONMENTAL SCIENCES DIV.
(Air pollution control, solid waste management, radiation control)
Administrator: Benjamin F. Wake
449-3454

WATER QUALITY BUREAU
Chief: Donald G. Willems
449-2407

Dept. of Natural Resources and Conservation
Sam W. Mitchell Bldg., Helena, Mont. 59601
406-449-3647
Director: Gary J. Wicks

FORESTRY DIV.
2705 Spurgin Rd., Missoula, Mont. 59801
406-728-4300
Administrator: Gareth C. Moon

OIL AND GAS CONSERVATION DIV.
325 Fuller Ave., Helena, Mont. 59601
406-449-2611
Administrator: Norman J. Beaudry

NEBRASKA

Dept. of Agriculture, Feed, Fertilizer, and Pesticide Div.
State House Sta., Lincoln, Nebr. 68509
402-471-5211
Section Head: C. E. McCurry

Dept. of Environmental Control
Box 94653, State House Sta., Lincoln, Nebr. 68509
402-471-2186
Director: James L. Higgins

AIR POLLUTION CONTROL DIV.
Chief: Dennis Grams
473-1553

ENVIRONMENTAL CONTROL COUNCIL
Secretary: James L. Higgins
402-471-2186

SOLID WASTE CONTROL DIV.
Chief: Gayle Lewis

WATER POLLUTION CONTROL DIV.
Chief: Ron Benson

Dept. of Health, Radiological Health Program
State House Sta., Lincoln, Nebr. 68509

402-477-5211
Director: H. Ellis Simmons

Dept. of Water Resources
Lincoln, Nebr. 68509
402-473-1663
Director: Dan S. Jones, Jr.

Game and Parks Commission
2200 N. 33 St., Box 30370, Lincoln, Nebr. 68503
402-434-0641
Director: Willard R. Barbee

Natural Resources Commission
Box 94725, State House Sta., Lincoln, Nebr. 68509
402-471-2081
Executive Secretary: Dayle E. Williamson

NEVADA

Dept. of Agriculture, Plant Industry Div.
350 Capitol Hill Ave., Box 1209, Reno, Nev. 89504
702-784-6401
(Pesticides regulation and information)
Chief Chemist: Harlan Specht

Dept. of Conservation and Natural Resources
Nye Bldg., Carson City, Nev. 89701
702-882-7482
Director: Elmo De Ricco

FORESTRY DIV.
State Forester: George Zappettini
882-7488

OIL AND GAS COMMISSION, BUREAU OF MINES
University Station, Reno, Nev. 89507
702-784-6987
Chairman: Arthur Baker, III

STATE PARKS DIV.
Administrator: Eric R. Cronkhite

WATER RESOURCES DIV.
State Engineer: Roland D. Westergard
882-7441

Dept. of Fish and Game
Box 10678, Reno, Nev. 89510
702-784-6214
Director: Frank W. Groves

Dept. of Health, Welfare, and Rehabilitation, Bureau of Environmental Health, Health Div.
201 S. Fall St., Carson City, Nev. 89701
(Air and water pollution control, solid waste management)
Chief: Ernest G. Gregory

Environmental Protection Commission, State Health Div.
201 S. Fall St., Carson City, Nev. 89701
702-882-7458
Chairman: Elmo J. De Ricco

Soil Conservation Committee
262 W. Winnie Lane, Carson City, Nev. 89701
Secretary: George Zappettini

NEW HAMPSHIRE

Conservation Committee
State House Annex, Concord, N.H. 03301
Chairman: Robert Hacket

Council of Resources and Development
State House Annex, Concord, N.H. 03301
603-271-2155
Chairman: Mary Louise Hancock

Dept. of Agriculture, Pesticide Section
State House Annex, Concord, N.H. 03301
603-271-3550
Pesticide Inspector: Durwood A. French

Dept. of Fish and Game
34 Bridge St., Concord, N.H. 03301
603-271-3421
Director: Bernard W. Corson

CONSERVATION, EDUCATION, AND INFORMATION DIV.
Chief: Richard V. Wentz

GAME MANAGEMENT AND RESEARCH DIV.
Chief: Hilbert R. Siegler

INLAND AND MARINE FISHERIES DIV.
Chief: Richard G. Seamans, Jr.

Dept. of Health and Welfare, Public Health Division
Concord, N.H. 03301
Director: Henry D. Smith, M.D.

AIR POLLUTION CONTROL AGENCY
61 S. Spring St., Concord, N.H. 03301
603-271-2281
Director: Forrest H. Bumford

AIR POLLUTION CONTROL COMMISSION
61 S. Spring St., Concord, N.H. 03301
603-271-2281
Executive Secretary: Forrest H. Bumford

SOLID WASTE MANAGEMENT
Civil Engineer: Thomas Sweeney

Dept. of Resources and Economic Development
State House Annex, Concord, N.H. 03301
603-271-2411
Commissioner: George Gilman

PARKS DIV.
Director: George T. Hamilton
271-3254

RESOURCES DEVELOPMENT DIV.
Director: Theodore Natti
271-2214

WATER RESOURCES BOARD
State House Annex, Concord, N.H. 03301
603-271-3406
Chairman: George M. McGee, Sr.

WATER SUPPLY AND POLLUTION CONTROL COMMISSION
Prescott Park, 105 Loudon Rd., Concord, N.H. 03301
603-271-3502
Executive Secretary: William A. Healy

NEW JERSEY

Dept. of Agriculture, Rural Resources Div.
Box 1888, Trenton, N.J. 08625
609-292-5532
Acting Director: Richard D. Chumney

Dept. of Environmental Protection
Labor and Industry Bldg., Box 1390, Trenton, N.J. 08625
609-292-2885
Commissioner: Richard J. Sullivan

ENVIRONMENTAL QUALITY DIV.
Acting Director: Richard D. Goodenough
292-5383

Air Pollution Control Bureau
Chief: William A. Munroe
292-6704

Noise Control Office
Head: Edward J. DiPolvere
292-7695

Pesticide Control Office
Head: George Beyer
292-5890

Radiation Protection Bureau
Chief: John Russo
292-5588

Solid Waste Management Bureau
Chief: Bernhardt Lind
292-8609

FISH, GAME, AND SHELLFISHERIES DIV.
Director: Russell A. Cookingham
292-2965

Fish and Game Coordination and Law Enforcement Bureau
Chief: John C. O'Dowd

Fisheries Management Bureau
Chief: Robert A. Hayford

Wildlife Management Bureau
Chief: George N. Alpaugh

MARINE SERVICES DIV.
Acting Director: Thomas O'Neill
292-2795

Marine Lands Management Bureau
Chief: Harold Barker
292-2614

PARKS AND FORESTRY DIV.
Director: Joseph J. Truncer
292-2733

Forestry Bureau
Chief: George R. Moorhead
292-2520

Parks Bureau
Chief: Frank H. Rigg
292-2772

WATER RESOURCES DIV.
Acting Director: George C. Friedel
292-2737
Assistant Director: Ernest Segesser
292-2722

Geology Bureau
Chief: Dr. Kemble Widmer
292-2576

Planning and Management Bureau
Chief: Robert Cyphers
292-2956

Potable Water Bureau
Chief: John Wilford
292-5550

Water Control Bureau
Chief: Dick C. Hofman
292-2373

Water Facilities Operations Bureau
Chief: Michael Galley
292-2298 or 201-638-6121

Water Pollution Control Bureau
Chief: Robert Vincent
292-4091

Soil Conservation Committee, Dept. of Agriculture
Box 1888, Trenton, N.J. 08625
609-292-5540
Executive Secretary: Samuel R. Race

NEW MEXICO

Bureau of Mines and Mineral Resources
Campus Station, Socorro, N. Mex. 87801
505-835-5420
Acting Director: Frank Kottlowski

Dept. of Agriculture, Div. of Inspection
Box 3150, Las Cruces, N. Mex. 88001
505-646-3007
(Pesticides regulation and information)
Chief: William P. Stephens

Dept. of Game and Fish
State Capitol, Santa Fe, N. Mex. 87501
505-827-2651
Director: Ladd S. Gordon

FISHERIES MANAGEMENT DIV.
Chief: R. L. Brashears

GAME MANAGEMENT DIV.
Chief: Walter A. Snyder

Dept. of State Forestry
Box 2167, Santa Fe, N. Mex. 87501
505-268-4374
State Forester: Manuel A. Ortiz

Environmental Improvement Agency
Box 2348, Santa Fe, N. Mex. 87501
505-827-2693
Director: Aaron L. Bond

GENERAL SANITATION SECTION
(Solid waste management)
Chief: Bryan E. Miller
827-2693

OCCUPATIONAL HEALTH, RADIOLOGICAL HEALTH, AND AIR QUALITY SECTION
Chief: Cubia Clayton
827-2813

WATER QUALITY SECTION
Chief: John R. Wright
827-2375

Office of the State Engineer
Bataan Memorial Bldg., Santa Fe, N. Mex. 87501
505-827-2127
(Water resources programs)
State Engineer: S. E. Reynolds

Park and Recreation Commission
Box 1147, Santa Fe, N. Mex. 87501
505-827-2726
Director: Dick Mutz

Soil and Water Conservation Committee
219 State Land Office Bldg., Santa Fe, N. Mex. 87501
505-827-5380
Executive Secretary: James A. Lee, Jr.

NEW YORK

Bureau of Environmental Protection, Dept. of Law, State of New York
80 Centre St., New York, N.Y. 10013
212-488-3475
(Institutes environmental legal actions in cases involving air and water pollution, wildlife, and scenic and natural resources)
Assistant Attorney General in Charge: Philip Weinberg
Environmental Engineer: Peter Skinner

Dept. of Environmental Conservation
50 Wolf Rd., Albany, N.Y. 12201
518-457-3446
Commissioner: James L. Biggane

Government Environmental Agencies

AIR RESOURCES DIV.
Director: Alexander Rihm, Jr.
457-7231

Abatement Planning
Chief: Edward Davis
457-6379

Air Quality Surveillance
Chief: Paul Berry
457-7235

Source Control
Chief: Sidney Marlow
457-5118

Technical Services
Chief: Gerard Blanchard
457-5276

COMMUNICATIONS AND EDUCATION OFFICE
Director: Robert L. McManus
457-2390
Educational Services Director: Holt Bodinson
457-3720

ENVIRONMENTAL ANALYSIS OFFICE
Chief: Terence Curran
457-2223

FISH AND WILDLIFE DIV.
Director: Herbert Doig
457-5690

GENERAL COUNSEL OFFICE
General Counsel: John Hanna
457-4416

LANDS AND FORESTS DIV.
Director: James Preston
457-7430

MARINE AND COASTAL RESOURCES
State University of New York, Bldg. 40, Stony Brook, N.Y. 11790
516-751-7900
Regional Supervisor: Albert Jensen

PLANNING AND RESEARCH
Director: Sidney Schwartz
457-1254

PROGRAM PLANNING OFFICE
Chief: Frederick Howell

PURE WATERS DIV.
Associate Director: Eugene Seebald
457-6674

Industrial Wastes
Chief: Salvatore Pagano
457-3967

Municipal Wastes
Chief: Frank O. Bogedain
457-7496

Water Quality Management
Chief: Donald B. Stevens
457-7360

QUALITY SERVICES DIV.
Director: William Bentley
457-4143

Mineral Resources Bureau
Chief: John Dragonetti
457-7480

Noise Control Bureau
Chief: Frederick Haag
457-1108

Pesticide Control Bureau
Chief: Charles Frommer
457-7482

Radiological Pollution Bureau
Chief: Thomas Cashman
457-6600

SOLID WASTES MANAGEMENT DIV.
Director: Maurice Feldman
457-6603

Recovery, Recycling, and Reuse
Chief: John Mathur
457-3199

WATER MANAGEMENT PLANNING DIV.
Director: Thomas Eichler
457-1952

Water Management Bureau
Chief: Eldred Rich
457-3157

Central Planning Office
Chief: Frederick Howell
457-2672

ENVIRONMENTAL FACILITIES CORP.
50 Wolf Rd., Albany, N.Y. 12201
President: George Humphreys
518-457-4222

State Government 63

Fish and Wildlife Management Board, Dept. of Environmental Conservation
50 Wolf Rd., Albany, N.Y. 12201
Secretary: Eugene Parks
518-457-4193

Office of Parks and Recreation
South Mall, Albany, N.Y. 12223
518-474-0443
Commissioner: Alexander Aldrich

Soil and Water Conservation Committee
142 Emerson Hall, Cornell University, Ithaca, N.Y. 14850
607-256-4420

NORTH CAROLINA

Dept. of Agriculture, Div. of Agricultural Chemistry, Pesticide Branch
Agriculture Bldg., Raleigh, N.C. 27611
919-829-3556
Administrator: William B. Buffaloe

Dept. of Human Resources, Board of Health
Box 2091, Raleigh, N.C. 27602
Director of Health Services: Jacob Koomen, M.D.
919-829-3446

RADIATION PROTECTION PROGRAM
Director: Dayne H. Brown
829-4283

SOLID WASTE AND VECTOR CONTROL, DIV. OF SANITARY ENGINEERING
Branch Head: Sidney H. Usry
829-3586

Dept. of Natural and Economic Resources
112 W. Lane St., Box 27687, Raleigh, N.C. 27611
919-829-4184
Secretary: James E. Harrington, Jr.

EARTH RESOURCES
Director: Stephen Conrad
829-3433

Commercial and Sports Fisheries Div.
Administration Bldg., Raleigh, N.C.
Chief: Ed McCoy

Mineral Resources Div.
Chief: Stephen Conrad
829-3633

Mining Div.
Chief: Craig McKenzie
829-3326

FOREST RESOURCES
Administration Bldg., Raleigh, N.C.
Director: Ralph C. Winkworth
829-4141

RECREATION RESOURCES
Director: James Stevens, Jr.
829-7701

State Parks Div.
Director: Thomas Ellis
829-4181

WATER AND AIR RESOURCES
Director: E. C. Hubbard
829-4740

Air Quality Div.
Chief: James McColman

Water Planning Div.
Chief: Tom Harton

Water Quality Div.
Chief: Darwin Coburn

Waterways and Seashore Program
Chief: R. J. B. Page

Soil and Water Conservation Committee, Dept. of Natural and Economic Resources
112 W. Lane St., Box 27687, Raleigh, N.C. 27611
919-829-4776
Director: S. Grady Lane

Wildlife Resources Commission
Albermarle Bldg., 325 N. Salisbury St., Box 27687, Raleigh, N.C. 27611
919-829-3391
Executive Director: Clyde P. Patton

NORTH DAKOTA

Air Pollution Control Advisory Council
c/o Basin Electric Power Corp., 316 N. 5 St., Bismarck, N. Dak. 58501
Chairman: Lloyd Ernest

Dept. of Game and Fish
2121 Lovett Ave., Bismarck, N. Dak. 58501

701-224-2180
Commissioner: Russell Stuart

Dept. of Health
State Capitol, Bismarck, N. Dak. 58501
701-224-2372
State Health officer: James R. Amos, M.D.

ENVIRONMENTAL ENGINEERING
(Air pollution control, radiation control, solid waste management)
Director: Gene A. Christianson
224-2374

ENVIRONMENTAL HEALTH AND ENGINEERING SERVICES
Chief: W. Van Heuvelen
224-2371

ENVIRONMENTAL SANITATION AND FOOD PROTECTION
Director: Kenneth W. Tardif
224-2382

WATER SUPPLY AND POLLUTION CONTROL
Director: Norman L. Peterson
224-2386

Dept. of Laboratories
Box 937, Bismarck, N. Dak. 58501
701-224-2485
(Pesticides Control Agency)
Director: Ailsa Simonson

Water Commission
State Office Bldg., Bismarck, N. Dak. 58501
701-224-2750
Secretary and State Engineer: Vernon Fahy

OHIO

Dept. of Agriculture, Div. of Plant Industry
Rte. 40, Reynoldsburg, Ohio 43068
614-866-6361
(Pesticides regulation and information)
Chief: Harold L. Porter

Dept. of Health, Radiological Health Program
Box 118, Columbus, Ohio 43216
614-466-8873
Engineer-in-Charge: James C. Wynd

Dept. of Natural Resources
Fountain Square, Columbus, Ohio 43224
614-466-3770
Director: William B. Nye

FORESTRY DIV.
Chief: Ernest J. Gebhart
466-7842

LANDS AND SOIL DIV.
Chief: Richard Jones
466-4910

OIL AND GAS DIV.
Chief: Lyman Dawe
466-3990

RECLAMATION DIV.
Chief: Raymond Lowrie
466-4850

WATER DIV.
Chief: Roy Winkle
466-2646

WATER PLANNING SECTION
Chief: Terry Wakeman
466-7803

WILDLIFE DIV.
1500 Dublin Rd., Columbus, Ohio 43212
614-469-4603
Chief: Dan Armbruster

Environmental Protection Agency
Box 1049, Columbus, Ohio 43216
Director: Ira L. Whitman
614-466-8318

OHIO ENVIRONMENTAL PROTECTION AGENCY
Box 1049, Columbus, Ohio 43216
Director: Ira L. Whitman
614-466-8318
Executive Assistant to the Director: John W. Kroeger
466-7785

Management and Analysis Office
Acting Chief: Toby Portman
466-7220

Ombudsman: Mrs. Adelle Mitchell
466-8972

Public Interest Center
Chief: David Milenthal
466-8508

State Government 65

ADMINISTRATIVE SERVICES
Deputy Director: Donald Britton
466-3743

ENVIRONMENTAL PROGRAMS
Deputy Director: Alan Levin
466-7210

POLICY DEVELOPMENT OFFICE
Deputy Director: Alan Farkas
466-6116

REGULATION AND ENFORCEMENT OFFICE
Deputy Director: Samuel Bleicher
466-8595

AIR AND NEW SOURCE PERMITS RECORDS DIV.
Chief: David Rome
466-3506

DATA SYSTEMS DIV.
Chief: Gaylord Whitney
466-5829

INTERGOVERNMENTAL ADMINISTRATION DIV.
Acting Chief: Robert France
466-8974

LITIGATION AND NPDES PERMIT RECORDS DIV.
Chief: Jack A. Wilson
466-8595

PLANNING DIV.
Chief: H. William Sellers
466-8866

SURVEILLANCE DIV.
Chief: Ernest C. Neal
466-2390

WASTE MANAGEMENT AND ENGINEERING DIV.
Chief: Paul Flanigan
466-8825

OKLAHOMA

Conservation Commission
Rm. 114, State Capitol, Oklahoma City, Okla. 73105
405-521-2384
Executive Director: Leonard A. Solomon

Corporation Commission
Jim Thorpe Bldg., Oklahoma City, Okla. 73105
405-521-2242
Manager, Pollution Abatement: Sam F. Shakely

Dept. of Agriculture
122 State Capitol, Oklahoma City, Okla. 73105
405-521-3868
(Pesticides regulation and information)
Chief, Regulatory Services: Clyde Bower

Dept. of Health
N. E. 10 and Stonewall, Oklahoma City, Okla. 73105
405-271-4200
Commissioner: R. LeRoy Carpenter, M.D.

ENVIRONMENTAL SERVICES
Deputy Commissioner: Loyd F. Pummill

Air Pollution Control Div.
Director: Robert V. Blanche

Radiological Health Program
Director: J. Dale McHard

Solid Waste Management Div.
Director: Calvin Grant

Water Quality Control Div.
Director: Charles D. Newton

Dept. of Pollution Control
N. E. 10 and Stonewall, Oklahoma City, Okla. 73105
405-271-4677
(Overall coordinating agency for state environmental affairs)

Dept. of Wildlife Conservation
1801 N. Lincoln, Box 53465, Oklahoma City, Okla. 73105
405-521-3851
Director: I. H. Standefer

Water Resources Board
2211 N.W. 10, Oklahoma City, Okla. 73112
405-528-7807
Executive Director: Forest Nelson

OREGON

Columbia River Gorge Commission
920 N.E. Seventh Ave., Portland, Oreg. 97232

Dept. of Agriculture, Laboratory Services
635 Capitol St. N.E., Salem, Oreg. 97301
503-364-2171
(Pesticides regulation and information)
Administrator: Virgil Hiatt

Dept. of Environmental Quality
1234 S.W. Morrison, Portland, Oreg. 97207
503-229-5696
Director: Diarmuid O'Scannlain

AIR QUALITY CONTROL DIV.
Director: H. M. Patterson

Dept. of Forestry
Box 2289, Salem, Oreg. 97310
503-378-2560
State Forester: J. E. Schroeder

Dept. of Geology and Mineral Industries
1069 State Office Bldg., Portland, Oreg. 97201
503-229-5580
State Geologist: Raymond E. Corcoran

Dept. of Human Resources, Environmental Health Section, Health Div.
Portland, Oreg.
(Solid waste management, radiation control)
Director: LaVerne S. Miller
Director, Radiological Health Program: Marshall W. Parrott

Environmental Quality Commission
1234 S.W. Morrison St., Portland, Oreg. 97205
503-229-5696
Chairman: B. A. McPhillips

Fish Commission
307 State Office Bldg., Portland, Oreg. 97201
502-229-5667
Director: Thomas E. Kruse

Marine Board
109 Agriculture Bldg., Salem, Oreg. 97310
503-378-3785
Director: Robert F. Rittenhouse

Natural Resources Planning Committee
State Capitol, Salem, Oreg. 97310
503-378-3109
Assistant to the Governor, Natural Resources: Kessler R. Cannon

Soil and Water Conservation Board
217 Agriculture Bldg., Salem, Oreg. 97310
503-378-3810
Director: Bud F. A. Svalberg

State Engineer
1178 Chemeketa St. N.E., Salem, Oreg. 97310
503-378-3740
State Engineer: Chris L. Wheeler

Chief, Hydrological and Climatological Data Collection Resource Inventory: Walter N. Perry
Chief, Watershed Planning: Darrell A. Learn

Water Resources Board
1158 Chemeketa St. N.E., Salem, Oreg. 97310
503-378-3671
Director: Fred D. Gustafson

PENNSYLVANIA

Dept. of Agriculture, Bureau of Foods and Chemistry
2301 N. Cameron St., Harrisburg, Pa. 17120
717-787-4315
(Pesticides regulation and information)
Director: Joseph E. Brennan

Dept. of Environmental Resources
202 Evangelical Press Bldg., Third and Reily Sts., Harrisburg, Pa. 17120
Secretary: Maurice K. Goddard
717-787-2814
Public Information Officer: John G. Hope
717-787-1323
Deputy for Environmental Protection and Regulation: Wesley E. Gilbertson
717-787-5027

AIR QUALITY AND NOISE CONTROL BUREAU
Director: Clark L. Gaulding
787-9702

COMMUNITY ENVIRONMENTAL CONTROL BUREAU
Director: William B. Middendorf
787-9036

FORESTRY BUREAU
Director: Samuel S. Cobb
787-2708

STATE PARKS BUREAU
Director: William C. Forrey
787-6640

WATER QUALITY MANAGEMENT BUREAU
Director: Walter A. Lyon
787-2666

Dept. of Health, Office of Radiological Health
Fulton Bank Bldg., Harrisburg, Pa. 17120
717-787-2480
Director: Thomas M. Gerusky

Fish Commission
Box 1673, Harrisburg, Pa. 17120
717-787-6593
Executive Director: Ralph W. Abele

Game Commission
Box 1567, Harrisburg, Pa. 17120
717-787-3633
Executive Director: Glenn L. Bowers

Conservation Commission, Dept. of Environmental Resources
2301 N. Cameron St., Harrisburg, Pa. 17120
717-787-5267
Executive Secretary: Walter N. Peechatka

RHODE ISLAND

Dept. of Health
Davis St., Providence, R.I. 02908
401-277-2234
Director: Joseph E. Cannon, M.D.

AIR POLLUTION CONTROL DIV.
Chief: Austin C. Daley
277-2808

ENVIRONMENTAL HEALTH SERVICES
Director: Walter J. Shea

RADIOLOGICAL HEALTH PROGRAM
401-277-2438
Chief: James P. Deery

WATER POLLUTION CONTROL DIV.
Director: Carleton A. Maine

Dept. of Natural Resources
83 Park St., Providence, R.I. 02903
401-277-2771
Director: Dennis Murphy, Jr.

COASTAL RESOURCES DIV.
Chief: Charles F. Replinger
277-2476

INFORMATION AND EDUCATION
Chief: Bradford W. Monahon
277-2776

FISH AND WILDLIFE DIV.
Chief: John Cronin
277-2784

FOREST ENVIRONMENT DIV.
Chief: Henry J. Deion, Jr.
277-3086

PARKS AND RECREATION DIV.
Chief: William H. Cotter, Jr.
277-2632

PLANNING AND DEVELOPMENT DIV.
Chief: Calvin B. Dunwoody
277-2776

Soil and Water Conservation Committee
935 E. Main Rd., Middletown, R.I. 02840
401-847-2585
Secretary: Antone E. Mendonca

Water Resources Board
265 Melrose St., Providence, R.I. 02907
401-277-2217
Chairman: Alex DiMartino

SOUTH CAROLINA

Board of Health, Radiological Health Div.
J. Marion Sims Bldg., Columbia, S.C. 29201
803-758-5548
Director: Heyward G. Shealy

Commission of Forestry
Box 287, Columbia, S.C. 29202
803-758-2261
State Forester: John R. Tiller

Dept. of Agriculture, Plant Pest Regulatory Service
Clemson University, Clemson, S.C. 29631
803-654-2421
(Pesticides regulation and information)
Director: L. H. Senn

Dept. of Wildlife Resources
1015 Main St., Box 167, Columbia, S.C. 29202
803-758-2561
Executive Director: James W. Webb

MARINE RESOURCES DIV.
217 Fort Johnson Rd., Box 12559, Charleston, S.C. 29407
803-795-6350
Director: James A. Timmerman, Jr.

Land Resources Conservation Commission
2414 Bull St., Columbia, S.C. 29201
803-758-2824
Director: John W. Parris

Pollution Control Authority
1321 Lady St., Box 11628, Columbia, S.C. 29211

803-758-2915
Executive Director: H. J. Webb
Public Information Officer: Michael A. Creel

AIR POLLUTION CONTROL DIV.
Chief: William G. Crosby

SOLID WASTE MANAGEMENT DIV.
Chief: Johnie W. Smith

WATER POLLUTION CONTROL DIV.
Chief: R. Kenneth Tinsley

Soil and Water Conservation Commission
2414 Bull St., Columbia, S.C. 29201
Chairman: W. B. Bennet, Jr.

Water Resources Commission
2414 Bull St., Columbia, S.C. 29201
803-758-2514
Executive Director: Clair P. Guess, Jr.

SOUTH DAKOTA

Committee on Water Pollution
Dept. of Health, Pierre, S. Dak. 57501
605-224-3351
Secretary and Executive Officer: Charles E. Carl

Conservation Commission, Department of Environmental Protection
Rm. 415, Bldg. No. 2, Pierre, S. Dak. 57501
605-224-3258
Secretary: Howard Geers

Dept. of Environmental Protection
Rm. 415, Bldg. No. 2, Pierre, S.Dak. 57501
605-224-3351
Secretary: Allyn O. Lockner

AIR QUALITY PROGRAM
Chief: Lyle Randen

PESTICIDES PROGRAM
Chief: Ronald Disrud

SOIL AND WATER CONSERVATION PROGRAM
Chief: Howard Geers

SOLID WASTE PROGRAM
Chief: Ronald Disrud

SURFACE MINING REGULATION PROGRAM
Chief: Howard Geers

WATER HYGIENE PROGRAM
Chief: John Hatch

WATER QUALITY PROGRAM
Chief: Blaine Barker

Dept. of Game, Fish, and Parks
State Office Bldg., Pierre, S.Dak. 57501
605-224-3387
Director: Robert A. Hodgins

Water Resources Commission
Bldg. No. 2, Pierre, S. Dak. 57501
605-224-3584
Chief Engineer and Executive Officer: Joseph W. Grimes

TENNESSEE

Dept. of Agriculture, Div. of Food and Drugs
Box 40627, Melrose Sta., Nashville, Tenn. 37204
615-741-1411
(Pesticides regulation and information)
Director: Eugene H. Holman

Dept. of Conservation
2611 West End Ave., Nashville, Tenn. 37203
615-741-2301
Commissioner: Granville Hinton

CONSERVATION EDUCATION DIV.
Director: James L. Bailey
741-2661

DEVELOPMENT PLANNING DIV.
Director: Walter L. Criley
741-1061

FORESTRY DIV.
Director: Max J. Young
741-3326

STATE PARKS DIV.
Director: W. T. Boswell
741-3251

STRIP MINING AND LAND RECLAMATION DIV.
Director: Chase Delony
741-1046

WATER RESOURCES DIV.
Director: Raleigh W. Robinson
741-2572

Dept. of Public Health, Environmental Health Services Bureau
349 Cordell Hull Bldg., Nashville, Tenn. 37219
615-741-3657
Director: J. L. Church

AIR POLLUTION CONTROL DIV.
Director: Harold E. Hodges
741-3931

INDUSTRIAL AND RADIOLOGICAL HEALTH DIV.
Director: Robert H. Wolle
741-3161

SANITARY ENGINEERING DIV.
Director: John W. Saucier
741-2281

SANITATION AND SOLID WASTE MANAGEMENT DIV.
320 Capitol Hill Bldg., Nashville, Tenn. 37219
615-741-2951
Director: James C. Ault

WATER QUALITY CONTROL DIV.
Director: S. Leary Jones
741-2275

Game and Fish Commission
Box 40747, Ellington Agricultural Center, Nashville, Tenn. 37220
615-741-1431
Acting Director: Harold Worvil

Soil Conservation Committee
Box 1071, Knoxville, Tenn. 37901
615-974-7208
Executive Secretary: James H. Robinson

Water Quality Control Board, Dept. of Public Health
621 Cordell Hull Bldg., Nashville, Tenn. 37219
615-741-2275
Technical Secretary: S. Leary Jones

TEXAS

Agriculture Experimental Station, Feed and Fertilizer Control Service
Texas A & M University, College Station, Tex. 77843
713-846-7707
(Pesticides regulation and information)
Director: Dr. Flake Fisher

Dept. of Health
1100 W. 49 St., Austin, Tex. 78756
512-454-3781
Commissioner: James E. Peavey, M.D.

AIR CONTROL BOARD
Executive Secretary: Charles Barden

AIR POLLUTION CONTROL SERVICES
Deputy Commissioner: Charles Barden

ENVIRONMENTAL HEALTH SERVICES
Deputy Commissioner: G. R. Herzik, Jr.

Environmental Development Program
(Solid waste management)
Chief: David Houston

Radiological Health Program
Director: Martin C. Wukasch

Sanitary Engineering Div.
Director: Charles K. Foster

Wastewater Technology and Surveillance Div.
Director: Henry L. Dabney

Dept. of Parks and Wildlife
John H. Reagan Bldg., Austin, Tex. 78701
512-475-2087
Executive Director: Clayton T. Garrison

FISH AND WILDLIFE DIV.
Director: Robert J. Kemp, Jr.

PARKS DIV.
Director: Paul E. Schlimper

Forest Service
College Station, Tex. 77843
713-845-2641
Director: Paul R. Kramer

Soil and Water Conservation Board
1018 First National Bldg., Temple, Tex. 76501
817-773-2250
Executive Director: Harvey D. Davis

Water Quality Board
314 W. 11 St., Austin, Tex. 78701
512-475-2651
Executive Director: Hugh C. Yantis

UTAH

Dept. of Natural Resources
438 State Capitol, Salt Lake City, Utah 84114
801-328-5357
Executive Director: Gordon E. Harmston

70 Government Environmental Agencies

OIL AND GAS CONSERVATION DIV.
1588 W. North Temple, Salt Lake City, Utah 84116
801-328-5771
Director: Cleon B. Feight

PARKS AND RECREATION DIV.
1596 W. North Temple, Salt Lake City, Utah 84114
801-328-6011
Director: Harold J. Tippetts

WATER RESOURCES DIV.
435 State Capitol Bldg., Salt Lake City, Utah 84114
801-328-5401
Director: Daniel F. Lawrence

WILDLIFE RESOURCES DIV.
1596 W. North Temple, Salt Lake City, Utah 84116
801-328-5081
Director: John E. Phelps

Dept. of Social Services, Div. of Health
44 Medical Dr., Salt Lake City, Utah 84113
801-328-6111
Director: Lyman J. Olsen, M.D.

ENVIRONMENTAL HEALTH BUREAU
Director: Howard M. Hurst
328-6121

Air Quality Section
Chief: Grant S. Winn, Ph.D.
328-6108

General Sanitation Section
Chief: Mervin R. Reid
328-6163

Radiation and Occupational Health Section
Chief: Dennis R. Dalley
328-6121

Water Quality Section
Chief: Calvin K. Sudweeks
328-6146

Soil Conservation Commission, Department of Agriculture
412 State Capitol Bldg., Salt Lake City, Utah 84114
801-328-5421
Executive Secretary: James D. Harvey

VERMONT

Agency of Environmental Conservation
Montpelier, Vt. 05602
802-828-3357
Secretary: Martin L. Johnson
Environmental Board Executive Officer: Kenneth E. Senecal
Environmental Conservation Planning Director: Forrest E. Orr
Environmental Protection Director: Donald W. Webster

AIR AND SOLID WASTE PROGRAMS
Chief: Reginald A. LaRosa

FISH AND GAME DEPT.
Commissioner: Edward F. Kehoe

FORESTS AND PARKS DEPT.
Commissioner: Arthur F. Heitmann
Forests Director: James E. Wilkinson, Jr.
Parks Director: Rodney A. Barber

WATER RESOURCES DEPT.
Commissioner: Gordon R. Pyper, P.E.

Management and Engineering Div.
Director: John E. Cerutti

Water Supply and Pollution Control Div.
Director: Reginald A. LaRosa

Engineering and Operations Section
Chief: William Brierley

Water Quality Section
Chief: David L. Clough

Dept. of Agriculture, Plant Pest Control Div.
Montpelier, Vt. 05602
802-828-2431
(Pesticides regulation and information)
Director: John W. Scott

Dept. of Health, Radiological Health Program
32 Spaulding St., Box 607, Barre, Vt. 05641
802-476-3171
Director: Harry B. Ashe

Natural Resources Conservation Council
State Office Bldg., Montpelier, Vt. 05602
802-828-3351
Executive Secretary: Linda Beaudoin

VIRGINIA

Air Pollution Control Board
Rm. 1106, 9 St. Office Bldg., Richmond, Va. 23219
703-770-2378
Executive Director: William R. Meyer

Dept. of Agriculture and Commerce
203 N. Governor St., Richmond, Va. 23219
703-770-3798
(Pesticides regulation and information)
Laboratory Director: L. M. Cox, Jr.

Dept. of Conservation and Economic Development
1100 State Office Bldg., Richmond, Va. 23219
703-770-2121
Director: Marvin M. Sutherland

FORESTRY DIV.
Box 3758, Charlottesville, Va. 22903
702-296-6174
State Forester: Wallace F. Custard

MINED LAND RECLAMATION DIV.
Drawer U, Big Stone Gap, Va. 24219
703-523-2925
Commissioner: William O. Roller

MINERAL RESOURCES DIV.
Box 3667, Charlottesville, Va. 22903
703-293-5121
State Geologist: James L. Calver

PARKS DIV.
1201 State Office Bldg., Richmond, Va. 23219
703-770-2132
Commissioner: Ben H. Bolen

Dept. of Health
James Madison Bldg., Richmond, Va. 23219
703-770-3561
Commissioner: M. I. Shanholtz, M.D.

ENGINEERING DIV.
(Solid waste management)
Director: Oscar H. Adams

RADIOLOGICAL HEALTH PROGRAM
James Madison Bldg., Richmond, Va. 23219
703-770-6285
Director: Bryce P. Schofield

Marine Resources Commission
Box 756, Newport News, Va. 23607
703-244-3572
Commissioner: James E. Douglas, Jr.
Conservation and Repletion Officer: Howard S. Judnall

Water Control Board
4010 W. Broad St., Box 11143, Richmond, Va. 23230
703-770-2241
Director: A. H. Paessler

WATER RESOURCES DIV.
11 S. 10 St., Richmond, Va. 23219
703-770-2111
Director: Julian M. Alexander
Executive Secretary: Eugene T. Jensen

WASHINGTON

Dept. of Agriculture, Grain and Agricultural Chemicals Div.
406 General Administration Bldg., Olympia, Wash. 98504
206-753-5064
(Pesticides regulation and information)
Supervisor: Errett Deck

Dept. of Ecology
Olympia, Wash. 98504
206-753-2800
Director: John A. Biggs
Deputy Director: Wesley A. Hunter

ADMINISTRATION AND PLANNING BRANCH
Executive Assistant Director: Robert L. Stockman

ADMINISTRATION OFFICE
Assistant Director: Jerry Gray

OPERATIONS OFFICE
Assistant Director: R. Jerry Bollen

PLANNING AND PROGRAM DEVELOPMENT OFFICE
Assistant Director: Fred D. Hahn

PUBLIC SERVICES BRANCH
Executive Assistant Director: James P. Behlke

TECHNICAL SERVICES OFFICE
Assistant Director: Peter Hildebrandt

Dept. of Fisheries
115 General Administration Bldg., Olympia, Wash. 98504
206-753-6600
Director: Thor C. Tollefson

Dept. of Game
600 N. Capitol Way, Olympia, Wash. 98504
206-753-5700
Director: Carl N. Crouse

Dept. of Natural Resources
Public Lands Bldg., Olympia, Wash. 98504
206-753-5327
Administrator: Bert L. Cole

FOREST LAND MANAGEMENT DIV.
Supervisor: Herb Grell
753-5315
Geology and Earth Resources Div.
Supervisor: Vaughn E. Livingston, Jr.
753-6183

SURVEYS AND MARINE LAND MANAGEMENT DIV.
Supervisor: Ralph Beswick
753-5324

Dept. of Social and Health Services, Health Services Div.
Box 1788, Olympia, Wash. 98501
Assistant Secretary: John A. Beare, M.D.

OFFICE OF ENVIRONMENTAL HEALTH PROGRAMS
(Solid waste management)
Chief: Sam Reed
206-753-5955

RADIATION CONTROL SECTION
Public Health Buildings, Olympia, Wash. 98501
206-753-3459
Head: Clifford G. Lewis

Parks and Recreation Commission
Box 1128, Olympia 98504
206-753-5755
Director: Charles H. Odegaard

Conservation Commission, Dept. of Ecology
Olympia, Wash. 98504
206-753-3894
Executive Secretary: G. C. Digerness
Conservation Field Representative: Gordon R. Burt

WEST VIRGINIA

Air Pollution Control Commission
4104A MacCockle Ave., Charleston, W. Va. 25304
304-348-2275
Executive Director: Carl G. Beard, II

Dept. of Agriculture, Consumer Protection Div.
State Capitol, Charleston, W. Va. 25305
304-349-2226
(Pesticides regulation and information)
Director: C. Harold Amick

Dept. of Health, Environmental Health Services
Charleston, W. Va. 25305
304-348-2981
(Solid waste management)
Director: Robert G. McCall

INDUSTRIAL HYGIENE
1800 E. Washington St., Charleston, W. Va. 25305
304-348-3526
(Administers radiological health program)
Director: Harvey J. Roberts

Dept. of Natural Resources
1800 Washington St. E., Charleston, W. Va. 25305
304-348-2754
Director: Ira S. Latimer, Jr.

FOREST SERVICE
State Forester: Lester McClung
348-2788

INFORMATION AND EDUCATION
Chief: Ed Johnson
348-3381

PARKS AND RECREATION
Chief: Kermit McKeever
348-2764

PLANNING AND DEVELOPMENT
Chief: J. D. Brackenrich
348-2775

RECLAMATION
Chief: Benjamin C. Greene
348-3267

WATER RESOURCES
Chief: Edgar N. Henry
348-2107

WILDLIFE RESOURCES
Chief: Dan E. Cantner
348-2771

WISCONSIN

Dept. of Agriculture
Rm. 208, Hill Farms State Office Bldg., Madison, Wis, 53702
608-266-2295
Administrator: K. P. Robert

Dept. of Health and Social Services, Radiological Health Program
Box 309, Madison, Wis. 53701
608-266-2295
Chief, Radiation Protection: William L. Lea

Dept. of Natural Resources
Box 450, Madison, Wis. 53701
608-266-2121
Secretary: L. P. Voight

ENVIRONMENTAL PROTECTION DIV.
Administrator: Thomas G. Frangos
266-2747

Air Pollution Control and Solid-Waste Disposal Bureau
Director: Edward Brooks Becker
266-0924

Air Pollution Control Section
Chief: Douglas W. Evans
266-1199

Solid-waste Disposal Section
Chief: John J. Reinhardt
266-0158

Environmental Impact Bureau
Director: Carroll D. Besadny
266-1327

Biological Investigation Section
Chief: L. A. Posekany
266-2178

Planning Bureau
Director: Arthur D. Doll
266-0818

Standards and Surveys Bureau
Director: F. H. Schraufnagel
266-3291

Laboratory Service Section
Chief: Lloyd Lueschow
266-0100

Surveillance Section
Chief: Stanton J. Kleinert
266-7721

Water Quality Evaluation Section
Chief: Jerome McKersie
266-2879

Water and Shoreland Management Bureau
Director: Vacant
266-2304

Floodplain and Shoreland Management Section
Chief: Thomas M. Lee
266-3093

Private Water Supply Section
Chief: Thomas A. Calabresa
266-3415

Water Regulation Section
Chief: Edmund M. Brick
266-1205

Water Resources Planning Section
Chief: John M. Cain
266-0157

Water Supply and Pollution Control Bureau
Director: Carl J. Blabaum
266-3910

Certification and Licensing Section
Chief: Alpheus W. Tandy
266-0151

Industrial Wastewater Section
Chief: Paul P. Didier
266-0289

Municipal Wastewater Section
Chief: Robert M. Krill
266-2427

Public Water Supply Section
Chief: Robert A. Baumeister
266-2299

FORESTRY, WILDLIFE, AND RECREATION DIV.
Administrator: J. R. Smith
266-2243

Fish Management Bureau
Assistant Director: C. W. Threinen
266-2194

Forest Management Bureau
Acting Director: H. J. Hovind
266-2196

Game Management Bureau
Director: John M. Keener
266-2175

Parks and Recreation Bureau
Director: Milton E. Reinke
266-2152

TOURISM AND INFORMATION DIV.
Administrator: Burton D. Loken
266-0837

Information and Education Bureau
Acting Director: James W. Taylor
266-3010

Environmental Education Council
Lowell Hall, 610 Langdon St., Madison, Wis. 53706
608-263-3327
Executive Secretary: David Walker

Geological and Natural History Survey
University Extension, University of Wisonsin, 1815 University Ave., Madison, Wis. 53706
608-262-1705
State Geologist and Director: N. A.

WYOMING

Dept. of Agriculture
2219 Carey Ave., Cheyenne, Wyo. 82001
307-777-7321
Commissioner: Glenn J. Hertzler

PLANT INDUSTRY DIV.
(Pesticides regulation and information)
Director: Walter H. Patch

Dept. of Economic Planning and Development
720 W. 18 St., Cheyenne, Wyo. 82001
307-777-7284
Executive Director: J. D. Brunk

INDUSTRIAL DEVELOPMENT
Chief: John C. Williams

MINERAL DEVELOPMENT
Chief: John T. Goodier

STATE PLANNING
Chief: David Ellis

WATER DEVELOPMENT
Chief: Myron Goodson

Dept. of Environmental Quality
State Office Bldg., Cheyenne, Wyo. 82001
307-777-7511
Director: Robert E. Sundin
AIR QUALITY DIV.
Administrator: Randolph Wood

LAND QUALITY DIVISION
Acting Administrator: Homer Derrer

WATER QUALITY DIV.
Administrator: Arthur E. Williamson

SANITARY ENGINEERING SERVICES
(Solid waste management)
Director: Arthur E. Williamson
777-7513

Forestry Div.
Capitol Bldg., Cheyenne, Wyo. 82001
307-777-7333
State Forester: Carl E. Johnson

Game and Fish Commission
Box 1589, Cheyenne, Wyo. 82001
307-777-7461
Commissioner and Director: James B. White

Soil and Water Conservation Committee
Capitol Bldg., Cheyenne, Wyo. 82001
Executive Secretary: Marvin H. Cronberg

2 Private Environmental Organizations

An increased public interest in the environment in recent years has been accompanied by the establishment of a remarkably large number of organizations concerned with environmental matters. Although these organizations differ widely in size, function, and interests, they generally serve three basic purposes: to furnish information, to initiate social and political action, and to act as a forum for concerned citizens.

The listings in this chapter are representative of the wide variety of environmental groups active in all regions of the United States. The organizations range from small local groups concerned with a single aspect of the environmental movement to large national groups dealing with a broad range of subjects and activities. Two basic categories of groups are listed in this chapter.

Citizens' organizations. Groups of interested private citizens form the heart of the environmental movement. Most of the organizations listed here are open to general public membership, and they are listed in two sections: national and international groups, and regional, state, and local groups.

Trade and professional organizations. These groups are composed of firms or individuals representing a particular occupation, industry, or profession. Although most of these organizations are not open to general public membership, they often cooperate with individuals and groups outside their professions, particularly in furnishing information about environmental matters.

A brief description of the purposes and activities is included in the listings to give readers a general idea of the character of each organization. Most groups offer highly informative descriptive literature, which will supply further information to prospective members.

The alphabetical index at the back of this book includes references to all organizations listed in this chapter.

This chapter concludes with a list of organizations that are either currently inactive or that have been disbanded. The small number of such groups indicates that the interest of Americans in environmental matters is not decreasing significantly.

CITIZENS' ORGANIZATIONS

NATIONAL AND INTERNATIONAL

African Wildlife Leadership Foundation, Inc.
1717 Massachusetts Ave. N.W., Washington, D.C. 20036
202-265-8394
Works for the conservation of African wildlife with major emphasis on wildlife conservation education, support of national parks and reserves, scientific research, and leadership. Founded: 1961. Nonmembership.
Chief Officer: John E. Rhea, Executive Director
Publication: *African Wildlife News*

Air Pollution Control Assn.
4400 Fifth Ave., Pittsburgh, Pa. 15213
412-621-1100
A nonprofit technical and educational organization dedicated to advancing the science and art of air pollution control. Its membership is balanced among industrial, scientific, government, and educational sectors. Founded: 1907. Membership: 6,500.
Chief Officer: David M. Benforado, President
Publication: *Journal of the Air Pollution Control Association*

American Assn. for the Advancement of Science
1515 Massachusetts Ave. N.W., Washington, D.C. 20005
202-387-7171
Works to further the work of scientists, to facilitate cooperation among them, to improve the effectiveness of science in the promotion of human welfare, and to increase public understanding and appreciation of the importance and promise of the methods of science in human progress. Founded: 1848. Membership: 127,500.
Chief Officer: William Bevan, Executive Officer
Publication: *Science*

American Assn. of State Highway Officials
341 National Press, Washington, D.C. 20004
202-628-2348
Fosters the development, operation, and maintenance of a nationwide highway system in cooperation with other agencies in consideration of the public need. Founded: 1914. Membership: Highway Departments of the individual states, Puerto Rico, District of Columbia; Federal Highway Administration.
Chief Officer: Henrik E. Stafseth, Executive Director
Publications: Over 40

American Assn. of University Women
2401 Virginia Ave. N.W., Washington, D.C. 20037
202-785-7700
Open to all women who hold baccalaureate or higher degrees from colleges or universities on the AAUW list of qualified institutions. Membership in AAUW enables women to continue their intellectual growth, further the advancement of women, and discharge their special responsibilities to society. Since 1969 the AAUW has directed much of its program toward the problem of environmental pollution and the use of natural resources. Founded: 1882. Membership: 175,000.
Chief Officer: Anne Campbell, President
Publication: *AAUW Journal*

American Cetacean Society
4725 Lincoln Blvd., Marina del Rey, Calif. 90291
213-823-7311
The threefold aim is conservation, education, and involvement with all matters aquatic. While concerned primarily with marine mammals, especially whales, dolphins, and porpoises, the society recognizes the interdependence of all marine life, and takes concerted action to protect and enjoy it. Founded: 1967. Membership: 400 (in seven countries).
Chief Officer: John Olguin, President
Publications: *The Whalewatcher*; fact sheets, newsletter

American Committee for International Wild Life Protection, Inc.
Suite S-176, 3900 Wisconsin Ave. N.W., Washington, D.C. 20016
202-363-2435
Coordinates the interests and activities of individuals and organizations concerned with safeguarding endangered and vanishing species. Founded: 1930. Membership: 60.
Chief Officer: Lee M. Talbot, Chairman
Publications: Various special publications

American Forest Institute
1619 Massachusetts Ave. N.W., Washington, D.C. 20036
202-667-7807
The information and education arm of the forest industry, representing manufacturers of wood and paper products in the United States. AFI administers the American Tree Farm System, a program to encourage management of privately owned woodlands. Founded: 1940. Membership: 105 companies.
Chief Officer: George C. Cheek, Executive Vice President
Publications: *Green America* (quarterly); *Tree Farm News* (quarterly)

American Forestry Assn.
1319 18 St. N.W., Washington, D.C. 20036
202-467-5810
Encourages intelligent management and use of forests, soil, water, wildlife, and all other natural resources necessary for a high-quality environment and citizens' well-being. Seeks to promote an enlightened public appreciation of natural resources and their effect on the social, recreational, and economic life of

the nation. Founded: 1875. Membership: 72,000.
Chief Officer: William E. Towell, Executive Vice President
Publication: *American Forests*

American Health Foundation
1370 Ave. of the Americas, New York, N.Y. 10019
212-489-8700
Nonprofit research foundation devoted to promoting preventive medicine through research in the major chronic diseases (particularly cancer and heart disease), through health motivation and education, and through health care (multiphasic health screening and follow-up clinics). All research is funded through grants and contracts from governmental agencies, private agencies, and private donations. Founded: 1968. Membership: None.
Chief Officer: Ernest L. Wynder, M.D.
Publications: *Preventive Medicine; AHF Newsletter*

American Humane Assn.
Box 1266, Denver, Colo. 80201
303-771-1300
National federation of the organizations dedicated to the prevention of cruelty to children and animals. Founded: 1877. Membership: 2,000,000 (in 1,050 societies).
Chief Officer: Thomas C. Justice, President
Publication: *The National Humane Review*

American Lung Assn.
1740 Broadway, New York, N.Y. 10019
212-245-8000
Works for prevention and control of lung disease. Conducts programs on the cause, treatment, and prevention of tuberculosis and other respiratory diseases; the elimination of cigarette smoking; the elimination of air pollution; and the improvement of community health and welfare. Founded: 1904. Membership: 6,431.
Chief Officer: Robert J. Anderson, M.D., Managing Director
Publications: *ALA Bulletin; American Review of Respiratory Disease*

The American Museum of Natural History
Central Park W. and 79 St., New York, N.Y. 10024
212-873-1300
Maintains and studies a 23 million-specimen collection; operates exhibitions (thirty-five permanent halls); conducts public education programs (classes, lectures, special exhibits, etc.); carries out long-range basic research in systematic zoology, anthropology, geology, animal behavior, and physiology. Founded: 1869. Membership: 300,000.
Chief Officer: Thomas D. Nicholson, Director
Publications (partial list): *Curator; Natural History* (magazine); *American Museum Novitates; Bulletin of the AMNH; Micropaleontology;* Annual Report

American Ornithologists Union, Inc.
National Museum of Natural History, Smithsonian Institution, Washington, D.C. 20560
202-183-5207
Furthers ornithological science. Founded: 1883. Membership: 3,200.
Chief Officer: Joseph J. Hickey, President
Publications: *The Auk; Monographs*

American Shore and Beach Preservation Assn.
10 Rickenbacker Causeway, Miami, Fla. 33149
305-350-7216
Fosters cooperation among agencies, interest groups, and individuals concerned with the protection and proper utilization of shores and beaches. Fosters sound, far-sighted, and economical development and preservation of these lands in order to benefit the most people. Founded: 1926. Membership: 700.
Chief Officer: M.P. O'Brien, President
Publications: *Shore & Beach Journal* (semiannual); *Newsletter* (monthly)

American Society of Planning Officials
1313 E. 60 St., Chicago, Ill. 60637
312-324-3400
Works for the improvement of community planning and development. Activities include planning advisory service, land-use controls service, and a sponsored research division. Conducts studies for governmental agencies, foundations, and others, and sponsors the annual National Planning Conference (3,000 participants). Founded: 1934. Membership: 10,000.
Chief Officer: Israel Stollman, Executive Director
Publications: *PAS Reports* (monthly); *Planning* (monthly magazine)

Assn. for Voluntary Sterilization, Inc.
14 W. 40 St., New York, N.Y. 10018
212-524-2344
Publicizes the benefits of voluntary sterilization in the solution of family and population problems, and works to make voluntary ster-

ilization freely available, regardless of age, marital status, number of children, race, religion, or income. Acts as a clearinghouse for information on sterilization practice and research and runs a nationwide referral service for men and women seeking sterilization. Educational efforts are directed toward both the layman and the professional. Founded: 1943. Membership: 28,000.
Chief Officer: Charles T. Faneuff
Publications: *AVS News* (quarterly newsletter); brochures

Bounty Information Service
Stephens College, Post Office, Columbia, Mo. 65201
314-442-0509
Aims to remove all bounties on wildlife through educational programs and support of appropriate legislation. Founded: 1965. Membership: Mailing list: 5,000.
Chief Officer: H. Charles Laun, Director
Publication: *Bounty News*

The Boy Scouts of America
National Council, North Brunswick, N.J. 08902
201-249-6000
The purpose of the Boy Scouts is to encourage boys to learn to do things for themselves and others. Character development, good citizenship, and mental and physical fitness are the Boy Scouts' goal. Founded: 1910. Membership: 4,903,969.
Chief Officer: Alden G. Barber, Chief Scout Executive
Publications: *Boys' Life*; *Scouting Magazine*; *Exploring* (magazine)

Camp Fire Girls, Inc.
1740 Broadway, New York, N.Y. 10019
212-581-0500
Directed toward helping young people grow as self-reliant, caring, and responsible individuals through experiences in groups. Individuals can explore, test, experiment, and grow in skills, self-reliance, and self-esteem. Members take part in community projects, go camping, traveling, enjoy crafts activities, make friends, and, in general, enjoy themselves. Founded: 1910. Membership: 600,000.
Chief Officer: Hester Turner, National Executive Director
Publication: *Camp Fire Leadership*

Center for Law and Social Policy
1751 N St. N.W., Washington, D.C. 20036
202-872-0679
A public interest law firm which represents the interests of previously unrepresented citizens before agencies and courts, analyzes legal institutions, particularly federal administrative agencies, and provides clinical education for law students. Founded: 1969.
Chief Officer: Joseph N. Onek, Director
Publications: Articles written by those working with the Center appear in various law journals

Citizens League Against the Sonic Boom
19 Appleton St., Cambridge, Mass. 02138
617-876-0764
Hopes to protect people and animals from the sonic boom of supersonic transport planes (SSTs) by seeing that such planes do not go into service. Activities include educating government officials, airline officials, the press, and the public about the extent to which sonic booms would damage property and annoy people and animals. Founded: 1967. Membership: 4,000.
Chief Officer: William A. Shurcliff, Director and Treasurer
Publications: Newsletter; various special publications

Committee for National Arbor Day
63 Fitzrandolph Rd., West Orange, N.J. 07052
Establishes the last Friday in April as National Arbor Day. Founded: 1939. Membership: 30.
Chief Officer: Edward H. Scanlon, National Chairman

Conservation and Environmental Studies Center, Inc.
R.D. 2, Box 2230, Browns Mills, N.J. 08015
609-893-9151
Nine environmental education consultants assist school districts in developing environmental education curriculums for all grades up through high school. CESC prepares environmental curriculum materials, conducts teacher training courses and workshops, and provides environmental programs for children. CESC also provides environmental assessment services for industries and public agencies. Founded: 1966. Membership: 331.
Chief Officer: V. Eugene Vivian, Director
Publications: *Sourcebook in Environmental Education*; other publications designed for use with CESC programs and workshops

Conservation Foundation
1717 Massachusetts Ave. N.W., Washington, D.C. 20036

202-265-8882

Its purposes are to promote greater knowledge about the earth's resources, to initiate research and education concerning these resources and their relation to each other, to ascertain the most effective methods of making them available and useful to people, to assess population trends and their effect upon environment, and to encourage human conduct to sustain and enrich life on earth. Founded: 1948.

Chief Officer: Arthur A. Davis, Vice President-Operations

Publication: *CF Letter*

Consumer Federation of America
Suite 901, 1012 14 St., Washington, D.C. 20005
202-737-3732

A federation of national, state, and local consumer organizations dedicated to consumer action and protection through legislation, information, and education. Founded: 1968. Membership: 200 consumer organizations.

Chief Officer: Erma Angevine, Executive Director

Publications: *Consumer News & Comment*; various special reports

Consumers' Research
Washington, N.J. 07882
201-689-3300

A public service organization dedicated to serve the consumer. Consumers' Research reports, in its magazine, laboratory and other tests on a wide range of ultimate-consumer goods and services. CR's testing is competent, independent, and unbiased. It is not supported by manufacturers, dealers, or government agencies. Founded: 1927. Subscribers: 100,000.

Chief Officer: F. J. Schlink, President and Technical Director

Publication: *Consumers' Research Magazine* (monthly)

Council on Population and Environment
Rm. 206, 100 E. Ohio, Chicago, Ill. 60611
312-787-1114

National Organization dealing with population, environment, transportation, housing, and energy issues.

Chief Officer: Janet H. Malone, Executive Director

Crusade for a Cleaner Environment
Suite 520, 2000 L St. N.W., Washington, D.C. 20036

202-296-2608

Works to promote, support, and conduct programs and activities relating to the problem of littering, pollution, and defilement of communities and lands, caused by indiscriminate discarding of trash and other solid waste materials. Founded: 1970. Membership: 100.

Chief Officer: T.J. Hamilton, Executive Secretary

Publications: *Litter Bits of News and Facts*; occasional fact sheets

Daughters of the American Revolution National Society
1776 D St. N.W., Washington, D.C. 20006
202-628-4980

Promotes historic preservation, education, patriotic endeavor. Founded: 1890. Membership: 196,000.

Chief Officer: Mrs. Donald Spicer, President General

Publication: *DAR Magazine*

Defenders of Wildlife
2000 N St. N.W., Washington, D.C. 20036
202-223-1993

An educational organization dedicated to the preservation of all forms of wildlife. Its objectives are to promote, through education and research, the protection and humane treatment of all mammals, birds, fish, and other wildlife, and to eliminate painful methods of trapping, capturing, and killing wildlife. Founded: 1925. Membership: 40,000.

Chief Officer: Mary Hazell Harris, Executive Director

Publication: *Defenders of Wildlife News*

Ducks Unlimited
Box 66300, Chicago, Ill. 60666
312-299-3334

Raises money for developing, preserving, restoring, and maintaining the waterfowl breeding grounds in Canada. Founded: 1937. Membership: 80,000.

Chief Officer: Herman Taylor, Jr., President

Publication: *Ducks Unlimited Magazine*

Elm Research Institute
Harrisville, N.H. 03450
603-827-3048

Established to fund research on Dutch elm disease and possible cures through membership dues, grants from foundations, and other contributions. Also aims to awaken public concern over the probable extinction of the American elm. Founded: 1967. Membership: 780.

Chief Officer: John P. Hansel, Executive Director
Publications: Annual progress report; *Specialized Elm Care* (brochure)

Environmental Action Foundation
720 Dupont Circle Bldg., Washington, D.C. 20036
202-293-6960
An environmental education organization which is primarily concerned with land use in sewage disposal, solid waste management, and energy. Founded: 1970.
Chief Officer: Richard C. Dalsemer, Director
Publications: Occasional papers

Environmental Defense Fund, Inc.
162 Old Town Rd., East Setauket, N.Y. 11733
516-751-5191
A public-interest coalition of scientists, lawyers, and citizens; emphasizes legal action and public education. Founded: 1967. Membership: 45,000.
Chief Officer: Roderick A. Cameron, Executive Director
Publications: *EDF Letter* (bimonthly)

Environmental Law Institute
Suite 620, 1346 Connecticut Ave. N.W., Washington, D.C. 20036
202-659-8037
Publishes the *Environmental Law Reporter*; conducts and sponsors research into the legal problems of conservation and resource utilization; maintains a clearinghouse for information regarding the law of the environment; and engages in related educational activities which include conducting classes, lectures, panels, and workshops. Founded: 1969.
Chief Officer: Thomas P. Alder, President
Publications: *Environmental Law Reporter*; others

Environmental Policy Center
324 C St. S.E., Washington, D.C. 20003
202-547-6500
Combines Washington lobbying with economic and political analyses of resource problems, specializing in energy, land-use planning, and water resources. Works against strip mining, offshore oil drilling, and environmentally damaging dredging and dam projects; and for safer and more efficient deep-mined coal production, development of solar and local control of land-use planning, and preservation of the Everglades. Supported by the sale of information and research services and by nondeductible donations. Works free on behalf of state and local citizens' groups. Nonmembership.
Chief Officer: Joe Browder, Executive Vice-President
Publications: Special publications on energy, water resources, and land-use issues.

Friends of Animals, Inc.
11 W. 60 St., New York, N.Y. 10023
212-247-8077
Works to protect animals, make abuses known, and propose solutions to end abuses. Founded: 1957. Membership: 45,000.
Chief Officer: Alice Herrington, President
Publication: *Actionline* (newsletter)

Friends of the Earth
529 Commercial Ave., San Francisco, Calif. 94111
415-391-4270
Works on the restoration and preservation of the earth's resources. Founded: 1969. Membership: 20,000.
Chief Officer: David R. Brower, President
Publication: *Not Man Apart*

Future Farmers of America
National FFA Center, Alexandria, Va. 22309
703-360-3600
An organization of agriculture students (to age 21) designed to encourage intelligent agricultural practices through practical work experience and traditional classroom study. Founded: 1928. Membership: 432,288.
Chief Officer: H.N. Hunsicker, National FFA Advisor
Publications: *Future Farmer Magazine*; Proceedings of national FFA conventions; official *FFA Manual*

Girl Scouts of the United States of America
830 Third Ave., New York, N.Y. 10022
212-751-6900
Girls and volunteer adults are involved in an ongoing partnership to help develop creative, responsible individuals with a deep sense of personal worth. Through a wide variety of projects in service, social and environmental action, youth leadership, and career exploration, girls are encouraged to develop personal, social, ethical, and individual values and skills, to gain a sense of oneness and interdependence with others, and to participate actively as citizens in their homes, communities, the nation, and the world. Founded: 1912. Membership: 3,726,000.
Chief Officer: Cecily C. Selby, National Executive Director

Publications: *The Girl Scout Leader*; *American Girl Magazine*; *The Brownie Reader*

International Assn. for Pollution Control
Suite 700, 4733 Bethesda Ave., Washington, D.C. 20014
301-652-3420
An interdisciplinary professional group that acts as a forum for evaluating federal, state, and local government action on pollution. Also holds annual international conferences on pollution control in the marine industries and monthly seminars with government speakers. Founded: 1970. Membership: 500.
Chief Officer: Thomas F.P. Sullivan, President
Publications: *Forum* (monthly newsletter); proceedings from conferences

International Assn. of Game, Fish and Conservation Commissioners
1709 New York Ave., N.W., #301, Washington, D.C. 20006
202-872-8866
Promotes the rational management of fish and wildlife, fosters the conservation of all natural resources by cultivating friendly relationships and mutual understanding, and coordinates the work of public conservation agencies in North America. Founded: 1902. Membership: 390.
Chief Officer: John S. Gottschalk, Executive Vice President
Publication: *International Association Convention Proceedings* (annual)

International Crocodilian Society
Box 217, Silver Springs, Fla. 32688
904-236-2210
Works for the preservation and conservation of crocodilians. Founded: 1967. Membership: 250.
Chief Officer: E. Ross Allen, President
Publications: Reprints relevant material from other sources

International Game Fish Assn.
3000 E. Las Olas Blvd., Fort Lauderdale, Fla. 33316
305-523-0161
Represents anglers in the regulation, preservation, and proper management of the species, their habitat, and the sport of angling. The group is setting up a library which will contain books, papers, statistics, photographs, and historical articles and artifacts. Founded: 1939. Membership: 700 member clubs (worldwide).
Chief Officer: William K. Carpenter, President

Publications: *World Record Marine Fishes*; *The International Marine Angler*

International Pacific Salmon Fisheries Commission
Box 30, New Westminster, B.C., Canada
604-521-3771
Manages sockeye and pink salmon runs of the Fraser River system. Founded: 1937. Membership: 6.
Chief Officer: A.C. Cooper, Director
Publications: Annual reports; bulletins; progress reports

Interprofessional Council on Environmental Design
National Society of Professional Engineers, 2029 K St. N.W., Washington, D.C. 20006
Works to develop the best in environmental design by coordinating the efforts of professionals, such as planners, architects, and engineers, that play a role in designing the environment. Founded: 1963. Membership: 7 organizations.

Izaak Walton League of America
Suite 806, 1800 N. Kent St., Arlington, Va. 22209
703-528-1818
A broadly based conservation organization which aims at the preservation and wise use of soils, woodlands, waters, wildlife, and air. Founded: 1922. Membership: 56,000.
Chief Officers: Roy B. Crockett, President; Raymond C. Hubley, Jr., Executive Director
Publication: *Outdoor America* (monthly tabloid)

League of Conservation Voters
324 C St. S.E., Washington, D.C. 20003
202-547-7200
The League publishes voting charts detailing the environmental voting records of U.S. Senators and Congressmen. During election years the organization raises money and support for environmentally oriented candidates running for Congressional and Gubernatorial races throughout the U.S. Founded: 1970. Nonmembership.
Chief Officer: Marion Edey, Chairman and Coordinator
Publications: *House Voting Chart* (1971, 1972); *Senate Voting Chart* (1971, 1972)

League of Women Voters of the United States
1730 M St. N.W., Washington, D.C. 20036
202-296-1770

Encourages informed and active participation of all citizens in government and politics. The national program devotes much of its efforts towards environmental quality, land use, and human resources. Founded: 1920. Membership: 160,000.
Chief Officer: Lucy Wilson Benson, President
Publications: *National Voter* (journal); many special publications

National Assn. of Counties Research Foundation
1001 Connecticut Ave. N.W., Washington, D.C. 20036
Conducts research for U.S. counties in the areas of manpower, transportation, environmental management, and health. Founded: 1935 (1955 for Research Foundation). Membership: 1,076 counties.
Chief Officer: Bernard F. Hillenbrand, Executive Director
Publications: *County News*; *American County*

National Audubon Society
950 Third Ave., New York, N.Y. 10022
212-832-3200
Works for the conservation and restoration of natural resources, with emphasis on wildlife and wildlife habitats; sponsors nature camps, tours, and lectures; maintains wildlife sanctuaries; and produces films and teaching materials. Founded: 1905. Membership: 261,000.
Chief Officer: Elvis J. Stahr, President
Publications: *Audubon*; *American Birds*; *Audubon Leader*; nature bulletins

National Council of State Garden Clubs, Inc.
4401 Magnolia Ave., St. Louis, Mo. 63110
314-776-7574
Benevolent, charitable, scientific, and educational purposes are served through extensive involvement in programs of beautification, civic development, conservation, education, environmental improvement, garden therapy, horticulture, landscape design, litter control, preservation, roadside development, scholarships, world gardening, and work with youth. Founded: 1929. Membership: 373,656.
Chief Officer: Mrs. Howard S. Kittel, President
Publication: *The National Gardener*

National Parks and Conservation Assn.
1701 18 St. N.W., Washington, D.C. 20009
202-265-2717

Devoted to the maintenance of a national park system and conservation. Founded: 1919. Membership: 48,000.
Chief Officer: Anthony Wayne Smith
Publication: *National Parks and Conservation Magazine*

National Reclamation Assn.
897 National Press Bldg., Washington, D.C. 20004
202-347-2672
Promotes balance in utilization and conservation of natural resources. Founded: 1932. Membership: 4,800.
Chief Officer: Carl H. Brown, Executive Director
Publication: *Water Life*

National Recreation and Park Assn.
1601 N. Kent St., Arlington, Va. 22209
703-525-0606
A service, research, and education organization providing services to professional and lay members in the park, recreation, and leisure fields. It is dedicated to the improvement of park and recreation leadership, programs, and facilities and the promotion of proper land use planning policies in every state. Founded: 1967. Membership: 18,000.
Chief Officer: Dwight F. Rettie, Executive Director
Publications: *NRPA: Washington Action Report*; *Parks and Recreation*; *Communique*; *The Journal of Leisure Research*; *Therapeutic Recreation Journal*

National Rifle Assn. of America
1600 Rhode Island Ave. N.W., Washington, D.C. 20036
202-783-6505
The National Rifle Association is a nonprofit organization of public-spirited citizens and clubs with an interest in guns, shooting, hunting, and conservation. The NRA fosters conservation of natural resources and promotes competitive and recreational shooting. Founded: 1871. Membership: Over one million.
Chief Officer: Maxwell E. Rich, Major General (Ret.), Executive Vice President
Publications: *The American Rifleman* (journal); *Tournament News* (quarterly); *NRA Hunting Annual*; *The Game Bag* (quarterly newsletter)

National Trust for Historic Preservation
740-748 Jackson Pl. N.W., Washington, D.C. 20006
202-382-3304
Organization chartered by Congress to further the national historic preservation policy; to

facilitate public preservation of districts, sites, buildings, structures, and objects; and to preserve and administer for public benefit properties significant in American history and culture. It sponsors workshops and seminars (regional basis), provides speakers and consultant services in areas such as law, architecture, museology, and historical research, and has matching grant and loan programs, photo collection, and archives. Founded: 1947. Membership: 40,000.
Chief Officer: James Biddle, President
Publications: *Preservation News* (monthly); *Historic Preservation* (quarterly); various books, brochures, pamphlets

National Waterfowl Council
Alabama Dept. of Conservation, Montgomery, Ala. 36104
205-269-6704
Represents the various states as an advisory group to the Bureau of Sports Fisheries and Wildlife. Founded: 1960. Membership: 52 states and provinces.
Chief Officer: W.L. Holland, Chairman

National Watershed Congress
Rm. 1105, 1025 Vermont Ave. N.W., Washington, D.C. 20005
202-347-5995
Holds an annual forum to discuss ways to advance and improve programs to conserve natural resources in the smaller, upstream tributary watersheds of the nation. Founded: 1954. Membership: 34 organizations.
Chief Officer: Gordon K. Zimmerman, Chairman
Publications: Annual proceedings

National Wildlife Federation
1412 16 St. N.W., Washington, D.C. 20036
202-483-1550
Dedicated to the conservation of soil, forests, waters, wildlife, and all natural resources. Founded: 1936. Membership: 3,500,000.
Chief Officer: Thomas L. Kimball, Executive Vice President
Publications: *National Wildlife*; *International Wildlife*; *Ranger Rick's Nature Magazine*

National Wildlife Federation Endowment, Inc.
1412 16 St. N.W., Washington, D.C. 20036
202-232-8004
Established as a perpetual endowment fund to finance conservation education and resource management programs of the National Wildlife Federation. Gifts and bequests are held inviolate; only the income from the sums invested is used. Founded: 1956. Membership: 7 (Board of Directors).
Chief Officer: Joseph D. Hughes, President

Natural Resources Council of America
Suite 911, 1025 Connecticut Ave. N.W., Washington, D.C. 20036
202-223-1536
Provides a forum for the discussion of conservation issues; disseminates information; seeks to effect cooperation between groups working to protect the environment; and makes available to members scientific data and technical findings. Founded: 1946. Membership: 43 organizations.
Chief Officer: Hamilton K. Pyles, Executive Secretary
Publication: News service

Natural Resources Defense Council, Inc.
15 W. 44 St., New York, N.Y. 10036
212-869-0150
National public-interest organization using legal and scientific techniques, including monitoring of major national legislation, to approach issues of broad concern, such as air, water, and noise pollution, energy, land use, and natural-resource utilization. Founded 1970. Membership: 15,000.
Chief Officer: John H. Adams, Executive Director
Publication: Newsletter (quarterly); occasional papers

The Nature Conservancy
1800 N. Kent St., Arlington, Va. 22209
Devoted solely to the preservation of significant natural land. Founded: 1917. Membership: 25,000.
Chief Officer: E.M. Woodman, President
Publications: *The Nature Conservancy News*

North American Family Campers Assn.
76 State St., Box 552, Newburyport, Mass. 01950
617-462-6455
Encourages development, expansion, and improvement of public and private campgrounds; cooperates with and advises government agencies on sound legislation for the improvement of camping; cooperates with and initiates conservation programs to protect and improve our camping environment; informs and educates membership in all phases of modern family camping; and provides a structure of camping fellowship. Founded: 1958. Membership: 60,000.

Chief Officer: Samuel R. Thoreson, Executive Director
Publications: *Campfire Chatter* (magazine); *Tips* (for new campers)

North American Wildlife Foundation
709 Wire Bldg., Washington, D.C. 20005
202-347-1775
Promotes and sponsors wildlife and natural resources research and management in the broad public interest. Founded: 1911. Membership: 1,712.
Chief Officer: C.R. Gutermuth, Secretary and Treasurer
Publications: Progress reports

Planned Parenthood World Population
810 7 Ave., New York, N.Y. 10019
212-541-7800
Provides leadership in making available to everyone effective means of voluntary fertility control, including contraception, abortion, and sterilization; aims to achieve a U.S. population of stable size in an optimum environment; stimulates relevant biomedical, socioeconomic, and demographic research; develops appropriate information, education, and training programs; and supports the efforts of others to achieve similar goals in the U.S. and throughout the world. Founded: 1942. Membership: 15,000 volunteers (national headquarters; 191 affiliates in 44 states).
Chief Officer: John C. Robbins, Chief Executive Officer
Publications: *Family Planning Perspectives* (quarterly); *Planned Parenthood Report* (bimonthly newsletter); *President's Letter* (monthly); *Family Planning Digest* (bimonthly newsletter).

Population Council
245 Park Ave., New York, N.Y. 10017
212-687-8330
Established for scientific training and study in the field of population. It works to advance knowledge about population by fostering research, training, and technical consultation and assistance in the social and biomedical sciences. Founded: 1952. Nonmembership.
Chief Officer: Bernard Berelson, President
Publications: Books; periodicals

Population Crisis Committee
1835 K St. N.W., Washington, D.C. 20006
202-659-1833
Worldwide distributor of the publications of the Victor-Bostrom Fund for the International Planned Parenthood Federation. Founded: 1965. Membership: 3,000.
Chief Officers: Joseph D. Tydings; Robert Wallace, Co-chairmen
Publications: *Population Crisis* (newsletter); Victor-Bostrom Fund Reports; various special publications and pamphlets

Population Reference Bureau, Inc.
1755 Massachusetts Ave. N.W., Washington, D.C. 20036
202-232-2288
Gathers, analyzes, interprets, and distributes information concerning population and related subjects on a scientific and educational basis. Founded: 1929. Membership: 10,000.
Chief Officer: Michael F. Brewer, President
Publications: Bulletins; data sheets

Rachel Carson Trust for the Living Environment, Inc.
8940 Jones Mill Rd., Washington, D.C. 20015
301-652-1877
Works to develop through research and education an awareness of the contamination of the environment and to serve as a clearinghouse of information on the ecology of the environment for both scientists and laymen. Founded: 1965. Nonmembership.
Chief Officer: John L. George, President

Radiation Research Society
4211 39 St. N.W., Washington, D.C. 20016
202-244-5787
Encourages advancement of research and cooperation between the sciences in their radiation investigations and promotes dissemination of knowledge about radiation. Founded: 1952. Membership: 1,500.
Chief Officer: Richard J. Burk, Jr., Executive Director
Publications: *Radiation Research*; *Memberandum* (newsletter)

Resources for the Future, Inc.
1755 Massachusetts Ave. N.W., Washington, D.C. 20036
202-462-4400
Encourages research and education in the development, conservation, and use of natural resources and improvement of the environment. Special attention is paid to maintaining or improving environmental quality, including the relationship of population and economic growth to the environment and use of resources. Urban problems are an important area of study because of their direct impact on the environment and their influence on land use and on the demand for many kinds of resource products. Founded: 1952.

Chief Officer: Joseph L. Fisher, President
Publication: *Resources* (newsletter)

Scientists' Institute for Public Information
30 E. 68 St., New York, N.Y. 10021
212-249-3200

A national clearinghouse for science information, as well as the national coordinating body for its affiliated local scientists' committees. SIPI's primary concern is to seek out, inform, and enlist scientists of all disciplines in public information programs and to promote the growth and proliferation of such programs. Founded: 1963. Membership: 120 fellows; 35,000 subscribers.
Chief Officer: Alan McGowan, President
Publications: *Environment*; environmental workbooks

Sierra Club
1050 Mills Tower, San Francisco, Calif. 94104
415-981-8634

Works to protect and conserve the natural resources of the Sierra Nevada in particular, and the United States and the world in general. Publishes scientific and educational studies concerning all aspects of man's environment and the natural ecosystems of the world. Seeks to educate all people about the need to preserve and restore the quality of that environment and the integrity of those ecosystems. Founded: 1892. Membership: 138,000.
Chief Officer: Michael McCloskey, Executive Director
Publications: *Sierra Club Bulletin* (monthly); *National News Report* (weekly); Sierra Club books

Sierra Club Foundation
220 Bush St., San Francisco, Calif. 94101
415-981-8637

Works to finance the educational, literary, and scientific projects of groups working on environmental problems across the country. Parcels of land are owned and preserved. Special regional or interest funds may be established by individuals or foundations. Founded: 1960.
Chief Officer: Colburn S. Wilbur, Executive Secretary
Publication: Annual report

Soil Conservation Society of America
7515 N.E. Ankeny Rd., Ankeny, Iowa 50021
515-289-2331

Works to advance the science and art of good land use. Activities include ten resource divisions that delve into areas of environmental and conservation management problems and purposes. Conducts an annual meeting, sponsors special conferences, and carries on its work through 135 local chapters. Founded: 1945. Membership: 15,500.
Chief Officer: H. Wayne Pritchard, Executive Vice President
Publication: *Journal of Soil and Water Conservation*

Sport Fishery Research Foundation
Suite 801, 608 13 St. N.W., Washington, D.C. 20005
202-737-2145

Helps finance the graduate-level training of promising fisheries scientists, and helps generate and support critically needed ecological research regarding aquatic ecosystems, water quality requirements of aquatic life, and fisheries resources conservation. Founded: 1962. Membership: 7,000.
Chief Officer: Robert G. Martin, Secretary

Sport Fishing Institute
Suite 801, 608 13 St. N.W., Washington, D.C. 20005
202-737-0668

Based on concept that "the quality of fishing reflects the quality of living," the institute works through integrated programs of ecological research, fish conservation education, and aquatic science advisory service to help ensure optimum productivity of marine and fresh water ecosystems and an abundance of high-quality associated amenities. Founded: 1949. Membership: 28,000.
Chief Officer: Richard H. Stroud, Executive Vice President
Publications: *SFI Bulletin*; research papers

Trout Unlimited
4260 E. Evans, Denver, Colo. 80222
303-757-7144

Works to protect, enhance, and restore the cold water fishery in North America. Founded: 1959. Membership: 17,600.
Chief Officer: R.P. Van Gytenbeek, Executive Director
Publications: *Trout* (magazine); *Action Line* (newsletter)

Urban Land Institute
1200 18 St. N.W., Washington, D.C. 20036
202-331-8500

Promotes the highest and best use of land with the least disruption to the surrounding envi-

ronment. Founded: 1936. Membership: 5,500.
Chief Officer: David E. Stahl, Executive Vice President
Publications: Special reports; research reports.

Washington Ecology Center
Rm. 612, 2000 P St. N.W., Washington, D.C. 20006
202-833-1778
Encourages distribution of information, education, and involvement in local environmental matters. Founded: 1970. Nonmembership.
Chief Officer: Gail Daneker; David McGrew, Co-directors
Publication: Newsletter (monthly)

Water Pollution Control Federation
3900 Wisconsin Ave. N.W., Washington, D.C. 20016
202-362-4100
Works to advance the knowledge of all aspects of water pollution control by dissemination of technical information in publications of the organization. Founded: 1928. Membership: 20,000.
Chief Officer: Robert A. Canham, Executive Secretary
Publications: *Journal Water Pollution Control Federation*; *Highlights*; *Deeds and Data*

The Wilderness Society
729 15 St. N.W., Washington, D.C. 20005
202-347-4132
Aims to preserve the wilderness; carries on an educational program concerning its value, use, and preservation in the public interest; makes and encourages scientific studies of the wilderness; and mobilizes cooperation in resisting its invasion. Founded: 1935. Membership: 77,000.
Chief Officer: Stewart M. Brandborg, Executive Director
Publication: *The Living Wilderness* (quarterly)

Wildlife Disease Assn.
Box 886, Ames, Iowa 50010
515-597-2527
Advances knowledge of the effects of diseases and environmental factors upon the health of free-living and captive wild animals. Founded: 1951. Membership: 900.
Chief Officer: Leslie A. Page, President
Publications: *Journal of Wildlife Diseases* (quarterly); *Wildlife Disease* (microfiche)

Wildlife Management Institute
709 Wire Bldg., Washington, D.C. 20005
202-347-1774
Works to promote the restoration and wise use of renewable natural resources. Founded: 1945.
Chief Officer: Daniel A. Poole, President
Publication: *Transactions North American Wildlife and Natural Resources Conference* (annual)

Zero Population Growth, Inc.
4080 Fabian Way, Palo Alto, Calif. 94303
415-327-2000
A nationwide organization formed to stabilize the population of the United States by voluntary means. Founded: 1968. Membership: 25,000.
Chief Officer: Larry Mires, Acting Director
Publications: *ZPG National Reporter; Equilibrium*

REGIONAL, STATE, AND LOCAL

Alabama

The Alabama Conservancy
1816 E. 28 Ave. S., Birmingham, Ala. 35209
205-871-0839
Works for improvement of all facets of Alabama's natural environment—air, water, land, and wildlife. Operates primarily through education of the public and its elected leaders. Founded: 1967. Membership: 2,500 individuals; 70 organizations.
Chief Officer: Rowland Burns, President
Publications: *ACT* (The Alabama Conservancy tabloid); *Spaceship Earth* (educational program—slides, script, tape)

Alabama Environmental Quality Council
Box 11000, Montgomery, Ala. 36111
205-281-6474
An umbrella organization that works to solve problems concerning man's relationship to his natural and man-made surroundings; encourages voluntary community improvement and environmental quality programs. Founded: 1967.
Chief Officer: John W. Bloomer, Chairman
Publication: *EnviroNews* (newsletter)

Alabama Wildlife Federation
660 Adams Ave., Montgomery, Ala. 36104
205-263-6565
The group is dedicated to the conservation of soil, forests, waters, wildlife, and all natural resources. Founded: 1936. Membership: 16,500.

Chief Officer: Reo Kirkland, Executive Director
Publication: *Alabama Out of Doors* (newspaper)

Birmingham Audubon Society
Box 314, Birmingham, Ala. 35201
205-871-4010
The society works for the conservation and protection of the state's natural resources, particularly wildlife and wildlife habitat; carries out education and action programs. Founded: 1947. Membership: 866.
Chief Officer: J. Russell Bailey, President
Publication: *Flicker Flashes*

League of Women Voters of Alabama
768 Cary Dr., Auburn, Ala. 36830
205-887-9895
Encourages informed and active citizen participation in government and politics; supports a physical environment beneficial to life; promotes wise use of water resources and improvement of water and air quality; supports active federal leadership in solid waste management, including reuse, reclamation, and recycling; and evaluates land-use policies and procedures and their relationship to human needs, population trends, and ecological and socioeconomic factors. Founded: 1947. Membership: 794.
Chief Officer: Phyllis E. Rea, President

Mobile Bay Audubon Society
Box U-581, Mobile, Ala. 36688
205-342-5051
Works for the conservation and protection of the state's natural resources, particularly wildlife and wildlife habitat; conducts field studies, action projects, and educational programs. Founded: 1969. Membership: 350.
Chief Officer: Alicia V. Linzey, President
Publication: Newsletter

National Speleological Society, Inc.
Cave Ave., Huntsville, Ala. 35810
205-852-1300
Promotes interest in and advances the study and science of speleology, the protection of caves and their natural contents, and promotes fellowship among those interested in speleology. Founded: 1941. Membership: 4,079.
Chief Officer: Rane L. Curl, President
Publications: *NSS Bulletin*; *NSS News*

Trout Unlimited, Alabama Chapter
979 Mansard Dr., Apt. 212, Birmingham, Ala. 35223
Works to protect, enhance, and restore cold water fishery in North America. Founded: 1959. Membership: 17,000.
Chief Officer: R.P. Van Gytenbeek, Executive Director
Publication: *Trout* (magazine)

Alaska

Alaska Conservation Society
Box 80192, College, Alaska 99701
907-452-2240
Works to secure the wise use of renewable and unrenewable resources and the protection and preservation of the scenic, scientific, recreation, wildlife, and wilderness values of Alaska. Founded: 1960. Membership: 1,000.
Chief Officer: Ernst W. Mueller, President
Publication: *Alaska Conservation Review* (quarterly)

Arizona

The Research Ranch, Inc.
Elgin, Ariz. 85611
602-455-5689
Sponsors ecological research, environmental education, and conservation of an 8,000-acre natural area. Founded: 1968. Membership: 350.
Chief Officer: Ariel B. Appleton, President
Publications: Annual reports; specific studies

Arkansas

Arkansas Ecology Center
1919 W. 7 St., Little Rock, Ark. 72202
501-374-6271
Engages in general environmental education and research into alternatives to the state's environmental problems. Has participated as party plaintiffs in two law suits questioning legality of federal water projects. Active in land use planning in eastern Arkansas. Founded: 1970. Membership: 5 (Board of Directors); mailing list: 1,200.
Chief Officer: Pratt Remmel, Jr., Director
Publication: *Arkansas Ecology Center Newsletter*

Arkansas Federation of Water and Air Users
Rm. 104, 1015 Louisiana, Little Rock, Ark. 72803

501-374-0810

Informs the public about the use of water, air, and land and what is being done to maintain and improve their quality; encourages exchange of information and cooperation between industry, municipalities, and various state agencies. Membership: 150.
Publication: *The Environmental News*

Arkansas Waterways Commission
138 National, Old Line Bldg., Little Rock, Ark. 72201
A state agency to promote, develop, and protect the navigable streams of the state. Founded: 1967. Membership: 7.
Chief Officer: Paul E. Adams

Four-States Wildlife Assn.
Box 1004, Texarkana, Ark. 75501
Devoted to aspects of hunting, fishing, and related subjects. Founded: 1923. Membership: 642.
Chief Officer: E.P. Reagan, President and Service Official
Publication: Bulletin

Ozark Society, Inc.
Box 2914, Little Rock, Ark. 72203
501-374-9429
Promotes the knowledge, enjoyment, and preservation of the scenic, scientific, ecological, historical, archaeological, recreational, and aesthetic qualities of the Ozark-Ouachita region and other scenic areas in Arkansas and adjoining states. Founded: 1962. Membership: 2,000.
Chief Officer: Joe F. Nix, President
Publication: *The Ozark Society Bulletin*

California

American Lung Assn. of Santa Clara-San Benito Counties
1144 N. 4 St., San Jose, Calif. 95112
408-295-3533
Works to prevent and control respiratory diseases through programs aimed at reducing community air pollution by the development of a balanced transportation system, the preservation of open space, the conservation of energy, land-use planning, and the enforcement of strong air pollution regulations. Supports medical research and professional education; carries out screening programs for the early detection of tuberculosis and respiratory diseases; and provides special programs for patients with respiratory diseases. Founded: 1911. Membership: 63.
Chief Officer: Richard S. Gaines, Executive Director
Publication: Local newsletter

California Academy of Sciences
Golden Gate Park, San Francisco, Calif. 94118
415-221-5100
Dedicated to research and public education in science. The public areas are devoted to dioramas and exhibits, including live animals in Steinhart Aquarium. Seven active research departments are completely operative. Founded: 1853. Membership: 6,880 (paying); 698 (nonpaying); 471 (junior academy).
Chief Officer: George E. Lindsay, Director
Publications: *Pacific Discovery* (bimonthly); *Newsletter* (monthly); scientific publications include occasional papers and proceedings

California Anti-Litter League
350 Sansome St., San Francisco, Calif. 94104
415-989-5900
Works to enhance the beauty and cleanliness of California by developing and putting into effect methods to avoid and correct the problems of litter; encourages the public to become aware of their private and public responsibility to dispose of litter properly and to avoid the creation of litter along streets, highways, and in recreation and similar areas. Founded: 1967. Membership: 48 companies.
Chief Officer: Paul D. Griem, President
Publication: *The Littergram*

California Roadside Council, Inc.
2636 Ocean Ave., San Francisco, Calif. 94132
415-681-6189
Works for highway and streetside beautification, sign control, and undergrounding of utilities. Freeway location and design as it relates to the environment of communities affected. Founded: 1929. Membership: 1,500.
Chief Officer: Yale Maxon, President
Publications: Bulletins (quarterly); *Signs in California* (handbook)

Committee for the Preservation of the Tule Elk
5502 Markland Dr., Los Angeles, Calif. 90022
213-723-2924
Activities include programs, lectures, participation in public forums, educational exhibits, and field trips, all with the aim of encouraging the protection of the Tule elk and disseminating information about it. Founded: 1960. Membership: 2,000.

Chief Officer: Lawrence R. Emme, President
Publications: *History of the California Tule Elk*; membership communications

Consumer Alliance, Inc.
Box 11773, Palo Alto, Calif. 94306
415-328-7771
Works to promote better quality, reliability, and environmental soundness of consumer goods. Founded: 1971. Membership: Several hundred.
Chief Officer: Roy Kiesling, Jr., President

Cooper Ornithological Society
Department of Zoology, University of California, Los Angeles, Calif. 90024
Works for observation and cooperative study of birds, spread of interest in bird study, conservation of birds and wildlife in general, and publication of ornithological knowledge. Founded: 1893. Membership: 1,607.
Chief Officer: William H. Behle, President
Publications: *The Condor*; *Pacific Coast Avifauna*

Council for Planning and Conservation
Box 228, Beverly Hills, Calif. 90213
213-276-2685
Works to develop environmental awareness and publicize developments in areas affecting environment. Founded: 1967.
Chief Officer: Ellen S. Harris, Executive Secretary
Publication: Periodic newsletter

Desert Protective Council, Inc.
Box 33, Banning, Calif. 92220
Works to safeguard desert areas that are of unique scenic, scientific, historical, spiritual, and recreational value. Founded: 1954. Membership: 700.
Chief Officer: Arthur B. Johnson, Executive Director
Publication: *El Paisano* (newsletter)

Ecology Center
2179 Allston Way, Berkeley, Calif. 94704
415-548-2220
A community environmental information center consisting of bookstore, reading room, library, telephone switchboard, research files, and meeting rooms. Informs the public on environmental problems and ecologically sound alternatives through information dissemination and community action projects. Founded: 1969. Membership: 200
Chief Officer: Richard D. Evans, Chairman
Publication: Newsletter

The Endangered Species Committee of Berkeley
c/o Ecology Center, 2179 Allston Way, Berkeley, Calif. 94704
415-548-2220
An action organization dedicated to the protection of wildlife with a major emphasis towards, but not limited to, endangered species. Through lobbying, letter writing, and active research, it seeks to involve the public in the decision-making processes affecting the survival of our wildlife. Founded: 1970. Membership: 300.
Chief Officer: Mark Palmer, Chairman
Publication: Newsletter

Environmental Defense Fund, Inc.
2728 Durant, Berkeley, Calif. 94704
415-548-8906
Preservation of natural environment through legal and administrative action based on scientific expertise. Founded: 1967. Membership: 37,000
Publication: *EDF Letter*

Forest History Society, Inc.
Box 1581, Santa Cruz, Calif. 95061
408-426-3770
Engages in and promotes research on the history of man's relation to the forest. Seeks original source materials and places them in archives in Santa Cruz or regional facilities for availability to scholars. Also maintains an oral history program. Founded: 1947. Membership: 1,196.
Chief Officer: Elwood R. Maunder, Executive Director
Publication: *Forest History*

Friends of the Sea Otter
Big Sur, Calif. 93920
408-667-2254
Aims to protect the sea otter and increase the public's knowledge about this animal. Founded: 1968. Membership: 2,950.
Chief Officer: Margaret Owings, President
Publication: *The Otter Raft*

League to Save Lake Tahoe
1176 Emerson St., Palo Alto, Calif. 94301
415-328-5313
Works to discourage urbanization of Lake Tahoe by reducing further development of major parcels of undeveloped lands. Membership: 7,000.
Chief Officer: Steven C. Brandt, President

Monterey Area Conservation Coordinating Council

325 Melrose, Pacific Grove, Calif. 93980
408-375-2740
Coordinates common interests of conservation organizations on the Monterey Peninsula; distributes information concerning events and news items relating to the environment; conducts studies of special conservation problems of the Monterey area. Founded: 1971. Membership: 15 organizations; 300 individuals.
Chief Officer: William Reese, Chairman
Publication: *MACCC Newsletter*

Monterey Bay Committee for Environmental Information
Monterey Peninsula College, 980 Fremont, Monterey, Calif. 93940
408-372-7798
Formed to supply the local community with scientific information of an unbiased nature concerning local environmental issues. Serves as a resource center for information and personnel on a wide variety of environmental problems in the area. Founded: 1969. Membership: 50.
Chief Officer: Peter L. Besag, Chairman
Publication: Newsletter

National Audubon Society Western Regional Office
555 Audubon Place, Sacramento, Calif. 95825
916-481-5332
Works for the conservation and protection of natural resources, particularly wildlife and wildlife habitat. The Regional Office represents California, Nevada, Oregon, Washington, Alaska, and Hawaii. Founded: 1905. Membership: 250,000.
Chief Officer: Paul Howard, Representative

The Nature Conservancy Western Regional Office
Suite 1118, 215 Market St., San Francisco, Calif. 94105
415-989-3056
Devoted to the preservation of ecologically significant land. Natural areas acquired and held by the Conservancy are managed for scientific and educational purposes. Founded: 1951. Membership: 25,000.
Chief Officer: Steven P. Steinhour (SF Office), Western Regional Director
Publication: *TNC News* (quarterly)

North American Assn. for the Preservation of Predatory Animals, Inc.
Mountain Place, Box 166, Doyle, Calif. 96109
415-526-5895 (evenings)
Works to educate the public regarding the value of predatory animals and promotes an intelligent policy for their management and protection. Founded: 1969. Membership: 800.
Chief Officer: John Harris, President
Publication: *NAAPPA Newsletter* (quarterly)

Northern California Committee for Environmental Information
Box 761, Berkeley, Calif. 94701
415-642-6707
Provides public with information on environmental problems. An affiliate of the Scientists' Institute for Public Information. Founded: 1968. Membership: 300.
Publication: *EnFo* (newsletter)

Peninsula Conservation Center
1176 Emerson, Palo Alto, Calif. 94301
415-328-5313
Works to protect the peninsula's ecological balance; serves as an educational and information center and coordinates efforts of other groups. Founded: 1969.
Chief Officer: Claire T. Dedrick, Executive Director
Publications: Fact sheets

Planned Parenthood Assn. of Santa Clara County, Inc.
28 N. 16 St., San Jose, Calif. 95112
408-294-3032
Engages in a program to encourage family planning. Founded: 1965. Membership: 700.
Chief Officer: Allene Soshea, President

Planning and Conservation League
Suite 310, 1225 8 St., Sacramento, Calif. 95814
916-444-8726
A public-interest lobby; sole business is promoting sound environmental legislation in California's State Legislature. Founded: 1965. Membership: 4,500 individuals; 90 organizations.
Chief Officer: Bill Press, Executive Director
Publication: *California Today* (monthly newsletter)

Public Advocates, Inc.
433 Turk St., San Francisco, Calif. 94102
415-441-8850
Emphasizes environmental actions as they relate particularly to urban, low-income, and minority issues. Activities include successful federal court injunctions against highways that destroy parks and low-income communities and utility rate structures that encour-

age excessive consumption and penalize low-income conservationist efforts. Also emphasizes broadening and democratizing of environmental movement to include black, Chicano, and other minority groups. Acts as legal counsel for the NAACP, Western Region, the League of United Latin American Citizens, various Asian, Filipino and native American organizations as well as representing environmental groups such as San Francisco Tomorrow and Sierra Club. Founded: 1971. Membership: 8 attorneys.
Chief Officer: Robert L. Gnaizda, Managing Attorney

Public Education Research Committee of California
Suite 305, 1760 Solano Ave., Berkeley, Calif. 94707
415-524-4261
Follows legislation, court cases, and administrative activity in California in the area of family planning. Provides expert testimony at public hearings when requested, and gives information on family planning to legislators when requested. Founded: 1971. Membership: 4 (3,500 mailing list).
Chief Officers: Nancy M. Jewel; Sarah Beserra, Co-directors
Publications: Special reports

San Francisco Planning and Urban Renewal Assn. (SPUR)
126 Post St., San Francisco, Calif. 94108
415-781-8726
Acts as a watchdog on issues which affect San Francisco and the Bay Area such as transportation, planning, regional affairs, social issues, housing, waterfront and urban design, and open space. Founded: 1959. Membership: 1,000.
Chief Officer: John H. Jacobs, Executive Director
Publication: *SPUR Reports*

Santa Clara County Bar Assn. Environmental Law Section
12 S. 1 St., #229, San Jose, Calif. 95113
408-288-8844
Works to develop improvements in the environmental law field and to contribute to the professional development of the members of the Santa Clara County Bar Association through seminars, programs, and distribution of informational materials. Founded: 1970. Membership: 100.
Chief Officer: Mary A. Davis, Executive Director

Save Our Valley Action Committee
11040 Enchanto Vista, San Jose, Calif. 95127
408-258-0655
Deals with environmental factors affecting the Santa Clara Valley, particularly the adverse effects created by explosive growth in commercial aircraft traffic and the resulting noise and air pollution. Founded: 1967. Membership: 800.
Chief Officer: Robert Gray, Director
Publication: Newsletter

Save the Redwoods League
Rm. 605, 114 Sansome St., San Francisco, Calif. 94104
415-362-2352
Works to preserve representative areas of our primeval forests; cooperates with the California State Park Commission, the National Park Service, and other agencies, in establishing redwood parks and other parks and reservations; purchases redwood groves by private subscription; cooperates with the California State Highway Commission and other agencies in assuring the preservation of trees and roadside beauty along highways; and supports reforestation and conservation of forest areas. Founded: 1918. Membership: 55,000.
Chief Officer: Newton B. Drury, President
Publication: Bulletin (biannual)

Society for the Preservation of Birds of Prey
Box 891, Pacific Palisades, Calif. 90272
Educates the public about the value of predatory birds; disseminates information and promotes communication among raptor enthusiasts; discourages the harvesting of birds of prey for research purposes; and legislates against the practice of falconry. Conducts a year-round banding program in Southern California and sponsors hawk watches at Mt. Peter and Hook Mt., New York. Founded: 1966. Membership: 200.
Chief Officer: J. Richard Hilton, President
Publication: *The Raptor Report* (quarterly)

Trustees for Conservation
251 Kearny St., San Francisco, Calif. 94108
415-392-2838
Raises funds to support legislative activities for proposals favoring conservation goals and opposing proposals which would adversely affect such goals. Founded: 1954. Membership: 75.
Chief Officer: Hilary H. Crawford, Jr., President

United New Conservationists
84 S. 5 St., San Jose, Calif. 95112
Activities include committees to study and identify pollution problems, camping and hiking environmental awareness groups, and recycling days. Aims to strengthen conservation efforts through a confederation of organizations and individuals, and maintains an up-to-date library of publications on environmental subjects. Founded: 1969. Membership: 12 organizations; 30 individuals.
Chief Officer: Lilyan Brannon, President
Publication: *Common Ground* (bimonthly)

Zero Population Growth, Inc., California Confederation
Suite 208-C, 100 W. Rincon Ave., Campbell, Calif. 95008
408-374-5444
Initiates and lobbies for legislation related to population and family planning. Founded: 1971. Membership: 500.
Chief Officer: Doug Graham, Chairman of the Board
Publication: Newsletter (monthly)

Colorado

American Assn. for Conservation Information
6060 Broadway, Denver, Colo. 80216
A loose-knit organization of state conservation agencies formed primarily to share knowledge and experiences to help member agencies do a better job. Founded: 1938. Membership: 45 agencies.
Chief Officer: Kliess Brown
Publication: *Balance Wheel*

Balarat Center for Environmental Studies
1521 Irving St., Denver, Colo. 80204
303-266-2255
Develops and operates a program of outdoor Environmental Education for pupils of the Denver public schools from kindergarten through 12th grade. Founded: 1968. Membership: 12 Denver public schools.
Chief Officer: Kenneth W. Horn, Administrator
Publications: *At Balarat* (newsletter); special publications

Colorado Citizens for Clean Air
1325 Delaware, Denver, Colo. 80203
303-573-9241
Promotes air pollution control legislation requiring high quality air standards; cooperates with federal, state, and local agencies in controlling air pollution; and educates the public to the dangers of air pollution. Founded: 1969. Membership: 150.
Chief Officer: Eugene R. Weiner
Publication: Newsletter (monthly)

Colorado Institute on Population Problems
Box 18291, Capitol Hill Station, Denver, Colo. 80218
303-781-1649
Works to gather and spread population information relevant to Colorado and publicize the consequences of overpopulation. Founded: 1969.
Chief Officer: Ruth M. Steel, President
Publications: Brochures; papers

Colorado Open Space Council, Inc.
1325 Delaware St., Denver, Colo. 80204
303-573-9241 or 573-7870
Coordinating council for citizen groups concerned with environmental issues; engages in education, study, and legislative action in areas such as pollution, highways and transportation, wilderness, land-use planning, energy, water resources, mining, and urban problems. Founded: 1965. Membership: 33 organizations (30,000).
Chief Officer: Marilyn Miller, Administrative Secretary
Publications: *COSC Legislative Bulletin* (weekly during legislative session); *COSC Newsletter*

Colorado Water Congress
Suite 328, Livestock Exchange Bldg., Denver, Colo. 80216
303-573-8572
Works to educate the public as to the proper uses of water, to store all of Colorado's water for future use, and to induce proper water- and land-use legislation in Colorado. Founded: 1958. Membership: 2,000.
Chief Officer: R.T. Edmondson, Executive Director
Publications: Monthly bulletin; newsletter

Colorado Wildlife Federation, Inc.
Box 1588, Denver, Colo. 80201
A state organization affiliated with the National Wildlife Federation. Dedicated to the conservation of soil, forests, waters, wildlife, and all natural resources. Founded: 1952.
Chief Officer: Hans W. Von Barby, President
Publication: *Colorado Wildlife Federation News*

Environmental Action Committee
1100 14 St., Denver, Colo. 80202
Serves as a research and consulting center, information clearinghouse, and catalyst for intelligent action by citizens. Founded: 1970. Membership: 7,000.
Chief Officer: Rick Speed
Publication: *REACT* (monthly)

Rocky Mountain Center on Environment
4260 E. Evans Ave., Denver, Colo. 80222
303-757-5439
Seeks rational solutions to environmental issues. Works with other groups, sponsors forums and speeches, and disseminates information. Founded: 1968. Nonmembership.
Chief Officer: Roger P. Hansen, Executive Director
Publication: *ROMCOE Forum*

Connecticut

Connecticut Assn. of Soil and Water Conservation Districts, Inc.
Goshen, Conn. 06756
Coordinates activities of the eight Connecticut Soil and Water Conservation Districts and is affiliated with the National Association of Conservation Districts to promote and coordinate programs and actions. Founded: 1947. Membership: 40.
Chief Officer: John Breakelli, President

Connecticut Conservation Assn.
Northrop St., Bridgewater, Conn. 06752
203-354-9325
Broad-spectrum environmental organization with emphasis on education of the public on environmental issues, problems, and their solutions. Founded: 1967. Membership: 5,000.
Chief Officer: Robert F. Kunz, Executive Vice President
Publications: *Reporter* (monthly); annual magazine

Connecticut Forest and Park Assn.
1010 Main St., Box 389, E. Hartford, Conn. 06108
203-289-3637
Works to conserve forests, scenery, and wildlife, and to improve environmental quality in Connecticut. Founded: 1895. Membership: 2,200.
Chief Officer: John E. Hibbard, Secretary-Forester
Publications: *Connecticut Woodlands* (quarterly); newsletters

Connecticut Wildlife Federation
Box 7, Middletown, Conn. 06457
203-347-1291
Dedicated to the conservation of soil, forests, waters, wildlife, and all natural resources. Founded: 1936.
Chief Officer: Walter Hylwa, President
Publication: *Connecticut Wildlife Flyer*

Conservation and Research Foundation, Inc.
Connecticut College, Box 1445, New London, Conn. 06320
203-442-5391 or 442-5306
Works to promote the conservation of natural resources, to encourage research in the biological sciences, and to deepen understanding of the relationship between man and his environment. Founded: 1953. Membership: 8 trustees.
Chief Officer: Richard H. Goodwin, President

Natural Science for Youth Foundation
763 Silvermine Rd., New Canaan, Conn. 06840
203-966-5643
Provides free counseling to community groups in the planning and development of environmental and natural science centers and museums which are designed particularly to meet the needs and interests of children and young people. Offers a training course in the management of small museums and nature centers, and conducts an annual conference as part of its widespread effort to promote professional excellence in environmental and natural science centers and museums. Founded: 1961. Membership: 306.
Chief Officer: John Ripley Forbes, President
Publication: Proceedings of annual conference

Wildlife Management Institute
200 Audubon Lane, Fairfield, Conn. 06430
203-259-1447
Representative of the Northeast region; provides service to states, towns, groups, and individuals in wildlife and general environmental services; provides technical knowledge for solution of practical problems. Founded: 1910.
Chief Officer: Daniel Poole, President
Publications: *North American Wildlife and Natural Resources Conference*; *Outdoor News Bulletin*; special publications

Delaware

Delaware Wildlife Federation
1011 Washington St., Wilmington, Del. 19801

302-654-9424
Dedicated to the conservation of soil, forests, waters, wildlife, and all natural resources.
Chief Officer: James C. Warren, President
Publication: Newsletter

District of Columbia

Central Atlantic Environment Center
1717 Massachusetts Ave., Washington, D.C. 20036
202-265-1587
Provides information on matters of environmental concern in Maryland, Delaware, Virginia, and the District of Columbia. It assists individuals, private organizations, public officials, members of the business community, and the press in their evaluation and action on environmental matters. Founded: 1967 (as Potomac Basin Center). Nonmembership.
Chief Officer: William E. Shands, Executive Director
Publication: *Central Atlantic Environment News* (monthly newsletter)

Florida

Citizen Action Against Pollution
Box 1721, Fort Myers, Fla. 33902
813-694-2121
Searches for ways to improve the environment and works to implement them. Founded: 1970. Membership: 20.
Chief Officer: J.K. Isley, Jr., M.D.

Concerned Citizens for Conservation
Box 12646, University Station, Gainesville, Fla. 32601
904-373-0668
Local and regional participation in environmental action and protection through clean-up campaigns, letter-writing campaigns, public displays, etc. Founded: 1969. Membership: 580.
Chief Officer: David H. Williams IV, Director

Environmental Advisory Board
City of Boca Raton, Boca Raton, Fla. 33432
305-395-1110
Advises City Council and administration officials on environmental problems; proposes policies and procedures to alleviate such conditions. Founded: 1972. Membership: 11.
Chief Officer: Edward W. Hassell, Chairman

Environmental Information Center of the Florida Conservation Foundation, Inc.
935 Orange Ave., Winter Park, Fla. 32789
305-644-5377
Encourages research and education about Florida's environment.
Founded: 1968. Membership: 25.

Florida Audubon Society
Drawer 7, Maitland, Fla. 32751
305-647-2615
Works for conservation and protection of the state's natural resources, particularly wildlife and wildlife habitat. Conducts environmental education programs, and manages many wildlife sanctuaries. Founded: 1900. Membership: 25,000. Chief Officer: Hal Scott, Executive Director
Publications: *Florida Naturalist*; *Conservation Digest*

Florida Council for Clean Air
Box 8217, Jacksonville, Fla. 32211
904-743-2933
Sponsored by the Florida Lung Association, it aims to provide information on air pollution control to the public and to work with official agencies and volunteers to represent the public in all regulatory matters involving air pollution. Founded: 1968. Membership: 360.
Chief Officer: Carl C. Booberg, Secretary
Publications: Occasional mailings; newsletter

Florida Defenders of the Environment, Inc.
Box 12063, Gainesville, Fla. 32601
904-372-6965
An organization of scientists, economists, attorneys, and other specialists who voluntarily research and compile data on potential threats to the quality of Florida's environment. Founded: 1969. Membership: 300.
Chief Officer: Marjorie H. Carr, President
Publication: Newsletter

Florida Forestry Assn.
Box 1696, Tallahassee, Fla. 32302
904-222-5646
An organization of industries, businesses, and individuals who encourage the promotion, development, and protection of Florida's forest resources. This is accomplished through a public information program including distribution of booklets, pamphlets, radio and television announcements, articles, and contacts with influential groups of all types. Founded: 1924. Membership: 1,000.
Chief Officer: Wm. Carroll Lamb, Executive Director

Publications: *Pines & Needles* (monthly newsletter); annual report

International Defenders of Animals, Inc.
71 Hialeah Dr., Box 172, Hialeah, Fla. 33011
305-887-0804
Takes an active interest in all problems concerning animals, both wild and domestic. Helps animals in distress and people with animal problems; finds homes for abandoned, stray, and unwanted dogs and cats. Founded: 1958. Membership: Over 500.
Chief Officer: Virginia Gillas, President
Publication: Newsletter (every two months)

Keep Florida Beautiful, Inc.
520 Seybold Bldg., Miami, Fla. 33132
Encourages the preservation of Florida's natural beauty through a program of environmental education with emphasis on litter prevention and control and water and air pollution control. Founded: 1972. Membership: 100.
Chief Officer: Jack Block, President

League of Women Voters of Florida
324 Datura St., West Palm Beach, Fla. 33401
305-655-9521
Works to promote active participation of citizens in government. Takes action on environmental concerns: wise use of water resources, improved water and air quality, solid waste management, and land-use policies. Founded: 1939. Membership: 4,000.
Chief Officer: Eleanor Weinstock, President
Publication: *Florida Voter*

Pollution Protective Assn.
Box 187, Palmetto, Fla. 33561
813-722-2600
Organized for the protection of growers in Hillsborough and Manatee Counties against industry pollution. It has since expanded to include civic groups interested in all forms of air and water pollution. Founded: 1964. Membership: 225.
Chief Officer: R.L. Council, Chairman
Publication: *Pollution Protective Reporter* (monthly)

Sierra Club Florida Chapter
12195 S.W. 90 Ave., Miami, Fla. 33156
Conservation organization actively involved with preserving and improving our natural environment. Founded: 1970. Membership: 1,200.
Chief Officer: Ellen Winchester, Chairperson
Publication: Bulletin

Georgia

Citizens for Clean Air
Georgia T. Bond RD Assn., 1383 Spring St. N.W., Atlanta, Ga. 30309
404-876-3601
Monitors state implementation plan, lobbies for air legislation during state session, and acts as air resource information center for other conservation organizations in Atlanta. Founded: 1970. Membership: 300.
Chief Officer: Executive Committee
Publication: Newsletter (quarterly)

The Georgia Conservancy, Inc.
Suite 402, 3376 Peachtree Rd. N.E., Atlanta, Ga. 30326
404-262-1967
A statewide organization concerned with preservation of natural areas and education on environmental issues. Founded: 1967. Membership: 5,300.
Chief Officer: James D. Landrum, President
Publications: Quarterly magazine; monthly newsletter; children's newsletter

Georgia Environmental Education Council
Box 819, Macon, Ga. 31202
912-746-3531
Coordinates the outdoor education efforts in Georgia, promotes and encourages outdoor education, and operates the Georgia Environmental Education Institute. Founded: 1964. Membership: 20.
Chief Officer: George D. Walker, Chairman

Georgia Forest Research Council
Box 828, Macon, Ga. 31202
912-746-3531
An independent agency of the State of Georgia which promotes research in forest resources for a quality forest environment. Founded: 1953.
Chief Officer: H.E. Ruark, Director
Publications: Research reports and papers

Georgia Tuberculosis and Respiratory Disease Assn.
1383 Spring St. N.W., Atlanta, Ga. 30309
404-876-3601
Engages in fund raising for research, scholarships, and patient aid, and conducts educational programs for the prevention of lung diseases; coordinates Citizens for Clean Air activities. Founded: 1913. Membership: 69.
Chief Officer: Flay W. Sellers, Managing Director for the TB-RD Assn.

Publications: *TB-RD News in Georgia; Airogram*

Save America's Vital Environment
Box 52652, Atlanta, Ga. 30305
404-237-5693
Aims to conserve resources through wise stewardship; to promote open space conservation; to control air, water, and noise pollution; to further the establishment of urban and rural amenities; to work towards solution of transportation problems; and to coordinate total environmental planning at state and other levels. Founded: 1970. Membership: 300.
Chief Officer: Landon Butler, President
Publication: *Assembly Record* (bulletin)

Southern Forest Institute
Suite 280, 1 Corporate Sq. N.E., Atlanta, Ga. 30329
404-633-5137
Works to encourage full development of forest lands for multiple uses. Programs include news service, forestry camps for youths, teacher workshops, conferences for private landowners, materials and films on forestry and the industry, and administration of the Southern Forest Disease and Insect Research Council and Southern Forest Resource Council. Founded: 1939 (formerly Southern Pulpwood Conservation Association). Membership: 70 companies.
Chief Officer: Benton H. Box, Executive Vice President
Publications: Newsletter (monthly); other special forestry publications

Hawaii

First Society of Whale Watchers
Box 10312, Honolulu, Hawaii 96816
808-734-8327
Engages in activities to encourage the preservation and protection of whales. Founded: 1952. Mailing list: 4,000.
Chief Officer: Gerald B. Burtnett

Hawaii Audubon Society
Box 5032, Honolulu, Hawaii 96814
808-988-6798
Works for the conservation and protection of the state's natural resources, particularly wildlife and wildlife habitat; holds field trips and meetings. Founded: 1939. Membership: 400.
Chief Officer: William P. Mull, President
Publication: *The Elepaio* (monthly)

Life of the Land
404 Piikoi St., Honolulu, Hawaii 96814
808-521-1300
Promotes environmental research and action; investigates, lobbies, testifies at public hearings, and litigates; and operates an environmental law program involving attorneys and law students that does background work for court cases. Founded: 1970. Membership: 700.
Chief Officer: Tony Hodges, Executive Director

The Outdoor Circle
Rm. 502, 200 N. Vineyard Blvd., Honolulu, Hawaii 96817
808-521-0074
Works to develop a more beautiful state, to conserve and develop its natural beauty, and to cooperate in educational and other efforts towards community welfare, health, sanitation, sightliness, and physical good order. Founded: 1912. Membership: 3,437.
Chief Officer: Mrs. Robert Creps, President
Publication: Newsletter (triannual)

Idaho

Idaho Environmental Council
Box 3371, University Station, Moscow, Idaho 83843
208-882-3511 or 882-6417
Works to stimulate an increased understanding and awareness of the impact of modern society and man on his environment; promotes the preservation and wise use of scenic, historic, open space, wildlife, wilderness, and outdoor recreational resources; and encourages citizen, legislative, and administrative action toward the protection and restoration of our natural and historic heritage and the creation of communities which reflect these values. Founded: 1968.
Chief Officer: Gerald A. Jayne, President
Publication: Newsletter (monthly)

Illinois

Bicycle Ecology
Box 66498, Chicago, Ill. 60666
312-468-1588
Promotes bicycling as a stimulus for needed transportation reforms. Founded: 1970. Membership: 590.
Chief Officer: Edward Abramic, Director

Publications: *Bicycle Ecology* (newsletter); *The Transportation Reform Bulletin*

Citizens Against Noise
2729 W. Lunt Ave., Chicago, Ill. 60645
312-274-0980
Works to reduce noise in our society. Founded: 1969. Membership: 200.
Chief Officer: Theodore Berland, President
Publication: *CANews*

Citizens for a Better Environment
Box 124, Dupo, Ill. 62239
Aims to stop air and noise pollution, and confronts specific local problems as they arise. Founded: 1969. Membership: About 40.
Chief Officer: Ray Fitzpatrick, Chairman

Citizens for Better Environment Research Department
Rm. 1101, 109 N. Dearborn, Chicago, Ill. 60602
312-263-5670
Raises and distributes funds for environmental purposes; identifies polluters and brings legal action against them; and studies urban problems and takes appropriate legal or public action. Founded: 1971. Mailing list: 3,000.
Chief Officer: Duane Lindstrom, Director of Research
Publication: *One* (newsletter)

Clean Air Coordinating Committee
1440 W. Washington St., Chicago, Ill. 60607
312-243-2000
Promotes measures to create a public awareness about the mounting threat of air pollution; coordinates activities between organizations and individuals interested in air pollution control; provides a clearinghouse for information on air pollution; and institutes step-by-step community action programs that focus on the problem of air pollution. Founded: 1969. Membership: 40 organizations; 1,500 individuals.
Chief Officer: Richard Kates, Chairman
Publications: *Chicagoland Air Monitor*; legislative newsletter

Committee on Lake Michigan Pollution
111 W. Washington St., Chicago, Ill. 60602
312-263-6630
Studies, publicizes, and lobbies to preserve Lake Michigan. Founded: 1967. Membership: 105.
Chief Officer: James D. Griffith, President
Publication: *Michigan Murk*

Eagle Valley Environmentalists, Inc.
Box 152, Apple River, Ill. 61001
815-594-2305
Aims to preserve wilderness areas throughout the nation and to educate the public as to why they should be preserved. Founded: 1971. Membership: 160.
Chief Officer: Terrence N. Ingram, President
Publication: *Eagle Valley News*

Environmental Forum, Inc.
Box 52, Peoria, Ill. 61602
Provides information and ideas for environmental improvement through seminars, conferences, and other educational media. Provides one large seminar a year and brings in many out-of-state speakers. Founded: 1970. Membership: 175.
Chief Officer: Ed Seibert, President

Environmental Parameters Research Organization
Rte. 1, Box 83, Elgin, Ill. 60120
312-741-9053
Conducts scientific research and educational activities in oceanography and the environmental sciences. Founded: 1969.
Chief Officer: John D. Harper, Executive Director

Garden Club of Illinois, Inc.—Environmental Improvement
1629 Garfield, Granite City, Ill. 62040
Organizes and helps garden clubs throughout Illinois; advances gardening; develops home grounds and civic beautification; stimulates an interest in cooperative gardening; aids in the protection of forests, wild flowers, and birds; exterminates obnoxious weeds; and improves highways. Founded: 1927. Membership: 10,482.
Chief Officer: Mrs. Eugene J. Tamillo, President
Publication: *Garden Glories*

Illinois Audubon Society
1017 Burlington Ave., Downers Grove, Ill. 60515
312-968-0744
Works for the conservation and protection of the state's natural resources, particularly wildlife and wildlife habitat. Founded: 1897. Membership: 3,000.
Chief Officer: Warren R. Dewalt, Executive Director
Publications: *The Audubon Bulletin; The Illinois Audubon Newsletter*

Illinois Citizens Clean Air League
725 S. 26 St., Box 2576, Springfield, Ill. 62708
217-528-3441
Distributes educational materials and supplies expertise for testimony for hearings. Founded: 1970. Membership: 100.
Chief Officer: Jeff Hartzler, Director of Special Programs

Illinois Planning and Conservation League
122 S. Michigan Ave., #1900, Chicago, Ill. 60603
312-341-0515
Supports and promotes good environmental legislation in the Illinois State Legislature. Founded: 1970. Membership: 300.
Chief Officer: Douglas Schroeder, President
Publication: *IPCLetter*

Illinois Prairie Path
616 Delles Rd., Box 1086, Wheaton, Ill. 60187
312-232-2558
A part of the National Trails System, the Path offers a variety of terrain for hiking, bicycling, horseback riding, as well as for photographers, rock-hounds, rail fans, birders, and ecologists. Founded: 1964. Membership: 1,200.
Chief Officer: F. Paul Mooring, President
Publications: *Newsletter* (quarterly); trail guides

Illinois Wildlife Federation
13005 S. Western Ave., Box 116, Blue Island, Ill. 60406
312-388-3995
Dedicated to the conservation of soil, forests, waters, wildlife, and all natural resources. Founded: 1936. Membership: 35,000.
Chief Officer: Ace Extrom, Executive Secretary
Publication: *Illinois Wildlife*

Institute of Environmental Sciences
940 E. N.W. Highway, Mount Prospect, Ill. 60056
312-255-1561
Promotes and encourages the acquisition and dissemination of knowledge pertaining to environmental sciences, environmental engineering, and related areas of interest for industry, science, and government; develops and promotes standards, research, simulation, testing, and design criteria in the environmental field; and sponsors curricula in the environmental sciences. Founded: 1953. Membership: 1,600.
Chief Officer: Betty L. Peterson, Executive Director

Publications: Various technical and special publications

Lake Michigan Federation
53 W. Jackson Blvd., Chicago, Ill. 60604
312-427-5121
Works to involve the public in all environmental decision-making to the fullest extent possible. Focus areas include nuclear power production, shoreland planning, and monitoring water quality enforcement procedures and activities. Founded: 1970. Membership: 250 organizations; 400 individuals.
Chief Officer: Mrs. Lee Botts, Executive Secretary
Publication: *Bulletin of the Lake Michigan Federation* (monthly newsletter)

Max McGraw Wildlife Foundation
Box 194, Dundee, Ill. 60118
312-741-8000
Works to further the welfare of wildlife and fisheries resources through programs of research, management, education, and cooperation with other agencies. Founded: 1962. Membership: 200.
Chief Officer: Crowdus Baker, President
Publications: Brochures and leaflets; reprints of technical research papers

Natural Land Institute
819 N. Main St., Rockford, Ill. 61103
815-964-6666
Promotes preservation of natural land, encourages study, establishes and maintains preserves, maintains a library, and disseminates information. Founded: 1958.
Chief Officer: George B. Fell, Chairman
Publications: Various special publications

O'Hare Area Noise Abatement Council
194 Sherwood Dr., Wood Dale, Ill. 60191
312-766-8620
Works through federal, state, and local agencies to relieve jet aircraft noise, and represents 31 municipalities adjacent to and surrounding O'Hare International Airport. At least one member appointed by the governing body of each municipality is a member of the group. Founded: 1969. Membership: 31 municipalities.
Chief Officer: George J. Franks, President

Open Lands Project
53 W. Jackson Blvd., Chicago, Ill. 60604
312-427-4256
Preserves and develops areas of natural beauty and scientific value in Illinois; develops urban

parks; conducts vast programs of environmental education at the elementary and secondary levels; works with community groups and senior citizens to beautify the city; and works in all areas of outdoor recreation. Founded: 1963. Membership: 1,200.
Chief Officer: Gunnar A. Peterson, Executive Director
Publication: Newsletter

The Nature Conservancy, Illinois Chapter
708 Church St., Evanston, Ill. 60201
312-328-0530
Acquires and manages natural areas for scientific, educational, and aesthetic uses. Founded: 1957. Membership: 1,025.
Chief Officer: Daniel E. Pike, Director
Publication: Newsletter

Planned Parenthood Assn.
185 N. Wabash Ave., Chicago. Ill. 60601
312-726-5134
Provides family planning services to the public: direct services, counseling, training, education, and referral services. Founded: 1946. Membership: 6,000.
Chief Officer: Benjamin F. Lewis, Executive Director
Publications: Newsletter; annual report

Sierra Club, Great Lakes Chapter
616 Delles, Wheaton, Ill. 60187
312-665-3939
Works for the appreciation and preservation of natural areas and the environment through education, legislation, and litigation. Founded: 1892. Membership: 3,900.
Chief Officer: Keith Olson, Chariman
Publication: *Lake and Prairie*

Water Quality Research Council
330 S. Naperville St., Wheaton, Ill. 60187
312-668-8892
Conducts or sponsors research and public education in water chemistry as it relates to pollution and human or animal health. Founded: 1957. Membership: 1,000.
Publication: *International Water Quality Symposia Proceedings*

Indiana

Acres, Inc.
1802 Chapman Rd., Huntertown, Ind. 46748
219-637-6264
Dedicated to the preservation of natural areas in northeastern Indiana. Founded: 1960. Membership: 450.
Chief Officer: Robert C. Weber, President
Publication: *Acres* (quarterly)

Columbus Water and Air Assn.
S. Pear, Box 170, Columbus, Ind. 47201
812-372-8861
Encourages proper use and treatment of the water supply and waste water.
Chief Officer: Clyde Spear, Manager

Indiana Conservation Council, Inc.
2128 E. 46 St., Indianapolis, Ind. 46205
317-251-1533
Works for the wise use of natural resources and the protection of our environment by all educational means. ICCI is the Indiana affiliate of the National Wildlife Federation. Founded: 1961. Membership: 5,000.
Chief Officer: Jim Jontz, Executive Director
Publication: *Hoosier Conservation*

Save the Dunes Council
1512 Park Dr., Munster, Ind. 46321
219-838-5843
Works for the protection of Indiana Dunes region. Part of objective was to establish the Indiana Dunes National Lakeshore (1966); it is now dedicated to enlarging Lakeshore, protecting it against a variety of threats and encroachments, and combating air and water pollution. Founded: 1952. Membership: 3,000.
Chief Officer: Sylvia Troy, President
Publication: Newsletter (monthly)

Iowa

J.N. "Ding" Darling Foundation, Inc.
c/o Central National Bank and Trust Co., Des Moines, Iowa 50304
515-243-8181
Works to initiate, coordinate, and expedite programs, research, and education on conservation and management of natural resources. Aims to improve and assure outdoor recreational opportunities now and for the future. Founded: 1962. Membership: 50 board members.
Chief Officer: Sherry R. Fisher, Chairman

Iowa Wildlife Federation, Inc.
Box 25, Mediapolis, Iowa 52637
319-394-3671

Dedicated to the conservation of soil, forests, waters, wildlife, and all natural resources; conducts youth educational programs. Founded: 1952. Membership: 2,000.
Chief Officer: John Creswell, President.
Publication: *Iowa Wildlife Newsletter* (monthly)

Upper Mississippi River Conservation Committee
314 Federal Bldg., Davenport, Iowa 52801
319-323-8129
Promotes the preservation, development, and wide utilization of the natural and recreational resources of the Upper Mississippi River. Founded: 1943. Membership: 63.
Chief Officer: Al Lopinot
Publications: Various special publications

Kansas

Kansas Wildlife Federation, Inc.
R.R. 1, Wamego, Kans. 66547
913-456-2500
Dedicated to the conservation of soil, forests, waters, wildlife, and all natural resources.
Chief Officer: Walt Snell, President
Publication: *The Kansas Sportsman*

Kentucky

Action for Clean Air, Inc.
10014 Foxboro Dr., Louisville, Ky. 40223
502-425-7022
Works to educate the public to the effects of air pollution; encourages public participation in public hearings and in regulatory processes of air pollution control; encourages individual conservation and proper use of resources; and cooperates with other environmentally oriented groups. Founded: 1968. Membership: 250 individuals; 8 organizations.
Chief Officer: Charles Hassett, President
Publication: *Action News* (newsletter)

The Izaak Walton League of Kentucky, Inc.
9 E. Southern Ave., Covington, Ky. 41015
606-491-5000
A broadly based conservation organization which aims at the preservation and wise use of soils, woodlands, waters, wildlife, and air.
Chief Officer: David F. Surber, President
Publication: Newsletter

Kentucky Audubon Council
1020 E. 20 St., Owensboro, Ky. 42301
502-685-1849
Coordinates activities of community chapters of the National Audubon Society to reflect the Society's aims of environmental protection and education. Founded: 1971. Membership: 4,000.
Chief Officer: Ralph Madison, Council President

Kentucky Lung Assn. (formerly the Kentucky TB and RD Assn.)
Box 8405, 4100 Churchman Ave., Louisville, Ky. 40208
502-363-2652
Works towards the prevention and control of disease and environmental threats to the human lung. Founded: 1909.
Chief Officer: Thomas P. Summers, Executive Director
Publications: *The Kentucky Lung Association Newsletter* (bimonthly); *The Kentucky Thoracic Society's News Notes* (quarterly)

League of Women Voters of Kentucky
3316 Braemer Dr., Lexington, Ky. 40502
606-278-8132
Acts as lobby and watchdog of administrative agencies, particularly at public hearings where statements are made. Active in the fields of air pollution, severance tax (advocates tax on coal and other minerals administered by state government), strip minings, and water resources. Founded: 1920. Membership: 1,090.
Chief Officer: Mrs. G.W. Schwert, President
Publication: *The Kentucky Voter*

Strategies for Environmental Control
City Hall, Rm. 105, 6 and Jefferson, Louisville, Ky. 40201
502-589-4230 Ext. 315
Activities include citizen action, legal and legislative research, watchdog on local government and industry, lobbying, and environmental education programs from kindergarten to adult levels. Works to actively promote environmental quality in the Louisville area by any appropriate means. Founded: 1970. Membership: 20 organizations; mailing list: 500.
Chief Officer: Gary F. Levy, Executive Director
Publication: Newsletter (monthly)

Louisiana

Committee on Environmental Quality
Box 44033, Capital Sta., Baton Rouge, La. 70804

504-389-2141
Conducts research on environmental quality in order to influence judgments on proposed environmental legislation. Founded: 1970. Membership: 9.
Chief Officer: Don Whittinghill, Director
Publications: Various special publications

Ecology Center of Louisiana
Box 15149, New Orleans, La. 70175
504-522-4008
Deals with the broad range of environmental issues, and provides a variety of information functions. Members serve as advisors to public and private agencies at all levels and, when necessary, assume the role of advocate on key environmental issues. Founded: 1969. Membership: 500.
Chief Officer: James R. Renner, President
Publications: Newsletter; issue papers

Louisiana Forestry Assn.
Box Drawer 5067, Alexandria, La. 71301
318-443-2558
Works to promote the orderly growth and development of Louisiana's 15 million acres of forestland. Founded: 1947. Membership: 2,200.
Chief Officer: William H. Matthews, President
Publications: *Forests and People*; newsletter; legislative reports

Maine

Applied Naturalist Guild
RFD Salem Township, Strong, Maine 04983
207-678-2841
Aims to educate people about finding and using products easily available in nature for food, tools, and shelter. Founded: 1964. Membership: 100.
Chief Officer: Jaro A. Konecny
Publication: Newsletter

Friends of Nature, Inc.
Brooksville, Maine 04617
Founded: 1954.
Chief Officer: Martin R. Haase, Executive Secretary and Treasurer
Publications: Various special publications

Maine Audubon Society, Penobscot Valley Chapter
2203 Broadway, Bangor, Maine 04401
207-942-7233
Works for the conservation and protection of the state's natural resources, particularly wildlife and wildlife habitat; conducts field trips, monthly meetings, and educational programs. Founded: 1967. Membership: 116.
Chief Officer: Edward J. Danforth, President
Publication: *The Northern Shrike* (monthly newsletter)

Maine Audubon Society, Portland Chapter
57 Baxter Blvd., Portland, Maine 04101
207-774-8282
Works for the conservation and protection of the state's natural resources, particularly wildlife and wildlife habitat. Founded: 1853. Membership: 2,000.
Chief Officer: Richard B. Anderson, Executive Director
Publication: Newsletter

Maine Federation of Women's Clubs
Box 149, Rockland, Maine 04841
207-594-4112
Works for conservation, education, and improved home life; aims to be informed on international affairs, the arts, and public affairs. Founded: 1892. Membership: 6,500.
Chief Officer: Mrs. George C. Harvey, President
Publication: Magazine (quarterly)

Natural Resources Council of Maine
20 Willow St., Augusta, Maine 04330
207-622-3101
Encourages the appropriate use and preservation of Maine's natural resources and the regulated development of the state's wildlands; also develops and distributes educational materials. Founded: 1959. Membership: 2,700.
Chief Officer: William Snow, President
Publications: *Maine Environment*; *Legislative Reporter*

Zero Population Growth, Bangor Chapter
Box 124, Orono, Maine 04473
Works to bring about the stabilization of the population first of the United States and then of the world. Activities include legislative lobbying, providing population/environmental educational activities and materials to schools and organizations, and cooperating with other organizations which have overlapping interests. Founded: 1969. Membership: 15.
Chief Officers: Lee Davis; Pattie Moore, Co-chairwomen

Maryland

Chesapeake Bay Foundation, Inc.
Box 1709, Annapolis, Md. 21404

301-268-8816
Works to involve citizens in the care of the natural resources of the Chesapeake Bay region. Administers three programs: (1) environmental education, emphasizing student exposure to the Bay estuarine system; (2) representational service to citizens, including biological field work and legal aid; and (3) preservation of natural areas acquired by the Foundation by gift. Founded: 1966. Membership: 3,000.
Chief Officer: Arthur W. Sherwood, Director
Publication: *CBF Reports* (bimonthly)

Conservation Education Council of Maryland
Natural Resources Institute, Box 3266, LaVale, Md. 21502
Promotes environmental education through workshops, scholarships, and coordinating other programs. Membership: 100.
Chief Officer: James A. Ruckert, Chairman
Publication: Quarterly bulletin

Maryland Environmental Trust
8 E. Mulberry St., Baltimore, Md. 21202
301-383-4264
Purposes are educational; conducts research and educational programs on key environmental issues including land-use control and watershed management. The Trust is developing a program of scenic or conservation easements. Founded: 1967. Membership: 100.
Chief Officer: Paul Allen, Director
Publications: Newsletter (monthly); brochures

Maryland Ornithological Society, Inc.
4915 Greenspring Ave., Baltimore, Md. 21209
Works to further the knowledge of wildlife, especially birds. Maintains a museum, library, and bookstore; owns four bird sanctuaries; and sponsors local lectures, several national Audubon lectures, field trips for all, junior nature club, and a camp for children. Founded: 1945. Membership: 2,200.
Chief Officer: Lawrence Zeleny
Publication: *Maryland Birdlife*

Maryland Wildlife Federation
3229 Avon Ave., Baltimore, Md. 21218
301-467-3200
Dedicated to the conservation of soil, forests, waters, wildlife, and all natural resources. Founded: 1961. Membership: 75,000.
Chief Officer: Paul M. Breidenbaugh, President
Publication: Newsletter

Remington Farms
Chestertown, Md. 21620
301-778-1565
Operated by Remington Arms Co., Inc., to demonstrate through wise land use how wildlife habitat can be improved in a manner compatible with normal farm operation. Founded: 1956.
Chief Officer: Clark G. Webster, Manager
Publications: Occasional papers

Massachusetts

American Lung Assn. of Boston, Boston Citizens for Clean Air Committee
131 Clarendon St., Boston, Mass. 02116
617-536-0935
Supports state and federal clean air legislation and promotes general understanding of health consequences of air pollution among citizens of Boston and surrounding communities. Founded: 1970. Membership: 22.
Chief Officer: Louis Carvelli, Executive Director

Appalachian Mountain Club
5 Joy St., Boston, Mass. 02108
617-523-0636
Works for the protection and recreational enhancement of the mountain country of the Northeast; maintains an extensive system of huts, trails, and shelters in the White Mountains. The eight chapters conduct varied programs of snowshoeing, skiing, canoeing, rock climbing, and hiking activities. Practical conservation is a prime interest in the effort to preserve and protect Northeastern wilderness. Founded: 1876. Membership: 17,000.
Chief Officer: C. Francis Belcher, Executive Director
Publications: *Appalachia Bulletin* (monthly); *Appalachia Journal* (biannual)

Assn. for Preservation of Cape Cod
Box 636, Orleans, Mass. 02653
617-255-4142
Founded to research, study, and find solutions to the problems threatening Cape Cod. Aims to spread these solutions throughout the Cape to its private citizens, conservation organizations and commissions, town governments and regional groups, and to all who are concerned with the life of the Cape. Founded: 1969. Membership: 1,600.
Chief Officer: Peter G. Brown, President
Publications: Membership and special publications

Berkshire Natural Resources Council, Inc.
8 Bank Row, Pittsfield, Mass. 01201
413-499-0596
Assists the cities and towns of Berkshire County through their conservation commissions in achieving a quality environment. Sponsors the Berkshire County Land Trust and Conservation Fund, a nonprofit citizens' land trust which seeks to preserve the open lands of Berkshire County. Founded: 1967. Membership: 600.
Chief Officer: George S. Wislocki, Executive Director
Publication: Newsletter

Boston Environment, Inc.
Rm. 710, 14 Beacon St., Boston, Mass. 02108
617-227-2669
Works to provide an independent environmental information service to those, especially in Massachusetts state and local government, working for the improvement of environmental quality. Founded: 1969. Membership: 500.
Chief Officer: John W. Putnam, Executive Officer
Publications: *Environmental Townsman* (monthly); *Environmental Action* (biweekly); *Highlights of Environmental Action* (biweekly); *Directory of Greater Boston Environmental Groups*; numerous small pieces on recycling

Boston Industrial Mission
56 Boylston St., Cambridge, Mass. 02138
617-491-6350
Especially concerned with social and ethical issues related to technological change; also works to promote ecojustice, i.e., ecology and social justice. Founded: 1964.
Chief Officer: Rev. Scott. I. Paradise
Publication: *Vectors*

Center for Environmental Studies
Williams Col., Williamstown, Mass. 02167
413-597-2346
Activities include undergraduate environmental education (coordinate program), student/faculty research, and Outreach—public activities (largely on regional problems and community education). Founded: 1967.
Chief Officer: Thomas C. Jorling, Director
Publications: Various special publications

Coalition for Environmental Quality
R.S.O. 347 Campus Center, Univ. of Massachusetts, Amherst, Mass. 01002
413-545-0618
An undergraduate student volunteer ecology group dedicated to increasing the ecological consciousness of the university community. Sponsors workshops, speakers, meetings, and films, organizes recycling in dorms, and cooperates in recycling in academic and administration buildings. Founded: 1970. Nonmembership.
Chief Officer: Douglas McCallum, President (1973-74)
Publication: *Effluent* (newsletter)

Cohasset Environmental Action
Box 31, Cohasset, Mass. 02025
617-383-1614
Examines the ecological crisis and explores how these problems can be solved by social change. The group is currently evaluating its purpose in terms of developing alternative lifestyles that allow the individual to develop his full potential as an expressive human being, working on practical utopian development for ourselves and society, and examining society's social values and social conditioning. Founded: 1969. Membership: 200.
Chief Officer: Erik Gjesteby, Facilitator
Publication: *Cohasset Environmental Action*

Connecticut River Watershed Council, Inc.
125 Combs Rd., Easthampton, Mass. 01027
413-584-0057
Preserves the natural resources of the four-state Connecticut River valley. Programs include land acquisition for conservation and recreation, water quality improvement, fisheries restoration, and scenic preservation. Founded: 1952. Membership: 1,200.
Chief Officer: Christopher Percy, Executive Director/Secretary
Publication: *The Valley Newsletter*

Conservation Law Foundation of New England, Inc.
506 Statler Office Bldg., Boston, Mass. 02116
617-542-1354
Aids conservation commissions, environmental groups, and individuals in the enforcement of environmental laws. Deals especially in dredge-and-fill violations, land preservation, and other land-use problems. CLF is also concerned with the energy crisis and the conduct of utilities companies in Massachusetts. Founded: 1966. Membership: 900.
Chief Officer: Morris K. McClintock, Executive Director
Publications: Monthly newsletter; *Gifts of Land for Conservation*, (tax pamphlet)

Conservation Services, Inc.
S. Great Rd., Lincoln, Mass. 01773
617-259-9500
A division of the Massachusetts Audubon Society which provides material, ideas, consultation, and other services, including management techniques and scientific reports, to other nonprofit conservation or environmental organizations and governmental units. Founded: 1966. Nonmembership.
Chief Officer: Allen H. Morgan, Director
Publications: Monthly news service for newsletters; annual publication

Environmental Law Society of Boston University
765 Commonwealth Ave., Boston, Mass. 02215
617-266-1561
Studies environmental law through lectures, library, and meetings; works with local groups and lawyers on various projects involving aspects of environmental law. Founded: 1968. Membership: 25.
Chief Officer: Andrew Wiessner, President

Greater Boston Committee on the Transportation Crisis
56 Boylston St., Cambridge, Mass. 02138
617-491-5215
Works to develop a strong pro-transit coalition and help community groups articulate and implement their needs and concerns. Founded: 1969. Membership: 500.
Chief Officer: Charles Turner, Chairman
Publication: *Transit Notes*

Harvard Environmental Law Society
Langdell Hall W. 131, Harvard Law Sch., Cambridge, Mass. 02138
617-495-3125
Conducts legal research. Founded: 1969.

Massachusetts Assn. of Conservation Commissions
506 Statler Office Bldg., Park Sq., Boston, Mass. 02116
617-542-1584
Fosters environmental quality and the conservation and wise use of natural resources by providing services to conservation commissions and related agencies in Massachusetts through public education, publicity, and publication, by advice and appropriate action on legislative and governmental affairs, and by promoting the formation of conservation commissions. Founded: 1961. Membership: 316 municipalities.
Chief Officer: Robert J. Ellis, President
Publications: Newsletters

Massachusetts Audubon Society, Inc.
S. Great Rd., Lincoln, Mass. 01773
617-259-9500
Works for the conservation and protection of the state's natural resources, particularly wildlife and wildlife habitat. Operates more than 40 sanctuaries; sponsors educational programs, natural history camps, and nature walks. Founded: 1896. Membership: 24,400.
Publications: *Man and Nature; The Massachusetts Audubon Newsletter*

Massachusetts Forest and Park Assn.
1 Court St., Boston, Mass. 02108
617-742-2553
Lobbies for conservation legislation. Founded: 1898. Membership: 3,000.
Chief Officer: Michael Ventresca, Executive Director
Publications: *Conservation Legislation Bulletin; Forest and Park News* (quarterly)

Massachusetts Roadside Council
74 North St., Lexington, Mass. 02173
617-862-2859
Works to prevent visual pollution along our highways and to preserve scenic and historic areas through education and legislation. Founded: 1954. Membership: 20 organizations.
Chief Officer: Mrs. Ralph H. Davis, Chairman

Massachusetts Wildlife Federation, Inc.
Box 343, Natick, Mass. 01760
617-653-3915
Dedicated to the conservation of soil, forests, waters, wildlife, and all natural resources. Founded: 1965. Membership: 65,000.
Publications: Membership publications.

Metropolitan Ecology Workshop
74 Joy St., Boston, Mass. 02114
617-723-2387 or 723-4699
Sponsors education, research, and community programs. Founded: 1971. Membership: 1,000.
Chief Officer: Richard D. Wimberly
Publication: Newsletter

New England Consortium on Environmental Protection
31 Wildwood Dr., Bedford, Mass. 01730
617-458-2501 Ext. 35
Conducts joint and cooperative action among member universities in educational research and other endeavors relating to environmental protection. Founded: 1970. Membership: 14 universities.

Chief Officer: James Halitsky, Chairman, Board of Directors

New England Forestry Foundation
1 Court St., Boston, Mass. 02108
617-742-5586
Works for education of the private woodland owner through service, conservation of forest land through Memorial Forest program, and general education for the public in the need to conserve and protect the forests and New England. Founded: 1944. Nonmembership.
Chief Officer: John T. Hemenway, Executive Director
Publication: *Foundation News*

New England Natural Resources Center
506 Statler Office Bldgs., Boston, Mass. 02116
617-542-9370
Provides a focal point for discussion and resolution of regional issues; serves as an intelligence center and "switchboard" for private citizen environmental interests; and establishes a secure and effective communications bridge between environmental groups, business, and government agencies within the six-state region. Founded: 1970. Nonmembership.
Chief Officer: Philip H. Hoff, Chairman of the Board
Publications: Various issue papers

Northeastern Bird-Banding Assn.
c/o Massachusetts Audubon Society, Lincoln, Mass. 01773
617-259-9500
Works to promote the study of birds and their habits, especially through bird-banding, and dissemination of the information obtained from this study. Founded: 1922. Membership: 800. Chief Officer: John Kennard, President
Publication: *Bird-Banding*

Nuttal Ornithological Club
c/o Museum of Comparative Zoology, Harvard Univ., Cambridge, Mass. 02138
617-495-2471
Works to promote ornithology through meetings, scientific publications, etc. Membership by invitation only. Founded: 1873. Membership: 125.
Chief Officer: Raymond A. Paynter, Jr.
Publication: *Publications of the Nuttall Ornithological Club* (monograph series)

Salt Pond Areas Bird Sanctuaries, Inc.
231 Main St., Falmouth, Mass. 02540
617-548-0711
Provides nature study for children, nature walks, and oceanographic research, and works to preserve the natural state and protect wildlife. Founded: 1961. Members: 1,050.
Chief Officer: Ermine Lovell, President
Publication: Brochure

Save Our Shores, Inc.
Box 103, North Quincy, Mass. 02171
617-328-5510
Works to preserve Boston Harbor, to establish a national recreation area and historic site with the cooperation of the Commonwealth of Massachusetts, and to carry on a shore alert program for major oil spills in the harbor. Founded: 1969. Membership: 250,000.
Chief Officer: Mrs. Nelson R. Saphir, President

Sherborn Forest and Trail Assn.
28 Mill St., Sherborn, Mass. 01770
Maintains trails; works for conservation education, and sponsors horse shows and clinics, nature walks, and family activities. Works closely with town officials. Founded: 1968. Membership: 180 families.
Chief Officer: H. Sossen, President
Publications: Trail maps

Sierra Club, Massachusetts Chapter
14 Beacon St., Boston, Mass. 02108
617-227-5339
Conservation organization actively involved with preserving and improving our natural environment. Founded: 1892. Membership: 140,000.
Chief Officer: Michael McCloskey, Executive Director
Publications: *Sierra Club Bulletin* (monthly); newsletter

Trustees of Reservations
224 Adams St., Milton, Mass. 02186
617-698-2066
Works to preserve places of natural beauty and historic interest in Massachusetts. Founded: 1891. Membership: 2,700.
Chief Officer: Charles E. Mason, Jr., President
Publications: Newsletter (quarterly); annual report

Union of Concerned Scientists
Box 289, MIT Branch Sta., Cambridge, Mass. 02139
617-253-7589
A public-interest group that advocates intelligent application of scientific knowledge. Founded: 1969.

Michigan

Detroit Area Coalition for the Environment
Rm. 100, 4866 Third, Detroit, Mich. 48201
313-577-3480
A coalition of groups and individuals concerned with urban environmental problems, which include air, water, and noise pollution, rats, garbage, transportation, the energy crisis, and nuclear power. Also concerned with occupational health and safety. Works for change through education, legislation, and by working for and against candidates for office. Founded: 1971. Membership: 300; mailing list: 2,000.
Chief Officer: Robert Magnuson, Chairperson
Publications: *Earth Watch* (monthly newsletter); various informational pamphlets

East Michigan Environmental Action Council
912 S. Woodward, Birmingham, Mich. 48011
313-642-1866
Acts as an umbrella organization for other groups and individuals interested in ecology. Activities include work on environmental education, local and state legislation, newspaper recycling; and maintaining a community office for questions, publication, and distribution of various booklets. Founded: 1971. Membership: 110 individuals; 35 organizations.
Chief Officer: Susan Cooper, Chairman of the Board
Publication: *Target: Earth*

Human Environment House
6634 N. Westnedge, Kalamazoo, Mich. 49001
616-382-5694
Acts as the environmental arm of the Kalamazoo Nature Center. Founded: 1970.
Chief Officer: James E. Gourley, Director

Michigan Audubon Society
7000 N. Westnedge Ave., Kalamazoo, Mich., 49007
616-381-1574
Works for the conservation and protection of the state's natural resources, particularly wildlife and wildlife habitat; operates seven wildlife sanctuaries and nature centers. Founded: 1904. Membership: 1,000.
Chief Officer: Robert Bradburn, President
Publications: *Michigan Audubon Newsletter; Jack-Pine Warbler*

Michigan Botanical Club, Inc.
1800 Dixboro Rd., Ann Arbor, Mich. 48105
Encourages the preservation of Michigan flora and dissemination of knowledge about it. Founded: 1941. Membership: 650.
Chief Officer: Wayne Flowers, President
Publication: *The Michigan Botanist*

Michigan Lake and Stream Associations, Inc.
9610 E. Shore Dr., Kalamazoo, Mich. 49002
616-327-3260
A statewide association of lake and stream associations interested in conserving and improving the inland waters of Michigan, the Great Lakes, and shorelands surrounding the waters. Holds an annual two-day seminar. Founded: 1962. Membership: 99 associations; 60,000 members.
Chief Officer: Sandra Mriscin, President
Publication: *The Michigan Riparian Inc.* (quarterly magazine)

Michigan Natural Resources Council
Dept. of Natural Resources, Mason Bldg., Lansing, Mich. 48926
517-373-1270
Endeavors to advance the intelligent use of natural resources, and encourages the application of scientific principles and sound management practices in their development. Apolitical, but serves as a public forum to evaluate issues, problems, and needs. Founded: 1956. Membership: 60.
Chief Officer: John Calkins, President
Publications: Reports of annual conference and scientific advisory committee

Michigan Student Environmental Confederation, Inc.
409 Seymour St., Lansing, Mich. 48933
517-484-7421
Works to coordinate, unite, and establish environmental leadership among Michigan's youth; works with educators to establish curricula and action projects; and lobbies for appropriate legislation. Founded: 1971. Membership: 130 organizations.
Chief Officer: Eric H. Bauman, Coordinator
Publication: *Michigan Earth Beat*

Michigan Tuberculosis and Respiratory Disease Assn.
403 Seymour Ave., Lansing, Mich. 48914
517-484-4541
Works to prevent and control respiratory disease. Activities include professional and public education, research, community service, and antismoking and air pollution control programs. Founded: 1909. Membership: 1,830.

Chief Officer: J. Irvin Nichols, Executive Director
Publications: *Health* (quarterly); *Report* (bimonthly)

Michigan United Conservation Clubs
Box 2235, Lansing, Mich. 48911
517-371-1041
Works to protect and enhance the environment and outdoor recreation areas through education, legislation, and litigation. Founded: 1937. Membership: 110,000.
Chief Officer: Paul J. Leach, Executive Director
Publication: *Michigan Out-of-Doors* (monthly)

Minnesota

Assn. of Midwest Fish and Game Commissioners
Dept. of Natural Resources, 658 Cedar St., St. Paul, Minn. 55101
621-221-2894
Custodian of Minnesota's natural resources responsible for the management and protection of Minnesota's game and fish, lands and forests, waters, soils, and minerals, as well as many recreational facilities. Membership: 1,200 staff; 2,000 seasonal and temporary; 1,800 volunteer fire wardens; 6,000 others.
Chief Officer: Robert L. Herbst, Commissioner
Publications: *Volunteer; Environmental Focus;* various membership publications

Brooklin Center Conservation Commission
6301 Shingle Creek, Brooklin Center, Minn. 55430
612-561-5440.
Advises the City Council on matters dealing with conservation, open space, and the environment. Founded: 1970. Membership: 7.
Chief Officer: Mary Ellen Vetter, Chairman

Clear Air, Clear Water Unlimited
Box 311, South St. Paul, Minn. 55075
612-451-6773
A citizen's action and lobbying group for environmental concerns; works towards general education of public for awareness of environmental problems.
Chief Officer: Gilbert Hamm, President
Publication: Newsletter

Committee on Urban Environment
301 M City Hall, Minneapolis, Minn. 55415
612-348-2104
Aims to improve the appearance of Minneapolis. Activities include design review of new development, historical preservation, and neighborhood improvement. Founded: 1968. Membership: 26.
Chief Officer: Edward A. Howe, Executive Director
Publications: *CUE Newsletter;* annual reports

Friends of the Wilderness
3515 E. 4 St., Duluth, Minn. 55804
218-724-7227
Works for the preservation of the wilderness character of the Boundary Waters Canoe Area of the Superior National Forest. Founded: 1949. Membership: 14,761.
Chief Officer: William H. Magie, Executive Secretary
Publication: Newsletter

Izaak Walton League, Minnesota Division
106 Times Bldg., 57 S. 4 St., Minneapolis, Minn. 55401
612-338-1418
A broadly based organization which aims at the preservation and wise use of soils, woodlands, waters, wildlife, and air. Founded: 1946. Membership: 3,200.
Chief Officer: Kenneth RockVam, President
Publication: *Waltonian*

Metro Clean Air Committee
1829 Portland Ave., Minneapolis, Minn. 55404
612-333-5463
A volunteer action group sponsored by the Minneapolis affiliate of the American Lung Association. It serves as an information resource center on air pollution; provides technical expertise and program development assistance to other agencies and organizations; analyzes proposed legislation, testifies, and reacts when necessary, conducts public education and community service projects; and provides materials and teaching aids to schools. Founded: 1966. Membership: 200.
Chief Officer: Sandi Knudson, Director
Publication: *Clearing the Air*

Metropolitan Aircraft Sound Abatement Council
6040 28 Ave. S., Minneapolis, Minn. 55450
612-726-9411
Works to propose, initiate, coordinate, and promote reasonable and effective methods for the control of aircraft noise. Founded: 1969. Membership: 24 regular; 24 alternate; 6 advisors.
Chief Officer: Stanley W. Olson, Chairman

Minnesota Assn. for Conservation Education
5400 Glenwood Ave., Golden Valley, Minn. 55422
612-544-8971
Provides a forum to promote conservation education; works to alert people to the need for conservation; and encourages endeavors aimed at the wise use of natural resources. Founded: 1965. Membership: 100.
Chief Officer: Carl Vogt, President

Minnesota Conservation Federation
790 Cleveland Ave. S., St. Paul, Minn. 55116
State affiliate of the National Wildlife Federation. With 110 affiliated clubs, the federation promotes wise use of all natural resources and special emphasis is given to the need for conservation education in schools. Founded: 1939. Membership: 12,000.
Chief Officer: John F. Rose, President
Publication: *Minnesota Out of Doors* (monthly)

Minnesota Environmental Control Citizens Assn.
Central Manor, 26 E. Exchange St., St. Paul, Minn. 55101
612-222-2998
Fights against depletion of resources and pollution of air, water, and soil. Acts on legislative, educational, and legal levels. Founded: 1968. Membership: 1,000.
Chief Officer: Paul H. Engstrom, President
Publication: *MECCA News*

Northern Environmental Council
601 Christie Bldg., Duluth, Minn. 55802
218-727-2424
Acts as a service center for members to foster cooperation and avoid duplication of effort in dealing with regional environmental problems. Founded: 1970. Membership: 45 organizations; 300 individuals.
Chief Officer: Walter L. Pomeroy, Executive Director
Publication: *NOREC Newsletter*

Mississippi

Jackson Audubon Society
3803 Rebecca Ct., Jackson, Miss. 39216
601-366-0623
Promotes the conservation of wildlife and the natural environment, and educates man regarding his relationship with, and his place within, the natural environment as an ecological system. These goals are implemented through monthly programs, field trips, education projects in the schools, workshops for adults, and community conservation projects. Founded: 1972. Membership: 145.
Chief Officer: Dudley Peeler, President
Publication: Monthly newsletter

Mississippi Forestry Assn.
1111 Standard Life Bldg., Jackson, Miss. 39201
601-354-4936
Works to conserve, develop, protect, and promote the forest and related natural resources of Mississippi for the best interest of this and succeeding generations. Founded: 1938. Membership: 1,400.
Chief Officer: Ben A. Davis, Jr., Executive Vice President
Publication: *The Voice of Forestry* (monthly newsletter)

Mississippi Lung Assn.
Box 9865, N. Sta., Jackson, Miss. 39206
601-362-5453
Participates in case-finding, prevention, medical education and research, and patient service programs and projects. Founded: 1912.
Chief Officer: Judson M. Allred, Jr., Executive Director

Mississippi Wildlife Federation
Box 1814, Jackson, Miss. 39205
601-353-6922
Dedicated to the conservation of soil, forests, waters, wildlife, and all natural resources. Active in conservation, environmental issues, legislation, and recognition of outstanding conservation work by individuals or groups. Founded: 1954. Membership: 7,000.
Chief Officer: Polly Anderson, Executive Director
Publication: *The Outdoor Watchdog* (monthly)

Missouri

Audubon Society of Missouri
40 Plaza Sq., Apt. 1106, St. Louis, Mo. 63130
Works for the conservation and protection of the state's natural resources, particularly wildlife and wildlife habitat. Founded: 1901. Membership: 450.
Chief Officer: James P. Jackson, President
Publication: *The Bluebird* (quarterly)

Conservation Federation of Missouri
312 E. Capitol Ave., Jefferson City, Mo. 65101
314-635-7188
Serves to unite and coordinate the activities of over 185 sportsmen and conservation clubs throughout Missouri. State affiliate of the National Wildlife Federation; promotes conservation of wildlife and natural resources. Founded: 1935. Membership: 23,000.
Chief Officer: Ed Stegner, Executive Director
Publication: *Missouri Wildlife*

Conservation Foundation of Missouri Charitable Trust
312 E. Capitol Ave., Jefferson City, Mo. 65101
314-635-7188
Established to inform the people of Missouri, through research and education, about important developments and needs in the fields of conservation, ecology, and environmental control. Aims specifically to establish a Conservation Education Center and Library. Founded: 1972.
Chief Officer: Carl Morrow, Chairman

Missouri Prairie Foundation
Box 200, Columbia, Mo. 65201
314-449-3761
Works to ensure the preservation of native prairies and associated plant and animal life by acquisition, management protection, control, and perpetuation of the prairie; carries on educational programs; and provides scientific research relevant to native prairies. Founded: 1966. Membership: 500.
Chief Officer: G. Andy Runge, President
Publication: *Prairie News*

St. Louis Committee for Environmental Information
438 N. Skinker Blvd., St. Louis, Mo. 63130
314-863-6560
Provides scientific information relevant to political and social issues, without bias or prejudice, in the belief that the dissemination of such information is necessary for a democratic society in a technological age. Founded: 1958. Membership: 200.
Chief Officer: Penelope H. Royse, Executive Director
Publication: *C. E. Eye* (newsletter)

Montana

Montana Conservation Council, Inc.
Drawer W, Missoula, Mont. 59801
Works for the wise use of Montana's natural resources. Founded: 1948.
Chief Officer: Richard McConnen
Publications: Occasional newsletters

Montana Environmental Quality Council
Capitol Bldg., Helena, Mont. 59601
406-449-3742
The arm of the Montana State Legislature responsible for administering the Montana Environmental Policy Act of 1971. Founded: 1971. Membership: 13.
Chief Officer: Fletcher E. Newby

Montana Wilderness Assn.
Box 578, Bozeman, Mont. 59715
406-586-9472
Works to preserve a system of wilderness areas for recreational, scenic, scientific, educational, conservation, and historical purposes. Founded: 1958. Membership: 800.
Publication: *Montana Wilderness Walks*

Montana Wildlife Federation
410 Woodworth, Missoula, Mont. 59801
406-543-6945
Dedicated to the conservation of soil, forests, waters, wildlife, and all natural resources. Operates as a coordinating and communicating organization for all of the active environmental organizations in the state and maintains communication with other regional and national organizations. Founded: 1935. Membership: 50 affiliated clubs.
Chief Officer: Robert Lynam, President
Publication: Monthly newspaper

Western Montana Scientists' Committee for Public Information
Univ. of Montana, Natural Science Bldg., Missoula, Mont. 59801
Provides environmental information and policy assessment. Founded: 1962. Membership: 20.
Chief Officer: Arnold J. Silverman, Chairman

Nebraska

Inland Bird Banding Assn.
Wisner, Nebr. 68791
Studies birds and bird-banding. Founded: 1922. Membership: 1,000.
Chief Officer: Mrs. John Lueshen
Publication: *Inland Bird Banding News*

Izaak Walton League of America, Nebraska Division
1570 33 Ave., Columbus, Nebr. 68601
402-564-1461
A broadly based conservation organization which aims at the preservation and wise use of soils, woodlands, waters, wildlife, and air. Membership: 2,560.
Chief Officer: Lyle Winkle, President

Nebraska Wildlife Federation
1111 Bellevue Blvd., Bellevue, Nebr. 68113
402-731-3140
Dedicated to the conservation of soil, forests, waters, wildlife, and all natural resources. Founded: 1970. Membership: 300.
Chief Officer: C. D. Pechler, President
Publication: *Prairie Blade*

Nevada

Colorado River Wildlife Council
4747 W. Vegas Dr., Las Vegas, Nev. 89108
Consists of the seven state fish and game and wildlife agencies located on the Colorado River drainage (Arizona, Nevada, California, Utah, Wyoming, New Mexico, and Colorado) and cooperating agencies (Bureau of Land Management, Forest Service, Bureau of Reclamation, National Park Service, Bureau of Indian Affairs, U.S. Coast Guard, Bureau of Sport Fisheries and Wildlife, and Army Corps of Engineers). The Council was formed to correlate the activities of the individual agencies and provides technical advice when needed. Founded: 1964. Membership: 7 state agencies and cooperating agencies.
Chief Officer: Wayne E. Kirch, Chairman
Publications: Annual minutes

Nevada Wildlife Federation, Inc.
Box 49, Sparks, Nev. 89431
702-358-7668
Dedicated to the conservation of soil, forests, waters, wildlife, and all natural resources. Supports appropriate legislation and carries out educational programs. Founded: 1946. Membership: 684.
Chief Officer: Wayne Capurro, President
Publications: Newsletter; legislative bulletin

New Hampshire

Air Pollution Control Agency Committee
61 S. Spring St., Concord, N.H. 03301
603-271-2281
Works for development, achievement, and maintenance of air pollution standards and registration, control, and abatement of air pollution sources. Founded: 1967. Membership: 15.
Chief Officer: Forrest H. Bumford, Director

Audubon Society of New Hampshire
3 Silk Farm Rd., Concord, N.H. 03301
603-224-1896
Works for conservation and protection of the state's natural resources, particularly wildlife and wildlife habitat; operates statewide environmental education programs, nine wildlife sanctuaries and nature centers, and year-round field trip program. Founded: 1914. Membership: 3,000.
Chief Officer: Tudor Richards, Executive Director
Publications: *N.H. Audubon News* (monthly); *N.H. Audubon Quarterly*

Environmental Law Council of N.H.
5 S. State St., Concord, N.H. 03301
Works on environmental law cases, drafts legislation, assists in litigation, and advises governmental units, conservation groups, etc. Acts as New Hampshire chapter of the Conservation Law Foundation. Founded: 1970. Membership: 20.
Chief Officer: Malcolm Taylor, Executive Secretary
Publication: Newsletter

Land Use Foundation of New Hampshire
7 S. State St., Concord, N.H. 03301
603-224-7615
Promotes better use of land in New Hampshire. Founded: 1967. Membership: 180.
Chief Officer: Robert E. Dunning, Jr., Executive Director
Publications: *The Critical Path* (newsletter); brochures

New Hampshire Natural Resources Council, Inc.
5 S. State St., Concord, N.H. 03301
603-224-9945
Promotes the far-sighted and wise use of soil, water, animal life, forest, and mineral resources. Founded: 1952. Membership: 150.
Chief Officer: Tudor Richards, Chairman

Society for the Protection of New Hampshire Forests
5 S. State St., Concord, N.H. 03301
603-224-9945

Dedicated to promoting wise use of the renewable natural resources. Carries out educational programs; supports legislation; and acts as legal advisor. Founded: 1901. Membership: 3,000.
Chief Officer: Lawrence W. Rathbun, President
Publications: *Forest Notes*; *Involvement*

New Jersey

Air Pollution Committee, Essex County Medical Society
Sub Professional Bldg., 2130 Millburn Ave., Maplewood, N.J. 07040
Works to acquaint physicians with the health hazards of air pollution; prepares articles for medical journals and talks for TV, radio, and lay and professional groups. Founded: 1816. Membership: 1,600.
Chief Officer: Arthur Bernstein, M.D., President
Publication: *Bulletin, Essex County Medical Society.*

American Littoral Society
Sandy Hook, Highlands, N.J. 07732
201-872-0200
Works for the study and conservation of the marine environment and the life it contains; holds seminars, field trips, and dive/study expeditions. Founded: 1961. Membership: 4,000.
Chief Officer: Nixon Griffis, President
Publications: *Underwater Naturalist*; newsletters; conservation alerts

American Lung Assn. of New Jersey
2441 Rte. 22 W., Union, N.J. 07083
201-687-9340
Works for the prevention and control of lung diseases, eradication of tuberculosis, control of respiratory diseases, elimination of cigarette smoking, air conservation, and improvement of community health and welfare; carries out educational, social, and other programs. Founded: 1906. Membership: 125.
Chief Officer: Joseph H. Furnari, Managing Director

Anti-Pollution League
77 Homewood Ave., Allendale, N.J. 07401
201-567-6443
Works to ban nuclear power plants through educating the public and lobby activities in the Northeast. Founded: 1966. Membership: 486.

Chief Officer: Sara Donahue, Chairman
Publication: Bulletin (monthly)

Assn. of New Jersey Environmental Commissions
Box 157, Mendham, N.J. 07945
201-539-7547
Coordinates the work of municipal conservation commissions; promotes intelligent use of natural resources through education and action. Founded: 1969. Membership: 700.
Chief Officer: Stephen Levy, President
Publication: *ANJEC* (newsletter)

Atlantic County Citizens Council on Environment, Inc.
137 S. Main St., Pleasantville, N.J. 08232
609-823-1733
Investigates environmental issues; prepares position papers; and gives testimony at public hearings and local governmental agencies. Founded: 1969. Membership: 500.
Chief Officer: John Williamson, President

Circle K Club
Fairleigh Dickinson, Madison, N.J. 07940
201-377-4700 Ext. 210
Works to recycle aluminum cans, glass, and paper through two campus depots. Paper is given to a paper-mill, and money goes to scholarships for those who work on the programs. Founded: 1973. Membership: 10.
Chief Officer: Neil Shapiro

Citizens Against Water Pollution
7 Oak Tree Lane, Rumson, N.J. 07760
201-842-1914
Promotes legal means to improve the water quality in, touching, or near Monmouth County, N.J. Holds meetings to inform the public with qualified speakers, writes position papers, and testifies at hearings. Also tests quality of water regularly. Founded: 1968. Membership: 50.
Chief Officer: William D. Reid, President
Publications: Occasional newsletters and position papers

Citizens Committee for Environmental Protection
47 Huntington St., New Brunswick, N.J. 08901
201-249-0044
Acts to protect the local urban and rural environment, and deals with specific problems, such as highway construction. Founded: 1971. Membership: 45.
Chief Officer: Bruce E. Newling, Chairman

Citizens for Conservation
11 Berta Pl., Basking Ridge, N.J. 07920
Concerned with the total environment. Encourages citizen participation in environmental affairs by promoting environmental education in the schools; participates in hearing procedures; and encourages development and enforcement of good laws and procedures. This organization has been represented at over one hundred hearings at every level of government on a wide range of environmental affairs. Founded: 1969. Membership: 250.
Chief Officer: Walter C. H. Stocker, President
Publications: Occasional papers; environmental alerts

Citizens for Environmental Action
49 Dogwood Lane, Berkeley Heights, N.J. 07922
201-464-0518
Activities include recycling drives, setting up permanent recycling center, land-use and natural resources survey, local flood control studies, gypsy moth control efforts, dedication of local parkland, and supporting environmental legislation. Works for public involvement in protecting the local environment by making citizens aware of environmental issues. Founded: 1970. Membership: 20.
Chief Officer: Donald A. Rudy, Chairman
Publication: Joint newsletter (monthly) with Citizens for Environmental Quality of New Providence, N.J.

Clean Air Council
John Fitch Plaza, Trenton, N.J. 08625
Serves as advisory body to the State Commissioner of Environmental Protection on all aspects of air pollution. Conducts annually at least one fact-finding public hearing. Founded: 1967. Membership: 17.
Chief Officer: Irwin Zonis, Chairman
Publications: Reports of hearings

Eco Center
529 Mattison Ave., Asbury Park, N.J. 07712
Assists individuals in improving the environment. Maintains a public hot line for help in getting action on environmental problems; investigates complaints and takes necessary action. Conducts research and sponsors public meetings. Founded: 1971.
Chief Officer: Martin S. Levetin, President
Publications: Air Pollution Survey of Monmouth County; Recycling Calendar for Monmouth County

Environmental Political Action
RPO 2994, Rutgers Univ., New Brunswick, N.J. 08903
201-247-1766 Ext. 6689
Works to end all kinds of pollution; takes an active role in local planning and improvement by supporting appropriate legislation. Founded: 1970. Membership: 40.
Chief Officer: Jan Sokol, Henry Hornbostel, Edith Lewis, Chairpersons
Publications: *E.P.A. Newsletter*; various special publications; reports of hearings

Essex Citizens Conservation Organization
496 Richmond Ave., Maplewood, N.J. 07040
201-763-4441
Works for development of a used-materials management system and general environmental concerns in the county. Founded: 1970. Membership: 80.
Chief Officer: Louis E. Schindel, Chairman

Friends of the Hudson
77 Homewood Ave., Allendale, N.J. 07401
201-327-3914
Works to protect the environment of the Hudson River Valley and Adirondack and Catskill preserves. Founded: 1964. Membership: 800.
Chief Officer: Larry Bogart, President
Publication: *The River and the Mountains* (quarterly)

League for Conservation Legislation
Box 605, Teaneck, N.J. 07666
201-836-5794
Works to halt deterioration in air, water, and noise quality, to further land-use policies that will preserve and extend open space, to control housing development in sparsely settled areas and wetlands, and to control industrial growth in vital ecological areas. Supports or opposes state and federal legislation, through correspondence and direct contact between legislators and a paid league agent. Founded: 1971. Membership: 250.
Chief Officer: Frank J. Oliver, President
Publication: Newsletter

League of Women Voters of New Jersey
400 Bloomfield Ave., Montclair, N.J. 07042
Promotes political responsibility through informed and active participation of citizens in government. Selects topics for study and then makes a position statement. Acts through education, organized effort, lobbying, and in conjunction with groups of similar viewpoints. Founded: 1920. Membership: 10,000.

Chief Officer: Nina McCall
Publication: *New Jersey Voter*

Morris County for Clean Air and Water
4 Spencer Ct., Morris Plains, N.J. 07950
Works against pollution and for consumer protection. Founded: 1968. Membership: 400.
Chief Officer: Stephen J. Roman, Chairman

New Jersey Audubon Society
790 Ewing Ave., Franklin Lakes, N.J. 07417
201-891-1211
Works for the conservation and protection of the state's natural resources, particularly wildlife and wildlife habitat. Operates sanctuaries, educational programs, and field trips; encourages sound conservation legislation. Founded: 1910. Membership: 3,500.
Chief Officer: Norman C. Fisher, Executive Director
Publication: *New Jersey Nature News* (quarterly)

New Jersey Citizens for Clean Air, Inc.
Suite 405, 144 S. Harrison St., East Orange, N.J. 07018
201-355-9450
Works to educate the public to the dangers of air pollution and to methods of improving air quality. Founded: 1966. Membership: 400.
Chief Officer: Barbara Eisler, President
Publication: *Clean Air Report* (triannual)

New Jersey Educational Assn., Environmental Education Commission
180 State St., Trenton, N.J. 08608
609-599-4561
Aims to develop a citizenry aware, active, and articulate in the improvement of our environment. Trains teachers; serves as a watchdog committee; keeps alert to new curricular developments in New Jersey and the nation; disseminates pertinent information to the members of NJEA; and identifies the controversial environmental issues. Founded: 1972. Membership: 14.

New Jersey State Council for Environmental Education
Montclair State Col., Upper Montclair, N.J. 07043
201-744-0362
Aims to implement a statewide master plan for environmental education which involves preparing a model environmental education curriculum, establishing local environmental education advisory committees, encouraging schools and colleges to initiate environmental education courses and adult education programs, and disseminating information on environmental education and curriculum materials. A multimedia library is in preparation. Founded: 1967. Membership: 13 staff.
Chief Officer: Edward J. Ambry, Director
Publications: Environmental education surveys

North Jersey Conservation Foundation
300 Mendham Rd., Morristown, N.J. 07960
201-539-7540
Founded: 1965. Membership: 2,000.
Chief Officer: David F. Moore, Executive Director
Publication: *Footprints* (periodical)

Ocean County Fish and Game Protective Assn.
21 Harley Blvd., Bayville, N.J. 08721
Works to improve the sports of hunting and fishing through education, conservation, management of open space, and pollution control; also promotes hunter safety. Founded: 1935. Membership: 100.
Chief Officer: John Moran, President
Publication: Newsletter (monthly)

Ocean Nature and Conservation Society
380 Luane Rd., Toms River, N.J. 08753
201-349-1275
Works for the enhancement of all facets of nature and the wise use and proper management of our natural resources. Founded: 1966. Membership: 500.
Chief Officer: Elizabeth D. Cooper, President
Publication: Newsletter (monthly)

Project Recycle
RPO 2994, Rutgers Univ., New Brunswick, N.J. 08903
201-247-1766 Ext. 6689
Runs a recycling center, and works to solve problem of solid waste disposal. Founded: 1970. Membership: 10.
Chief Officer: Tim Deacon, Chairman

TB-Respiratory Disease Assn. of Central New Jersey, Inc.
1457 Raritan Rd., Clark, N.J. 07066
Works for the prevention and control of tuberculosis and other respiratory diseases including emphysema, chronic bronchitis, and asthma. Seeks aims through promotion of adequate treatment, diagnosis, rehabilitation facilities, education of the public, professional persons, and public officials, as well as demonstration of new programs. Promotes control of air pollution through official agencies and community education. Serves Hudson,

Union, and Monmouth counties. Founded: 1904.
Chief Officer: Annette Riordan, Managing Director

New Mexico

Albuquerque Wildlife Federation
Box 1234, Albuquerque, N. Mex. 87103
505-344-1428
Dedicated to the conservation of soil, forests, waters, wildlife, and all natural resources. Gives courses in hunter safety. Founded: 1914. Membership: 423.
Chief Officer: Doc H. Burnett, President
Publications: *Outdoor Reporter*; newsletter (monthly)

Bernalillo County Planned Parenthood Assn.
113 Montclaire Dr. S.E., Albuquerque, N. Mex. 87108
505-265-3722
Works to help make every child a wanted child through medical contraceptive and sterilization services, a broad community education program, and related counseling and referral services. Founded: 1964. Membership: 7,000 patients.
Chief Officer: Gail Montgomery, Executive Director
Publication: *Planned Parenthood Happenings*

New Mexico Citizens for Clean Air and Water
113 Monte Rey Dr. N., Los Alamos, N. Mex. 87544
505-672-9792
Active at state regulatory hearings in areas of air and water pollution, strip mining, and subdivisions; engages in legal actions, lobbying activities, and educational efforts. Founded: 1969. Membership: 2,300.
Chief Officer: John R. Bartlit, State Chairman
Publication: Newsletter

New Mexico Conservation Coordinating Council
Box 142, Albuquerque, N. Mex. 87103
505-265-4244
Coordinates efforts in all areas of environmental concern in New Mexico. Active in problems of energy development, environmental quality, wildlife conservation, land-use planning, and federal agency projects. Founded: 1967. Membership: 22 organizations.
Chief Officer: Larry T. Caudill, President
Publication: *Environmental News*

New Mexico Wildlife Conservation Assn.
714 La Pablano, Albuquerque, N. Mex. 87107
505-344-1428
Works for the betterment of conservation and wildlife. Founded: 1914. Membership: 380.
Chief Officer: Doc H. Burnett
Publication: *Outdoor Reporter*

New Mexico Wildlife Federation
Box 1542, Santa Fe, N. Mex. 87501
505-983-8459
Dedicated to the conservation of soil, forests, waters, wildlife, and all natural resources. Founded: 1914. Membership: 2,000.
Chief Officer: William F. Brockwell, Executive Director
Publication: *Outdoor Reporter*

Roswell Branch-Citizens for Clean Air and Water
700 N. Missouri, #37, Roswell, N. Mex. 88201
505-622-2258
Aids state organization in lobbying at state capitol. Locally, works to keep the city and environs clean and to develop a recycling program. Founded: 1971. Membership: 23.
Chief Officer: Ralph A. Milligan, Chairman
Publication: News sheet

Students for Environmental Action
Student Union, Univ. of New Mexico, Albuquerque, N. Mex. 87131
505-277-2738
Sponsors research and public action, and coordinates distribution of information about New Mexico's environment. Founded: 1970. Membership: 150.
Chief Officer: Tony Wolfe, President
Publication: *S.E.A. Newsletter*

Trout Unlimited, Rio Grande Chapter
9809 Dorothy Pl. N.E., Albuquerque, N. Mex. 87111
505-299-1369
Works for the preservation and enhancement of cold water fisheries.
Founded: 1971. Membership: 100.
Chief Officer: Pete Test, President

Zero Population Growth, Santa Fe Chapter
Rte. 3, Box 131, Santa Fe, N. Mex. 87501
Works for family planning and increased awareness of the dangers of overpopulation. Founded: 1971. Membership: 50.
Chief Officer: Sally Rodgers, Chairman
Publication: Newsletter

New York

Adirondack Trail Improvement Society
St. Hubers, N.Y. 12943
518-576-4411
Helps support measures that will preserve and protect the Adirondack region. Maintains over 90 miles of trails that are kept open for the public for hiking only, and conducts education and recreation programs for children. Founded: 1897. Membership: 325.
Chief Officer: William P. Dunham, President
Publications: Annual report and trail guide; special geodetic survey maps with trail overlays

Canandaigua Lake Pure Waters, Ltd.
Box A1, Canandaigua, N.Y. 14424
315-232-6500
Studies and informs members and the public about methods to conserve, improve, and protect the natural resources and environment of the watershed at Canandaigua Lake; works to control water, land, and air pollution in order to enhance the health, safety, and welfare of the people who reside and seek recreation in that watershed; and fosters, promotes, creates, and maintains conditions under which man and nature can thrive in harmony with each other and achieve social and economic progress for future generations. Founded: 1969. Membership: 500.
Chief Officer: John E. Swett, President
Publication: Newsletter

Citizens Ecology Committee
Box 143, New Hartford, N.Y. 13413
Studies environmental problems and alerts the public to them; follows New York State environmental legislation and reacts appropriately; and encourages recycling and use of recycled paper. Founded: 1970. Membership: 30.
Chief Officer: Mrs. John Sammon, Chairwoman

Citizens for a Better Environment
Box 1341, New Rochelle, N.Y. 10802
914-834-4925
Deals mostly with local environmental issues and some national environmental issues. Aims to inform the public on environment, recycling, solid waste disposal and consumer issues. Founded: 1969. Membership: 400.
Chief Officer: Ira Gulker
Publication: *CBE Bulletin*

Citizens for a Clean Environment
23 Deer Path Rd., Central Islip, N.Y. 11722
516-234-3112
Fights air, water, noise, and visual pollution; lobbies for local ordinances on litter, signs, banning throwaway bottles, etc.; and sponsors exhibits and various recycling drives. Founded: 1970. Membership: 50.
Chief Officer: Nancy Manfredonia, Chairman
Publication: Newsletter (bimonthly)

Citizens for Clean Air, Inc.
572 Madison Ave., New York, N.Y. 10022
212-935-1454
Conducts a program of public education about the causes and consequences of air pollution and motivates public action to abate air pollution in the New York metropolitan area. Maintains energy conservation project. Founded: 1965. Membership: 3,000.
Chief Officer: Lewis Kruger, Esq., Chairman of the Board

Ecology Center
Rm. 330, 1265 Broadway, New York, N.Y. 10001
212-684-1912 Ext. 330
An information-gathering group which dispenses data to organizations that require it. Founded: 1971. Membership: 5.
Chief Officers: Harry Kaye; Shirley Kaye

Environmental Action Coalition, Inc.
235 E. 49 St., New York, N.Y. 10017
212-486-9550
Encourages recycling programs, provides educational materials through its library, and organizes tenant education workshops. Founded: 1970. Membership: 500.
Chief Officer: Karen N. Dumont, Executive Director
Publications: *Eco-News* (newsletter); *Cycle* (membership newsletter)

Environmental Clearing House Organization, Inc.
Buffalo Museum of Science, Humboldt Park, Buffalo, N.Y. 14211
716-896-5200
Acts as a center for distribution of information and correlation of activities. Sponsors speakers and education courses, and provides material for grades five through high school. Clearinghouse for recycling points, etc. Founded: 1970. Membership: 750.
Chief Officer: Robert A. Smith, Executive Director
Publication: *ECHO Issues*

Environmental Commission of the Incorporated Village of Roslyn
199 E. Broadway, Roslyn, N.Y. 11576
516-621-1506
A municipal commission which advises elected village board of trustees. Interests include recycling, sewage treatment, pollution of harbor, traffic pollution, solid waste, and park development. Founded: 1971. Membership: 6.
Chief Officer: Leonard Shaw, Chairman

Environmental Conservation Advisory Board Incorporated Village of Port Jefferson
121 W. Broadway, Port Jefferson, N.Y. 11777
516-473-4724
Serves as advisory board to trustees of Village of Port Jefferson on environmental matters. Founded: 1973. Membership: 7.
Chief Officer: Murrey D. Goldberg, Chairman

Environmental Planning Lobby
211 E. 43 St., New York, N.Y. 10017
211-661-1360
Helps to shape laws and policies for sound environmental planning. Founded: 1970. Membership: 750 individuals, 80 groups.
Chief Officer: David Sive, Chairman of the Board
Publications: *New York Environmental Voters' Guide*; occasional papers

Federation of New York State Bird Clubs, Inc.
Mary Ann Sunderlin, Corresponding Secretary, 505 Bay Rd., Webster, N.Y. 14580
Furthers the study of birds, bird life, and bird lore; disseminates knowledge and appreciation of birds; works to preserve and protect birds and other wildlife and their environment; encourages the establishment and maintenance of sanctuaries and protected areas for birds and other wildlife; and educates the public on the need to conserve natural areas and resources. Founded: 1947. Membership: 36 clubs; 400 individuals.
Chief Officer: Gordon M. Meade, M.D., President
Publications: *The Kingbird* (quarterly); *New York Birders* (newsletter)

Friends of Africa in America
330 S. Broadway, Tarrytown, N.Y. 10591
914-631-5168
Conducts educational programs organized and presented by volunteers in the U.S., especially at the community level, intended to develop American cooperation with Africans on wildlife conservation. Founded: 1963. Non-membership.
Chief Officer: Clement E. Merowit, Director
Publications: Occasional newsletter

Genesee Valley Environment Assn.
Box 242, Geneseo, N.Y. 14454
716-243-2455
Works to protect, preserve, and enhance the physical environment within the Genesee River environs; to educate the public toward appreciating, protecting, and improving this environment; and to promote greater consciousness of the worldwide nature of the environmental crisis. Founded: 1971. Membership: 40.
Chief Officer: Judy Egelston, Chairman

Herkimer County Board of Cooperative Educational Services
132 W. German St., Herkimer, N.Y. 13350
315-866-1781
Provides services of an environmental education consultant, inservice teacher training programs, films and other teaching aids, and summer field programs for educators in local schools. Founded: 1970. Membership: 12 school districts.
Chief Officer: Donald F. Tuttle, Director
Publication: *Environdex*

Housewives to End Pollution
7052 West Lane, Eden, N.Y. 14057
716-649-3493
Works to make the public more aware of local environmental and consumer problems, and to get involved in solving them at the local level. Specific accomplishments include organizing recycling programs, help in passing phosphate ban, and lobby for a state law. Founded: 1970. Membership: 200.
Chief Officer: Mrs. William Shadle, Chairman
Publication: Newsletter

Izaak Walton League, New York Division
101 Grace St., Penn Yan, N.Y. 14527
315-536-3252
A broadly based conservation organization which aims at the preservation and wise use of soils, woodlands, waters, wildlife, and air. Founded: 1926. Membership: 328.
Chief Officer: Allan Christopher, President
Publication: *Empire State Newsletter* (bimonthly)

Laboratory of Ornithology
Cornell Univ., 159 Sapsucker Woods, Ithaca, N.Y. 14850

607-256-5056

Promotes the science of ornithology through research and teaching; serves as a center for the study of birds, especially their behavior and ecology; and acts as a center for the cultural appreciation of birds. Promotes the conservation of bird life; disseminates information about birds. Activities include field courses, extension service to handle questions about birds, exhibits on bird paintings and photographs, maintenance of a 180-acre sanctuary and library. Founded: 1955. Membership: 2,500.
Chief Officer: Douglas A. Lancaster, Director
Publications: *The Living Bird* (annual scientific journal); newsletter (quarterly)

League of Women Voters of New York State
817 Broadway, New York, N.Y. 10003
212-677-5050
Works towards increased citizen participation in government. Founded: 1919. Membership: 14,516.
Chief Officer: Ruth Robbins, President
Publication: *New York State Voter*

Long Island Environmental Council, Inc.
95 Middleneck Rd., Port Washington, N.Y. 11050
516-883-4725
Works to protect and restore the natural and historic heritage, and create an environment that reflects conservation awareness. Accomplishes aims through public education and cooperation among citizens, industry, government, and educational institutions. Founded: 1969. Membership: 100 organizations; 500 individuals.
Chief Officer: Claire Stern, Executive Director
Publication: *ALERT* (newsletter)

Monroe County Environmental Management Council
305 County Bldg., Rochester, N.Y. 14614
716-454-7200 Ext. 536
Advises the county legislature, conducts open-space survey of county, and deals with other environmental matters as they occur. Founded: 1971. Membership: 39.
Chief Officer: Clarence R. Gehris, Chairman
Publications: *EnviroNews*; special bulletins; directory of environmental groups.

The Nature Conservancy Central New York Chapter
Box 175, Ithaca, N.Y. 14850
607-272-6499
Works to identify, acquire, preserve, and manage valuable natural areas. Cooperates with federal, state, and local governments to acquire natural areas and, with safeguards, to put them in governmental hands. Also cooperates with other naturalist organizations for the same objectives. Founded: 1966. Membership: 249.
Chief Officer: Frank L. Eldridge, Chairman
Publications: *Natural Areas* (bulletin); newsletter

New York Scientists' Committee for Public Information, Inc.
30 E. 68 St., New York, N.Y. 10021
An organization of elected scientists, physicians, engineers, and other professionals who seek to interpret for the general public technical issues with social implications. Subcommittees are active in areas of occupational health, noise pollution, air and water pollution, transportation, energy, solid waste, lead poisoning, drug use, and concepts of race. Founded: 1961. Membership: Elected.
Chief Officer: Philip Siekewitz, President
Publication: Newsletter (monthly)

New York Zoological Society
The Zoological Park, Bronx, N.Y. 10160
212-933-1500
Purposes include recreation, education, and research in wild animals; operates New York Zoological Park (Bronx Zoo), New York Aquarium, Field Center for Conservation Research, and Osborn Laboratories of Marine Sciences. Founded: 1895. Membership: 7,200.
Chief Officer: Robert G. Goelet, President
Publications: *Animal Kingdom* (bimonthly); *Zoologica* (quarterly)

Peoples Environmental Program
Box 5028; FDR Sta., New York, N.Y. 10022
212-755-1816
Recycles as many materials as possible and uses money from them to plant trees and build a park. Founded: 1970. Membership: 45.
Chief Officer: Roslyn K. Baldassare, President
Publication: Newsletter

Progress Without Pollution
67 Stanridge Ct., Rochester, N.Y. 14617
716-342-8398
Sponsors recycling and clean-up campaigns; actively supports environmentally sound legislation and projects. Founded: 1970. Membership: 15
Publications: Information sheets

Protect Your Environment Club of Albany
Rm. FA218, 1400 Washington Ave., Albany, N.Y. 12203
518-457-3913
Engages in community environmental action including pollution abatement, land use, education, and environmental research. Founded: 1969. Membership: 50.
Chief Officer: Ann Dizard

Recycling Information
50 W. Main St., Rochester, N.Y. 14614
Conducts program of environmental education in solid waste. Founded: 1973. Membership: 12
Chief Officer: Byrna P. Weir, Director
Publication: *Environmental Self-guide* (booklet)

Rochester Committee for Scientific Information
Box 5236, River Campus Sta., Rochester, N.Y. 14627
Publishes information on local environmental problems, researched, compiled, and interpreted by scientists, and distributed to members, the public, and appropriate officials. Founded: 1964. Membership: 370.
Chief Officer: Mrs. Robert L. Fredette, Executive Secretary
Publication: *The R.C.S.I. Bulletins* (irregular)

Saint Hubert Society of America, Inc.
Studio One, 5 Tudor City Pl., New York, N.Y. 10017
212-986-2989
Devoted to the principles of good sportsmanship, good hunting, the promulgation of the lore of wildlife and the outdoors, and the preservation of wildlife and wildlife habitat. Founded: 1958. Membership: 100.
Chief Officer: George V. Lenher, President

Scenic Hudson Preservation Conference
545 Madison Ave., New York, N.Y. 10022
212-755-3082
Works for the preservation of the Hudson area, and educates people about the heritage and value of the Hudson area. Founded: 1963. Mailing List: 23,000.

Soil Conservation Service Farm and Home Center
4487 Lake Ave., Lockport, N.Y. 14094
713-434-4949
Assists landowners in planning and carrying out measures to control erosion, pollution, and siltation of streams; encourages proper land use according to capability of soils; assists planning boards; and assists the Niagara County Soil and Water Conservation District in furnishing technical assistance to District cooperators. Founded: 1954.

Staten Island Science Information Committee
Institute of Arts and Sciences, 75 Stuyvesant Pl., Staten Island, N.Y. 10301
Provides references, resources, and assistance to community groups and others gathering information about the local environment; especially helps individuals and groups maintain the local environment and keep it usable in the best interests of the residents. Founded: 1967. Membership: 700.
Chief Officer: G. K. Schneider, Pro tem Secretary
Publications: Proceedings (triannual)

Sterling Forest Pollution Control
Tuxedo, N.Y. 10987
914-351-2151
A private utility that owns and operates sewer systems and sewage treatment plants. Founded: 1962.
Chief Officer: Miles P. Shanahan, President

Town of Avon Commission for Conservation
Avon, N.Y. 14414
716-926-2770
Serves as advisory council for the Town Board on environmental concerns. Founded: 1971. Membership: 9.
Chief Officer: Irene W. Swanton, Chairman

Upper Hudson Environmental Action Committee
Riparius, N.Y. 12862
518-998-2209
Takes any action necessary for a better environment; supports state and national causes; works locally for the protection of the Upper Hudson River region and the Adirondack Mountains; carries out monthly educational programs and field trips; encourages land-use planning in the Adirondacks; and works against overpopulation and litter. Founded: 1970. Membership: 55.
Chief Officer: Louis C. Curth, Chairman
Publication: *The Duff—Environmental News at the Grassroots Level*

Wild Flower Preservation Society
c/o New York Botanical Gardens, Bronx, N.Y. 10458
212-933-9400
Dedicated to the preservation of endangered habitats of plants through the distribution of

educational information. Founded: 1914. Membership: 75.
Chief Officer: Larry G. Purdue, Assistant Vice President

Zero Population Growth, New York State Federation
374 Rugby Ave., Rochester, N.Y. 14619
716-328-5022
Works towards education of the public on the overpopulation problem. Lobbies for laws or removal of restrictions on current laws to make limited families possible by making contraceptives more available and increasing family planning facilities. Founded: 1970. Membership: 1,900.
Chief Officer: Mary Spurrier, President
Publication: Newsletter

North Carolina

Carolina Bird Club, Inc.
Box 1220, Tryon, N.C. 28782
Nonprofit educational and scientific organization whose membership is open to those interested in birds, natural history and conservation, and ornithology. Founded: 1937. Membership: 1,500.
Chief Officer: Frederick M. Probst, President
Publications: *CHAT* (quarterly); bimonthly newsletters

Conservation Council of North Carolina
Box 1066, Chapel Hill, N.C. 27514
919-942-2263
Initiates, participates in, and coordinates statewide action in conservation and environmental education. A paid lobbyist in the State Legislature monitors bills and keeps affiliated organizations in the state informed on specific issues. Founded: 1968. Membership: 700 individuals; 90 organizations.
Chief Officer: Wallace Kaufman, President
Publication: *Carolina Conservationist*

Keep America Beautiful, Inc.
3238 Reynolds Rd., Winston Salem, N.C. 27106
919-722-3972
Serves as a promotional, educational, advisory, and coordinating agency for the beautification of North Carolina; cooperates with and augments the efforts of existing local, state, and national groups. Founded: 1972. Membership: 170.
Chief Officer: Mrs. W.C. Landolina, Sr., President
Publication: Newsletter (quarterly)

League of Women Voters of North Carolina
Box 925, Elon College, N.C. 27244
919-834-2114
Active in environmental quality efforts as well as other areas. Founded: 1934. Membership: 2,000.
Chief Officer: Mrs. Edward Wiser, President
Publication: *State Government*

North Carolina Wildlife Federation
109 S. Main St., Box 948, Rocky Mount, N.C. 27801
919-442-2212
Dedicated to the conservation of soil, forests, waters, wildlife, and all natural resources. Founded: 1945. Membership: 21,000.
Chief Officer: Turner W. Battle, Executive Director
Publication: *Friend o'Wildlife*

North Dakota

Association of Midwest Fish and Game Commissioners
c/o North Dakota Game and Fish Commissioner, 2121 Lovett Ave., Bismarck, N. Dak. 58501
701-224-2180
A group of game and fish management agencies from Midwest states and Canadian provinces which discusses and solves problems concerning game and fish management and the environment which are common to the Midcontinent. Founded: 1934. Membership: 15 states; 3 Canadian provinces.
Chief Officer: Russell W. Stuart, Chairman
Publications: Proceedings of annual conference

North Dakota Natural Science Society
Box 1672, Jamestown, N. Dak. 58401
701-252-5363
Encourages the recording and preservation of observations of nature in North Dakota; also serves as a means of communication among those who are concerned about the wonder, enjoyment, and safekeeping of the natural world. Founded: 1967. Membership: 349.
Chief Officer: William Barker, President
Publication: *The Prairie Naturalist* (quarterly)

North Dakota Wildlife Federation
Suite 9, 200 W. Main St., Bismarck, N. Dak. 58501
701-223-8741
Dedicated to the conservation of soil, forests, waters, wildlife, and all natural resources. Founded: 1936. Membership: 7,000.
Chief Officer: Konrad Norstog, President
Publication: *Flickertales*

Ohio

Citizens for Clean Air and Water, Inc.
312 Park Bldg., 140 Public Sq., Cleveland, Ohio 44114
216-781-0880
Deals with pollution of the environment, particularly nuclear pollution; participates in air and water hearings; and distributes educational information. Founded: 1968. Membership: 500.
Chief Officer: Evelyn Stebbins
Publication: Newsletter

Clean Air
Box 265, Berea, Ohio 44017
216-331-2003
Disseminates public information on ecology; takes social action in legislation and hearings, with special emphasis on local and national issues, such as nuclear power, jetports, mass transit, highways, noise, pesticides, land use, and air and water pollution control. Founded: 1967. Membership: 100.
Chief Officer: David Gitlin, M.D., Chairman
Publications: Occasional bulletins

Institute for Environmental Education
8911 Euclid Ave., Cleveland, Ohio 44106
A teacher-student graduate credit and noncredit summer and in-service year training and curriculum development program. Designated a National Demonstration Project by the U.S. Office of Environmental Education, IEE contracts with 18 school systems in northeast Ohio to send a cadre of in-service environmental education specialists throughout these schools. IEE then shares these experiences in other communities so that they may learn how to incorporate appropriate components, techniques, skills, etc. into their community and educational system. Founded: 1971. Membership: 215 summer program graduates; 500 workshop participants; mailing list: 4,000.
Chief Officer: Joseph H. Chadbourne, President
Publication: *Investigator* (monthly newsletter)

Lake Erie Watershed Conservation Foundation
621 Superior Bldg., Cleveland, Ohio 44114
216-696-3340
Works to improve our natural resources and their use by bringing together the efforts of industry, commerce, education, government, conservation, and civic communities. Founded: 1951.
Chief Officer: R. Livingston Ireland, President and Chairman
Publication: *Notes of Interest*

Ohio Forestry Assn., Inc.
Neil House, Columbus, Ohio 43215
614-221-6671
Carries out educational programs for youth and adults in forestry and related fields. Founded: 1903. Membership: 1,200.
Chief Officer: T.M. Higgins, Executive Director
Publications: *Ohio Woodlands*; *Forestry Bulletin*

Protect Our Environment
2600 S. Park Blvd., Cleveland, Ohio 44120
Sponsors solid waste recycling programs. Founded: 1971. Membership: 450.
Chief Officer: Jack Reed
Publication: *POE Newsletter*

Oklahoma

Midcontinent Environment Center Assn.
1111 Petroleum Club, Tulsa, Okla. 74119
Encourages research, development, management, education, and planning for a better environment. Founded: 1970. Membership: 14.
Chief Officer: George R. Waller, President
Publications: Various special publications

Oklahoma Coalition for Clean Air
2442 Walnut, Box 53303, Oklahoma City, Okla. 73105
405-524-8471
An affiliate of the Oklahoma Lung Association concerned with maintaining clean air in the state. Founded: 1970. Membership: 1,000.
Chief Officer: Lois Blanche, Executive Secretary
Publication: *OCCA Newsletter*

Oklahoma Environmental Information and Media Center
East Central State Col., Ada, Okla. 74820
405-332-8000 Ext. 3088
Funded by the Environmental Protection Agency as a prototype organization, the group works for cooperation among federal, state, and local agencies and individuals. Helps set up educational programs for schools, and generally makes information available to those who need it. Founded: 1971. Membership: volunteers.
Chief Officer: Robert V. Garner, Director
Publication: *ECO Systems*

Oklahoma Ornithological Society
Rte. 1, Box 256, Harrah, Okla. 73045
405-964-3476
Encourages conservation education; promotes field trips; participates in nationally sponsored projects such as the Christmas Bird Census, the Nest Record Program, and Breeding Bird Survey; and publicizes the need to protect endangered species. Founded: 1950. Membership: 600.
Chief Officer: Jack Tyler, President
Publications: *The Scissortail* (newsletter); *Oklahoma Ornithological Society* (scientific bulletin)

Oklahoma Wildlife Federation
Box 1262, Norman, Okla. 73069
405-364-3609
Dedicated to the conservation of soil, forests, waters, wildlife, and all natural resources. Founded: 1952. Membership: 30,000.
Chief Officer: William W. Howard, Executive Director
Publication: *Outdoor News*

Oregon

Western Forestry and Conservation Assn.
1326 American Bank Bldg., Portland, Oreg. 97205
503-226-4562
Works to advance forest resource management and utilization by furthering cooperation among public and private forestry interests of western United States and western Canada. Its membership includes corporations, private woodland owners, public and private foresters, partnerships, and others with an interest in forest conservation. Founded: 1909. Membership: 550.
Chief Officer: Steele Barnett, Forest Counsel

Publications: Proceedings of annual conference and standing committees.

Pennsylvania

Academy of Natural Sciences
19 and Benjamin Franklin Pkwy., Philadelphia, Pa. 19103
215-567-3700
Runs a natural-science museum open to the public; sponsors educational programs and scientific research. Founded: 1812. Membership: 3,450.
Chief Officer: William W. Marvel, President
Publications: *Academy News; Frontiers*

American Institute of Medical Climatology
1023 Welsh Rd., Philadelphia, Pa. 19115
215-673-8368
Studies the relationship between weather and climate and life in all phases. Conducts courses, meetings, seminars, and lectures. Founded: 1958. Membership: 100.
Chief Officer: Helmut E. Landsberg
Publications: Membership mailings

Environmental Planning and Information Center
313 S. 16 St., Philadelphia, Pa. 19102
215-732-1958
An environmental planning and information center which provides information, training, education, and research services, and coordinates efforts of other groups and individuals. Founded: 1970.
Chief Officer: Thomas Dolan IV, President and Executive Director

Izaak Walton League of America, Pennsylvania Division
1146 E. Poplar St., New York, Pa. 17403
717-854-4517
A broadly based organization which aims at the preservation and wise use of soils, woodlands, waters, wildlife, and air. Founded: 1926. Membership: 1,544.
Chief Officer: Kenneth Fahnestock, President

Pennsylvania Environmental Council, Inc.
313 S. 16 St., Philadelphia, Pa. 19102
215-735-0966
Works for stronger legislation to protect the environment and to secure stricter enforcement of present environmental protection laws. Founded: 1970. Membership: 1,000.
Chief Officer: Curtin Winsor, President

Publications: *News and Views*; legislative summaries; and news alerts

Pennsylvania Forestry Assn.
5221 E. Simpson St., Mechanicsburg, Pa. 17055
717-766-5371
Dedicated to environmental protection and wise use of natural resources. Main thrust of activities is environmental education and improvement. Founded: 1886. Membership: 2,000.
Chief Officer: John C. Fralish, Executive Director
Publication: *Pennsylvania Forests* (quarterly)

Pennsylvania Roadside Council, Inc.
34 Palmers Mill Rd., Media, Pa. 19063
215-356-0539
Encourages local roadside improvement programs, building rest areas, and campaigns against littering supports appropriate legislation; and distributes education materials. Founded: 1939. Membership: 1,000.
Chief Officer: Birchard Clothier, President
Publications: Newsletter (bimonthly); others

Western Pennsylvania Conservancy
204 5 Ave., Pittsburgh, Pa. 15222
412-288-2777
Dedicated to furthering the public welfare through education, conservation, and preservation of land, forests, and waters. Founded: 1931. Membership: 5,300.
Chief Officer: Joshua C. Whetzel, President
Publication: *CONSERVE (Water, Land, and Life)*

Puerto Rico

Puerto Rico Assn. of Soil and Water Conservation Districts
Apartado 1921, Ponce, P.R. 00731
Devoted to the conservation and development of soil and water resources; carries on activities which stimulate public concern about the need to conserve those natural resources. Founded: 1946. Membership: 85.
Chief Officer: Israel Rivera, President

Puerto Rico Pollution Control Assn.
Apartado 7066, BO Obrero Sta., Santurce, P.R. 00916
809-765-3072
Studies, promotes, and encourages improved sanitation of waterways; advances knowledge in design, construction, operation, and management of waterborne waste systems, treatment, and reclamation works; and promotes sound legislation relating to the water pollution control field. Founded: 1947. Membership: 150.
Chief Officer: Gines Flaque Garces, Treasurer
Publication: *Noticias de Ingenieria*

Rhode Island

Audubon Society of Rhode Island
40 Bowen St., Providence, R.I. 02903
401-521-1670
Works to foster conservation and protection of the state's natural resources, particularly wildlife and wildlife habitat. Operates statewide environmental education programs, nine wildlife sanctuaries and nature centers, and a year-round field trip program. Founded: 1897. Membership: 2,180.
Chief Officer: Alfred L. Hawkes, Executive Director
Publications: *Man and Nature*; *Rhode Island Audubon Report*

Ecology Action for Rhode Island
286 Thayer St., Providence, R.I. 02906
401-274-9429
Involved in environmental education and citizen action, with groups working to aid the Environmental Protection Agency in their determination of water discharge permits and training citizens around the state to act as monitors once those permits are granted. Provides speakers and materials for teachers and environmental groups.
Chief Officer: Richard Green, President
Publication: *EARI Newsletter*

Environment Council of Rhode Island
40 Bowen St., Providence, R.I. 02903
401-521-1670
Coordinates intrastate action and information of member groups in the environmental field. Makes available information on environmental legislation in the Rhode Island Assembly. Founded: 1970. Membership: 28 organizations; 95 individuals.
Chief Officer: Wilfrid L. Gates, Jr., President
Publication: Newsletter

South Carolina

Beaufort Environmental Protection Assn.
Box 5, Beaufort, S.C. 29902

Encourages protection and improvement of the environment in Beaufort County, with primary interest in preventing the unnecessary pollution of air, land, and water. Founded: 1971. Membership: 175.
Chief Officer: J.B. Heles, Executive Director

South Carolina Forestry Assn.
Box 274, Columbia, S.C. 29202
803-796-6490
Works to promote, develop, protect, and wisely use the forests of South Carolina through the establishment of conservation and education programs directed toward government, private, and public interests. Founded: 1968. Membership: 700.
Publication: Newsletter

South Carolina TB and Respiratory Disease Assn.
1817 Gadsden St., Columbia, S.C. 29201
803-254-7692
Works for the prevention of tuberculosis and respiratory disease and improvement of air quality.
Chief Officer: Herman F. Allen, Executive Director

South Dakota

South Dakota Assn. of Conservation Districts
Box 1031, Pierre, S. Dak. 57501
Works towards the conservation, orderly development, and beneficial use of lands, water, and other resources; relies primarily on local initiative and self-government. Founded: 1940. Membership: 70 districts.
Chief Officer: Leonard Schultz, President
Publication: Quarterly newsletters

Tennessee

Greater Knoxville Area Audubon Society
Box 1213, Knoxville, Tenn. 37901
615-523-9730
Works for the conservation and protection of the state's natural resources, particularly wildlife and wildlife habitat. Organizes various educational programs, and confronts specific problems as they arise. Founded: 1969. Membership: 700.
Chief Officer: D. M. Manley, President
Publications: *Environmental Alert*; occasional brochures

Oak Ridge Conservation Club
Box 192, Oak Ridge, Tenn. 37830
615-483-5555
Works for conservation of natural resources, cooperation with state and federal agencies in enforcement of game and fish laws, and conservation education. Founded: 1953. Membership: 25.
Chief Officer: E.W. Means, President
Publication: Newsletter

Tennessee Beautiful, Inc.
2611 W. End Bldg., Nashville, Tenn. 37203
Encourages private action to fight litter and pollution; promotes educational programs; serves as advisory and coordinating agency; and disseminates information. Founded: 1972.
Chief Officer: Helen Keith, President

Tennessee Citizens for Wilderness Planning
130 Tabor Rd., Oak Ridge, Tenn. 37830
615-482-2153
Works for the preservation of wilderness and natural areas, free-flowing rivers, strip-mine control, land-use planning, and environmental education. Founded: 1966. Membership: 600.
Chief Officer: William L. Russell, President
Publication: *The TCWP Newsletter*

Tennessee Environmental Council
Tennessee Botanical Gardens, Cheek Rd., Nashville, Tenn. 37205
615-356-3306
Works to coordinate the ideas, manpower, and resources of members to fight the threat of unplanned urban growth and industrial exploitation. Currently working to develop an environmental study center including a library and information clearinghouse. Founded: 1970. Membership: 28 organizations; 40 individuals.
Chief Officer: Douglas Henry, Jr., President
Publication: Newsletter

Tennessee Forestry Assn.
2020 21 Ave. S., Box 12429, Nashville, Tenn. 37212
615-383-2356
Promotes the development and wise use of Tennessee's forest resources. Founded: 1952. Membership: 500.
Chief Officer: Charles E. Cheston, President
Publications: *Tennescene Newsletter; TFA Legislative Bulletin*

124 Private Environmental Organizations

Tennessee Scenic Rivers Assn.
Box 3104, Nashville, Tenn., 37219
Works to help preserve and protect Tennessee's scenic rivers, educate the public about them, and emphasize river safety through sponsored canoe trips, canoe training sessions, and personal contacts. Founded: 1966. Membership: 500 families.
Chief Officer: William H. McLean, President
Publication: *TSRA Newsletter*

Texas

Bayou Preservation Assn., Inc.
1200 Bissonnet, Houston, Tex. 77005
713-524-0607
Seeks alternatives to concrete channelization of bayous. Founded: 1966.
Chief Officer: George P. Mitchell, President

Citizens Environmental Coalition
1200 Bissonnet, Houston, Tex. 77005
713-524-7451
A coordinating group which aims to avoid duplication of effort of 34 member organizations. Library, educational, and public information services are available. Founded: 1971. Membership: 20,000.
Chief Officer: P. Burgess Griesenbeck, Executive Secretary
Publication: *Eco-alition News*

Citizens for a Better Environment
705 S. Texas Bldg., San Antonio, Tex. 78205
Organizes recycling programs and encourages general community environmental education. Founded: 1971. Membership: 400.
Publication: *Environmental Reporter* (monthly)

Citizens for Hike and Bike
11937 Memorial Dr., Houston, Tex. 77024
713-181-1393
Works to stimulate interest in promoting and installing bicycle trails and paths to connect colleges, libraries, parks, schools, and shopping centers in Houston. Founded: 1970. Membership: 25.
Chief Officer: Sandra Maxfield, President

City Planners Assn. of Texas
Box 231, Arlington, Tex. 76010
817-275-3271 Ext. 321
A division of the Texas Municipal League that works to promote better city planning in Texas, including greater awareness of the environmental impact of all forms of development. Founded: 1950. Membership: 140.
Chief Officer: Ross Wilhite, Director
Publications: Various special publications

Earth Awareness Foundation
Suite 209, 1730 Nasa Blvd., Houston, Tex. 77058
713-333-3101
Assists students in their efforts to become environmentally literate and involved in community projects, leading to improved environmental quality. Founded: 1970. Membership: 70 clubs.
Chief Officer: Eugene E. Horton, President-National Director
Publication: *Earth, I Care* (newsletter)

Ecology Action of Austin
4502-1/2 Ave. H, Austin, Tex. 78751
512-452-0004
Responsible for Austin's recycling centers. Founded: 1970. Membership: 825.
Publication: *Ecology Action Newsletter*

Environmental Consumers' Education Council
Box 10716, El Paso, Tex. 79997
915-779-3737
Serves as a clearinghouse, plans and sponsors educational programs, and pursues improvement of dialogue between government, industry, and citizens. Founded: 1971. Membership: 33.
Chief Officer: James Milson

League of Women Voters, Environmental Quality Committee
Box 491, Irving, Tex. 75060
214-351-4125
Conducts studies on air and water quality and solid wastes; will begin shortly a land-use study. Also lobbies for adequate standards and enforcement in these areas. Membership: 88.
Chief Officer: Anne Pfaff, President
Publications: *Irving Voter* (monthly); occasional publications

Pesticide Task Force
6505 Northwood, Dallas, Tex. 75225
214-363-8182
Works for strong pesticide regulations statewide, and educates the public on the safe use of pesticides and the challenge of organic gardening. Founded: 1970. Mailing list: 1100.
Chief Officer: Judy Thayer, Chairman
Publication: *PTF News*

Sportsmen's Club of Texas, Inc.
311 Vaughn Bldg., Austin, Tex. 78701
512-472-2267
Promotes and fosters a general and continued movement for the conservation, utilization, restoration, protection, and scientific supervision of all game, fish, fowl, and other wildlife in its natural habitat; promotes the observance and enforcement of laws for the protection of fish, game, and other wildlife, and their natural foods, forests, marshes, streams, lakes, and waters; and promotes sportsmanlike methods in hunting and fishing and proper respect for the rights of landowners. Founded: 1956. Membership: 90,000.
Chief Officer: Cecil Reid, Executive Director
Publication: *SCOT Wildlife News*

Texas Bar Assn., Environmental Law Section
201 W. 15 St., Austin, Tex. 78701
Provides educational services to the State Bar of Texas on environmental law. Founded: 1969. Membership: 500.
Chief Officer: Elbert Hooper, Chairman
Publication: Newsletter

Texas Forestry Assn.
Box 1488, Lufkin, Tex. 75901
713-634-5523
Works to advance the cause of forestry; to develop public appreciation of the value of Texas forests; to assist in determining and securing the adoption of the most beneficial forest policy within Texas; to give encouragement and assistance in the growing, production, processing, storage, transporation, and use of forest products; to foster and maintain ethical practices and high standards in the forest products industry of Texas; to promote air and water pollution research; and, by all practical means, to encourage the multiple use, expansion, protection, proper management, and wise use of all forest and related resources. Founded: 1914. Membership: 2,000.
Publication: *Texas Forestry*

Utah

National Mustang Assn., Inc.
Newcastle, Utah 84756
801-439-2272
Works for the preservation and perpetuation of mustangs; owns a 44,000-acre ranch at Clover Valley, Nevada, for a preserve. Founded: 1965. Membership: 17,000 (plus 12,000 supporting).
Chief Officer: Kent Gregersen, First Vice President
Publication: Monthly

Utah Air Conservation Committee
632 17 Ave., Salt Lake City, Utah 84103
801-364-5077
An official control group established by state law; members are appointed by the Governor. Passes rules, regulations, and standards to control air pollution which have the effect of law. The Committee, a part of the State Division of Health, is a government agency, not a citizen organization. Founded: 1967. Membership: 11.
Publications: Many special reports

Utah Assn. of Soil Conservation Districts
Morgan, Utah 84050
801-829-3378
A legal subdivision of State Government that looks after and cares for the natural resources of the state, particularly on private land; cooperates with all other groups and agencies. Inventory, planning, and programming conservation activities are the main functions. Founded: 1937. Membership: 15,000.
Chief Officer: Frank W. Bohman, President

Utah Environmental Center
1247 Wilmington Ave., Salt Lake City, Utah 84106
801-467-0433
Serves as a sounding board for environmental concern and a clearinghouse for environmental information. Provides a forum for environmental dialogue and tries to involve all segments of society in making ecologically sound decisions. Founded: 1971. Mailing list: 2,500.
Chief Officer: Verne Huser, Executive Director
Publication: Newsletter (monthly)

Vermont

Conservation Society of Southern Vermont
Box 256, Townshend, Vt. 05353
802-365-7754
Aims to protect natural resources; plans and administers programs devoted to the wise use of land, forests, and water. Founded: 1966. Membership: 1,200.
Chief Officer: John W. Stevens, Director
Publication: *The Conserver* (newsletter); staff reports

Merck Forest Foundation, Inc.
Rupert, Vt. 05768
Maintains a 2600-acre environmental demonstration area using fields and forests for a variety of activities directed towards increased awareness of natural systems and ways man can live or work within them; conducts in-school programs and community projects for nearby towns; gives special slide shows and lectures as requested. Founded: 1957. Membership: 200.
Chief Officer: Duncan A. Campbell, Director
Publications: Brochures; guidesheets

Vermont Natural Resources Council
26 State St., Montpelier, Vt. 05602
802-223-2328
Primarily educates and informs the public on environmental concerns; takes an active interest in legislation that will affect environment. Founded: 1963. Membership: 1,400 individuals; 60 organizations; 20 businesses.
Chief Officer: Seward Weber, Executive Director
Pubication: *Vermont Environmental Report*

Virgin Islands

Caribbean Conservation Assn.
Box 4187, St. Thomas, V.I. 00801
809-775-3225
Ascertains and coordinates the conservation needs of the area, encourages the creation of national and other conservation organizations in each island and country, and helps to foster in the people of the Caribbean a greater awareness of the value of their natural and cultural resources. Founded: 1967. Membership: 150.
Chief Officer: Mahamad Hanif, Executive Director
Publication: Newsletter (monthly)

Island Resources Foundation, Inc.
Box 4187, St. Thomas, V.I. 00801
809-775-3225
An independent research center for the study of island systems, dedicated to improved resources management, comprehensive planning, and conservation of cultural, physical, and natural resources. Founded: 1970. Nonmembership.
Chief Officer: Edward L. Towle, President

League of Women Voters of the Virgin Islands
St. Thomas, V.I. 00801
809-774-4742
Promotes citizen participation in government. Founded: 1968.
Publications: *The V.I. Voter*; educational publications

Virginia

Northern Virginia Conservation Council
Box 304, Annandale, Va. 22003
Deals with all environmental problems affecting northern Virginia. Problems include transportation, water quality, air pollution, solid waste management, land use, etc. Founded: 1966. Membership: 350.
Chief Officer: Mrs. Doann Haines, President

Virginia Forests, Inc.
1 N. 5 St., Richmond, Va. 23219
703-644-8462
Encourages the development and wise use of the forest and related resources of Virginia for the best interests of this and succeeding generations. Activities include meetings and forums, exhibits and displays, talks and illustrated lectures, publicity, conducted tours, scholarships, forestry training camps, and various special programs. Founded: 1943. Membership: 1,100.
Chief Officer: William E. Cooper, Executive Director
Publications: *Virginia Forests Magazine* (quarterly); bulletins (usually monthly)

Virginia Wildlife Federation, Inc.
4021 Locust St., Fairfax, Va. 22030
703-273-0288
Dedicated to the conservation of soil, forests, waters, wildlife, and all natural resources. Founded: 1950. Membership: 8,000.
Chief Officer: James F. Miles, Jr., President
Publication: *Federation Record*

Washington

Good Outdoor Manners Assn.
Box 7095, Seattle, Wash. 98133
206-325-7798
Organized to prevent vandalism and abuse of outdoor resources. Founded: 1960. Membership: 200.
Chief Officer: Mrs. Karl E.E. Mehrer, President
Publication: *Howdy's Happenings* (quarterly newsletter)

Student Conservation Assn., Inc.
Olympic View Dr., Rte. 1, Box 573A, Vashon, Wash. 98070
206-567-4798
Conducts and operates the Student Conservation Program in cooperation with the National Park Service, U.S. Forest Service, and the Merck Forest Foundation. The Program, one of work and conservation education for youth, enlists the voluntary services of conservation-minded students (high school, college, and graduate men and women) to work and learn during their summer vacations. Founded: 1957. Membership: 2,000.
Chief Officer: Jack Dolstad, Executive Director
Publications: Brochures; occasional newsletters

Washington Environmental Council, Inc.
107 S. Main St., Seattle, Wash. 98104
206-623-1483
Dedicated to the promotion of citizen, legislative, and administrative action toward providing a better environment. Founded: 1968. Membership: 1,200 individuals; 80 organizations.
Chief Officer: Joan Thomas, President
Publications: *WEC Report; Legislative Newsletter*

Washington State Sportsmen's Council, Inc.
Box 569, Vancouver, Wash. 98660
206-693-0826
Works to protect, propagate, and increase fish and game and the natural foods thereof; to improve wildlife habitat; to acquire and develop wildlife habitat; to ensure enactment of conservation laws; and to foster conservation education. Founded: 1933. Membership: 8,500 (in 104 units).
Chief Officer: Albert M. Stanley, President
Publications: Newsletters; press releases; minutes of meetings

West Virginia

Appalachian Trail Conference
Box 236, Harpers Ferry, W. Va. 25425
304-535-6331
Founded: 1925.
Chief Officer: Stanley A. Murray
Publications: 10 guidebooks on the Trail (sectional); *Trailway News* (quarterly); other publications pertaining to Trail use and maintenance

West Virginia Wildlife Federation
Box 275, Paden City, W. Va. 26159
304-337-9282
Dedicated to the conservation of soil, forests, waters, wildlife, and all natural resources. Founded: 1952. Membership: 42,508 (142 clubs).
Chief Officer: David Brantner, President
Publication: *Wildlife Notes*

Wisconsin

Center for Environmental Communication and Education Studies
602 State St., Madison, Wis. 53703
608-262-2115/6
Acts as a convener and catalyst for university scholars and students devoted to instruction, investigation, and outreach in a variety of fields concerned with interpreting environmental issues to many publics. Founded: 1969. Membership: 9.
Chief Officer: Clay Schoenfeld, Chairman
Publication: *The Journal of Environmental Education*

Citizens Natural Resources Assn. of Wisconsin, Inc.
Rte. 1, Box 390, Stevens Point, Wis. 54481
715-341-0494
Works toward solution of environmental problems such as use of chemicals, water pollution, and protection of unusual ecological habitats. Founded: 1953. Membership: 425.
Chief Officer: George Becker, President.
Publications: *The CNRA Bulletin*; occasional bulletins on specific problems

Earth Action
4141 N. 64 St., Milwaukee, Wis. 53218
Sponsors recycling drives and environmental education. Founded: 1970. Membership: 30.

Environmental Awareness Committee
225 N. Adams St., Green Bay, Wis. 54301
414-437-5445
Works to get people to do something about the unnatural and unconscious destruction of their surroundings by making them more aware of their environment. Founded: 1970.
Chief Officer: Kenneth J. Steliga, Chairman

Environment Wisconsin
114 N. Carroll St., Madison, Wis. 53703
608-256-0565
Serves as clearinghouse for environmental information for citizens throughout Wisconsin, and coordinates efforts of environmental organizations in the state. Founded: 1971. Membership: 31 organizations.

Chief Officer: Susan Harris, Executive Director
Publications: *Eco-Echo* (monthly); *Legislative Newsletter* (bimonthly)

Izaak Walton League, Wisconsin Division
Box 303, Green Bay, Wis. 54305
414-435-8471
This is a broadly based conservation organization which aims at the preservation and wise use of soils, woodlands, waters, wildlife, and air. Activities include adult and youth education, legislation, and watchdog activities. Founded: 1922. Membership: 1,500.
Chief Officer: William Fisk, President
Publication: *Wisconsin Waltonian*

League of Women Voters of Wisconsin, Environmental Quality Program
536 La Plant St., Green Bay, Wis. 54302
414-432-7189
Promotes citizen participation in government. Environmental Quality is one of 12 programs with specific study and action activities. The EQ program promotes a quality environment for living, publishes materials for members, and holds meetings and seminars. Members appear as observers, and through the consensus process, agree to support or oppose legislation through writing letters, attending hearings, and making statements. Founded: 1922. Membership: 3,300.
Chief Officer: Mrs. Richard Whalen, President
Publication: *Forward*

Society of Tympanuchus Cupido Pinnatus
Box 1156, Milwaukee, Wis. 53201
414-272-6200
Dedicated to the preservation of the prairie chicken. Founded: 1961. Membership: 1,500.
Chief Officer: Willis G. Sullivan, President
Publication: *BOOM* (quarterly)

Southeastern Wisconsin Regional Planning Commission
916 N. East Ave., Box 769, Waukesha, Wis. 53186
414-547-6721
The official areawide planning agency for the 2,689-square-mile Southeastern Wisconsin Region which is charged by law with preparing a comprehensive plan designed to resolve the developmental and environmental problems of this rapidly urbanizing region. The Commission's work program has addressed itself to such major problem areas as planning for the protection of the environment, for the movement of people and goods, for land use and housing, and for community development. Founded: 1960. Membership: 21.
Chief Officer: Kurt W. Bauer, Executive Director
Publications: Various special and technical reports

Trees for Tomorrow, Inc.
Box 216, Eagle River, Wis. 54521
715-479-6456
Strives to educate the public about the need to bring about a better environment. Groups study soil, water, and forests, and discuss topical urban and recreational problems, pollution, etc. Founded: 1944. Membership: 13 staff; 15 paper and power industries.
Chief Officer: M. N. Taylor, Executive Director

Washington County Environmental Council
Box 537, West Bend, Wis. 53095
Deals with environmental concerns. Current projects include land-use plan for county, study of energy crisis, and solid waste disposal for county. Founded: 1967. Membership: 50.
Chief Officer: Albert Schroeder, Chairman
Publication: Newsletter

Wilderness Watch
Box 3184, Green Bay, Wis. 54303
414-499-9131
Dedicated to the sustained use of America's sylvan lands and waters, with particular emphasis on ecological considerations. Decisions are based upon the advice of a scientific advisory staff of experts in the behavioral and physical sciences. Founded: 1969.
Chief Officer: Jerry Gandt, President
Publication: *Watch It!*

Wisconsin Committee for Environmental Information
114 N. Carroll St., Madison, Wis. 53703
Provides factual scientific support to other environmental groups and to the public. Founded: 1970. Membership: 40.
Chief Officer: Alwyn Scott, President

Wisconsin Ecological Society
Box 514, Green Bay, Wis. 54305
414-435-5121
Works to see that technological advances do the least possible harm to the environment. Aims to preserve natural areas for future generations by halting degradation of present areas. Founded: 1969. Membership: 25.
Chief Officer: John F. Wilson, President

Wisconsin Park and Recreation Assn.
610 Langdon St., 230 Lowell Hall, Madison, Wis. 53706
608-262-3735
Provides educational services to develop and improve the knowledge and skills of those interested in the park and recreation fields. Activities include annual conference, regional workshops, summer sessions, in-depth clinics, promotion of desirable legislation, and professional certification of qualified members. Founded: 1965. Membership: 900.
Chief Officer: Fred E. Lengfeld, Executive Secretary
Publication: *Wisconsin Park and Recreation Newsletter*

Zero Population Growth, Marinette-Menominee Branch
Univ. of Wisconsin Center, Marinette County, Marinette, Wis. 54143
715-735-7477
A nationwide organization formed to stabilize the population of the United States by voluntary means. Founded: 1969. Membership: 15.
Chief Officer: Vida Yazdi Ditter, President

Wyoming

Wyoming Assn. of Conservation Districts
Big Piney, Wyo. 83113
Works to protect and conserve natural resources through wise use. Founded: 1941. Membership: 6,000.
Chief Officer: Dan S. Budd, President
Publication: *From the Ground Up*

Wyoming Wildlife Federation
Box 1406, Casper, Wyo. 82601
307-234-5212
Dedicated to the conservation of soil, forests, waters, wildlife, and all natural resources; a liaison with state and federal agencies and legislators. Founded: 1948. Membership: 2,500.
Chief Officer: John J. Wantulok, President
Publication: Newsletter

TRADE AND PROFESSIONAL ORGANIZATIONS

Acoustical and Insulating Materials Assn.
205 W. Touhy Ave., Park Ridge, Ill. 60068
312-692-5178
Concerned with combating noise pollution and providing protection from excessive heat and cold in buildings; strives to provide a quiet, comfortable environment through technology. Founded: 1968. Membership: 14 manufacturers.
Chief Officer: James E. Nolan, CAE, Executive Vice President

Acoustical Society of America
335 E. 45 St., New York, N.Y. 10017
212-685-1940
Works to increase and diffuse the knowledge of acoustics and promote its practical applications. Founded: 1929. Membership: 4,800.
Chief Officer: Edgar A. G. Shaw, President.
Publication: *Journal of the Acoustical Society of America*

American Academy of Environmental Engineers
Box 1278, Rockville, Md. 20850
301-762-7797
Certifies professional engineers as to their competence in the field of environmental engineering; also encourages its members to provide an engineering input into legislative decision-making. Founded: 1954. Membership: 1,400.
Chief Officer: Frank Bowerman, President.
Publication: *The Diplomate*

American Assn. for Health, Physical Education and Recreation
1201 16 St., N.W., Washington, D.C. 20036
202-833-5541
A voluntary professional organization dedicated to improving the quality of life through programs in health, physical education, and recreation, including fields such as environment, leisure, and outdoor education. Founded: 1885. Membership: 50,000.
Chief Officer: Carl A. Troester, Jr., Executive Secretary
Publications: *Journal of Health, Physical Education, and Recreation; School Health Review; Research Quarterly; AAHPER Update* (newsletter)

American Camping Assn., Inc.
Bradford Woods, Martinsville, Inc. 46151
317-342-8456
Professional organization for camp leaders; conducts standards program for 3,000 member camps and leadership training. Also provides legislative information service and research program. Founded: 1910. Membership: 7,500.
Chief Officer: Ernest F. Schmidt, Executive Vice President
Publications: *Camping Magazine; Camping Law Abstract*

American Chemical Society
1155 16 St. N.W., Washington, D.C. 20036
202-872-4600
Encourages in the broadest and most liberal manner the advancement of chemistry in all its branches; the promotion of research in chemical science and industry; the improvement of the qualifications and usefulness of chemists through high standards of professional ethics, education, and attainments; the increase and diffusion of chemical knowledge; and by its meetings, professional contacts, reports, papers, discussions, and publications. Also promotes scientific interests and inquiry, thereby fostering public welfare and education, aiding the development of our country's industries, and adding to the material prosperity and happiness of our people. Founded: 1876. Membership: 108,000.
Chief Officer: Robert W. Cairns, Executive Director
Publications: *Chemical and Engineering News; Environmental Science and Technology*

American Fisheries Society
1319 18 St. N.W., Washington, D.C. 20036
202-872-8282
Works to advance fisheries research and management in all its branches. It represents professional and nonprofessional workers in fisheries science and practice, and is concerned with the conservation, development, and wise utilization of all aquatic resources. The Society disseminates scientific knowledge and technical information through its journal and newsletter. Activities cover a broad spectrum: aquatic biology, economics, engineering, fish culture, limnology, marine ecology, oceanography, and technology. Founded: 1870. Membership: 6,125.
Chief Officers: Charles J. Campbell, President; Richard A. Wade, Executive Director
Publications: *Transactions of The American Fisheries Society; Journal of Ichthyology; Hydrobiological Journal;* newsletter

American Gas Assn.
1515 Wilson Blvd., Arlington, Va. 22209
703-524-2000
National trade association for the natural gas industry. Founded: 1919. Membership: 6,500.
Chief Officer: F. Donald Hart, President
Publications: *A. G. A. Monthly;* many technical publications

American Industrial Hygiene Assn.
66 S. Miller Rd., Akron, Ohio 44313
216-836-9537
World's largest professional society of industrial hygienists. Founded: 1939. Membership: 1,600.
Chief Officer: William E. McCormick, Managing Director
Publication: *American Industrial Hygiene Association Journal*

American Institute of Planners
1776 Massachusetts Ave. N.W., Washington, D.C. 20036
202-872-0611
The national organization of professional urban and regional planners in America whose members work for city, county, regional, state, and national government, as well as with private consulting firms. Its main concerns are with the critical issues of urban growth and change, as well as environmental and social balance, and it aims to encourage orderly growth and development responsive to the needs and problems of society. Founded: 1917. Membership: 7,800.
Chief Officer: John R. Joyner, Executive Director
Publications: *Journal of the American Institute of Planners;* newsletter; *Planners Notebook*

American Iron and Steel Institute
150 E. 42 St., New York, N.Y. 10017
212-697-5900
Conducts research and disseminates information on ferrous (iron and steel) recovery from household refuse and recycling. Founded: 1865. Membership: 2,100.
Chief Officer: J. P. Roche, President

American Mining Congress
1100 Ring Bldg., 1200 18 St. N.W., Washington, D.C. 20036
202-331-8900
A trade association serving as the industry's spokesman on matters such as environmental quality, public lands, mined land reclamation, safety and health, and energy resources. Founded: 1897. Membership: 600.

Chief Officer: J. Allen Overton, Jr., President
Publication: *Mining Congress Journal*

American National Cattlemen's Assn.
Box 569, Denver, Colo. 80201
303-266-2142
Engages in all activities necessary for the betterment of the cattle industry in the U.S., and serves as a clearinghouse for the accumulation and dissemination of information concerning the industry. Founded: 1898. Membership: 10,000.
Chief Officer: John Trotman, President
Publication: *Beef Business Bulletin*

American Paper Institute
260 Madison Ave., New York, N.Y. 10016
212-889-6200
National Trade Association of U.S. Pulp, Paper and Paperboard Manufacturers, the organization has a Department of Environmental Affairs. Founded: 1964. Membership: 200.
Chief Officer: Edwin A. Locke, Jr., President
Publications: *API Report*; other monthly and annual reports

American Petroleum Institute
1801 K St. N.W., Washington, D.C. 20006
202-833-5600
A trade association that concerns itself with all matters affecting the petroleum industry, and seeks cooperation between government and the industry. Founded: 1919. Membership: 8,000.
Chief Officer: Frank N. Ikard, President
Publication: *Petroleum Today*

American Public Gas Assn.
2600 Virginia Ave. N.W., Washington, D.C. 20037
202-338-0044
Founded: 1960. Membership: 250.
Chief Officer: Charles F. Wheatley, Jr., General Manager; General Counsel
Publication: Newsletter

American Society of Limnology and Oceanography
Box 853, Gaithersburg, Md. 20760
301-973-4155
Encourages study and understanding of limnology, oceanography, and related sciences; publishes results of such investigations. Founded: 1936. Membership: 2,700.
Chief Officer: George W. Saunders, Jr., Secretary
Publication: *Limnology and Oceanography*

American Trucking Assn.
1616 P St. N.W., Washington, D.C. 20036
202-269-3212
A national trade association for the trucking industry. Founded: 1933. Membership: 51 affiliated state associations, including the District of Columbia; 13 affiliated conferences.
Chief Officer: William A. Bresnahan, President
Publication: *Transport Topics*

American Water Resources Assn.
905 W. Fairview, Box 434, Urbana, Ill. 61801
217-367-9695
Encourages interdisciplinary communication between professionals working on all aspects of water resources problems.
Chief Officer: William Whipple, Jr., President
Publications: Several journals; special publications and reprints

Asbestos Textile Institute
131 N. York Rd., Box 471, Willow Grove, Pa. 19090
215-658-5007
Member companies are engaged in the manufacture of asbestos textiles. Founded: 1944. Membership: 7 regular; 10 associate.
Chief Officer: Doris M. Fagan, Executive Secretary
Publications: Publications dealing with special areas of asbestos textile production

Assn. of American Pesticide Control Officials
1615 S. Harrison Rd., East Lansing, Mich. 48823
517-332-0885
A group of state and federal law enforcement officials which controls the sale and application of pesticides and to some extent pesticide applicators; develops and publishes uniform definitions, official policies, and model pesticide laws and regulations; and attempts to provide a uniform legislation of pesticides. Founded: 1948. Membership: 50 states, Federal government, Canada, and Puerto Rico.
Chief Officer: L. H. Senn, President
Publication: *Association of American Pesticide Control Officials Official Publication*

Assn. of Conservation Engineers
Wisconsin Dept. of Natural Resources, Box 450, Madison, Wis. 53701
Works to encourage the educational, social, and economic interests of engineering practices, and to promote recognition of the importance of sound practices in fish, wildlife, and recreation development. Founded: 1962. Membership: 150.

Chief Officer: Allen I. Lewis, President
Publication: *ACE Newsletter* (biannual)

Assn. of Interpretive Naturalists
International Business Office, 6700 Needwood Rd., Derwood, Md. 20855
301-948-8844
A professional organization serving park naturalists, teachers of natural science, historians, camp leaders, anthropologists, geologists, and media specialists whose primary responsibility is interpretation of the natural environment. It is an outgrowth of the Bradford Woods Interpretive Workshop established at Martinsville, Indiana, in 1955. Founded: 1961. Membership: 800.
Chief Officer: Robert L. Young, Secretary-Treasurer
Publications: Pamphlets; research papers

Bituminous Coal Research, Inc.
350 Hochberg Rd., Monroeville, Pa. 15146
412-327-1600
Engages in a program of coal research. Founded: 1936.
Chief Officer: James R. Garvey, President

Chemical Specialties Manufacturers Assn.
50 E. 41 St., New York, N.Y. 10017
212-685-8722
Represents the chemical specialties industry and is active in areas of legislation, product testing, marketing, labeling, and ecology. Founded: 1914. Membership: 500 companies.
Chief Officer: A. A. Mulliken, Executive Director
Publications: *CSMA Outlook*; various reports and bulletins

Cooling Tower Institute
3003 Yale St., Houston, Tex. 77018
713-861-5328
A technical association dedicated to improvement in technology, design, performance, and maintenance of cooling towers. Founded: 1950. Membership: 88.
Chief Officer: Dorothy Garrison, Executive Secretary
Publications: *CTI News* (quarterly newsletter); various special publications

Dairy Research, Inc.
6300 N. River Rd., Rosemont, Ill. 60018
312-696-1870
Aims to extend the use of dairy products through the development of new markets, processes, and products. Founded: 1969.
Chief Officer: Richard E. Farrar, Executive Vice President
Publication: *Dairy Research Digest*

Edison Electric Institute
90 Park Ave., New York, N.Y. 10016
212-986-4100
Works to advance the art of electric supply in the public interest. Founded: 1933.

Engine Manufacturers Assn.
111 E. Wacker Dr., Chicago, Ill. 60601
312-644-6610
A trade association that conducts research, recommends technical standards, serves as a voice for the industry, and acts as a forum for exchanging information. Founded: Reorganized in 1968 from the Internal Combustion Engine Institute. Membership: 16.
Chief Officer: Thomas C. Young, Executive Director
Publication: *Lube Oil Data Book*

Farm Electrification Council
666 Fifth Ave., New York, N.Y. 10019
212-489-4631
Coordinates all segments of the electrical industry encourage the beneficial use of electricity for agricultural production and countryside living. Membership: 400 companies.
Chief Officer: Hugh Hansen, Executive Manager
Publications: Newsletters; information sheets

Food and Drug Law Institute
1750 Pennsylvania Ave. N.W., Washington, D.C. 20006
202-333-2230
An educational organization, which aims to improve understanding of the nature and scope of laws and regulations applicable to the food, drug, cosmetic and related industries. Founded: 1949. Membership: 100 firms.
Chief Officer: Laurence I. Wood, President
Publications: *Food Drug Cosmetic Law Journal*; casebooks and textbooks

Glass Container Manufacturers Institute
1800 K St., N.W., Washington, D.C. 20006
202-872-1280
Trade association of glass container manufacturers. Founded: 1945. Membership: 70.
Chief Officer: Leif Oxaal, President

Gulf and Caribbean Fisheries Institute
10 Rickenbacker Causeway, Miami, Fla. 33149
305-350-7533
Holds an annual meeting to transmit informa-

tion from the scientific world of fisheries to the fishing industry and to inform the scientists of the types of information required by industry. Founded: 1948. Membership: 600.
Chief Officer: James B. Higman, Executive Director
Publications: Proceedings of meetings held

Hardwood Research Council
610 Stearns Bldg., Box 961, Statesville, N.C. 28677
704-873-6356
Promotes research and education in both hardwood forest management and utilization. Activities include meetings, demonstrations, exhibits, and publishing special literature and news releases; also gives advice to landowners and operators, youth groups, etc. Founded: 1953. Membership: 130.
Chief Officer: Howard J. Doyle, Council Forester
Publication: *Hardwood Forestry Bulletin* (monthly)

Incinerator Institute of America
2425 Wilson Blvd., Arlington, Va. 22201
703-528-0663
Encourages the manufacture of environmentally acceptable, technologically sound thermal reduction systems which would assist in dealing with the increasing national solid waste disposal problem. Founded: 1950. Membership: 50.
Chief Officer: Richard P. Harper, Secretary-Treasurer
Publications: Various technical publications

Industrial Health Foundation, Inc.
5231 Centre Ave., Pittsburgh, Pa. 15232
412-687-2100
Works for the advancement of healthful working conditions in industry. Services to member companies include information (publications, literature searches, and data retrieval), industrial hygiene and safety surveys, consultations in occupational medicine, and toxicological studies. Founded: 1935. Membership: 309 companies.
Chief Officer: Daniel C. Braun, M.D., President
Publications: *Industrial Hygiene Digest; Memos to Members;* technical bulletins (medical, nursing, legal, engineering, and chemical-toxicological)

Institute of Paper Chemistry
1043 E. South River St., Appleton, Wis. 54911
414-734-9251
A graduate school, information center, and research community particularly concerned with the education of scientific generalists. The research divisions include a Division of Industrial and Environmental Systems and a Division of Information Services that provide information, consultation, and research in environmental matters. Founded: 1929.
Chief Officer: John Strange, President
Publications: Bulletin; various special publications

Inter Industry Emission Control Program
Ford Motor Co., American Rd., Dearborn, Mich. 48121
313-332-4888
Formed by Ford Motor Co. and the Mobil Oil Corp. as a cooperative research effort on automotive emission control. Conducts joint research studies on experimental hardware and fuel systems to meet low emission targets. Founded: 1967. Membership: 11 companies.
Chief Officer: Donald R. Tope, Vice President
Publications: Technical reports

International Air Transport Assn.
1155 Mansfield St., Montreal 113, Que., Canada
514-866-1011
Works to promote safe, regular, economical air transport, studies the problems of air transport, and promotes cooperation among groups involved in air transport. Founded: 1945. Membership: 108 airlines.
Chief Officer: Knut Hammarskjöld, Director General
Publications: proceedings; symposia; various special reports

Land Improvement Contractors of America
435 N. Michigan Ave., Chicago, Ill 60611
312-321-9044
Trade association of land improvement contractors. Founded: 1961. Membership: 2,000.
Chief Officer: Paul A. Bucha, Executive Secretary
Publication: Newsletter

Manufacturing Chemists Assn.
1825 Connecticut Ave. N.W., Washington, D.C. 20009
202-483-6126
Founded: 1872. Membership: 180.
Chief Officer: William J. Driver, President

Milk Industry Foundation
910 17 St. N.W., Washington, D.C. 20006
Deals with all problems affecting the fluid milk

industry including pollution, waste disposal (liquid and solid), energy conservation, noise control, and air pollution. Founded: 1900. Membership: 500.
Chief Officer: Robert H. North, Executive Vice President
Publications: Various special publications

National Academy of Sciences/National Research Council
2101 Constitution Ave. N.W., Washington, D.C. 20418
202-961-1234
An organization of scientists and engineers dedicated to the furtherance of science and its use for the general welfare, and chartered by the U.S. Congress to provide advisory services to agencies of the Federal government. Activities are carried out through more than 500 boards and committees. One of these, the Environmental Studies Board, is concerned with environmental problems. The Academy does not have facilities to handle general inquiries from the public, but does publish some monographs for professional groups. Founded: 1863. Membership: 1,000.
Chief Officer: Philip Handler, President, National Academy of Sciences.
Publications: *Proceedings* (monthly); *News Report* (ten times a year); monographs (irregular)

National Assn. of Conservation Districts
1025 Vermont Ave. N.W., Washington, D.C. 20005
202-347-5995
Works to advance the cause of soil, water, and related natural resource conservation through locally organized and managed conservation districts created in accordance with state legislation. Founded: 1946. Membership: 3,019 conservation districts.
Chief Officer: Gordon K. Zimmerman, Executive Secretary
Publications: *Tuesday Letter*; various reports and special publications

National Assn. of State Park Directors
Division of State Parks, Oklahoma Tourism and Recreation Dept., Rm. 500, W. Rogers Memorial Bldg., Oklahoma City, Okla. 73105
405-521-3414
Chief Officer: Chris Terrell Delaporte

National Automotive Muffler Assn.
Box 579, West Covina, Calif. 91793
213-338-2417
A group of muffler installers that has been active in the area of producing and installing mufflers that give better performance. The Association has done considerable study in reducing exhaust noise emission, and is presently introducing legislation which will permit static noise testing stations. Founded: 1954. Membership: 225.
Chief Officer: A. J. Esposito, Executive Director
Publication: *NAMA News*

National Canners Assn.
1133 20 St. N.W., Washington, D.C. 20036
202-331-7070
An organization of packers of food processed in hermetically sealed containers and sterilized by heat; aims to improve the efficiency of operations of its members and to promote the acceptance and use of these foods. Founded: 1907. Membership: 540.
Chief Officer: Charles J. Carey, President
Publications: Various publications; audiovisual aids

National Dairy Council
111 N. Canal St., Chicago, Ill. 60606
312-372-3156
Works to achieve optimal health through nutrition research and education based on the concept of a balanced diet, including milk and milk products, in accordance with scientific recommendations, thus strengthening the dairy industry and American agriculture. Founded: 1915.
Chief Officer: M. F. Brink, President
Publications: Special reports; educational materials; teaching aids

National Environmental Health Assn.
1600 Penn St., Denver, Colo. 80203
303-222-4456 or 222-5118
An organization of professionally trained men and women working to control environmental hazards and permit attainment of the highest possible human health standards. Members are administrators, environmentalists, sanitarians, and technicians employed by federal, state, and local government, schools, medical care facilities, the military, and industry. Educators and students of environmental health are an important segment of NEHA membership. Founded: 1937. Membership: 6,000.
Chief Officer: Nicholas Pohlit, Executive Director
Publication: *Journal of Environmental Health*

National Flexible Packaging Assn.
12025 Shaker Blvd., Cleveland, Ohio 44120
216-229-6373
Trade association for flexible packaging. Founded: 1950. Membership: 200.
Chief Officer: E. C. Merkle, Managing Director
Publications: Bulletins

National Industrial Zoning Committee
2459 Dorset Rd., Columbus, Ohio 43221
614-488-4433
Works to improve the techniques and practice of zoning as applied to land for industry as a part of comprehensive planning. Also concerned with ecological problems (especially those facing industry) in water, noise, and air pollution. Founded: 1948. Membership: 11 trade associations.
Chief Officer: Albert E. Redman, Secretary
Publications: Various special publications

National Petroleum Refiners Assn.
1725 DeSales St. N.W., Washington, D.C. 20036
202-638-3722
A national trade association of petroleum refiners. Founded: 1961. Membership: 115 companies.
Chief Officer: Donald C. O'Hara, President
Publications: Various special and technical reports

Outdoor Writers Assn. of America, Inc.
4141 W. Bradley Rd., Milwaukee, Wis. 53209
414-354-9690
A professional and educational organization through which members strive to improve themselves in the art and media of their craft and increase their knowledge in support of conservation of natural resources. Holds workshops and maintains a scholarship program in environmental journalism. Founded: 1927. Membership: 1,400
Chief Officer: Edwin W. Hanson, Executive Director
Publication: *Outdoor Unlimited*

The Packaging Institute, U.S.A.
342 Madison Ave., New York, N.Y. 10017
212-687-8874
National nonprofit professional packaging society. Founded: 1939. Membership: 2,123.
Chief Officer: Paul B. Reuman
Publications: *The PI-USA* (journal); *Pack-Info Newsletter*

Petroleum Industry Research Foundation
60 E. 42 St., New York, N.Y. 10017
212-867-0052
Carries out economic research on oil and related matters. Founded: 1944.
Chief Officer: John H. Lichtblau, Executive Director
Publications: Occasional reports

Plastic Container Manufacturers Institute
54 Apple St., New Shrewsbury, N.J. 07724
201-741-3800
Encourages plastic bottle recycling. Founded: 1960.
Chief Officer: R. E. Hartung

Pulp Chemicals Assn.
60 E. 42 St., New York, N.Y. 10017
212-697-4816
Trade association representing producers of tall oil and turpentine. Founded: 1947. Members: 16.
Chief Officer: Douglas E. Campbell, Secretary-Treasurer

Rubber Reclaimers Assn.
63 Radnor Ave., Naugatuck, Conn. 06770
203-729-2460
Works to improve the quality and usefulness of reclaimed rubber through jointly sponsored research, and to promote the use of reclaimed rubber in present and new applications. Founded: 1930. Membership 7.
Chief Officer: T. H. Fitzgerald, Secretary-Treasurer

Single Service Institute, Inc.
250 Park Ave., New York, N.Y. 10017
212-697-4545
National trade association for manufacturers of disposable products for food service and packaging. Founded: 1933. Membership: 43.
Chief Officer: Robert W. Foster
Publication: *Environment News Digest*

Soap and Detergent Assn.
475 Park Ave. S., New York, N.Y. 10016
212-725-1262
A national trade group representing the detergents produced in the U.S. It serves as a communications crossroads of the industry and channels information to and from the consumer, public, media, and government. Founded: 1926. Membership: 115 companies.
Chief Officer: Theodore E. Brenner, President and Secretary

Publication: *Water in the News* (bimonthly newsletter)

Technical Assn. of the Pulp and Paper Industry
1 Dunwoody Pk., Atlanta, Ga. 30341
404-457-6352

Promotes research and educational programs in the pulp and paper industry. Founded: 1915. Membership: 13,000.
Chief Officer: P.E. Nethercut, Executive Secretary
Publication: *Tappi*

DISBANDED AND INACTIVE ORGANIZATIONS

Disbanded

Community Pride Recycling Center, Denver, Colo.
Conservation Associates, San Francisco, Calif.
Ecology Action of Florida, Inc., Miami, Fla.
Environmental Information Center, Milwaukee, Wis.
Food Forum, Albuquerque, N. Mex.
Hawaii Wildlife Federation, Honolulu, Hawaii
Hugh Moore Fund, New York, N.Y.
North Jersey Anti-Pollution League, Mountain Lakes, N.J.
Pollution Underground, Frankfort, N.Y.
Potomac Basin Center, Washington, D.C. (now Central Atlantic Environment Center)
Prairie Chicken Foundation of Illinois, Centralia, Ill.
Pulp Manufacturers Research League, Appleton, Wis. (merged into Effluent Processes Group of the Division of Industrial and Environmental Systems of The Institute of Paper Chemistry)
Quality Environment Group, Miami Beach, Fla.
Transportation Research Foundation, Washington, D.C.
Vermont Environmental Center, Ripton, Vt.
Zero Population Growth, Brunswick, Maine
Zero Population Growth, South Jersey Center, Mount Holly, N.J.
Zero Population Growth, Fort Worth, Tex.

Inactive

Asbestos Cement Products Assn., New York, N.Y.
Citizens for Clean Air and Water, Tucumcari, N. Mex.
Illinois Woman's Conservation, Blue Island, Ill.
International Institute for Environmental Affairs, New York, N.Y. (headquarters being moved to London, England)
Manforce, Washington, D.C.
Open Space Institute, New York, N.Y.
Zero Population Growth, Terre Haute, Ind.

3 Environmental Consultants

Solution of most environmental problems requires consultation with experts who are familiar with the complex theoretical and technological aspects of environmental activities. This chapter lists environmental consultants alphabetically by state, and it indicates the consultants' environmental specialties.

Both individuals and corporations are included. Each type offers distinctly different services.

Individual consultants. Most individual consultants are employed in the academic area, and they offer consultation to government agencies, private corporations, and civic groups. Individual consultants often give advice and conduct surveys on projects that will eventually require larger staffs and resources. In addition, they frequently advise civic groups of the relevant questions that should be asked about a particular problem. Sometimes a private consultant furnishes his services free to nonprofit organizations or charges them only for expenses incurred; the words "paid" or "unpaid" in the listings indicate the payment policy.

Consulting corporations. The typical environmental consulting corporation has available a large group of skilled people and extensive laboratory and field survey equipment. Such companies are employed by government and private organizations for planning major construction projects. Consulting corporations always charge a fee for their consultation services, and the costs are often substantial. The word "manufacturing" is used at the end of corporation listings if the firm manufactures and sells equipment used in environmental projects.

Alabama

Dr. J.H. Carney
Dept. of Chemistry, Univ. of Alabama
University, Ala. 35486
205-348-5957
Specialty: water
Unpaid

George M. Lamb
Dept. of Geology, Univ. of Southern Alabama
Mobile, Ala. 36688
205-460-6381
Specialties: solid waste, water
Unpaid

Marathon Equipment Co., Inc.
1312 Borden Ave., Leeds, Ala. 35094
Specialties: air, noise, solid waste, water
Manufacturing

The Rust Engineering Co.
1130 S. 22 St., Box 101, Birmingham, Ala. 35201
205-323-6551
Specialties: air, noise, solid waste, water

Southern Research Institute
2000 9 Ave. S., Birmingham, Ala. 35205
205-323-6592
Specialties: air, noise, water

Dr. Ervin R. Van Artsdalen
Dept. of Chemistry, Box H, Lloyd Hall, Univ. of Alabama
University Ala. 35486
205-348-5954
Specialties: air, radiation
Unpaid

Alaska

Dr. Jack M. Van Hyning
Dept. of Wildlife and Fisheries, Univ. of Alaska
Fairbanks, Alaska 99701
907-479-7177
Specialties: conservation and recreation, fish and wildlife, water
Paid/unpaid

Arizona

Virgil B. Hawk
10871 Santa Fe Dr., Sun City, Ariz. 85351
602-977-3459
Specialties: conservation and recreation, land use, plant materials
Unpaid

Timothy G. O'Keefe
Faculty Box 4098, Northern Arizona Univ.
Flagstaff, Ariz. 86001
602-523-3031
Specialties: conservation and recreation, forestry, land use
Paid

Eric G. Walther
Executive Director, Colorado Plateau Environmental Advisory Council and Coordinator of Environmental Studies
Museum of Northern Arizona
Box 1389, Flagstaff, Ariz. 86001
602-774-8572
Specialty: air
Paid

Arkansas

John Kenneth Beadles
Div. of Biological Sciences, Arkansas State Univ.
State University, Ark. 72467
501-972-3082
Specialties: conservation and recreation, fish and wildlife, land use, solid waste, water, commercial fish farming, disease problems
Unpaid

George L. Harp
Div. of Biological Sciences, Arkansas State Univ.
State University, Ark. 72467
Specialties: conservation and recreation, fish and wildlife, water
Unpaid

California

Acurex Corp.
485 Clyde Ave., Mt. View, Calif. 94040
415-964-3200
Specialty: air
Manufacturing

Agri Development Co.
3 Fleetwood Court, Orinda, Calif. 94563
415-254-0789
Specialties: air, solid waste, water

Ambient Purification Technology, Inc.
Box 71, Riverside, Calif. 92502
714-682-6211
Specialties: air, water

Gery F. Anderson
Geomechanics, Inc
5431 Diablo Dr., Sacramento, Calif. 95842
916-331-8640
Specialties: land use, solid waste, water
Paid

BC Laboratories
3016 Union Ave., Bakersfield, Calif. 93305
714-325-7475
Specialties: solid waste, water

Bechtel Corp.
50 Beale St., San Francisco, Calif. 94119
415-764-5000
Specialties: air, noise, radiation, solid waste, water

Hal D. Boley
El Dorado Nature Center
7550 E. Spring St., Long Beach, Calif. 90815
213-425-8569
Specialties: conservation and recreation, nature center program development
Paid

Richard E. Cale
12904 E. Oak Crest, Cerritos, Calif. 90701
213-926-6149
Specialty: air
Paid

Camp Dresser and McKee, Inc.
283 S. Lake Ave., Pasadena, Calif. 91101
Specialties: air, solid waste, water

Dr. Ju Chin Chu
Tech Resources, Inc.
Box 3517, Orange, Calif. 92665
714-639-4941
Specialties: air, radiation, solid waste, thermal problems
Paid

Combustion Power Co., Inc.
1346 Willow Rd., Menlo Park, Calif. 94025
415-324-4744
Specialty: solid waste
Manufacturing

Cook Research Laboratories, Inc.
Edison Way at 11 Ave., Box 2266, Menlo Park, Calif. 94025
415-368-3329
Specialties: air, noise, solid waste, water

Copley International Corp.
7817 Herschel Ave., La Jolla, Calif. 92037
714-454-0391
Specialties: air, noise, solid waste, water

James F. Cotter, Consulting Ecologist
D.C. Services Co.
Box 253, Westwood, Calif. 96137
916-256-3517
Specialties: air, conservation and recreation, environmental law, fish and wildlife, forestry, land use, noise, pesticides, radiation, solid waste, thermal problems, water, environmental impact reports
Paid

Terrence Cullinan
Lassen Volcanic National Park Co.
Manzanita Lake, Calif. 96060
916-335-4400
Specialties: conservation and recreation, land use
Paid

Ronald S. Daniel
Dept. of Biological Sciences, California State Polytechnic Univ.
Pomona, Calif. 91768
714-598-4440
Specialty: electron microscopy in all environmental applications
Paid

Stuart L. Deutsch
Sch. of Law, Univ. of Santa Clara
Santa Clara, Calif. 95053
408-984-4140
Specialties: environmental law, land use
Paid

William A. Dickinson, Jr.
Chevron Chemical Co.
Box 743, La Habra, Calif. 90631
213-694-2131
Specialty: use of fertilizers and soil amendments
Unpaid

Dillingham Environmental Co.
Box 1560, La Jolla, Calif. 92037
714-453-2390
Specialties: solid waste, water

Dynamic Development
Box 2084-D, Pasadena, Calif. 91105
213-335-5483
Specialty: air

Ecotech
Box 458, Cardiff, Calif. 92007
714-753-6391
Specialties: solid waste, water
Manufacturing

Energex, Ltd.
7998 Miramar Rd., San Diego, Calif. 92126
714-271-4880
Specialty: solid waste
Manufacturing

Envirodyne, Inc.
1180 S. Beverly Dr., Los Angeles, Calif. 90035
Specialties: air, noise, radiation, solid waste, water
Manufacturing

Enviro-Engineers, Inc.
150 E. Foothill Blvd., Arcadia, Calif. 91006
213-359-9381
Specialties: air, noise, solid waste, water

Environics, Inc.
1430-B Village Way S., Santa Ana, Calif. 92705
714-541-3693
Specialties: air, solid waste, water
Manufacturing

Environmental Engineering Lab., Inc.
3467 Kurtz St., San Diego, Calif. 92110
714-224-2885
Specialties: air, noise, solid waste, water

Environmental Measurements, Inc.
215 Leidesdorff St., San Francisco, Calif. 94111
415-398-7664
Specialty: air
Manufacturing

Environmental Quality Analysts, Inc.
66 Mint St., San Francisco, Calif. 94103
415-982-2442
Specialties: solid waste, water

Environmental Quality Engineering, Inc.
3661 Grand Ave., Oakland, Calif. 94610
415-465-5727
Specialties: air, solid waste, water
Manufacturing

W.L. Faith
2540 Huntington Dr., San Marino, Calif. 91108
213-287-9383
Specialty: air

Fluor Corp.
2500 S. Atlantic Blvd., Los Angeles, Calif. 90040
213-262-6111
Specialties: air, noise, solid waste, water

Sidney R. Frank Group
1500 Cecil Cook Rd., Drawer 580, Santa Barbara Airport, Goleta, Calif. 93017
805-964-4477
Specialties: air, noise, radiation, solid waste, water

Frederiksen Engineering Co., Inc.
1755 Broadway, Oakland, Calif. 94612
415-465-0644
Specialties: air, noise, radiation, solid waste, water

Garratt-Callahan Co.
111 Rollins Rd., Millbrae, Calif. 94030
415-697-5811
Specialty: water
Manufacturing

Geomet, Inc. (Calif.)
2814a Metropolitan Pl., Pomona, Calif. 91767
714-593-1318
Specialty: air
Manufacturing

George L. Harper
1540 Marsh St., San Luis Obispo, Calif. 93401
805-544-1132
Specialties: air, noise, radiation, water
Paid

Ray W. Hawksley Co., Inc.
220 Cutting Blvd., Richmond, Calif. 94804
415-235-5780
Specialties: solid waste, water

Hirt Combustion Engineers
931 S. Maple Ave., Montebello, Calif. 90640
213-723-8294
Specialty: air
Manufacturing

The Ben Holt Co.
521 E. Green St., Pasadena, Calif. 91101
213-684-2541
Specialties: air, noise, solid waste, water

Hydro Combustion Corp.
22805 S. Avalon Blvd., Carson, Calif. 90744
213-835-5691
Specialties: air, solid waste, water
Manufacturing

Industrial Noise Services
543 Bryant St., Palo Alto, Calif. 94301
415-321-7911
Specialty: noise

Kaiser Engineers, Div. of Kaiser Industries Corp.
300 Lakeside Dr., Oakland, Calif. 94604
415-271-4245
Specialties: air, noise, radiation, solid waste, water

Kennedy Engineers, Inc.
657 Howard St., San Francisco, Calif. 94105
415-362-6065
Specialties: air, noise, radiation, solid waste, water
Manufacturing

Koebig and Koebig, Inc.
1053 Sunset Blvd., Los Angeles, Calif. 90053
Specialties: solid waste, water

Irving P. Krick Associates, Inc.
Suite 216, 611 S. Palm Canyon Dr., Palm Springs, Calif. 92262

LFE Corp., Trapelo Div.
2030 Wright Ave., Richmond, Calif. 94804
415-235-2633
Specialties: air, noise, radiation, solid waste, water

Decker G. McAllister, Jr., Consulting Engineers
122 W. 5 St., Long Beach, Calif. 90812
213-436-1708
Specialties: air, solid waste, water
Manufacturing

Richard U. McConnell
Hugh Carter Engineering Corp.
236 E. 3 St., Long Beach, Calif. 90812
213-432-7477
Specialties: air, solid waste, thermal problems, water
Paid

Malcolm H. McVickar
Chevron Chemical Co.
200 Bush St., San Francisco, Calif. 94120
415-894-2531
Specialties: land use, solid waste, water (for company or company customers)
Unpaid

Marvin H. Malone
Dept. of Physiology and Pharmacology, Univ. of the Pacific
Stockton, Calif. 95204
209-946-2487
Specialties: pesticides, water
Paid

Prof. Kenneth A. Manaster
Sch. of Law, Univ. of Santa Clara
Santa Clara, Calif. 95053
408-984-4319
Specialties: air, conservation and recreation, environmental law (principal area), land use, noise, pesticides, radiation, solid waste, thermal problems, water
Paid

Mee Industries, Inc.
4939 N. Earle St., Rosemead, Calif. 91770
213-287-9631
Specialty: air
Manufacturing

Metronics Associates, Inc.
3201 Porter Dr., Stanford Industrial Park, Palo Alto, Calif. 94304
415-493-5632
Specialties: air, noise, water
Manufacturing

Micrographics, Inc.
3855 Birch St., Newport Beach, Calif. 92660
714-540-8494
Specialty: air
Manufacturing

James M. Montgomery, Consulting Engineers, Inc.
555 E. Walnut St., Pasadena, Calif. 91101
213-796-9141
Specialties: air, solid waste, water

North American Weather Consultants
Santa Barbara Municipal Airport, Goleta, Calif. 93017
805-967-1246
Specialties: air, noise, radiation, water
Manufacturing

Oilwell Research, Inc.
1439 W. 16 St., Long Beach, Calif. 90813
213-436-4254
Specialty: water
Manufacturing

Pacific Environmental Laboratory
657 Howard St., San Francisco, Calif. 94105
Specialties: air, noise, solid waste, water

Edward L. Pack Associates
101 Main St., Los Altos, Calif. 94022
415-948-9157
Specialty: noise

Norman H. Parker, Engineers/Constructors
5448 Briggs Ave., La Crescenta, Calif. 91214
213-248-6669
Specialties: air, solid waste, water

Ralph M. Parsons Co.
617 W. 7 St., Los Angeles, Calif. 90017
213-629-2484
Specialties: air, solid waste, water

Philip E. Peterson
Nature Center Program Development, El Dorado Nature Center
7550 E. Spring St., Long Beach, Calif. 90815
213-429-5782
Specialties: conservation and recreation, fish and wildlife, land use
Unpaid

Pollution Research and Control Corp.
616 E. Colorado St., Glendale, Calif. 91205
213-240-0515
Specialties: air, noise, water
Manufacturing

Pollution Solutions, Inc.
Suite 200, 14225 Ventura Blvd., Sherman Oaks, Calif. 91403
213-981-7107
Specialties: air, noise, radiation, solid waste, water
Manufacturing

James A. Pomerening
Plant and Soil Science Dept., California State Polytechnic Univ.

142 Environmental Consultants

Pomona, Calif. 91768
714-598-4116
Specialties: conservation and recreation, land use (soil classification and survey)
Paid

Pomeroy, Johnston, and Bailey
660 S. Fair Oaks, Pasadena, Calif. 91105
213-795-7553
Specialties: solid waste, water

Pulsco-AAF, Div. of American Air Filter Co., Inc.
126 W. Santa Barbara St., Santa Paula, Calif. 93060
805-525-6641
Specialty: noise
Manufacturing

Earl Pye
Chemistry Dept., California State Polytechnic Univ.
Pomona, Calif. 91768
714-598-4411/4498
Specialties: radiation, water, corrosion products
Paid (expenses only)

Rhombic Rents
10459 Roselle St., San Diego, Calif. 92121
714-453-8421
Specialties: air, noise, radiation, solid waste, water
Manufacturing

Science Spectrum, Inc.
1216 State St., Santa Barbara, Calif. 93101
805-963-8605
Specialty: air
Manufacturing

Ralph Stone and Co., Inc.
10954 Santa Monica Blvd., Los Angeles, Calif. 90025
213-879-1115
Specialties: air, noise, radition, solid waste, water

Systems Applications, Inc.
9418 Wilshire Blvd., Beverly Hills, Calif. 90212
213-278-5410
Specialties: air, water

Richard Terry and Associates, Environmental Science and Services
116 N. Carousel St., Anaheim, Calif. 92806
714-630-2930
Specialties: air, noise, radiation, solid waste, water

Jim Thorup
Box 5458, Fresno, Calif. 93755
209-224-2513
Specialty: soil fertility and related problems

Toups Engineering, Inc.
1801 N. College Ave., Santa Ana, Calif. 92706
714-541-4431
Specialties: solid waste, water

Truesdail Laboratories, Inc.
4101 N. Figueroa St., Los Angeles, Calif. 90065
213-225-1564
Specialties: air, noise, solid waste, water

URS Research Co.
155 Bovet Rd., San Mateo, Calif. 94402
415-574-5001
Specialties: air, noise, radiation, solid waste, water

Sanford L. Werner
21031 Blythe St., Canoga Park, Calif. 91304
213-341-8893
Specialties: conservation and recreation, pesticides, radiation, solid waste, thermal problems, water, liquid waste problems
Paid/unpaid

Wilsey and Ham
1035 E. Hillsdale Blvd., San Mateo, Calif. 94404
Specialties: solid waste, water

Wilson, Ihrig and Associates, Inc.
5606 Ocean View Dr., Oakland, Calif. 94618
415-658-6386
Specialty: noise

Larry Wood
6161 Castle Dr., Oakland, Calif. 94611
415-531-0977
Specialties: conservation and recreation, forestry, land use
Paid

Jerry Yudelson
Environmental Systems
Box 1145, Santa Cruz, Calif. 95060
408-423-3560
Specialties: conservation and recreation, land use, solid waste, water, environmental design, ecological planning

Zimmey Corp.
134 E. Pomona Ave., Box 1268, Monrovia, Calif. 91016
213-357-2291

Specialty: air
Manufacturing

COLORADO

Accu-Labs Research, Inc.
9170 W. 44 Ave., Wheat Ridge, Colo. 80033
303-423-2766
Specialties: air, solid waste, water
Manufacturing

American Sportsman Club, Inc.
650 S. Lipan, Denver, Colo. 80223
303-744-1881
Specialties: conservation and recreation, fish and wildlife, forestry, land use
Paid

Jay E. Anderson
Biological Sciences Curriculum
Box 930, Boulder, Colo. 80302
303-666-6558
Specialties: conservation and recreation, fish and wildlife, land use, pesticides, water
Paid

John R. Bagby, Jr.
Institute of Rural Environmental Health, Colorado State Univ.
Fort Collins, Colo. 80521
303-491-6228
Specialties: pesticides, solid waste
Unpaid

Dr. Clark N. Crain
Dept. of Geography, Univ. of Denver
Denver, Colo. 80210
303-753-2763
Specialties: conservation and recreation, land use
Paid

Richard N. Denney
The American Humane Assn.
Box 1266, Denver, Colo. 80201
303-771-1300
Specialties: conservation and recreation, environmental law, fish and wildlife, forestry, land use
Paid

Douglas L. Gilbert
Col. of Forestry and Natural Resources, Colorado State Univ.
Fort Collins, Colo. 80521
303-491-5402

Specialties: conservation and recreation, fish and wildlife, land use, public relations in natural resources management
Paid/unpaid

George S. Innis
Natural Resource Ecology Laboratory, Colorado State Univ.
Fort Collins, Colo. 80521
303-491-5571
Specialties: fish and wildlife, forestry, land use
Paid

Johns-Manville
Greenwood Plaza, Denver, Colo. 80217
303-770-1000
Specialties: air, noise, solid waste, water
Manufacturing

Parry A. Larsen
Natural Resource Management, Colorado Mountain Col.
Glenwood Springs, Colo. 81601
303-945-8391
Specialties: fish and wildlife (primary field), conservation and recreation (secondary field), land use
Paid (expenses only)

Prof. Bruce L. Papier
Univ. of Denver
University Park, Denver, Colo. 80210
303-753-3650
Specialty: visual pollution and graphic design
Paid

Elmar R. Reiter
Dept. of Atmospheric Science, Colorado State Univ.
Fort Collins, Colo. 80521
303-491-8555
Specialty: air
Paid

Douglas B. Seba
National Field Investigations, Denver Office of Enforcement
Rm. 410, U.S. Environmental Protection Agency Bldg., Denver, Colo. 80225
303-234-4661
Specialties: air, conservation and recreation, environmental law, fish and wildlife, pesticides, thermal problems, water
Paid

Sierra Research Corp., Environmental Systems Div.
Box 3007, Boulder, Colo. 80303

303-443-0384
Specialty: air
Manufacturing

Peter C. Sinclair
Dept. of Atmospheric Science, Colorado State Univ.
Fort Collins, Colo. 80521
303-491-8679
Specialty: air
Paid/unpaid

Stearns-Roger Corp.
700 S. Ash, Denver, Colo. 80217
303-758-1122
Specialties: air, noise, solid waste, water

Thomas H. Vonder Harr
Dept. of Atmospheric Science, Colorado State Univ.
Fort Collins, Colo. 80521
303-491-8566
Specialties: air, radiation, thermal problems
Paid

CONNECTICUT

Albertson Sharp and Associates
33 East Ave., Norwalk, Conn. 06851
Specialties: solid waste, water

American Chemical and Refining Co., Inc.
36 Sheffield St., Waterbury, Conn. 06714
203-757-9231
Specialties: air, noise, radiation, solid waste, water
Manufacturing

Aqualogic Inc.
32 Main St., Seymour, Conn. 06483
203-888-3533
Specialties: solid waste, water
Manufacturing

Crawford and Russell, Inc.
733 Canal St., Stamford, Conn. 06904
203-327-1450
Specialties: air, noise, solid waste, water

DeBell and Richardson, Inc.
Water St., Enfield, Conn. 06082
203-749-8371
Specialty: solid waste

Engineered Environments
Box 747, Waterbury, Conn. 06720
203-757-2021
Specialties: air, noise, radiation, solid waste, water

F and J Scientific
79 Far Horizon Dr., Monroe, Conn. 06468
203-268-3335
Specialty: air
Manufacturing

W.F. Heneghan Associates
289 Greenwich Ave., Greenwich, Conn. 06830
203-661-7928
Specialties: air, water

Industrial Pollution Control, Inc.
45 Riverside Ave., Westport, Conn. 06880
203-227-8497
Specialties: solid waste, water

Liberty Industries, Inc.
598 Deming Rd., Berlin, Conn. 06037
203-828-6361
Specialty: air
Manufacturing

Harold R. Mull, Bell and Associates
80 Danbury Rd., Wilton, Conn. 06897
203-762-8393
Specialty: noise

Olin Corp.
120 Long Ridge Rd., Stamford, Conn. 06904
203-356-2000
Specialty: water
Manufacturing

Pollution Control Industries, Inc.
507 Canal St., Stamford, Conn. 06902
203-325-1326
Specialties: air, solid waste, water
Manufacturing

Resource Control, Inc.
145 Orange Ave., Box 420, West Haven, Conn. 06516
203-934-6621
Specialty: water
Manufacturing

Slickbar, Inc.
Box 295, Saugatuck Sta., Westport, Conn. 06880
Specialty: water
Manufacturing

Sunshine Chemical Corp., Eastern Div.
Box 17041, West Hartford, Conn. 06117
203-232-9227

Specialty: water
Manufacturing

United Acoustic Consultants
124 Hebron Ave., Glastonbury, Conn. 06033
203-633-0225
Specialty: noise

Delaware

Brandt Associates, Inc.
50 Blue Hen Dr., Newark, Del. 19711
302-731-1550
Specialties: solid waste, water

E.I. du Pont de Nemours and Co., Inc.
1007 Market St., Wilmington, Del. 19898
302-774-2421
Specialty: noise
Manufacturing

Vytautas Klemas
Col. of Marine Studies, Univ. of Delaware
Newark, Del. 19711
302-737-8312
Specialties: land use, thermal problems, water
Paid

John C. Miller
Delaware Geological Survey, 101 Penny Hall, Univ. of Delaware
Newark, Del. 19711
302-738-2833
Specialties: land use, solid waste, water, hydrogeology (no private consultation in Delaware)
Unpaid

Rollins-Purle, Inc.
Box 1791, Wilmington, Del. 19899
302-478-5150
Specialties: solid waste, water
Manufacturing

John Thornton, Jr.
Rollins Environmental Services
Box 2349, Wilmington, Del. 19899
302-658-8541
Specialties: pesticides, solid waste, industrial waste problems
Paid

District of Columbia

Dennis A. Dutterer
Suite 602, 1700 K St. N.W., Washington, D.C. 20006
Specialty: noise

Joseph Gillman Associates
1700 K St. N.W., Washington, D.C. 20006
202-296-4940
Specialties: air, solid waste

Richard A. Kenney
George Washington Univ. Medical Center
1339 H St. N.W., Washington, D.C. 20005
202-331-6553
Specialty: thermal problems
Unpaid

Man Mohan Varma
Sch. of Engineering, Howard Univ.
Washington, D.C. 20001
202-636-6574
Specialties: pesticides, radiation, thermal problems, water
Paid/unpaid

Wapora, Inc.
1725 DeSales St. N.W., Washington, D.C. 20036
202-833-8510
Specialties: air, radiation, solid waste, water

Paul E. Whittington
Dept. of the Army
USAMC Bldg. T-7, Washington, D.C. 20315
202-697-8301
Specialty: water

Stephen Wiel
6220 32 Pl. N.W., Washington, D.C. 20015
202-363-8840
Specialties: air, land use, environmental management, impact statements
Paid/unpaid

Florida

Aquatic Sciences, Inc.
2624 N.W. 2 Ave., Boca Raton, Fla. 33432
305-391-0091
Specialty: water

Black, Crow, and Eidsness, Inc.
Drawer 1329, Gainesville, Fla. 32601
Specialties: air, solid waste, water

Briley, Wild and Associates
Drawer D, Daytona Beach, Fla. 32018
904-253-1644
Specialties: solid waste, water

Brockway, Owen and Anderson Engineers, Inc.
Guaranty Bldg., Box 3331, West Palm Beach, Fla. 33402

305-833-2535
Specialties: solid waste, water

John B. Cook
Jacksonville Univ.
Box 28, Jacksonville Univ. Sta. Jacksonville, Fla. 32211
904-744-3950
Specialty: environmental education
Paid/unpaid

Ecological Science Corp.
20215 N.W. 2 Ave., Miami, Fla. 33169
305-624-9601
Specialties: air, noise, solid waste, water
Manufacturing

Environmental Engineering, Inc.
2324 S.W. 34 St., Gainesville, Fla. 32601
904-372-3318
Specialties: air, noise, radiation, solid waste, water

K.L. Hicks
1308 E. Parker St., Lakeland, Fla. 33801
813-688-1900
Specialties: land use, farm and ranch layout planning
Paid/unpaid

DeSoto B. McCabe
480 Biltmore Way, Coral Gables, Fla. 33134
305-444-2372
Specialties: land use, solid waste, water, sewage and wastewater treatment
Paid

Malcolm E. McLouth, P.E.
Brevard Engineering Co.
8660 Astronaut Blvd., Cape Canaveral, Fla. 32920
305-783-1320
Specialties: air, land use, noise, radiation, solid waste, water
Paid

Eugene H. Man
Univ. of Miami
Box 8293, Coral Gables, Fla. 33124
305-284-4541
Specialty: conservation and recreation
Unpaid

Mason and Hanger
Silas Mason Co., Inc.
33 S. Hogan St., Jacksonville, Fla. 32202
904-353-1793
Specialties: air, noise, radiation, solid waste, water

Stephen E. Newman
Dept. of Transportation
Box 1249, Bartow, Fla. 33830
813-533-8161
Specialties: conservation and recreation, fish and wildlife, environmental impact statements
Unpaid

Orlando Laboratories, Inc.
90 W. Jersey St., Box 8025-A, Orlando, Fla. 32806
305-424-5606
Specialties: air, noise, solid waste, water

William M. Partington, Jr.
Center of Florida Conservation Foundation, Inc.
Suite E, 935 Orange Ave., Winter Park, Fla. 32789
Specialties: conservation and recreation, fish and wildlife, forestry, land use, water
Paid/unpaid

William B. Pearce
5107 S. Westshore Blvd., Box 13228, Tampa, Fla. 33611
813-831-1211
Specialties: land use, dredge and fill problems
Unpaid

Pollution Control Engineering, Inc.
794 W. 84 St., Hialeah, Fla. 33014
305-822-8460
Specialties: air, noise, solid waste, water
Manufacturing

Reynolds, Smith and Hills
4019 Blvd. Center Dr., Box 4850, Jacksonville, Fla. 32201
904-396-2011
Specialties: air, solid waste, water

H.J. Ross Associates, Inc.
2660 Brickell Ave., Miami, Fla. 33129
305-854-1900
Specialties: air, noise, solid waste, water
Manufacturing

Smith-Davis and Associates, Inc.
2512 S.W. 34 St., Gainesville, Fla. 32601
904-372-6338
Specialties: air, solid waste, water

Southern Fish Culturists, Inc.
Box 251, Leesburg, Fla. 32748
904-787-1360
Specialty: biology-ecology

Wellman-Power Gas, Inc.
Box 2436, Lakeland, Fla. 33803
813-646-5011
Specialty: air

Georgia

Wayne A. Bough
Food Science, Univ. of Georgia Experimental Sta.
Experiment, Ga. 30212
404-227-9471
Specialties: solid waste, water, food processing wastes
Unpaid

Lester Laboratories, Inc.
2370 Lawrence St., Atlanta, Ga. 30344
404-767-0277
Specialty: water
Manufacturing

Optimal Systems, Inc.
1375 Peachtree St. N.E., Atlanta, Ga. 30309
404-892-1570
Specialties: air, noise

Robert & Co. Associates
96 Poplar St. N.W., Atlanta, Ga. 30303
404-525-8411
Specialties: air, solid waste, water

Rossnagel and Associates
2517 Lake Flair Ct. N.E., Atlanta, Ga. 30345
404-636-9641
Specialties: air, noise, water

A.L. Shewfelt
Food Science, Univ. of Georgia Experimental Sta.
Experiment, Ga. 30212
404-227-9471
Specialties: fish and wildlife, land use, solid waste, water
Unpaid

Owens J. Smith
Institute of Natural Resources and Institute of Government, 203 Forestry Bldg., Univ. of Georgia
Athens, Ga. 30601
404-542-1666
Specialty: environmental law
Paid

Southeast Laboratories, Inc.
1490 Mecaslin St. N.W., Atlanta, Ga. 30309
404-873-1896
Specialties: solid waste, water
Manufacturing

The T. E. Stivers Organization, Inc.
Box 1008, Decatur, Ga. 30031
404-378-1392
Specialties: air, noise, solid waste

Mrs. Rebecca C. Trooboff
Sch. of Nursing, Medical Col. of Georgia
126 W. Trinity Pl., Decatur, Ga. 30030.
404-373-2525
Specialty: community nutrition
Paid

Hawaii

Austin, Smith and Associates, Inc.
850 Richards St., Honolulu, Hawaii 96813
Specialties: solid waste, water

Idaho

David C. Campbell
Dept. of Economics, Univ. of Idaho
Moscow, Idaho 83843
208-885-6294
Specialties: air, conservation and recreation, fish and wildlife, forestry, land use, noise, solid waste, water
Paid

Frederick D. Johnson
Col. of Forestry, Univ. of Idaho
Moscow, Idaho 83843
208-885-6444
Specialties: conservation and recreation, forestry, land use, water
Paid/unpaid

Fenton C. Kelley
Dept. of Biology, Boise State Col.
1907 Campus Dr., Boise, Idaho 83707
208-385-1526
Specialties: fish and wildlife, water
Unpaid

Illinois

Alvord, Burdick and Howson
20 N. Wacker Dr., Chicago, Ill. 60606
Specialties: solid waste, water

148 Environmental Consultants

Ted F. Andrews
Col. of Environmental and Applied Sciences, Governors State Univ.
Park Forest South, Ill. 60466
312-563-2211
Specialties: conservation and recreation, water, environmental planning
Paid

ArRo Laboratories, Inc.
Box 686, Joliet, Ill. 60434
815-727-5436
Specialties: solid waste, water
Manufacturing

The Austin Co., Process Div.
2001 Rand Rd., Des Plaines, Ill. 60016
312-774-7900
Specialties: air, radiation, solid waste, water
Manufacturing

Carus Chemical Co., Inc.
1500 8 St., La Salle, Ill. 61301
815-223-1500
Specialties: air, noise, solid waste, water
Manufacturing

Albert L. Caskey, Ph.D.
Dept. of Chemistry and Biochemistry, Southern Illinois Univ.
Carbondale, Ill. 62901
618-453-5721
Specialty: water
Paid

Homer L. Chastain and Associates
5 N. Country Club Rd., Box 1587, Decatur, Ill. 62521
217-422-8544
Specialties: solid waste, water

The Chemitrol Co.
5318 W. 95 St., Oak Lawn, Ill. 60453
312-636-5354
Specialty: water
Manufacturing

Chicago Aerial Survey
10265 Franklin Ave., Franklin Park, Ill. 60131
312-678-0380
Specialty: water

Clark, Dietz and Associates-Engineers, Inc.
211 N. Race St., Urbana, Ill. 61801
217-367-6661
Specialties: air, noise, radiation, solid waste, water

Commercial Testing and Engineering Co.
226 N. LaSalle St., Chicago, Ill. 60201
312-726-8434
Specialties: air, noise, solid waste, water

Dearborn Chemical Div., Chemed Corp.
300 Genesee St., Lake Zurich, Ill. 60047
312-527-5700
Specialties: solid waste, water
Manufacturing

William R. Edwards
Illinois Natural History Survey
Urbana, Ill. 61801
217-333-6856
Specialties: conservation and recreation, fish and wildlife, land use
Unpaid

E.T. Erickson
Water Technology Consultants
333 N. Michigan Ave., Chicago, Ill. 60601
312-943-4100
Specialties: solid waste, water
Manufacturing

Rodney J. Fink
Dept. of Agriculture, Western Illinois Univ.
Macomb, Ill. 61455
309-295-3534
Specialties: conservation and recreation, land use, pesticides
Paid/unpaid

Freeman Laboratories, Inc.
9290 Evenhouse Ave., Rosemont, Ill. 60018
312-696-3360
Specialties: air, solid waste, water
Manufacturing

Geo-Engineering Laboratories, Inc.
Box 781, Mt. Vernon, Ill. 62864
618-242-6175
Specialties: solid waste, water

GPE Controls Div., Singer Co.
6511 Oakton, Morton Grove, Ill. 60053
312-966-4000
Specialty: air
Manufacturing

Robert E. Greenberg
Illinois Natural History Survey, Section of Wildlife Research
Urbana, Ill. 61801
217-333-6856
Specialties: conservation and recreation, fish and wildlife, forestry, land use, pesticides
Paid

Charles W. Greengard Associates, Inc.
1374 Old Skokie Rd., Highland Park, Ill. 60035
312-831-3380
Specialties: solid waste, water

Gurnham and Associates, Inc.
223 W. Jackson Blvd., Chicago, Ill. 60606
312-939-0568
Specialties: solid waste, water

IIT Research Institute
10 W. 35 St., Chicago, Ill. 60616
312-225-9630
Specialties: air, noise, radiation, solid waste, water

Illinois Water Treatment Co.
840 Cedar St., Rockford, Ill. 61105
815-968-9691
Specialties: solid waste, water
Manufacturing

Industrial Filter and Pump Mfg. Co.
5900 W. Ogden Ave., Cicero, Ill. 60650
312-656-7800
Specialties: solid waste, water
Manufacturing

Ion Exchange Products, Inc.
4500 N. Clark St., Chicago, Ill. 60640
312-784-4100
Specialty: water
Manufacturing

Efon K. Kamarasy
Southern Illinois Univ.
Carbondale, Ill. 62901
618-536-2371
Specialties: environmental law, land use, environmental administration and policy formulation
Unpaid

Lester B. Knight and Associates, Inc.
549 W. Randolph St., Chicago, Ill. 60606
312-346-2100
Specialties: air, noise, radiation, solid waste, water

Ronald F. Labisky
Illinois Natural History Survey
Urbana, Ill. 61801
217-333-6767
Specialties: fish and wildlife, land use
Paid outside Illinois

Laicon, Inc.
1038 S. La Grange Rd., La Grange, Ill. 60525
312-354-9630
Specialties: solid waste, water

Laramore, Douglass and Popham
332 S. Michigan Ave., Chicago, Ill. 60604
312-427-8486
Specialties: air, water

Robert S. Levi and Associates
8929 Neenah Ave., Morton Grove, Ill. 60053
312-965-5411
Specialties: air, noise, solid waste, water

Walter C. McCrone Associates, Inc.
493 E. 31 St., Chicago, Ill. 60616
312-842-7100
Specialty: air

James J. McGrath
Peoria Sch. of Medicine
Peoria, Ill. 61601
309-674-8477
Specialty: biomedical effects of environmental contaminants
Paid

Thomas J. Maloney
Dept. of Anthropology, Southern Illinois Univ.
Edwardsville, Ill. 62025
618-692-2138
Specialty: economic problems in developing nations
Paid (expenses only)

Master Leakfinding Co.
273 Glenview Ave., Elmhurst, Ill. 60126
312-832-8795
Specialties: air, noise, radiation, solid waste, water
Manufacturing

Robert H.G. Monninger, M.D., D.Sc.
Lake Forest Medical Center
320 E. Vine Ave., Lake Forest, Ill. 60045
312-234-4440
Specialties: air, environmental law, ocular irritants and pathology
Unpaid

Monsanto Enviro-Chem Systems, Inc.
10 S. Riverside Plaza, Chicago, Ill. 60606
312-782-5041
Specialties: air, solid waste, water
Manufacturing

Nalco Chemical Co.
180 N. Michigan Ave., Chicago, Ill. 60601
312-782-2035

Specialties: air, solid waste, water
Manufacturing

National Loss Control Service Corp.
Long Grove, Ill. 60049
312-540-2400
Specialties: air, noise, radiation, solid waste, water

NU-AG, Inc.
U.S. 51 S., Box 239, Rochelle, Ill. 61068
815-562-6060
Specialty: water

P and W Engineers, Inc.
309 W. Jackson Blvd., Chicago, Ill. 60606
312-427-2700
Specialties: air, solid waste, water

Particle Data Laboratories, Ltd.
Box 265, Elmhurst, Ill. 60126
312-832-5653
Specialties: air, noise, water
Manufacturing

Peabody Welles
Box J, Roscoe, Ill. 61073
815-623-2111
Specialty: water
Manufacturing

Polytechnic, Inc.
2600 S. Michigan Ave., Chicago, Ill. 60616
312-326-6440
Specialties: air, noise

Procon Inc.
30 UOP Plaza, Algonquin and Mt. Prospect, Des Plaines, Ill. 60016
312-391-3512
Specialties: air, noise, solid waste, water

Rempe Sharpe and Associates, Inc.
324 W. State St., Geneva, Ill. 60134
312-232-0827
Specialties: air, noise, radiation, solid waste, water

Rosner-Hixson Laboratories
7737 S. Chicago Ave., Chicago, Ill. 60619
312-734-0142
Specialties: solid waste, water

M.F. Rupp
De Leuw Cather and Co.
165 W. Wacker Dr., Chicago, Ill. 60601
312-346-0424
Specialties: air, conservation and recreation, fish and wildlife, forestry, land use, solid waste, water
Paid

Tenco Hydro-Aero Sciences, Inc.
5220 East Ave., Countryside, Ill. 60625
312-482-7200
Specialties: air, noise, solid waste, water
Manufacturing

INDIANA

Charles W. Alliston
Dept. of Animal Sciences, Purdue Univ.
Lafayette, Ind. 47907
317-493-9798
Specialties: noise, thermal problems, environmental physiology
Unpaid

Aquatic Control, Inc.
Rte. 5, Seymour, Ind. 47274
812-643-2011

Curtis H. Ault
Indiana Geological Survey
611 N. Walnut Grove, Bloomington, Ind. 47401
812-337-2687
Specialties: land use, environmental geology
Paid outside Indiana

George S. Austin
Indiana Geological Survey
611 N. Walnut Grove, Bloomington, Ind. 47401
812-337-2687
Specialties: conservation and recreation, land use, solid waste
Paid outside Indiana

Leroy E. Becker
Indiana Geological Survey
611 N. Walnut Grove, Bloomington, Ind. 47401
812-337-5412
Specialty: subsurface disposal of industrial wastes
Paid outside Indiana

Maurice E. Biggs
Indiana Geological Survey
611 N. Walnut Grove, Bloomington, Ind. 47401

812-337-2862
Specialty: land use
Paid outside Indiana

Ned K. Bleuer
Indiana Geological Survey
611 N. Walnut Grove, Bloomington, Ind. 47401
812-337-7428
Specialties: land use, solid waste
Paid outside Indiana

Don E. Bloodgood
334 Leslie Ave., West Lafayette, Ind. 47906
317-743-2216
Specialty: water
Paid

Richard D. Brown
Life Science Dept., Indiana State Univ.
Terre Haute, Ind. 47809
812-232-6311
Specialty: water
Paid

Donald D. Carr
Indiana Geological Survey
611 N. Walnut Grove, Bloomington, Ind. 47401
812-337-2687
Specialties: conservation and recreation, land use, solid waste, mineral resources
Paid outside Indiana

Chas. W. Cole and Son, Inc.
3600 E. Jefferson Blvd., South Bend, Ind. 46615
219-288-9131
Specialties: air, solid waste, water

H. Dan Corbin
Lambert Gym, Purdue Univ.
Lafayette, Ind. 47907
317-493-9392
Specialty: conservation and recreation
Paid/unpaid

Environmental Consultants, Inc.
391 Newman., Ave., Box 37, Clarksville, Ind. 47150
812-282-8481
Specialties: air, noise, radiation, solid waste, water

Henry H. Gray
Indiana Geological Survey
611 N. Walnut Grove, Bloomington, Ind. 47401
812-337-7428
Specialties: conservation and recreation, land use, solid waste, water
Unpaid (Indiana only)

Edwin J. Hartke
Indiana Geological Survey
611 N. Walnut Grove, Bloomington, Ind. 47401
812-337-7428
Specialty: land use
Unpaid

John R. Hill
Indiana Geological Survey
611 N. Walnut Grove, Bloomington, Ind. 47401
812-337-7428
Specialties: solid waste, water
Unpaid

Richard K. Leininger
Indiana Geological Survey
611 N. Walnut Grove, Bloomington, Ind. 47401
812-337-2504
Specialties: land use, solid waste, water
Paid outside Indiana

David W. Malone
Center for Large Scale Systems, Duncan Annex, Purdue Univ.
Lafayette, Ind. 47907
317-749-2365
Specialties: air, land use, long-range planning
Unpaid

Mitchell and Associates, Inc.
Box 5345, Evansville, Ind. 47715
812-477-2381
Specialties: solid waste, water
Manufacturing

Erskine V. Morse, D.V.M., Ph.D.
Sch. of Veterinary Science, Environmental Health Institute, Purdue Univ.
Lafayette, Ind. 47907
317-494-4006 or 317-743-3790
Specialties: fish and wildlife, veterinary medicine
Paid/unpaid

Frederick B. Morse
Sch. of Mechanical Engineering, Purdue Univ.
Lafayette, Ind. 47906
317-493-9720
Specialty: air
Paid

Robert H. Shaver
Indiana Geological Survey
611 N. Walnut Grove, Bloomington, Ind. 47401
812-337-7428
Specialty: general geological problems
Unpaid

Toufiq A. Siddiqi
Sch. of Public and Environmental Affairs, Indiana Univ.
Bloomington, Ind. 47401
812-337-8485
Specialties: air, noise, radiation
Unpaid

Charles E. Wier
Indiana Geological Survey
611 N. Walnut Grove, Bloomington, Ind. 47401
812-337-7785
Specialties: air, land use, water, coal-mined land reclamation
Unpaid

Vance P. Wiram
Indiana Geological Survey
611 N. Walnut Grove, Bloomington, Ind. 47401
812-337-7785
Specialties: air, water, coal combustion and mining problems
Unpaid

IOWA

Fred Brinkerhoff
Chevron Chemical Co.
6567 University Ave., Des Moines, Iowa 50311
515-274-4681
Specialties: land use, solid waste, water, agricultural fertilizers and amendments
Unpaid

Brown Engineering Co.
508 10 St., Des Moines, Iowa 50309
Specialties: air, solid waste, water

Richard W. Coleman
Box 156, Fayette, Iowa 52142
319-425-3654
Specialty: plant-invertebrate environmental interrelationships
Unpaid

Corning Laboratories Inc.
1004 Main St., Box 625, Cedar Falls, Iowa 50613
319-277-2401
Specialties: air, noise, water
Manufacturing

DeWild Grant Reckert and Associates Co.
315 1 Ave., Rock Rapids, Iowa 51246
712-472-2531
Specialties: solid waste, water

James W. Eckblad
Biology Dept., Luther Coll.
Decorah, Iowa 52101
319-382-3621
Specialty: water
Paid

P.J. Kingsbury
Dept. of Biology, Drake Univ.
Des Moines, Iowa 50311
515-271-3765
Specialty: water
Paid

Robert E. Kribel
Physics Dept., Drake Univ.
Des Moines, Iowa 50311
515-271-3750
Specialties: radiation, thermal problems
Unpaid

Marve H. Lavin, Ph.D.
Univ. of Iowa, C-212, East Hall
Iowa City, Iowa 52240
319-353-5178
Specialties: pesticides, food, drugs, and cosmetics adulterants
Unpaid

James G. Lindberg
Drake Univ.
Des Moines, Iowa 50311
515-271-2827
Specialty: air
Unpaid

George T. Peckham
415 Oakhurst Dr., Clinton, Iowa 52732
319-242-5098
Specialties: solid waste, water
Paid

George Skadron
Dept. of Physics, Drake Univ.
Des Moines, Iowa 50311
515-271-3141

Specialty: energy resources and energy usage
Unpaid

Stanley Consultants, Inc.
Stanley Bldg., Muscatine, Iowa 52761
319-263-9494
Specialties: air, solid waste, water

Donald C. Stouse and Associates, P.C.
Rte. 1, Box 134-A, Dubuque, Iowa 52001
319-588-1544
Specialties: solid waste, water

Tailor & Co., Inc.
2403 State St., Bettendorf, Iowa 52722
319-355-2621
Specialties: air, solid waste, water
Manufacturing

Richard M. Thorup
Box 282, Fort Madison, Iowa 52627
319-372-6012
Specialties: water, plant nutrition, soil fertility, nutrient movement and accumulation in the soil
Unpaid

Charles C. Wunder
Univ. of Iowa, Col. of Medicine
Iowa City, Iowa 52240
319-353-3457
Specialty: space, gravity, weightlessness, and acceleration as related to living organisms
Paid (expenses only)

Kansas

Bucher and Willis, Consulting Engineers, Planners and Architects
605 W. North St., Box 1287, Salina, Kans. 67401
913-827-3603
Specialties: air, solid waste, water

Deady Chemical Co., Olin Corp., Chemicals Group
3155 Fiberglas Rd., Kansas City, Kans. 66115
913-321-0200
Specialty: water
Manufacturing

Langston Laboratories Inc.
3000 W. 135 St., Leawood, Kans. 66209
913-681-2361

Specialties: air, environmental law, noise, pesticides, solid waste, water, laboratory testing, analytical chemistry
Paid

Van Doren-Hazard-Stallings-Schnacke
2910 Topeka Ave., Box 719, Topeka, Kans. 66601
Specialties: solid waste, water

Kentucky

Howard K. Bell, Consulting Engineers, Inc.
Box 546, Lexington, Ky. 40501
606-252-7771
Specialties: solid waste, water

Industrial Services of America, Inc.
3901 Atkinson Dr., Atkinson Sq., Louisville, Ky. 40218
502-459-7600
Specialty: solid waste

Johnson, Depp, and Quisenberry
2625 Frederica St., Owensboro, Ky. 43201
502-683-2444
Specialties: solid waste, water

Kenco Associates Inc.
Box 1004, Ashland, Ky. 41101
606-324-6315
Specialties: air, solid waste, water

Klenz-Aire, Inc.
Box 99326, Louisville, Ky. 40299
502-267-1783
Specialties: air, noise, solid waste, water
Manufacturing

Marvin Thompson
Dept. of Biological Sciences, Eastern Kentucky Univ.
Richmond, Ky. 40475
606-622-2949
Specialties: conservation and recreation, fish and wildlife, land use
Paid/unpaid

Watkins and Associates, Inc.
446 E. High St., Lexington, Ky. 40508
606-252-4951
Specialties: solid waste, water

Environmental Consultants

LOUISIANA

Rhesa M. Allen, Jr.
Col. of Engineering, Louisiana Tech Univ.
Ruston, La. 71270
318-257-4648
Specialties: land use, water
Paid

Bovay Engineers, Inc.
10305 Airline Hwy., Baton Rouge, La. 70815
Specialties: air, noise, radiation, solid waste, water

Paul Y. Burns
Sch. of Forestry and Wildlife, Louisiana State Univ.
Baton Rouge, La. 70803
504-388-4131
Specialty: forestry
Unpaid

John V. Conner
Sch. of Forestry and Wildlife, Louisiana State Univ.
Baton Rouge, La. 70803
504-388-6051
Specialties: fish, thermal problems, water
Paid/unpaid

deLaureal Engineers, Inc.
1512 International Trade Mart, 2 Canal St., New Orleans, La. 70130
Specialties: air, noise, solid waste, water

Demopulos and Ferguson, Inc.
220 Johnson Bldg., Shreveport, La. 71101
318-423-7117
Specialties: solid waste, water

Domingue, Szabo and Associates, Inc.
Box 52115, Lafayette, La. 70501
318-234-4566
Specialties: solid waste, water

B.M. Dornblatt and Associates, Inc.
826 Lafayette St., New Orleans, La. 70113
504-524-5774
Specialties: air, solid waste, water

M. David Egan, P.E.
6950 Milne Blvd., New Orleans, La. 70124
504-288-7509
Specialty: noise
Paid

Framherz Engineers
1539 Jackson Ave., New Orleans, La. 70130
504-529-7661
Specialties: air, solid waste, water

Harold E. Garrett, Ph.D.
Sch. of Forestry, Louisiana Tech Univ.
Ruston, La. 71270
318-255-4571
Unpaid

W.B. Gurney Associates
1439 Arlington Ave., Baton Rouge, La. 70808
504-343-0769
Specialty: water

Harold G. Hedrick
Col. of Life Sciences, Louisiana Tech Univ.
Box 5708, Tech Sta. Ruston, La. 71270
318-255-4758
Specialties: pesticides, water, health safety
Paid/unpaid

William H. Herke
Sch. of Forestry and Wildlife, Louisiana Cooperative Fishery Unit
Baton Rouge, La. 70803
504-388-6051
Specialties: conservation and recreation, fish and wildlife
Unpaid

Guy H. Johnston Associates
211 Clegg St., Rayne, La. 70578
Specialty: solid waste

Kem-Tech Laboratories, Inc.
16550 Highland Rd., Rte. 3, Baton Rouge, La. 70808
504-766-3050
Specialties: air, solid waste, water
Manufacturing

Gerald C. Kerr
625 Pine St., New Orleans, La. 70118
Specialty: noise
Paid

Ludwig Consulting Engineers
12495 E. Millburn Ave., Baton Rouge, La. 70815
504-275-3490
Specialties: air, noise, solid waste, water

Pavia-Byrne Engineering Corp.
431 Graier St., New Orleans, La. 70130
504-581-9451
Specialties: air, solid waste, water

Pyburn and Odom, Inc.
8178 G.S.R.I. Ave., Box 267, Baton Rouge, La. 70821
504-776-6330
Specialties: solid waste, water

F.C. Schaffer and Associates, Inc.
185 Bellewood Dr., Baton Rouge, La. 70806
504-926-2541
Specialties: air, noise, solid waste, water
Manufacturing

Joe R. Wilson
Col. of Engineering, Louisiana Tech Univ.
Ruston, La. 71270
318-255-2381 or 257-2244
Specialties: land use, solid waste, water, wastewater treatment problems
Paid

MAINE

Edward C. Jordan Co., Inc.
379 Congress St., Portland, Maine 04111
201-774-0313
Specialties: solid waste, water

Jaro A. Konečny
Salem Township P.O., Strong, Maine 04983
207-678-2841
Specialties: conservation and recreation, naturalist
Paid (expenses only)

James W. Sewall Co.
147 Center St., Old Town, Maine 04468
207-827-4456
Specialties: solid waste, water

MARYLAND

Frank D. Arnold, Ph.D.
Health Care Facilities Service, HSMHA Public Health Service
Parklawn Bldg., Rockville, Md. 20852
301-443-1155
Specialty: institutional environmental control training
Unpaid

Biospheric, Inc.
4928 Wyaconda Rd., Rockville, Md. 20852
301-946-3300
Specialties: air, radiation, solid waste, water
Manufacturing

Thomas E. Burnett
National Institutes of Health
Rm. 2905, Bldg. 13
Bethesda, Md. 20014
301-496-2345
Specialty: air
Paid

Willard R. Calvert, Chemical Engineering Consultant Services
809 Teakwood Dr., Severna Park, Md. 21146
301-647-6094
Specialties: air, solid waste, water

Hittman Associates, Inc.
9190 Red Branch Rd., Columbia, Md. 21043
301-730-7800
Specialties: air, radiation, solid waste, water
Manufacturing

IBM, Federal Systems Div.
18100 Frederick Pike, Gaithersburg, Md. 20760
301-840-0111
Specialties: air, solid waste, water

Lyon Associates, Inc.
6707 Whitestone Rd., Baltimore, Md. 21207
301-944-9112
Specialties: air, solid waste, water
Manufacturing

J. Murray Mitchell, Jr.
NOAA Environmental Data Service
Rm. 612, Gramax Bldg., 8060 13 St., Silver Spring, Md. 20910
301-495-2203
Specialties: air, man's impact on climate
Unpaid

NUS Corp.
4 Research Pl., Rockville, Md. 20850
301-948-7010
Specialties: air, radiation, solid waste, water

Sprinkle and Associates
Box 10, Kensington, Md. 20795
301-942-7755
Specialty: noise

Veracity Corp.
Glen Echo, Md. 20768
202-223-3384
Specialty: water

Manfred von Ehrenfried
The Ehrenfried Corp.
15300 Rosecroft Rd., Rockville, Md. 20853
301-929-1271

Specialties: air, radiation, thermal problems
Paid

Whitman, Requardt and Associates
1304 St. Paul St., Baltimore, Md. 21202
301-727-3450
Specialties: air, noise, radiation, solid waste, water

MASSACHUSETTS

Badger Co., Inc.
1 Broadway, Cambridge, Mass. 02142
617-492-7400
Specialty: solid waste

A.W. Banister Co., Inc.
21 Charles St., Cambridge, Mass. 02141
617-876-2940
Specialty: air
Manufacturing

Barnstead Co.
225 Rivermoor St., Boston, Mass. 02132
617-327-1600
Specialty: water
Manufacturing

Billings and Gussman, Inc.
1254 Main St., Waltham, Mass. 02154
617-891-9380
Specialty: air
Manufacturing

Cambridge Acoustical Associates, Inc.
1033 Massachusetts Ave., Cambridge, Mass. 02138
617-491-1421
Specialty: noise

Camp Dresser and McKee, Inc.
1 Center Plaza, Boston, Mass. 02108
617-742-5151
Specialties: air, solid waste, water

Cavanaugh and Copley
112 Newtonville Ave., Newton, Mass. 01760
617-969-2871
Specialty: noise

Judith H. Clausen, Ph.D.
Box 203, Lexington, Mass. 02173
617-646-0220
Specialties: air, solid waste, water
Paid

Coffin and Richardson, Inc.
141 Milk St., Boston, Mass. 02109
Specialties: solid waste, water

Arthur Edward Driscoll
Biology Dept., Westfield State Col.
Westfield, Mass. 01085
413-568-3311
Specialties: land use, water
Paid/unpaid

Richard Enright
Dept. of Geology, Bridgewater State Col.
Bridgewater, Mass. 02324
617-697-6161
Specialties: solid waste, water, geological research
Paid

Environmental Management, Inc.
9 Kettle Pond Rd., Amherst, Mass. 01002
413-253-5926
Specialties: air, solid waste, water

Foxboro Co.
Neponset Ave., Foxboro, Mass. 02035
617-543-8750
Specialties: air, water
Manufacturing

Arnold Friedmann
Professor of Environmental Arts
Skinner Hall, Univ. of Massachusetts
Amherst, Mass. 01002
413-545-2274
Specialty: design
Unpaid

GCA Technology Div.
Burlington Rd., Bedford, Mass. 01730
617-275-9000
Specialties: air, solid waste, water
Manufacturing

Haley and Ward, Inc.
25 Fox Rd., Waltham, Mass. 02154
617-890-3980
Specialty: water

Hayden, Harding and Buchanan, Inc.
1340 Soldier's Field Rd., Boston, Mass. 02135
617-254-6930
Specialties: air, noise, radiation, solid waste, water

Heath Consultants, Inc.
100 Tosca Dr., Stoughton, Mass. 02072
617-344-1400

Specialty: water
Manufacturing

IKOR, Inc.
2 Ave., Burlington, Mass. 01803
617-272-4400
Specialties: air, noise
Manufacturing

Interex Corp.
66 Woerd Ave., Waltham, Mass. 02154
617-899-9145
Specialty: radiation
Manufacturing

JBF Scientific Corp.
2 Ray Ave., Burlington, Mass. 01803
617-273-0270
Specialties: noise, solid waste, water
Manufacturing

John C. Jahoda
Dept. of Biology, Bridgewater State Col.
Bridgewater, Mass. 02324
617-697-6161
Specialties: conservation and recreation, fish and wildlife, land use, solid waste
Paid

Joseph L. Levit, Ph.D.
Ecology Center of Environmental Sciences, Office of the Administrator
Camelot, R.D. 2, Central Shaft Rd., Florida, Mass. 01247
413-663-6060
Specialties: conservation and recreation, fish and wildlife, forestry, land use, water
Unpaid

Arthur D. Little, Inc.
Acorn Pk., Cambridge, Mass. 02140
Specialties: air, solid waste, water

Charles T. Main, Inc.
S.E. Tower, Prudential Center, Boston, Mass. 02199
617-262-3200
Specialties: air, noise, solid waste, water

David Martin
Champion Research
636 Beacon St., Boston, Mass. 92215
617-536-9700
Specialties: conservation and recreation, forestry
Unpaid

Metcalf and Eddy
Statler Bldg., Boston, Mass. 02116
617-423-5600
Specialties: air, solid waste, water

National Research Corp.
70 Memorial Dr., Cambridge, Mass. 02142
617-354-5400
Specialty: noise
Manufacturing

James W. Phillips
Westfield State Col.
Westfield, Mass. 01085
413-568-1055
Specialties: fish and wildlife, water
Unpaid

Reclamation Systems Inc.
Box 29, Cambridge, Mass. 02141
617-742-8147
Specialty: solid waste
Manufacturing

Sanitas Technology and Development Corp.
Suite 4550, Prudential Tower, Boston, Mass. 02199
617-262-7980
Specialty: solid waste
Manufacturing

Swift Laboratories, Inc.
Box 164, Waltham, Mass. 02154
617-894-2995
Specialties: air, solid waste, water
Manufacturing

Thorstensen Laboratory
66 Littleton Rd., Westford, Mass. 01886
617-692-8395
Specialties: air, solid waste, water
Manufacturing

Tighe and Bond
211 Bowers St., Holyoke, Mass. 01040
413-533-3991
Specialties: air, solid waste, water

Walden Research Corp.
359 Allston St., Cambridge, Mass. 02139
617-868-3940
Specialty: air
Manufacturing

Wallace-Fisher Instrument Co.
Box 4, South Sta., Swansea, Mass. 02777
617-673-4744
Specialty: air
Manufacturing

Weston and Sampson, Consulting Engineers
10 High St., Boston, Mass. 02110
617-357-5995
Specialties: air, solid waste, water

Michigan

Bigelow-Liptak Corp.
Northwestern Hwy. and 10 Mile Rd., Southfield, Mich. 48076
313-353-5400
Specialty: solid waste
Manufacturing

Emmy Booy
Dept. of Geology and Geological Engineering, Michigan Tech Univ.
Houghton, Mich. 49931
906-487-2531
Specialties: conservation and recreation, land use
Paid

Daniel A. Bronstein
312 Natural Resources Bldg., Michigan State Univ.
East Lansing, Mich. 48823
517-353-5326
Specialties: environmental law, energy
Paid/unpaid

Calcinator Corp.
28 and Water Sts., Bay City, Mich. 48706
517-894-4543
Specialty: water
Manufacturing

Carpart Corp.
520 Parkdale Ave., Owosso, Mich. 48867
517-725-5144
Specialty: air
Manufacturing

Centri-Spray Corp.
39001 Schoolcraft Rd., Livonia, Mich. 48150
313-534-7000
Specialties: air, noise, radiation, solid waste, water
Manufacturing

George D. Clayton and Associates
25711 Southfield Rd., Southfield, Mich. 48075
313-352-3120
Specialties: air, noise, radiation, solid waste, water

Commonwealth Associates Inc.
209 E. Washington Ave., Jackson, Mich. 49201
517-787-6000
Specialties: air, radiation, noise, solid waste, water

Contamination Control Laboratories, Inc.
13324 Farmington Rd., Livonia, Mich. 48151
313-427-8450
Specialty: air
Manufacturing

Detroit Testing Laboratory
12800 Northend Ave., Detroit, Mich. 48237
313-398-2100
Specialties: air, noise, water

Philip A. Doepke
Dept. of Biology, Northern Michigan Univ.
Marquette, Mich. 49855
906-277-3740
Specialty: water
Paid

Fillmore, C.F. Earney
Dept. of Geography, Northern Michigan Univ.
Marquette, Mich. 49855
906-227-2500
Specialty: mining and the environment
Unpaid

Environmental Engineers, Inc.
123 Main St., Royal Oak, Mich. 48067
313-545-0200
Specialties: air, solid waste, water

The Hinchman Co.
304 Francis Palms Bldg., Detroit, Mich. 48201
Specialty: corrosion

Hoad Engineers Inc.
1159 E. Michigan Ave., Ypsilanti, Mich. 48197
313-482-0920
Specialties: air, noise, solid waste, water

B. Ray Horn
Univ. of Michigan
555 E. William St., Ann Arbor, Mich. 48108
313-764-1410
Specialty: conservation and recreation
Unpaid

Hubbell, Roth and Clark, Inc.
2323 Franklin Rd., Bloomfield Hills, Mich. 48013
313-338-9241
Specialties: air, solid waste, water

Hydro Research Laboratories Div., Vulcan Laboratories, Inc.
408 Auburn Ave., Pontiac, Mich. 48058
313-334-1630
Specialties: solid waste, water
Manufacturing

Hydromation Filter Co.
39201 Amrhein Rd., Livonia, Mich. 48150
313-464-0600
Specialties: solid waste, water
Manufacturing

Johnson and Anderson, Inc.
2300 Dixie Hwy., Box 1066, Pontiac, Mich. 48056
313-334-9901
Specialties: air, solid waste, water

National Sanitation Foundation Testing Laboratory, Inc.
3475 Plymouth Rd., Box 1468, Ann Arbor, Mich. 48105
313-663-8581
Specialties: solid waste, water
Manufacturing

Prenco Manufacturing Co.
29800 Stephenson Hwy., Madison Heights, Mich. 48071
313-549-2700
Specialties: solid waste, water
Manufacturing

William I. Rose
Dept. of Geology, Michigan Tech Univ.
Houghton, Mich. 49931
906-487-2367
Specialty: geological research
Unpaid

Salem Laboratories
Box 135, Plymouth, Mich. 48170
Specialties: air, water

George E. Snyder Associates, Inc.
714 W. Michigan Ave., Jackson, Mich. 49201
Specialties: solid waste, water

Charles M. Spooner
Dept. of Geology, Michigan State Univ.
East Lansing, Mich. 48823
517-353-9768
Specialties: radiation, water
Unpaid

Williams and Works
250 Michigan St. N.E., Grand Rapids, Mich. 49503
616-451-4511
Specialties: solid waste, water

Theodore E. Winkler, P.E.
15933 Glastonbury, Detroit, Mich. 48223
313-835-7548
Specialties: air, water
Paid

Minnesota

American Pipe Services, Inc.
2231 Edgewood Ave., Minneapolis, Minn. 55426
612-545-0271
Specialties: solid waste, water
Manufacturing

Donaldson Co., Inc.
1400 W. 94 St., Minneapolis, Minn. 55431
612-888-7981
Specialty: noise
Manufacturing

Environmental Research Corp.
3725 N. Dunlap St., St. Paul, Minn. 55112
612-484-8591
Specialty: air
Manufacturing

FluiDyne Engineering Corp.
5901 Olson Memorial Hwy., Minneapolis, Minn. 55422
612-544-2721
Specialty: air

E. A. Hickok and Associates
545 Indian Mound, Wayzata, Minn. 55391
612-473-4224
Specialties: air, solid waste, water

International Acoustical Testing Laboratories, Inc.
Box 8049, St. Paul, Minn. 55113
612-633-8434
Specialty: noise

Lyon Chemicals, Inc.
2313 Wycliff St., St. Paul, Minn. 55114
612-646-1351
Specialty: water
Manufacturing

Markley Laboratories, Inc.
1853 Old Hwy. 8, New Brighton, Minn. 55112
612-633-5477
Specialties: air, solid waste, water

Jerome C. Peltier
Brainerd Area Vocational Tech Sch.
Brainerd, Minn. 56401
218-829-4653
Specialty: conservation and recreation
Unpaid

Pollution Curbs, Inc.
502 N. Prior Ave., St. Paul, Minn. 55104
Specialties: air, noise, solid waste, water

Earl Ruble and Associates, Inc.
217 S. Lake Ave., Duluth, Minn. 55802
218-722-3953
Specialties: air, noise, radiation, solid waste, water
Manufacturing

SERCO Laboratories
3105 E. 42 St., Minneapolis, Minn. 55406
612-722-6661
Specialties: solid waste, water

Roger H. Smith
Environmental Institute, Box 007, Mankato State Col.
Mankato, Minn. 56001
507-389-6425
Specialties: air, conservation and recreation, fish and wildlife, forestry, land use, noise, pesticides, solid waste, thermal problems, water, environmental management, planning, and design

Solids Conversion Systems, Inc.
6340 Industrial Dr., Hopkins, Minn. 55343
612-941-1744
Specialty: solid waste
Manufacturing

Twin City Testing and Engineering Laboratories, Inc.
662 Cromwell Ave., St. Paul, Minn. 55114
612-645-3601
Specialties: air, noise, solid waste, water

Mississippi

Bahngrell Walter Brown
2407 Mamie St., Hattiesburg, Miss. 39401
601-582-0107
Specialties: land use, mineral industry
Paid

Dr. G. C. Gupta
J. H. Comprehensive Health Center
Box 173, Utica, Miss. 39175
601-885-6021
Specialties: air, pesticides, solid waste, thermal problems, water, environmental health
Paid

Missouri

Richard J. Baldauf, Ph.D.
Director of Education, Kansas City Museum
Kansas City, Mo. 64123
816-483-8300
Specialties: conservation and recreation, fish and wildlife, water, environmental education
Paid/unpaid

Bendy Engineering Co.
1530 Page Industrial Blvd., St. Louis, Mo. 63132
314-429-7911
Specialties: air, noise, solid waste, water

Black and Veatch
1500 Meadow Lake Pkwy., Kansas City, Mo. 64114
816-361-7000
Specialties: air, noise, radiation, solid waste, water

Richard A. Boutwell
Biology Dept., Missouri Western Col.
4525 Downs Dr., St. Joseph, Mo. 64507
816-233-7192
Specialties: air, conservation and recreation, fish and wildlife, water
Unpaid

Burns and McDonnell Engineering Co.
Box 173, Kansas City, Mo. 64141
Specialties: air, solid waste, water

Alden B. Carpenter
Dept. of Geology, Univ. of Missouri
Columbia, Mo. 65201
314-449-9202
Specialties: solid waste, water
Unpaid

William Cate
Box 8002, University Sta., St. Louis, Mo. 63108

Specialty: water
Unpaid

Donald P. Duncan
Sch. of Forestry, Univ. of Missouri
Columbia, Mo. 65201
314-882-6446
Specialties: conservation and recreation, forestry
Paid

Robert M. Eastman
1066 E.E. Bldg., Columbia, Mo. 65201
314-449-9570
Specialty: project evaluation and organization, management of conservation functions
Paid

Engineering Dynamics International
225 N. Meramec, Clayton, Mo. 63130
Specialty: noise

Gordon S. Griffin
Charleston R. 1. H.S.
Charleston, Mo. 63834
314-683-3761
Specialties: conservation and recreation, environmental education
Unpaid

Haskins, Sharp and Ordelheide
1009 Baltimore, Kansas City, Mo. 64105
816-471-7730
Specialties: solid waste, water

Horner and Shifrin, Inc.
5200 Oakland Ave., St. Louis, Mo. 63110
314-531-4320
Specialties: solid waste, water

Howard, Needles, Tammen and Bergendoff
1805 Grand Ave., Kansas City, Mo. 64108
Specialties: solid waste, water

Ju Chang Huang
Dept. of Civil Engineering, Univ. of Missouri
Rolla, Mo. 65401
314-341-4461
Specialties: pesticides, water, industrial and municipal wastes
Paid

C. G. Lewis
9291 Watson Rd., St. Louis, Mo. 63126
314-968-3850
Specialties: air, pesticides, solid waste, thermal problems, water
Unpaid

Edward S. Macias
Dept. of Chemistry, Washington Univ.
St. Louis, Mo. 63130
314-863-0100
Specialty: radiation
Paid/unpaid

Midwest Research Institute
425 Volker Blvd., Kansas City, Mo. 64110
816-561-0202
Specialties: air, noise, solid waste, water

Donald Miles
Div. of Biological Sciences, Univ. of Missouri
Columbia, Mo. 65201
314-449-8331
Specialty: trace metals
Paid/unpaid

Monsanto Research Corp.
800 N. Lindbergh Blvd., St. Louis, Mo. 63166
Specialties: air, noise, radiation, solid waste, water
Manufacturing

Edward J. Peloquin
Health Maintenance Systems
700 Glendale, Jefferson City, Mo. 65101
314-635-8573
Specialties: environmental law, environmental impact statements and planning
Paid (expenses only)

Riddle Engineering, Inc.
3947 State Line, Kansas City, Mo. 64111
816-753-2300
Specialties: solid waste, water

Ryckman, Edgerley, Tomlinson and Associates
12161 Lackland Rd., St. Louis, Mo. 63141
314-434-6960
Specialties: air, noise, solid waste, water

St. Louis Testing Laboratories, Inc.
2810 Clark Ave., St. Louis, Mo. 63103
Specialties: solid waste, water
Manufacturing

Richard C. Smith
Sch. of Forestry, Univ. of Missouri
Columbia, Mo. 65201
314-882-3445
Specialty: forestry
Paid

Sverdrup, Parcel and Associates, Inc.
800 N. 12 Blvd., St. Louis, Mo. 63101
314-436-7600
Specialties: air, solid waste, water

Oktay Ural
Dep. of Civil Engineering, Univ. of Missouri
Rolla, Mo. 65401
314-341-4472
Specialties: land use, environmental planning and housing
Unpaid

Montana

Daniel H. Henning
Eastern Montana Col.
Billings, Mont. 59101
406-657-2138
Specialties: conservation and recreation, fish and wildlife, forestry, land use, governmental and intergovernmental problems
Paid/unpaid

Murray G. Klages
Plant and Soil Science Dept., Montana State Univ.
Bozeman, Mont. 59715
406-994-4601
Specialties: land use, water
Paid/unpaid

Northern Testing Laboratories
Box 1561, Great Falls, Mont. 59401
406-453-1641
Specialties: air, solid waste, water

Kenneth J. Tiahrt
Statistical Laboratory, Dep. of Mathematics, Montana State Univ.
Bozeman, Mont. 59715
406-994-3601
Specialties: air, conservation and recreation, fish and wildlife, forestry, land use, water, statistics
Paid

Wenzel and Co.
4035 10 Ave. S., Great Falls, Mont. 59403
406-453-5478
Specialties: air, noise, radiation, solid waste, water

Nebraska

Walter T. Bagley
102 Plant Industry, Col. of Agriculture
Lincoln, Nebr. 68503
402-472-2854
Specialties: conservation and recreation, forestry, land use
Unpaid

Leo A. Daly Co.
8600 Indian Hills Dr., Omaha, Nebr. 68114
402-391-8111
Specialties: air, solid waste, water

Harris Laboratories, Inc.
624 Peach St., Box 80837, Lincoln, Nebr. 68501
402-432-2811
Specialties: solid waste, water

Larry C. Holcomb
Environmental Consulting Team
3717 S. 116 St., Omaha, Nebr. 68144
402-334-1366
Specialties: air, conservation and recreation, environmental law, fish and wildlife, forestry, land use, noise, pesticides, radiation, solid waste, thermal problems, water, environmental education, organic gardening and farming
Paid

Kirkham, Michael and Associates
7300 Woolworth Ave., Omaha, Nebr. 68124
402-393-5630
Specialties: air, solid waste, water

Nebraska Testing Laboratories
4453 S. 67 St., Box 6075, Elmwood Park Sta., Omaha, Nebr. 68106
402-331-4453
Specialties: air, noise, radiation, solid waste, water

Nevada

Richard Gordon Miller
Foresta Institute for Ocean and Mountain Studies
R.R. 1, Box 620, Carson City, Nev. 89701
702-882-6361
Specialties: air, conservation and recreation, forestry, land use, water
Paid/unpaid

New Hampshire

Normandeau Associates, Inc.
686 Mast Rd., Manchester, N.H. 03102
603-669-7911
Specialty: water

New Jersey

Air Pollution Industries, Inc. (Air Pol)
95 Cedar La., Englewood, N.J. 07631
201-871-3855
Specialties: air, water
Manufacturing

Seymour Barer
1424 Laurelwood Ave., Lakewood, N.J. 08701
201-363-0714
Specialties: air, solid waste, water

Louis Berger, Inc.
100 Halsted St., East Orange, N.J. 07019
201-678-1960
Specialties: solid waste, water

Biometric Testing, Inc.
661 Palisade Ave., Englewood Cliffs, N.J. 07632
201-568-0224
Specialties: air, radiation, water

Clinton Bogert Associates
2083 Center Ave., Fort Lee, N.J. 07024
201-944-1676
Specialties: solid waste, water

Buck, Seifert and Jost
429 Sylvan Ave., Englewood Cliffs, N.J. 07632
201-567-8990
Specialties: solid waste, water

Burns and Roe, Inc.
700 Kinderkamack Rd., Oradell, N.J. 07649
210-265-2000
Specialties: air, noise, radiation, solid waste, water

Dr. Leonard L. Ciaccio
55 Yardley Ct., Glen Rock, N.J. 07452
201-652-3677
Specialties: air, water
Paid

Drew Chemical Corp., Process Chemicals Div.
701 Jefferson Rd., Parsippany, N.J. 07054
201-887-9300
Specialties: solid waste, water
Manufacturing

Engelhard Minerals and Chemicals Corp., Engelhard Industries Div.
430 Mountain Ave., Murray Hill, N.J. 07974
201-242-2700
Specialties: air, radiation, solid waste, water
Manufacturing

Engineering Chemical Services, Inc.
40 Fulton St., New Brunswick, N.J. 08902
201-846-4181
Specialties: solid waste, water
Manufacturing

Gamlen Chemical Co.
4 Midland Ave., East Paterson, N.J. 07503
201-796-5292
Specialties: air, water
Manufacturing

Martin Gilwood Associates
40 Fulton St., New Brunswick, N.J. 08902
201-846-4121
Specialites: air, solid waste, water

Gollob Analytical Service, Inc.
47 Industrial Rd., Berkeley Heights, N.J. 07922
Specialties: air, radiation, solid waste, water

Robert J. Haefeli, Consulting Engineers
707 Raritan Ave., Highland Park, N.J. 08904
201-574-1321
Specialties: solid waste, water

Industrial Process Engineers, Process Plants Div.
8-10 Lister Ave., Newark, N.J. 07105
201-589-4400
Specialties: air, solid waste, water
Manufacturing

International Hydronics Corp.
Box 910, R-4, Princeton, N.J. 08540
201-329-2361
Specialties: air, solid waste, water

Lacz Associates, Inc.
662 Goffle Rd., Hawthorne, N.J. 07506
201-423-0350
Specialties: air, noise, water

W. B. Middleton and Associates
152 Brookfield Ave., Paramus, N.J. 07652
201-845-9318
Specialties: air, noise, solid waste, water

Noyes Data Corp.
Mill Rd. and Grand Ave., Park Ridge, N.J. 07656
201-391-8484
Specialties: air, noise, radiation, solid waste, water

164   Environmental Consultants

Ostergaard Associates
10 Glenwood Way, West Caldwell, N.J. 07006
201-228-0523
Specialty: noise

James C. Pierce, Jr.
Van Note Harvey Associates
1101 State Rd., Princeton Research Pk., Bldg.
   N, Princeton, N.J. 08540
609-924-0413
Specialty: water
Paid

Princeton Aqua Science
789 Jersey Ave., New Brunswick, N.J. 08902
201-846-8800
Specialty: water
Manufacturing

Princeton Chemical Research, Inc.
Box 652, Princeton, N.J. 08540
609-924-3035
Specialties: air, noise, solid waste, water

Recon Systems, Inc.
Cherry Valley Rd., Princeton, N.J. 08540
609-921-2112
Specialties: air, noise, solid waste, water
Manufacturing

Regenerative Heat Corp.
91 W. Allendale Ave., Allendale, N.J. 07401
201-327-2882
Specialty: air
Manufacturing

Research-Cottrell, Inc.
Box 750, Bound Brook, N.J. 08805
201-356-2600
Specialties: air, solid waste, water
Manufacturing

John G. Reutter Associates
9 and Cooper Sts., Camden, N.J. 08101
609-966-1202
Specialties: air, noise, solid waste, water

Scientific Gas Products Inc.
513 Raritan Center, Edison, N.J. 08817
201-225-1100
Specialty: air
Manufacturing

Strobic Air Corp.
213 Bunting Ave., Trenton, N.J. 08611
609-695-0308
Specialties: air, noise
Manufacturing

Wells Laboratories, Inc.
25-27 Lewis Ave., Jersey City, N.J. 07306
201-653-6036
Specialties: solid waste, water

Wyssmont Co., Inc.
1476 Bergen Blvd., Fort Lee, N.J. 07024
201-947-4600
Specialty: air
Manufacturing

NEW MEXICO

Victor R. Bickel
Dep. of Environmental Health
Box 1293, Albuquerque, N. Mex. 87103
505-766-7451
Specialties: noise, solid waste
Unpaid

Philip A. Buscemi
Dep. of Biological Sciences, Eastern New Mexico Univ.
Portales, N. Mex. 88130
505-562-2241
Specialties: conservation and recreation, fish
   and wildlife, land use, water
Paid

Controls for Environmental Pollution, Inc.
1925 Rosina St., Box 5351, Santa Fe, N. Mex.
   87501
505-982-9841
Specialties: air, radiation, solid waste, water

Channing R. Kury
Sch. of Law, Univ. of New Mexico
Albuquerque, N. Mex. 87106
505-277-2146
Specialties: conservation and recreation, environmental law, fish and wildlife, land use
Unpaid

William M. Turner
Hydrotechnics
Box 4061, Albuquerque, N. Mex. 87106
505-243-4301
Specialties: thermal problems, water, geothermal resources
Paid

NEW YORK

Advanced Acoustical Research Corp.
1211 Stewart Ave., Bethpage, N.Y. 11714

516-938-6640
Specialty: noise
Manufacturing

Alken-Murray Corp.
111 5 Ave., New York, N.Y. 10003
212-777-6560
Specialty: water
Manufacturing

Ambient Systems Inc.
Box 234, Hastings-on-Hudson, N.Y. 10706
914-693-5812
Specialties: air, water
Manufacturing

Ambionic Designs, Inc.
162 E. 64 St., New York, N.Y. 10021
212-421-8707
Specialties: solid waste, water

American Environmental Systems Co.
35-10 Broadway, Long Island City, N.Y. 11106
212-286-9095
Specialties: air, noise, radiation, solid waste, water

American Standards Testing Bureau, Inc.
40 Water St., New York, N.Y. 10004
212-943-3156
Specialties: air, noise, radiation, solid waste, water

Andco Environmental Processes, Inc.
51 Anderson Rd., Buffalo, N.Y. 14225
716-896-8181
Specialties: air, solid waste, water
Manufacturing

Anderson and Angevine, Inc.
484 Main St., East Aurora, N.Y. 14052
716-652-0282
Specialty: noise

Automated Environmental Systems, Inc.
135 Crossways Park Dr., Woodbury, N.Y. 11797
516-364-0200
Specialties: air, water
Manufacturing

Baldwin and Cornelius Co.
101 S. Bergen Pl., Freeport, N.Y. 11520
516-378-6760
Specialties: air, solid waste, water

Bruce Bell
1188 Grand Concourse, Bronx, N.Y. 10456
212-293-7555
Specialties: lake studies, wastewater treatment
Paid

Beltran Associates, Inc.
1133 E. 35 St., Brooklyn, N.Y. 11210
212-338-3311
Specialties: air, noise, radiation, solid waste, water
Manufacturing

Bilbyrne Corp.
335 Broadway, New York, N.Y. 10013
212-227-3902
Specialties: air, noise, radiation, solid waste, water

Olin C. Braids
U.S. Geological Survey
1505 Kellum Pl., Mineola, N.Y. 11501
516-746-3750
Specialties: solid waste, water, soils, pollution and waste disposal
Unpaid

Dayton T. Brown, Inc.
Church St., Bohemia, N.Y. 11716
516-589-6300
Specialties: noise, radiation, solid waste, water

Buffalo Testing Laboratories, Inc.
902 Kenmore Ave., Buffalo, N.Y. 14216
716-873-2302
Specialties: air, noise, solid waste, water

Raul Cardenas, Jr., Ph.D.
Assistant Professor of Civil Engineering (Sanitary)
66 Pine Tree La., Tappan, N.Y. 10983
914-359-1184
Specialties: water, ecology, environmental impact studies and evaluation, lake studies, microbiology
Paid

Chem Systems, Inc.
866 3 Ave., New York, N.Y. 10022
212-421-9460
Specialties: air, solid waste, water

Chemec Process Systems, Inc.
501 Rte. 303, Tappan, N.Y. 10983
914-359-3008
Specialties: air, solid waste, water
Manufacturing

Chemico
320 Park Ave., New York, N.Y. 10022

212-751-3900
Specialties: air, solid waste, water
Manufacturing

Consolidated Technology, Inc.
410 Boston Post Rd., Larchmont, N.Y. 10538
914-834-7168
Specialty: solid waste
Manufacturing

Noel J. Cutright
Dept. of Natural Resources, Cornell Univ.
Ithaca, N.Y. 14850
607-256-2106
Specialties: conservation and recreation, fish and wildlife, pesticides
Paid/unpaid

Dames and Moore
100 Church St., New York, N.Y. 10007
Specialties: air, solid waste, water

Joseph Danto
City Univ. of New York
Convent Ave. at 138 St., New York, N.Y. 10031
212-621-2383
Specialty: noise
Paid

Charles Davidoff
198 Broadway, New York, N.Y. 10038
212-349-3917
Specialties: air, solid waste, water
Manufacturing

Peter A. Dykeman
F.D. Roosevelt High Sch.
Hyde Park, N.Y. 12538
914-229-7101
Specialties: conservation and recreation, education, interpretive programs
Unpaid

Ecologic Instruments Corp.
597 Old Willets Path, Hauppauge, N.Y. 11787
516-582-4110
Specialties: solid waste, water
Manufacturing

Ecology and Environment, Inc.
Box D, Buffalo, N.Y. 14225
716-632-4491
Specialties: air, noise, solid waste, water

Ecolotrol, Inc.
1211 Stewart Ave., Bethpage, N.Y. 11714
516-938-6622
Specialties: solid waste, water
Manufacturing

Empire Blower Co., Inc.
60 Lenriet St., Rochester, N.Y. 14615
716-865-7584
Specialty: air
Manufacturing

Environistics, Div. of Instrument Systems Corp.
410 Jericho Turnpike, Jericho, N.Y. 11753
516-822-4200
Specialties: air, noise, solid waste, water
Manufacturing

Environmental Research and Applications, Inc.
60 E. 42 St., New York, N.Y. 10017
212-687-2207
Specialties: solid waste, water
Manufacturing

Environmental Service Center, Inc.
220 Delaware Ave., Buffalo, N.Y. 14202
716-854-5532
Specialties: air, solid waste, water

Martin Henry Garrell
Dept. of Physics, Adelphi Univ.
Garden City, N.Y. 11530
516-294-8700
Specialties: fish and wildlife, radiation, solid waste, thermal problems
Unpaid

Gold-Marc Industries, Inc.
Box 350, E. Broadway, Monticello, N.Y. 12701
914-794-1700
Specialty: water
Manufacturing

John I. Green
St. Lawrence Univ.
Canton, N.Y. 13617
315-379-5650
Specialties: fish and wildlife, land use, conservation education
Paid/unpaid

Frederic R. Harris, Inc.
300 E. 42 St., New York, N.Y. 10017
212-986-2700
Specialties: air, noise, solid waste, water

Heen and Flint Associates
285 Mt. Read Blvd., Rochester, N.Y. 14611
716-436-4160
Specialties: air, noise, solid waste, water

Heyward-Robinson Co., Inc.
100 Church St., New York, N.Y. 10007
212-964-7566
Specialties: solid waste, water

Holzmacher, McLendon and Murrell, P.C.
500 Broad Hollow Rd., Melville, N.Y. 11746
516-694-3040
Specialties: solid waste, water

Walter G. Hoydysh
New York Univ. Res. Bldg. 1
1 W. 177 St. and Harlem River, Bronx, N.Y. 10453
212-584-0700
Specialties: air, land use, noise, solid waste, thermal problems
Paid

Industrial Acoustics Co., Inc.
380 Southern Blvd., Bronx, N.Y. 10454
212-292-0180
Specialty: noise
Manufacturing

William T. Ingram
7 North Dr., Whitestone, N.Y. 11357
212-353-8690
Specialties: air, solid waste, water
Paid

Michael J. Kodaras, Inc.
75-02 51 Ave., Elmhurst, N.Y. 11373
Specialty: noise

Lockwood Greene Engineers, Inc.
200 Park Ave., New York, N.Y. 10017
212-687-0630
Specialties: air, noise, radiation, solid waste, water

Harold J. McKenna
City Col., Sch. of Education, Klapper Hall, Rm. 301
135 St. and Convent Ave., New York, N.Y. 10031
212-621-2470
Specialties: conservation and recreation, fish and wildlife, noise, pesticides, environmental education programs
Unpaid

C.T. Male Associates, P.C.
3000 Troy Rd., Schenectady, N.Y. 12309
518-785-0976
Specialties: solid waste, water

Microchemical Research Institute
Box 73, Little Neck, N.Y. 11050
516-883-4560
Specialties: air, solid waste, water

Monsanto Biodize Systems, Inc.
510 Northern Blvd., Great Neck, N.Y. 11021
516-466-5511
Specialty: water
Manufacturing

Marie Morisawa
Geology Dept., State Univ. of New York
Binghamton, N.Y. 13901
607-798-2453
Specialties: conservation and recreation, water (rivers), aesthetics, erosion, sedimentation
Unpaid

Nalews-Weston
1044 Northern Blvd., Roslyn, N.Y. 11576
516-484-2480
Specialties: air, solid waste, water

New York Testing Laboratories, Inc.
81 Urban Ave., Westbury, L.I., N.Y. 11590
516-334-7770
Specialties: air, noise, solid waste, water

Newing Laboratories, Inc.
260 Islip Ave., Islip, N.Y. 11751
516-581-3729
Specialties: air, radiation, solid waste, water

Nussbaumer and Clarke, Inc.
310 Delaware Ave., Buffalo, N.Y. 14202
716-853-7582
Specialties: solid waste, water

O'Brien and Gere, Engineers, Inc.
1050 W. Genessee St., Syracuse, N.Y. 13201
315-472-6251
Specialties: solid waste, water

Offshore/Sea Development Corp.
99 Nassau St., New York, N.Y. 10038
212-267-2532
Specialty: water
Manufacturing

Olin Water Service Laboratories
615 W. 131 St., New York, N.Y. 10027
212-368-1000
Specialty: water
Manufacturing

Donald Osterberg
Dept. of Biology, State Univ. Col.
Potsdam, N.Y. 13676
315-268-2996
Specialty: fish and wildlife
Paid/unpaid

Donald F. Othmer
Polytechnic Institute
333 Jay St., Brooklyn, N.Y. 11201

Environmental Consultants

212-625-1845
Specialties: forestry, land use, solid waste, thermal problems, water
Unpaid

Pamispa, Inc.
Box 129, Grand Island, N.Y. 14072
Specialty: water
Manufacturing

Parsons, Brinkerhoff, Quade, and Douglas, Inc.
111 John St., New York, N.Y. 10035
212-233-6300
Specialties: air, solid waste, water

Glenn L. Paulson, Ph.D.
110 Riverside Dr., New York, N.Y. 10024
212-595-3859
Specialties: air, pesticides, water, power, occupational health

Perolin Co., Inc.
350 5 Ave., New York, N.Y. 10001
212-947-8987
Specialties: solid waste, water
Manufacturing

Malcolm Pirnie, Inc.
266 Westchester Ave., White Plains, N.Y. 10602
914-428-1000
Specialties: air, solid waste, water

Polyphase Chemical Service, Inc.
180 Hempstead Turnpike, West Hempstead, N.Y. 11552
516-485-6161
Specialty: water
Manufacturing

Pope, Evans, and Robbins, Inc.
11 E. 36 St., New York, N.Y. 10016
212-889-5800
Specialties: air, noise, solid waste, water

Power Applications, Inc.
41-06 Bell Blvd., Bayside, N.Y. 11361
212-631-7784
Specialty: water
Manufacturing

Sol Raboy
Dept. of Physics, State Univ. of New York
Binghamton, N.Y. 13901
607-798-2217
Specialty: radiation
Paid

Sanderson and Porter, Inc.
25 Broadway, New York, N.Y. 10004
212-344-5550
Specialties: air, noise, solid waste, water

Schore Automations, Inc.
73 Rushmore St., Westbury, N.Y. 11590
Specialty: water
Manufacturing

Scientific Design Co., Inc.
2 Park Ave., New York, N.Y. 10016
212-689-3000
Specialties: air, solid waste, water

Seelye, Stevenson, Value and Knecht
99 Park Ave., New York, N.Y. 10016
212-867-4000
Specialties: air, radiation, solid waste, water

Stein, Hall and Co., Inc.
605 3 Ave., New York, N.Y. 10016
212-867-8484
Specialty: solid waste
Manufacturing

Syracuse Univ. Research Corp.
Merrill La., University Heights, Syracuse, N.Y. 13210
315-477-8562
Specialties: air, solid waste, water

Terra Marine Scoop Co., Inc.
Box 603, Geneva, N.Y. 14456
315-789-7352
Specialties: solid waste, water
Manufacturing

Tisdel Associates
111 Main St., Canton, N.Y. 13617
315-386-8542
Specialties: air, solid waste, water

Tri-Aid Sciences, Inc.
161 Norris Dr., Rochester, N.Y. 14610
716-461-1660
Specialties: air, noise, radiation, solid waste, water
Manufacturing

Charles R. Velzy Associates, Inc.
350 Executive Blvd., Elmsford, N.Y. 10523
914-592-4750
Specialties: solid waste, water

Leonard S. Wegman Co., Inc.
101 Park Ave., New York, N.Y. 10017
212-686-0500
Specialties: air, radiation, solid waste, water

Wendel Associates
7405 Canal Rd., Lockport, N.Y. 14094
716-433-5993
Specialties: solid waste, water

Western New York Nuclear Research Center, Inc.
Power Dr., Buffalo, N.Y. 14214
716-831-2826
Specialty: radiation

Fred E. Winch, Jr.
New York State Col. of Agriculture and Life Sciences, Cornell Univ.
114 Fernow Hall, Ithaca, N.Y. 14850
607-256-2114
Specialties: forestry, land use
Paid/unpaid

World Ecology Systems
75 E. North St., Geneva, N.Y. 14456
315-789-4522
Specialties: air, solid waste, water
Manufacturing

NORTH CAROLINA

Aeronca, Inc., Environmental Control Group
200 Rodney St., Pineville, N.C. 28134
704-889-7281
Specialty: air
Manufacturing

Henry S. Brown
Geological Resources, Inc.
Box 12424, Raleigh, N.C. 27605
919-828-2218
Specialties: land use, solid waste, water, mineral resources information, land stabilization and reclamation
Paid

Byron Instruments, Inc.
520-1-2 S. Harrington st., Raleigh, N.C. 27601
919-832-7502
Specialties: air, noise, radiation, solid waste, water
Manufacturing

Walter A. Gardner, P.E.
506 Picadilly Circle, Gastonia, N.C. 28052
704-865-4666
Specialties: solid waste, water
Paid

Richter H. Moore, Jr.
Dept. of Political Science, Appalachian State Univ.
Boone, N.C. 28607
704-262-3086
Specialties: recreation, environmental law, land use
Paid/unpaid

Dan J. Pitillo
Dept. of Biology, Western Carolina Univ.
Cullowhee, N.C. 28723
704-293-7244
Specialty: conservation of natural areas
Paid

Richard A. Stephenson
Dept. of Geography, East Carolina Univ.
ECU Sta., Box 2723, Greenville, N.C. 27834
919-758-6230
Specialties: conservation and recreation, land use, water
Paid

P. Aarne Vesilind
Dept. of Civil Engineering, Duke Univ.
Durham, N.C. 27706
919-684-2434
Specialties: solid waste, water
Paid

James E. Wuenscher
Sch. of Forestry, Duke Univ.
Durham, N.C. 27706
919-684-2421
Specialties: conservation and recreation, land use
Paid

OHIO

Aircon Corp.
201 Carrousel Towers, Cincinnati, Ohio 45237
513-821-1996
Specialty: air
Manufacturing

Aquarium Systems Inc.
33208 Lakeland, Eastlake, Ohio 44094
216-946-9180
Specialty: water
Manufacturing

Barnebey-Cheney Co.
835 N. Cassady Ave., Columbus, Ohio 43219
614-258-9501
Specialties: air, radiation, water
Manufacturing

Bartlett-Snow
6200 Harvard Ave., Cleveland, Ohio 44105
216-883-5700
Specialty: solid waste
Manufacturing

Leo E. Bendixen
Dept. of Agronomy, Ohio State Univ.
1885 Neil Ave., Columbus, Ohio 43210
614-422-2247
Specialty: pesticides
Unpaid

Bonham, Grand and Brundage, Ltd.
4955 Arbor Village Dr., Columbus, Ohio 43214
614-888-3100
Specialties: solid waste, water

Robert A. Busser
Trott and Bean Associates
50 W. Broad St., Columbus, Ohio 43215
614-221-1469
Specialties: land use, solid waste, water
Paid/unpaid

CWC Industries, Inc.
2750 Grand Ave., Cleveland, Ohio 44104
216-721-4747
Specialties: air, solid waste, water
Manufacturing

Jot D. Carpenter
Div. of Landscape Architecture, Ohio State Univ.
Columbus, Ohio 43210
614-422-8263
Specialties: conservation and recreation, land use, environmental impact statements and assessments
Paid/unpaid

Columbus Water and Chemical Testing Laboratory
4628 Indianola Ave., Columbus, Ohio 43214
614-262-4372
Specialties: solid waste, water
Manufacturing

Compact Air Samplers
825 Belmonte Pk. N., Dayton, Ohio 45405
513-278-3891
Specialties: air, solid waste, water

Crobaugh Laboratories
3800 Perkins Ave., Cleveland, Ohio 44114
216-881-7320
Specialties: air, solid waste, water

Earth Science Laboratories, Inc.
3020 Vernon Pl., Cincinnati, Ohio 45219
Specialty: solid waste

H.K. Ferguson Co.
1 Erieview Plaza, Cleveland, Ohio 44114
216-523-5600
Specialties: air, noise, solid waste, water

Ferro Corp.
1 Erieview Plaza, Cleveland, Ohio 44114
216-641-8580
Specialty: noise
Manufacturing

J.R. Geisman
2001 Fyffe Court, Ohio State Univ.
Columbus, Ohio 43210
614-422-5169
Specialties: pesticides, water, food processing wastes
Paid outside Ohio

Hale and Kullgren Associates, Inc.
613 E. Tallmadge, Akron, Ohio 44310
Specialties: air, solid waste, water

Heil Process Equipment Corp.
12901 Elmwood Ave., Cleveland, Ohio 44111
216-252-4141
Specialties: air, solid waste, water
Manufacturing

Charles E. Hendendorf
Center for Lake Erie Area Research, Ohio State Univ. 484 W. 12 Ave., Columbus, Ohio 43210
614-422-8949
Specialties: environmental law, fish and wildlife, thermal problems, water, shore erosion problems
Paid

Herron Testing Laboratories, Inc.
5405 Schaaf Rd., Cleveland, Ohio 44131
216-524-1450
Specialties: solid waste, water

Hytek International Corp.
1035 Industrial Pkwy., Medina, Ohio 44256
216-725-4592
Specialties: solid waste, water
Manufacturing

Brian M. Jones
Dept. of Plant Pathology, Ohio Agricultural Research and Development Center
Wooster, Ohio 44691

216-264-1021
Specialty: pesticides
Unpaid

Jones and Henry, Engineers, Ltd.
2000 W. Central Ave., Toledo, Ohio 43606
419-479-7801
Specialties: solid waste, water

Raphael Katzen Associates
1050 Delta Ave., Cincinnati, Ohio 45208
513-321-8403
Specialties: air, solid waste, water

A.M. Kinney, Inc.
2912 Vernon Pl., Cincinnati, Ohio 45219
Specialties: air, solid waste, water

Kral, Zepf, Freitag and Associates
3021 Vernon Pl., Cincinnati, Ohio 45219
Specialties: air, noise, radiation, solid waste, water

Lau, Inc.
2027 Home Ave., Dayton, Ohio 45407
513-263-3591
Specialties: air, noise, radiation, solid waste, water
Manufacturing

Lombard Corp.
639 Wick Ave., Youngstown, Ohio 44501
216-747-3535
Specialty: solid waste
Manufacturing

Garry D. McKenzie
Dept. of Geology, Ohio State Univ.
Columbus, Ohio 43210
614-422-0655
Specialty: land use
Paid/unpaid

Robert M. Miller
Dept. of Agronomy, Ohio State Univ.
1885 Neil Ave., Columbus, Ohio 43210
614-422-2247
Specialty: sludge disposal and land disposal of secondary effluents
Paid/unpaid

Mogul Corp.
Chagrin Falls, Ohio 44022
216-247-5000
Specialties: air, noise, solid waste, water
Manufacturing

Nalin Laboratories
2641 Cleveland Ave., Columbus, Ohio 43211
614-263-3588
Specialties: air, noise, solid waste, water

Natural Resources Management Corp.
Box 526, Worthington, Ohio 43085
614-888-9978
Specialty: water
Manufacturing

PEDCo-Environmental Specialists
Suite 8, Atkinson Sq., Cincinnati, Ohio 45246
513-771-4330
Specialties: air, noise, solid waste, water
Manufacturing

E.S. Preston Associates, Inc.
939 Goodale Blvd., Columbus, Ohio 43212
614-221-7505
Specialties: solid waste, water

E.L. Quarantelli
Disaster Research Center, Ohio State Univ.
127 W. 10 Ave., Columbus, Ohio 43201
614-422-5916
Specialties: air, water, general disasters
Paid

Rackoff Associates, Inc.
867 S. James Rd., Columbus, Ohio 43227
Specialties: solid waste, water

Merle D. Schmid
Dept. of Industrial and Systems Engineering, Univ. of Dayton
Dayton, Ohio 45409
513-229-3621
Specialty: total systems: interaction of programs with current or proposed activities
Unpaid

Schneider Instrument Co.
8115 Camargo Rd., Cincinnati, Ohio 45243
513-561-6803
Specialty: water
Manufacturing

Geoffrey Stanford
Hunatech Foundation
240 W. South College St., Yellow Springs, Ohio 45387
Specialty: solid waste
Paid

Dennis P. Stombaugh
Agricultural Engineering Dept., Ohio Agricultural Research and Development Center
Wooster, Ohio 44691

216-264-1021
Specialties: solid waste, thermal problems
Unpaid

TBW International Inc.
1902 Carew Tower, Cincinnati, Ohio 45202
513-721-1828
Specialties: air, water

Tek-Air Inc.
13405 York Rd., North Royalton, Ohio 44133
216-237-8060
Specialty: air
Manufacturing

TraDet, Inc.
930 Kinnear Rd., Box 5093, Columbus, Ohio 43212
614-299-9229
Specialties: air, water

Vari-Systems, Inc.
1295 W. 78 St., Cleveland, Ohio 44102
216-651-7708
Specialties: air, solid waste
Manufacturing

Vulcan-Cincinnati, Inc.
1329 Arlington St., Cincinnati, Ohio 45225
513-542-7000
Specialty: air
Manufacturing

T. Craig Weidensaul
Laboratories for Environmental Studies, Ohio Agricultural Research and Development Center
Wooster, Ohio 44691
216-264-1021
Specialties: air, forestry
Paid

Lynn B. Willett
Ohio Agricultural Research and Development Center
Wooster, Ohio 44691
216-264-1021
Specialty: pesticides
Paid

OKLAHOMA

Benham-Blair and Affiliates, Inc.
6323 N.W. Grand Blvd., Oklahoma City, Okla. 73118
405-848-6631
Specialties: air, noise, solid waste, water

Michael A. Chartock
Dept. of Zoology and Science and Public Policy Program, Univ. of Oklahoma
Norman, Okla. 73069
405-325-2554
Specialties: fish and wildlife, thermal problems
Paid

Fram Corp., Industrial Div.
2929 E. Apache St., Tulsa, Okla. 74110
918-939-5451
Specialty: solid waste
Manufacturing

Edwin H. Klehr
Sch. of Civil Engineering and Environmental Science, Univ. of Oklahoma
Norman, Okla. 73069
405-325-5914
Specialties: water, radio tracer technology
Paid

Midcontinent Environmental Center Associates
406 Public Service Bldg., Box 201, Tulsa, Okla. 74102
918-587-0500
Specialties: air, noise, radiation, solid waste, water

Moutrey and Associates, Inc.
5509 N. Pennsylvania Ave., Oklahoma City, Okla. 73112
405-848-3321
Specialties: air, noise, solid waste, water
Manufacturing

Elroy L. Rice
Dept. of Botany and Microbiology, Univ. of Oklahoma
Norman, Okla. 73069
405-325-4034
Specialties: conservation and recreation, pesticides
Unpaid

Paul W. Santelmann
Agronomy Dept., Oklahoma State Univ.
Stillwater, Okla. 74074
405-372-6211
Specialty: pesticides
Paid

Robert C. Summerfelt
Cooperative Fishery Unit, Oklahoma State Univ.
Stillwater, Okla. 74074
405-372-6211
Specialty: fish and wildlife
Paid

Technology Research and Development, Inc.
4619 N. Santa Fe, Oklahoma City, Okla. 73118
405-528-7016
Specialties: air, noise, solid waste, water
Manufacturing

United States Pollution Control, Inc.
2000 Classen Center, 200 S, Oklahoma City, Okla. 73106
405-524-9844
Specialties: solid waste, water
Manufacturing

Williams Brothers Waste Control, Inc.
321 S. Boston, Resource Sciences Center, Tulsa, Okla. 74103
918-585-2261
Specialties: air, solid waste, water
Manufacturing

John Zink Co., Pollution Research Div.
4401 S. Peoria, Tulsa, Okla. 74105
917-747-1371
Specialties: air, solid waste, water
Manufacturing

OREGON

Clark and Groff Engineers, Inc.
3276 Commercial St. S.E., Salem, Oreg. 97302
Specialties: solid waste, water

Haner, Ross and Sporseen, Inc.
220 S.W. Alder St., Portland, Oreg. 97204
503-226-6193
Specialties: solid waste, water

Metallurgical Engineers, Inc.
2340 S.W. Canyon Rd., Box 1048, Portland, Oreg. 97207
503-228-9663
Specialties: air, noise, radiation, solid waste, water

W.F. Perley and Associates
805 Dekum Bldg., Portland, Oreg. 97204
Specialties: solid waste, water

Victor H. Prodehl
Consulting Engineer
2670 Englewood N.E., Salem, Oreg. 97301
503-581-5198
Specialties: air, noise, solid waste, water
Paid

Sandwell International, Inc.
1618 S.W. 1 Ave., Portland, Oreg. 97201
503-226-1321
Specialties: air, noise, solid waste, water

Stevens, Thompson and Runyan, Inc.
5505 S.E. Milwaukie Ave., Portland, Oreg. 97202
503-234-0721
Specialties: solid waste, water
Manufacturing

Robin M. Towne and Associates, Inc.
208 Mohawk Bldg., Portland, Oreg. 97204
503-221-0210
Specialty: noise

PENNSYLVANIA

Alpha Laboratories, Inc.
Box 95, Elverson, Pa. 19520
215-286-5131
Specialties: air, solid waste, water

AMSCO Industrial Co.
2820 W. 23 St., Erie, Pa. 16512
814-838-6511
Specialty: water
Manufacturing

Applied Technology Corp.
135 Delta Dr., Pittsburgh, Pa. 15238
412-782-0682
Specialties: air, solid waste, water

Apt, Bramer, Conrad and Associates, Inc.
5100 Centre Ave., Pittsburgh, Pa. 15232
412-687-1958
Specialties: air, noise, radiation, solid waste, water

Michael Baker, Jr., Inc.
Box 280, Beaver, Pa. 15009
412-495-7711
Specialties: air, noise, solid waste, water

B.B. Barefoot and Associates, Inc.
Box 274, Monroeville, Pa. 15146
412-327-1159
Specialty: noise
Manufacturing

Beco Engineering Co.
1312 Rte. 8, Glenshaw, Pa. 15116
412-486-4900
Specialty: air
Manufacturing

174 Environmental Consultants

Betz Environmental Engineers, Inc., Subdiv. of Betz
Somerton Rd., Trevose, Pa. 19047
215-355-3300
Specialties: air, solid waste, water
Manufacturing

Brandywine Valley Sales Co.
Icedale Rd., Honey Brook, Pa. 19344
215-273-2841
Specialties: solid waste, water
Manufacturing

Calgon Corp.
Box 1346, Pittsburgh, Pa. 15230
412-923-2345
Specialties: solid waste, water
Manufacturing

Catalytic, Inc.
1528 Walnut St., Philadelphia, Pa. 19102
215-545-7500
Specialties: air, radiation, solid waste, water
Manufacturing

Craig C. Chase
Environmental Education, Slippery Rock State Col.
Slippery Rock, Pa. 16057
412-794-7503
Specialties: conservation and recreation, noise, water

Chester Engineers, Inc.
845 4 Ave., Coraopolis, Pa. 15108
412-262-1035
Specialties: air, solid waste, water

Combustion Unlimited, Inc.
Box 8856, Elkins Park, Pa. 19117
Specialties: air, noise, solid waste

Craig Chemical Consulting Services, Inc.
120 Stout Rd., Ambler, Pa. 19002
215-643-7682
Specialty: literature searches and evaluation services

Environmental Sciences, Inc.
2901 Banksville Rd., Pittsburgh, Pa. 15216
412-343-8800
Specialties: air, solid waste
Manufacturing

Environmental Tectonics Corp.
County Line Industrial Pk., Southampton, Pa. 18966
215-355-9100
Specialties: air, water
Manufacturing

Ferro-Tech, Inc.
1231 Banksville Rd., Pittsburgh, Pa. 15216
412-344-8700
Specialty: water

E.L. Foerster, Sr.
Box 779, Harrisonburg, Pa. 22801
703-434-0160
Specialties: solid waste, water

Frumerman Associates, Inc.
5423 Darlington Rd., Pittsburgh, Pa. 15217
412-521-5640
Specialties: air, solid waste, water

Gannett Fleming Corddry and Carpenter, Inc.
Box 1963, Harrisburg, Pa. 17105
717-238-0451
Specialties: air, solid waste, water
Manufacturing

Gilbert Associates, Inc.
Box 1498, Reading, Pa. 19603
215-376-3873
Specialties: air, radiation, solid waste, water

Hemeon Associates
6025 Broad St. Mall, Pittsburgh, Pa. 15206
412-441-6660
Specialty: air
Manufacturing

Holley, Kenney, Schott, Inc.
921 Penn Ave., Pittsburgh, Pa. 15222
412-471-5348
Specialties: air, solid waste, water

Huth Engineers, Inc.
37 N. Duke St., Lancaster, Pa. 17602
717-393-5821
Specialties: air, solid waste, water

Morris Knowles Inc.
300 6 Ave., Pittsburgh, Pa. 15222
412-281-3882
Specialties: solid waste, water

Kuljian Corp.
1200 N. Broad St., Philadelphia, Pa. 19121
Specialties: air, solid waste, water

Lancy Laboratories, Div. of Dart Industries, Inc.
525 W. New Castle St., Zelienople, Pa. 16063
412-452-9360

Specialty: solid waste
Manufacturing

Andrew S. McCreath and Son, Inc.
610 Willow St., Box 1453, Harrisburg, Pa. 17105
Specialties: air, water

A.W. Martin Associates, Inc.
900 W. Valley Forge Rd., King of Prussia, Pa. 19406
Specialties: solid waste, water

Matrix Engineering, Inc.
2961 W. Liberty Ave., Pittsburgh, Pa. 15216
412-344-9600
Specialties: air, noise, solid waste, water

George B. Mebus, Inc.
1560 York Rd., Abington, Pa. 19001
215-657-3700
Specialties: solid waste, water

Ovitron Chemical Process Div.
Birch St., East Stroudsburg, Pa. 18301
717-421-5100
Specialties: air, solid waste
Manufacturing

Puricons
16 Central Ave., Berwyn, Pa. 19312
215-644-5488
Specialties: air, solid waste, water
Manufacturing

Radiation Management Corp
Suite 30, Science Center Bldg. No. 2, 3508 Market St., Philadelphia, Pa. 19104
215-386-1805
Specialty: radiation

Eileen C. Raizen
Dept. of Biological Science, Duquesne Univ.
Pittsburgh, Pa. 15219
412-434-6317
Specialty: water
Paid/unpaid

Sadtler Research Laboratories, Inc.
3316 Spring Garden St., Philadelphia, Pa. 19104
215-382-7800
Specialties: solid waste, water
Manufacturing

Sanders and Thomas, Inc.
First Federal Bldg., High and Hanover Sts., Pottstown, Pa. 19464

Specialties: air, noise, radiation, solid waste, water

Scott Research Laboratories, Inc.
Box D-11, Plumsteadville, Pa. 18949
215-766-8861
Specialty: air
Manufacturing

Marcus Sittenfield and Associates
1405 Locust St., Philadelphia, Pa. 19102
215-735-5788
Specialties: air, water
Manufacturing

Smith, Miller and Associates
189 Market St., Kingston, Pa. 18704
717-288-4567
Specialties: solid waste, water
Manufacturing

Spotts, Stevens and McCoy, Inc.
345 N. Wyomissing Blvd., Wyomissing, Pa. 19610
215-376-6581
Specialties: air, noise, solid waste, water

Swindell-Dressler Co.
441 Smithfield St., Pittsburgh, Pa. 15222
412-562-7501
Specialties: air, noise, solid waste, water
Manufacturing

Teck Labs
Box 489, Bradford, Pa. 16701
814-368-6087
Specialties: air, solid waste, water
Manufacturing

Thermal Research and Engineering Corp., A Cordon International Co.
Brook Rd., Conshohocken, Pa. 19428
215-828-5400
Specialty: solid waste
Manufacturing

J. Fred Triggs and Associates
1601 Penn Ave., Pittsburgh, Pa. 15221
412-242-5255
Specialties: solid waste, water

Warner Co.
1721 Arch St., Philadelphia, Pa. 19103
215-563-3900
Specialties: air, solid waste
Manufacturing

Roy F. Weston, Inc.
Lewis La., West Chester, Pa. 19380
215-692-3030
Specialties: air, noise, solid waste, water

Zurn Industries, Inc.
1801 Pittsburgh Ave., Erie, Pa. 16512
814-455-0921
Specialties: air, noise, solid waste, water
Manufacturing

Puerto Rico

Etienne R. Dusart
Suite 504, Empire Bldg., 316 De Diego Ave., Santurce, Puerto Rico 00909
809-723-2687
Specialties: conservation and recreation, land use
Paid

Rhode Island

Norwood Engineers
Meetinghouse La., Little Compton, R.I. 02837
413-734-7034
Specialty: water
Manufacturing

Orgonics, Inc.
Box 543, Slatersville, R.I. 02876
401-766-3530
Specialty: solid waste
Manufacturing

South Carolina

Hahn Laboratories
1111 Flora St., Box 1177, Columbia, S.C. 29202
803-252-3445
Specialty: solid waste

J.E. Sirrine Co.
216 S. Pleasantburg Dr., Box 5456, Greenville, S.C. 29606
803-233-2531
Specialties: air, noise, solid waste, water

Thermo-Kinetics, Inc.
716 E. Fairfield Rd., Box 6747, Greenville, S.C. 29606
Specialties: air, noise
Manufacturing

South Dakota

J.T. Banner and Associates, Inc.
1024 6 St., Brookings, S. Dak. 57006
605-692-6342
Specialties: solid waste, water

John H. Davidson, Jr.
Sch. of Law, Univ. of South Dakota
Vermillion, S. Dak. 57069
605-677-5492
Specialties: environmental law, land use
Paid

Yvonne A. Greichus
Experiment Sta. Biochemistry, South Dakota State Univ.
Brookings, S. Dak. 57006
605-688-5171
Specialties: fish and wildlife, pesticides, water
Paid/unpaid

James Heidinger
Univ. of South Dakota
Vermillion, S. Dak. 57069
605-677-5211
Specialties: solid waste, heavy metals pollution
Paid/unpaid

George Hoffman
Univ. of South Dakota
Vermillion, S. Dak. 57069
605-677-5211
Specialty: air
Paid/unpaid

Perry H. Rahn
201 Franklin St., Rapid City, S. Dak. 57701
605-394-2464
Specialties: land use, water
Paid

James Schmulbach
Univ. of South Dakota
Vermillion, S. Dak. 57069
605-677-5211
Specialties: fish and wildlife, water
Paid/unpaid

Webster H. Sill, Jr.
Center for Environmental Studies, Univ. of South Dakota
Vermillion, S. Dak. 57069

605-677-5211
Specialties: conservation and recreation, fish and wildlife, land use, solid waste
Paid/unpaid

Ted VanBruggen
Univ. of South Dakota
Vermillion, S. Dak. 57069
605-677-5211
Specialties: forestry, land use
Paid/unpaid

TENNESSEE

Allen and Hoshall, Consulting Engineers
2430 Poplar Ave., Memphis, Tenn. 38112
901-327-8222
Specialties: solid waste, water

Barrow-Agee Laboratory, Inc.
650 New York St., Memphis, Tenn. 38101
901-278-2000
Specialties: solid waste, water

Sanford M. Brown, M.P.H., Ph.D.
Dept. of Environmental Health, East Tennessee Univ.
Johnson City, Tenn. 37601
615-929-4268
Specialties: conservation and recreation, solid waste, environmental planning, administration, and management
Paid

Geo. S. Campbell and Associates, Inc.
701 E. 4 St., Chattanooga, Tenn. 37403
615-267-9718
Specialties: air, radiation, solid waste, water

Carborundum Co., Pollution Control Div
Box 1269, Middlebrook Industrial Pk., Knoxville, Tenn. 37901
615-588-8585
Specialties: air, water
Manufacturing

Chemical Separations Corp.
Box 549, Oak Ridge, Tenn. 37830
615-483-7426
Specialties: air, solid waste, water
Manufacturing

David Allen Conner
Div. of Engineering, Univ. of Tennessee
Chattanooga, Tenn. 37401
615-755-4680
Specialties: air, noise, radiation, frequency spectrum pollution
Paid

Dempster Brothers, Inc.
Box 3127, Knoxville, Tenn. 37917
615-524-1671
Specialty: solid waste

W. Wesley Eckenfelder, Jr.
Box 6222, Station B, Vanderbilt Univ., Nashville, Tenn. 37235
Specialty: water
Paid

Environmental Science and Engineering Corp.
Box 3655, Nashville, Tenn. 37217
615-758-5858
Specialties: air, radiation, solid waste, water

Henry August Fribourg
Dept. of Plant and Soil Science, Univ. of Tennessee
Knoxville, Tenn. 37916
615-974-7161
Specialties: conservation and recreation, land use
Paid/unpaid

Ovid M. McMillion
Dept. of Geography, Middle Tennessee State Univ.
Murfreesboro, Tenn. 37130
Specialties: conservation and recreation, forestry, land use
Unpaid

Steelcraft Corp.
Box 12408, Memphis, Tenn. 38112
901-324-2151
Specialty: air
Manufacturing

Stewart Laboratories, Inc.
820 Tulip Ave., Knoxville, Tenn. 37921
615-525-1123
Specialties: air, solid waste, water

Sverdrup and Parcel and Associates, Inc.
2120 8 Ave. S., Nashville, Tenn. 37204
615-297-3547
Specialties: solid waste, water

Wymer Wiser
Dept. of Biology, Middle Tennessee State Univ.
Murfreesboro, Tenn. 37130
615-898-2842
Specialties: radiation, water
Unpaid

Frank W. Woods
Dept. of Forestry, Box 1071, Univ. of Tennessee
Knoxville, Tenn. 37901
615-974-7126
Specialties: conservation and recreation, forestry, land use
Paid/unpaid

TEXAS

Bovay Engineers, Inc.
5009 Caroline St., Houston, Tex. 77004
Specialties: air, noise, radiation, solid waste, water

Kirk W. Brown
Soil and Crop Sciences Dept., Texas A and M Univ.
College Station, Tex. 77843
713-845-5251
Specialties: pesticides, solid waste, water
Unpaid

Brown and Root, Inc.
Box 3, Houston, Tex. 77001
713-228-8811
Specialties: air, solid waste, water

Horace R. Byers
Dept. of Meteorology, Texas A and M Univ.
College Station, Tex. 77843
713-845-6344
Specialties: air, water
Paid

Maurice Carroll
Suite 400, First Bank and Trust Bldg., Richardson, Tex. 75080
214-238-8271
Specialties: conservation and recreation, land use
Unpaid

Henry Chafetz
Geology Dept., Univ. of Houston
Houston, Tex. 77004
713-748-6600
Specialties: conservation and recreation, land use, geology of the coastal environment
Paid/unpaid

Dayle M. Clark
Dept. of Civil Engineering, Univ. of Texas
Arlington, Tex. 76010
817-261-8461

Specialties: conservation and recreation, land use, noise, solid waste, water, urban planning and transportation
Paid/unpaid

Coastal Ecosystems Management, Inc.
3550 Hulen, Fort Worth, Tex. 76107
817-731-3727
Specialty: water

Core Laboratories, Inc.
Box 10185, Dallas, Tex. 75207
214-631-8270
Specialties: air, solid waste, water
Manufacturing

Detailed Engineered Equipment Corp.
Box 66626, Houston, Tex. 77006
713-523-1344
Specialties: air, solid waste
Manufacturing

Robert S. Dewers
Rm. 310, 203 W. Nueva, San Antonio, Tex.
512-220-2774
Specialties: conservation and recreation, forestry, land use
Unpaid

Ecology Audits, Inc., Subsidiary of Core Laboratories, Inc.
7501 Stemmons Expressway, Dallas, Tex. 75207
214-631-8270
Specialties: air, water

Edminster Hinshaw and Associates, Inc.
5051 Westheimer #1580, Houston, Tex. 77027
713-621-8500
Specialties: solid waste, water

Howard E. Erdman
Biology Dept., Texas Woman's Univ.
Denton, Tex. 76204
817-387-6266
Specialties: conservation and recreation, radiation
Unpaid

Filters, Inc.
6319 Eppes, Houston, Tex. 77017
713-644-1509
Specialties: air, noise, water

W.L. Fisher
Bureau of Economic Geology
Box X, Univ. Sta., Austin, Tex. 78712
512-471-1534

Specialties: land use, solid waste
Paid outside Texas

Raymond A. Gerdes
Biology Dept., Texas Woman's Univ.
Denton, Tex. 76204
817-382-3443
Specialties: conservation and recreation, pesticides, mutagenicity of environmental contaminants
Paid/unpaid

Gulf States Pollution Control, Inc.
Hwy. 79 W., Jacksonville, Tex. 75766
214-586-2408
Specialties: air, solid waste
Manufacturing

Albert H. Halff Associates, Inc.
3636 Lemmon Ave., Dallas, Tex. 75219
214-526-8309
Specialties: solid waste, water

Houston Research Inc.
8330 Broadway, Houston, Tex. 77017
713-641-0331
Specialties: solid waste, water

Institute for Research, Inc.
1714 Rice Blvd., Houston, Tex. 77005
713-526-4093
Specialties: air, noise, radiation, solid waste, water
Manufacturing

Institute for Storm Research
3812 Montrose Blvd., Houston, Tex. 77006
713-529-4891
Specialties: air, noise, radiation, solid waste, water

International Pollution Control, Inc.
5455 Old Spanish Trail, Houston, Tex. 77023
713-923-9781
Specialties: solid waste, water
Manufacturing

Wesley P. James
Civil Engineering Dept., Texas A and M Univ.
College Station, Tex. 77843
713-845-3011
Specialty: water
Unpaid

Delmar L. Janke
Dept. of Educational Curriculum and Instruction, Texas A and M Univ.
College Station, Tex. 77843

713-845-6811
Specialty: environmental education
Unpaid

Bernard Johnson Engineers, Inc.
5050 Westheimer, Houston, Tex. 77027
713-622-1400
Specialties: air, noise, solid waste, water

K-N-B Inc.
3908 Colgate St., Houston, Tex. 77017
713-643-6513
Specialty: air
Manufacturing

M.W. Kellogg Co.
1300 3 Greenway Plaza E., Houston, Tex. 77046
713-626-5600
Specialties: air, noise, solid waste, water

Frank J. Kelly
Mason and Hanger Corp.
Box 647, Amarillo, Tex. 79105
806-335-1581
Specialties: air, noise, pecticides, radiation, thermal problems, water
Paid

Kemlon Products and Development Co.
Box 14666, Houston, Tex. 77021
Specialties: radiation, solid waste, water

Lace Engineering
8829 N. Lamar, Austin, Tex. 78753
512-836-5606
Specialty: air
Manufacturing

Lockwood, Andrews and Newman, Inc.
1010 Waugh Dr., Houston, Tex. 77019
713-526-1781
Specialties: air, noise, solid waste, water

Harry E. Malley
307 Dwyer Ave., San Antonio, Tex. 78285
512-225-5511
Specialties: radiation, thermal problems
Unpaid

Walter W. Melvin, Jr.
USAF Environmental Health Laboratory
Kelly Air Force Base, Tex. 70229
512-925-5198
Specialties: air, noise, pesticides, thermal problems, water
Unpaid

180 Environmental Consultants

Municipal Engineering Co.
1730 S. Richey St., Pasadena, Tex. 77502
713-473-7655
Specialties: solid waste, water

Douglas Muster
4615 O'Meara Dr., Houston, Tex. 77035
713-723-6849
Specialty: noise
Paid

Oceanography International Corp.
512 W. Loop, College Station, Tex. 77840
713-846-7721
Specialties: solid waste, water
Manufacturing

Oceanonics, Inc
6204 Evergreen St., Houston, Tex. 77036
713-771-5731
Specialties: solid waste, water

Pace Co.
3700 Buffalo Speedway, Houston, Tex. 77006
713-626-2020
Specialties: air, noise, solid waste, water

Pan American Laboratories, Inc.
Box 3051, Brownsville, Tex. 78520
512-831-4266
Specialty: water

R.E. Quinn
405 Academic Bldg., Texas A and M Univ.
College Station, Tex. 77843
713-845-6811
Specialty: environmental education, curriculum development and instructional statistics
Paid/unpaid

Radian Corp.
8500 Shoal Creek Blvd., Box 9948, Austin, Tex. 78757
512-454-9535
Specialties: air, noise, water

S and B Engineers
7820 Park Place Blvd., Houston, Tex. 77032
713-645-4141
Specialties: air, solid waste, water

San Jacinto Drilling and Disposal Co.
San Jacinto Bldg., Houston, Tex. 77002
713-227-5353
Specialties: solid waste, water

Scientific and Educational Services, Inc.
Box 20421, Astrodome Sta., Houston, Tex. 77025
Specialties: air, noise, solid waste, water

Dudley T. Smith
Texas Agricultural Experimental Sta.
College Station, Tex. 77843
713-845-3711
Specialty: pesticides
Unpaid

Southwest Research Institute, Central Proposal Office
8500 Culebra Rd., San Antonio, Tex. 78228
512-684-2000
Specialties: air, noise, solid waste, water
Manufacturing

Speller and Associates, Inc.
788 The Petroleum Bldg., Tyler, Tex. 75701
214-593-9401
Specialties: solid waste, water

Royal Jay Swenson
Chevron Chemical Co.
Suite 400, First Bank and Trust Bldg., Richardson, Tex. 75080
214-238-8271
Specialties: conservation and recreation, land use
Paid

Tracor, Inc.
6500 Tracor La., Austin, Tex. 78721
512-926-2800
Specialties: air, noise, water
Manufacturing

Turner, Collie and Braden, Inc.
Box 13089, Houston, Tex. 77019
713-528-6361
Specialties: air, solid waste, water

Victor W. Ward
Urban Management Planners
4927 Gaston, #208, Dallas, Tex. 75214
214-824-8653
Specialty: urban economics
Paid

Wepco, Inc.
Hwy. 69 S., Box 1525, Jacksonville, Tex. 75766
214-586-2409
Specialties: air, solid waste

William Bernard Whitney, Sr.
Chemistry Dept., Texas Woman's Univ.,
Denton, Tex. 76204
817-382-9662
Specialty: air
Unpaid

F.R. Young Co.
5402 Bell Ave., Houston, Tex. 77023
713-928-3771
Specialties: air, noise
Manufacturing

Utah

AIR, Inc. (Aerostatics Instrumentation and Research, Inc.)
1081 E. 2200 North, Logan, Utah 84321
801-752-3323
Specialty: air
Manufacturing

EcoDynamics, Inc.
82 W. Louise Ave., Salt Lake City, Utah 84109
801-487-5706
Specialties: solid waste, water
Manufacturing

Miles C. Labrum
Bldg. 306, Univ. of Utah
Salt Lake City, Utah 84112
801-581-6711
Specialties: conservation and recreation, land use, noise
Paid

R.I. Corp.
Box 389, Ogden, Utah 84402
801-392-6212
Specialty: noise

Paul J. Riley
Utah Water Research Laboratories, Utah State Univ.
Logan, Utah 84321
801-752-4100
Specialties: conservation and recreation, forestry, land use, water
Paid/unpaid

Stanley L. Welsh
Rm. 113-B49, Herbarium, Brigham Young Univ.
Provo, Utah 84601
801-374-1211

Specialties: air, conservation and recreation, land use, plant inventory of selected habitats, plant and geological formation correlation
Paid

Neil E. West
Col. of Natural Resources, Utah State Univ.
Logan, Utah 84321
801-752-4100
Specialties: conservation and recreation, fish and wildlife, forestry, land use, computer retrieval of environmental literature
Paid/unpaid

Vermont

Frank Harris Armstrong
Dept. of Forestry, Univ. of Vermont
Burlington, Vt. 05401
802-656-2620
Specialty: forestry
Unpaid

Ian A. Worley
Botany Dept., Univ. of Vermont
Burlington, Vt. 05401
802-656-2930
Specialty: botanical ecology
Paid

Virginia

Leo Alpert
4120 N. 34 St., Arlington, Va. 22207
703-527-1585
Specialty: air
Paid

CH$_2$M/Hill
1930 Isaac Newton Sq. E., Reston, Va. 22070
703-471-4151
Specialties: air, noise, solid waste, water

Commonwealth Laboratory, Inc.
2209 E. Broad St., Richmond, Va. 23223
703-648-8358
Specialties: air, noise, water

Edwin Cox Associates
2209 E. Broad St., Richmond. Va. 23223
703-648-8358
Specialties: air, noise, radiation, solid waste, water
Manufacturing

General Environments Corp.
6840 Industrial Rd., Springfield, Va. 22151
703-354-2000
Specialties: air, noise, radiation, solid waste, water

Griffith Engineering
450 W. Broad St., Falls Church, Va. 22046
703-534-8844
Specialty: solid waste
Manufacturing

Hazleton Laboratories, Inc.
9200 Leesburg Turnpike, Vienna, Va. 22180
Specialties: air, noise, radiation, solid waste, water

Inter Technology Corp.
Box 340, Warrenton, Va. 22186
703-347-7900
Specialties: air, solid waste, water
Manufacturing

Karl S. Landstrom
510 N. Edison St., Arlington, Va. 22203
703-527-0968
Specialties: environmental law, land use
Paid

Langley, McDonald and Overman
Box 12047, Norfolk, Va. 23502
Specialties: solid waste, water

McCallum Inspection Co.
1808 Hayward Ave., Box 13266, Chesapeake, Va. 23325
703-420-2520
Specialties: air, solid waste, water

Marine Advisory and Associated Services
716 Kentland Dr., Herndon, Va. 22070
703-450-4884
Specialty: water
Manufacturing

Harold G. Marshall
Dept. of Biology, Old Dominion Univ.
Norfolk, Va. 23508
703-489-8000
Specialties: conservation and recreation, fish and wildlife, coastal wetlands
Paid

Lawrence E. Schlesinger
National Children's Rehabilitation Center, Box 1260, Leesburg, Va. 22075
703-777-3485
Specialties: environmental psychology, design research, man-environment relations
Paid

The Stanwick Corp.
Box 9184, Rosslyn Sta., Arlington, Va. 22209
703-524-6126
Specialties: air, solid waste, water

Sydnor Hydrodynamics, Inc.
1305 Brook Rd., Richmond, Va. 23212
703-643-2725
Specialties: solid waste, water

Robert M. Yancey
8104 Fort Hunt Rd., Alexandria, Va. 22308
703-768-4585
Specialty: fish and wildlife
Paid

WASHINGTON

R.W. Beck and Associates
200 Tower Bldg., Seattle, Wash. 98101
206-MA2-5000
Specialties: air, noise, solid waste, water

Bovay Engineers, Inc.
E. 808 Sprague Ave., Spokane, Wash. 99202
Specialties: air, noise, radiation, solid waste, water

Philip C. Dumas
Dept. of Biological Sciences, Central Washington State Col.
Ellensburg, Wash. 98926
509-963-2731
Specialties: conservation and recreation, fish and wildlife, land use
Unpaid

EKONO
410 104 Ave. S.E., Bellevue, Wash. 98004
206-455-5969
Specialties: air, solid waste, water

Frankfurter and Associates, Inc.
1930 6 Ave. S., Seattle, Wash. 98134
Specialties: air, solid waste, water

Bernard H. Frerichs
Dept. of Economics, Western Washington State Col.
Bellingham, Wash. 98225
206-676-3910
Specialty: land use
Paid/unpaid

Benjamin A. Jayne
Col. of Forest Resources, Univ. of Washington
Seattle, Wash. 98195
206-543-2730
Specialties: forestry, land use
Paid

Moore, Wallace and Kennedy, Inc.
1915 1 Ave., Seattle, Wash. 98101
206-624-2623
Specialties: solid waste, water

Saxton and Kennedy, Inc.
W. 1625 4 Ave., Spokane, Wash. 99204
509-838-6466
Specialties: solid waste, water

James A. Sewell and Associates
Box 160, Newport, Wash. 99156
509-447-3626
Specialties: solid waste, water

Robin M. Towne and Associates, Inc.
105 N.E. 56 St., Seattle, Wash. 98105
206-523-3350
Specialty: noise

Valentine, Fisher and Tomlinson
520 Lloyd Bldg., Seattle, Wash. 98101
206-623-0717
Specialties: air, noise, solid waste, water

West Virginia

D.J. Horvath
Agricultural Science Bldg., West Virginia Univ.
Morgantown, W. Va. 26506
304-293-2406
Specialty: heavy metals in sewage and other recycled materials
Paid/unpaid

Edward S. Neuman
Dept. for Civil Engineering, West Virginia Univ.
Morgantown, W. Va. 26506
304-293-5580
Specialty: systems planning
Paid

Willem A. Van Eck
Div. of Plant Sciences, West Virginia Univ.
Morgantown, W. Va. 26506
304-293-2219
Specialties: conservation and recreation, environmental law, forestry, land use, water, soil-related problems
Paid/unpaid

Wisconsin

Daniel M. Benjamin
Dept. of Entomology, Univ. of Wisconsin
Madison, Wis. 53706
608-262-1125
Specialty: forest entomology
Paid/unpaid

Jack M. Bostrack
Dept. of Biology, Univ. of Wisconsin
River Falls, Wis. 54022
715-425-6701
Specialties: solid waste, water
Paid

George Mallory Boush
Dept. of Entomology, 643 Russell Laboratory, Univ. of Wisconsin
Madison, Wis. 53706
608-262-1269
Specialty: pesticides
Paid/unpaid

Allen A. Denio
Dept. of Chemistry, Univ. of Wisconsin
Eau Claire, Wis. 54701
715-836-3712
Specialties: air, radiation, water
Paid

Foth and Van Dyke and Associates, Inc.
1970 S. Broadway, Green Bay, Wis. 54301
414-432-0655
Specialties: solid waste, water

Thomas A. Heberlein
Dept. of Rural Sociology, 240 Agriculture Hall, Univ. of Wisconsin
Madison, Wis. 53706
608-262-1510
Specialties: conservation and recreation, environmental social psychology
Paid

John W. Hill
Dept. of Chemistry, Univ. of Wisconsin
River Falls, Wis. 54022
715-425-6701
Specialties: land use, solid waste
Unpaid

184 Environmental Consultants

John D. Hudson
Dept. of Biology, Univ. of Wisconsin
River Falls, Wis. 54022
715-425-6701
Specialties: fish, water
Paid

Harold J. Jebens
Univ. of Wisconsin
Platteville, Wis. 53818
608-342-1557
Specialty: water
Unpaid

Limnetics, Inc.
6132 W. Fond Du Lac Ave., Milwaukee, Wis. 53218
414-461-9500
Specialties: air, noise, solid waste, water

Alden McLellan, IV
Space Science and Engineering Center, Univ. of Wisconsin
Madison, Wis. 53706
608-262-0119
Specialties: air, land use, water, remote sensing and mapping by satellites
Unpaid

Stanley A. Nichols
1815 University Ave., Madison, Wis. 53706
608-262-3686
Specialties: conservation and recreation, land use, water
Unpaid

Lawrence A. Nutter
Univ. of Wisconsin
La Crosse, Wis. 54601
608-785-1800
Specialties: air, water
Paid

Arthur H. Ode
2949 S. 90 St., West Allis, Wis. 53227
414-543-1176
Specialties: conservation and recreation, land use
Paid

Paragon Electric Co., Inc.
1600 12 St., Two Rivers, Wis. 54241
414-793-1161
Specialties: air, noise, radiation, solid waste, water
Manufacturing

Stephen C. Smith
Sch. of Natural Resources, Univ. of Wisconsin
1450 Linden Dr., Madison, Wis. 53706
608-262-6968
Specialties: conservation and recreation, environmental law, forestry, land use, water, environmental and resource management policy problems dealing with organizational issues
Paid/unpaid

Charles H. Stoddard
Wolf Springs Forest
Minong, Wis. 54859
218-727-2424
Specialties: conservation and recreation, environmental law, fish and wildlife, forestry, land use, solid waste, water
Paid

H.G. Swope and Associates
Box 1254, Madison, Wis. 53701
608-238-9966
Specialties: radiation, solid waste, water

Terra-Cology Services
Box 29, Stoughton, Wis. 53589
608-873-7750
Specialties: air, noise

Daniel O. Trainer
Dean of Col. of Natural Resources, Univ. of Wisconsin
Stevens Point, Wis. 54481
715-346-4617
Specialties: conservation and recreation, fish and wildlife, pesticides, disease
Paid/unpaid

Milan W. Wehking
Dept. of Chemistry, Univ. of Wisconsin
River Falls, Wis. 54022
715-425-6629
Specialties: air, water
Paid/unpaid

Edward J. Zeimet
Univ. of Wisconsin
1705 State St., La Crosse, Wis. 54601
608-785-1800
Specialty: noise
Unpaid

WYOMING

Robert L. Streeter
1945 Westwood Hill, Box 2030, Casper, Wyo. 82601
307-234-5759
Specialties: solid waste, water

4 Environmental Officers of U.S. Corporations

JANET Y. WILLEN

The information in this chapter was obtained from the presidents of the companies on the *Fortune* 500 list and the presidents of the fifty largest utility companies in the United States. They were asked to provide the names and corporate positions of the individuals in their firms who handle environmental affairs. Over 72 percent identified such a person.

In many major U.S. corporations, the individuals responsible for handling environmental affairs occupy high positions in the corporate structures. This, and the fact that better than 72 percent of the companies queried responded, suggests that environmental matters are very important to American business.

The following listings are alphabetically arranged within the 30 industrial classifications listed below. The president or other chief executive is given for each company, followed by the name or names of the people who handle environmental affairs. If no environmental affairs officer is listed, inquiries should be directed to the company president.

Aircraft and Parts
Apparel
Appliances and Electronics
Beverages
Broadcasting and Motion Pictures
Chemicals
Farm and Industrial Machinery
Food
Furniture
Glass, Cement, Gypsum, and Concrete
Jewelry and Silverware
Leather and Leather Products
Measuring, Scientific, and Photographic Equipment
Metal Manufacturing
Metal Products
Mining

Miscellaneous Manufacturing
Motor Vehicles and Parts
Musical Instruments, Toys, and Sporting Goods
Office Machinery and Computers
Paper and Wood Products
Petroleum Refining
Pharmaceuticals
Publishing and Printing
Rubber
Shipbuilding, Railroad Equipment, and Mobile Homes
Soaps and Cosmetics
Textiles
Tobacco
Utilities

AIRCRAFT AND PARTS

Automation Industries, Inc.
1901 Bldg., Century City, Los Angeles, Calif. 90067
213-879-2222
John J. Burke, President

Avco Corp.
1275 King St., Greenwich, Conn. 06830
203-552-1800
James R. Kerr, President

Boeing Co.
Box 3707, Seattle, Wash. 98124
206-655-2121

185

Malcolm T. Stampler, President
Arnold Goldburg, Director, Science and Technology, Mail Stop 13-41

Curtiss-Wright Corp.
1 Passaic St., Wood Ridge, N.J. 07075
201-777-2900
T. Roland Berner, President

Fairchild Industries
Fairchild Dr., Germantown, Md. 20767
301-948-9600
Edward G. Uhl, President
James J. Greeves, Program Manager

General Dynamics Corp.
Pierre Laclede Center, St. Louis, Mo. 63105
314-862-2440
Hilliard W. Paige, President
Algie A. Hendrix, Vice President, Industrial Relations

Grumman Corp.
S. Oyster Bay Rd., Bethpage, N.Y. 11714
516-575-0574
E. Clinton Towl, Chairman
William T. Schwendler, Jr., Executive Vice President and Treasurer, Grumman Ecosystems Corp.

Lockheed Aircraft Corp.
2555 N. Hollywood Way, Burbank, Calif. 91503
213-847-6121
A. Carl Kotchian, President
E. G. Mattison, Vice President, Industrial Relations

McDonnell Douglas Corp.
Box 516, St. Louis, Mo. 63166
314-232-0232
Sanford N. McDonnell, President
George B. Sloan, Director, Environment and Strategic Planning

Martin Marietta Corp.
277 Park Ave., New York, N.Y. 10017
212-826-5050
J. Donald Rauth, President
Dr. George W. Morgenthaler, Director, Research and Development

North American Rockwell Corp.
1700 E. Imperial Hwy., El Segundo, Calif. 90245
213-647-5000
Robert Anderson, President

W. B. Ericson, Manager, Environmental Control, North American Rockwell Corp., 600 Grant St., Pittsburgh, Pa. 15219

Northrop Corp.
1800 Century Pk. E., Century City, Los Angeles, Calif. 90067
213-553-6262
Thomas V. Jones, President
Ward B. Dennis, Vice President, Forward Planning

Rohr Industries, Inc.
Foot of H St., Chula Vista, Calif. 92010
714-426-7111
Frank E. McCreery, President
Lawrence Borbolla, Chairman, Environmental Control Committee

Textron, Inc.
10 Dorrance St., Providence, R.I. 02903
401-421-2800
G. William Miller, President

Thiokol Chemical Corp.
Box 27, Bristol, Pa. 19007
215-946-9150
Robert E. Davis, President
Dr. James T. Grey, Jr., Assistant to the President, Research and Development

TRW, Inc.
23555 Euclid Ave., Cleveland, Ohio 44117
216-383-2121
Dr. Ruben F. Mettler, President
K. C. White, Vice President, Manufacturing Staff

United Aircraft Corp.
400 Main St., East Hartford, Conn. 06118
203-565-4321
Harry J. Gray, President
Dale Van Winkle, Vice President

APPAREL

Blue Bell, Inc.
335 Church St., Greensboro, N.C. 27401
919-275-9392
Rodger S. LeMatty, President

Cluett, Peabody & Co., Inc.
510 5 Ave., New York, N.Y. 10036
212-697-6100
Henry H. Henley, Jr., President

Genesco, Inc.
111 7 Ave. N., Nashville, Tenn. 37202
615-747-7000
J. Owen Howell, President

Hanes Corp.
Box 5416, Winston-Salem, N.C. 27103
919-767-3200
Robert E. Elberson, President
Robin L. Hinson, Vice President; General Counsel

Hart Schaffner and Marx
36 S. Franklin St., Chicago, Ill. 60606
312-372-6300
Jerome S. Gore, President

Kayser-Roth Corp.
640 5 Ave., New York, N.Y. 10019
212-757-9600
Alfred P. Slaner, President

Kellwood Co.
9909 Clayton Rd., St. Louis, Mo. 63124
314-994-9200
Fred W. Wenzel, President

Jonathan Logan, Inc.
3901 Liberty Ave., North Bergen, N.J. 07047
212-695-4440
Richard J. Schwartz, President

Manhattan Industries, Inc.
1271 Ave. of the Americas, New York, N.Y. 10020
212-265-3700
Laurence C. Leeds, Jr., President

Phillips-Van Heusen Corp.
417 Fifth Ave., New York, N.Y. 10016
212-689-3700
Lawrence S. Phillips, President
Stuart H. Green, Vice President and Secretary

Rapid-American Corp.
711 5 Ave., New York, N.Y. 10022
212-752-0100
M. Riklis, President

Levi Strauss & Co.
98 Battery St., San Francisco, Calif. 94111
415-321-6200
Peter E. Haas, President

U.S. Industries, Inc.
250 Park Ave., New York, N.Y. 10017
212-697-4141
Charles E. Selecman, President

V F Corp.
1047 N. Park Rd., Wyomissing, Reading, Pa. 19610
215-376-7201
Manford O. Lee, President

Warnaco
325 Lafayette St., Bridgeport, Conn. 06604
203-333-1151
John W. Field, President
John J. Maloney, Public Relations Director

APPLIANCES AND ELECTRONICS

Admiral Corp.
3800 Cortland St., Chicago, Ill. 60647
312-292-2600
Ross D. Siragusa, Jr., President
Robert B. Lukingbeal, Senior Vice President, Operations

AMP Inc.
Eisenhower Blvd., Harrisburg, Pa. 17105
717-564-0101
Joseph D. Brenner, President
Joseph Gouhin, Project Manager, Air, Noise, and Water Pollution

Ampex Corp.
401 Broadway, Redwood City, Calif. 94063
415-367-2011
Arthur H. Hausman, President
William G. Anderson, Manager, Facilities Engineering

Avnet, Inc.
767 5 Ave., New York, N.Y. 10022
212-980-3300
Simon Sheib, President

Bendix Corp.
Bendix Center, Southfield, Mich. 48075
313-352-5000
W. Michael Blumenthal, President
B. B. Burton, Staff Assistant, Environmental Protection

Bunker Ramo Corp
1200 Harger Rd., Oakbrook N., Oak Brook, Ill. 60521
312-654-3100
George S. Trimble, President
F. E. Tweed, Director, Facility Engineering

Champion Spark Plug Co.
Box 910, Toledo, Ohio 43601

419-536-3711
K. C. Schoettley, President
Charles E. Heckert, Industrial Engineer

Collins Radio Co.
1200 N. Alma Rd., Dallas, Tex. 75215
214-235-9511
Robert C. Wilson, President
Carl Weaver, Manager, Facilities and Maintenance Dept.

Cutler-Hammer, Inc.
4201 N. 27 St., Milwaukee, Wis. 53216
414-442-7800
Donald M. Miller, President

Eltra Corp.
2 Pennsylvania Plaza, New York, N.Y. 10001
212-695-1600
J. A. Keller, President
James Barry, Director, Corporate Planning

Emerson Electric Co.
8100 W. Florissant Ave., St. Louis, Mo. 63136
314-553-2000
Edward L. O'Neill, President

ESB Inc.
5 Penn Center Plaza, Philadelphia, Pa. 19103
215-564-4030
Frederick J. Port, President
W. M. Pallies, Manager, Environmental Control

Essex International
1601 Wall St., Fort Wayne, Ind. 46804
219-743-0311
Paul W. O'Malley, President
T. P. Sharples, Assistant to the President

Fairchild Camera and Instrument Corp.
464 Ellis St., Mountain View, Calif. 94040
415-962-5011
Dr. C. Lester Hogan, President
Gene Amato, Manager, Engineering Services

Fedders Corp.
Woodbridge Ave., Edison, N.J. 08817
201-549-7200
Salvator Giordano, President

General Electric Co.
570 Lexington Ave., New York, N.Y. 10022
212-750-2000
Reginald H. Jones, President
Dr. E. L. Simons, Manager, Environmental Information Center

General Instrument Corp.
65 Gouverneur St., Newark, N.J. 07104
201-485-2100
Frank G. Hickey, President
Sam Karch, Director, Plant Engineering

General Signal Corp.
280 Park Ave., New York, N.Y. 10017
212-752-1000
Harold A. Strickland, Jr., President
P. R. Fortune, Chairman of the Executive Committee

Gould, Inc.
8550 W. Bryn Mawr Ave., Chicago, Ill. 60631
312-693-2550
William T. Ylvisaker, President
Dr. David L. Douglas, Vice President and Director, Gould Laboratories

Harris-Intertype Corp.
55 Public Sq., Cleveland, Ohio 44114
216-861-7900
Joseph A. Boyd, President
Robert G. Dyke, Vice President, Manufacturing

Hewlett-Packard Co.
1501 Page Mill Rd., Palo Alto, Calif. 94304
415-493-1501
William R. Hewlett, President
R. Glenn Affleck, Environmental Control Coordinator

Hoover Co.
101 E. Maple St., North Canton, Ohio 44720
216-499-9200
Felix N. Mansager, President
D. C. Krammes, Vice President, Engineering

International Telephone and Telegraph Corp.
320 Park Ave., New York, N.Y. 10022
212-752-6000
Harold S. Geneen, President

I-T-E Imperial Corp.
1900 Hamilton St., Philadelphia, Pa. 19130
215-561-1500
William Musham, President

Lear Siegler Inc.
3171 S. Bundy Dr., Santa Monica, Calif. 90406
213-391-0666
Robert T. Campion, President
Dr. Phillips W. Smith, Vice President and General Manager, Environmental Technology Center, 32 Denver, Technological Center, Englewood, Colo. 80110

Appliances and Electronics

Magnavox Co.
345 Park Ave., New York, N.Y. 10022
212-758-6600
Robert H. Platt, President

McGraw-Edison Co.
333 W. River Rd., Elgin, Ill. 60120
312-741-8900
Edward J. Williams, President

Motorola, Inc.
9401 W. Grand Ave., Franklin Park, Ill. 60131
312-451-1000
William J. Weisz, President
Walter B. Scott, Vice President

North American Philips Corp.
100 E. 42 St., New York, N.Y. 10017
212-697-3600
Pieter C. Vink, President

H. K. Porter Co., Inc.
601 Grant St., Pittsburgh, Pa. 15219
412-391-1800
J. S. Morrow, President

Raytheon Co.
141 Spring St., Lexington, Mass. 02173
617-862-6600
Thomas L. Phillips, President
James K. Rogers, Manager, Environmental Quality

RCA Corp.
30 Rockefeller Plaza, New York, N.Y. 10020
212-265-5900
Anthony L. Conrad, President
Samuel M. Convissor, Director, Urban Affairs and Community Relations

Reliance Electric Co.
24701 Euclid Ave., Cleveland, Ohio 44117
216-266-7000
B. Charles Ames, President
Edward F. Lannigan, Vice President, Employee and Community Relations

Republic Corp.
1900 Ave. of the Stars, Century City, Calif. 90067
213-553-3900
Roderick M. Hills, Acting Chief Executive Officer
George A. F. Weida, Vice President, Industrial Relations

Roper Corp.
1905 W. Court St., Kankakee, Ill. 60901
815-939-3641
Charles M. Hoover, President
R. Seagrave, Vice President, Manufacturing Services

Singer Co.
30 Rockefeller Plaza, New York, N.Y. 10020
212-581-4800
Donald P. Kircher, President
Andrew W. Nelson III, Director, Corporate Information

Square D Co.
Executive Plaza, Park Ridge, Ill. 60068
312-774-9200
Mitchell P. Kartalia, President

Studebaker Worthington, Inc.
530 5 Ave., New York, N.Y. 10036
212-697-2345
Leslie T. Welsh, President
Malcolm L. Land, Vice President, Technology

Sunbeam Corp.
5400 W. Roosevelt Rd., Chicago, Ill. 60650
312-854-3500
W. J. Pfeif, President
Thomas H. Sheehan, Vice President, Manufacturing Operations

Teledyne, Inc.
1901 Ave. of the Stars, Los Angeles, Calif. 90067
213-277-3311
George A. Roberts, President

Texas Instruments Inc.
13500 N. Central Expressway, Dallas, Tex. 75222
214-238-2011
Mark Shepherd, Jr., President
Jim Wissemann, Vice President

Varian Associates
611 Hansen Way, Palo Alto, Calif. 94304
415-493-4000
Norman F. Parker, President
Robert E. Worcester, Director, Plant Facilities and Land Management

Western Electric Co.
195 Broadway, New York, N.Y. 10007
212-571-2345
Donald E. Procknow, President
D. R. Chittick, Director of Environmental Control, Western Electric Co., Box 900, Princeton, N.J. 08540

Westinghouse Electric Corp.
3 Gateway Center, Pittsburgh, Pa. 15222
412-255-3800
D. C. Burnham, Chairman
S. W. Herwald, Vice President, Engineering
S. F. Miketic, Vice President, Manufacturing

Whirlpool Corp.
Lake Shore and Monte Rd., Benton Harbor, Mich. 49022
616-926-5000
John H. Platts, President
Thomas H. Goodgame, Director of Environmental Control

Zenith Radio Corp.
1900 N. Austin Ave., Chicago, Ill. 60639
312-745-2000
John J. Nevin, President
Charles R. Hogan, Director, Properties Management

Beverages

Anheuser-Busch, Inc.
721 Pestalozzi St., St. Louis, Mo. 63118
314-577-0577
Richard A. Meyer, President
Edward L. Miles, Corporate Ecology Coordinator

Coca Cola Co.
310 N. Ave. N.W., Atlanta, Ga. 30313
404-897-2121
Charles W. Duncan, Jr., President
Howard H. Hyle, Manager, Environmental Planning, Coca Cola, U.S.A., Drawer 1734, Atlanta, Ga. 30301

Heublein, Inc.
330 New Park Ave., Hartford, Conn. 06101
203-233-7531
Stuart D. Watson, President
John L. Brunen, Director, Facilities, Planning, and Engineering

National Distillers and Chemical Corp.
99 Park Ave., New York, N.Y. 10016
212-697-0700
Drummond C. Bell, President
James G. Couch, Vice President, Engineering

Pabst Brewing Co.
917 W. Juneau, Milwaukee, Wis. 53233
414-271-0230
James C. Windham, President

PepsiCo Inc.
Purchase, N.Y. 10577
914-253-2000
Andrall E. Pearson, President
L. Curtiss, Vice President, Environmental Affairs

Rheingold Corp.
41 E 42 St., New York, N.Y. 10017
212-687-0790
Robert W. Beeler, President
Eugene F. Kelly, Financial Vice President

F and M Schaefer Brewing Co.
430 Kent Ave., Brooklyn, N.Y. 11211
212-387-7000
John T. Morris, President
Henry Fliegler, Manager, Production Operations

Joseph Schlitz Brewing Co.
235 W. Galena St., Milwaukee, Wis. 53201
414-224-5000
Robert A. Uihlein, Jr., President
Dr. J. M. Bennett, Director, Environmental Affairs

Joseph E. Seagram & Son, Inc.
375 Park Ave., New York, N.Y. 10022
212-572-7000
Jack Yogman, President
Marion G. Clower, Chief Ecology Engineer, Joseph E. Seagram & Son, Inc., Box 240, Louisville, Ky. 40201

Broadcasting and Motion Pictures

American Broadcasting Companies
1330 Ave. of the Americas, New York, N.Y. 10019
212-581-7777
Elton H. Rule, President
Robert Sammon, Director, Real Estate, Construction, and General Services

Columbia Broadcasting System, Inc.
51 W. 52 St., New York, N.Y. 10019
212-765-4321
Arthur R. Taylor, President
Clarence Hopper, Vice President, Facilities

Columbia Pictures Industries, Inc.
711 5 Ave., New York, N.Y. 10022
212-751-4400
Leo Jaffe, President
Joseph A. Fischer, Vice President

MCA Inc.
100 Universal City Plaza, Universal City, Calif. 91608
213-985-4321
Lew R. Wasserman, President
Albert A. Dorskind, Vice President

Warner Communications
10 Rockefeller Plaza, New York, N.Y. 10020
212-586-0800
Steven J. Ross, President

CHEMICALS

Air Products and Chemicals Co.
Box 538, Allentown, Pa. 18105
215-395-4911
Edward J. Donley, President
John H. Arnold, Vice President, Corporate Engineering

Airco, Inc.
85 Chestnut Ridge Rd., Montvale, N.J. 07645
212-682-6700
Richard V. Giordano, President
Dr. Gordon J. Arquette, Director, Corporate Planning

Akzona
Asheville, N.C. 28802
704-253-6851
Claude S. Ramsey, President
F. van Haaren, Technical Vice President, American Enka Co., Enka, N.C. 28728

Allied Chemical Corp.
1411 Broadway, New York, N.Y. 10018
212-736-7000
Frederick L. Bissinger, President

American Cyanamid Co.
859 Berdan Ave., Wayne, N.J. 07470
201-831-1234
H. C. Levin, President
John M. Fasoli, Chairman, Environmental Health Coordinating Committee

Armour-Dial, Inc. (Subsidiary of Greyhound Corp.)
111 W. Clarendon, Phoenix, Ariz. 85077
602-248-4000
D.L. Duensing, President
J. C. Hesler, Manager, Corporate Environmental Control Dept., Law Division, Greyhound Corp.

Cabot Corp.
125 High St., Boston, Mass. 02110
617-423-6000
Robert A. Charpie, President
W. F. Greeley, Vice President

Celanese Corp.
522 5 Ave., New York, N.Y. 10036
212-867-2000
John W. Brooks, President
Robert L. Dietrich, Vice President, Manufacturing and Technology

Chemetron Corp.
840 N. Michigan Ave., Chicago, Ill. 60611
312-565-5000
John P. Gallagher, President

Dart Industries, Inc.
8480 Beverly Blvd., Los Angeles, Calif. 90048
213-658-2000
Justin W. Dart, President

De Soto, Inc.
1700 S. Mt. Prospect Rd., Des Plaines, Ill. 60018
312-296-6611
George A. Nichols, President
Douglas K. Larsen, Corporate Environmental Engineer

Diamond Shamrock Co.
300 Union Commerce Bldg., Cleveland, Ohio 44115
216-621-6100
C. A. Cash, President
J. S. Abdnor, Vice President

Dow Chemical Co.
2030 Dow Center, Midland, Mich. 48640
517-636-1000
C. Benson Branch, President
Chester E. Otis, Manager, Environmental Affairs

E. I. DuPont de Nemours & Co.
DuPont Bldg., Wilmington, Del. 19898
302-774-2421
Charles B. McCoy, President
John A. Georges, Director, Environmental Affairs

Ethyl Corp.
330 S. 4 St., Richmond Va. 23219
703-644-6081
Bruce C. Gottwald, President

GAF Corp.
140 W. 51 St., New York, N.Y. 10020
212-582-7600
Dr. Jesse Werner, President

W. R. Grace & Co.
7 Hanover Sq., New York, N.Y. 10005
212-344-1200
Felix E. Larkin, President

Hercules, Inc.
910 Market St., Wilmington, Del. 19899
302-656-9811
Werner C. Brown, President
John R. Ryan, Vice President

Inmont Corp.
1133 Ave. of the Americas, New York, N.Y. 10036
212-765-1100
William R. Barrett, Sr., President
Jack M. Derr, Director of Engineering, Inmont Corp., 609 Lafayette Ave., Hawthorne, N.J. 07506

International Minerals and Chemical Corp.
5401 Old Orchard Rd., Skokie, Ill., 60076
312-362-8100
Richard A. Lenon, President

Koppers Co., Inc.
1301 Koppers Bldg., Pittsburgh, Pa. 15219
412-391-3300
Douglas Grymes, Jr., President
David L. Eynon, Jr., Vice President, Environmental Resources

Lubrizol Corp.
29400 Lakeland Blvd., Wickliffe, Ohio 44092
216-943-4200
Dr. Thomas W. Mastin, President

Monsanto Co.
800 N. Lindbergh Blvd., St. Louis, Mo. 63166
314-694-1000
John W. Hanley, President

Nalco Chemical Co.
180 N. Michigan Ave., Chicago, Ill. 60601
312-822-1200
Robert T. Powers, President
Dr. J. C. Calandra, President, Industrial Bio-Test Div., 1810 Frontage Rd., Northbrook, Ill. 60062

NL Industries, Inc.
111 Broadway, New York, N.Y. 10006
212-732-9400
John B. Henrich, President

Pennwalt Corp.
Pennwalt Bldg., 3 Parkway, Philadelphia, Pa. 19102
215-587-7000
William P. Drake, President
J. Drake Watson, Director, Environmental Affairs and Safety

Reichhold Chemicals, Inc.
525 N. Broadway, White Plains, N.Y. 10603
914-948-6200
Dr. Stefan H. Baum, President

Rohm and Haas Co.
Independence Mall W., Philadelphia, Pa. 19105
215-592-3000
Vincent L. Gregory, President
C. J. Prizer, Vice President

SCM Corp.
299 Park Ave., New York, N.Y. 10017
212-752-2700
Paul H. Elicker, President

Sherwin-Williams Co.
101 Prospect Ave. N.W., Cleveland, Ohio 44115
216-566-2000
Walter O. Spencer, President
F. C. Gaugush, Director, Environmental Control

Stauffer Chemical Co.
Westport, Conn. 06880
212-421-5000
H. Barclay Morley, President
Dr. Myron V. Anthony, Vice President, Environmental Affairs, Stauffer Chemical Co., 1612 K St. N.W., Washington, D.C. 20006

Union Carbide Corp.
270 Park Ave., New York, N.Y. 10017
212-551-3763
William S. Sneath, President
P. P. Huffard, Jr., Director, Environmental Affairs

Witco Chemical Corp.
277 Park Ave., New York, N.Y. 10017
212-826-1000
William Wishnick, President

FARM AND INDUSTRIAL MACHINERY

A-T-O Corp.
4420 Sherwin Rd., Willoughby, Ohio 44094

216-946-9000
Alfred V. Gangnes, President
Jack F. Polgar, Design Engineer

Alco Standard
Valley Forge, Pa. 19481
215-666-0760
Myron S. Gelbach, Jr., President
Dr. Onslow B. Hager, Associate Research and Development Director, Alco Standard Corp., 4 Olney Ave., Cherry Hill, N.J. 08003

Allis Chalmers Corp.
1204 S. 70 St., Milwaukee, Wis. 53214
414-475-2000
David C. Scott, President
Charles W. Parker, Jr., Staff Executive and Vice President

Babcock and Wilcox Co.
161 E. 42 St., New York, N.Y. 10017
212-687-6700
George Zipf, President
Carl Claus, Vice President

Bangor Punta Corp.
1 Greenwich Plaza, Greenwich, Conn. 06830
203-661-3900
David W. Wallace, President
Dudley Phillips, Vice President

Black and Decker Manufacturing Co.
701 E. Joppa Rd., Towson, Md. 21204
301-828-3940
Francis P. Lucier, President
John M. Connelly, Director, Facilities Engineering

Briggs and Stratton Corp.
3300 N. 124 St., Wauwatosa, Wis. 53201
414-461-1212
Vincent R. Shicly, President

Brunswick Corp.
69 W. Washington St., Chicago, Ill. 60602
312-982-6000
K. B. Abernathy, President
J. A. Anthony, Director, Manufacturing

Bucyrus Erie Co.
1100 Milwaukee Ave., South Milwaukee, Wis. 53172
414-762-0900
Eugene P. Berg, President
H. J. Row, Director, Public Relations

Carrier Corp.
Carrier Pkwy., Syracuse, N.Y. 13201
315-463-8411

William J. Bailey, President
William Westlake, Manager, Air Quality Systems

Caterpillar Tractor Co.
100 N.E. Adams St., Peoria, Ill. 61602
309-675-1000
Lee L. Morgan, President
W. W. Dodge, Manager, Environmental Control

Cincinnati Milacron, Inc.
4701 Marburg Ave., Cincinnati, Ohio 45209
513-841-8100
James A. D. Geier, President
Harold V. Edwards, Vice President, Personnel and Community Relations

Clark Equipment Co.
324 E. Dewey Ave., Buchanan, Mich. 49107
616-697-8000
Bert E. Phillips, President
L. A. Jarvis, Environmental Control Coordinator

Cooper Industries, Inc.
First National City Bank Bldg., Houston, Tex. 77002
713-224-9181
E. L. Miller, President
Each division is responsible for its own environmental matters.

Cummins Engine Co., Inc.
1000 5 St., Columbus, Ind. 47201
812-372-7211
Henry B. Schacht, President
David E. Wulfhorst, Director, Environmental Management

Deere & Co.
John Deere Rd., Moline, Ill. 61265
309-792-8000
Ellwood F. Curtis, President

Dresser Industries, Inc.
Box 718, Dallas, Tex. 75221
214-748-6411
John V. James, President
V. Rock Grundman, Attorney

Ex-Cell-O Corp.
Box 386, Detroit, Mich. 48232
313-868-3900
Edward J. Giblin, President
Carl Roberts, Industrial Engineer

Federal-Mogul Corp.
Box 1966, Detroit, Mich. 48235

313-444-8800
Thomas F. Russell, President
Jerry E. Cardillo, Vice President, Engineering and Manufacturing

FMC Corp.
1105 Coleman Ave., San Jose, Calif. 95110
408-289-0111
Robert H. Malott, President
Raymond M. Porter, Division Manager, FMC Corp., Environmental Equipment Div., 2240 W. Diversey Ave., Chicago, Ill. 60647

Foster-Wheeler Corp.
100 S. Orange Ave., Livingston, N.J. 07039
201-533-1100
Frank A. Lee, President
William F. Bischoff, Manager, Environmental Systems Dept.

Gardner Denver Co.
Gardner Expressway, Quincy, Ill. 62301
217-222-5400
C. H. Rieman, President
Joe Holloway, Legal Counsel

Hobart Manufacturing Co.
711 Pennsylvania Ave., Troy, Ohio 45373
513-335-7171
David B. Meeker, President
Richard L. Lenox, Director, Facilities Engineering

Hyster Co.
2902 N.E. Clackamas, Portland, Oreg. 97232
503-288-5011
William H. Kilkenny, President

Ingersoll Rand Co.
Box 636, Woodcliff Lake, N.J. 07675
201-573-0123
D. Wayne Hallstein, President
M. W. Grant, Vice President

Joy Manufacturing Co.
Oliver Bldg., Pittsburgh, Pa. 15222
412-471-2140
James W. Wilcock, President

Walter Kidde & Co., Inc.
9 Brighton Rd., Clifton, N.J. 07012
201-777-6500
Fred R. Sullivan, President

Koehring Co.
780 N. Water St., Milwaukee, Wis. 53202
414-273-2300
Orville R. Mertz, President

E. C. Brekelbaum, Vice President, Manufacturing

Midland and Ross Corp.
55 Public Sq., Cleveland, Ohio 44113
216-771-4800
Harry J. Bolwell, President

Otis Elevator Co.
260 11 Ave., New York, N.Y. 10001
212-244-8000
Ralph A. Weller, President

Outboard Marine Corp.
100 Pershing Rd., Waukegan, Ill. 60085
312-689-6200
William C. Scott, President
Howard F. Larson, Vice President, Environmental Affairs, Outboard Marine Corp., 4143 N. 27 St., Milwaukee, Wis. 53201

Rex Chainbelt, Inc.
111 E. Wisconsin Ave., Milwaukee, Wis. 53201
414-384-3000
Robert V. Krikorian, President
George H. Woodland, Vice President, Operations

Sundstrand Corp.
4751 Harrison Ave., Rockford, Ill. 61101
815-226-6200
Carl L. Sadler, President
Leo E. Keenan, Corporate Director, Fire, Safety, and Security

Tecumseh Products Co.
E. Patterson and S. Ottawa Sts., Tecumseh, Mich. 49286
313-423-7411
William E. Macbeth, President
C. G. Desmet, Corporate Environmental Control Dept.

Timken Co.
1835 Dueber Ave. S.W., Canton, Ohio 44706
216-453-4511
H. E. Markley, President
J. E. Lieser, Chairman, Environmental Control Committee

Trane Co.
3600 Pammel Creek Rd., La Crosse, Wis. 54601
608-782-8000
Thomas Hancock, President
Robert Staley, Corporate Development

USM Corp.
140 Federal St., Boston, Mass. 02107
617-542-9100
Herbert W. Jarvis, President
T. L. Williams, Corporate Coordinator, OSHA and Pollution Control

Wean United Inc.
3 Gateway Center, Pittsburgh, Pa. 15222
412-261-4534
Raymond J. Wean, Jr., President
R. M. Reisacher, Senior Vice President

White Consolidated Industries, Inc.
11770 Berea Rd., Cleveland, Ohio 44111
216-252-3700
Roy H. Holdt, President

Food

Agway, Inc.
333 Butternut Dr., Syracuse, N.Y. 13214
315-477-7061
Harold G. Soper, President
Norwood K. Talbert, Director, Environmental Quality and Engineering, Agway, Inc., Box 1333, Syracuse, N.Y. 13201

Allied Mills, Inc.
110 N. Wacker Dr., Chicago, Ill. 60606
312-346-5060
Roy E. Folck, Jr., President
G. M. Patton, Director, Manufacturing

American Bakeries Co.
10 S. Riverside Plaza, Chicago, Ill. 60606
312-645-7400
L. Arthur Cushman, Jr., President

American Beef Packers
7000 W. Center Rd., Omaha, Nebr. 68106
402-391-4700
Frank R. West, President

Amstar Corp.
1251 Ave. of the Americas, New York, N.Y. 10020
212-489-9000
Robert T. Quittmeyer, President
Thomas W. Baker, Manager, Environmental Technology, Corporate Quality Assurance Dept.

Anderson, Clayton & Co.
Tennessee Bldg., Houston, Tex. 77002
713-224-6641
Thomas J. Barlow, President
W. A. Jacob, Vice President

Archer-Daniels-Midland Co.
4666 Faries Pkwy., Decatur, Ill. 62525
217-423-2571
Donald B. Walker, President

Associated Milk Producers, Inc.
800 N.W. Loop 410, San Antonio, Tex. 78216
512-341-8651
John Butterbrodt, President
Bob Lilly

Beatrice Foods Co.
120 S. LaSalle St., Chicago, Ill. 60603
312-782-3820
Don L. Grantham, President
Dr. Peter Noznick, Director, Research

Borden, Inc.
277 Park Ave., New York, N.Y. 10017
212-573-4000
Augustine Marusi, President
Louis Janik, Corporate Coordinator, Environmental Quality, Borden, Inc., 1840 Mackenzie Dr., Columbus, Ohio 43220

Campbell Soup Co.
375 Memorial Ave., Camden, N.J. 08101
609-964-4000
Harold A. Shaub, President
Louis C. Gilde, Director, Environmental Engineering

Campbell Taggart, Inc.
6211 Lemmon Ave., Dallas, Tex. 75209
214-352-4861
C. B. Lane, President

Carnation Co.
5045 Wilshire Blvd., Los Angeles, Calif. 90036
213-931-1911
H. E. Olson, President
Clarke Nelson, Vice President

Castle and Cooke, Inc.
130 Merchant St., Honolulu, Hawaii 96802
805-848-6611
Malcolm MacNaughton, President
Frederick C. Gross, Director, Environmental Standards, c/o Waialua Sugar Co.

Central Soya Co., Inc.
1300 Fort Wayne Bank Bldg., Fort Wayne, Ind. 46802
219-422-8541
Joseph F. Jones, President

Jack Rosenberger, Vice President, Manufacturing

Conagra Corp.
500 Kiewit Plaza, Omaha, Nebr. 68131
402-346-8004
J. Allan Mactier, President

Consolidated Foods
135 S. LaSalle St., Chicago, Ill. 60603
312-726-6414
William Teets, President

CPC International, Inc.
International Plaza, Englewood Cliffs, N.J. 07632
201-894-2410
James W. McKee, Jr., President

Dairylea Cooperative
1250 Broadway, New York, N.Y. 10001
212-594-4200
James Donnan, President
Ernest Ellison, Manager, Control Department; Chairman, Environmental Committee

Del Monte Corp.
215 Fremont St., San Francisco, Calif. 94119
415-781-7760
Richard G. Landis, President
A. W. Hansen, Director, Consumer and Environmental Protection

DiGiorgio Corp.
1 Maritime Plaza, San Francisco, Calif. 94111
415-362-8972
Robert C. McCracken, President

Peter Eckrich & Sons, Inc.
3515 Hobson Rd., Fort Wayne, Ind. 46805
219-484-0761
Donald P. Eckrich, President
Bernard Kaminski, Chief Mechanical Engineer

Fairmont Foods Co.
3201 Farnam St., Omaha, Nebr. 68101
405-345-9500
LeRoy Melcher, Sr., President
W. E. Logan, Vice President, Administration

Federal Co.
Sterick Bldg., Memphis, Tenn. 38103
901-525-7382
W. L. Taylor, President

General Foods Corp.
250 North St., White Plains, N.Y. 10605
914-694-2500

C. W. Cook, President
David E. James, Director, Corporate Quality Assurance

General Host Corp.
245 Park Ave., New York, N.Y. 10017
212-661-5300
Edward H. Hoornstra, President
Louis A. Guzzetti, Corporate Counsel

General Mills, Inc.
9200 Wayzata Blvd., Minneapolis, Minn. 55440
612-540-2311
James A. Summer, President
Donald J. Thimsen, Chief Environmental Control Engineer

Gerber Products Co.
445 State St., Fremont, Mich. 49412
616-928-2000
Arthur J. Frens, President
Paul F. Leavitt, Assistant Chief Engineer

Gold Kist Corp.
3348 Peachtree Rd., Atlanta, Ga. 30301
404-237-2251
Warren P. Sewell, President
Joe Cox, Director, Engineering
G. A. Burson, Executive Vice President

Great Western United Corp.
Equitable Bldg., Denver, Colo. 80202
303-893-4300
Robert G. Everett, President
Bruce Ducker, Vice President, Legal Affairs

Green Giant Co.
1200 Commerce St., LeSueur, Minn. 56058
612-665-3515
C. J. Tempas, President
J. G. Martland, Vice President, Research and Development

Greyhound Corp.
Greyhound Tower Bldg., Phoenix, Ariz. 85004
602-248-4000
Raymond F. Shaffer, President
J. C. Hesler, Manager, Corporate Environmental Control Dept.

H. J. Heinz Co.
1062 Progress St., Pittsburgh, Pa. 15212
412-231-5700
R. Burt Gookin, President

Hershey Foods Corp.
19 E. Chocolate Ave., Hershey, Pa. 17033

717-534-4200
Harold S. Mohler, President
Dr. Paul W. Hess, Manager, Environmental Affairs

George A. Hormel & Co.
501 16 Ave. N.E., Austin, Minn. 55912
507-437-5611
I. J. Holton, President
C. D. Nyberg, Secretary

Hygrade Food Products, Inc.
11801 Mack Ave., Detroit, Mich. 48214
313-355-1100
Richard T. Berg, President

International Multifoods Corp.
1200 Investors Bldg., Minneapolis, Minn. 55402
612-339-8444
William G. Phillips, President
Darrell M. Runke, Executive Vice President, Operations

Interstate Brands Corp.
12 E. Armour Blvd., Kansas City, Mo. 64111
816-561-6600
Ernest B. Hueter, President
Karl M. Ellington, Chief Engineer, Cake Operations
John W. Glover, Chief Engineer, Bread Operations

Iowa Beef Processors, Inc.
Dakota City, Nebr. 68731
402-494-2061
J. Fred Haigler, President
Jimmie Chittenden, Manager, Technical Services

Kane-Miller Corp.
355 Lexington Ave., New York, N.Y. 10017
212-687-3920
Daniel Kane, President

Keebler Co.
677 Larch Ave., Elmhurst, Ill. 60126
312-833-2900
Edwin L. Cox, President
John D. Thomas, Vice President, Industrial Relations

Kraftco Corp.
Kraftco Court, Glenview, Ill. 60025
312-998-2000
William O. Beers, President
Mr. K. S. Watson, Director, Environmental Control, Kraftco Corp., 801 Waukegan Rd., Glenview, Ill. 60025

Land O'Lakes
614 McKinley Pl., Minneapolis, Minn. 55413
612-331-6330
D. H. Henry, President
Philip F. Stocker, Vice President, General Services

Libby-McNeill and Libby
200 S. Michigan Ave., Chicago, Ill. 60604
312-341-4111
Douglas B. Wells, President

Thomas J. Lipton, Inc.
800 Sylvan Ave., Englewood Cliffs, N.J. 07632
201-567-8000
W. Gardner Barker, President
Jack W. Riehm, Vice President, External Affairs

LTV Corp.
Box 5003, Dallas, Tex. 75222
214-742-9555
Paul Thayer, President
R. L. Dahlberg, Director, Corporate Material and Services

Oscar Mayer & Co.
910 Mayer Ave., Madison, Wis. 53701
608-241-3311
P. Goff Beach, President
A. Paul Bowman, Group Vice President

Missouri Beef Packers, Inc.
Amarillo Bldg., Amarillo, Tex. 79105
806-373-6621
David LaFleur, President

Monfort of Colorado
Box G, Greeley, Colo. 80603
303-353-8200
Kenneth W. Monfort, President

Nabisco, Inc.
425 Park Ave., New York, N.Y. 10022
212-751-5000
Robert M. Schaeberle, President
E. A. Otocka, Senior Vice President, Facility Planning

National Industries, Inc.
510 W. Broadway, Louisville, Ky. 40202
502-583-7602
Stanley R. Yarmuth, President
George Veach, Corporate Director, Facilities

Needham Packing Co.
220 Badgeraw Bldg., Sioux City, Iowa 51101
712-252-4457

James R. McDonald, Chairman
John Lindquist, Plant Manager, Sioux By-Products Div.

Norton Simon, Inc.
277 Park Ave., New York, N.Y. 10017
212-832-1000
David J. Mahoney, President
Jill Flores, Social Action Coordinator

Pet, Inc.
400 4 St., St. Louis, Mo. 63102
314-621-5400
Boyd F. Schenk, President

Pillsbury Co.
608 2 Ave. S., Minneapolis, Minn. 55402
612-330-4966
Terrance Hanold, Chairman of the Executive Committee
Dean McNeal, Group Vice President

Quaker Oats Co.
Merchandise Mart Plaza, Chicago, Ill. 60654
312-222-7111
Robert D. Stuart, Jr., President
Thomas E. Mole, Manager, Environmental Control

Ralston Purina Co.
835 S. 8 St., St. Louis, Mo. 63102
314-241-3600
Warren M. Shapleigh, President
F. J. Lane, Chairman, Corporate Committee on Environment

Rath Packing Co.
Elm and Sycamore, Waterloo, Iowa 50703
319-235-8900
Harry G. Slife, President

Spencer Foods, Inc.
Box 512, Spencer, Iowa 51301
712-262-4250
Jerry P. Kozney, President

A. E. Staley Manufacturing Co.
Eldorado at 22 St., Decatur, Ill. 62525
217-423-4411
Donald E. Nordlund, President
William P. Hagenbach, Director, Environmental Sciences

Standard Brands, Inc.
625 Madison Ave., New York, N.Y. 10022
212-759-4400
Henry Weigl, President
W. C. Neumann, Director, Environmental Control

Stokely-Van Camp, Inc.
941 N. Meridian St., Indianapolis, Ind. 46204
317-631-2551
Alfred J. Stokely, President
Fred Laird, Legal Dept.

Swift & Co.
115 W. Jackson Blvd., Chicago, Ill. 60604
312-431-2000
Robert W. Reneker, President
Lawrence E. Klinger, Director, Public Responsibility

United Brands Co.
245 Park Ave., New York, N.Y. 10017
212-697-7560
Eli M. Black, President

Ward Foods, Inc.
2 Penn Plaza, New York, N.Y. 10001
212-594-5400
Jeff Jaffe, President

William Wrigley Jr. Co.
410 N. Michigan Ave., Chicago, Ill. 60611
312-644-2121
William Wrigley, President

FURNITURE

National Service Industries, Inc.
1180 Peachtree St. N.E., Atlanta, Ga. 30309
404-892-2400
Edwin Zaban, President

Simmons Co.
280 Park Ave., New York, N.Y. 10022
212-697-2300
Joseph V. Quarles, President

GLASS, CEMENT, GYPSUM, AND CONCRETE

Anchor Hocking Glass Corp.
109 N. Broad St., Lancaster, Ohio 43130
614-653-3131
Roger H. Hetzel, President
Charles J. Arnsbarger, Director, Public Affairs

Brockway Glass Co., Inc.
McCullough Ave., Brockway, Pa. 15824
814-268-3015
Stuart Holmquest, President
H. Taylor Winner, Director, Environmental Affairs

Glass, Cement, Gypsum, and Concrete

Carborundum Co.
Box 337, Niagara Falls, N.Y. 14302
716-278-2000
William H. Wendel, President
Henry H. Hemenway, Group Vice President, Environment Systems

Ceco Corp.
5601 W. 26 St., Chicago, Ill. 60650
312-242-2000
Ned A. Ochiltree, Jr., President
E. L. Lasser, Plant Engineer, Lemont Manufacturing Co., Lemont, Ill. 60439

Certain-teed Products Corp.
Valley Forge, Pa. 19481
215-687-5000
Malcolm Meyer, President
Stephen E. Monoky, Environmental Control and Safety Director

Corning Glass Works
Corning, N.Y. 14830
607-962-4444
Dr. Thomas C. MacAvoy, President
Mr. Hugh L. Kline, Pollution Abatement Consultant, Facilities Div.

Flintkote Co.
400 Westchester Ave., White Plains, N.Y. 10604
914-761-7400
James D. Moran, President
John R. Szal, Manager, Corporate Engineering

Ideal Basic Industries
821 17 St., Denver, Colo. 80202
303-222-5661
Mayfield L. Shilling, President
J. L. Gilliland, Technical Director

Interpace Corp.
260 Cherry Hill Rd., Parsippany, N.J. 07054
201-335-1111
Hugh F. Kennison, President

Johns-Manville Corp.
Greenwood Plaza, Denver, Colo. 80217
303-770-1000
W. Richard Goodwin, President
Internal: Jack Hesse, Senior Vice President, Production and Engineering
External: Jack Solon, Vice President, Environmental Affairs

Libby-Owens-Ford Co.
811 Madison Ave., Toledo, Ohio 43624
419-242-5781
Robert G. Wingerter, President
Richard E. Warren, Vice President, Engineering

Lone Star Industries, Inc.
1 Greenwich Plaza, Greenwich, Conn. 06830
203-661-3100
John Kringel, President
F. E. Purcell, Vice President; Assistant to the President

National Gypsum Co.
325 Delaware Ave., Buffalo, N.Y. 14202
716-852-5880
Darwin D. Tucker, President
F. H. Zimmerman, Corporate Director, Safety and Environmental Health

Norton Co.
1 New Bond St., Worcester, Mass. 01606
617-853-1000
Robert Cushman, President
Richard S. Johnson, Coordinator, Environment, Health, and Safety

Owens Corning Fiberglas Corp.
Box 901, Toledo, Ohio 43601
419-259-3000
William Boeschenstein, President
S. H. Thomas, Director, Environmental Services

Owens-Illinois, Inc.
Box 1035, Toledo, Ohio 43601
419-242-6543
Edwin D. Dodd, President
K. G. VanTine, Vice President, Director, Environmental Affairs

PPG Industries, Inc.
1 Gateway Center, Pittsburgh, Pa. 15222
412-434-3131
Joseph A. Neubauer, President
William Carpenter, Vice President, Corporate Relations

United States Gypsum Co.
101 S. Wacker Dr., Chicago, Ill. 60606
312-321-4000
Edward W. Duffy, President
J. F. Schroeder, Manager, Environmental Protection

Vulcan Materials Co.
1 Office Park Circle, Birmingham, Ala. 35223
205-879-0421
John M. Lambert, President
Ben Greene, Environmental Relations Manager

Jewelry and Silverware

Insilco Corp.
1000 Research Pkwy., Meriden, Conn. 06450
203-634-2000
Durand B. Blatz, President
Henry E. Bartels, Vice President, Operations

Leather and Leather Products

Brown Group
8400 Maryland Ave., St. Louis, Mo. 63105
314-997-7500
W. L. H. Griffin, President
Herbert M. Patton, Jr., Vice President, Research and Development

Interco, Inc.
10 S. Broadway, St. Louis, Mo. 63102
314-231-1100
John K. Riedy, President

U.S. Shoe Corp.
1658 Herald Ave., Cincinnati, Ohio 45212
513-731-5010
Philip Barach, President
Robert Stix, Vice President and Director, Administration

Measuring, Scientific, and Photographic Equipment

Becton, Dickinson & Co.
Stanley St., East Rutherford, N.J. 07073
201-939-9000
Fairleigh S. Dickinson, Jr., President
Leon R. Becker, Corporate Director, Safety and Loss Prevention

Bell and Howell Co.
7100 McCormick Rd., Chicago, Ill. 60645
312-262-1600
Henry E. Bowes, President
Charles G. Weigand, Corporate Director, Industrial Engineering

Cenco Instruments Corp.
2600 S. Kostner Ave., Chicago, Ill. 60623
312-277-8300
Ralph C. Read, President

Eastman Kodak Co.
343 State St., Rochester, N.Y. 14608
716-325-2000
Walter A. Fallon, President

Johnson and Johnson
501 George St., New Brunswick, N.J. 08903
201-524-0400
Richard B. Sellars, President
John J. Heldrich, Corporate Vice President, Administration

Johnson Service Co.
507 E. Michigan St., Milwaukee, Wis. 53202
414-276-9200
F. L. Brengel, President

Minnesota Mining and Manufacturing
3M Center, St. Paul, Minn. 55101
612-733-1110
Raymond H. Herzog, President
Dr. Joseph T. Ling, Director, Environmental Engineering and Pollution Control

Polaroid Corp.
549 Technology Sq., Cambridge, Mass. 02139
617-864-6000
Edwin H. Land, President

Sybron Corp.
1100 Midtown Tower, Rochester, N.Y. 14604
716-546-4040
William G. von Berg, President
Theodore B. Roessel, Patent Counsel, Assistant Secretary, and Technical Administrator

Talley Industries, Inc.
3500 N. Greenfield Rd., Mesa, Ariz. 85201
602-969-7411
Franz G. Talley, President

Metal Manufacturing

Allegheny Ludlum Industries
537 Smithfield St., Pittsburgh, Pa. 15222
412-261-5300
Robert J. Buckley, President
John D. Paulus, Vice President, Public Relations and Public Affairs, Allegheny Ludlum Industries, Inc., Oliver Bldg., Pittsburgh, Pa. 15222

Aluminum Co. of America
1501 Alcoa Bldg., Pittsburgh, Pa. 15219
412-553-4545
W. H. Krome George, President
Miles D. Colwell, M.D., Vice President, Health and Environment

American Metal Climax, Inc.
1270 Ave. of the Americas, New York, N.Y. 10020
212-757-9700
Donald J. Donahue, President
Donald F. Stephens, Manager, Environmental Services Group, American Metal Climax, Inc., 4704 Harlan, Denver, Colo. 80212

American Smelting and Refining Co.
120 Broadway, New York, N.Y. 10005
212-732-9500
Ralph L. Hennebach, President
K. W. Nelson, Director, Dept. of Environmental Sciences, ASARCO, 700 West, Salt Lake City, Utah 84119

Amsted Industries, Inc.
3700 Prudential Plaza, Chicago, Ill. 60601
312-645-1700
Goff Smith, President

Anaconda Co.
25 Broadway, New York, N.Y. 10004
212-422-6300
John B. M. Place, President
George W. Wunder, Vice President, Technology

Armco Steel Corp.
703 Curtis St., Middletown, Ohio 45042
513-425-6541
Donald E. Reichelderfer, President
John E. Barker, Director, Environmental Engineering

Bethlehem Steel Corp.
701 E. 3 St., Bethlehem, Pa. 18016
215-694-2424
Lewis W. Foy, President
Dr. David M. Anderson, Manager of Environmental Quality Control, Industrial Relations Dept.

Cerro Corp.
300 Park Ave., New York, N.Y. 10022
212-688-8822
C. Gordon Murphy, President
Irving Hauser, Director of Engineering, Cerro Mining Co.

Chromalloy American Corp.
111 S. Meramec, Clayton, Mo. 63105
314-721-8163
I. A. Shepard, President
Kurt Roth, Executive Vice President

Commercial Metals Co.
3000 Diamond Park Dr., Dallas, Tex. 75247
214-631-4120
Charles W. Merritt, President

Cyclops Corp.
650 Washington Rd., Pittsburgh, Pa. 15228
412-343-4000
William H. Knoell, President
D. Kinker, Director, Environmental Controls Empire, Detroit Steel Corp., Portsmouth, Ohio 45662

Diversified Industries, Inc.
7701 Forsyth Blvd., Clayton, Mo. 63105
314-862-8200
Sam Fox, President
Phillip Marr, Manager, Manufacturing, Engineering

EASCO Corp.
201 N. Charles St., Baltimore, Md. 21201
301-837-9550
Richard P. Sullivan, President

General Cable Corp.
730 3 Ave., New York, N.Y. 10017
212-986-3800
Robert P. Jensen, President
D. C. Searls, Vice President, Secretary, and General Counsel

Howmet Corp.
475 Steamboat Rd., Greenwich, Conn. 06830
203-661-4600
Jean L. Loyer, President
T. Operhall, Vice President, Gas Turbine Components Group
J. P. Altorffer, Vice President, Aluminum Group
Marcel Paul, Vice President, Aluminum Reduction Group

Illinois Central Industries, Inc.
135 E. 11 Pl., Chicago, Ill. 60605
312-939-5313
Stanley E. G. Hillman, President
A. J. Dolby, Pollution Control Engineer, Illinois Central Gulf Railroad Co.

Inland Steel Co.
30 W. Monroe St., Chicago, Ill. 60603
312-346-0300
Michael Tenebaum, President
John R. Brough, Director, Air and Water Control

Interlake, Inc.
310 S. Michigan Ave., Chicago, Ill. 60604
312-663-1700

Reynold C. MacDonald, President
F. K. Armour, Vice President, Engineering and Research

Kaiser Aluminum and Chemical Corp.
300 Lakeside Dr., Oakland, Calif. 94612
415-271-2211
Cornell C. Maier, President
W. R. (Bill) Smith, Manager, Environmental Control

Kaiser Steel Corp.
300 Lakeside Dr., Oakland, Calif. 94612
415-271-2211
Jack J. Carlson, President
John D. Saussaman, Vice President and General Manager, Resources Div.

Keystone Consolidated Industries, Inc.
411 Hamilton Blvd., Peoria, Ill. 61602
309-676-8000
John R. Sommer, President
Warren G. Reynolds, Corporate Secretary

Lykes-Youngstown
821 Gravier St., New Orleans, La. 70112
504-522-6661
Frank Nemec, President

McLouth Steel Corp.
300 S. Livernois, Detroit, Mich. 48217
313-843-3000
Thomas J. Johnson, President
William V. Murphy, Assistant Vice President, Public Affairs and Public Relations

National Steel Corp.
2800 Grant Bldg., Pittsburgh, Pa. 15219
412-471-5600
George A. Stinson, President
Fred E. Tucker, Vice President, Environmental Control

Northwest Industries, Inc.
400 W. Madison St., Chicago, Ill. 60606
312-263-4200
Ben W. Heineman, President

NVF Co.
Maryland and Beach, Wilmington, Del. 19899
302-239-5281
Walter E. Gregg, President
James K. McCauley, Vice President, Environmental Control

Olin Corp.
120 Long Ridge Rd., Stamford, Conn. 06904
203-356-2000

James F. Towey, President
Everett Bellows, Vice President; Chairman, Environmental Control Resources Council

Penn-Dixie Cement Corp.
1345 Ave. of the Americas, New York, N.Y. 10019
212-687-5000
Jerome Castle, President

Phelps Dodge Corp.
300 Park Ave., New York, N.Y. 10022
212-751-3200
George B. Munroe, President
Dr. James D. Forrester, Director, Environmental Engineering and Research, Phelps Dodge Corp., Box 2265, Tucson, Ariz. 85701

Republic Steel Corp.
25 Prospect Ave. W., Cleveland, Ohio 44115
216-574-7100
W. B. Boyer, President
Perry E. Miller, Director, Environmental Control

Revere Copper and Brass, Inc.
605 3 Ave., New York, N.Y. 10016
212-687-4111
William F. Collins, President
J. M. Kennedy, Vice President

Reynolds Metals Co.
6601 W. Broad St., Richmond, Va. 23261
703-282-2311
Richard S. Reynolds, Jr., President
R. B. Newman, Vice President, Corporate Operating Services

St. Joe Minerals Corp.
250 Park Ave., New York, N.Y. 10017
212-986-7474
John C. Duncan, President
Peter B. Nalle, Vice President

Scovill Manufacturing Co.
99 Mill St., Waterbury, Conn. 06720
203-757-6061
John C. Helies, President

Signode Corp.
3600 W. Lake Ave., Glenview, Ill. 60025
312-724-6100
J. Milton Moon, President
James O. Kovar, Administrative Assistant to Vice President, Manufacturing

U.S. Steel Corp.
71 Broadway, New York, N.Y. 10006

212-558-4444
Edgar B. Speer, President
Earl W. Mallick, Vice President, Environmental Control, U.S. Steel Corp., 600 Grant St., Pittsburgh, Pa. 15234

UV Industries
235 E. 42 St., New York, N.Y. 10017
212-682-0800
Martin Horowitz, President

Wheeling Pittsburgh Steel Corp.
4 Gateway Center, Pittsburgh, Pa. 15222
412-471-3600
Robert E. Lauterbach, President

Metal Products

Allied Products Corp.
208 S. LaSalle St., Chicago, Ill. 60604
312-261-3556
S. S. Sherman, President
Larry D. Hansbarger, Vice President, Manufacturing and Physical Resources, 223 E. Bacon St., Hillsdale, Mich. 49242

American Can Co.
American La., Greenwich, Conn. 06830
212-972-4700
Harry S. Howard, Jr., President
H. Blair Smith, Vice President, Environmental Affairs

American Chain and Cable Co., Inc.
929 Connecticut Ave., Bridgeport, Conn. 06602
203-335-2511
Wilmot F. Wheeler, Jr., President
C. Lawrence Warwick, Director, Governmental Agency Relations

American Standard Inc.
40 W. 40 St., New York, N.Y. 10018
212-484-5100
William A. Marquard, President

Chicago Bridge and Iron Co.
901 W. 22 St., Oak Brook, Ill. 60523
312-654-1700
Marvin G. Mitchell, President

City Investing Co.
767 5 Ave., New York, N.Y. 10022
212-759-5300
George T. Scharffenberger, President
John Silver, Vice President, Corporate Communications

Colt Industries, Inc.
430 Park Ave., New York, N.Y. 10022
212-980-3500
David I. Margolis, President
Dr. Andrew C. Hilton, Executive Vice President

Combustion Engineering Inc.
277 Park Ave., New York, N.Y. 10017
212-826-7100
Arthur J. Santry, Jr., President
John H. Fernandes, Coordinator, Environmental Control Systems

Container Corp. of America
1 First National Plaza, Chicago, Ill. 60670
312-786-5500
F. S. Cripler, President
Paul E. Trout, Director, Environmental Control, Container Corp. of America, Oaks, Pa. 19456

Continental Can Co., Inc.
633 3 Ave., New York, N.Y. 10017
212-551-7000
Robert S. Hatfield, President
Donald V. Earnshaw, Vice President, Environmental Affairs

Crane Co.
300 Park Ave., New York, N.Y. 10022
212-752-3600
Dante C. Fabiani, President

Crown Cork and Seal Co., Inc.
9300 Ashton Rd., Philadelphia, Pa. 19136
215-673-5100
John F. Connelly, President

Eagle-Picher Industries, Inc.
American Bldg., Cincinnati, Ohio 45202
513-721-7010
William D. Atteberry, President
Donald R. Carter, Director, Environmental Standards

Emhart Corp.
950 Cottage Grove Rd., Bloomfield, Conn. 06002
203-242-8551
T. Mitchell Ford, President
Walter A. Jaeger, Vice President, Manufacturing Services

Gillette Co.
Prudential Tower Bldg., Boston, Mass. 02199
617-261-8500
William G. Salatich, President
Paul O'Friel, Director, Public Affairs

Gulf and Western Industries
1 Gulf and Western Plaza, New York, N.Y. 10023
212-333-7000
David N. Judelson, President

Harsco Corp.
Camp Hill, Pa. 17011
717-233-8771
J. G. Underwood, President
Fred J. Mattscheck, Vice President, Administration

Hoover Ball and Bearing Co.
Box 1003, Ann Arbor, Mich. 48106
313-429-2552
John F. Daly, President

National Can Corp.
5959 S. Cicero Ave., Chicago, Ill. 60638
312-735-2400
Frank W. Considine, President
Clifford Klotz, Manager, Environmental Affairs, National Can Corp., Midway Center, Chicago, Ill. 60638

Norris Industries, Inc.
5215 S. Boyle Ave., Los Angeles, Calif. 90058
213-588-7111
Kenneth T. Norris, Jr., President

Parker-Hannifin Corp.
17325 Euclid Ave., Cleveland, Ohio 44112
216-531-3000
Patrick S. Parker, President

H. H. Robertson Co.
2 Gateway Center, Pittsburgh, Pa. 15222
412-281-3200
Douglas A. Jones, President
Dr. F. G. Singleton, Senior Vice President; Director

Rockwell Manufacturing Co.
400 N. Lexington Ave., Pittsburgh, Pa. 15208
412-214-8400
Louis Putze, President
E. I. Henning, Vice President

Stanley Works
195 Lake St., New Britain, Conn. 06052
203-225-5111
D. W. Davis, President

Universal Oil Products Co.
30 Algonquin Rd., Des Plaines, Ill. 60016
312-824-1155
J. O. Logan, President
R. N. Speer, Vice President, Manufacturing

Wallace-Murray Corp.
299 Park Ave., New York, N.Y. 10017
212-758-4000
Fred R. Raach, President
Joseph A. Abbott, Vice President, Corporate Communications

Whittaker Corp.
10880 Wilshire Blvd., Los Angeles, Calif. 90024
213-475-9411
Joseph F. Alibrandi, President
S. L. Spiller, Corporate Administrative Services

MINING

Coastal States Gas Producing Co.
Petroleum Tower, Corpus Christi, Tex. 78403
512-883-5211
Harry G. Fair, President
Harry A. Brown, President, Coastal States Petrochemical Co., Corpus Christi, Tex.

Cyprus Mines Corp.
523 W. 6 St., Los Angeles, Calif. 90014
213-629-5771
Kenneth Lieber, President

Eastern Gas and Fuel Associates
2900 Prudential Tower, Boston, Mass. 02199
617-262-3500
Eli Goldston, President

Hanna Mining Co.
100 Erieview Plaza, Cleveland, Ohio 44114
216-523-3111
Walter A. Marting, President
M. J. Doyle, Director, Environmental Affairs

Newmont Mining Corp.
300 Park Ave., New York, N.Y. 10022
212-753-4800
Plato Malozemoff, President
Robert H. Ramsey, Assistant to the President

Texas Gulf, Inc.
200 Park Ave., New York, N.Y. 10017
212-972-5000
Charles F. Fogarty, President
Dr. James R. West, Vice President, Research and Engineering

MISCELLANEOUS MANUFACTURING

Armstrong Cork Co.
Liberty and Charlotte Sts., Lancaster, Pa. 17603

717-397-0611
J. H. Binns, President
Milton D. Ford, Vice President, Technical Services

Bath Industries, Inc.
2100 N. Mayfair Rd., Milwaukee, Wis. 53226
414-778-2100
Robert R. Greenwalt, President

MOTOR VEHICLES AND PARTS

American Motors Corp.
14250 Plymouth Rd., Detroit, Mich. 48232
313-493-2000
William V. Luneburg, President
Frank G. Armstrong, Vice President, Environmental and Civic Affairs

Arvin Industries, Inc.
1531 E. 13 St., Columbus, Ind. 47201
812-372-7271
Eugene I. Anderson, President

Borg-Warner Corp.
200 S. Michigan Ave., Chicago, Ill. 60604
312-663-2111
James F. Bere, President
W. M. DuVall, Director of Public Affairs

Budd Co.
2450 Hunting Park Ave., Philadelphia, Pa. 19132
215-225-9100
Gilbert F. Richards, President
James H. McNeal, Vice President, Manufacturing Services

Chrysler Corp.
341 Massachusetts Ave., Detroit, Mich. 48203
313-956-5252
John J. Riccardo, President
S. L. Terry, Vice President, Environmental and Safety Relations

Dana Corp.
Box 1000, Toledo, Ohio 43601
419-531-7333
Gerald B. Mitchell, President
Von R. Kaufman, Director, Manufacturing, Research, and Development

Eaton Corp.
100 Erieview Plaza, Cleveland, Ohio 44114
216-523-5000
William A. Mattie, President

S. K. Lightfoot, Staff Engineer, Environmental Control, Eaton Corp., Technical Center, 4160 Mayfield, Rd., Cleveland, Ohio 44121

Ford Motor Co.
American Rd., Dearborn, Mich. 48121
313-322-3000
Lee A. Iacocca, President
Herbert L. Misch, Vice President, Environmental and Safety Engineering

Fruehauf Corp.
10900 Harper Ave., Detroit, Mich. 48213
313-921-2410
Robert D. Rowan, President
Richard T. Fujioka, Director, Environmental Services

General Motors Corp.
3044 W. Grand Blvd., Detroit, Mich. 48202
313-556-5151
Edward N. Cole, President
Ernest S. Starkman, Vice President, Environmental Activities Staff

Houdaille Industries, Inc.
1 M and T Plaza, Buffalo, N.Y. 14203
716-854-3456
Gerald C. Saltarelli, President
Each division president is responsible for environmental affairs in his division.

International Harvester Co.
401 N. Michigan Ave., Chicago, Ill. 60611
312-527-0200
Brooks McCormick, President

Kelsey Hayes Co.
38481 Huron River Dr., Romulus, Mich. 48174
313-941-2000
W. D. MacDonnell, President
Edward J. Hayes, Vice President, Engineering, Research, and Development

Maremont Corp.
168 N. Michigan Ave., Chicago, Ill. 60601
312-263-7676
Richard D. Abelson, President
John W. Mills, Vice President; General Counsel

Paccar
777 106 Ave. N.E., Bellevue, Wash. 98004
206-455-0520
C. M. Pigott, President

Purolator, Inc.
970 New Brunswick Ave., Rahway, N.J. 07065

201-388-4000
Paul Cameron, President

Questor Corp.
1801 Spielbusch Ave., Toledo, Ohio 43601
419-244-7424
P. M. Grieve, President

Sheller-Globe Corp.
1505 Jefferson Ave., Toledo, Ohio 43624
419-255-8840
Chester Devenow, President

Signal Oil and Gas Co.
Box 94193, Houston, Tex. 77018
713-688-9261
W. H. Thompson, Jr., President
Harold E. Nissen, Manager, Environmental Conservation

A. O. Smith Corp.
Box 584, Milwaukee, Wis. 53201
414-873-3000
Urban Kuechle, President
S. K. Rudorf, Vice President, Manufacturing and Engineering

White Motor Corp.
100 Erieview Plaza, Cleveland, Ohio 44114
216-523-5800
S. E. Knudsen, President
James G. Musser, Jr., Vice President, Engineering

Musical Instruments, Toys, and Sporting Goods

AMF Inc.
777 Westchester Ave., White Plains, N.Y. 10604
914-694-9000
John L. Tullis, President
Stanley Groner, Vice President, Group Services

Mattel, Inc.
5150 Rosecrans Ave., Hawthorne, Calif. 90250
213-644-0411
Ruth Handler, President
Spencer Boise, Vice President, Corporate Affairs

Office Machinery and Computers

Addressograph-Multigraph Co.
Tower E., Shaker Heights, Ohio 44021
216-283-3000
Charles L. Davis, President
John R. Lenox, Vice President, Administration Staff

Burroughs Corp.
2 Ave. and Burroughs Pl., Detroit, Mich. 48232
313-972-7000
Ray W. Macdonald, President
Martin F. Fleming, Director, Safety and Environmental Control

Control Data Corp.
8100 34 Ave. S., Minneapolis, Minn. 55420
612-888-5555
William C. Norris, President
Norbert Berg, Vice President, Administration

Honeywell, Inc.
2701 4 Ave. S., Minneapolis, Minn. 55408
612-332-5222
Stephen F. Keating, President
Richard J. Boyle, Director, Environmental and Urban Control Systems

International Business Machines Corp.
Old Orchard Rd., Armonk, N.Y. 10504
914-765-1900
Frank T. Cary, President
R. H. Howe, President, Real Estate and Construction Div., IBM, 1000 Westchester Ave., White Plains, N.Y. 10604

Litton Industries, Inc.
360 N. Crescent Dr., Beverly Hills, Calif. 90210
213-273-7860
Roy L. Ash, President

National Cash Register Co.
Main and K Sts., Dayton, Ohio 45409
513-449-2000
William E. Anderson, President
P. E. Fleming, Manager, Facilities Management

Pitney Bowes, Inc.
Walnut and Pacific Sts., Stamford, Conn. 06902
203-356-5000
Fred T. Allen, President
Frederick A. Groesbeck, Vice President, Administration

Sperry Rand
1290 Ave. of the Americas, New York, N.Y. 10019
212-956-2121
Robert E. McDonald, President

Bert T. Oakley, Vice President, working with J. Paul Lyet, Chairman of the Board and Chief Executive Officer

Xerox Corp.
1200 High Ridge Rd., Stamford, Conn. 06904
203-329-8711
Archie R. McCardell, President
Frederick Wickstead, Vice President, Manufacturing and Logistics

Paper and Wood Products

Bemis Co., Inc.
800 Northstar Center, Minneapolis, Minn. 55402
612-332-7151
Richard A. Young, President
R. A. Bold, Chief, Buildings, Real Estate, and Environmental Affairs

Boise Cascade Corp.
114 S. 10 St., Boise, Idaho 87306
208-384-6161
John B. Fery, President

Champion International Corp.
777 3 Ave., New York, N.Y. 10017
212-935-3500
Thomas F. Willers, President
James M. Quigley, Vice President, Environmental Quality

Crown Zellerbach Corp.
1 Bush St., San Francisco, Calif. 94104
415-823-5000
Charles R. Dahl, President
Dr. Herman R. Amberg, Director, Environmental Services

Diamond International Corp.
733 3 Ave., New York, N.Y. 10017
212-697-1700
Richard J. Walters, President
Ray Dubrowin, Vice President, Public Affairs

Evans Products Co.
1121 S.W. Salmon St., Portland, Oreg. 97205
503-222-5592
Sheldon Kaplan, President

Fibreboard Corp.
55 Francisco St., San Francisco, Calif. 94133
415-362-6900
Melvin L. Levine, President
Walter Simon, Manager, Water Resources and Effluent Control

Georgia-Pacific Corp.
900 S.W. 5th Ave., Portland, Oreg. 97204
503-222-5561
Robert B. Pamplin, President
Matthew Gould, Director, Environmental Control

Great Northern Nekoosa Corp.
75 Prospect St., Stamford, Conn. 06901
203-359-4000
Samuel A. Casey, President
Robert Hellendale, Executive Vice President

Hammermill Paper Co.
Box 1440, Erie, Pa. 16512
814-456-8811
Albert F. Duval, President
R. W. Brown, Vice President, Research

Hoerner Waldorf Corp.
Box 3260, St. Paul, Minn. 55101
612-645-0131
John H. Myers, President
Milton L. Knoll, Jr., Vice President, Employee Relations and Public Affairs

Inland Container Corp.
120 E. Market St., Indianapolis, Ind. 46204
317-633-0100
Henry C. Goodrich, President
Dr. John M. Vaughn, Vice President, Engineering and Environmental Activities

International Paper Co.
220 E. 42 St., New York, N.Y. 10017
212-682-7500
Paul A. Gorman, President
A. P. Foster, Vice President, Engineering and Environmental Management

Kimberly Clark Corp.
N. Lake St., Neenah, Wis. 54956
414-729-1212
Darwin E. Smith, President
Richard M. Billings, Director, Environmental Control

Masonite Corp.
29 N. Wacker Dr., Chicago, Ill. 60606
312-372-5642
Samuel S. Greeley, President
James Leker, Environmental Administrator

Mead Corp.
118 W. 1 St., Dayton, Ohio 45402
513-222-9561
Paul V. Allemang, President
Peter E. Wrist, Vice President

National Homes Corp.
Earl and Wallace, Lafayette, Ind. 47902
317-447-3131
George E. Price, President
George D. Washington, Director, Corporate Industrial Engineering

Potlatch Forests, Inc.
Box 3591, San Francisco, Calif. 94119
415-981-5980
Richard B. Madden, President
John Hanson, Public Information Manager (San Francisco)
J. R. Ripper, Corporate Environmental Engineer (Lewiston, Idaho)
William G. Gray, Vice President, Engineering (San Francisco)

Riegel Paper Corp.
260 Madison Ave., New York, N.Y. 10016
212-883-5600
William J. Scharffenberger, President

St. Regis Paper Co.
150 E. 42 St., New York, N.Y. 10017
212-697-4400
William E. Caldwell, President
B. W. Recknagel, Executive Vice President

Saxon Industries, Inc.
450 7 Ave., New York, N.Y. 10001
212-736-3663
Myron P. Berman, President

Scott Paper Co.
Scott Plaza, Philadelphia, Pa. 19113
215-724-2000
G. Willing Pepper, President
L. V. Forman, Vice President

Southwest Forest Industries, Inc.
3443 N. Central Ave., Phoenix, Ariz. 85012
602-279-5381
Raymond E. Baker, President
R. M. Sternberger, Vice President

Union Camp Corp.
1600 Valley Rd., Wayne, N.J. 07470
201-628-9000
Samuel M. Kinney, Jr., President
V. E. Kelly, Director, Environmental Protection

Jim Walter Corp.
1500 N. Dale Mabry Hwy., Tampa, Fla. 33607
813-876-4181
Frank J. Pizzitola, President

Westvaco Corp.
299 Park Ave., New York, N.Y. 10017
212-688-5000
David L. Luke III, President

Weyerhaeuser Co.
11 and A Sts., Tacoma, Wash. 98402
206-924-2345
George H. Weyerhaeuser, President
John L. McClintock, Director, Environmental Resources

Willamette Industries, Inc.
3800 First National Bank Tower, Portland, Oreg. 97201
503-227-5585
Gene D. Knudson, President
William Swindells, Jr., Senior Vice President

PETROLEUM REFINING

Amerada Hess Corp.
1 Hess Plaza, Woodbridge, N.J. 07095
212-581-2910
Philip Kramer, President

American Petrofina, Inc.
Box 2159, Dallas, Tex. 75221
214-747-7011
Richard I. Galland, President
Rene Brown, Vice President, Research, Cosden Div.

Ashland Oil, Inc.
1409 Winchester Ave., Ashland, Ky. 41101
606-324-1111
Robert Yancey, President
David C. Williams, Vice President, Environmental Affairs and Safety

Atlantic Richfield Co.
717 5 Ave., New York, N.Y. 10022
212-758-2345
T. F. Bradshaw, President
William B. Halladay, Director, Environmental Protection Dept.

Cities Service Co.
60 Wall St., New York, N.Y. 10005
212-422-1600
Charles J. Waidelich, President
Charles P. Goforth, Manager, Environmental Affairs

Clark Oil and Refining Corp.
8530 W. National Ave., Milwaukee, Wis. 53227
414-321-5100
Owen L. Hill, President
Robert H. Bruggink, Director, Environmental Control

Commonwealth Oil Refining Co.
245 Park Ave., New York, N.Y. 10017
212-986-6191
Norman C. Keith, President

Continental Oil Co.
High Ridge Pk., Stamford, Conn. 06904
203-359-3500
John G. McLean, President
T. R. Samsell, Director, Environmental Conservation, Continental Oil Co., 1130 17 St. N.W., Washington, D.C. 20036

Crown Central Petroleum Corp.
1 N. Charles St., Baltimore, Md. 21203
301-539-7400
Henry A. Rosenberg, Jr., President
A. J. Morris, Executive Vice President

Exxon Corp.
1251 Ave. of the Americas, New York, N.Y. 10020
212-974-3000
C. C. Garvin, President
Dr. Raymond W. Winkler, Environmental Conservation Coordinator

Farmers Union Central Exchange, Inc.
1185 N. Concord St., South St. Paul, Minn. 55075
612-455-8571
Thomas H. Steichen, President

Farmland Industries, Inc.
3315 N. Oak Trafficway, Kansas City, Mo. 64116
816-453-1400
E. T. Lindsey, President

Getty Oil Co.
Pennsylvania Bldg., Wilmington, Del. 19899
213-381-7151
J. Paul Getty, President
Albert H. Zinkand, Washington Representative, Getty Oil Co.
1701 Pennsylvania Ave. N.W., Washington, D.C. 20006

Gulf Oil Corp.
Gulf Bldg., Box 1166, Pittsburgh, Pa. 15230
412-391-2400
B. R. Dorsey, President
Ernest Cotton, Air and Water Advisor, Gulf Oil Corp., Pittsburgh
H. A. Bailey, Manager, Air and Water Conservation, Gulf Oil Co.—U.S., Houston, Tex.

Kerr-McGee Corp.
Kerr-McGee Bldg., Oklahoma City, Okla. 73102
405-236-1313
F. C. Love, President
Dr. Thomas L. Hurst, Technical Advisor to Chief Executive Officer, Environmental Services

Marathon Oil Co.
539 S. Main St., Findlay, Ohio 45840
419-422-2121
Harold D. Hoopman, President
T. J. Challoner, Manager, Environmental Control Div.

Mobil Oil Corp.
150 E. 42 St., New York, N.Y. 10017
212-883-4242
William P. Tavoulareas, President
C. G. Cortelyou, Coordinator, Air and Water Conservation

Occidental Petroleum Corp.
10889 Wilshire Blvd., Los Angeles, Calif. 90024
213-879-1700
Dr. Armand Hammer, President
Each division and subsidiary has its own organization to deal with environmental issues and activities.

Phillips Petroleum Co.
Phillips Bldg., Bartlesville, Okla. 74003
918-661-6600
W. F. Martin, President
W. A. Roberts, Executive Vice President

Shell Oil Co.
1 Shell Plaza, Houston, Tex. 77002
Harry Bridges, President
H. R. Kemmerer, General Manager, Environmental and Safety Affairs, Public Affairs Dept.

Standard Oil Co. of California
225 Bush St., San Francisco, Calif. 94104
415-894-7700
H. J. Haynes, President
E. D. Kane, Vice President

Standard Oil Co. (Indiana)
910 S. Michigan Ave., Chicago, Ill. 60605
312-356-6111
Robert C. Gunness, President
R. C. Mallatt, Manager, Air and Water Conservation

Standard Oil Co. of Ohio
Midland Bldg., Cleveland, Ohio 44115
216-575-4141
Alton W. Whitehouse, Jr., President
R. E. Farrell, Director, Environmental Affairs

Sun Oil Co.
1608 Walnut St., Philadelphia, Pa. 19103
215-985-1600
H. Robert Sharbaugh, President
Harold F. Elkin, Coordinator, Environmental Conservation

Tenneco, Inc.
Box 2511, Tenneco Bldg., Houston, Tex. 77002
713-229-2131
R. E. McGee, President
Dr. Casey E. Westell, Jr., Director, Industrial Ecology

Texaco, Inc.
135 E. 42 St., New York, N.Y. 10017
212-953-6000
John K. McKinley, President
Dr. W. J. Coppoc, Vice President, Environmental Protection Dept., Texaco, Inc., Box 509, Beacon, N.Y. 12508

Union Oil Co. of California
461 S. Boylston, Los Angeles, Calif. 90017
213-486-7600
Fred L. Hartley, President
Dr. Carleton B. Scott, Director, Environmental Sciences

PHARMACEUTICALS

Abbott Laboratories
14 St. and Sheridan Rd., North Chicago, Ill. 60064
312-688-6100
Edward J. Ledder, President
David Schwarz, Director, Corporate Environmental Control

American Home Products Corp.
685 3 Ave., New York, N.Y. 10017
212-986-1000
William F. Laporte, President

Baxter Laboratories, Inc.
6301 Lincoln Ave., Morton Grove, Ill. 60053
312-267-6900
John J. Kimbell, President
Lincoln R. Dowell, Director, Public Affairs

Bristol-Myers Co.
345 Park Ave., New York, N.Y. 10022
212-644-2100
Richard L. Gelb, President
Patrick F. Crossman, Director, Public Affairs

Eli Lilly & Co.
307 E. McCarty St., Indianapolis, Ind. 46206
317-636-2211
Richard D. Wood, President
Richard G. Weldele, Director, Corporate Engineering Services

Merck & Co., Inc.
126 E. Lincoln Ave., Rahway, N.J. 07065
201-381-5000
Dr. Antonie T. Knoppers, President
H. N. Fiaccone, Senior Vice President

Miles Laboratories, Inc.
1127 Myrtle St., Elkhart, Ind. 46514
219-264-8111
Dr. Walter A. Compton, President
Elmer E. Hartgerink, Director, Corporate Environmental Control

Morton-Norwich Products, Inc.
110 N. Wacker Dr., Chicago, Ill. 60606
312-621-5200
Daniel Peterkin, Jr., President

Pfizer, Inc.
235 E. 42 St., New York, N.Y. 10017
212-573-2323
Gerald D. Laubach, Ph.D., President
Bernard J. Quinn, Vice President, Corporate Production and Engineering

Richardson-Merrell Inc.
122 E. 42 St., New York, N.Y. 10017
212-697-3800
H. R. Marschalk, President

Schering-Plough Corp.
60 Orange St., Bloomfield, N.J. 07003
201-743-6000
W. H. Conzen, President
Herbert Kaplan, Director, Corporate Engineering

G. D. Searle & Co.
Searle Pkwy., Skokie, Ill. 60076

312-673-3200
Wesley M. Dixon, President

Smith Kline and French Laboratory
1500 Spring Garden St., Philadelphia, Pa. 19101
215-564-2400
Robert F. Dee, President
Benoit L. McMahen, Director, Corporate Engineering

Squibb Corp.
40 W. 57 St., New York, N.Y. 10019
212-489-2000
R. M. Furlaud, President
Norman R. Ritter, Vice President, Public Affairs

Sterling Drug, Inc.
90 Park Ave., New York, N.Y. 10016
212-972-4141
David J. Fitzgibbons, President
Donald S. Shepherd, Vice President, Plants and Production

Upjohn Co.
7000 Portage Rd., Kalamazoo, Mich. 49002
616-382-4000
Robert M. Boudeman, President
Bruce S. Lane, Vice President, Engineering

Warner-Lambert Co.
201 Tabor Rd., Morris Plains, N.J. 07950
201-285-0234
E. Burke Giblin, President
Harold Jensen, Manager, Environmental Control

Publishing and Printing

Arcata National Corp.
2750 Sand Hill Rd., Menlo Park, Calif. 94025
415-854-5222
J. Frank Leach, President
William D. Walsh, Vice President, Administration

R. R. Donnelley & Sons Co.
2223 Martin Luther King Dr., Chicago, Ill. 60616
312-326-8000
Charles W. Lake, Jr., President
J. B. Schwemm, Vice President and General Counsel

Gannett Co., Inc.
55 Exchange St., Rochester, N.Y. 14614
716-232-7100
Allen H. Neuharth, President
Ronald A. White, Vice President, Production

Grolier, Inc.
575 Lexington Ave., New York, N.Y. 10022
212-751-3600
William J. Murphy, President
Basil F. Harrison, Vice President, Special Projects

Knight Newspapers, Inc.
1 Herald Plaza, Miami, Fla. 33132
305-350-2921
Lee Hills, President
James Keeley, Research Director

McGraw-Hill, Inc.
1221 Ave. of the Americas, New York, N.Y. 10020
212-997-1221
Shelton Fisher, President

Macmillan, Inc.
866 3 Ave., New York, N.Y. 10022
212-935-2000
Raymond C. Hagel, President

New York Times Co.
229 W. 43 St., New York, N.Y. 10036
212-556-1234
Arthur Ochs Sulzberger, President

Time, Inc.
Time and Life Bldg., Rockefeller Center, New York, N.Y. 10020
212-586-1212
James R. Shepley, President
Charles Terranella, Assistant to the Vice President, Administration

Times Mirror Co.
Times Mirror Sq., Los Angeles, Calif. 90053
213-625-2345
Albert V. Casey, President
Samuel J. Robinson, Vice President

Washington Post Co.
1515 L St. N.W., Washington, D.C. 20005
202-223-6000
Katharine Graham, President

Western Publishing Co.
1220 Mound Ave., Racine, Wis. 53404
414-633-2431
Gerald J. Slade, President
J. W. (Bill) Hall, Manager, Corporate Facilities, Engineering

Rubber

Dayco Corp.
333 W. 1 St., Dayton, Ohio 45402
513-461-3700
Richard J. Jacob, President

Firestone Tire and Rubber Co.
1200 Firestone Pkwy., Akron, Ohio 44301
216-379-7000
Richard A. Riley, President
J. R. Laman, Corporate Manager, Environmental Engineering

General Tire and Rubber Co.
1 General St., Akron, Ohio 44305
216-798-3000
M. G. O'Neil, President
William C. Lang, Manager, Chemical Engineering

B. F. Goodrich Co.
500 S. Main St., Akron, Ohio 44311
216-379-2000
H. B. Warner, President
Dr. R. W. Strassburg, Director, Environmental Affairs

Goodyear Tire and Rubber Co.
1144 E. Market St., Akron, Ohio 44305
216-794-2121
Charles J. Pilliod, Jr., President
Frank R. Tully, Director, Manufacturing Services

Uniroyal, Inc.
1230 Ave. of the Americas, New York, N.Y. 10020
212-247-5000
George R. Vila, President
Robert C. Niles, Director, Environmental Control, Uniroyal, Inc., Oxford Management and Research Center, Middlebury, Conn. 06749

Shipbuilding, Railroad Equipment, and Mobile Homes

ACF Industries, Inc.
750 3 Ave., New York, N.Y. 10017
212-986-8600
Henry A. Correa, President
W. A. Buchanan, Corporate Manager, Capital Budgets

Fuqua Industries, Inc.
First National Bank Bldg., Atlanta, Ga. 30303
404-521-0204
Carl L. Patrick, President

General American Transportation Corp.
120 S. Riverside Plaza, Chicago, Ill. 60606
312-621-6200
J. Richard Scanlin, President
Harlan J. Thompson, Vice President

Ogden Corp.
161 E. 42 St., New York, N.Y. 10017
212-972-2200
M. Lee Rice, President

Pullman, Inc.
200 S. Michigan Ave., Chicago, Ill. 60604
312-939-4262
Samuel B. Casey, Jr., President
Thomas P. Conroy, Manager, Environmental Solutions

Skyline Corp.
2520 By Pass Rd., Elkhart, Ind. 46514
219-523-2380
Dale Swikert, President

Trans Union Corp.
111 W. Jackson Blvd., Chicago, Ill. 60604
312-431-3111
J. W. Van Gorkom, President
T. P. O'Boyle, President, Ecodyne Corp.

Soaps and Cosmetics

Avon Products, Inc.
9 W. 57 St., New York, N.Y. 10019
212-593-4017
David W. Mitchell, President
Donald J. Steller, Manager, Public Affairs

Chesebrough-Pond's, Inc.
485 Lexington Ave., New York, N.Y. 10017
212-697-4900
Ralph E. Ward, President
P. D. Lindholm, Vice President, Manufacturing

Colgate Palmolive Co.
300 Park Ave., New York, N.Y. 10022
212-751-1200
David R. Foster, President
William Dorn, Director, Corporate Relations

Lever Brothers Co.
390 Park Ave., New York, N.Y. 10022
212-688-6000
Thomas S. Carroll, President

James W. Flynn, General Manager, Engineering, Development, and Coordination Div.

Max Factor & Co.
1655 N. McCadden Pl., Hollywood, Calif. 90028
213-462-6131
Alfred Firestein, President

Procter and Gamble Co.
301 E. 6 St., Cincinnati, Ohio 45202
513-421-3100
Edward G. Harness, President

Purex Corp. Ltd.
5101 Clark Ave., Lakewood, Calif. 90712
213-636-0431
William R. Tincher, President

Revlon, Inc.
767 5 Ave., New York, N.Y. 10022
212-758-5000
Charles Revson, Chairman
Sol Levine, Executive Vice President, Operations

TEXTILES

Burlington Industries, Inc.
301 N. Eugene St., Greensboro, N.C. 27401
919-379-2000
Ely Callaway, Jr., President
Charles A. McLendon, Senior Vice President

Cannon Mills Co.
Box 7, Kannapolis, N.C. 28081
704-933-1221
Don S. Holt, President

Collins and Aikman Corp.
210 Madison Ave., New York, N.Y. 10016
212-689-3900
Albert Laughey, President
Leigh C. Woodall, Jr., Manager, Environmental Affairs

Cone Mills Corp.
4 and Maple Sts., Greensboro, N.C. 27405
919-379-6220
Lewis S. Morris, President
W. O. Leonard, Vice President

Dan River, Inc.
Box 6126, Sta. B, Greenville, S.C. 29606
803-242-5950
Robert S. Small, President

M. A. Cross, Vice President, Public and Industrial Relations

Fieldcrest Mills, Inc.
Stadium Rd., Eden, N.C. 27288
919-623-2123
William C. Battle, President
Dr. L. H. Hance, Vice President, Research and Engineering

Indian Head, Inc.
111 W. 40 St., New York, N.Y. 10018
212-695-1260
Richard J. Powers, President
Jerry R. Bishop, Vice President, Engineering Services

Kendall Co.
225 Franklin St., Boston, Mass. 02110
617-482-3030
Willard M. Bright, President

Lowenstein & Sons, Inc.
1430 Broadway, New York, N.Y. 10018
212-560-5000
Joseph H. Anderer, President
Geoff Lund, Director, Research and Development

Mohasco Industries, Inc.
57 Lyon St., Amsterdam, N.Y. 12010
518-843-2000
Herbert L. Shuttleworth, President
Edgar L. Pinel, Jr., Director, Corporate Research and Engineering

Spring Mills, Inc.
Fort Mill, S.C. 29715
803-547-2901
Peter G. Scotese, President
J. Dixon Lesslie, P.E., Director, Utilities Services

J. P. Stevens & Co., Inc.
1185 Ave. of the Americas, New York, N.Y. 10036
212-575-2000
Whitney Stevens, President
Dr. Edward D. Harrison, Executive Vice President

United Merchants and Manufacturers, Inc.
1407 Broadway, New York, N.Y. 10018
212-564-6000
Martin J. Schwab, President

West Point-Pepperell Inc.
Box 71, West Point, Ga. 31833

404-645-1111
John P. Howland, President
Grady Webb, Jr., Vice President, Manufacturing

Tobacco

American Brands, Inc.
245 Park Ave., New York, N.Y. 10017
212-557-7000
Robert K. Heimann, President
Richard H. Stinnette, Assistant to the Chairman

Liggett and Myers, Inc.
630 5 Ave., New York, N.Y. 10020
212-246-0500
Milton E. Harrington, President

Loews Corp.
666 5 Ave., New York, N.Y. 10019
212-586-4400
Preston R. Tisch, President

Philip Morris, Inc.
100 Park Ave., New York, N.Y. 10017
212-679-1800
Joseph F. Cullman III, Chief Executive Officer; Chairman of the Board
Richard D. Robertson, Vice President

R. J. Reynolds Industries, Inc.
Winston-Salem, N.C. 27102
919-748-4000
David S. Peoples, President

Universal Leaf Tobacco Co.
Hamilton St. at Broad, Richmond, Va. 23230
703-359-9311
Gordon L. Crenshaw, President

Utilities

Allegheny Power System, Inc.
320 Park Ave., New York, N.Y. 10022
212-752-2121
Charles B. Finch, President
Francis J. McAlary, Vice President

American Electric Power Co., Inc.
2 Broadway, New York, N.Y. 10004
212-422-4800
Donald C. Cook, Chairman and Chief Executive Officer

John A. Tillinghast, Senior Executive Vice President, Engineering and Construction, American Electric Power Service Corp.

American Natural Gas Co.
30 Rockefeller Plaza, New York, N.Y. 10020
212-247-4630
Wilber H. Mack, President

American Telephone and Telegraph Co.
195 Broadway, New York, N.Y. 10007
212-393-9800
Robert D. Lilley, President
William A. Horton, Manager, Environmental Programs

Baltimore Gas and Electric Co.
Lexington and Liberty Sts., Baltimore, Md. 21203
301-234-5000
C. Edward Utermohle, Jr., President
John W. Stout, Jr., Chief Environmental Engineer, Electric Engineering Dept.

Carolina Power and Light Co.
336 Lafayetteville St., Raleigh, N.C. 27602
919-828-8211
Shearon Harris, President
D. V. Menscer, Manager, Special Services Dept., Engineering and Operating Group

Central and South West Corp.
300 Delaware Ave., Wilmington, Del. 19801
302-655-1526
S. B. Phillips, Jr., President

Columbia Gas System, Inc.
20 Montchanin Rd., Wilmington, Del. 19807
302-429-5000
Bernard J. Clarke, President
Edward D. Callahan, Vice President, Environmental Affairs Dept.

Commonwealth Edison Co.
1 First National Plaza, Chicago, Ill. 60690
312-294-4321
Thomas G. Ayers, President
Joseph P. McCluskey, Director, Environmental Affairs

Consolidated Edison Co.
4 Irving Pl., New York, N.Y. 10003
212-460-4600
Louis H. Roddis, Jr., President
Harry G. Woodbury, Executive Vice President, Environmental Affairs

Consolidated Natural Gas Service Co.
30 Rockefeller Plaza, New York, N.Y. 10020
212-245-5100
Robert E. Seymour, President

Consumers Power Co.
212 W. Michigan Ave., Jackson, Mich. 49201
517-788-0550
Alphonse Aymond, President
Roy A. Wells, Jr., Executive Director, Environmental Activities

Continental Telephone Corp.
Box 400, Merrifield, Va. 22116
703-661-2100
J. P. Maguire, President

Detroit Edison Co.
2000 2 Ave., Detroit, Mich. 48226
313-962-2100
William G. Meese, President
Oslin D. Whiddon, Manager, Environmental Affairs

Duke Power Corp.
422 S. Church St., Charlotte, N.C. 28202
704-332-8521
Carl Horn, Jr., President
Charles A. Dewey, Jr., Principal Environmental Engineer

Duquesne Light Co.
435 6 Ave., Pittsburgh, Pa. 15219
412-471-4300
Stanley G. Schaffer, President
S. L. Pernick, Manager, Environmental Affairs Dept.

El Paso Natural Gas Co.
Box 1492, El Paso, Tex. 79999
915-543-2600
Hugh F. Steen, President
Charles R. Bowman, Manager, Environmental Affairs

Florida Power and Light Co.
4200 W. Flagler St., Miami, Fla. 33134
305-445-6211
Marshall McDonald, President
Robert J. Gardner, Vice President, Environmental Affairs

General Public Utilities Corp.
80 Pine St., New York, N.Y. 10005
212-943-5600
William G. Kuhns, President

John R. Thorpe, Manager, Environmental Affairs, GPU Service Corp., 260 Cherry Hill Rd., Parsippany, N.J. 07054

General Telephone and Electronics Corp.
730 3 Ave., New York, N.Y. 10017
212-551-1000
Theodore F. Brophy, President
John J. Davin, Vice President, Materials and Facilities, GTE Sylvania Inc.

Gulf States Utilities Co.
285 Liberty Ave., Beaumont, Tex. 77701
713-838-6631
Floyd R. Smith, President

Houston Lighting and Power Co.
611 Walker Ave., Houston, Tex. 77002
713-228-9211
Carl B. Sherman, President
Mr. DeSimmons, Vice President, Environmental Affairs

Long Island Lighting Co.
250 Old Country Rd., Mineola, N.Y. 11501
516-747-1000
Edward C. Duffy, President
Dr. Mathew C. Cordaro, Manager, Environmental Engineering

Middle South Utilities, Inc.
280 Park Ave., New York, N.Y. 10017
212-687-7181
Floyd W. Lewis, President
W. M. Brewer, Vice President, Engineering and Operations

New England Electric System
20 Turnpike Rd., Westboro, Mass. 01581
617-366-9011
Guy W. Nichols, President
Edward A. Plumley, Vice President, New England Power Co.

Niagara Mohawk Power Corp.
300 Erie Blvd. W., Syracuse, N.Y. 13202
315-474-1511
James A. O'Neill, President
Thomas J. Brosnan, Vice President; Chief Engineer

Northeast Utilities
176 Cumberland Ave., Wethersfield, Conn. 06109
203-529-7471
Lelan F. Sillin, Jr., President

Northern Natural Gas Co.
2223 Dodge St., Omaha, Nebr. 68102
402-348-4000
Willis A. Strauss, President
Karl H. Frantzen, Environmental Supervisor

Northern States Power Co.
414 Nicollett Ave., Minneapolis, Minn. 55401
612-330-5500
David F. McElroy, President
A. E. Hassinger, Vice President, Environmental and Consumer Affairs

Ohio Edison Co.
47 N. Main St., Akron, Ohio 44308
216-762-9661
D. Bruce Mansfield, President
James H. Carson, General Production, Environmental, and Performance Engineer

Pacific Gas and Electric Co.
245 Market St., San Francisco, Calif. 94105
415-781-4211
Shermer L. Sibley, President
Wallace B. Allen, Director, Environmental Quality

Pacific Lighting Corp.
810 S. Flower St., Los Angeles, Calif. 90017
213-620-0360
Joseph R. Rensch, President
Reine J. Corbeil, Manager, Environmental Affairs, Southern California Gas Co. (a subsidiary of PLC)

Pacific Power and Light Co.
920 S.W. 6 Ave., Portland, Oreg. 97204
503-226-7411
Don C. Frisbee, President
C. P. (Ted) Davenport, Vice President

Panhandle Eastern Pipe Line Co.
Box 1642, Houston, Tex. 77001
713-664-3401
Richard L. O'Shields, President
L. E. Hanna, Vice President, Box 1348, Kansas City, Mo. 64141

Pennsylvania Power and Light Co.
901 Hamilton St., Allentown, Pa. 18101
215-821-5151
Jack K. Busby, President

Pennzoil United, Inc.
900 Southwest Tower, Houston, Tex. 77002
713-228-8741
William C. Liedtke, Jr., President
N. O. Wade, Vice President

Peoples Gas Co.
122 S. Michigan Ave., Chicago, Ill. 60603
312-431-4000
Robert M. Drevs, President
John H. Miller, Manager, Technical and Environmental Control Services

Philadelphia Electric Co.
1000 Chestnut St., Philadelphia, Pa. 19107
215-841-4000
James L. Everett, President
Walter E. Rosengarten, Jr., Engineer in Charge, Environmental Engineering Section, Philadelphia Electric Co., 2301 Market St., NZ-1, Philadelphia, Pa. 19101

Potomac Electric Power Co.
929 E St. N.W., Washington, D.C. 20004
202-872-2000
W. Reid Thompson, President
Fred J. Grozinger, Environmental Engineer

Public Service Electric and Gas Co.
80 Park Pl., Newark, N.J. 07101
201-622-7000
Edward R. Eberle, President
Clyde C. Ruffle, General Manager, Environmental Affairs

Southern California Edison Co.
Box 800, Rosemead, Calif. 91770
213-572-1212
T. M. McDaniel, Jr., President
David J. Fogarty, Vice President

Southern Co.
64 Perimeter Center E., Atlanta, Ga. 30346
404-252-6112
Alvin W. Vogtle, Jr., President
William B. Harrison, Vice President, Southern Services, Inc., 300 Office Park Dr., Birmingham, Ala. 35202

Texas Eastern Transmission Corp.
Box 2521, Houston, Tex. 77001
713-224-7961
Dr. George F. Kirby, President
Roland E. Moore, Vice President and Chief Engineer, Texas Eastern Transmission Corp., Box 1612, Shreveport, La. 71130

Texas Utilities Co.
1506 Commerce St., Dallas, Tex. 75201
214-742-4742
T. L. Austin, Jr., President
P. G. Brittain, Executive Vice President, Texas Utilities Services, Inc.

Utilities

Transcontinental Gas Pipe Line Corp.
3100 Travis St., Houston, Tex. 77001
713-524-6351
G. Montgomery Mitchell, President
Russell J. Judah, Director, Environmental and
  Industry Affairs

Union Electric Co.
1 Memorial Dr., St. Louis, Mo. 63166
314-621-3222
Charles J. Dougherty, President
E. K. Dille, Executive Vice President

United Telecommunications, Inc.
Box 11315, Plaza Sta., Kansas City, Mo. 64112
913-236-9900
Paul H. Henson, President
J. F. McCarthy, Vice President, Corporate
  Communications

Virginia Electric and Power Co.
700 E. Franklin St., Richmond, Va. 23219
703-771-3000
T. Justin Moore, Jr., President
J. D. Ristroph, Executive Director, Environmental Control

Western Union Telegraph Co.
60 Hudson St., New York, N.Y. 10013
212-577-4321
Earl D. Hilburn, President
Herbert E. Salter, Vice President, Resources

Wisconsin Electric Power Co.
231 W. Michigan St., Milwaukee, Wis. 53201
414-273-1234
John G. Quale, President
N. A. Ricci, Assistant Vice President

5 Labor Unions and the Environment

GLENN PAULSON, Ph.D.
Staff Scientist, Natural Resources Defense Council, Inc.

There are several reasons for surveying in this directory the role played by American labor organizations in current environmental activities. First, in general, one can say that the two groups of individuals who know the most about the environmental impact of any given industrial facilities are the people who own and run the facilities (the corporations) and the people who work in them. Each group has its own perspective on the environmental impact of an industry's activities. Thus, both groups can provide valuable information, based on their differing perspectives, on any given industrial facility.

Second, American workers, in addition to their general civic responsibilities, have a history and tradition of organizing themselves for common goals and making these goals known to the broader public through a wide variety of techniques. Included in these techniques are extensive capabilities that workers and their unions have in organizing people, in lobbying, and in other activities. As general public awareness of environmental problems has grown, so has the awareness of many workers and their representatives. As a result, there has been a growing number of coalitions between different labor organizations, as well as between labor organizations and other organizations, on environmental issues of common concern.

Third, workers have their own individual environmental problems, namely the conditions inside the facilities in which they spend their working day. This is often called "in-plant pollution." The general problem of occupational health and safety is, of course, an important one in its own right. In addition it has broader environmental ramifications because, as a general rule, any steps taken to improve the quality of the working environment will benefit the surrounding environment as well. Similarly, any steps imposed to lessen the overall environmental impact of a facility will tend to improve working conditions within the facility. This interrelationship is not often explicitly recognized, but it can be extremely significant.

In several major metropolitan areas, local union groups have joined in a variety of activities designed to reduce air pollution levels in the community. At the national level, unions often participate in ad hoc coalitions with environmental organizations in support of major legislative proposals before Congress, or to insist on strong implementation of laws affecting such diverse issues as the preservation of open space or abatement of water pollution. In this context it should be noted that both during the legislative debate that resulted in the Occupational Safety and Health Act of 1970, and during subsequent implementation activities called for by this Act, prominent environmental organizations have given their support to labor organizations in requesting action to protect the health of workers.

This is not to say that workers and their unions always agree with any group of other organizations, such as corporate groups, broadly based citizen organizations, or governmental or quasi-governmental organizations, on an issue. Since unions have their own perspective, their actual positions on issues will be developed on the basis of that perspective as well as the specific issues under consideration. But whatever their stance, the size of unions and the number of citizens involved in them gives them an important position in the overall scope of environmental activities in the United States.

It is not possible to list here every chapter or local of every union in the country, although many are actively involved in environmental issues. This chapter lists the major national unions that have in the recent past shown some active involvement in one or more environmental issues at the national level. The entries are arranged alphabetically by "key word," which sometimes involves inverting the union's title. Each entry includes the name and title of the staff member responsible for environmental affairs. If no such person has been designated, the name of the union president is provided, and any queries should be directed to him.

Aerospace and Agricultural Implement Workers of America - UAW, United
8000 E. Jefferson Ave., Detroit, Mich. 48214
313-926-5000
Olga M. Madar, Director, Conservation and Resource Development

Bakery and Confectionery Workers International Union of America
1828 L St. N.W., Washington, D.C. 20036
202-466-2500
Vaughn Ball, Research Director

Building and Construction Trades Dept., AFL-CIO
Rm. 603, 815 16 St. N.W., Washington, D.C. 20006
202-347-1461
Frank Bonadio, President

Carpenters and Joiners of America, United Brotherhood of
101 Constitution Ave. N.W., Washington, D.C. 20001
202-546-6206
Paul Connelley, Health and Safety Director

Cement, Lime, and Gypsum Workers International Union, United
7830 W. Lawrence Ave., Chicago, Ill. 60656
312-774-2217
Don Spatz, Research Director

Chemical Workers, International
1655 W. Market St., Akron, Ohio 44313
216-867-2444
Lawrence J. Ahern, Director, Collective Bargaining

Clothing Workers of America, Amalgamated
15 Union Sq., New York, N.Y. 10003
212-255-7800
Arthur M. Goldberg, General Counsel

Communications Workers of America
1925 K St. N.W., Washington, D.C. 20006
202-337-7711
Joseph Hafkenschiel, Safety Coordinator

Electrical, Radio, and Machine Workers, International Union of
1126 16 St. N.W., Washington, D.C. 20036
202-296-1200
Jack Suarez, Safety Director

Electrical Workers, International Brotherhood of
1125 15 St. N.W., Washington, D.C. 20005
202-833-7000
Charles Tupper, Safety Director

Engineers, International Union of Operating
1125 17 St. N.W., Washington, D.C. 20036
202-347-8560
Allen Burch, Safety Director

Glass and Ceramic Workers of North America, United
556 E. Town St., Columbus, Ohio 43215
614-221-4465
Ralph Rieser, President

Government Employees, American Federation of
1325 Massachusetts Ave. N.W., Washington, D.C. 20005
202-737-8700
Clyde M. Webber, President

Graphic Arts International Union
1900 L St. N.W., Washington, D.C. 20036
202-833-3190
John A. Stagg, Director, Education
William Schroeder, Vice President

Heat and Frost Insulators and Asbestos Workers, International Assn. of

1300 Connecticut Ave. N.W., Washington, D.C. 20036
202-785-2388
Andrew T. Haas, President

Industrial Union Dept., AFL-CIO
815 16 St. N.W., Washington, D.C. 20006
202-637-5000
Sheldon Samuels, Director, Occupational Safety, Health, and Environmental Affairs

Industrial Workers of America, International Union, Allied
3520 W. Oklahoma Ave., Milwaukee, Wis. 53215
414-645-9500
John Zalusky, Research Director

Laborers' International Union of North America
905 16 St. N.W., Washington, D.C. 20006
202-737-8320
W. Vernie Reed, Vice President

Longshoremen's Assn., International
17 Battery Place, New York, N.Y. 10004
212-425-1200
Joseph Leonard, Safety Director

Machinists and Aerospace Workers, International Assn. of
1300 Connecticut Ave. N.W., Washington, D.C. 20036
202-785-2525
Angelo Cefalo, Assistant to the President

Marine and Shipbuilding Workers of America, Industrial Union of
1126 16 St. N.W., Washington, D.C. 20036
202-223-0902
Eugene McCabe, President

Meat Cutters and Butcher Workmen of North America, Amalgamated
2800 N. Sheridan Rd., Chicago, Ill. 60657
312-248-8700
Jessie Prosten, Vice President

Metal Trades Dept., AFL-CIO
815 16 St. N.W., Washington, D.C. 20006
202-347-7255
Paul Hutchings, Research Director

Molders and Allied Workers Union, AFL-CIO, International
1225 E. McMillan St., Cincinnati, Ohio 45206
513-221-1525
James Wolfe, Research Director

Newspaper Guild
1125 15 St. N.W., Washington, D.C. 20005
202-296-2990
Yetta Reisel, Assistant to the President

Oil, Chemical, and Atomic Workers International Union
1636 Champa St., Box 2812, Denver, Colo. 80201
303-266-0811
Anthony Mazzocchi, Citizenship-Legislative Director

Painters and Allied Trades, International Brotherhood of
1750 New York Ave. N.W., Washington, D.C. 20006
202-872-1444
John Pecoraro, Director, Legislative Activities

Paperworkers International Union, United
163-03 Horace Harding Expressway, Flushing, N.Y. 11362
212-762-6000
William Casamo, Assistant to the President

Printing Pressmen and Assistants Union of North America, International
1730 Rhode Island Ave. N.W., Washington, D.C. 20036
202-293-2185
William Martin, Health and Safety Director

Retail, Wholesale, and Department Store Union
101 W. 31 St., New York, N.Y. 10001
212-947-9303
Alvin E. Heaps, Secretary-Treasurer

Rubber, Cork, Linoleum, and Plastic Workers of America, United
87 S. High St., Akron, Ohio 44308
216-376-6181
Louis Beliczky, Director, Industrial Hygiene

Service Employees International Union
900 17 St. N.W., Washington, D.C. 20006
202-296-5940
Rudolph Oswald, Research Director

Slate, Tile, and Composition Roofers, Damp and Waterproof Workers Assn., United
1125 17 St. N.W., Washington, D.C. 20036
202-638-3228
Charles D. Aquadro, President

State Employees and Moving Picture Machine Operators of the U.S. and Canada, International Alliance of Theatrical
Suite 1900, 1270 Ave. of the Americas, New York, N.Y. 10020
212-245-4369
Richard F. Walsh, President

State, County, and Municipal Employees, Federation of
1155 15 St. N.W., Washington, D.C. 20005
202-223-4460
Jerry Wurf, President

Steelworkers of America, United
1500 Commonwealth Bldg., Pittsburgh, Pa. 15222
412-471-5254
John J. Sheehan, Legislative Director
Adolph Schwartz, Safety Director

Teachers, American Federation of
1012 14 St. N.W., Washington, D.C. 20005
202-737-6141
David Selden, President

Textile Workers Union of America
99 University Pl., New York, N.Y. 10003
212-673-1400
George Perkel, Research Director

Utility Workers Union of America
Suite 1717, Grant-Deneau Tower, Dayton, Ohio 45402
513-223-0123
Marshall M. Hicks, Secretary-Treasurer

Woodworkers of America, International
1622 N. Lombard St., Portland, Oreg. 97217
503-285-5281
Ronald F. Roley, President

6 Environmental Employment

ODOM FANNING

Free-lance writer on environmental affairs; author of Opportunities in Environmental Careers; *editor-in-chief of the federal government's "First Annual Report on Environmental Quality" (1970)*

As recently as the late 1960s, few people recognized the need for trained men and women to engage in such pursuits as managing the environment. Even the professionals—scientists, engineers, technicians, aides, economists, managers, teachers, lawyers, and journalists—who were involved in environmental problems seldom considered themselves environmentalists.

The Santa Barbara oil spill in January 1969 and Earth Day in April 1970 dramatized an environmental movement that had started quietly, much earlier, probably with the publication of Rachel Carson's *Silent Spring* in 1962. Whatever the origins of the public concern over the environmental crisis, the Congress, the President, and the courts had begun to respond to public demand by the beginning of the 1970's. Stronger environmental laws were passed; federal environmental agencies were reorganized; federal funding for environmental programs climbed sharply. And, in lawsuit after lawsuit, courts ruled that environmental considerations must be given equal weight with economic concerns in public policy decisions.

Such ferment created a demand for environmental manpower which society and its educational institutions were ill prepared to supply. The immediate solution lay in efforts to retrain existing specialists. Next, educational institutions and their curricula were reoriented to meet potential labor market needs. The environmental movement is now forcing individuals and institutions to reshape their thinking and to revise policies and programs of environmental employment and education. Both jobs and training for jobs are becoming more relevant to both labor market needs and to the solving of pressing social problems.

KINDS OF ENVIRONMENTAL JOBS

In its literature, the United States Environmental Protection Agency (EPA) lists more than seventy disciplines in which it employs personnel in research and monitoring activities. These fall largely into three categories: biological and health sciences; physical, engineering, mathematical, and computer sciences; and the social and behavioral sciences.

Environmental management is the term applied to the field in which environmental personnel work, in industry or government. An *environmental manager* is someone who works at the professional or paraprofessional level in a program whose purpose is to manage the human environment. Science and technology are common denominators in much, but not all, environmental management. The environmental manager could be a social or behavioral scientist, medical or nursing practitioner, public or business administrator, architect or planner, journalist, or almost any other trained person whose job involves managing the human environment. Two professional areas in which there are rapidly increasing opportunities are environmental teaching and the practice of environmental law.

I have arbitrarily divided the field of environmental management into six broad categories as follows.

Ecologists are scientists of varying backgrounds concerned with the functioning organism on the one hand and the influencing environment on the other. Ecology often is called the science of the interrelationships of nature. One ecologist might be studying the increase of disease-carrying snails believed to come from the building of the Aswan High Dam on the River Nile. Another might be studying the disappearance of oysters from San Francisco Bay. Another might be in the Peace Corps in Colombia studying the destruction of birdlife, which has resulted from advances in agriculture. Virtually all ecologists have college degrees, most have advanced degrees, and many have doctorates. Ecology is the smallest specialty in environmental management.

Earth scientists are also known as geologists, geophysicists, geographers, meteorologists, oceanographers, and the like. Their work concerns the solid ground, the oceans, the poles, weather and climate, minerals, sun and outer space, and living and nonliving things. Earth scientists are college graduates and often have advanced degrees.

Resource conservationists are individuals concerned with the outdoors and man's use and enjoyment of it. Their interests often are ecological in nature, having to do with the balance of organisms and the influencing environment; therefore, some of them are ecologists as well. Their province includes the soil, water, forests, minerals, wildlife, and grazing lands. A few job titles in this category are forester, fish hatchery manager, wildlife refuge manager, and park ranger. Here we have a wide range of educational requirements. Many outdoor jobs for aides and technicians require only on-the-job training. All the professional positions require at least four years of college, and many require graduate education.

Recreationists may work for public parks departments, the armed forces, industry, resorts, hospitals, schools, or even prisons. The activity specialist, who may or may not have two years of college education, conducts programs such as archery, baseball, basketball, horseshoes, and volleyball. A bachelor's degree in parks and recreation qualifies the recreationist for supervisory and quasi-administrative positions. Advanced degrees are becoming requirements for many recreation positions.

Architects and *planners* are concerned with man's use of the land and with his "built" environment. Architecture is the art and science of designing buildings and the spaces between them. Landscape architecture combines knowledge of plants with the design and blending of buildings and natural features. City and regional planning is concerned with the physical use of space on a large scale. Nearly all architects and planners have college degrees in their specialty.

Environmental health specialists are responsible for protecting man from diseases and blight caused by pollution or associated with social activities. The field may be called public health, sanitation, environmental protection, environmental medicine, or something else. The use of so many terms is symbolic of the identity crisis all environmentalists or environmental managers are experiencing today. Practitioners may be physicians, scientists, engineers, sanitarians, industrial hygienists, inspectors, technicians, aides, nurses, or even laymen or nonscientific specialists.

EDUCATION FOR AN ENVIRONMENTAL CAREER

Because science and technology are at the heart of most environmental management functions, two or more years of college training are needed at the paraprofessional or professional levels. A person who aspires to a career in environmental management should plan to go to college. He should choose a college on the basis of his test scores, preferred geographic location, the expense factor, and the advice of parents, teachers, and counselors. There are many publications in high school or public libraries, including annual college and university guides and catalogs, which describe available courses in environmental studies. A selection of college and university environmental programs is listed in Chapter 7.

While in high school, a student should visit a few college campuses and discuss his needs and aspirations with admissions personnel. During his first two years in college, he will have the opportunity to take introductory courses in ecology and environmental studies, as well as basic liberal arts and sciences. By the end of his sophomore year he should have a better idea of his goals. He might decide to transfer to another college or university for the B.S. or B.A. degree. Before making any move, however, he should discuss his plans with, and seek the advice of, a guidance counselor, faculty advisor, or major professor.

The educational hierarchy is rapidly responding to the environmental challenge. Almost every college and university is developing new courses to try to improve its contributions to local or national environmental needs. Most schools of engineering have reshaped sanitary engineering or agricultural engineering curricula into more comprehensive environmental engineering programs. The graduate schools of public health have deemphasized biology and medicine and reemphasized ecology and man. Other schools— of agriculture, education, home economics, public administration, law, economics, recreation, and natural resources, among others—are taking broader ecological approaches to their traditional disciplines.

A few colleges and universities have emerged with comprehensive environmental studies as specialties: the University of Wisconsin at Green Bay, the University of California at Santa Barbara, Huxley College of Western Washington State College at Bellingham, and College of the Atlantic at Bar Harbor, Maine. Other institutions have won reputations through the presence on their staff of prominent ecologists; for example, Washington University at St. Louis with its Center for the Biology of Natural Systems, headed by Barry Commoner. The major urban universities specialize in problems of the urban environment—housing and rat control, air and water pollution, community action and public interest law, and geography—and in regional development and international environmental programs.

COMPENSATION IN ENVIRONMENTAL JOBS

When the new graduate or trainee begins work in any field, he rarely has any leverage for salary demands upon the employer. But he has ready access to information about salary levels from recruiters who visit his campus, from his classmates, and from published information. Table 1 indicates starting salaries for engineers, including those in environmental specialties, are climbing, and average from $647 to $1,396 per month.

Salary information beyond starting levels is more difficult to obtain, as companies want to negotiate separately with each potential employee. Job advertisements are seldom precise, preferring such expressions as "excellent salaries, commensurate with experience and abilities, plus outstanding benefits." Out of 250 recent ads for environmental jobs in the *New York Times*, only twenty-five mentioned salaries. For example:

Manager, Air Pollution, $23,000. (blind ad, New York)

Outdoor Camping Conservation Education Administrator, $22,000. (Long Island)

Table 1
AVERAGE ENGINEERING
STARTING SALARIES, 1972 GRADUATES

Degree Level	Monthly salary offered	% change from 1971
Associate degree in technology (2 years)	$647	+1.6
Bachelor's degree in engineering (4 or 5 years)	$892	+1.7
Master's degree in engineering (1 or 2 years in addition to B.S.)	$1,024	+1.4
Doctor's degree in engineering (3 to 5 years in addition to B.S.)	$1,396	+4.2

Source: Engineering Manpower Commission of Engineers Joint Council

Noise Pollution Control Specialist, $11,000–$14,000. (Pittsburgh)

Wastewater Pollution Control Project Engineer, $18,000. (agency, Newark)

In those and other ads which specified salaries, the levels seem to be comparable to federal salaries, slightly above most local agencies, and significantly above state agencies.

If one enters federal government service upon graduating from a four-year environmental science or engineering curriculum, he can expect to be rated at the GS-9 level ($12,167 per year), a full grade higher and about $1,000 more than the common entrance salary in federal service for a nonscience or nonengineering college graduate. Federal government salaries and benefits generally are superior to those in private industry, unless, of course, one achieves a vice presidency of a large industrial firm or a partnership in a successful consulting firm, where a high salary might be augmented with profit-sharing and stock options. Another advantage of federal service is that the government will pay an employee to get his master's degree, to study for the doctorate, and even, in some cases, for postdoctoral work. The government's exceptionally liberal annual and sick leave and retirement benefits are other advantages of civil service over private industry. With good performance ratings, one can expect to advance, within five years of graduation, to a GS-12 grade, starting at $17,497; within ten years, to a GS-14 grade, starting at $24,247; and within fifteen years, to a GS-15 grade, starting at $28,263. (Figures are 1974 pay scale).

In response to stricter pollution abatement standards and regulations, private industry is constantly seeking more people for environmental management. Most of the ads cited from the *New York Times* are from manufacturing companies, consulting engineering firms, or employment agencies with unspecified clients.

MANPOWER DEMAND: TODAY AND TOMORROW

Herbert Bienstock, New York regional director of the Bureau of Labor Statistics, in speaking of the job prospects for the rest of the 1970s, recently observed: "In a tight job market it may well be that the college graduate whose academic studies have been more relevant to labor market needs and requirements will experience less difficulty in job adjustment in his immediate post-college years."

Environmental studies are, indeed, relevant to labor market needs and requirements, and there is a growing demand for many types of scientists and engineers, particularly for programs in great public demand. The *Wall Street Journal* recently reported: "Additional engineering jobs have been created by the growing national efforts to increase productivity and to deal with energy demands, pollution problems and industrial health and safety hazards."

The Engineering Manpower Commission of Engineers Joint Council surveyed the placement officers of 260 colleges and universities and concluded: "Despite the slowdown in hiring that resulted from the economic recession of 1970-1971 .... graduates from engineering and technological programs at all levels did not find a general shortage of jobs. Compared to graduates of other curricula, engineers and technicians compiled an outstanding record of finding employment or pursuing other chosen plans."

What about the immediate future? In the same survey of placement officers, "64 percent said the employment situation for new graduates was better this year (1972) than last, 27 percent thought it was about the same, and only nine percent felt it was not as good. In response to a similar question about job prospects for experienced alumni, these same officials were almost as positive."

What about the long-range future? Not one college placement director among the 260 in the survey thought that the employment picture "four to five years from now would be unsatisfactory in any way." Universally, they felt that job prospects would be "good to outstanding." Many pointed to current declines in enrollment as leading inevitably to a shortage of graduates, and therefore excellent job prospects, in the years ahead.

Some typical comments in this survey (with the states in which the university is located) were:

"There will be an emphasis on new specialties relating to the new national goals in environment and urban problems." (Connecticut)

"We need more women and blacks enrolling in engineering and science." (Missouri)

"Anticipate decided need for engineers in environmentally related work." (Texas)

On what basis are university placement officers so optimistic about environmental management? The primary reason is that federal and private spending for environmental control is increasing so rapidly. In 1972 American business investment in air and water pollution abatement equipment increased more than 50 percent over 1971, to an estimated $4.9 billion—$2.9 billion for air quality improvement and $2 billion for water quality improvement.

The *U.S. Industrial Outlook, 1973*, published by the Department of Commerce, reported: "Spending in both public and private sectors is expected to rise further in 1973, assisted by federal funds to be provided under the Clean Waters Act enacted in October 1972. Expenditures for 1973 air and water pollution abatement are expected to exceed $5.9 billion, 20 percent over 1972 levels."

With growing markets for pollution abatement equipment, the Council on Environmental Quality (CEQ) estimates that $274 billion needs to be spent in this decade to clean up the environment. Of this, a third will go into new capital equipment and the remainder into operating costs.

A final, crucial question: How many jobs will this spending for environmental improvement create in the field of environmental management between now and 1980?

Table 2
ENVIRONMENTAL MANAGEMENT EMPLOYMENT, 1973
AND ESTIMATED MANPOWER NEEDS, 1980

Field	Employed 1973 (or latest year surveyed)	Needed by 1980
Ecology	4,800	14,400
Earth sciences	39,400	95,800
Resource conservation	99,500	146,300
Recreation	215,790	260,000
Environmental design (architecture and planning)	89,500	162,700
Environmental health (or environmental protection)	242,000	665,000
Total	690,990	1,344,200

Source: Opportunities in Environmental Careers

Manpower projections are notably unscientific and unreliable. Throughout the 1960s projections on environmental management were so conservative that they foresaw fewer than one-fifth of the individuals actually found, later, to be employed in environmental disciplines. Federal funding is determined by the President and the Congress one year at a time; therefore, any projection of activities for the next five to ten years, which depends on funding, is understandably a guess.

Yet both industrial and government leaders foresee a significant, continuing demand for trained manpower, lasting until the end of this decade and beyond. The Environmental Protection Agency predicts that water pollution control will require additional highly trained sanitary or environmental engineers plus technicians with two years in a qualified community college program in air, water, solid wastes, or possibly estuarine or marine technology.

The most comprehensive picture of environmental management manpower needs can be derived by combining censuses of present employment, plotting curves over the past three years, and making an educated guess about the continuation of manpower demands. In this process, one makes certain assumptions, notably the avoidance of war, an ever-growing economy, and no slackening of public demand for environmental enhancement. In my studies I identify manpower for the six categories of environmental management now numbering approximately 700,000. Furthermore, I believe that the nation will need, by 1980, virtually a doubling—to 1.4 million, as shown in Table 2.

To achieve the goals of our national and international environmental management programs, much of this nation's employment and education must be reoriented. Fortunately for the student interested in an environmental career, as well as for the country, we are in the midst of a reorientation towards relevance. By that I mean that both environmental employment and environmental education are rapidly becoming more relevant to the needs and requirements of the labor market and of society in general.

For further information on environmental careers, consult Odom Fanning, *Opportunities in Environmental Careers*, published 1971, 1972, and 1973 by Vocational Guidance Manuals, 235 E. 45 St., New York, N.Y. 10017, at $5.75.

7 Environmental Education Programs

This chapter lists enviromental studies programs currently in operation or being planned by U.S. colleges and universities. The listings reflect a restructuring of traditional educational programs that has resulted from increased public and institutional awareness of environmental problems.

The essence of the new programs is a reorganization of curricula into departments that cut across former disciplinary lines and employ faculty from many academic fields. Such programs frequently combine the social sciences, humanities, physical and biological sciences, and engineering.

This chapter does not describe environmental courses in detail; but it indicates the general scope and emphases of the programs. Many programs are in an experimental stage; therefore, it is likely that general goals and specific course work will be modified. Readers interested in a given program may obtain detailed information from the person or office in charge of program inquiries.

ALABAMA

Univ. of South Alabama
307 Gaillard Dr., Mobile, Ala. 36608
205-460-6141
Proposed degree in recreation.
Program Inquiries: Chairman, Dept. of Health, Physical Education, and Recreation
Proposed interdisciplinary degree in environmental control studies.
Program Inquiries: Dr. F. H. Mitchell, Dept. of Physics

ALASKA

Univ. of Alaska
College, Alaska 99701
907-479-7211
Graduate programs (M.S., M.A., Ph.D.) in biological sciences, wildlife management, land resources, and teaching (biology).
Program Inquiries: Dean, Col. of Biological Sciences and Renewable Resources

CALIFORNIA

California Institute of Technology
1201 E. California Blvd., Pasadena, Calif. 91109
213-795-6841
Interdisciplinary graduate program in environmental engineering.
Program Inquiries: Chairman, Div. of Engineering and Applied Science

California State Col., Bakersfield
9001 Stockdale Hwy., Bakersfield, Calif. 93309
805-833-2011
Interdepartmental program emphasizing environmental relationships with human health.
Program Inquiries: Dean, Sch. of Natural Sciences

California State Col., Hayward
25800 Hillary St., Hayward, Calif. 94542
415-884-3723
Graduate program in elementary curriculum with an option in environmental education.
Program Inquiries: Dr. Esther P. Railton, Dept. of Teacher Education

California State Col., Long Beach
6101 E. 7 St., Long Beach, Calif. 90840
213-498-4111
Undergraduate and graduate programs (B.S., M.S.) in biology, including marine science.
Program Inquiries: Chairman, Biology Dept.

California State Polytechnic Institute
3801 W. Temple Ave., Pomona, Calif. 91768
213-964-6424
Courses in environmental design, biology, and water resource management.
Program Inquiries: Admissions Office

California State Univ., Fresno
Shaw and Cedar Aves., Fresno, Calif. 93710
209-487-9011
Programs of instruction and research in marine environment; interdisciplinary programs in environmental studies and ecology. Program Inquiries: Dean, Sch. of Natural Sciences

Chico State Col.
Chico, Calif. 95926
916-345-5011
Undergraduate and graduate programs (B.A., M.A.) in park and recreation administration with an emphasis on outdoor education and camping.
Program Inquiries: Dr. Donald Hall, Administration Bldg.

Humboldt State Col.
Arcata, Calif. 95521
707-826-3011
Undergraduate program (B.S.) in natural resources with emphasis on conservation education; minor in natural resources for students majoring in other fields, particularly education.
Program Inquiries: Sch. of Natural Resources

Sacramento State Col.
6000 J St., Sacramento, Calif. 95819
916-454-6011
Undergraduate program (B.S.) in biological conservation.
Program Inquiries: Chairman, Dept. of Biological Sciences
Undergraduate and graduate programs (B.A., M.A.) in ecological studies to fill the need for broadly trained people in this area.
Program Inquiries: Director, Ecological Studies Program
Undergraduate program (B.S.) in environmental resources with concentrations in park administration, park interpretation, park planning, and resource management.
Program Inquiries: V. Aubrey Neasham, Chairman, Dept. of Environmental Resources

San Diego State Col.
5402 College Ave., San Diego, Calif. 92115
714-286-5000
Graduate programs (M.A., M.S., Ph.D.) in ecology with emphasis on research and teaching.
Program Inquiries: Chairman, Dept. of Biology
Graduate program (M.A.) in geography with specialization in conservation.
Program Inquiries: Chairman, Dept. of Geography

San Fernando Valley State Col.
18111 Nordhoff St., Northridge, Calif. 91324
213-885-1200
Undergraduate program (B.S.) in recreation resources administration; proposed graduate program (M.S.) in outdoor recreation and resources administration.
Program Inquiries: Talmage W. Morash, Dept. of Recreation

San Francisco State Col.
1600 Holloway Ave., San Francisco, Calif. 94132
415-469-9123
Graduate program (M.A.) in education with a concentration in outdoor education.
Program Inquiries: Dept. of Ecology and Systematic Biology

San Jose State Col.
125 S. 7 St., San Jose, Calif. 95114
408-294-6414
Undergraduate programs in environmental studies (B.A.) and environmental sciences (B.S.).
Program Inquiries: Dr. Donald W. Aitken, Chairman, Dept. of Environmental Studies

Univ. of California, Davis
Davis, Calif. 95616
916-752-2065
Interdisciplinary graduate programs (M.S., Ph.D.) in ecology; research-oriented programs with emphasis on interdisciplinary approaches to current problems of environmental quality.
Program Inquiries: Chairman, Graduate Group in Ecology, Institute of Ecology

Univ. of California, Irvine
Irvine, Calif. 92664
714-833-5414

Graduate programs (M.S., Ph.D.) in population studies and environmental biology.
Program Inquiries: Dr. Howard A. Schneiderman, Dean, Sch. of Biological Sciences

Univ. of California, Los Angeles
405 Hilgard Ave., Los Angeles, Calif. 90024
415-845-6000
Undergraduate programs (B.A.) in geography and analysis and conservation of ecosystems.
Program Inquiries: Chairman, Dept. of Geography

Univ. of California, Riverside
Riverside, Calif. 92502
415-845-6000
Graduate programs in environmental health service training.
Program Inquiries: Chairman, Dept. of Biology

Univ. of California, San Diego
La Jolla, Calif. 92037
415-845-6000
Graduate programs in oceanography.
Program Inquiries: Scripps Institution of Oceanography

Univ. of California, Santa Barbara
Santa Barbara, Calif. 93106
805-961-3231
Undergraduate interdisciplinary degree program (B.S.) in environmental sciences.
Program Inquiries: Chairman, Environmental Studies Committee

Univ. of California, Santa Cruz
Santa Cruz, Calif. 95060
415-845-6000
Undergraduate program (B.A.) in environmental studies.
Program Inquiries: Chairman, Environmental Studies Program

Univ. of Southern California
Los Angeles, Calif. 90007
213-746-2311
Nondegree program of research and training for improved understanding and control of urban and environmental programs.
Program Inquiries: Institute of Urban Ecology

COLORADO

Adams State Col.
Alamosa, Colo. 81101
303-589-7321
Undergraduate program in environmental sciences; undergraduate selected studies program in which individual students work out a program of studies best suited to their needs under an adviser's guidance.
Program Inquiries: Dr. James H. Craft, Dept. of Biology

Colorado State Univ.
Fort Collins, Colo. 80521
303-491-5321
Undergraduate and graduate programs in recreation and watershed resources. An outdoor recreation program offers studies in parks and recreation, planning, and environmental interpretation.
Program Inquiries: Arthur T. Wilcox, Head, Dept. of Recreation Resources

Univ. of Colorado
Boulder, Colo. 80302
303-443-2211
Undergraduate program (B.A.) in conservation education; graduate programs (M.A., Ph.D.) in geography with an emphasis on conservation.
Program Inquiries: Tim K. Kelley, Dept. of Geography

Univ. of Denver
Denver, Colo. 80210
303-753-2036
Undergraduate and graduate programs in environmental sciences.
Program Inquiries: Director, Environmental Science and Technology Center

Univ. of Northern Colorado
Greeley, Colo. 80639
303-351-1890
Interdisciplinary graduate program in outdoor education.
Program Inquiries: Dr. Vince A. Cyphers, Coordinator, Outdoor Education Program

CONNECTICUT

Univ. of Connecticut
Storrs, Conn. 06268
203-429-3311
Undergraduate program (B.S.) in secondary education with emphasis on outdoor education.
Program Inquiries: Dr. Herbert Tag, Sch. of Education

Undergraduate program (B.S.) in natural resources conservation.
Program Inquiries: Prof. Miklos Gratzer, Col. of Agriculture and Natural Resources
Graduate programs (M.A., M.S., Ph.D.) in systematic and environmental biology.
Program Inquiries: Prof. Henry N. Andrews, Systematic and Environmental Biology

Yale Univ. School of Forestry
205 Prospect St., New Haven, Conn. 06511
203-787-3131
Graduate program in forestry science; students may elect to concentrate in conservation education
Program Inquiries: Admissions Office

Delaware

Univ. of Delaware
Newark, Del. 19711
302-738-2000
Undergraduate program (B.S.) in agricultural engineering with emphasis on soil and water conservation.
Program Inquiries: Prof. Ely Scarborough, Dept. of Agricultural Engineering
Undergraduate and graduate programs (B.S., M.S.) in entomology with an option in ecology.
Program Inquiries: Dr. W. E. McDaniel, Dean, Col. of Agricultural Science
Graduate program (M.Ed.) in population-environmental education.
Program Inquiries: Population Curriculum Study, Col. of Education

District of Columbia

George Washington Univ.
Washington, D.C. 20006
202-676-6000
Graduate program in environmental science, with emphasis on solving policy problems in government.
Program Inquiries: Director, Natural Resources Policy Center

Florida

Florida Atlantic Univ.
Boca Raton, Fla. 33432
305-395-5100
Undergraduate program (B.A.) in conservation biology with emphasis on field studies and their practical application.
Program Inquiries: Chairman, Dept. of Biological Sciences

Univ. of Florida
Gainesville, Fla. 32601
904-392-1365
Graduate programs (M.A., Ph.D.) in teaching and research in areas of environmental concern.
Program Inquiries: Admissions Office

Univ. of Jacksonville
Jacksonville, Fla. 32211
904-744-3950
Undergraduate and graduate programs in freshwater and salt-water life.
Program Inquiries: Center for Estuarine Studies

Univ. of West Florida
Pensacola, Fla. 32504
904-476-9500
Proposed interdisciplinary environmental science program; proposed master's degree program in recreation with emphasis on outdoor recreation, conservation, and nature interpretation.
Program Inquiries: Dr. Herman C. Kranzer, Faculty of Elementary Education

Georgia

The Univ. of Georgia
Athens, Ga. 30601
404-542-4040
Interdisciplinary graduate and undergraduate programs to promote research and application of principles of environmental science.
Program Inquiries: Institute of Ecology; Institute of Natural Resources

Idaho

Col. of Idaho
Caldwell, Idaho 83605
208-459-5011
Proposed undergraduate program in environmental science.
Program Inquiries: Director, Regional Environmental Center

Illinois

Eastern Illinois Univ.
Charleston, Ill. 61920
217-581-2223
Undergraduate program (B.S.) in environmental biology, including practical work experience with an agency concerned with environmental quality.
Program Inquiries: Dr. Leonard Durham, Director, Div. of Life Sciences

George Williams Col.
555 31 St., Downers Grove, Ill. 60515
312-964-3100
Undergraduate and graduate programs (B.S., M.S.) in applied behavioral science and recreation studies with emphasis on camping and outdoor education.
Program Inquiries: Dr. Lyle K. Johnson, Director, Div. of Applied Behavioral Science

Two-year master's degree program in camping and outdoor education administration; includes field work.
Program Inquiries: Nelson E. Wieters, Graduate Dept., Camping and Outdoor Education Administration

Illinois Institute of Technology
Chicago, Ill. 60616
312-225-9600
Graduate programs (M.S., Ph.D.) in air, water, and health engineering.
Program Inquiries: Environmental Engineering Center

Kankakee Community Col.
R.R. 1, River Rd., Box 888, Kankakee, Ill. 60901
815-933-9311
One-year certificate program in outdoor education.
Program Inquiries: Dr. David L. Ferris, Continuing Education

Northern Illinois Univ.
Lorado Taft Field Campus, DeKalb, Ill. 60115
815-753-1000
Graduate program (M.S. Ed.) in outdoor teacher education.
Program Inquiries: Dr. Donald R. Hammerman, Head, Dept. of Outdoor Teacher Education

Northwestern Univ.
Evanston, Ill. 60201
312-492-3741
Graduate programs (M.S., Ph.D.) in biology with a major program of study in environmental biology.
Program Inquiries: Dr. Lawrence I. Gilbert, Chairman, Dept. of Biology

Southern Illinois Univ.
Carbondale, Ill. 62901
Graduate program (M.S. Ed.) in conservation and outdoor education.
Program Inquiries: Paul F. Nowak, Chairman, Dept. of Conservation and Outdoor Education

Undergraduate and graduate (B.S., M.S.) in outdoor recreation resources management with concentrations in social science, biological science, managerial science, and natural science.
Program Inquiries: Ray Mischon, Dept. of Forestry

Undergraduate and graduate programs (B.S., M.S., Ph.D.) in recreation with an option in outdoor education.
Program Inquiries: Dr. William E. O'Brien, Chairman, Dept. of Recreation

Univ. of Illinois
104 Huff Gymnasium, Champaign, Ill. 61820
217-333-1000
Undergraduate and graduate programs (B.S., M.S.) in recreation with specialization in outdoor recreation and education; Ph.D. program in physical education with an option in recreation and specialization in outdoor recreation and education.
Program Inquiries: Prof. Allen V. Sapora, Head, Dept. of Recreation and Park Administration

Indiana

Ball State Univ.
Muncie, Ind. 47306
317-289-1241
Undergraduate and graduate programs (B.A., B.S., M.A., M.S.) in natural resources with options in resource geography, fishery resources, communications, and general natural resources; a number of courses have been developed especially for these programs.
Program Inquiries: Director, Natural Resources Institute

Indiana State Univ.
Terre Haute, Ind. 47809

812-232-6311

Graduate programs in life sciences (M.A., Ph.D.) and secondary school teaching of life sciences (M.S.—nonthesis, M.A.—thesis). Both programs have specializations in ecology.

Program Inquiries: Dr. Christopher P. Sword, Chairman, Dept. of Life Sciences

Indiana Univ.
Bloomington, Ind. 47401
812-332-0211

Undergraduate and graduate programs (B.S., M.S. Rc. Dir., Rc.D.) in recreation with emphasis on camping and outdoor education; includes a teaching minor.

Program Inquiries: Dr. Theodore Deppe, Chairman, Dept. of Recreation and Park Administration

Purdue Univ.
Lafayette, Ind. 47907
915-749-8111

Undergraduate and graduate programs (B.S., M.S., Ph.D.) in conservation and conservation education. Areas of emphasis include general conservation, outdoor recreation, management, nature interpretation, and international conservation.

Program Inquiries: W.C. Bramble, Head, Dept. of Forestry and Conservation

Bachelor's degree program in environmental science; graduate program in this area is being developed.

Program Inquiries: Ronald L. Giese, Director, Natural Resources and Environmental Science Program

Iowa

Iowa State Univ.
Ames, Iowa 50010
515-294-4111

Interdisciplinary courses for graduates and qualified undergraduates in water resources management.

Program Inquiries: Admissions Office

Univ. of Iowa
Iowa City, Iowa 52240
319-353-3452

Graduate program in comparative medicine (M.S.) and industrial hygiene (Ph.D.); both research-oriented.

Program Inquiries: Director, Institute of Agricultural Medicine

Kansas

Kansas State Teachers Col.
Emporia, Kans. 66801
316-343-1200

Undergraduate program (B.A.) in biology with emphasis in ecology.

Program Inquiries: Thomas A. Eddy, Dept. of Biology

Kansas State Univ., College of Agriculture
Manhattan, Kans. 66502
913-532-6011

Undergraduate program (B.S.) in natural resource conservation and use with options in economics of conservation, soil, and water conservation and conservation of recreational areas. Programs are tailored to each student's objectives.

Program Inquiries: Natural Resource Conservation and Use, Col. of Agriculture

Louisiana

Louisiana Polytechnic Institute
Ruston, La. 71270
318-257-2641

Nondegree program in water resources management and interpretation.

Program Inquiries: Water Resources Center

Louisiana State Univ.
Baton Rouge, La. 70803
504-388-5475

Undergraduate and graduate programs in environmental design.

Program Inquiries: Dean, Sch. of Environmental Design

Northwestern State Univ.
Natchitoches, La. 71457
318-357-6171

Graduate program (M.S. Ed.) in outdoor education. Program may be designed to fit individual needs.

Program Inquiries: Dr. Warren R. Evans, Chairman, Div. of Outdoor Education and Recreation, Dept. of Health, Physical Education, and Recreation

Tulane Univ.
New Orleans, La. 70118
504-865-7711

Graduate programs (M.S., Ph.D.) in biology; training and research in environmental biology, including ecology and systematics.

Program Inquiries: Prof. Volpe, Chairman, Dept. of Biology

MAINE

Col. of the Atlantic
Box 3, Bar Harbor, Maine 04609
Bachelor's degree program in human ecology.
Program Inquiries: Admissions Office.

Univ. of Maine
Orano, Maine 04473
207-866-7011
Graduate programs as environmental education specialist (M.Ed., Ed.D.) and as classroom teacher (M.Ed.) with emphasis on conservation education.
Program Inquiries: Dr. D.W. Bishop, Col. of Education
Bachelor's degree program in natural resource management with options in conservation, engineering, soil and water conservation, forest resources, and resource economics; Associate of Science degree in resource and business management.
Program Inquiries: Dr. Winston E. Pullen, Col. of Life Science and Agriculture
Proposed program in recreation education including outdoor education.
Program Inquiries: Director, Physical Education and Athletics

MARYLAND

Johns Hopkins Univ.
Baltimore, Md. 21218
301-366-3300
Graduate programs to study the operation and interrelationships of the environment and to work out engineering and administrative solutions.
Program Inquiries: Chairman, Dept. of Geography and Environmental Engineering

Univ. of Maryland
College Park, Md. 20742
301-454-0100
Undergraduate and graduate programs (B.S., M.A.) in recreation with emphasis on outdoor education; graduate program includes a summer outdoor education workshop.
Program Inquiries: Dr. Ellen E. Harney, Head, Dept. of Recreation, Col. of Physical Education, Recreation, and Health

MASSACHUSETTS

Boston Col.
Chestnut Hill, Mass. 02167
617-969-0100
Interdisciplinary undergraduate and graduate programs in environmental science.
Program Inquiries: Admissions Office

Boston Univ.
765 Commonwealth Ave., Boston, Mass. 02215
617-353-2100
Undergraduate and graduate programs (B.S. in Ed., M.Ed., Ed.D.) in outdoor education and school camping.
Program Inquires: Dr. James A. Wylie, Sch. of Education

Eastern Nazarene Col.
Quincy, Mass. 02170
617-773-6350
Undergraduate teacher training program in marine and terrestrial environmental biology.
Program Inquiries: Sch. of Education

Harvard Univ.
Cambridge, Mass. 02138
617-868-7600
Program in environmental science.
Program Inquiries: Chairman, Dept. of Environmental Sciences and Engineering

Springfield Col.
Springfield, Mass. 01109
413-781-2200
Bachelor's degree programs in environmental studies.
Program Inquiries: Joel Cohen, Chairman, Biology Dept.
Bachelor's degree programs in outdoor education; graduate programs (M.Ed.) in outdoor education and community and outdoor recreation.
Program Inquiries: Dr. Robert E. Markarian, Director, Div. of Community Education
Certificate of Advanced Study in teacher education with specialization in school camping and outdoor education.
Program Inquiries: Director, Graduate Teacher Education

Univ. of Massachusetts
Amherst, Mass. 01002
413-545-0222
Bachelor's degree program in recreation with options in environmental interpretation and natural history interpretation.

Program Inquiries: Dr. W. E. Randall, Head, Dept. of Recreation

Program in environmental science.

Program Inquiries: Prof. John A. Naegele, Dept. of Environmental Science

Proposed program in natural resources ecology.

Program Inquiries: Joseph Larson, Dept. of Forestry and Wildlife

Williams Col.
Williamstown, Mass. 02167
413-458-7131

Undergraduate programs in environmental science.

Program Inquiries: Center for Environmental Studies

MICHIGAN

Central Michigan Univ.
Mount Pleasant, Mich. 48858
517-774-3151

Five-year combined undergraduate and graduate program in natural resources and liberal arts; two-year preparatory curriculum in forestry and conservation. A conservation minor may be obtained with one of several major programs.

Program Inquiries: Chairman, Dept. of Biology

Michigan State Univ.
East Lansing, Mich. 48823
517-355-1855

Graduate programs (master's and doctoral) in outdoor education with workshops, seminars, and independent study.

Program Inquiries: Dr. Julian W. Smith, Dept. of Administration and Higher Education, Col. of Education

Undergraduate and graduate programs (B.S., M.S., Ph.D.) in conservation education.

Program Inquiries: Dr. Gilbert W. Monser, Dept. of Fisheries and Wildlife

Undergraduate and graduate programs in park and recreation resources (B.S., M.S.) and natural resources (Ph.D.).

Program Inquiries: Dr. Louis Tvardzik, Dept. of Park and Recreation Resources, Sch. of Natural Resources

Northern Michigan Univ.
Marquette, Mich. 49855
906-227-1000

Offers a minor in conservation or conservation education; two-year programs in preparation for studies in forestry, conservation, or resource education.

Program Inquiries: Dr. Henry Heimonen, Head, Dept. of Geography, Earth Science, and Conservation

Univ. of Michigan
Ann Arbor, Mich. 48103
313-764-1817

Undergraduate and graduate programs in conservation (B.S., M.S.), conservation and teaching (B.S., M.S.), and naturalist (B.S.).

Program Inquiries: Dean, Sch. of Natural Resources

Graduate programs (M.A., Ph.D.) in environmental education.

Program Inquiries: Dr. William B. Stapp, Director, Environmental Education Programs, Sch. of Natural Resources

Graduate programs (M.S., Ph.D.) in resource planning and conservation with emphasis in ecology, economics, policy, and institutions; graduate programs in natural resources administration (M.S.) and natural resource economics (Ph.D.).

Program Inquiries: Admissions Office, Horace H. Packham Sch. of Graduate Studies

Western Michigan Univ.
Kalamazoo, Mich. 49001
616-383-1630

Bachelor's degree program in environmental studies.

Program Inquiries: Dr. Robert W. Kaufman, Dept. of Political Science, Institute for Public Affairs

MINNESOTA

Bemidji State Col.
Bemidji, Minn. 56601
218-755-2020

Bachelor's degree program in elementary education with a concentration in outdoor education and secondary education and a minor in outdoor education.

Program Inquiries: Dr. Robert A. Montebello, Dept. of Health, Safety, and Recreation

Mankato State Col.
Mankato, Minn. 56001
507-389-1111

Undergraduate programs (B.S., B.S. Teaching) in environmental studies coordinated with second major in biology, chemistry, geography, recreation and park administration, or sociology.

Program Inquiries: Dr. Theodore L. Nydahl, Chairman, Environmental Studies Program Committee, Sch. of Arts and Sciences

Univ. of Minnesota
Minneapolis, Minn. 55455
612-373-2851
Graduate programs (M.S., Ph.D.) in ecology; minimal required course work with programs tailored to individual needs.
Program Inquiries: Dr. John R. Tester, Director of Graduate Studies, Dept. of Ecology and Behavioral Biology

Winona State Col.
Winona, Minn. 55987
507-457-2002
Undergraduate and graduate (master's degree only) in river research.
Program Inquiries: River Research Foundation

Mississippi

Mississippi State Univ.
State College, Miss. 39762
601-325-2022
Graduate programs in space and environmental sciences.
Program Inquiries: Director, Institute for Space and Environmental Sciences and Engineering

Univ. of Southern Mississippi
Hattiesburg, Miss. 39401
601-266-7011
Undergraduate and graduate programs (B.S., M.S.) in recreation with emphasis on outdoor education.
Program Inquiries: Dr. John M. King, Dept. of Recreation

Missouri

Central Missouri State Col.
Warrensburg, Mo. 64093
816-747-8141
Undergraduate programs (B.A., B.S.) in biology with concentration in conservation.
Program Inquiries: Dr. Oscar Hawksley, Dept. of Biology

Northeast Missouri State Col.
Kirksville, Mo. 63501
816-665-5121
Undergraduate program (B.S. in Ed.) in environmental science for students wishing to become accredited earth science teachers.
Program Inquiries: Dean A. Rosebery, Head, Science Div.

Univ. of Missouri
Columbia, Mo. 65201
314-449-9221
Undergraduate and graduate programs in environmental science.
Program Inquiries: Environmental Health Center

Montana

Univ. of Montana
Missoula, Mont. 59801
406-243-0211
Master's and doctoral degrees in environmental education.
Program Inquiries: Dr. Ray C. White, Sch. of Education
Bachelor's and master's degree programs in resource conservation with specialization in conservation education or environmental interpretation.
Program Inquiries: Dean, Sch. of Forestry
Master's degree programs in environmental studies.
Program Inquiries: W. Leslie Pengelly, Coordinator, Environmental Studies Program, Sch. of Forestry

Nebraska

Chadron State Col.
Chadron, Nebr. 69337
308-432-5571
Bachelor's program in recreation with emphasis on outdoor education.
Program Inquiries: Mack Peyton, Dept. of Health, Physical Education, and Recreation

Univ. of Nebraska
Lincoln, Nebr. 68503
402-472-7211
Undergraduate program (B.S.) in natural resources with options in soil conservation and survey, range management, recreational resources management, and water resources management.
Program Inquiries: Donald F. Burzlaff, Col. of Agriculture

Univ. of Nebraska at Omaha
Omaha, Nebr. 68101
402-553-4700
Undergraduate program (B.S.) in recreation with emphasis on outdoor education.
Program Inquiries: Ernie Gorr, Dept. of Health, Physical Education, and Recreation

NEVADA

Univ. of Nevada
Reno, Nev. 89507
702-784-6865
Bachelor's degree program in renewable natural resources with options in forestry, game management, range science, recreation area management, watershed management, and conservation.
Program Inquiries: C. M. Skau, Chairman, Renewable Natural Resources Div., Col. of Agriculture
Undergraduate program (B.S.) in elementary education with concentration in environmental science.
Program Inquiries: Dept. of Elementary Education, Col. of Education
Undergraduate program (B.S.) in secondary education with teaching minor in environmental science.
Program Inquiries: Dr. John Trent, Dept. of Secondary Education, Col. of Education

NEW HAMPSHIRE

Dartmouth Col.
Hanover, N.H. 03755
603-646-1110
Program in environmental studies.
Program Inquiries: Director, Environmental Studies Program

Univ. of New Hampshire
Durham, N.H. 03824
603-862-1360
Graduate program in water resources.
Program Inquiries: Water Resource Research Center
Nondegree program in resource development and use.
Program Inquiries: Resources Development Center
Undergraduate and graduate programs in engineering design.
Program Inquiries: Engineering Design and Analysis Laboratory

NEW JERSEY

Glassboro State Col.
Glassboro, N.J. 08028
609-881-8400
Master's degree program in environmental education.
Program Inquiries: Dr. Thomas J. Rillo, Professor of Outdoor Education

Montclair State Col.
Upper Montclair, N.J. 07043
201-893-4000
Interdepartmental master's degree program in environmental education.
Program Inquiries: Dr. Edward J. Ambry, Associate Dean, Graduate Studies

Rutgers Univ.
New Brunswick, N.J. 08903
201-247-1766
Undergraduate program (B.S.) in environmental science education which includes student teaching.
Program Inquiries: Director of Resident Instruction, Col. of Agriculture and Environmental Science

NEW MEXICO

New Mexico Institute of Mining and Technology
Socorro, N. Mex. 87801
505-835-5424
Graduate programs (M.S., Ph.D.) in physics or geophysics specializing in cloud research.
Program Inquiries: Director, Cloud Physics Center, Langmuir Laboratory

Univ. of New Mexico
Albuquerque, N. Mex. 87107
505-277-0111
Undergraduate and graduate programs in recreation (B.A., M.S., Ph.D.) with options in outdoor education and natural resource management.
Program Inquiries: D. Warder, Dept. of Recreation

NEW YORK

Alfred Univ.
Alfred, N.Y. 14802
607-587-8157

Interdepartmental program in environmental studies.
Program Inquiries: Admissions Office

Briarcliff Col.
Briarcliff Manor, N.Y. 10510
914-941-6400
Program in biology with emphasis on environmental science.
Program Inquiries: Walter Chinziusky

City Univ. of New York
New York, N.Y. 10031
212-621-2541
Graduate programs (M.S., Ph.D.) in biology with ecology concentration.
Program Inquiries: Chairman, Dept. of Biology

Col. of New Rochelle
New Rochelle, N.Y. 10801
914-632-5300
Undergraduate program in marine environment.
Program Inquiries: Environmental Science Center

Columbia Univ.
Broadway and W. 116 St., New York, N.Y. 10027
212-280-1754
Five-year Ph.D. program in ecological anthropology.
Program Inquiries: Prof. Andrew Vayda, Dept. of Anthropology

Community Col. of the Finger Lakes
Canandaigua, N.Y. 14424
315-394-3500
Associate degree in natural resource conservation; program prepares for career in conservation or transfer to four-year institution.
Program Inquiries: Director, Natural Resource Conservation Program

Cornell Univ
Ithaca, N.Y. 14850
607-273-4321
Graduate programs (M.S., M.A., Ph.D.) in conservation with courses in aquatic science, fishery science, forest conservation, natural resources conservation, and wildlife science.
Program Inquiries: Chairman, Dept. of Conservation
Graduate programs (M.S., M.A., Ph.D.) in ecology and evolutionary biology with courses in aquatic ecology, community and ecosystem ecology, environmental physiology, evolutionary biology, general ecology, paleontology, parasitology, population ecology, terrestrial ecology, and vertebrate zoology.
Program Inquiries: Chairman, Dept. of Ecology and Evolutionary Biology
Undergraduate and graduate programs (B.S., B.A., M.S., M.A.T., Ph.D.) in environmental education.
Program Inquiries: Dr. Richard B. Fischer, Environmental Education, Div. of Conservation Education, Dept. of Education.
Undergraduate program (B.S.) in natural resources, including wildlife science, fishery science, forestry science, outdoor recreation, and environmental conservation; master's degree program in natural resources, including fishery biology, wildlife science, and natural resources conservation.
Program Inquiries: Chairman, Dept. of Natural Resources, Col. of Agriculture

Manhattan Col.
Bronx, N.Y. 10471
212-548-1400
Graduage program in water pollution control; part of the sanitary engineering program.
Program Inquiries: Admissions Office

Mercy Col.
Dobbs Ferry, N.Y. 10522
914-693-4500
Programs to study effects of thermal effluents and algal and bacterial species and their role.
Program Inquiries: Director, Ecological Training and Research Center

New York Univ.
Rm. 675, Education Bldg., New York, N.Y. 10003
212-598-1212
Programs in camping education (M.A., sixth-year certificate, Ph.D., Ed.D.) with specialization in outdoor education and environmental education.
Program Inquiries: Dr. Edith L. Ball, Director, Recreation and Camping Education Area, Div. of Health, Physical Education, and Recreation

New York University Medical Center
New York, N.Y. 10003
Graduate program in health as it is affected by the environment.
Program Inquiries: Institute of Environmental Medicine

Polytechnic Institute of Brooklyn
Brooklyn, N.Y. 11201

212-643-5000
Graduate programs in urban environment field.
Program Inquiries: Director, Center for Urban Environmental Studies

Queens Col.
65-30 Kissena Blvd., Flushing, N.Y. 11367
212-445-7500
Proposed graduate and undergraduate programs in environmental studies.
Program Inquiries: Dr. John Loret, Director, Environmental Studies

Rensselaer Polytechnic Institute
Troy, N.Y. 12181
518-270-6000
Graduate program in urban environment field.
Program Inquiries: Admissions Office

State Univ. College at Buffalo
1300 Elmwood Ave., Buffalo, N.Y. 14222
716-862-4000
Master's degree program in biology with emphasis on environmental biology.
Program Inquiries: George M. Lang, Dept. of Biology

State Univ. College at Fredonia
Fredonia, N.Y. 14063
716-673-3251
Program for environmental research on the Great Lakes.
Program Inquiries: Director, Lake Erie Environmental Studies

State Univ. College of Forestry
Syracuse, N.Y. 13210
315-848-2566
Master's degree program in forest resources management.
Program Inquiries: Prof. Russell Getty, Chairman, Forest Resources Management

State Univ. of New York at Albany
Albany, N.Y. 12200
518-457-3300
Program in environmental studies.
Program Inquiries: Eugene McLaren, Coordinator, Environmental Studies Program

State Univ. of New York at Purchase
Purchase, N.Y. 10577
914-253-5000
Interdepartmental undergraduate program in environmental science. Interfaces with urban studies in the division of social sciences (Dean John Howard).

Program Inquiries: Curtis A. Williams, Dean of Natural Sciences

State Univ. of New York at Stony Brook
Stony Brook, N.Y. 11790
516-246-5000
Program in problems of estuaries and ocean waters.
Program Inquiries: Marine Sciences Research Center

Union College and Univ.
Schenectady, N.Y. 12308
518-346-8751
Graduate programs in environmental sciences; goals are research and teaching.
Program Inquiries: Admissions Office

North Carolina

North Carolina State Univ. at Raleigh
Raleigh, N.C. 27600
919-755-2191
Bachelor's degree programs in natural resources, recreation management, and conservation.
Program Inquiries: Dr. LeRoy C. Saylor, Assistant Dean, Sch. of Forest Resources

Univ. of North Carolina
Chapel Hill, N.C. 27541
919-933-2304
Graduate programs in air pollution control and environmental health.
Program Inquiries: Institute for Environmental Health Studies

Wake Forest Univ.
Winston-Salem, N.C. 27109
919-725-9711
Graduate programs (M.A., Ph.D.) in biology with opportunities for research in physiological ecology and population ecology.
Program Inquiries: Dr. Ralph D. Amen, Chairman, Dept. of Biology

North Dakota

Univ. of North Dakota
Grand Forks, N. Dak. 58201
701-777-2011
Research projects, seminars, and symposia on ecological studies and the environmental sciences.

Program Inquiries: Director, Institute for Ecological Studies

OHIO

Antioch Col.
Yellow Springs, Ohio 45387
513-767-7331
Bachelor's degree program in environmental studies. Programs are individually tailored and include work programs in the United States or abroad.
Program Inquiries: Dr. Robert Bieri, Chairman, Environmental Studies Center

Kent State Univ.
Kent, Ohio 44241
216-672-2444
Program in recreational leadership with specialization in interpretive ecology.
Program Inquiries: Glenna Williams, Dept. of Recreation, Sch. of Health, Physical Education, and Recreation

Miami Univ.
Oxford, Ohio 45056
513-529-2161
Master's degree program in environmental science.
Program Inquiries: Dr. Gary W. Barrett

Ohio State Univ.
124 W. 17 Ave., Columbus, Ohio 43210
614-422-1321
Bachelor's degree programs in conservation and outdoor education, double degree with education (B.S. in Agriculture and B.S. in Ed.), and interpretive work. Master's degree programs in conservation, outdoor education, and environmental education.
Program Inquiries: Dr. Carl S. Johnson, Sch. of Natural Resources
Undergraduate program (B.S. in Ed.) in recreation and outdoor education.
Program Inquiries: Dr. Charles L. Mand, Sch. of Health, Physical Education, and Recreation

Univ. of Cincinnati
Cincinnati, Ohio 45221
513-475-8000
Graduage programs in environmental health, air pollution control, industrial hygiene, occupational medicine, biostatistics (M.S.); toxicology (Ph.D.).
Program Inquiries: Director, Institute of Environmental Health

OKLAHOMA

Oklahoma State Univ. of Agriculture and Applied Science
Stillwater, Okla. 74074
405-372-6211
Master's degree program in environmental science.
Program Inquiries: Dean, Sch. of Civil Engineering and Environmental Science

Univ. of Oklahoma
Norman, Okla. 73069
405-325-2558
Master's degree program in environmental science.
Program Inquiries: Dean, Sch. of Civil Engineering and Environmental Science

OREGON

Oregon State Univ.
346 Waldo Hall, Corvallis, Oreg. 97331
503-754-0123
Undergraduate and graduate programs (B.S., M.Ed.) in education with concentrations in ecological education and outdoor recreation.
Program Inquiries: Dr. Edward H. Heath, Head, Dept. of Leisure Science and Environmental Resources

Southern Oregon Col.
Ashland, Oreg. 97520
503-482-3311
Master's degree program in general studies and outdoor education.
Program Inquiries: Dr. Ronald Lamb, Director of Outdoor Education

Univ. of Oregon
Eugene, Oreg. 97401
503-686-3201
Bachelor's and master's degree programs in recreation and park administration with emphasis on outdoor education.
Program Inquiries: Chairman, Dept. of Recreation and Park Administration

PENNSYLVANIA

California State Col.
California, Pa. 15417
412-938-2281
Bachelor's degree programs in conservation and environmental science; education with emphasis on environmental science.

Program Inquiries: Dr. W. LeRoy Black, Head, Conservation and Recreation

Cedar Crest Col.
Allentown, Pa. 18100
215-437-4471
Interdisciplinary program in environmental studies.
Program Inquiries: Robert A. Scott, Dept. of Biology

Drexel Univ.
32 and Chestnut Sts., Philadelphia, Pa. 19104
215-387-2400
Graduate Programs (M.S., Ph.D.) in environmental science.

Lehigh Univ.
Bethlehem, Pa. 18015
215-867-5071
Nondegree interdisciplinary research in marine science, ocean engineering, and environmental science.
Program Inquiries: Center for Marine and Environmental Studies

Mercyhurst Col.
Erie, Pa. 16501
814-864-0681
Undergraduate program in environmental science and research.
Program Inquiries: Environmental Science Center

Pennsylvania State Univ.
Recreation Bldg., University Park, Pa. 16802
814-865-4700
Undergraduate program (B.S.) in recreation and parks with options in camping and outdoor education.
Program Inquiries: Dr. Fred Coombs, Recreation and Parks Program
Graduate programs in recreation and parks (M.S., M.Ed.) and physical education-recreation (Ph.D., D.Ed.).
Program Inquiries: Dr. Betty VanDer Smissen, Recreation and Parks Program

Slippery Rock State Col.
Slippery Rock, Pa. 16057
412-794-7203
Master's degree program in environmental education; proposed bachelor's degree program.
Program Inquiries: Dr. Craig Chaise, Director, Environmental Education Program

Wilkes Col.
Wilkes-Barre, Pa. 18703
717-824-4651
Undergraduate program in environmental science.
Program Inquiries: Director, Environmental Science Research Institute

RHODE ISLAND

Univ. of Rhode Island
Kingston, R.I. 02881
401-792-1000
Undergraduate and graduate programs in natural resources.
Program Inquiries: Dr. John Kupa, Col. of Resource Development

SOUTH CAROLINA

Clemson Univ.
Clemson, S.C. 29631
803-656-2285
Bachelor's degree program in recreation and park administration.
Program Inquiries: Dept. of Recreation and Park Administration

SOUTH DAKOTA

South Dakota Sch. of Mines and Technology
Rapid City, S. Dak. 57701
605-394-2414
Graduate program in atmospheric science (rainfall, hailstorms).
Program Inquiries: Institute of Atmospheric Sciences

TENNESSEE

Univ. of Tennessee
408 10 St., Knoxville, Tenn. 37916
615-974-0111
Graduate programs (M.S., Ph.D.) in ecology.
Program Inquiries: Director, Graduate Program in Ecology

Vanderbilt Univ.
Nashville, Tenn. 37203
615-322-2561
Graduate programs (M.S., Ph.D.) in environmental engineering and water resources.
Program Inquiries: Chairman, Environmental and Water Resources Engineering Dept.

Texas

Baylor Univ.
Waco, Tex. 76706
817-755-1011
Undergraduate and first-year graduate program in environmental geology.
Program Inquiries: Admissions Office

Lamar Univ.
Beaumont, Tex. 77700
713-838-6671
Bachelor's degree program in environmental science.
Program Inquiries: Dr. Edwin S. Hayes, Dean, Sch. of Sciences

Rice Univ.
Houston, Tex. 77001
713-528-4141
Graduate programs in environmental science and engineering.
Program Inquiries: Admissions Office

Texas A and M University
College Station, Tex. 77843
713-845-4331
Bachelor's degree program in recreation and parks with option in environmental interpretation; master's degree program in recreation and resources development; master's and doctoral degree programs in natural resources development.
Program Inquiries: Dr. Leslie M. Reid, Head, Dept. of Recreation and Parks

Univ. of Houston
Houston, Tex. 77004
713-748-6600
Undergraduate programs in environmental science and engineering.
Program Inquiries: Dean, Cullen Col. of Engineering

Univ. of Texas
Austin, Tex. 78712
512-471-1233
Research programs in conservation and water resources.
Program Inquiries: Center for Research in Water Resources

Utah

Univ. of Utah
Salt Lake City, Utah 84112
801-322-7211
Graduate programs (M.A., M.S., Ph.D.) in environmental biology.
Program Inquiries: Chairman, Dept. of Biology

Utah State Univ.
Logan, Utah 84321
801-752-4100
Graduate program in ecology for teachers, researchers, and professionals.
Program Inquiries: Center of Ecology
Interdisciplinary research projects in pollution.
Program Inquiries: Center for Pollution Research

Vermont

Middlebury Col.
Middlebury, Vt. 05753
802-388-4929
Bachelor's degree programs in ecology, earth science, and human ecology.
Program Inquiries: Admissions Office

Univ. of Vermont
Morrill Hall, Burlington, Vt. 05401
802-656-3131
Bachelor's and master's degree programs in natural resource management.
Program Inquiries: Dr. Gerald Donovan, Recreation Resource Management Curriculum

Virginia

Sweet Briar Col.
Sweet Briar, Va. 24595
703-381-5525
Undergraduate research in human ecology.
Program Inquiries: Director, Center of Human Ecology

Virginia Polytechnic Institute and State Univ.
Blacksburg, Va. 24061
703-552-6232
Bachelor's degree program in forestry and related renewable natural resources with specialization in environmental conservation.
Program Inquiries: Dr. John F. Hosner, Director, Div. of Forestry and Wildlife Sciences

Washington

Olympic Col.
Bremerton, Wash. 98310

206-377-3891
Associate degree program in health, physical education, recreation, and outdoor education.
Program Inquiries: John M. Stenhjem, Chairman, Health, Physical Education, Recreation, and Outdoor Education Dept.

Univ. of Washington
Seattle, Wash. 98105
206-543-2100
Graduate program (M.Ed.) in environmental education.
Program Inquiries: Dr. Roger G. Olstad, Col. of Education

Washington State Univ.
Pullman, Wash. 99163
509-335-3564
Bachelor's and master's degree programs in environmental science; options in agricultural ecology, biological science, cultural ecology, environmental health, natural resources, and physical science.
Program Inquiries: Chairman, Program in Environmental Science

Western Washington State Col.
Bellingham, Wash. 98225
206-676-3440
Undergraduate degree (B.S.) in environmental studies; concentrations in ecological systems; analysis, environmental control, planning, hunger, food, and malnutrition, marine resources, and population dynamics. Proposed graduate program.
Program Inquiries: Huxley Col. of Environmental Studies

WEST VIRGINIA

West Virginia Univ.
Morgantown, W. Va. 26505
304-293-2124
Graduate-level extension division environmental health program.
Program Inquiries: Appalachian Center for Environmental Health

WISCONSIN

Northland Col.
Ashland, Wis. 54806
715-682-4531
Bachelor's degree program in environmental studies.
Program Inquiries: Dean of Admissions

Univ. of Wisconsin
253 Education Bldg., Madison, Wis. 53706
608-262-1234
Graduate programs (M.S., Ph.D.) in environmental education.
Program Inquiries: Dr. Milton O. Pella, Professor of Science Education

Univ. of Wisconsin, Green Bay
Green Bay, Wis. 54302
414-435-3211
Undergraduate programs (B.A., B.S.) in environmental sciences; options in environmental control or ecosystems analysis.
Program Inquiries: Dr. Thomas H. McIntosh, Col. of Environmental Sciences

Univ. of Wisconsin, Madison
Madison, Wis. 53706
608-262-1234
Bachelor's degree program in natural resources, conservation, and conservation journalism.
Program Inquiries: Dean, Col. of Agricultural and Life Sciences
Master's degree programs in environmental education and communications.
Program Inquiries: Director, Center for Environmental Communications and Education Studies
Bachelor's degree program in biological aspects of conservation.
Program Inquiries: Dr. John W. Thomson, 236 Birge Hall

Wisconsin State Univ., River Falls
River Falls, Wis. 54022
715-425-6701
Undergraduate program in environmental management.
Program Inquiries: Admissions Office

Wisconsin State Univ., Stevens Point
Stevens Point, Wis. 54481
715-346-2441
Bachelor's degree program in resource management with emphasis in conservation education; outdoor education minor.
Program Inquiries: James A. Bowles, Col. of Natural Resources

Wisconsin State Univ., Whitewater
Whitewater, Wis. 53190
414-472-1440
Undergraduate degree (B.S.) in elementary education; minor in outdoor education with emphasis on environmental studies.
Program Inquiries: J. Homer Englund, Chairman, Health, Physical Education, and Recreation for Men

Wyoming

Univ. of Wyoming
Laramie, Wyo. 82070
307-766-1121

Bachelor's and master's degree programs in recreation and park administration; option in outdoor recreation resource management.
Program Inquiries: Dr. John H. Schultz, Dept. of Recreation and Park Administration

8 Environmental Libraries

The number of publications on environmental subjects is increasing rapidly. Most general libraries have neither the facilities nor the funds to maintain comprehensive collections of the new environmental books, journals, and technical reports. Fortunately, however, many academic, government, and private organizations are establishing extensive collections in this area.

This list of special environmental libraries was compiled primarily by the staffs of the Library Systems Branch of the U.S. Environmental Protection Agency (EPA) and the national EPA libraries. The list is not intended to be complete at this point, since it represents only the initial results of a continuing survey of environmental collections. This chapter, which lists the libraries alphabetically by state, includes only libraries that are primarily oriented toward environmental material. However, readers may also wish to consult the many general public and university libraries that may include much helpful material in their holdings.

ALABAMA

Medical Center Library, Univ. of Alabama
Birmingham, Ala. 35233
205-934-4229

ARIZONA

Dept. of Library and Archives, State of Arizona
3rd Floor, Capitol, Phoenix, Ariz. 85007
602-271-5031

Div. of Water Pollution Control, Arizona State Dept. of Health
1624 W. Adams St., Phoenix, Ariz. 85007
602-271-5455

ARKANSAS

Dept. of Pollution Control and Ecology Library, State of Arkansas
7209 Acorn Pl., Little Rock, Ark. 72209
501-565-1054

CALIFORNIA

Agriculture Library, Univ. of California
Berkeley, Calif. 94720
415-642-4493

California Dept. of Fish and Game, Marine Technical Information Center
320 Golden Shore, Long Beach, Calif. 90802
213-435-7741

California State Resources Agency Library
Rm. 117, 1416 9 St., Sacramento, Calif. 95814
916-445-7752

Ecology Information Center
1221 20 St., Sacramento, Calif. 95821
916-444-3174

Environmental Information Clearinghouse, c/o Ecology Center
2179 Allston Way, Berkeley, Calif. 94704
415-548-2220

Hopkins Marine Station Library, Stanford Univ.
Pacific Grove, Calif. 93950
408-373-0464

Lake Tahoe Area Council
Box 3475, South Lake Tahoe, Calif. 95705
916-544-5294

Oceanic Library and Information Center
Box 2369, La Jolla, Calif. 92037
714-292-1515

Oil Spill Information Center, Marine Science Institute, Univ. of California, Santa Barbara
Santa Barbara, Calif. 93106
805-961-3948

Scripps Institute of Oceanography, Univ. of California, San Diego
La Jolla, Calif. 92037
714-453-2000

Tabershaw-Cooper Associates, Inc., Information Center
Box 772, Berkeley, Calif. 94701
415-845-3355

Water Resources Archives, Univ. of California
Berkeley, Calif. 94720
415-642-4493

COLORADO

Conservation Library Center, Denver Public Library
1357 Broadway, Denver, Colo. 80203
303-573-5152

CONNECTICUT

Col. of Agriculture, Univ. of Connecticut
Wilbur Cross Library Bldg., Box 5, Storrs, Conn. 06268
203-429-3311

Connecticut State Library
231 Capitol Ave., Hartford, Conn. 06115
203-566-5295

Yale Univ. School of Forestry
205 Prospect St., New Haven, Conn. 06473
203-436-0440

DELAWARE

Office of Information and Education, Dept. of Natural Resources and Environmental Control of Delaware
Dover, Del. 19901
302-678-4506

DISTRICT OF COLUMBIA

Education Div., American Chemical Society
1155 16 St. N.W., Washington, D.C. 20030
202-737-3337

Conservation Foundation Library
1250 Connecticut Ave. N.W., Washington, D.C. 20036
202-659-2180

Dept. of Environmental Services Library
Rm. 306, 415 12 St. N.W., Washington, D.C. 20004
202-629-3011

Frazier Memorial Library, National Wildlife Federation
1412 16 St. N.W., Washington, D.C. 20036
202-483-1550

National Center for Resource Recovery
1211 Connecticut Ave. N.W., Washington, D.C. 20036
202-223-6154

National Park and Conservation Assn.
1701 18 St. N.W., Washington, D.C. 20009
202-265-2717

National Park Foundation
Dept. of the Interior Bldg., C St., between 18 and 19 Sts., Washington, D.C. 20240
202-343-6578

Resources for the Future, Inc.
1755 Massachusetts Ave. N.W., Washington, D.C. 20036
202-462-4400

FLORIDA

Div. of Interior Resources Library, Dept. of Natural Resources
Larson Bldg., Tallahassee, Fla. 32301
904-488-6286

Environmental Information Center
Box 922, Sarasota, Fla. 33578
813-355-6967

Escambia County Health Dept. Library
Box 1869, Pensacola, Fla. 32502
904-438-8571

Florida State Library
Supreme Court Bldg., Tallahassee, Fla. 32304
904-222-2374

Naval Aerospace Medical Institute Library
Code 12, Naval Aerospace Medical Center, Pensacola, Fla. 32512
904-452-2256

Medical Library, Univ. of Miami
Miami, Fla. 33152
305-350-6679

Georgia

A. W. Calhoun Medical Library, Emory Univ.
Atlanta, Ga. 30322
404-377-9201

Georgia Conservancy, Inc.
Suite 402, 3376 Peachtree Rd. N.W., Atlanta, Ga. 30326
404-262-1967

Information Exchange Center, Price Gilbert Memorial Library, Georgia Institute of Technology
Atlanta, Ga. 30332
404-894-4511

Medical Col. of Georgia Library
Augusta, Ga. 30902
404-724-7111

Illinois

Cooperative Wildlife Research Laboratory, Southern Illinois Univ.
806 South Marion St., Carbondale, Ill. 62901
618-453-2875

Institute for Environmental Quality
309 W. Washington St., Chicago, Ill. 60606
312-793-3870

Metropolitan Sanitary District of Greater Chicago
100 E. Erie St., Chicago, Ill. 60611
312-751-5600

Morton Arboretum
Lisle, Ill. 60532
312-968-0074

Municipal Reference Library
Rm. 1004, City Hall, Chicago, Ill. 60602
312-744-4992

North Shore Ecology Center, Inc.
747 Central, Highland Park, Ill. 60035
312-432-1440

Northwest Students for a Better Environment
2321 Sheridan Rd., Evanston, Ill. 60201
312-491-9627

Open Lands Project
Suite 1009, 53 W. Jackson Blvd., Chicago, Ill. 60604
312-427-4256

Indiana

Engineering Library, Univ. of Notre Dame
Notre Dame, Ind. 46556
219-283-6665

Environmental Systems Application Center, Poplars Research and Conference Center, Indiana Univ.
Bloomington, Ind. 47401
812-337-8260

Geology Library, Univ. of Notre Dame
Notre Dame, Ind. 46556
219-283-6686

Life Sciences Research Library, Univ. of Notre Dame
Notre Dame, Ind. 46556
219-283-7209

Jacob T. Oliphant Library, State Board of Health Bldg.
1330 W. Michigan St., Indianapolis, Ind. 46206
317-633-4360

Iowa

Iowa State Water Resources Research Institute Library, Dept. of Agronomy, Iowa State Univ. of Science and Technology
Ames, Iowa 50010
515-294-4264

KANSAS

Kansas State Geological Survey Library
Lawrence, Kans. 66044
913-874-3101

KENTUCKY

State Dept. of Health Library
275 E. Main St., Frankfort, Ky. 40601
502-564-3796

LOUISIANA

Bureau of Environmental Health, Louisiana State Dept. of Health
Box 60630, New Orleans, La. 70160
504-527-5111

State of Louisiana, Stream Control Commission
Drawer FC, Univ. Sta., Baton Rouge, La. 70803
504-389-5309

MAINE

Bureau of Water Pollution Control Library, Maine Environmental Improvement Commission
Augusta, Maine 04330
207-289-2591

MARYLAND

Dept. of Health and Mental Hygiene Library
301 W. Preston St., Baltimore, Md. 21201
301-383-2634

MASSACHUSETTS

Marine Biological Laboratory Library
Woods Hole, Mass. 02543
617-548-3705

Massachusetts Audubon Society, Environmental Education Curriculum Materials Center
Rte. 117, Lincoln, Mass. 01773
617-259-9500

Massachusetts Dept. of Public Health
600 Washington St., Boston, Mass. 02111
617-727-2665

Museum of Science, Science Park
Boston, Mass. 02114
617-742-1410

Technical Guidance Center, Univ. of Massachusetts
Marshall Hall, Amherst, Mass. 01002
413-545-0347

Woods Hole Oceanographic Institution
Woods Hole, Mass. 02543
617-548-1400

MICHIGAN

Atomic Energy Library, Phoenix Memorial Laboratory, Univ. of Michigan
2301 N. Campus, Ann Arbor, Mich. 48104
313-764-5298

Dept. of Natural Resources, Information and Education Div.
Stevens T. Mason Bldg., Lansing, Mich. 48926
517-373-1214

Engineering/Transportation Library, Univ. of Michigan
312 Undergraduate Library, Ann Arbor, Mich. 48104
313-764-7494

Great Lakes Basin Commission
City Center Bldg., 220 E. Huron St., Ann Arbor, Mich. 48108
313-769-7431

Great Lakes Research Div. Library, Univ. of Michigan
1077 N. University Bldg., Ann Arbor, Mich. 48104
313-764-2420

Institute of Public Affairs, Environmental Studies Program, Western Michigan Univ.
Kalamazoo, Mich. 49001
616-383-3983

Kalamazoo Nature Center
700 N. Westnedge Ave., Kalamazoo, Mich. 49007
616-381-1574

Kresge Library, Science Dept. Oakland Univ.
Rochester, Mich. 48063
313-377-2474

Natural Science/Natural Resources Library, Univ. of Michigan
3140 Natural Science Bldg., 830 N. University St., Ann Arbor, Mich. 48104
313-764-1494

Science and Technology Div. University Library, Eastern Michigan Univ.
Ypsilanti, Mich. 48197
313-487-1849

State Library, Michigan Dept. of Education
735 E. Michigan Ave., Lansing, Mich. 48913
517-373-1593

Van Oosten Library, Great Lakes Fishery Commission
1451 Green Rd., Ann Arbor, Mich. 48105
313-663-3331

Minnesota

Environmental Conservation Library, Minneapolis Public Library
300 Nicollet Mall, Minneapolis, Minn. 55401
612-372-6609

Geology Library, Univ. of Minnesota
Rm. 204, Pillsbury Bldg., Minneapolis, Minn. 55455
612-373-4052

Midwest Environmental Education and Research Assn. (MEERA)
295 Summit Ave., St. Paul, Minn. 55102
612-222-3350

North Central Environmental Council, Moorhead State Col. Library
Moorhead, Minn. 56560
218-236-2922

Mississippi

Mississippi Research and Development Center
Drawer 2470, 3825 Ridgewood Rd., Jackson, Miss. 39205
601-982-6110

NASA/MTF Technical Library, Mississippi Test Facility
Bay St. Louis, Miss. 39520
601-688-4123

Rowland Medical Library, Univ. of Mississippi Medical Center
Jackson, Miss. 39216
601-362-4411

Missouri

Committee for Environmental Information
438 N. Skinker Blvd., St. Louis, Mo. 63130
314-863-6560

Missouri Clean Water Commission Library, Dept. of Public Health and Welfare
Rm. 102, State Capitol Bldg., Box 154, Jefferson City, Mo. 65101
314-635-9117

Montana

Carroll Col. Library, Environmental Studies Div.
Helena, Mont. 59601
406-442-1295

Montana State Dept. of Health and Environmental Sciences
Helena, Mont. 59601
406-449-3459

Nevada

Desert Research Institute, Center for Water Resources Research, Univ. of Nevada
Reno, Nev. 89507
702-784-6955

Nevada State Library
Carson City, Nev. 89701
702-882-7372

New Hampshire

Dana Biomedical Library, Dartmouth Col.
Hanover, N.H. 03755
603-646-2858

Water Supply and Pollution Control Commission Library

Prescott Pk., 105 London Rd., Box 95, Concord, N.H. 03301
603-271-3502

New Jersey

Health–Agriculture Library
John Fitch Plaza, Trenton, N.J. 08625
609-292-5693

River and Harbor Library, Princeton Univ.
Engineering Quadrangle, Princeton, N.J. 08540
609-452-3237

New Mexico

Central Clearing House
338 E. DeVargas St., Santa Fe, N. Mex. 87501
505-982-4349

New York

Col. of Environmental Science and Forestry Library, State Univ. of New York at Syracuse
Syracuse, N.Y. 13210
315-476-3151

Engineering Library, Cornell Univ.
Ithaca, N.Y. 14850
607-256-4318

Environmental Medicine Library, New York Univ.
University Valley in Sterling Forest, Tuxedo, N.Y. 10979
914-351-4232

International Institute of Environmental Affairs
600 5 Ave., New York, N.Y. 10020
212-765-2786

National Audubon Society
1130 5 Ave., New York, N.Y. 10028
212-369-2100

Div. of Laboratories and Research Library, New York State Dept. of Health
New Scotland Ave., Albany, N.Y. 12201
518-474-6173

New York State Library
State Education Bldg., Washington Ave., Albany, N.Y. 12210
518-474-7381

Science and Engineering Library, State Univ. of New York at Buffalo
Bldg. 6, Buffalo, N.Y. 14214
716-837-2000

Scientists' Institute for Public Information
30 E. 68 St., New York, N.Y. 10021
212-249-3200

Water Resources Research Center, Cornell Univ.
Ithaca, N.Y. 14850
607-256-2385

North Dakota

North Dakota State Dept. of Health Library
Bismarck, N. Dak. 58501
701-224-2367

Ohio

Battelle Memorial Institute Library
505 King Ave., Columbus, Ohio 43212
614-299-3151

Botany and Zoology Library, Ohio State Univ.
1735 Neil Ave., Columbus, Ohio 43210
614-422-1744

Ecological Information Analysis Center, Battelle Memorial Institute
505 King Ave., Columbus, Ohio 43212
614-299-3151

Lake Erie Study Collection, Sears Library, Case Western Reserve Univ.
10900 Euclid Ave., Cleveland, Ohio 44106
216-368-4150

Northwestern Ohio Great Lakes Research Center, Bowling Green State Univ.
214-A Graduate Bldg., Bowling Green, Ohio 43403
419-372-2474

Ohio River Basin Commission
Rm. 208-20, 36 E. 4 St., Cincinnati, Ohio 45202
513-684-3831

Ohio State Dept. of Natural Resources
65 S. Front St., Columbus, Ohio 43215
614-369-3770

Oklahoma

Oklahoma Dept. of Libraries
109 State Capitol, Oklahoma City, Okla. 73105
405-521-3651

Oklahoma Environmental Information and Media Center, East Central State Col.
Box D-2, Ada, Okla. 74820
405-332-8000

Oregon

Environmental Education Center, Portland State Univ.
Rm. 373, Lincoln Hall, Portland, Oreg. 97207
503-229-4682

Pennsylvania

Earth and Mineral Sciences Library, Pennsylvania State Univ.
105 Dieke Bldg., University Park, Pa. 16802
814-865-9517

Environmental Engineering Library, Drexel Univ.
32 and Chestnut Sts., Philadelphia, Pa. 19104
215-895-2000

Technical Reference Library, Bureau of Water Quality Management
Rm. 1023, Health and Welfare Bldg., 7 and Forster Sts., Harrisburg, Pa. 17120
717-787-3220

Puerto Rico

Environmental Div., Dept. of Health
1259 Ponce de Leon Ave., Santurce, Puerto Rico 00908
809-722-2050

Medical Sciences Campus Library, Univ. of Puerto Rico
San Juan, Puerto Rico 00905
809-723-8139

Rhode Island

Biological Sciences Library, Brown Univ.
Providence, R.I. 02912
401-863-3346

Health Library, Rhode Island Dept. of Health
Rm. 407, Health Bldg., Providence, R.I. 02908
401-277-2506

New England Marine Resources Information Program, Narragansett Bay Campus, Univ. of Rhode Island
Narragansett, R.I. 02882
401-792-6211

Pell Marine Science Library, Narragansett Bay Campus, Univ. of Rhode Island
Narragansett, R.I. 02882
401-792-6161

Rhode Island State Library, The State House
Rm. 208, Providence, R.I. 02903
401-277-2473

South Carolina

Clemson Univ. Libraries, Dept. of Interdisciplinary Studies
Clemson, S.C. 29631
803-656-3052

Medical Univ. of South Carolina Library
Charleston, S.C. 29401
803-792-2371

Tennessee

Environmental Mutagen Information Center, Biology Div., Oak Ridge National Laboratory
Box Y, Oak Ridge, Tenn. 37830
615-483-8611

Medical Center Library, Vanderbilt Univ.
Nashville, Tenn. 37203
615-322-2292

Meharry Alumni Library, Meharry Medical Col.
Nashville, Tenn. 37208
615-327-6318

Mooney Memorial Library, Medical Units, Univ. of Tennessee
Memphis, Tenn. 38103
901-527-6641

Tennessee Valley Authority, Technical Library
500 Union Ave., Knoxville, Tenn. 37902
615-637-0101

TEXAS

City of Dallas Urban Planning Dept., Urban Design Div.
Suite 200B, 500 S. Ervay, Dallas, Tex. 75201
214-744-4371

Coastal Ecosystems Management, Inc.
3600 Hulen St., Fort Worth, Tex. 76107
817-731-3727

Community Living Dept., Environmental Section, Dallas Public Library
1954 Commerce, Dallas, Tex. 75202
214-748-9071

Davis Conservation Library
404 E. Main St., Box 776, League City, Tex. 75573
713-932-2535

Geology Library, Univ. of Texas
University Sta., Austin, Tex. 78712
512-471-1257

Marine Science Institute, Univ. of Texas
Port Aransas, Tex. 78373
512-749-5281

North Texas Council of Governments
Box 5888, Arlington, Tex. 76011
817-261-3333

Rob and Bessie Welder Wildlife Foundation
Box 1400, Sinton, Tex. 78387
512-364-2643

Science and Industrial Library, Southern Methodist Univ.
Dallas, Tex. 75222
214-792-2275

Southwest Research Institute
8500 Culebra Rd., San Antonio, Tex. 78228
512-684-5111

Texas Air Pollution Control Services, Technical Information File Room, Texas State Dept. of Health
820 E. 53 St., Austin, Tex. 78751
512-454-3781

Texas Parks and Wildlife Dept.
715 S. Bronte St., Rockport, Tex. 78382
713-764-2348

Texas State Dept. of Health Library
1100 W. 49 St., Austin, Tex. 78756
512-454-3781

Texas State Library
Drawer DD, Capitol Sta., Austin, Tex. 78711
512-475-4355

Texas Water Development Board Library
Box 12387, Capitol Sta., Austin, Tex. 78711
512-475-3783

Texas Water Quality Board
314 W. 11 St., Box 13246, Capitol Sta., Austin, Tex. 78711
512-475-2651

WASHINGTON

State of Washington, Dept. of Ecology Library
Olympia, Wash. 98504
206-753-2959

WEST VIRGINIA

Div. of Water Resources Library, West Virginia Dept. of Natural Resources
Charleston, W. Va. 25305
304-348-2107

WISCONSIN

Water Resources Center, Univ. of Wisconsin
116 Hydraulics Laboratory, Madison, Wis. 53702
608-262-3577

WYOMING

Science Library, Univ. of Wyoming
Laramie, Wyo. 82070
307-766-5165

9 Environmental Fund-Raising

JOSEPH WILLEN
Executive Consultant and Former Executive Vice President, Federation for the Support of Jewish Philanthropies of New York

The problem of funding any organized group incorporated to deal with environmental problems should be distinguished from the efforts of citizens' groups organized to solve a single problem in the community. Citizens' organizations are rarely incorporated, and their fund-raising problems are likely to be short-term and to be resolved by members and their immediate friends and by special events, such as theater parties. The following suggestions are almost entirely for incorporated groups that have substantial budgets.

The chief executive officer of the organization should be advised that one of his principal responsibilities is to organize and oversee a fund-raising department. Unfortunately, many executives, when engaged for an environmental program, are told that financing will not be their major reponsibility, and that it will be carried on by others. They quickly find, however, that at times it is the key to the job. Therefore, no one should assume the chief executive position of a nongovernmental environmental agency without a clear understanding of his fund-raising obligation.

Members of the board should also be aware that their responsibility involves giving dollar contributions to the agency as well as fund-raising activities.

If possible, an experienced director of development should be hired to help the head of the organization acquire funds. Although such a person can assume important administrative responsibilities for fund-raising, the ultimate responsibility still remains with the chief executive.

PRINCIPAL SOURCES OF FUNDS

Board members should solicit contributions personally from their well-to-do contacts. Each trustee should carefully review all his contacts, professional and social. It is unwise to ask a member of a board to solicit funds from an individual he does not know.

Additional important sources of funds are government, foundations, Community Chests, labor unions, and corporations. Applications to unions and corporations are best handled through individual contacts. Approaches to the three other sources may be made in the following ways.

Government Grants

Many federal, state, and local departments of government contribute to environmental programs. The chief executive of the environmental organization should acquaint himself with trends in the field, which may very well be his most important fund-raising responsibility.

The U.S. Government Printing Office publishes the *Catalog of Federal Domestic*

Assistance, which is available on a subscription basis from the Superintendent of Documents, U.S. Government Printing Office, Washington, D.C. 20402.

The availability and requirements of government funding change frequently; therefore, the chief executive should be familiar with current literature on the subject and should consult friends in the various communities about the programs that are being developed and encouraged. It is in this area that the executive of an agency must, in effect, be expert, guide, and philosopher. He should, if possible, spend some time in Washington or in the capital of the state in which his organization is located to get the latest possible information. Neither names nor past experience can substitute for a knowledge of current developments. Lawyers, distinguished environmentalists, and political leaders at the various levels of government can be of help. It is well to use them, and in most instances, they wish to be used.

Federal grants for the environmental field are administered primarily by the U.S. Environmental Protection Agency (EPA). Recently, thirty-four grant programs were listed by the EPA, including planning, development, training, research, and technical assistance programs in water and air pollution control, solid waste management, and pesticide and radiation control. The majority of such grants are available only to state and local government agencies, colleges, hospitals, and similar nonprofit institutions. Individuals are eligible for some training programs.

Inquiries about EPA grant applications and procedures may be directed to the Grants Administration Division, Environmental Protection Agency, Washington, D.C. 20460.

Potential applicants are also encouraged to communicate with the appropriate EPA Regional Administrator. A list of these administrators is found in Appendix A at the end of this chapter.

Foundation Grants

A study of the current giving pattern of foundations should be made. Excellent library services and effective research are offered by The Foundation Center, whose headquarters are at 888 Seventh Ave., New York, N.Y. 10019 and 1001 Connecticut Ave. N.W., Washington, D.C. 20036. The Center does not direct applicants for funds to particular foundations, arrange introductions to foundation officials, or assist persons seeking foundation positions. It is simply a resource for information. The headquarters can furnish basic literature describing the Center's facilities and services.

The Center maintains eight regional repositories of foundation information, whose addresses are listed in Appendix B at the end of this chapter. It is best to contact them directly for assistance in making a study of foundations that have made donations to environmental groups in recent years or in the current year.

Community Chests

It might be advisable for an environmental group that is incorporated and has tax-exempt status to approach the local Community Chest or United Fund for inclusion in its annual appeal. It sometimes takes several years before an application for inclusion is approved.

Community awareness of pollution problems and other environmental hazards has grown enormously in recent years, but the identification of a crisis is only the first step toward its solution. Action is required, and action depends on the availability of funds. Local leaders should be forcefully reminded that the health and comfort of a population is directly dependent on the quality of its environment.

When several groups with similar aims exist in the same city, it is advantageous for them to approach the fund as a group rather than as individual agencies. The environmental groups should stress that they are as vital to the health and welfare of a community as are more traditional agencies.

PROFESSIONAL ASSISTANCE

An important source of information on professional fund-raising firms is The American Association of Fund Raising Counsel, Inc., which is located at 500 Fifth Avenue, New York, N.Y. 10036. Approximately twenty-five fund-raising firms are members; they are among America's most experienced and well-managed firms, and are noted for maintaining ethical standards and practices in their client relationships.

The Association's member firms do business only on the basis of a specified fee, determined prior to beginning the campaign; they will not serve clients for a percentage or commission of the sums raised. They maintain this ethical standard also by not profiting, directly or indirectly, from disbursements for advertising or other purposes.

Executives of the local Community Chest or United Fund may also be helpful in aiding the executive of the environmental agency to choose competent fund-raising firms, which may or may not belong to the Association. But it is important to remember that professional fund-raisers can only furnish their knowledge and experience of how to organize for this undertaking; they will not relieve the environmental organization of the ultimate responsibility of asking for the money.

A more specialized type of professional assistance is offered by direct-mail solicitation companies, which are, as a rule, also known to the executives of the local Community Chest or United Fund. Most professional fund-raising concerns also specialize in the direct-mail approach. This method should definitely be considered but it should only be undertaken for long-term plans and should not be used to achieve an immediate objective. An organization is fortunate if a direct-mail campaign turns out to be self-liquidating in the first year or two of its use. Under no condition should this venture be undertaken to solve a current fiscal problem.

SUMMARY

The chief executive officer as well as the other officers and members of the board should be informed that fund-raising is one of their main responsibilities. Personal solicitation is the primary source of funding.

Research in the area of government and foundation grants is also vitally important in addition to an alliance with Community Chest activities in the local area.

The primary factor, however, is personal solicitation, and it should never be forgotten that most potential donors of funds have their spending impulses under careful control, making the personal approach a necessity. People most often give money to other people rather than to a cause, no matter how deserving the cause.

APPENDIX A. U.S. ENVIRONMENTAL PROTECTION AGENCY REGIONAL ADMINISTRATORS

REGION I

(Connecticut, Maine, Massachusetts, New Hampshire, Rhode Island, Vermont)
Regional Administrator: John A. S. McGlennon
Rm. 2303, John F. Kennedy Federal Bldg., Boston, Mass. 02203
617-223-7210

REGION II

(New Jersey, New York, Puerto Rico, Virgin Islands)
Regional Administrator: Gerald M. Hansler
Rm. 908, 26 Federal Plaza, New York, N.Y. 10007
212-264-2525

REGION III

(Delaware, District of Columbia, Maryland, Pennsylvania, Virginia, West Virginia)
Regional Administrator: Edward W. Furia, Jr.
Curtis Bldg., 6 and Walnut Sts., Philadelphia, Pa. 19106
215-597-9800

REGION IV

(Alabama, Florida, Georgia, Mississippi, Kentucky, North Carolina, South Carolina, Tennessee)
Regional Administrator: Jack E. Ravan
1421 Peachtree St. N.E., Atlanta, Ga. 30309
404-526-5727

REGION V

(Illinois, Indiana, Minnesota, Michigan, Ohio, Wisconsin)
Regional Administrator: Francis T. Mayo
Post Office Bldg., 433 W. Van Buren St., Chicago, Ill. 60607
312-353-5250

REGION VI

(Arkansas, Louisiana, New Mexico, Oklahoma, Texas)
Regional Administrator: Arthur W. Busch
Suite 1100, 1600 Patterson, Dallas, Tex. 75201
214-749-1962

REGION VII

(Iowa, Kansas, Missouri, Nebraska)
Regional Administrator: Jerome H. Svore
Rm. 249, 1735 Baltimore Ave., Kansas City, Mo. 64108
816-374-5493

REGION VIII

(Colorado, Montana, North Dakota, South Dakota, Utah, Wyoming)
Regional Administrator: John Green
1860 Lincoln St., Denver, Colo. 80203
303-837-3895

REGION IX

(Arizona, California, Hawaii, Nevada, Guam, American Samoa)
Regional Administrator: Paul DeFalco, Jr.
100 California St., San Francisco, Calif. 94111
415-556-2320

REGION X

(Alaska, Idaho, Oregon, Washington)
Regional Administrator: James L. Agee
1200 6 Ave., Seattle, Wash. 98101
206-442-1220

APPENDIX B. THE FOUNDATION CENTER REGIONAL INFORMATION REPOSITORIES

Associated Foundation of Greater Boston
Suite 948, 1 Boston Place, Boston, Mass. 02108
617-742-8084

Cleveland Foundation
700 National City Bank Bldg., Cleveland, Ohio 44114
216-861-3810

Newberry Library
60 W. Walton St., Chicago, Ill. 60610
312-943-9090

Danforth Foundation
222 S. Central Ave., St. Louis, Mo. 63105
314-862-6200

Foundation Library Collection, Atlanta Public Library
126 Carnegie Way N.W., Atlanta, Ga. 30303
404-522-9363

Regional Foundation Library, Hogg Foundation for Mental Health, Univ. of Texas
Austin, Tex. 78712
512-471-5041

Foundation Collection, Reference Dept., Univ. Research Library, Univ. of California
Los Angeles, Calif. 90024
213-825-1457

San Francisco Public Library, Business Branch
530 Kearny St., San Francisco, Calif. 94108
415-558-3946

10 The Environment and the Law

ANGUS MACBETH
Staff Attorney, Natural Resources Defense Council, Inc.

This chapter focuses primarily on federal laws and regulations that allow citizens to affect the quality of the environment they live in. The primary emphasis is upon major federal legislation and the interpretation that the courts have put on the federal statutes that govern the environmental area. The procedural rules regulating citizen action are mentioned only for the most important acts, and very little state legislation is discussed. Compilations of environmental laws and regulations of the federal and state governments are available in the *Environment Reporter*, published by the Bureau of National Affairs, and the *Environmental Law Reporter*, published by the Environmental Law Institute. Both publications may be consulted in law libraries.

THE COMMON LAW

Over the centuries, the courts have fashioned remedies for environmental problems that have not been recognized or regulated by the legislature. The most important common law doctrine in the environmental field is that of public nuisance. Any unreasonable invasion of the rights common to the public is a public nuisance, and a suit may be brought for damages or to enjoin future invasions. Air pollution and water pollution are public nuisances, as are loan-sharking and the keeping of a bawdy house. But success in a public nuisance suit is difficult for a citizen for a number of technical legal reasons.

First, traditionally, if a nuisance affects the general public rather than particular persons, a suit can be brought only by the state, usually the attorney general. Individuals are limited to suits in which they have suffered an injury different from the injury to the general public. For example, a private citizen could sue if he broke his leg by falling in a pothole in a public road, but he could not sue as a sports fisherman against the pollution of a lake in which he and many others have fished.[1] In recent years, courts have generally become more liberal in allowing citizens to sue for nonfinancial injuries. The first signs of such liberalized standing requirements are present in the public nuisance area, but they have not gone far. The present drafts of the American Law Institute's Restatement (Second) of Torts would allow private citizens and representatives of the public to sue to abate or enjoin a public nuisance, but not for damages.[2]

The second major bar to relief in a public nuisance suit has been the process of balancing equities, which the court undertakes after it has established that there is an unreasonable invasion of the rights common to the public. Essentially, the judge weighs the costs and benefits of the relief, measuring the utility of the defendant's conduct against the harm inflicted on the plaintiff. If the utility of the defendant's course of action outweighs the harm to the plaintiff, the nuisance will rarely be enjoined although damages may be given to the plaintiff. Thus, in a suit against a cement plant that created dirt, smoke, and vibrations that injured the plaintiffs, a New York court refused to prohibit the operation of the plant because the plant was a net social benefit; nevertheless, it did grant damages to the plaintiffs.[3]

The process of weighing and balancing is one that depends on the facts of each situation; therefore, it is impossible to predict in a difficult case how the courts will decide. "The law of nuisance affords no rigid rule to be applied in all instances. It is elastic. It undertakes to require only that which is fair and reasonable under all circumstances."[4] The uncertainty of the outcome makes the common law of nuisance difficult for citizens to handle. Nevertheless, public nuisance does offer a possible remedy in areas such as harm from excessive noise or aesthetic damage where there is no comprehensive statutory law to protect citizens such as there is in air or water pollution.[5]

THE NATIONAL ENVIRONMENTAL POLICY ACT

The bedrock for environmental control by the federal government is the National Environmental Policy Act (NEPA),[6] signed into law on January 1, 1970. At the heart of the act lies the requirement that every federal agency proposing an action that will significantly affect the quality of the human environment must draw up a statement on the environmental impact of the proposed action. This requirement is crucial, because it applies to all federal agencies and requires a broad analysis of the proposed agency action. The statement must include the following elements:
1. The environmental impact of the proposed action.
2. Any adverse environmental effects that cannot be avoided should the proposal be implemented.
3. Alternatives to the proposed action.
4. The relationship between local short-term uses of man's environment and the maintenance and enhancement of long-term productivity.
5. Any irreversible and irretrievable commitments of resources that would be involved in the proposed action should it be implemented.[7]

NEPA applies to agencies, such as the Army Corps of Engineers, that directly undertake projects affecting the environment, such as dam building. It is also pertinent to agencies like the Atomic Energy Commission, which licenses activities of private parties, such as the operation of nuclear plants. Thus prior to NEPA, the AEC had no jurisdiction to consider nonradiological environmental matters, such as the effect on aquatic biota of passage through the cooling system of a nuclear plant. Agencies only indirectly involved in environmental matters through their administrative powers have been required to file NEPA statements as part of their process of consideration and review. For example, the ICC must produce NEPA statements on the abandonment of railway lines.[8]

At the present time, the only major exception to the NEPA statement requirement is contained in the Federal Water Pollution Control Act Amendments of 1972,[9] which excuses the federal Environmental Protection Agency from filing NEPA statements on discharge permits authorized by that act, and prohibits other agencies from imposing effluent limitations other than those established under the act. In addition, the Trans-Alaska Pipeline Authorization Act bars further judicial review of the NEPA statement analyzing the effects of the pipeline, but the act does allow a judicial challenge to the Pipeline Act itself.[10]

These requirements of the act have raised a number of questions that demanded judicial resolution. The courts have ruled that one of the fundamental aims of the statute is to provide the information on which rational decisions can be made, not only to the agency, but also to the President, Congress, and the public.[11] Most of the problems faced by the courts have been resolved within this broad context and have raised questions of statutory construction that cannot be answered with rigid or simple definitions. The courts have ruled that the agency must look beyond its own jurisdiction in examining alternatives to the proposed agency action. For instance, when considering offshore oil drilling, an agency must consider alternatives, such as changes in the oil-import quota system, which it cannot directly effect itself.[11] Regarding the proper bounds of the agency's proposed action, the Department of Transportation has not been allowed to break roads into small segments to mask the total environmental impact of a larger road project.[11a] Similarly, the Corps of Engineers has been required to view at one time its entire scheme of development for a river basin.[12] The threshold of actions that will "significantly affect the quality of the human environment" is impossible to define, but the courts have interpreted the phrase liberally. For instance, the construction of a sixteen-story apartment building has required a NEPA statement.[13]

The agencies have been required to prepare the NEPA statements themselves, resulting, as far as possible, in a public and impartial analysis of the proposal rather than the self-serving critique that might be prepared by the applicant for a license.[14]

The Council on Environmental Quality was also established under the National Environmental Policy Act. This council is responsible for establishing the guidelines under which environmental impact statements are drawn up.[15] The present system requires the preparation of a draft impact statement which the federal agency then circulates for comments to other state and federal agencies with expertise in the area under analysis. The draft statement is also available to the public for comment, usually for ninety days.

Following the comment period, the agency drafts the final environmental impact statement which then accompanies the proposal through the agency review process. The review process varies enormously from agency to agency. For example, when the Atomic Energy Commission licenses nuclear power plants, the commission conducts a review, modelled on court procedures, that requires testimony under oath and examination and cross-examination of witnesses. On the other hand, hearings of the Army Corps of Engineers on permits to undertake construction in navigable waters are on a legislative model, allowing numerous position statements but neither following rules of evidence nor permitting thorough cross-examination of the agency's experts.[16]

On the basis of the final environmental impact statement and the agency review, the decision on a particular proposal is made and whatever environmental protection the agency imposes, becomes part of the course of action. The courts assure that the procedural requirements of NEPA are met, but, except in clear cases of abuse, they are unwilling to substitute their judgment on substantive matters for that of an agency deemed expert in the matters it considers. For this reason, working within the administrative process by which the statements are drawn up and reviewed is crucial to citizens who wish to influence the environmental aspects of any proposal that must pass through the hands of a federal agency.

A number of states, such as California and Montana, have passed "little NEPAs." These acts require state agencies, like federal agencies under NEPA, to conduct an environmental review on matters that come before them.[17]

AIR POLLUTION

Between 1955 and 1970 Congress enacted a series of air pollution statutes. The failure of administrative agencies at the state and federal level to act forcefully under these statutes resulted in the passage of the Clean Air Act Amendments of 1970.[18] The 1970 amendments focus power and responsibility over the nation's entire air pollution control effort in the federal Environmental Protection Agency (EPA), with broad new standard-setting and enforcement powers.[19] Reflecting the experience of previous legislation, the amendments circumscribe the discretionary powers of both state and federal agencies by setting strict deadlines and procedures, articulating clear standards for decisions, and giving citizens the right to sue to prevent administrative laxity at both state and federal levels.

The Clean Air Act requires the EPA to set two types of national ambient air quality standards.[20] Primary standards must be set at levels that are adequate to protect human health. These standards must be achieved within three years of the approval of a plan implementing them (not later than 1975 for most states). Secondary standards must be imposed at levels to protect human "welfare" values. Congress intended these secondary standards to safeguard all values other than health, including visibility, plant and animal life, building, and materials. Secondary standards must be achieved within a "reasonable" time period, whose length is not specified. National standards are expressed as permissible annual average concentrations of pollutants, with short-term maximum concentrations which may occur only a certain number of times a year.

Ambient standards for hydrocarbons, sulfur oxides, photochemical oxidants, carbon monoxide, particulates, and nitrogen oxides have been set.[21] The EPA administrator must add to this list any other pollutant he finds dangerous to public health or welfare. Within one year after a pollutant has been listed, he must propose standards for that pollutant.

In effect, the standards represent a federal ceiling on pollution. They are an effort to make pollution control uniform and to set adequate bases for abatement. They do not, however, prevent states from setting more stringent standards if their regions require them. In addition, the language and the legislative history of the amendments prohibit the states from permitting the significant degradation of air quality in regions where the air is already of higher quality than necessary to meet the requirements of the secondary standards.[22]

The Clean Air Act requires each state to formulate an air pollution abatement plan for each air quality control region in the state, or in the case of a region that crosses state boundaries, for the part that lies within the state boundaries.[23] These implementation plans must describe in detail how the state intends to achieve and maintain the national ambient air quality standards, both primary and secondary, in the required time. The states submitted their plans for approval by the EPA in 1972. The implementation plans must demonstrate that the state has the legal authority and sufficient personnel to carry out and enforce the plan.

There are three other crucial elements to the state plans. First, there is the control strategy, which must include a survey of each region's existing air quality and a detailed inventory of the emissions from all pollution sources in the region to determine what kind of air pollution problem exists. The control strategy must set forth all the measures that will be taken to assure that the region's air quality meets the national standards. These measures must include emission limitations on particular sources and other control procedures, such as process changes, fuel controls, and land use and transportation controls, if they are necessary to meet the standards. The control strategy must also give timetables for compliance with its control measures. Second, the plan must include both a system for monitoring emissions from individual sources and a network for sampling ambient air quality. This information must be reported and made available to the public. Finally, the state must be able to review new sources and their effects on ambient air quality and to revise its strategy as control techniques and air quality standards change in the future.

The guidelines require submission of two series of reports, beginning after a state's implementation plans are approved by the EPA. Quarterly reports must contain information on current ambient air quality. Semiannual reports must describe current progress in carrying out the approved implementation plans and any revisions of rules, regulations, or compliance schedules made in the plan.[24]

In 1972, the EPA administrator reviewed the state implementation plans, approving and disapproving parts of the submitted schemes. These state implementation plans are the basic blueprint for the control of air pollution in the various regions, and the administrator's decisions are being hotly contested, mostly by industry, in approximately seventy suits across the country.[25] One notable battle has been over the administrator's grant of an extension of time to a number of states to submit the transportation control segments of their plans and a parallel extension to 1977 given to all states that asked for it in order to meet the national standards initially set for 1975. These extensions were granted without a showing by the states that they could not attain the standards by 1975. On that basis, the Court of Appeals for the District of Columbia Circuit reversed the administrator's decision and required the immediate preparation of state transportation control plans.[26] Those plans are presently being produced and are undergoing review by the EPA. That decision also required the administrator to approve only those plans that provided for the maintenance of air quality standards. This has required the EPA to analyze further the effect of land development, such as sports complexes and shopping centers, to assure that the pollution generated by the traffic to and from such complex sources does not violate air quality standards.

The transportation plans are vitally important in determining future patterns of life, since they may contain wide-ranging strategies. Short-term strategies for improving public transportation include fare reductions, improved routing and scheduling of buses, establishment of exclusive or preferential bus lanes, and the provision of shared taxis. In order to encourage the development and use of mass transit, vehicle restraints are being proposed: bridge and road toll increases, parking restrictions, parking fee increases, auto-free zones, and increased gasoline taxes. In addition, emission-control devices are being suggested to reduce pollution from privately owned vehicles.

In addition to the state implementation plans, the Clean Air Act Amendments contain three other important provisions for the reduction of air pollution.

First, the amendments require massive reductions in the amounts of pollutants emitted by automobiles. By model year 1975, there must be a 90 percent reduction in the emissions of carbon monoxide and hydrocarbons from the model year 1970 levels, and by model year 1976 there must be a 90 percent reduction in the emissions of nitrogen oxides from the levels of model year 1971.[27] The manufacturers may apply to the EPA administrator for one-year extensions of those deadlines. A partial extension has been granted for carbon monoxide and hydrocarbons, and the EPA has also granted an extension of the deadline for reduction of nitrogen oxides.

Second, the administrator has the power under the act to promulgate and add to a list of hazardous air pollutants that may cause or contribute to death or serious irreversible or incapacitating illness. For such hazardous pollutants, standards are to be established that provide an ample margin of safety to protect public health. New sources of emissions must comply with those standards, and old sources are to conform with the standard within a maximum period of two years.[28] Presently, asbestos, beryllium, and mercury have been put on the hazardous pollutants list.

Third, the EPA may exercise control over new stationary sources by establishing performance standards for various categories of sources.[29] This provision assures that new sources produce no further pollution of the air than is necessary. The latter two provisions contain clauses whereby the administrator may delegate to the states the implementation and enforcement of the provisions when they submit an adequate plan.[30]

The Clean Air Act Amendments were written with a broad provision for suits brought by citizens. Any person has the right to sue in the federal district court to enjoin violations of the act and the state implementation plans under it.[31] Thus, a suit may result from violation of an emission standard or limitation in effect under the act, infringement of an order issued by the federal administrator or state concerning such standards or limitations, or the failure of the administrator to perform a nondiscretionary duty. These broad rights are limited in three ways. Most importantly, a citizen may not sue for damages, but only to enjoin an illegal act or to force a nondiscretionary duty, though the act does not prevent a suit for damages under any other law. Further, if the administrator or the state is diligently prosecuting a suit in the federal courts, a citizen may not institute a separate suit, but he may intervene and become a party to the suit. Finally, the citizen may not sue in a state in which he does not reside. The act also requires that reports of monitoring are to be available to the public,[32] and provides for the payment of litigation costs, including attorney and expert witness fees at the discretion of the court;[33] therefore, the act has built into it a very effective mechanism for enforcement by individual citizens and groups who wish to assure that the law is fully carried out.

WATER POLLUTION

In October 1972, dissatisfied with the pace of water cleanup under acts passed during the preceding decade, Congress enacted the Federal Water Pollution Control Act Amendments of 1972[34] as the new comprehensive statute governing the country's water quality. The new amendments aim "to restore and maintain the chemical, physical, and biological integrity of the Nation's waters. In order to achieve this objective . . . it is the national goal that the discharge of pollutants into the navigable waters be eliminated by 1985."[35] To this end, the amendments set two standards by which water pollution is to be measured and controlled: industry by industry standards of allowable discharge, and standards for water quality. The amendments add special provisions for particular pollutants such as toxic substances and heat. The whole is contained within a federalistic scheme requiring federal-state cooperation.

The amendments establish two national deadlines for the achievement of pollution control from all major point sources of pollution.[36] Industrial sources of pollution must achieve the "best practicable control technology currently available" by July 1977. Municipal sources of pollution (publicly owned waste treatment facilities) must achieve secondary treatment by the same date.

A second round of pollution control is to be instituted after 1977, requiring that by July 1983, industries install the "best available control technology economically available" and municipal facilities must attain "best practical waste treatment technology."

Within one year of the passage of the amendments, the EPA administrator must publish guidelines establishing the best practicable and best available control technology. He must also specify the factors—including the cost of application, engineering, and age of the facilities—which are to be considered in deciding on the control measures for particular plants. These guidelines may include both end-of-the-pipe controls which purify polluted water and process changes which will avoid the initial polluting action. Best available control-technology standards are also to be imposed on future or "new" sources by another section of the amendments, with its independent requirement for the establishment of standards.[37]

To reduce municipal waste discharge, the amendment provision of large sums of federal money for the construction of municipal waste treatment plants was crucial. Congress, therefore, authorized $18 billion for such construction over a three-year period to be provided on a 75 percent federal—25 percent local basis.[38] In November 1972, President Nixon impounded most of those funds. In a case brought by the City of New York, the district court struck down this impoundment and required allotment, though not obligation, of the funds. However, the federal government has appealed the decision.[39]

Standards for water quality are also set out in the amendments.[40] The national standard aimed at is a sufficiently high water quality to assure protection of public water supplies and of agricultural and industrial uses; to assure the protection and propagation of a balanced population of shellfish, fish, and wildlife; and to allow recreational activities in and on the water.

If the water quality standards set for the river or stream will demand a higher level of pollution control from the sources of pollution on the waterway than the national technological controls, those stricter standards must be required.[41] The amendments require that any more stringent limitations required by water quality standards must be achieved by the mid-1977 deadline. All states have water quality standards that are federally approved for interstate waters. Many states have water quality standards for intrastate waters as well. States are allowed to set more stringent limitations than the federal minimums required by technological controls. Therefore, if a state water quality standard for a particular stream will require greater than the best practicable technology in order to achieve that standard, the stricter state standards apply.

Present water quality standards must be reviewed and upgraded at least once every three years with public hearings required before a state revision of standards.[42]

Toxic pollutants are given special attention in the new law. Toxic discharges will be regulated through national effluent standards set by the EPA. These standards may prohibit the discharge, and must be achieved within a year of their promulgation by any source discharging the poisonous substances. These toxic standards will be based on the adverse effects of these substances to aquatic, human, and other life.[43] The first toxic effluent limitation was proposed by the EPA in July, 1973.

Thermal discharges are also specially treated.[44] Whenever a party discharging heated water can show that a balanced, indigenous population of fish, shellfish, and wildlife may be maintained in the water body with a greater thermal discharge than allowed by the technological control standards, the EPA may allow an appropriately greater thermal discharge. In addition, in reviewing thermal discharges, the EPA must assure that the location, design, construction, and capacity of cooling water intake structures reflect the best technology available for minimizing adverse environmental impact.

The amendment's discharge control scheme is to be operated and enforced through permits for discharges granted under the National Pollutant Discharge Elimination System.[45] The permits granted to industries and publicly owned treatment facilities will embody the effluent control deadlines for 1977 and 1983, the toxic effluent requirements, the new source standards, and requirements based on water quality standards. The permits will also contain compliance schedules for construction of abatement equipment or process changes. Industries discharging into municipal systems do not require a permit, but must conform to pretreatment regulations so that the burden of abatement is not simply shifted from private to municipal hands.

Enforcement of the effluent control deadlines is through the permit requirements.

Violation of a permit is a violation of the amendments. Monitoring requirements will also be imposed upon each source to require periodic reporting of effluent discharges and their composition; these reports must be available to the public.

In order to give the EPA time to gear up its regulatory machinery and produce the necessary standards and permits, no action can be taken until December 31, 1974, against a discharger who has applied for a permit.

Throughout the process of permit issuance there is opportunity for full public participation. Public notice of each permit application will be given, and all interested parties must be informed; if there is sufficient public interest, a public hearing will be held to examine the issues raised by the proposed permit.

The amendments contain provisions under which the EPA will delegate the administration of the amendments to states that meet basic requirements. The state must have authority to issue appropriate permits and to enforce the law against violators. The state also must have an approved continuing planning process. In addition, a state permit program must meet certain guidelines, such as monitoring and reporting requirements (including procedures to make information available to the public) and funding, personnel, and manpower qualifications.

The Federal Water Pollution Control Act Amendments provide for citizens suits on essentially the same terms as the Clean Air Act Amendments, except that suits are limited to persons "having an interest which is or may be adversely affected."[46] Thus, a general, but unaffected interest in water pollution control would not be a sufficient basis for a lawsuit.

REGULATION OF WATERWAYS

There is no comprehensive scheme by which the state or federal government regulates the use and development of the nation's waters, but two recent statutes are establishing regional or national standards and procedures. In 1965, under the Water Resources Planning Act,[47] Congress set up a cabinet-level Water Resources Council, with responsibility for assessing the adequacy of water supplies, studying the administration of water resources, and developing principles, standards, and procedures for federal participants in the preparation of comprehensive regional or river basin plans. The same act established the framework of state and federal cooperation through a series of river basin commissions (RBCs) whose principal activity is the production of development plans for the basins under their jurisdiction. A number of such commissions have been formed—the Pacific Northwest RBC, the Great Lakes RBC, the Souris-Red-Rainy RBC, and the New England RBC. Reports on the commissions' work are available directly from the individual commissions.

In 1968, Congress established the National Water Commission.[48] With seven members appointed by the President, the water commission is to make a broad review of present and anticipated national water resource problems and consider the alternatives for meeting future needs. The commission must consider the conservation, esthetic, economic, and social consequences of possible modes of water resource development. A final report by the commission, which will require extensive action by both executive agencies and Congress for its implementation, was published in June 1973.

Pending establishment of a national scheme for water use and development, a number of federal agencies exercise extensive power over the nation's waters. The Army Corps of Engineers has the authority to grant permits for construction, dredging, and filling in the navigable waters under the Rivers and Harbors Act.[49] Hundreds of these permits are granted annually for everything from the laying of a telephone cable to the filling in of large areas for development. As a matter of regulatory practice, the Corps holds public hearings on the large or controversial projects that stir public interest.[50]

A number of federal agencies grant licenses for or financially assist projects that directly alter the natural movement of water by dams, diversions, stream channelization, and similar methods. The principal goals of these projects are flood control, irrigation and agricultural improvement, and power production. The Army Corps of Engineers has built a large number of dams, primarily for flood control purposes, and has done extensive dredging and canalizing for navigation purposes. The dam building projects are undertaken primarily under the authority of the flood control acts,[51] which require that the projects be based on a cost-benefit analysis showing a net benefit to society.[52] These projects are generally approved by Congress on a case-by-case basis.[53]

The Soil Conservation Service has carried out an extensive stream channelization program to assist local soil conservation districts by "furthering the conservation, development, utilization and disposal of water."[54] The Bureau of Reclamation, particularly in the West, has been responsible for a series of water diversion projects aimed at providing water for irrigation. Beyond the authority of the federal reclamation laws,[55] and amendments thereto, these projects are generally initiated by Congress on a case-by-case basis.[56]

The Federal Power Commission has the authority to license dams and pumped storage projects for hydroelectric power, in accordance with the requirements of the Federal Power Act [57] that the project be "best adapted to a comprehensive plan for improving or developing a waterway . . . for the use or benefit of interstate or foreign commerce, for the improvement and utilization of water-power development, and for other beneficial public uses, including recreational purposes. . . ."[58]

All of these programs have been under attack by environmental interests, which complain that the agencies have not given sufficient weight to environmental values, as required by statute. The focus of these controversies has varied from esthetics through loss of recreational free-flowing streams to adverse effects on fisheries.[59]

REGULATION OF LAND USE

State and Local Regulation

Most land in the United States is owned by entities other than the federal government, and the use of that land is regulated by state and local government. The typical pattern is for the state to enact a statute which in turn allows the cities and towns to establish their own zoning regulations or land use plans. Zoning laws and land use plans vary widely from locality to locality, and it is impossible to provide a detailed analysis of these local laws beyond a description of the basic principles on which they rest.

State regulation of land use is founded on the power of the state to legislate for the promotion of the public health, safety, morals, or general welfare. This so-called "police power" is limited by the federal and state constitutional prohibitions against the taking of property except for a public purpose and with just compensation. The state courts test particular land use laws on a case-by-case basis. The way in which the requisite constitutional tests are framed varies from state to state, as do the results that are acceptable under the tests; nevertheless, four general standards are usually applied: the regulation must be reasonably related to a valid exercise of the police power; it must not unfairly discriminate between similar parcels; it cannot reduce the value of the parcel to the level of confiscation; and it must provide a benefit to the public by preventing harm that would be caused by particular uses of the property rather than a benefit normally acquired by condemnation. If the zoning regulation amounts to a taking, the regulation will be struck down, but the government may take the property and pay just compensation so long as the taking is for a valid public purpose.

The four standards can be illustrated by the example of a state regulation prohibiting fill in private marshland. Presumably, the ordinance would be judged a valid conservation measure designed to ensure continued nutrient production in the marshland for the sustenance of aquatic biota.[60] But if the state allowed fill of some marshes and barred development of adjacent marshes, it would be required to offer compelling justification for the discrimination, such as proof that filling the latter would have significantly greater impact on marine life.[61] Barring outright seizure, determining when regulation effectively becomes a taking will depend on a court's judgment about such factors as the extent to which use and value of property may properly be restricted, the method of determining property value, the burden a landowner must sustain in proving reduction in value, and the extent to which the judiciary should defer to legislative judgments.[62]

Finally, where the proposed regulation does not abate or prevent an external harm (air pollution, a decrease in adjacent property values, or an increase in traffic), but rather requires property to provide benefits to the public at significant expense to the individual landowner (such as sustaining marine life), some courts will require that the benefits be achieved by condemnation.[63] For a fuller understanding of regulation of private land by state and local governments, readers should consult Robert M. Anderson's *American Law of Zoning*.

In recent years some states have taken a more direct hand in regulating the use of land to assure that local communities do not serve their own interests to the detriment of the citizens of the state. For example, New York, which has protected large areas of the Adirondacks for more than fifty years under the "forever wild" clause of the state constitution, has established the Adirondack Park Agency to insure that local zoning and state policies in the protected areas are in harmony.[64] Vermont has established a scheme of statewide land planning, and California has passed an initiative measure that directs careful protection of the state's coastline.[65] With the increasing leisure and mobility of the population and the consequent pressure on the scenic and undeveloped regions of the country, the states can be expected to expand this direct control in the coming years.

FEDERAL REGULATION

Federal influence on the regulation and development of land is found in two general areas: first, the use of land directly under federal control; and second, federal requirements accepted as part of programs that are largely initiated and managed by the states or their subdivisions but that receive a considerable part of their financing from the federal government.

Forest Service

Approximately a third of the nation's land, primarily in the western states and Alaska, is owned by the federal government. This land is primarily administered by the Department of Agriculture through the Forest Service, which manages the 187 million acres of the national forests, and by the Department of the Interior through the Bureau of Land Management, which controls approximately 60 percent of the public domain.

The Forest Service manages the national forests under two principal acts, the Organic Act of 1897, which was the first comprehensive act governing the management of the national forests, and the Multiple Use–Sustained Yield Act of 1960. Under the Organic Act,[66] national forests were to be established to provide favorable conditions of water flow and to furnish a continuous supply of timber for the use of American citizens. These purposes were enlarged by the Multiple Use–Sustained Yield Act[67] to include outdoor recreation, range, timber, watershed, and fish and wildlife purposes. These interests are to be managed on a sustained yield basis which means "the achievement and maintenance in perpetuity of a high-level annual or regular periodic output of the various renewable resources."[68] In making management decisions, the Forest Service is to give "due consideration . . . to the relative values of the various resources in particular areas."[69] The main goal of the multiple-use law is to produce

> . . . management of all the various renewable surface resources of the national forests so that they are utilized in the combination that will best meet the needs of the American people; making the most judicious use of the land for some or all of these resources or related services over areas large enough to provide sufficient latitude for periodic adjustments in use to conform to changing needs and conditions.[70]

Various clauses in the Organic Act of 1897 may be interpreted as restraints on the Forest Service—the requirement that timber must be marked and designated before being sold and the language restricting sale to "dead, matured, or large growth of trees."[71] Suits aimed at establishing selective cutting and more careful forest management through the enforcement of those requirements are presently before the courts and have not been finally adjudicated.[72]

Under the terms of the Multiple Use–Sustained Yield Act, the Forest Service draws up multiple use plans for the National Forests on a segment-by-segment basis, and these plans then govern management decisions on matters such as sale of timber, method of timber harvest, or watershed protection. There is considerable debate on whether these decisions have in fact served the broad purposes of the act and whether the terms of the Multiple Use–Sustained Yield Act are so discretionary that virtually no standards are imposed on the Forest Service by Congress.[73]

Bureau of Land Management

There is no comprehensive, organic act regulating the vast holdings of the federal government that are within the jurisdiction of the Bureau of Land Management (BLM). In 1964 Congress established the Public Land Law Review Commission to analyze the law governing the public domain and recommend to Congress what changes in the statutes should be made to best serve the public benefit.[74] Congress has not acted on the commission's recommendations, but there is some possibility that Congress will pass an organic act in the not too distant future.

The historic policy of the United States towards the public lands has been for use by private parties or outright disposal. There have been many laws in favor of private use or disposal, and most remain on the statute books. Thus, hundreds of pages of the U.S. Code describe the Homestead Laws,[75] the great charter by which so much nineteenth-century settlement took place, and the grants of land for railroad construction, which were of great importance in an earlier era.[76]

Today a limited number of the crazyquilt of laws governing the public lands have immediate relevance and importance. The Taylor Grazing Act,[77] has allowed the use of large areas for livestock grazing under a fee-and-permit system, in order to promote the best use of public lands pending their disposal. The laws governing mining and mineral leasing still embody the century-old policy encouraging private exploitation of extractive resources on the public lands.[78]

These specific statutory policies must be viewed in light of the discretionary powers given the executive in the management of public lands. The President has the authority to withdraw public lands from the normal claims for use or possession which citizens might make on it.[79] In fact, most vacant public lands are withdrawn from entry, selection, and location under the nonmineral land laws or are administered for grazing under the Taylor Grazing Act.[80]

Over the past several years, the Interior Department has been engaged in the gigantic task of classifying the lands of the public domain for disposal and management purposes, primarily under the now expired Multiple Use–Classification Act.[81] Management, which the BLM is now favoring over disposal, will be conducted on a multiple use–sustained yield basis, though the number of classified uses will far exceed the Forest Service's mandated list of five.[82] This work is undertaken under regulations which set forth high and generalized goals. For instance, all classifications "will give due consideration to ecology, priorities of use, and the relative values of the various resources in particular areas."[83] It is still too early to know whether the BLM can or will give those terms a meaning that will satisfy many members of the American public.

National Park Service

The federal government holds other lands for special purposes and uses decreed by statute. The system of National Parks and Seashores is administered by the National Park Service under the Department of the Interior. The parks are governed by particular statutes that generally aim to maintain the land in its natural state but that differ in the details of management.[84]

Wilderness Act

Under the Wilderness Act[85] Congress has asked the Secretaries of Agriculture and Interior to review the appropriate areas under their jurisdiction in the national parks and national forests for suitability for inclusion in a national wilderness preservation system so that a heritage of natural lands substantially untouched by man may be preserved for future generations. Much of the review has taken place, and it is to conclude in 1974. This process includes public notice and hearing, and requires that after designation by the executive, Congress must act to include such lands in the wilderness system.

Other Programs

There is a whole range of programs under which federal financing of programs initiated or managed by the states directly influences the use of land across the country.

Detailed descriptions of any of these programs is beyond the scope of this chapter, but several examples should be provided. The most obvious is the federal highway program, which has pumped enormous quantities of money into local coffers for the construction both of interstate highways and smaller federal aid highways, with profound effects on land use.[86] Particular areas of the country have received special attention. The Coastal Zone Management Act,[87] passed in 1972, provides grants to encourage the states to establish management programs for land and water resources of the coastal zone. Such programs are to give full consideration to ecological, cultural, historic, and esthetic values, as well as to needs for economic development. The establishment of regional action planning commissions[88] in economically depressed areas of the country, such as New England and the Ozarks, has inevitably produced planning for schemes, such as economic-development highways, that directly influence the use of land in the region. Finally, the requirements of NEPA have meant that grants for land planning from the Department of Housing and Urban Development must now include assessments of the environmental impact of the proposed plan.[89]

There are many more such programs and it must be clearly recognized that while the federal government rarely exerts direct power over the uses of land held in private hands, it has a very considerable indirect influence that is exerted through the power of the purse by approving, rejecting, or forcing further analysis of the plans brought to it for funding.

SOLID WASTE

There are two federal statutes dealing with the problems of solid waste: the Solid Waste Disposal Act[90] and the National Materials Policy Act of 1970.[91]

The Solid Waste Disposal Act authorizes the EPA to conduct research, training, and demonstration projects dealing with the effects on health and welfare of releasing materials present in solid waste; with the operation and financing of solid waste disposal programs; with the reduction of solid waste; with improvements in its collection and processing; and with the identification and recovery of materials and energy from solid waste.

Throughout the act there is heavy emphasis on financial and other assistance to appropriate public and private agencies and individuals to perform these studies. The legislation also stresses federal encouragement of state, local, and regional cooperation, and gives the EPA a role through the publication of guidelines in seeing that federal agencies have responsible waste management programs. Thus, the act does not set standards, but it mandates research for the preparation of programs that are expected to be carried out principally on a state and local basis.

The National Materials Policy Act established the National Materials Policy Commission, with seven members from government service and the private sector who were chosen for their competence in materials policy. The members were appointed by the President. The commission was charged to study and investigate, among other things, future materials requirements in relation to both population size and environmental quality, to recommend means for the use of materials that can be recycled or that are self-destroying, and to consider which federal agency should have responsibility for the national materials policy. Over the last few years the commission has issued a series of reports on the issues within its congressional mandate, which are available from the commission in Washington, D.C. A final report was published in June 1973.

Comparatively little has been done by the states and localities to control the production of solid waste. Even regulations aimed at greater use of returnable containers have not been frequent.[92] Further information on possible forms of regulation in this field—taxes, deposits, and prohibitions—is available in "State and Local Regulations of Nonreturnable Beverage Containers," *Wisconsin Law Review* (1972): 536 ff.

NOISE

To promote an environment free from noise that jeopardizes health or welfare, Congress passed the Noise Control Act of 1972.[93] Under the act, the EPA is to undertake a series of investigations leading to noise control.

In the summer of 1973, the EPA published criteria on the effects of noise on public health and welfare. These are to be followed in the fall of 1973 with information on the noise levels that must be met to protect public health and welfare with an adequate margin of safety. In 1974, the EPA is to propose standards for the major sources of noise in the construction, transportation, and motor and electric sectors; however, aircraft, trucks, and trains are separately regulated. The standards are to be based on the best available technology and the cost of compliance, as well as health and welfare. The standards will be enforced by requiring the manufacturer to warrant to the ultimate purchaser that the product complies with the standards. The states will be preempted from setting standards other than the federal ones.

The EPA is undertaking a special study of aircraft noise, including the regulations of the Federal Aviation Administration.[94] It reported to Congress on that problem in the summer of 1973.[95] Regulations for trucks and trains are to be developed, using essentially the same guidelines as for other regulated areas, but are to be done in consultation with the Secretary of Transportation and to be promulgated in the fall of 1973.[96]

RADIATION

Man-made radiation is produced in various forms by nuclear-power generating plants, X-ray diagnosis and therapy, industrial X-ray cabinets, microwave ovens, television sets, lasers, and a variety of other electronic products. The federal government is involved in radiation control under a maze of standards, regulations, and guidelines in terms of emission control, performance standards, and occupational standards. Responsibility for setting standards and enforcing them is dispersed among the Environmental Protection Agency, the Atomic Energy Commission, the Bureau of Mines of the Department of the Interior, the Bureau of Radiological Health within the Department of Health, Education and Welfare, and the Department of Transportation. However, the major statutory authority for radiation control is the Radiation Control for Health and Safety Act of 1968 and the Atomic Energy Act of 1954.

Most man-made radiation comes from diagnostic X-ray and other treatment devices in the dental and medical fields. Pursuant to the Radiation Control for Health and Safety Act,[97] the Bureau of Radiological Health in the Department of Health, Education and Welfare has authority for setting performance standards, prescribing maximum allowable radiation levels, and other approaches to control radioactive emissions without specifying design features. Maximum emission standards for diagnostic X-ray systems, radiographic equipment, and fluoroscopic equipment were published in 1972 but do not take effect until August 1, 1974.[98]

The EPA has authority to establish generally applicable standards for the protection of the environment from radioactive materials.[99] The EPA has the dual responsibility (1) to formulate basic federal policies on radiation protection and on development of radiation protection guidelines, which are to be followed by all federal agencies concerned with radiation control; and (2) to establish environmental protection standards, which limit radiation levels in the general environment outside the boundaries of nuclear power plants or other radiation-producing installations. The agency plans to develop standards for the total uranium and plutonium fuel cycles in nuclear power generation, running from mining through use to final waste disposal, and to work out a method for assessing risks, costs and benefits, site criteria, and emergency preparedness.

The Atomic Energy Commission (AEC) has been given a broad mandate for promoting peaceful use of the atom.[100] It has authority to set standards governing the possession and use of special nuclear material in order to promote the common defense and security or to minimize danger to health, life, or property.[101] For the operation of the facilities it licenses, the commission has established general standards to protect the public from the effects of radiation.[102] Recently, the AEC has markedly reduced the limits of permissible emission from nuclear facilities. The AEC also publishes detailed guides for general design, construction, and operating requirements for nuclear power plants, as well as requirements for obtaining a permit to construct and a license to operate a nuclear plant.[103]

Transportation of radioactive materials, which represents an environmental health hazard, is subject to regulation by the Department of Transportation.[104] Some of this authority has recently passed to the AEC pursuant to a memorandum of understanding, which provides that while the Department of Transportation will continue to regulate handling and shipping, the AEC will set package standards and approve all containers for fissionable materials and large quantities of other radioactive materials.

Citizen concern for the relationship of the AEC to the nuclear power industry has grown in recent years as a result of questions about the bases and flexibility of guidelines and regulations where such great risk is involved. There have been an increasing number of interventions by citizens groups at the hearings on construction permits and operating licenses that the AEC must hold before allowing a power-producing nuclear plant to go on line.[105] Some of the dangers of this form of energy have been concisely summarized by Nobel Laureate Hannes Alfven:

> Fission energy is safe only if a number of critical devices work as they should, if a number of people in key positions follow all their instructions, if there is no sabotage, no hijacking of the transports, if no reactor fuel processing plant or reprocessing plant or repository anywhere in the world is situated in a region of riots or guerrilla activity, and no revolution or war—even a "conventional one"—takes place in these regions. The enormous quantities of materials must not get into the hands of ignorant people or desperadoes. No acts of God can be permitted. (*Science and Public Affairs*, vol. 28, 1972, p. 6.)

NOTES

1. E.g., *Kuehn v. City of Milwaukee*, 83 Wis. 583, 53 N.W. 912 (1892); *Bouquet v. Hackensack Water Co.*, 90 N.J.L. 203, 101 A.397 (1917).

The Environment and the Law   273

2. Restatement (Second) of Torts, Tentative Draft No. 17, §821C.
3. *Boomer v. Atlantic Cement, Inc.*, 26 N.Y. 2d 219, 257 N.E. 2d 870, 309, N.Y.S.2d 312 (1970).
4. *Stevens v. Rockport Granite*, 216 Mass. 486, 488, 104 N.E. 371, 373 (1914).
5. Further background on this complicated and changing area of the common law is available in Bryson & Macbeth, *Public Nuisance, the Restatement (Second) of Torts, and Environmental Law*, 2 Ecology Law Quarterly 241 (1972).
6. 42 U.S.C. §4321 *et seq.*
7. 42 U.S.C. §4332 (2)(C).
8. *City of New York v. U.S.*, 337 F.Supp 150, 334 F.Supp 929 (E.D.N.Y. 1972).
9. 33 U.S.C. § 1371(C)(2).
10. 87 Stat. 57b, § 203(d).
11. *NRDC v. Morton*, 458 F.2d 827 (D.C. Cir. 1972).
11a. *Named Individual Members of the San Antonio Conservation Society v. Texas Highway Department*, 446 F.2d 1013 (5th Cir. 1971).
12. *Sierra Club v. Froehlke*, —F.Supp—, 5 ERC 1033 (S.D. Tex 1973).
13. *Goose Hollow Foothills League v. Romney*, 334 F.Supp 877 (D. Ore. 1971).
14. *Greene County Planning Board v. FPC*, 455 F.2d 417 (2d Cir.), *cert. denied*, 409 U.S. 849 (1972).
15. The professional and administrative staff of CEQ is provided by the Office of Environmental Quality, which under the Environmental Quality Act of 1970, 42 U.S.C. §§4371-74, also has the responsibility of assisting other federal agencies in appraising their programs and undertaking analysis, research, and evaluation in the environmental field.
16. See *Citizens for Clean Air v. Corps of Engineers*, 349 F.Supp 696 (S.D.N.Y. 1972).
17. California Environmental Quality Act of 1970, Cal. Pub. Res. Code §21000 *et seq.* (West 1970); Montana Environmental Policy Act, Ch. No. 283, 1971 Session Laws at 984 *et seq.*
18. 42 U.S.C. Sts. §1857 *et seq.*
19. 42 U.S.C. §§1857c-4 to c-9.
20. 42 U.S.C. §1857c-4.
21. 40 C.F.R. Part 50.
22. 42 U.S.C. §1857(b)(1); (1); *Sierra Club v. Ruckelshaus*, 344 F.Supp 253 (D.D.C. 1972), *aff'd.* — F.2d —, 4 ERC 1815 ((D.C. Cir.), *aff'd. sub nom Fri v. Sierra Club* — U.S. —, 5 ERC 1417 (1973).
23. 42 U.S.C. §1857c-5.
24. 40 C.F.R. §51.7.
25. E.g., NRDC v. EPA, — F.2d —, 3 ELR 20375 (1st Cir. 1973).
26. NRDC v. EPA, 475 F.2d 968, (D.C. Cir. 1973).
27. 42 U.S.C. §1857f-1 (b)(1).
28. 42 U.S.C. §1857c-7.
29. 42 U.S.C. §1857c-6.
30. 42 U.S.C. §§1857c-7(d), 1857c-6(c).
31. 42 U.S.C. § 1857h-2.
32. 42 U.S.C. §1857c-9.
33. 42 U.S.C. §1857h-2.
34. 33 U.S.C. §1251 *et seq.*
35. 33 U.S.C. §1251a.
36. 33 U.S.C. §1311.
37. 33 U.S.C. §1316.
38. 33 U.S.C. §§1285, 1287.
39. *City of New York v. Ruckelshaus*, — F.Supp —, 5 ERC 1305 (D.D.C. 1973).
40. 33 U.S.C. §1312-1313.
41. 33 U.S.C. §1312-1313.
42. 33 U.S.C. §1313.
43. 33 U.S.C. §1317.
44. 33 U.S.C. §1326.
45. 33 U.S.C. §1342.
46. 33 U.S.C. §1365.
47. 42 U.S.C. §1962a *et seq.*
48. 82 Stat. 868 (see 42 U.S.C. §1962a note).
49. 33 U.S.C. §403.
50. 33 C.F.R. §209.120(g).
51. 33 U.S.C. §701 *et seq.*
52. 33 U.S.C. §701a.
53. E.g., Tennessee-Tombigbee Waterway, 60 Stat. 634 (1946).
54. 16 U.S.C. §§1001-09.
55. 32 Stat. 388.
56. E.g., Auburn-Folsom South Unit, Central Valley Project, California, 43 U.S.C. §§616aaa, 616ccc, 616ff-1 and 2.
57. 16 U.S.C. § 791a *et seq.*
58. 16 U.S.C. §803(a).
59. E.g., *EDF v. Corps of Engineers*, 470 F.2d 289 (8th Cir. 1972); *NRDC v. Grant*, 341 F.Supp 356; (E.D.N.C. 1972); 355 F.Supp 280 (E.D.N.C. 1973) (Soil Conservation Service); *NRDC v. Pafford*, C.A. No. S2663 (E.D. Cal.) (Bureau of Reclamation); *Scenic Hudson Preservation Conference v. FPC*, 453 F.2d 463 (2d Cir. 1971), *cert. denied*, 407 U.S. 926 (1972).

60. *Commissioner of Natural Resources v. S. Volpe & Co.*, 349 Mass. 104, 206 N.E. 2d 666, 669 (1965).
61. *Vernon Park Realty v. City of Mount Vernon*, 307 N.Y. 493, 121 N.E. 2d 517 (1954).
62. See *Volpe, supra*, note 60, at 671.
63. See *Morris County Land Improvement Co. v. Township of Parsippany-Troy Hills*, 40 N.J. 539, 193, A.2d 232 (1963).
64. N.Y. Const., Art XIV, §1; N.Y. Exec. Law, §§800-810 (McKinney 1971).
65. Vt. Stat. Ann., Tit. 10, §§6001 *et seq.* (Supp/1971); Cal. Pub. Res. Code §27000 *et seq.* (West 1973).
66. 16 U.S.C. §475.
67. 16 U.S.C. §528-531.
68. 16 U.S.C. §531(b).
69. 16 U.S.C. §529.
70. 16 U.S.C. §531(a).
71. 16 U.S.C. §476.
72. *Sierra Club v. Hardin*, 325 F.Supp 99 (D. Alas. 1971); *West Va. Div. of Isaac Walton League of America v. Butz*, civ. no. 73-68-E (N.D.W.Va.).
73. *Sierra Club v. Morton*, 405 U.S. 727, 748 (1972) (Douglas dissenting); Reich, "Public and the Nation's Forests," 50 Cal. L. Rev. 381 (1962).
74. 43 U.S.C. §§1393-94.
75. 43 U.S.C. §§161-302.
76. 43 U.S.C. §§881-914.
77. 43 U.S.C. §315 *et seq.*
78. E.g., 30 U.S.C. §§21-54, 241 *et seq.*
79. 43 U.S.C. §141.
80. 43 C.F.R. §2400.0-3.
81. 43 U.S.C. §§1411-18.
82. 43 C.F.R., Parts 2400, 2410, 2420.
83. 43 C.F.R. §2410.1.
84. E.g., Yellowstone, 16 U.S.C. §21 *et seq.*; Cape Cod, 16 U.S.C. §459b *et seq.*; Fire Island, 16 U.S.C. §459e *et seq.*
85. 16 U.S.C. §§1131-36.
86. 23 U.S.C. §101 *et seq.*
87. 16 U.S.C. §§1451-64.
88. 42 U.S.C. §3181 *et seq.*
89. 40 U.S.C. §461; 24 C.F.R. § 600. 65.
90. 42 U.S.C. §§3251-3259.
91. Public Law 91-512, §§201-206 (see 42 U.S.C. §3251 note).
92. E.g., Ore. Laws 2015.
93. 42 U.S.C. §§4901-18.
94. 14 C.F.R. Part 36.
95. 42 U.S.C. §4906.
96. 42 U.S.C. §§4916-17.
97. 42 U.S.C. §§263b-n.
98. 37 F.R. 16461, 38 F.R. 15444.
99. 42 U.S.C. §2021(h); 35 F.R. 1562.
100. 42 U.S.C. §2011.
101. 42 U.S.C. §2201.
102. 10 C.F.R. Part 20.
103. 10 C.F.R. Part 50.
104. 49 U.S.C. §1655(e)(4).
105. 42 U.S.C. §§2133, 2235, 2239.

11 Environmental Conferences and Meetings

One of the most informative activities of environmental organizations is the sponsorship of periodic meetings, conferences, and exhibitions. This chapter presents a representative listing of such events.

The listings are organized under alphabetically arranged subject headings and the specific meetings cited under each subject category are in chronological order. An explanation of the parenthetical codes preceding each entry and an alphabetical index of sponsoring organizations are included at the end of the chapter.

The individual entries specify the date, title, and place of each meeting as well as the name and address of a person or group that can furnish additional information about the events and exhibits included in the meeting. Many of the gatherings cover a wide range of topics; therefore, it is suggested that further information be requested from the sponsoring group about the emphasis given to specific environmental topics.

AIR POLLUTION

(A-1) May 12–16, 1974
Incinerator Conference and Exhibition
Miami Beach, Fla. (Carillon Hotel)
Inquiries: P. Drummond, American Society of Mechanical Engineers, 345 E. 47 St., New York, N.Y. 10017

(A-2) May 12–17, 1974
American Industrial Hygiene Conference
Miami, Fla. (Fontainebleau Hotel)
Inquiries: American Industrial Hygiene Assn., 210 Haddon Ave., Westmont, N.J. 08108

(A-3) June 9–13, 1974
Air Pollution Control Assn. Annual Meeting and Exhibition
Denver, Colo. (Convention Center)
Inquiries: Dr. L. H. Rogers, Air Pollution Control Assn., 4400 5 Ave., Pittsburgh, Pa. 15213

(A-4) June 11–15, 1974
International Exhibition and Technical Meetings for Environmental Sanitation
Basle, Switzerland
Inquiries: Swiss Industries Fair, Postfach 4021, Basle, Switzerland

(A-5) July 1–5, 1974
International Congress of Medicine, Biology and Environment
Paris, France
Inquiries: S. O. C. F. I., 7, rue Michel Ange, 75016 Paris, France

(A-6) Oct. 7–10, 1974
American Mining Congress Convention and Exposition
Las Vegas, Nev.
Inquiries: R. W. Van Evera, American Mining Congress, Ring Bldg., Washington, D.C. 20036

BIOLOGICAL CONTAMINATION

(B-1) May 12–17, 1974
American Society for Microbiology Annual Meeting
Chicago, Ill.
Inquiries: R. W. Sarber, American Society for Microbiology, 1913 I St. N.W., Washington, D.C. 20006

275

Conservation

(C-1) Apr. 25–27, 1974
Ohio Academy of Science Annual Meeting
Wooster, Ohio (Col. of Wooster)
Inquiries: J. H. Melvin, Ohio Academy of Science, 445 King Ave., Columbus, Ohio 43201

(C-2) Apr. 26–27, 1974
Iowa Academy of Science Annual Session
Fayette, Iowa
Inquiries: R. W. Hanson, Iowa Academy of Science, c/o Univ. of Northern Iowa, Cedar Falls, Iowa 50613

(C-3) Week of June 24, 1974 (approx.)
American Society of Agricultural Engineers Annual Meeting
Stillwater, Okla. (Oklahoma State Univ.)
Inquiries: J. L. Butt, American Society of Agricultural Engineers, Box 229, St. Joseph, Mich. 49085

Energy

(E-1) Apr. 1–5, 1974
Insitute of Electrical and Electronics Engineers Power Engineering Society Conference on Underground Power Transmission and Distribution
Dallas, Tex. (Dallas Convention Center)
Inquiries: C. O. Love, Texas Power and Light Co., Box 6331, Dallas, Tex. 75222

(E-2) June 9–11, 1974
International Conference on Nuclear Reactors
Montreal, Canada (Bonaventure Hotel)
Inquiries: J. A. Weller, Canadian Nuclear Assn., Suite 1120, 65 Queen St. W., Toronto M5H 2M5, Ontario, Canada

(E-3) Aug. 26–30, 1974
Ninth Intersociety Energy Conversion Engineering Conference
San Francisco, Calif.
Inquiries: A. D. Tonelli, McDonnell Douglas Astronautics Co., Biotechnology and Power Dept. 833, MS 22-2, 5301 Bolsa Ave., Huntington Beach, Calif. 92647

(E-4) Sept. 22–27, 1974
Ninth World Energy Conference
Detroit, Mich. (Cobo Convention Hall)
Inquiries: E. Ruttley, World Energy Conference, 5 Bury St., London SW1, England

Fish and Wildlife

(FW-1) Mar. 31–Apr. 3, 1974
North American Wildlife and Natural Resources Conference
Denver, Colo.
Inquiries: Dr. L. R. Jahn, Wildlife Management Institute, 709 Wire Bldg., Washington, D.C. 20005

(FW-2) Sept. 8–14, 1974
American Fisheries Society Annual Meeting
Honolulu, Hawaii (Sheraton-Waikiki Hotel)
Inquiries: Dr. R. A. Wade, American Fisheries Society, 1319 18 St. N.W., Washington, D.C. 20036

Forestry

(F-1) June 23–28, 1974
Forest Products Research Society Annual Meeting
Chicago, Ill. (LaSalle Hotel)
Inquiries: K. E. Huddleston, Forest Products Research Society, 2801 Marshall Ct., Madison, Wis. 53705

(F-2) Sept. 23–26, 1974
Society of American Foresters National Convention
New York, N.Y. (Hilton Hotel)
Inquiries: H. R. Glascock, Jr., Society of American Foresters, 1010 16 St. N.W., Washington, D.C. 20036

General Environment and Ecology

(G-1) Mar. 1974
Texas Academy of Science Annual Meeting
Denton, Tex. (North Texas State Univ.)
Inquiries: Dr. E. N. Drake, Texas Academy of Science, Dept. of Chemistry, Angelo State Univ., San Angelo, Tex. 76901

(G-2) Apr. 22–26, 1974
Ninth International Symposium on Remote Sensing of Environment
Ann Arbor, Mich. (Univ. of Michigan)
Inquiries: J. J. Cook, Univ. of Michigan, Willow Run Laboratories, Box 618, Ann Arbor, Mich. 48107

(G-3) Apr. 28–May 2, 1974
Institute of Environmental Sciences Technical Meeting and Equipment Exposition
Washington, D.C. (Shoreham Hotel)
Inquiries: Betty L. Peterson, Institute of Environmental Sciences, 940 E. Northwest Hwy., Mt. Prospect, Ill. 60056

(G-4) June 16–21, 1974
Ecological Society of America Annual Meeting
Tempe, Ariz. (Arizona State Univ.)
Inquiries: C. Malone, National Academy of Sciences, Natural Resources Council, Office of Information, 2101 Constitution Ave., Washington, D.C. 20418

(G-5) July 1–5, 1974
International Congress of Medicine, Biology and Environment
Paris, France
Inquiries: S. O. C. F. I., 7, rue Michel Ange, 75016 Paris, France

(G-6) Mar. 1975 (dates to be announced)
Texas Academy of Science Annual Meeting
Huntsville, Tex. (Sam Houston State Univ.)
Inquiries: Dr. E. N. Drake, Texas Academy of Science, Dept. of Chemistry, Angelo State Univ., San Angelo, Tex. 76901

Environmental Health and Safety

(HS-1) Mar. 1974
Conference on Rural Health
Michigan (city to be announced)
Inquiries: B. Bible, American Medical Assn., 535 N. Dearborn St., Chicago, Ill. 60610

(HS-2) Apr. 2–5, 1974
American Col. Health Assn. Meeting
Dallas, Tex. (Adolphus Hotel)
Inquiries: V. Arthur Stevens, American Col. Health Assn., 2807 Central St., Evanston, Ill. 60201

(HS-3) May 12–17, 1974
American Industrial Hygiene Conference
Miami, Fla. (Fontainebleau Hotel)
Inquiries: American Industrial Hygiene Assn., 210 Haddon Ave., Westmont, N.J. 08108

(HS-4) July 1–5, 1974
International Congress of Medicine, Biology and Environment
Paris, France
Inquiries: S. O. C. F. I., 7, rue Michel Ange, 75016 Paris, France

(HS-5) Feb. 6–8, 1975
National Western Mining Conference and Exhibition
Denver, Colo. (Denver Hilton)
Inquiries: D. R. Cole, Colorado Mining Assn., 402 Majestic Bldg., 209 16 St., Denver, Colo. 80202

Land Use

(L-1) May 1–4, 1974
American Assn. for the Advancement of Science, Southwestern and Rocky Mountain Div. Meeting
Laramie, Wyo. (Univ. of Wyoming)
Inquiries: Dr. M. G. Anderson, Secretary, American Assn. for the Advancement of Science, Southwestern and Rocky Mountain Div., c/o New Mexico State Univ., Box 3AF, Las Cruces, N. Mex. 88003

(L-2) Week of June 24, 1974 (approx.)
American Society of Agricultural Engineers Annual Meeting
Stillwater, Okla. (Oklahoma State Univ.)
Inquiries: J. L. Butt, American Society of Agricultural Engineers, Box 229, St. Joseph, Mich. 49085

(L-3) Sept. 9–16, 1974
International Federation of Surveyors Congress
Washington, D.C. (Washington Hilton Hotel)
Inquiries: J. Battley, Box 14262, Washington, D.C. 20004

(L-4) Oct. 7–10, 1974
American Mining Congress Convention and Exposition
Las Vegas, Nev.
Inquiries: R. W. Van Evera, American Mining Congress, Ring Bldg., Washington, D.C. 20036

Natural Resources

(NR-1) Mar. 31–Apr. 3, 1974
North American Wildlife and Natural Resources Conference
Denver, Colo.
Inquiries: Dr. L. R. Jahn, Wildlife Management Institute, 709 Wire Bldg., Washington, D.C. 20005

(NR-2) Apr. 1–3, 1974
American Assn. of Petroleum Geologists and Society of Economic Paleontologists and Mineralogists Annual Meeting
San Antonio, Tex. (Convention Center)
Inquiries: M. O. Turner, 2113 Alamo National Bldg., San Antonio, Tex. 78205

(NR-3) Apr. or May 1974 (dates to be announced)
Society of American Value Engineers Annual Meeting
Chicago, Ill. (Marriott Motor Hotel)
Inquiries: F. J. Johnson, Society of American Value Engineers, 2550 Hargrove Dr., Smyrna, Ga. 30080

(NR-4) May 5–8, 1974
American Mining Congress Coal Convention
Pittsburgh, Pa.
Inquiries: R. W. Van Evera, American Mining Congress, Ring Bldg., Washington, D.C. 20036

(NR-5) May 19–22, 1974
Geological Assn. of Canada Annual Meeting
St. John's, Canada (Memorial Univ.)
Inquiries: C. R. Barnes, Geological Assn. of Canada, Dept. of Earth Sciences, Univ. of Waterloo, Waterloo, Ontario, Canada

(NR-6) Sept. 29–Oct. 3, 1974
Symposium on Offshore Petroleum and Canada's Continental Margins
Calgary, Ontario, Canada
Inquiries: E. E. Gilbert, Coseka Research, Suite 602, 1 Calgary Pl., T2P OL4, Calgary, Alberta, Canada

(NR-7) Oct. 7–10, 1974
American Mining Congress Convention and Exposition
Las Vegas, Nev.
Inquiries: R. W. Van Evera, American Mining Congress, Ring Bldg., Washington, D.C. 20036

(NR-8) Feb. 6–8, 1975
National Western Mining Conference and Exhibition
Denver, Colo. (Denver Hilton)
Inquiries: D. R. Cole, Colorado Mining Assn., 402 Majestic Bldg., 209 16 St., Denver, Colo. 80202

NOISE

(N-1) May 12–17, 1974
American Industrial Hygiene Conference
Miami, Fla. (Fontainebleau Hotel)
Inquiries: American Industrial Hygiene Assn., 210 Haddon Ave., Westmont, N.J. 08108

(N-2) June 11–15, 1974
International Exhibition and Technical Meetings for Environmental Sanitation
Basle, Switzerland
Inquiries: Swiss Industries Fair, Postfach 4021, Basle, Switzerland

(N-3) July 1–5, 1974
International Congress of Medicine, Biology and Environment
Paris, France
Inquiries: S. O. C. F. I., 7, rue Michel Ange, 75016 Paris, France

PESTICIDES

(PE-1) Mar. 3–7, 1974
Society of Toxicology Annual Scientific Meeting
Washington, D.C.
Inquiries: Dr. R. A. Scala, Society of Toxicology, c/o Medical Research Div., Esso R and E Co., Linden, N.J. 07036

POPULATION

(PO-1) Apr. 18–20, 1974
Population Assn. of America Annual Meeting
New York, N.Y. (Commodore Hotel)
Inquiries: J. W. Brackett, Population Assn. of America, Box 14182, Benjamin Franklin Sta., Washington, D.C. 20044

(PO-2) Aug. 19–30, 1974
World Population Conference
New York, N.Y.
Inquiries: A. Carrillo Flores, Secretary-General, World Population Conference 1974, United Nations, New York, N.Y. 10017

(PO-3) 1974 (dates to be announced)
Eighth World Congress of Fertility and Sterility
Rio de Janeiro, Brazil
Inquiries: International Federation of Fertility Societies, University Col. Hospital, London WC1, England

Radiation

(R-1) May 12–17, 1974
American Industrial Hygiene Conference
Miami, Fla. (Fontainebleau Hotel)
Inquiries: American Industrial Hygiene Assn., 210 Haddon Ave., Westmont, N.J. 08108

(R-2) June 9–11, 1974
International Conference on Nuclear Reactors
Montreal, Canada (Bonaventure Hotel)
Inquiries: J. A. Weller, Canadian Nuclear Assn., Suite 1120, 65 Queen St. W., Toronto M5H 2M5, Ontario, Canada

(R-3) July 1–5, 1974
International Congress of Medicine, Biology and Environment
Paris, France
Inquiries: S. O. C. F. I., 7, rue Michel Ange, 75016 Paris, France

(R-4) July 14–20, 1974
Fifth International Congress of Radiation Research
Seattle, Wash.
Inquiries: Dr. W. K. Sinclair, Argonne National Laboratories, Argonne, Ill. 60439

Solid Waste

(SW-1) June 11–15, 1974
International Exhibition and Technical Meetings for Environmental Sanitation
Basle, Switzerland
Inquiries: Swiss Industries Fair, Postfach 4021, Basle, Switzerland

Transportation

(T-1) Sept. 1974 (dates to be announced)
Traffic Control and Transportation Systems Conference
Cote d'Azur, France
Inquiries: French Assn. for Cybernetic Applications and Technology (AFCET), Centre Dauphine, Place du Maréchal de Lattre de Tassigny, Paris 16, France

(T-2) Sept. 1974 (dates to be announced)
Twelfth International Study Week in Traffic Engineering and Safety
Belgrade, Yugoslavia
Inquiries: World Touring and Automobile Organization (OTA), 32 Chesham Pl., London SW2X 8HF, England

Urban Environment

(U-1) Apr. 22–24, 1974
Urban Land Institute Spring Meeting
Orlando, Fla. (Disney World)
Inquiries: Carla C. Sobala, Urban Land Institute, 1200 18 St. N.W., Washington, D.C. 20036

Water Resources and Pollution

(W-1) May 1974 (dates to be announced)
Tercentary of Hydrology
Location to be announced
Inquiries: J. A. DaCosta, International Hydrological Decade, UNESCO, Place de Fontenoy, Paris 7, France

(W-2) May 5–8, 1974
Annual Offshore Technology Conference
Houston, Tex. (Astrohall and Astroworld)
Inquiries: S. Houston, Offshore Technology Conference, 6200 N. Central Expressway, Dallas, Tex. 75206

(W-3) May 6–10, 1974
American Society of Lubrication Engineers Annual Meeting
Cleveland, Ohio
Inquiries: Executive Secretary, American Society of Lubrication Engineers, 838 Busse Hwy., Park Ridge, Ill. 60068

(W-4) May 19–22, 1974
Geological Assn. of Canada Annual Meeting
St. John's, Canada (Memorial Univ.)
Inquiries: C. R. Barnes, Geological Assn. of Canada, Dept. of Earth Sciences, Univ. of Waterloo, Ontario, Canada

(W-5) June 11–15, 1974
International Exhibition and Technical Meetings for Environmental Sanitation
Basle, Switzerland
Inquiries: Swiss Industries Fair, Postfach 4021, Basle, Switzerland

(W-6) June 16–21, 1974
American Water Works Assn. Annual Conference

Boston, Mass.
Inquiries: E. F. Johnson, American Water Works Assn., 2 Park Ave., New York, N.Y. 10016

(W-7) Week of June 24, 1974 (approx.)
American Society of Agricultural Engineers Annual Meeting
Stillwater, Okla. (Oklahoma State Univ.)
Inquiries: J. L. Butt, American Society of Agricultural Engineers, Box 229, St. Joseph, Mich. 49085

(W-8) July 1-5, 1974
International Congress of Medicine, Biology and Environment
Paris, France
Inquiries: S. O. C. F. I., 7, rue Michel Ange, 75016 Paris, France

(W-9) Summer 1974
National Symposium on Water Resources Problems Relating to Mining
Golden, Colo.
Inquiries: American Water Resources Assn., 206 E. University Ave., Urbana, Ill. 61801

(W-10) Sept. 8-14, 1974
American Fisheries Society Annual Meeting
Honolulu, Hawaii (Sheraton-Waikiki Hotel)
Inquiries: Dr. R. A. Wade, American Fisheries Society, 1319 18 St. N.W., Washington, D.C. 20036

(W-11) Sept. 29-Oct. 3, 1974
Symposium on Offshore Petroleum and Canada's Continental Margins
Calgary, Canada
Inquiries: E. E. Gilbert, Coseka Research, Suite 602, 1 Calgary Pl., T2P OL4, Calgary, Alberta, Canada

(W-12) Oct. 6-11, 1974
Water Pollution Control Federation Annual Conference
Denver, Colo.
Inquiries: R. A. Canham, Water Pollution Control Federation, 3900 Wisconsin Ave. N.W., Washington, D.C. 20016

(W-13) Oct. 7-10, 1974
American Mining Congress Convention and Exposition
Las Vegas, Nev.
Inquiries: R. W. Van Evera, American Mining Congress, Ring Bldg., Washington, D.C. 20036

(W-14) Oct. 13-17, 1974
American Society of Sanitary Engineering Annual Meeting
New Orleans, La. (Monteleone Hotel)
Inquiries: S. Schwartz, American Society of Sanitary Engineering, 960 Illuminating Bldg., Cleveland, Ohio 44113

(W-15) Fall 1974 (dates to be announced)
Tenth Annual American Water Resources Conference
San Juan, Puerto Rico
Inquiries: American Water Resources Assn., 206 E. University Ave., Urbana, Ill. 61801

(W-16) 1974 (dates to be announced)
Third International Conference on Groundwater Tracing
Ljubljana, Yugoslavia
Inquiries: K. Gospodaric, Postojna (YU), Titov Trg. 2, Yugoslavia

SPONSORING ORGANIZATIONS

The organizations sponsoring the preceding conferences and meetings are specified below. Following the name of each sponsoring organization is a parenthetical key number which identifies the specific meeting or meetings sponsored by each group. The key numbers begin with a code letter referring to the subject categories used in the main listings. For example, the code A-1 refers to the first listing in the category "air pollution." The code letters and their equivalent categories are listed here.

A—Air pollution
B—Biological contamination
C—Conservation
E—Energy

FW—Fish and wildlife
F—Forestry
G—General environment and ecology
HS—Environmental health and safety

L—Land use
NR—Natural resources
N—Noise
PE—Pesticides
PO—Population

R—Radiation
SW—Solid waste
T—Transportation
U—Urban environment
W—Water resources and pollution

Index to Sponsors

Air Pollution Control Assn. (A-3)
Alberta Society of Petroleum Geology (NR-6; W-11)
American Assn. for the Advancement of Science, Southwestern and Rocky Mountain Div. (L-1)
American Assn. of Petroleum Geologists (NR-2)
American Chemical Society (E-3)
American Col. Health Assn. (HS-2)
American Fisheries Society (FW-2; W-10)
American Industrial Hygiene Assn. (A-2; HS-3; N-1; R-1)
American Medical Assn. (HS-1)
American Mining Congress (A-6; L-4; NR-7; W-13)
American Society for Microbiology (B-1)
American Society of Agricultural Engineers (C-3; L-2; W-7)
American Society of Lubrication Engineers (W-3)
American Society of Mechanical Engineers (A-1; E-3)
American Society of Sanitary Engineering (W-14)
American Water Resources Assn. (W-9; W-15)
American Water Works Assn. (W-6)
Canadian Nuclear Assn. (E-2; R-2)
Colorado Mining Assn. (HS-5; NR-8)
Ecological Society of America (G-4)
European Community (A-5; G-5; HS-4; N-3; R-3; W-8)
Forest Products Research Society (F-1)
French Assn. for Cybernetic Applications and Technology (AFCET) (T-1)
Geological Assn. of Canada (NR-5; W-4)
Institute of Electrical and Electronics Engineers (E-1; E-3)

Institute of Environmental Sciences (G-3)
International Assn. of Medicine and Biology of Environment (A-5; G-5; HS-4; N-3; R-3; W-8)
International Assn. of Radiation Research (R-4)
International Conference on Groundwater Tracing (W-16)
International Federation of Fertility Societies (PO-3)
International Federation of Surveyors (L-3)
International Hydrological Decade (W-1)
Iowa Academy of Science (C-2)
Offshore Technology Conference (W-2)
Ohio Academy of Science (C-1)
Population Assn. of America (PO-1)
Radiation Research Society (R-4)
Society of American Foresters (F-2)
Society of American Value Engineers (NR-3)
Society of Economic Paleontologists and Mineralogists (NR-2)
Society of Toxicology (PE-1)
Swiss Industries Fair (A-4; N-2; SW-2; W-5)
Texas Academy of Science (G-1; G-6)
UNESCO (A-5; G-5; HS-4; N-3; R-3; W-8)
Univ. of Michigan Center for Remote Sensing (G-2)
Urban Land Institute (U-1)
U.S. Environmental Protection Agency (A-5; G-5; HS-4; N-3; R-3; W-8)
Water Pollution Control Federation (W-12)
Wildlife Management Institute (FW-1; NR-1)
World Energy Conference (E-4)
World Health Organization (WHO) (A-5; G-5; HS-4; N-3; R-3; W-8)
World Population Conference (PO-2)
World Touring and Automobile Organization (OTA) (T-2)

12 Films

Environmental topics have been treated extensively in films in recent years. The films described in this chapter are a representative cross section of those readily available to the general public for purchase or rental in 16mm format. Prices are those in effect at the time of writing, and are subject to change by their distributors.

The listings cover a broad spectrum of environmental topics, from the effects of ionizing radiation, to how weather is controlled, to the near-extinction of a type of Hawaiian wild goose. The films are organized into subject categories, but there is some overlap among the categories. For example, many of the films listed under Natural Resources might have also been included under Conservation. A similar overlap exists between Land Use and Natural Resources.

This listing of films is by no means comprehensive; it represents a selection of the more interesting and unusual films. Although a few of the films are fairly old, the material contained in them is not easily dated; for example, fission nuclear reactors still operate by the same principle as they did in the 1950s.

Some films abstracted here are not strictly environmental; they have been included because they can stimulate discussion. A number of films classified as General concern the difficulties of modern life; these films may lead to informative discussions of how one's perceived environment helps to formulate his view of things.

In general, no attempt was made to indicate the quality of the films listed, but an effort was made to include only films that achieve some degree of excellence. Films dealing with controversial environmental issues vary considerably in their viewpoints and degree of objectivity. Cases of noticeable bias are mentioned in the film descriptions.

The film listings are arranged alphabetically within each category, and include a short abstract about the film's content; information on the length of the film; whether it is in color or black and white (b&w); the purchase and/or rental price; the release date; and the name of the film distributor. Addresses for all distributors mentioned may be found immediately following the film descriptions.

Films are listed alphabetically by title under the following subject categories.

Air Pollution
Conservation
Energy
Environmental Education
Forestry
General Environment and Ecology
Land Use
Miscellaneous
Natural Resources

Noise
Pesticides
Population
Radiation
Solid Waste
The Urban Environment
Water Resources and Pollution
Weather Modification
Wildlife

AIR POLLUTION

Air Pollution. 11 ½ min.; color. Purchase $135; rental $10. 1969. Journal Films, Inc.
Considers the adverse health effects and billions of dollars damage that results annually from air pollution. Discusses dollars and commitment needed to change these conditions.

Air Pollution. 10 min.; color. Purchase $135. 1970. Sterling Educational Films
Surveys air pollution in the city and country. Discusses ongoing research in control devices. Asks children to join the fight against pollution through learning and discussions.

Air Pollution and Plant Life. 20 min.; color. Purchase $81.75; free loan. 1971. General Services Administration, National Archives and Records Service
Gives technical discussion of effects of sulphur oxides, nitrogen oxides, fluorides, ozone, and PAN on vegetation in the United States. Details vegetative injury in Tennessee, Alabama, Florida, West Virginia, Maryland, and California.

Air Pollution: Take a Deep Breath, Parts I, II, and III. 54 min.; color. Purchase $610; rental $40. 1968. Contemporary/McGraw Hill Films
Each unit is complete in itself and can be shown separately. Part I deals with what air pollution is. Part II deals with the efforts of a town in West Virginia to clean up its air. Part III considers citizen involvement.

The Answer Is Clear. 14 min.; color. Free loan. Modern Talking Picture Service, Inc.
Wally Cox, a bus driver, knows more about air pollution than his passengers, and pleads for more research to reduce even the pollution from diesel engines.

Beware the Wind. 22 min.; color. Purchase $89.75; free loan. 1967. General Services Administration, National Archives and Records Service
Begins with an animation of the creation of the earth and the immediately existing threat of air pollution; goes on to illustrate how air pollution is affecting the major cities of the world. Includes descriptions of the major sources of air pollution.

Collection of Particulate Matter and the Control of Air Pollution. 25 min.; color. Purchase $93.75; free loan. 1971. General Services Administration, National Archives and Records Service
Illustrates how particulate emissions can be reduced. Presents descriptions of five different abatement devices, and gives technical details of how the devices work.

Dead Earth. 20 min.; color. Purchase $240; rental $25. 1970. Films for Social Change
Barry Commoner narrates an overview of "Rush City," an East St. Louis slum, where Monsanto's chemical plant exudes quantities of 245-T, a defoliant, into the air. Commoner urges students to use their knowledge to improve lives in slum areas.

The Deluge. 4 min.; color. Purchase $75. rental $7. 1971. Creative Film Society
A cartoon which dramatizes the effects of air pollution. A child playing in the countryside is gradually overcome by the fumes and smog that result from a master planner's development of the area. Questions the benefits of misguided attempts at progress.

Don't Leave It to the Experts. 16 min.; color. Purchase $66; free loan. 1971. General Services Administration, National Archives and Records Service
Examines the most important sections of the Clean Air Act, and describes how citizens can, under the act, ensure clean air for the U.S.

First Mile Up. 28 min.; b&w. Purchase $200; rental $14. 1963. Contemporary/McGraw Hill Films
Presents examples of air, radiation, water, and chemical pollution. Offers some suggestions for abatement.

From the Face of the Earth. 16 min.; color. Purchase $195; rental $20. 1970. Holt, Rinehart and Winston, Inc.
Shows a family living beneath the crust of the earth. The child, wearing a gas mask, is taken to the earth's surface to observe its condition.

Garbage in the Sky. 8 min.; color. Purchase $175; rental $15. 1972. CCM Films, Inc.
Designed to help young children understand that air pollution is a serious problem. Discusses what causes air pollution and what individuals can do to help stop it.

The Great Clean Air Car Race. 25 min.; color. Free loan. 1970. U.S. Environmental Protection Agency, Office of Public Affairs

Gives a documentary of the 1970 clean-air car race, sponsored by California Institute of Technology and Massachusetts Institute of Technology. Depicts the race, and examines some of the cars entered—innovative cars that were propelled by steam, gas turbines, electricity, modified internal combustion engines, and hybrids. The object of the race was for cars to emit as few pollutants as possible while also being judged on speed and reliability. Narrated by Orson Welles.

LP Gas—The Clean Air Fuel. 13 min.; color. Free loan. Modern Talking Picture Service, Inc.

Shows environmental advantages (reduction of air pollution) of using propane (liquid petroleum gas).

Man and the Environment: Air Pollution. 29 min.; b&w. Purchase $90; rental $7. 1970. Univ. of Michigan Television Center

Diagnoses the problems of air pollution. Gives minimal consideration to solutions.

Our Poisoned World: Air. 30 min.; color. Purchase $300. Rental $30. 1970. Time-Life Films

Gives a case study of Grand Rapids, Michigan, with reactions of industries to Michigan's Air Pollution Control Act and how to comply with its provisions, particularly those dealing with automobiles.

The Poisoned Air. 50 min.; b&w. Rental $35. 1966. Carousel Films, Inc.

Shows cause and effect of air pollution. Also deals with air pollution abatement procedures. Notes special problems of Los Angeles and New York. Gives industry attitudes towards tighter federal controls.

Pollution Front-Line. 46 min.; b&w. Purchase $275; rental $30. 1970. National Film Board of Canada

Examines the serious air pollution problem in Hamilton, Ontario, Canada. Views the city's difficulties as part of a national crisis, and points out the reluctance of local government to deal effectively with the problem.

Problems of Conservation: Air. 15 min.; color and b&w. Purchase c $167, b&w $86; rental c $8, b&w $5.55. 1968. Encyclopaedia Britannica Educational Corp.

Describes air pollution as a constant health problem. Examines some abatement procedures.

Race for Clean Air. 27 min.; color. Purchase $375; rental $37.50. 1970. Perennial Education, Inc.

Explains environmental effects of automobile's internal combustion engine. Examines other propulsion systems and fuels. Takes a look at noise pollution from cars and the electric car.

Runaround. 17 ½ min.; color. Free loan. 1969. National Tuberculosis and Respiratory Disease Assn.

Shows the frustrations and futility experienced by an individual whose home, plants, and health are threatened by effects of air pollution. Discusses with the polluters (electric utility and incinerator operator) what can be done.

The Slow Guillotine. 53 min.; color. Purchase $500; rental $25. 1969. NBC Educational Enterprises

Shows how air pollution and population growth could destroy our environment. Asks for corporate responsibility. Gives examples of destruction, including disappearance of the bald eagle and strangulation of the ponderosa pine.

Something in the Air. 28 min.; color. Free loan. 1972. Modern Talking Picture Service, Inc.

Reviews causes and effects of air pollution. Cites the internal combustion engine as the main cause of air pollution. Suggests consideration of social, medical, and economic factors and a change to nonfossil-fueled engines.

Tall Stacks TF-111. 20 min.; color. Purchase $69.25; free loan. 1972. General Services Administration, National Archives and Records Service

Produced for technically proficient audiences. Reports on a five-year study being conducted by the Environmental Protection Agency to investigate the effects of large power plants on atmospheric gaseous and particulate concentrations at varying elevations and distances from tall stack installations. Includes discussion of meteorological influences.

To Live and Breathe. 11 min.; color. Free loan. 1971. Aetna Life and Casualty

Shows man with emphysema trying to breathe the polluted air. He struggles, fails, and dies.

To Set the Record Straight. 29 ½ min.; color. Free loan. 1971. Ethyl Corp.
The Ethyl Corp. discusses lead additives in gasoline. Concludes that lead anti-knock compounds are not harmful, and the use of lead-free gas would increase other pollutants.

Toward Cleaner Air. 15 min.; color. Free loan. Association-Sterling Films
Examines what industry is doing to help combat air pollution. Describes in general terms the kinds of controls used to trap noxious gases, dust, and wastes. Explains that good air pollution control can benefit industry by providing in-plant ventilation and dust control.

What on Earth? 10 min.; color. Purchase $145; rental $14.50. 1966. Contemporary/McGraw Hill Films
Portrays in an amusing, brief film the "view from Mars" towards life on Earth. Gives a revealing description of our ordinary routines—humans who need gasoline to live and species that require poisonous gases in the atmosphere to breathe.

Your Car and Clean Air. 13 min.; color. Free loan. 1970. Motor Vehicle Manufacturers Assn., Inc.
Presents a detailed account of auto manufacturers' attempt to control air pollution through research.

CONSERVATION

The American Elm: Plan for Survival. 28 min.; color. Free loan. 1970. Modern Talking Picture Service, Inc.
Presents a straightforward approach to what is happening to the American elm tree as a result of the Dutch elm disease. Explains that money spent on research for the prevention and cure of the disease is only a minute fraction of the amount spent to remove damaged or killed trees. Points out which sprays for bark beetles (carriers of elm disease) are the least environmentally damaging.

Big Four. 25 min.; color. Rental $7.50. 1960. Cornell Univ. Films
A wildlife expert explains the four basic principles of wildlife ecology. Also discusses some widely held, erroneous beliefs about wildlife management.

A Certain Distance. 29 min.; color. Price on request; free loan to certain groups. 1970. General Services Administration, National Archives and Records Service
Surveys scientists' use of technology to protect the land from environmental damage. Includes case studies on surveillance of bark beetle populations and use of sophisticated devices to detect smog damage to plants.

Conservation for Beginners. 11 min.; color and b&w. Purchase c $130, b&w $65. 1967. Coronet Instructional Films
Designed for young children. Concerns soil conservation. Shows children studying problems of erosion, the advantages of contour plowing, and fertilization.

Journey into Summer. 51 min.; color. Purchase $575. 1970. Xerox Films
Presents a travelogue through American wildernesses, emphasizing both extinct and endangered species. Notes particularly species that seem to have been saved from extinction by legislation.

Life in the Grasslands (North America). 17 min.; color and b&w. Purchase c $135, b&w $70; rental c $6.50, b&w $5.50. 1969. Encyclopaedia Britannica Educational Corp.
Gives an introduction to the ecology of the prairie. Explains interrelationships of plants and animals on the prairie.

Life in the Woodlot. 17 min.; color. Purchase $225; rental $15. 1963. Contemporary/McGraw Hill Films
Provides narration by a farmer who takes the viewer on a tour of the woodland that has been in the farmer's family for generations. During the tour, the narrator explains some of nature's balances.

Life on the Tundra. 14 min.; color and b&w. Purchase c $167.50, b&w $86; rental c $8, b&w $5.50. 1965. Encyclopaedia Britannica Educational Corp.
Presents an introduction to the adaptation of plants and animals to life on the tundra—a generally cold, usually hostile environment.

The Meaning of Conservation. 11 min.; color and b&w. Purchase c $130, b&w $65. Coronet Instructional Films
Describes for junior high school students what is being done to conserve the nation's natural resources; includes discussion of wildlife conservation, flood control, forest conservation, and soil conservation.

Mojave Desert: Fragile and Enduring. 25 min.; color. Purchase $265; rental $16. 1972. Films Inc.

Explores the Mojave Desert. Explains how vegetation that has survived thousands of years of a hostile environment may finally be destroyed by air pollution.

Problems of Conservation: Forest and Range. 14 min.; color and b&w. Purchase c $167.50, b&w $86; rental c $8, b&w $5.50. 1969. Encyclopaedia Britannica Educational Corp.

Explores how both forests and rangeland areas can be conserved. Includes a section on what the U.S. Forest Service is doing to protect what remains of American forests.

Problems of Conservation: Soil. 14 min.; color and b&w. Purchase c $167, b&w $86; rental c $8, b&w $5.50. 1969. Encyclopaedia Britannica Educational Corp.

Presents in easily understood terms how soil is formed, how it can be abused by man, and what man can do to conserve the soil.

Succession: From Sand Dune to Forest. 16 min.; color and b&w. Purchase c $200, b&w $102.50; rental c $8, b&w $4.50. 1960. Encyclopaedia Britannica Educational Corp.

Gives an introduction to biological succession. Uses the shore of Lake Michigan to explain the different life forms starting with the sand shore and working back to a forest environment. Includes discussion of the types of soil in different areas and the kinds of organisms inhabiting the various areas.

West Chichagof. 20 ½ min.; color. Purchase $285; free loan. 1971. Association-Sterling Films

Presents plea to save as a wilderness area part of an Alaskan island known as West Chichagof. Considers a number of species of animals that will be endangered if planned logging operations are allowed in the area.

The World at Your Feet. 22 min.; color. Purchase $265; rental $15. International Film Bureau, Inc.

Presents a study of the soil in an award-winning film. Depicts the many organisms that live in the soil, including animals, plants, and insects. Explains how all these organisms work together to form a natural balance.

ENERGY

Basic Principles of Power Reactors. 8 ½ min.; color. Free loan. 1962. U.S. Atomic Energy Commission

Discusses the basic work of nuclear reactors that operate on the fission principle. Describes fission, how chain reactions occur, and functions of the major reactor components.

Energy and Living Things. 10 ½ min.; color. Purchase $145. 1972. Centron Educational Films

Effectively and simply explains for elementary school students the concepts of matter and energy—the living creature's need for energy, the way dead organisms decompose, and the use for fossil fuels. Pauses in the narration to allow time for thought or response. Illustrates experiments which could be performed by a child at home.

Energy and Matter. 9 min.; color. Purchase $120; rental $6. 1967. Contemporary/McGraw Hill Films

Combines color photography and animation with an intelligent script to create an excellent introduction to some basic ideas about energy. Demonstrates that the sun is the source of all energy, that energy is able to change from one form to another, and that energy and matter are essentially the same.

Energy from the Sun. 17 min.; color. Purchase $210; rental $15. 1966. Contemporary/McGraw Hill Films

Explains how the sun's energy is produced—through fusion of hydrogen atoms. Discusses the essential need of the sun's energy on earth—without sunlight plants could not grow, and all animals depend on plants, either directly or indirectly, for their own energy.

Energy in Our Rivers. 11 min.; color and b&w. Purchase c $130, b&w $65. Coronet Instructional Films

Explains for junior high school grades how man has harnessed the energy of rivers throughout history. Includes descriptions of water use, from simple water wheels to modern hydroelectric power plants. Illustrates how dams help to provide electricity.

Fusion Research. 22 min.; color. Purchase $74.75; free loan. 1964. General Services Administration, National Archives and Records Service

Energy 287

Gives a rather advanced explanation of fusion reaction to reveal the process of achieving controlled thermonuclear reaction—the most efficient known form of energy production. Describes the process as complex and difficult, requiring high densities and temperatures of 1,000,000° F. Shows other features of fusion reaction and fusion research. Some knowledge of nuclear physics would be helpful to the viewer.

Great River. 28 min.; color. Free loan. 1963. U.S. Dept. of the Interior, Bureau of Reclamation
Shows the many possible uses of the Columbia River in the northwestern United States. Indicates that the river has more than 140 dams. Reveals that the largest dam, the Grand Coulee, providing a continuous flow of more than 2 million kilowatts of power, has attracted much industry to the Pacific Northwest, including more than one third of the U.S. production of aluminum. Shows how irrigation has also greatly increased population. States that "energy is the life blood of our economy."

The Magic of the Atom. 22 min.; color. Purchase $265. 1972. Handel Film Corp.
Reveals some of the peaceful uses of the atom, but omits some dangers inherent in these uses, which will disturb better informed viewers. Indicates that the atom in atomic and nuclear energy form can help preserve and restore the environment, and that less atmospheric pollution will be produced by nuclear power plants. Makes no mention of thermal pollution or the problem of storing radioactive wastes.

The Mighty Atom. 27 min.; color. Purchase $325. rental $18. 1967. Contemporary/McGraw Hill Films
Considers the beneficent possibilities in "the mighty atom" rather than its powers of destruction. Explores the potential peaceful uses of nuclear energy as a part of CBS 21st Century series. Illustrates the atom's use in medical research and healing. Demonstrates the possibility of digging canals with atomic power. Reveals that Glenn Seaborg, the 1967 AEC chairman, reported that more than half the AEC's budget was allocated to developing the atom's peaceful uses, and he imagined a day when ten billion inhabitants of the earth would satisfy their power needs with a network of giant nuclear reactors. Gives no attention to the dangers inherent in such reactors nor to the possible development of the atom for politically hostile purposes.

No Greater Challenge. 14 min.; color. Purchase $48.50; free loan. 1969. General Services Administration, National Archives and Records Service
Considers the possible role of atomic energy in alleviating environmental problems. Indicates the threats in a greatly increased population, an inadequate environment, and generally reduced resources. Considers the need for skillful planning in both agriculture and industry where atomic energy will be a prime necessity.

Nuclear Power and the Environment. 14 min.; color. Purchase $53; free loan. 1969. General Services Administration, National Archives and Records Service
Suggests that citizens visit nuclear power plants to see how cleanly and efficiently they operate. Focuses attention on architecturally pleasing nuclear power plants and attractive environmental scenes, including fresh streams, to reassure viewers of the safety of nuclear power. Omits mention of the possibility of radioactive leaks or the necessity of radioactive waste disposal.

Pipeline to Japan. 25 ½ min.; color. Free loan. 1970. Marathon Oil Co.
Presents a documentary about the export of natural gas from Alaska to Japan. Explains how gas is liquefied and then shipped to its destination. Includes brief discussion about the eventual uses of the gas.

Power from Fusion. 30 min.; color. Purchase $375; rental $16. 1968. Contemporary/McGraw Hill Films
Presents a careful step-by-step delineation of the process of nuclear fusion. Illustrative material includes diagrams of atomic forces and pictures of atomic equipment. Some knowledge of the fusion process will be advantageous for viewers.

Principles of Thermal, Fast, and Breeder Reactors. 9 min.; color. Free loan. 1963. U.S. Atomic Energy Commission
Describes the principle of fission nuclear reactors, including general discussions of fast and thermal reactors and a brief introduction to the concept of breeder reactors (the type of reactor the Nixon Administration is depending on for producing a large portion of our energy by the 1980s).

Putting the Atom to Work. 15 min.; color. Purchase $180. 1969. Doubleday Multimedia

Raises a number of questions, such as whether the benefits of nuclear power plants outweigh their potential dangers, and if it would be more profitable to eliminate air pollution from the burning of fossil fuels. Examines the dangers of radioactive leaks, radioactive waste disposal, and thermal pollution of adjacent waterways. Reveals that expensive U235 fuel is being used up, and its price may become prohibitive. Asks why the government has financed atomic power plants so generously. Questions if electricity can be generated atomically at reasonable cost to man and the environment and whether fission can be controlled safely.

Refinery Processes. 20 min.; color. Free loan. Shell Film Library

Describes modern oil refining. Shows how crude oil is separated into fractions which have diverse burning characteristics. Includes discussion of the catalysts' role in the refining process.

Solar Cookers: Something New under the Sun. 25 min.; color. Purchase $240; rental $8.25. Univ. of Wisconsin Films

Discusses the work of the University of Wisconsin Solar Energy Laboratory in developing solar cookers for rural Mexico where conventional sources of energy are not available. Details the collaboration between engineers and anthropologists in attempting to fit modern technology to the needs and cultural traditions of a rural people.

Solar Cookers: Technological Innovation. 13 min.; color. Purchase $110; rental $4.50. Univ. of Wisconsin Films

Details the production of solar cookers in a rural Mexican village. Shows how the inhabitants of the village were trained by engineers and anthropologists to make the cookers as a means of using an available, but unused, energy source—the sun.

The Sun Serves Niger. 18 min.; color. Purchase $210; rental $12. 1969. CCM Films, Inc.

Shows the Niger River, lying in the southern part of the Sahara Desert, which suffers from the blazing sun nine months of the year. Indicates that most kinds of agriculture and industry have been impossible. Shows that solar batteries are used to pump the river's waters into irrigation ditches and to activate local TV and radio transmitters. Indicates that the solar energy stations are nonpolluting and cost less to operate than nuclear power plants. Reveals that per acre, the sun produces the power equivalent to four tons of coal. Also tells much about African culture.

The Terrible News. 30 min.; color. Purchase $300. 1972. Bitterroot Films, Inc.

Quotes from Brecht to set the tone: "The man who is laughing has not been told the terrible news." Reveals the "terrible news" as an analysis of the effect of burning fossil fuel in industrial plants. Uses Montana as an example, where a copper smelter pours forth 654 tons of SO_2 per day and the death rate from lung cancer is twice the national average. Reveals that near a lead smelting plant, accumulations of lead on garden lettuce are 446 ppm, compared with 5 ppm elsewhere in Montana, and lead accumulations in children's hair are more than five times the average. Reveals other alarming facts. Planned for Montana distribution; also available in a version five minutes shorter and less directly concerned with Montana.

ENVIRONMENTAL EDUCATION

An Approach to School Site Development. 22 min.; color. Purchase $250; rental $15. International Film Bureau, Inc.

Uses the Ann Arbor (Michigan) High School to illustrate the benefits of school sites planned to provide an understanding and appreciation of natural resources. Shows how to select a good site, what natural features to look for, and how to blend nature with utility in school development.

Conservation: A Job for Young America. 19 min.; color. Purchase $250; rental $15. 1968. Contemporary/McGraw Hill Films

Stimulates children's interest in environmental activity. Shows how a group of children go to work on a debris-littered beach. They are appalled at first by the job before them, but they soon get into the swing of it. They are so pleased with their achievement that they plant trees, build bird houses, and create a small dam to help clean up a stream. The children's chatter and pleasant music by Patrick Sky add to the interest of this convincing film.

Conservation for the First Time. 9 min.; color. Purchase $130; rental $13. 1969. Contemporary/McGraw Hill Films

A group of children invited to "help shoot a movie of the city" produced this absorbing film, which will interest children and adults alike. Although it skillfully depicts the principal features of a city, it is not basically an environmental film. Does not stress pollution or manmade defects in the environment, but encourages viewer to study his environment—the first step toward becoming an environmentalist.

Discovery! 21 min.; color. Free loan. 1967. Tennessee Valley Authority

Reports on a week's visit by an elementary school group to the TVA's Conservation Education Center. Shows how to plan and carry out such a field trip, and is helpful to educators interested in such a venture. Indicates that the Tennessee center is within 500 miles of one third of the U.S. population, and is an excellent place for children to learn about nature. Promotes the center as a desirable recreational area for public use.

Environmental Enrichment—What You Can Do about It. 21 min.; color. Purchase $280; rental $28. 1972. Centron Educational Films

Shows how the decision by an intermediate class in a Michigan school to do something about improving the environment—besides just talking about it—led to the formation of a committee of concerned pupils, parents, and teachers. Indicates how plans were made to improve the school's immediate surroundings. Tells how money was raised by cake sales and Saturday car washes for the purchase of trees, shrubs, and equipment for a creative playground. Indicates that the joint effort resulted in a distinct improvement in the school environment—an activity that should be an inspiration to other schools.

The Environmental School. 7 min.; color. Purchase $38; free loan. 1971. U.S. Dept. of Agriculture

Shows a Detroit elementary school, which has an "outdoor laboratory" where children can visit natural habitats and build nature trails. Indicates some of the projects carried out by the teachers and children—landscaping of the school grounds and researching soil samples of ponds. Shows how the environmental education of even first grade pupils can begin under the tutelage of older students. Of particular benefit to schools with potential "outdoor laboratories."

From Start to Finish. 10 min.; color. Purchase $135. 1971. ACI Films, Inc.

An ecological film that also provides reading aids by printing increasingly complex key sentences on the screen as the narration proceeds. The narrator is a little girl, and the story tells of her visit to a nature center with her older brother and her parents. They explore different wilderness habitats, and see the animals that live in them. Stresses that while nature recycles all living things, it cannot take care of waste, such as bottles and cans.

Islands of Green. 24 min.; color. Purchase $115; rental $6. 1965. National Audubon Society

Pictures and describes nature centers established by the Audubon Society as "Islands of Green." Shows that while the centers were not planned for purposes of recreation, they are used as laboratories to study local wildlife and plant life and as outdoor classrooms. Faithfully covers its subject matter, contributes to environmental education, but is rather undramatic.

Nature Next Door. 28 min.; color. Purchase $315. 1962. Association-Sterling Films

Reveals the wonders of a wilderness area through the eyes and ears of children. The exploring children handle, examine, and photograph plants, insects, frogs, and snakes. They also ask interesting questions: Why are butterfly wings so colorful? How do bees communicate? How do tadpoles breathe? Warns that if we want to preserve natural beauties, we must be active in their defense.

The Sense of Wonder. 53 min.; color. Purchase $600; rental $35. 1969. Contemporary/McGraw Hill Films

Narrated by Helen Hayes, and based on Rachel Carson's two best-selling books: *The Sense of Wonder* and *The Edge of the Sea.* Indicates to adults techniques they may use in interesting children in the wonders of nature. The narration uses many quotations from Miss Carson's books, and the photography is splendid.

To Live on Earth. 15 min.; color. Purchase $95; rental $3.65. 1970. Northern Illinois Univ. Film Library

Aids classroom instructors by encouraging environmental awareness among elementary school students. Outlines methods of setting up a natural resources curriculum. Depicts several model classrooms in DeKalb County, Illinois, and uses discussion and visuals to encourage a comprehensive understanding of the environment and a sensible use of natural resources. Sets forth the basic features of the proposed curriculum, including the compatability of living things, environmental changes, and a description of resource materials.

What Ecologists Do. 15 ½ min.; color. Purchase $210; rental $21. 1971. Centron Educational Films

Explains for younger audiences the functions of an environmentalist. Shows researchers studying the effect an environment has on the life cycles of organisms in it. Clearly explains important aspects of an ecosystem. The pictorial and narrative elements will encourage students to learn about the earth sciences.

FORESTRY

The Changing Forest. 18 min.; color. Purchase $245; rental $15. 1958. Contemporary/McGraw Hill Films.

Presents an introduction to the ecology of a deciduous forest. Depicts the harmony and conflicts of the inhabitants of the forest and the type of organisms most likely to survive their environment for very long time spans. A National Film Board of Canada film.

The Coniferous Forest Biome. 16 min.; color and b&w. Purchase c $200, b&w $102.50; rental c $9, b&w $5.50. 1969. Encyclopaedia Britannica Educational Corp.

Examines the natural balances and variety of life in coniferous forests. Includes information on the function of forests in flood control.

Forest Regions of Canada. 17 min.; color. Purchase $200; rental $15. Purchase: National Film Board of Canada. Rental: Contemporary/McGraw Hill Films

Explores how modern technology is changing lumbering in Canada. Shows how machines can strip branches from trees, cut through the trunk of the tree, and finally lower the tree onto a waiting timber carrier. Also explains what is being done for long-term reforestation.

The Forest Tent Caterpillar. 17 min.; color. Purchase $200; rental $15. Purchase: National Film Board of Canada. Rental: Contemporary/McGraw Hill Films

Examines the habits and functions of the forest tent caterpillar—a creature that can do great harm to deciduous forests. Explains how the tent caterpillar population is controlled by natural forces.

Forest—Trees and Logs. 15 min.; color. Purchase $200; rental $20. 1971. American Educational Films

Presents an emotional appeal for forest conservation. Concentrates on showing the beauties of forests; offers little factual information. Contrasts virgin forests with lumbered areas.

Foresters. 14 min.; color. Purchase $200; rental $20. 1972. Centron Educational Films

Explains the importance of forests to an entire area, and discusses the environmental and economic value of forests on a national scale. Briefly describes how foresters manage forest resources.

New Man in the Forest. 26 min.; color. Purchase $335; rental $20. 1971. International Film Bureau Inc.

Presents an introduction to forest management. Describes a man and his son—new owners of a small forest. Shows how they learn to care for the forest while using it for both profit and enjoyment.

One Fortieth of a Federal Forest. 28 min.; color. Purchase $315; free loan. 1971. CCM Films, Inc.

Presents a response to the U.S. Forest Service's proposal to allow lumbering on 97 percent of the Tongass National Forest in southeastern Alaska. Suggests that one fortieth of the National Forest should be preserved as a wilderness area to prevent disruption to a number of species of wild animals.

The Redwoods. 20 min.; color. Purchase $250; free loan. 1968. Association-Sterling Films; CCM Films, Inc.

Depicts eloquently the fate of the redwoods in North America. Explains that redwood forests are being destroyed by logging and that rapid timbering may soon make the redwoods extinct. The narration, primarily by a logger who loves the forests, is simple but informative.

Redwoods—Saved? 3 ½ min.; color. Purchase $47.50; free loan. 1969. Association-Sterling Films, CCM Films, Inc.
Presents a very brief survey of the majesty of the redwoods. Includes a jarring contrast of a redwood standing next to a clearcut area.

The Temperate Deciduous Forest. 17 min.; color and b&w. Purchase c $200, b&w $102.50; rental c $9, b&w $5.50. 1962. Encyclopaedia Britannica Educational Corp.
Designed for students through high school age. Explains the web of life in deciduous forests and how life changes with the seasons. Presents a good introduction to ecology.

To Touch the Sky. 28 ½ min.; color. Free loan. Modern Talking Picture Service, Inc.
Explains high yield forestry, a method in which cut trees are replaced by seedlings, and growth is carefully planned so that the trees do not have low branches that complicate lumbering. Does not include discussions of why such methods might be dangerous, such as the particular susceptibility of monocultures (plantations of a single species) to infestation and disease. Sponsored by the Weyerhauser Company.

Treasure of the Forest. 13 min.; b&w. Purchase $81.25; rental $12. Coronet Instructional Films
Explores the benefits that accrue to industry through exploitation of the forest. Uses the rain forests of Canada's British Columbia to illustrate how giant trees are felled, transported, and made into usable products. Briefly discusses planned forest management and reforestation.

GENERAL ENVIRONMENT AND ECOLOGY

Alone in the Midst of the Land. 27 min.; color. Purchase $330; rental $15. 1970. NBC Educational Enterprises
Concerns the visit of a future being to the Chicago Academy of Sciences to view a historic film of the 1970s. The film-within-a-film catalogs the damage we are presently doing to our environment.

Ark. 20 min.; color. Purchase $250. 1970. National Council of Churches
Pictures a contemporary Noah who is trying to save plants and animals from pollution. This cinematic parable warns that our modern ark (Earth) may not be able to ride out the current storm.

Beach and Tidepool Life. 17 min.; color. Purchase $210; rental $10. 1968. International Film Bureau, Inc.
Presents an introduction to marine ecology, and explains how food chains work. Explores the ecological relationships of various organisms that live in open water, tidepools, or sandy and rocky shores.

Boomsville. 11 min.; color. Purchase $150; rental $15. 1969. Learning Corp. of America
Gives an indictment of unplanned industrial growth, and surveys briefly American development and its unforeseen consequences.

Cave Ecology. 13 min.; color. Purchase $175. 1970. Centron Educational Films
Presents a brief study of the interrelationships among organisms found in caves. Useful as an introduction to ecology because of its defined spatial limitations.

A Child's Garden of Pollution. 12 min.; color. Purchase $155; rental $15. 1972. ABC Media Concepts
Depicts a child who goes with his father to discover the natural world and finds only pollution. Designed for older persons. Describes in some technical detail both air and water pollution.

Ecology Checks and Balances: The Ladybug and the Aphid. 14 min.; color. Purchase $175; rental $15. 1970. Pyramid Films
Gives an excellent introduction to the concept of ecosystems. Deals with the way aphids are kept in check naturally by ladybugs. Uses such a simple relationship to explain a complex system.

Ecology Primer. 18 min.; color. Purchase $260; rental $25. 1972. American Educational Films
Designed for students through high school. Presents logical discussions of pollution, waste disposal, and population.

The Environment: Everything around Us. 14 min.; color. Purchase $167.50; rental $8. Encyclopaedia Britannica Educational Corp.
Designed for younger children. Pictures different types of environments. Shows two boys exploring various environments. The boys are surprised to find that man's alterations of his environment can substantially pollute his world.

Environmental Awareness. 5 ½ min.; color. National Park Service Bookstore

Attempts to get the viewer to look more carefully at his environment by showing him the environment of a character drawn in finger paints. Honored by the U.S. Industrial Film Festival for "outstanding achievement in the creation of visual communications."

A Fable for Fleas. 4 min.; b&w. Purchase $50; rental $7. 1970. Creative Film Society

A cartoon about fleas who abuse their host by soiling, overpopulating, and thereby causing the demise of the host. An obvious allegory.

The Food Cycle and Food Chains. 11 min.; color and b&w. Purchase c $130; b&w $65. Coronet Instructional Films

Uses both animation and live action photography to describe how food chains work. Relates food chains to natural cycles, including the oxygen-carbon dioxide and nitrogen cycles.

For Your Pleasure. 4 min.; color. Purchase $100; rental $10. 1971. Mass Media Associates

A cartoon concerned with unplanned growth, which leads to both industrial and people pollution. Excellent animation.

The Great Swamp. 29 min.; color. Purchase $240; rental $10. 1967. Indiana Univ. Audio-Visual Center

Designed for younger children. Tells about a boy who has left his urban home for the first time. The boy paddles a canoe through the Great Swamp National Wildlife Refuge in New Jersey, and with the help of a cooperative ranger, learns about the ecology of the swamp.

Home. 29 min.; color. Purchase $300. 1972. Swain Wolf, Southern Baptist Convention

Compares American Indian philosophy with white man's actions. Uses as narration a reading of a speech given by Chief Seattle in 1855; the speech preached the sanctity of the land. Shows, in contrast, man's destruction of the earth. Gives a moving tribute to the culture and foresight of the Indian.

How Man Adapts to His Physical Environment. 20 min.; color. Purchase $285; rental $25. 1970. Contemporary/McGraw Hill Films

Discusses how man has been able to live in a wide variety of environments. Makes little attempt to describe the effects that man has had on his surroundings.

Island of Dreams. 10 min.; color. Purchase $135; rental $15. 1972. Texture Films Inc.

An animated film of a man who escapes "civilization" with its attendant horrors (such as noise, congestion, and filth) to a desert island. Gifted with the power to produce whatever he wants, the hero proceeds to create a world similar to the one he has just rejected. There is no moralizing; the film speaks for itself.

Life in a Vacant Lot. 10 min.; color and b&w. Purchase c $135, b&w $70; rental c $8, b&w $5.50. 1966. Encyclopaedia Britannica Educational Corp.

Describes for urban dwellers the diversity of natural life. Examines the multitudes of species that live in a lot between two apartment buildings.

Man and the Environment: Primitives to Present. 29 min.; b&w. Purchase $90; rental $7. 1970. Univ. of Michigan Television Center.

A documentary which describes how man has historically treated his environment. Emphasizes that the more "civilized" man becomes, the more damage he does to his environment. Depicts contrasts between industrial societies and the Maring, a primitive tribe in New Guinea that lives in careful balance with its habitat.

Man and the Environment: Who Governs Nature? 29 min.; b&w. Purchase $90; rental $7. 1970. Univ. of Michigan Television Center

Produced before the creation of the Environmental Protection Agency. Contains some interesting discussion about who should be responsible for regulating pollution sources and what the role of government at all levels should be.

Man's Effect on the Environment. 13 ½ min.; color. Purchase $175; rental $10. 1970. BFA Educational Media

Shows the relationship between industrialization and pollution. Includes sections on air and water pollution, land use in cities, and exploitation of natural resources.

A Matter of Attitudes. 28 min.; color. Purchase $250; rental $17. 1968. National Film Board of Canada

Based on a survey of Canadians by two reporters. The reporters question people about their attitudes about pollution; the answers raise some fascinating points regarding the role of ethics and politics in environmental issues.

Multiply and Subdue. 8 min.; color. Purchase $120; rental $12. 1970. Pyramid Films

A brief film, which reverently presents the natural glories of the world. Also shows how pollution is damaging the earth.

The Myths and the Parallels. 28 min.; b&w. Purchase $150; rental $10. Association-Sterling Films

Analyzes American myths that have colored the way we have in the past viewed our environment. Explains that the initial myth (the myth of unlimited resources) was replaced by the myth of technology: no job was too big for an innovative mechanical design. Draws parallels with a termite colony and the lemming to show the consequences of these myths.

No Deposit—No Return. 10 min.; color. Purchase $150; rental $15. 1971. Centron Educational Films

Surveys pollution, overpopulation, and environmental destruction. Originally produced for ABC-TV. Includes poetry by Mark Van Doren, singing by Buffy Sainte Marie, and presentations by Kim Hunter.

No Turning Back. 10 min.; b&w. Purchase $100; rental $10. 1969. NBC Educational Enterprises

A brief documentary dealing with the way we live our lives with no thought of how we are polluting the world.

Our Poisoned World: The New Ones. 30 min.; color. Purchase $300; rental $30. 1970. Time-Life Films

Gives a brief introduction to the problems of solid waste, noise, and thermal pollution. Explains the similarities of some of the problems. Viewers should note that some new laws on these topics have been passed since this film was made.

People Who Fight Pollution. 18 min.; color. Purchase $210. 1971. Churchill Films

Concerns three people who are helping to clean up the environment: an air pollution inspector, a foreman of a glass recycling project, and a sanitation man. Points out that all sorts of people can help clean up pollution.

Persistent and Finagling. 56 min.; b&w. Price available on request. 1971. National Film Board of Canada

A documentary of how a "persistent and finagling" Montreal environmental group developed a successful project to increase environmental awareness in Montreal. Useful for other groups planning projects.

Problems of Conservation: Natural Resources. 11 min.; color and b&w. Purchase c $135, b&w $70; rental c $8, b&w $5.50. 1970. Encyclopaedia Britannica Educational Corp.

An introductory film to the problems of pollution, population, and resource conservation. Advocates recycling, planned land use, and wildlife management.

The Second Genesis. 16 min.; color. Purchase $200; rental $20. 1972. Perennial Education, Inc.

Surveys how man has polluted his world, and discusses how man must now clean it up. States that pollution abatement should not be accomplished by closing factories, but rather by innovation and creative use of modern technology.

Smile While You Can. 90 min.; b&w. Purchase and rental prices on request. 1970. International Film Bureau, Inc.

A French comedy with English subtitles for the small amount of dialogue. Illustrates humorously the pressures of overpopulation, pollution, and modern life in general.

State of the Environment: What Progress (if Any) Have We Made? 12 min.; color. Free loan. 1972. Modern Talking Picture Service, Inc.

Produced by the Georgia-Pacific Corporation. Shows the efforts of Georgia-Pacific to reduce pollution caused by the manufacture of paper products.

A Strand Breaks. 17 min.; color. Purchase $200; rental $9. 1950. Encyclopaedia Britannica Educational Corp.

Explains the function of natural balances, including two classic examples of what happens when a balance is upset. An old film, but not outdated.

The Time of Man. 50 min.; color. Purchase $450. 1969. Holt, Rinehart and Winston, Inc.

Points out that man is a relatively recent introduction in the world, and that perhaps nature made a mistake because man has altered his environment to make it nearly unliveable. Contrasts the ways in which primitive and industrial man view their surroundings.

Tom Lehrer Sings: Pollution. 3 min.; color. Purchase $29.95. 1967. Environmental Educators, Inc.
Written, narrated, and sung by Tom Lehrer. A very brief film which gives a humorous introduction to environmental problems.

Tomorrow Is Maybe. 60 min.; color. Purchase $550; rental $20.50. 1972. Indiana Univ. Audio-Visual Center
Gives a cogent analysis of why man has disregarded the destruction of his environment—explains it as a psychological need to avoid facing the threat of disaster. Advocates, as an alternative to the "head-in-the-sand" approach, reducing the population rather than returning to a kind of pretechnological existence.

Tomorrow Will Not Wait—Air, Water and Land Conservation. 13 min.; color. Purchase $54.50. 1970. General Services Administration, National Archives and Records Service
Accuses all of us of polluting the environment. Points out what the U.S. Air Force is doing to abate pollution.

The Tree. 10 min.; color and b&w. Purchase c $120; b&w $60. 1963. Churchill Films
Produced for young children as a good introduction to ecology. Presents the meaning of ecology through the eyes of a boy who goes to a forest and learns of the interrelationships among living things.

Warning, Warning. 23 min.; color. Purchase $200; rental $35. 1970. American Documentary Films, Inc.
Warns that unless there is effective legislation, environmental destruction will continue as long as there is profit in it. Gives examples of corporate disregard for the environment. Advocates careful planning in addition to strict legislation.

What Are We Doing to Our World? Parts I and II. 50 min.; color. Purchase $700; rental $36. 1969. Contemporary/McGraw Hill Films
Examines the nature of ecosystems. Explains that they are very resilient, but they can reach a point where they cannot tolerate any increased disruptions of natural balances. Presents a number of examples of ecosystems stretched to their breaking points. Interviews with ecologists such as Barry Commoner add clarity to the concepts explored.

Which Is My World? 9 ¼ min.; color. Purchase $120; rental $8. BFA Educational Media
Explores the root of pollution—the affluent lifestyle. Explains that the consumer is primarily responsible for much of the damage being done to the environment. Prods viewers to find solutions to the dilemma of affluence and pollution.

Work in Progress: Steel and the Environment. 28 ½ min.; color. Free loan. 1972. American Iron and Steel Institute
Sponsored by the American Iron and Steel Institute. Explains various pollution control devices that are used by the iron and steel industry. Uses some technical explanations.

You Don't Have to Buy War, Mrs. Smith. 30 min.; color. Purchase $95; rental $35. 1970. American Documentary Films, Inc.
Produced by Another Mother for Peace. Records a speech delivered by Bess Myerson, former Commissioner for the New York City Department of Consumer Affairs, in which Ms. Myerson decries biological warfare, pollution, disregard for ghettos, etc.

Your Environment Is the Earth. 13 min.; color. Purchase $165; rental $12. 1969. Journal Films, Inc.
An introduction to ecology for children through junior high school. Concentrates on the relationships among plants and animals. Examines a number of different types of environments.

LAND USE

Airports in Perspective. 15 min.; color. Purchase $51.75. 1968. Federal Aviation Administration
Examines the problem of airport siting; considers the benefits and liabilities a new airport can bring to an area.

Alaska: End of the Last Frontier. 11 min.; color. Purchase $140; rental $15. 1970. ABC Media Concepts
An ABC documentary. Discusses the trade-offs of quick money and traditional ways of life (including preservation of the land) that Alaskans have to choose between in deciding whether or not they want an oil pipeline built through their state. Shows that preliminary work on the pipeline has already altered the way a number of Alaskans live—some of the

changes are for the better, but most, according to the film, are for the worse.

Alaska: Settling a New Frontier. 22 min.; color. Purchase $265; rental $14. 1966. Films Inc.
Explains how Alaska is being exploited for its mineral riches, and discusses the attempts being made to preserve vast areas of land from development. Excellent photography of The National Geographic Society contributes to depicting the rugged beauty of America's last frontier.

The American Island. 29 min.; color. Purchase $117.50; rental $12.50. 1970. General Services Administration, National Archives and Records Service
Includes segments on such American islands as Isle Royal, Santa Catalina, and Mt. Desert Island. Presents the islands as some of America's last remaining unspoiled areas, and as reason enough for careful planning for preservation and potential recreational use of these areas.

America's Wildernesses. 53 min.; color. Purchase $500; rental $25. 1971. NBC Educational Enterprises
Gives an encompassing examination of America's wilderness areas. Discusses laws that regulate use and development of these areas. Describes the timber industry, which is allowed to operate in national parks with the cooperation of the U.S. Forest Service. Explores the problem of overcrowding in national parks.

Barrier Beach. 20 min.; color. Purchase $250. 1971. ACI Films, Inc.
Gives an excellent picture of a natural barrier between a fresh water lagoon and the ocean, showing how the barrier was built up over time and the effects of sand erosion.

Big Thicket: A Vanishing Wilderness. 21 min.; color and b&w. Purchase c $270, b&w $135. 1972. Coronet Instructional Films
Examines the ecology of The Big Thicket, a wilderness area in southeastern Texas. Explains how parts of the area are now being ruined by approaching developments.

Breaking the Web. 11 min.; color. Purchase $100; rental $10. 1968. Pictura Films Distribution Corp.
Briefly discusses what happens when man's developments interfere with nature's design. Gives a basic introduction to ecology. Explains the results of tampering with a carefully balanced system.

Bulldozed America. 25 min.; b&w. Purchase $135. 1965. Carousel Films, Inc.
Reveals that land-use policies must be reevaluated in light of the destruction of irreplaceable natural features. Concentrates on California's redwoods as an excellent example of how lack of planning can obliterate resources before people realize they are gone.

But the Dutch Made Holland. 25 min.; color. Purchase $280; rental $16. 1970. Films Inc.
Presents a somewhat superficial view of the intricate dike system that has allowed the Dutch to greatly expand the useable land area of their country, the most densely populated in the world. Tells the story of massive, but carefully planned changes in an area's ecology.

Cash Register in the Rockies. 14 min.; color. Purchase $180; rental $10. 1971. NBC Educational Enterprises
Presents the conflict between the preservation and development of land in the Rocky Mountains. Tends to side with preservationists, but does examine the question of marginal farmers selling their land at inflated costs to developers. Shows that economically, development makes a lot of sense to these people. Gives no solutions to the conflict.

The City and Its Region. 28 min.; b&w. Purchase $160. 1964. Sterling Educational Films
Based on Lewis Mumford's theories of the ideal relationship of cities to countryside. Explains that physical growth of cities should be limited so that all of a city's inhabitants can use undeveloped land surrounding the dense urban area. Indicates that what sounds like a novel concept is actually based on the design of medieval cities.

Conservation in Action. 15 min.; color. Purchase $118; rental $5. 1964. Portland Cement Assn.
An educational film, which actually treats a more restricted subject than the title implies. Deals with small dams that have been constructed in Nebraska to reduce erosion and stop the formation of dangerous gullies.

Cry of the Marsh. 12 min.; color. Purchase $155. 1971. Bill Snyder Films, Inc.
Gives a strong statement about the effect of development on the natural inhabitants of a

marsh. Shows the entrance of a bulldozer into a marsh, fires set to get rid of weeds, and the consequences for wildlife. Presents an emotional appeal for preservation.

The Dam Builders. 30 min.; color. Purchase $350; rental $18. 1969. Contemporary/McGraw Hill Films

Presents a case study of the Kariba Dam in Rhodesia. Examines how the dam was built, with careful testing of the needed technology, but lack of foresight to realize the environmental impact of the dam. Explains how the dam delivers power to the distant city of Salisbury, but has caused sickness among the natives living around the lake created by the dam, and has upset the environmental balance of animals living in the area. Gives the dam as an excellent example of the consequences of development when planners forget to consider environmental factors.

The Desert. 28 min.; color. Purchase $290; rental $16. 1971. Films Inc.

Examines the Saguaro National Monument, a park in Arizona. Shows the desert abounding in wildlife, with each species adapted to its unique environment. Mentions, but does not thoroughly explore, the effects of man's intrusion into the desert.

Dust Bowl. 26 min.; b&w. Purchase $160; rental $14. 1960. Contemporary/McGraw Hill Films

Explains how those who were dependent on the southwestern plains destroyed them and turned them into the Dust Bowl. Presents one of the classic cases of unforeseen ecological destruction.

Dust is Dying. 13½ min.; color. Rental $5. 1962. Cornell Univ. Films

Explains how farmers and ranchers of the Great Plains are working to insure that another Dust Bowl is not created. Illustrates the techniques being used to secure the soil, even during extreme droughts. Sponsored by the U.S. Department of Agriculture.

Erosion. 10 ½ min.; color. Purchase $125; rental $6.50. 1968. BFA Educational Media

Gives a brief introduction to erosion, with clear pictures of some of the more interesting natural wonders that have been formed by erosion.

Erosion—Leveling the Land. 14 min.; color and b&w. Purchase c $167.50, b&w $86; rental c $8, b&w $5.50. 1964. Encyclopaedia Britannica Educational Corp.

Gives a cogent analysis of erosion, including the effect of air and rain. Time-lapse photography helps give the viewer a clear understanding of the effects of erosion.

The Everglades. 28 min.; color. Purchase $290; rental $16. 1970. Films Inc.

The most important section comes toward the end, which explores the effect land developers will have on the Everglades. Particularly noteworthy is the discussion of poor land management practices of most developers, resulting in environmental destruction of an area.

The Everglades: Conserving a Balanced Community. 11 min.; color and b&w. Purchase c $135; b&w $70; rental c $8, b&w $5.50. 1968. Encyclopaedia Britannica Educational Corp.

Explores the various segments of life that make up the richness of the Florida Everglades. Describes how those segments interrelate, and explains life cycles. Designed as an educational film, and flashes on the screen any unfamiliar words used in the narration.

A Family Adventure: Wild River. 25 min.; color. Purchase $280; rental $16. 1970. Films Inc.

Shares an adventure with the Frank and John Craighead families as they travel down the Salmon River in Idaho. The Craigheads, both naturalists, know how to live with the wilderness, not in conflict with it. The viewer shares the families' feeling of oneness with nature.

For All to Enjoy. 20 ½ min.; color. Purchase $140; rental $10. 1968. Conservation Foundation

Begins by satirically extolling the glories of overcrowded campsites, caged animals, etc. Goes on to explain that national parks were designed as much for preservation of nature as for recreation. Shows how current overuse of some parks threatens to ruin them. Gives a good examination of the problems currently facing our national park system.

Glen Canyon. 26 min.; color. Purchase $315; free loan. 1966. Association-Sterling Films; CCM Films, Inc.

Depicts Glen Canyon, a portion along the Colorado River, before and after it was flooded by a hydroelectric dam. Clearly calls for help in blocking other projects that will destroy natural areas. Could be provocative basis of discussion of the trade-offs between power production and land preservation.

Grand Canyon. 28 min.; color. Purchase $290; rental $16. 1961. Films Inc.
Shows a tour through the Grand Canyon led by the late naturalist Joseph Wood Krutch. Krutch eloquently points out the beauties of the canyon in its small details as well as in its vastness. Serves primarily as a kind of travelogue, with only the last few minutes of the film devoted to conservation of natural wonders.

Grassland Ecology—Habitats and Change. 13 min.; color. Purchase $175; rental $17.50. 1971. Centron Educational Films
Examines the ecology of the prairie. Discusses extensively how man's tampering with the delicately balanced system has caused unforeseen damage.

The Great Swamp: A Last Wilderness. 28 min.; color. Purchase $325; rental $16. 1969. Compemorary/McGraw Hill Films
Explores The Great Swamp, located in northern New Jersey, less than thirty miles from mid-town New York. Reveals that The Great Swamp is the last undeveloped wetlands in the New York metropolitan area, and is a refuge for many species of wildlife. Tells that although a number of plans have been proposed that would impinge on the swamp, so far the area has not been subject to modern development.

How Gering Valley Saved Itself from Disaster. 25 ½ min.; color. Purchase $180.77; rental $5. 1967. Portland Cement Assn.
Explores Gering Valley, an agricultural area in western Nebraska, which had been subject to erosion, floods, and poor management. Details how through combined local, state, and federal efforts, the valley was saved by careful planning.

In Search of Space. 30 min.; color. Purchase $240; rental $10. 1968. Indiana Univ. Audio-Visual Center
Designed for young audiences. Looks at urban ills from schoolchildren's points of view. Shows children first looking at ways in which the urban environment is deteriorating and then beginning to predict ways in which future urban living could be made more enjoyable and fulfilling.

Land in Jeopardy. 28 ½ min.; color. Rental $7.50. 1969. Cornell Univ. Films
Reveals that the agriculture industry is being harmed by new developments on agricultural land. Describes the need for careful planning of development so that valuable farm land is not indiscriminately used for highways, housing, or industry.

Landforms and Human Use. 11 min.; color and b&w. Purchase c $130, b&w $65. Coronet Instructional Films
Describes how man's use of land around the world has historically depended on how the land was shaped. Shows that with increasing technological expertise, man has begun to change his patterns of land-use to fit his desires. Does not detail the consequences of such alterations of the environment, but offers a good basis for class discussion.

Louisiana Story. 77 min.; b&w. Purchase $400; rental $75. 1948. Contemporary/McGraw Hill Films
Shows a quest for oil in a Louisiana bayou and a Cajun boy's help, through magic, in locating the oil. Could give rise to discussion of how attitudes have changed in favor of the environment and the trade-offs between fuel exploration and protection of nature. Perhaps useful, although somewhat dated.

Man Makes a Desert. 10 ½ min.; color and b&w. Purchase c $120, b&w $60; rental c $6.50, b&w $6.50. 1964. BFA Educational Media
Traces the fate of a land area in the Southwest, first overgrazed, then overplanted, and finally abandoned. Indicates efforts are now underway to reclaim the land. Depicts the progression well.

Man Uses and Changes the Land. 11 min.; color and b&w. Purchase c $130, b&w $65. Coronet Instructional Films
Describes for young students how man uses the land for food, clothing, and shelter. Also discusses ways in which man has attempted to make his environment more suitable to his needs. Warns that because land is limited, its use must be well planned.

The Marsh Community. 11 min.; color and b&w. Purchase c $135, b&w $70; rental c $6.50, b&w $4.50. 1966. Encyclopaedia Britannica Educational Corp.

Discusses the ecology of marshes, offering details of how various plants and animals have adapted to their unique environment. Explains how food chains work.

Mud. 20 min.; color. Purchase $225; rental $22.50. 1968. Stuart Finley Inc.

Depicts ways in which land developers can build in environmentally sound ways. Graphically shows the effects of poor development, and explains that damage need not have occurred.

Mountains: A First Film. 9 min.; color. Purchase $125; rental $7. 1969. BFA Educational Media

Designed for introducing young children to the ecology of mountains. Includes weather patterns and animal habits.

Multiply...and Subdue the Earth. 67 min.; color and b&w. Purchase c $450, b&w $270; rental c $18.50, b&w $13.50. 1969. Indiana Univ. Audio-Visual Center

Gives an exposition of how land is despoiled in the United States. Tends to concentrate on Ian McHarg, a Scottish environmental planner now affiliated with the University of Pennsylvania. Reveals McHarg's view of the United States as an anthropomorphic place, too often forgetting its rich natural heritage.

No Room for Wilderness? 26 min.; color. Purchase $315; free loan. 1968. Association-Sterling Films; CCM Films, Inc.

Explores what happens to wilderness areas when the natural ecological balance is upset, either by introduction of alien species or when any species becomes overly abundant. Focuses on a South African area that was ruined by civilization, emphasizing the need for thoughtful planning. Ends with a clear message about the need for population control.

Open Space. 11 min.; color. Purchase $150. 1970. ACI Films, Inc.

Gives a concise plea for careful land-use planning. Contrasts undeveloped areas with what has been done to the land with subdivisions, highways, etc.

Our Wilderness. 10 min.; color. Purchase $130; rental $10. 1971. NBC Educational Enterprises

A shortened, classroom version of *America's Wilderness*. Discusses how man has upset the natural balances of many areas, and why such areas should be preserved. Also briefly touches on the problem of species extinction.

Pave It and Paint It Green. 27 min.; color. Purchase $325; rental $25. 1970. Univ. of California

Gives an eloquent statement of how people are destroying Yosemite National Park. Excellently depicts campers who so often require the comforts of home and hardly appreciate the surrounding beauty of the national parks. No narration.

The People's Heritage. 16 min.; color. Purchase $150; rental $15. 1968. Pictura Films Distribution Corp.

Calls to people to appreciate and support national parks as the last reserves of wilderness. Points out the spiritual need of humans for wild areas. Does not give solutions to destruction of such areas.

A Place to Land. 21 min.; color. Purchase $72.50. 1967. Federal Aviation Administration

Surveys the potential of Vertical and Short Take-off and Landing airplanes, focusing on their proposed use in crowded urban areas such as New York. Reveals that these planes may possibly solve the problem of airport siting in metropolitan areas by taking up much of the commuter traffic now congesting large commercial airports. Does not discuss the problems of pollution and noise from these planes.

Point Pelee. 28 min.; color. Purchase $290; rental $16. 1970. Films Inc.

Examines the dilemma of keeping unique wildlife areas free from human encroachment. Depicts Point Pelee, a small national park in eastern Canada, as a magnificent area that tourists may spoil and make uninhabitable for some of the wildlife found there. Implicitly favors the preservation of the park. Also does an excellent job of depicting ecological succession.

Pollution is a Matter of Choice. 53 min.; color. Purchase $500; rental $25. 1970. NBC Educational Enterprises

Takes an objective look at the conflict between economic progress and environmental preservation. Presents the cases of Machiasport, Maine, which was to be the site of a deep-water oil tanker port, and of the Florida Everglades, at one time slated to host Florida's newest jetport. Reveals that both projects made sense economically for their inhabitants, but would destroy natural areas that are in increasingly short supply. Concludes that development must be tempered by careful planning with an eye to preserving natural areas which cannot be replaced.

Pollution—It's Up to You! 10 min.; color. Purchase $130; rental $10. 1971. NBC Educational Enterprises
An edited version of *Pollution is a Matter of Choice*, adapted for school use. Also includes discussion of pollution in Gary, Indiana. Presents excellent base for discussion of the conflict between the environment and economic growth.

Preserving Our American Wilderness. 10 min.; color. Purchase $130; rental $10. 1971. NBC Educational Enterprises
Presents the conflict between developing wilderness areas for their natural resources and saving irreplaceable land. States that the economic value of natural resources cannot be ignored, but asks what we are giving up when we destroy our nonrenewable wildernesses.

Progress, Pork Barrel, and Pheasant Feathers. 27 min.; b&w. Purchase $175; rental $17.50. 1970. Contemporary/McGraw Hill Films
Presents a study of the Cross Florida Barge Canal before the project was halted on Presidential orders. Examines the reasons why environmentalists fought the project, and why many people in Florida wanted the canal built. Reveals how the temporary defeat of the project has become a classic environmental story.

Prudhoe Bay—Or Bust! 30 min.; color. Purchase $315; rental $11.50. 1970. Indiana Univ. Audio-Visual Center
Presents an unbiased picture of the problems and hazards of transporting crude oil from Prudhoe Bay in northern Alaska to the southern part of the state where the oil can be shipped to the "lower forty-eight." Discusses both an above-ground pipeline and one buried in the ground, and explores the attendant advantages and environmental hazards of both. Also touches on the economics of the proposed pipeline, particularly in regard to the petroleum companies' impatience with numerous delays.

The Ravaged Earth. 27 min.; color. Purchase $330; rental $15. 1969. NBC Educational Enterprises
Takes a thorough look at how strip mining wreaks havoc with the land, explaining how strip mining can cause serious water and air pollution. Does not offer solutions.

The Ravaged Land. 14 ½ min.; color. Purchase $180; rental $25. 1971. John Wiley & Sons, Inc.
Examines strip mining in West Virginia. Explains that although some strip mining companies have felt morally obligated or have been forced to reclaim some ravaged land, reclamation does not restore the earth to the state in which it was found. Enhanced by interviews with Henry Caudill, author of excellent books and articles on strip mining.

The Rocky Mountains. 28 min.; color. Purchase $290; rental $16. 1971. Films Inc.
Shows how the Rockies are being threatened: through overuse by campers and tourists, land development, and air pollution. Emphasizes the need to plan for, if not limit, tourist use. Also mentions the life cycles of indigenous wildlife.

Room to Breathe. 26 min.; color. Purchase $330; rental $15. 1969. NBC Educational Enterprises.
Presents an objective documentary of the Tocks Island Project, which has been currently halted by the governor of New Jersey. Shows how the project, if implemented, would create a vast recreation area in the Northeast, but would include several environmental hazards. Gives a good case study of the need for open space for people versus environmental preservation.

Sanctuary. 5 min.; color. Purchase $45; rental $10. 1971. Jon Royer
Gives a visual plea for the preservation of wildlife sanctuaries from bulldozers and pile-drivers. Depicts the destruction of a bird-and-fish sanctuary. Does not explain why the sanctuary is being destroyed or with what it will be replaced.

Sand: The Desert in Motion. 10 min.; color. Purchase $135; rental $6.50. 1969. BFA Educational Media
A brief film explaining how sand is formed and what then happens to it. Gives excellent pictures of a wide variety of desert regions. Presents easily understood discussion of the formation of sand dunes.

Sharing the Land. 27 min.; color. Purchase $300; rental $30. 1971. Cinema Associate Productions, Inc.

Examines the need for rational land-use planning. Ends with startling comparison of land destruction in the United States and Vietnam, indicating that the only difference is in the speed of destruction. Presents some interesting concepts, but, photographically, is not particularly good.

Siberia: Russia's Frontier. 27 min.; color. Purchase $300; rental $16. 1970. Films Inc.

A National Geographic film about the USSR's far northern frontier. Explains how the Russians developed a nearly barren land into what are becoming economically productive settlements. Particularly focuses on the city of Irkutsk to show that fur trading has given way to major mining, timber production, and growing industrialization. Conservation, though, is not the prime interest of the film.

Stop Destroying America's Past. 22 min.; color. Purchase $295; rental $26. 1971. Contemporary/McGraw Hill Films

Tells how a university professor struggles to preserve the ruins of Cahokia, an ancient American Indian city in Illinois. Developers are paving over land which is rich in the artifacts of Indian culture. The professor has had some help from local residents who have been awakened to the benefits of preserving the past.

Stop Ruining America's Past. 21 min.; b&w. Purchase $125; rental $5.50. 1968. Indiana Univ. Audio-Visual Center

Gives a call to preserve the remains of ancient native American culture. A black-and-white version of *Stop Destroying America's Past.*

Strip Mine Trip. 11 min.; color. Purchase $130. 1972. Churchill Films

Shows aerial shots of strip-mined land to impress the viewer with the utter destruction of the earth below. Somewhat repetitive, but a worthwhile introduction to the effects of strip mining.

Survival on the Prairie. 54 min.; color. Purchase $500; rental $25. 1970. NBC Educational Enterprises

Beautifully depicts the richness of the prairie, in which a variety of wildlife, from prairie dogs to buffalo, live. Emphasizes the beauty of the prairie somewhat at the expense of a thorough explanation of how man is tampering with the survival of remaining prairies and what the consequences of that tampering might be.

They Care for the Land: Mission Possible. 53 min.; color. Purchase $610; rental $47. 1971. Contemporary/McGraw Hill Films

Examines the conflict between environmentalists and developers regarding the now-halted jetport that was to be located in the Everglades. Concentrates heavily on Joe Browder, who was leader of the fight to defeat the jetport. Ostensibly objective, but seems to side with Browder in advocating the need to save America's dwindling open spaces.

The Treehouse. 9 min.; color. Purchase $140; rental $15. 1970. Holt, Rinehart and Winston, Inc.

A short film of a boy and his treehouse versus the bulldozer. Eloquently pictures the joys of treehouses in conflict with "progress."

Urban Sprawl vs. Planned Growth. 22 min.; color. Purchase $200; rental $15. 1968. Stuart Finley Inc.

Explores the benefits of urban planning, pointing out recent planning techniques, particularly those that consider potential environmental damage.

Vacant Lot. 21 min.; color. Purchase $225; rental $15. International Film Bureau, Inc.

Gives an introduction to ecological concepts to which urban children can relate. Describes relationships among organisms that are commonly found in a vacant lot, so that natural balance becomes an understandable idea.

Wilderness River Trail. 28 min.; color. Purchase $315; free loan. 1972. Association-Sterling Films; CCM Films, Inc.

A Sierra Club film designed to convince the viewer of the value in preserving Utah's Dinosaur National Park. Indicates that the park is threatened by plans to dam the Yampe river, which flows through the park. Shows that the dam will create a large reservoir, flooding an area particularly known for its dinosaur fossils and rugged scenery.

Will the Gator Glades Survive? 30 min,; color. Purchase $315; rental $11.50. 1970. Indiana Univ. Audio-Visual Center

Examines man's encroachment into the Everglades, dealing with land developers, water projects, and animal poachers. Devotes much of the film to the plight of the alligator.

MISCELLANEOUS

Auto—Environment. 15 min.; color. Purchase $250; rental $12. 1972. Media for the Urban Environment

Surveys the impact of the automobile on cities, particularly New York. Suggests that we have given our cities to our cars and forgotten about people. Advocates banning cars in certain areas, creating bike paths, and improving mass transit.

Before the Mountain Was Moved. 58 min.; color. Purchase $495. 1971. Contemporary/McGraw Hill Films

Shows how a group of West Virginia coal miners banded together to persuade the state to pass new legislation making mining safer and less destructive to the environment. Makes excellent use of actual miners, showing them in striking contrast to the smooth politicians with whom the miners must deal. An Academy Award-nominated documentary.

Happy Anniversary. 12 min.; b&w. Purchase $75; rental $7.50. 1962. Trans-World Films, Inc.

A charming French comedy with environmental overtones. Describes a man trying vainly to get home on time for his anniversary, only to be caught in traffic jams, have his nerves rattled by noise, and be thwarted in finding a place to park.

Industrial Hygiene—The Science of Survival. 9 min.; color. Rental $12.50. 1970. New York Univ. Film Library

Designed as a guidance film. Introduces the viewer to problems encountered in the workplace environment, including toxic chemicals, dust, intense light, and excessive noise.

Isotopes in Environmental Control. 14 min.; color. Purchase $54.50; free loan. 1971. General Services Administration-National Archives and Records Service

Explains in fairly technical terms how radioactive tracers can be used to track sources of pollution and to study how various organisms function.

Leaded vs. Unleaded Gas—The Facts and Myths. 27 min.; color. Free loan. 1970. Ethyl Corp.

Ethyl Corporation presents its claim that lead additives in gasoline do not make more smog, but adding aromatics does. Also states that lead in gasoline does not present a health hazard.

Pollution Control—The Hard Decisions. 30 min.; color. Purchase $265; rental $60. BNA Communications Inc.

Designed for industrial managers. Provokes thought on what the manager as a professional and as an individual can do to lessen the environmental effects of industry. Suggests that environmental improvements are trade-offs in terms of risks against costs, benefits, and jobs. Narrated by a former president of the Boise Cascade Corporation.

Research: The Common Denominator. 27 min.; color. Free loan. Association-Sterling Films

Describes highways as the "keystone to transportation." Discusses how research has helped to solve highway problems, such as noise, congestion, and some kinds of accidents. Might be a useful film to contrast with other concepts involving mass transit. Narrated by Rod Serling.

The Secrets of Secrecy. 49 min.; color. Purchase $470; rental $23. 1969. NBC Educational Enterprises

Surveys the hazards of experimenting with chemical and biological warfare techniques in the United States and England. The film helped bring about the U.S. ban of such research and the destruction of CB stockpiles.

A Trip to Chicago. 25 min.; color. Purchase $325; rental $18. 1967. Contemporary/McGraw Hill Films

Predicts what travel will be like in the year 2000. Slightly dated because of the defeat of the U.S. SST and because the film does not examine the environmental impact of the kinds of transport the producers foresee.

Turbo. 23 min.; color. Free loan. Association-Sterling Films

A documentary on the turbine-powered passenger trains that run between Toronto and Montreal, Canada. Offers a concept that could be expanded as the need for improved mass transit becomes more obvious.

Valley of Darkness. 18 min.; color. Purchase $240; rental $10. 1970. NBC Educational Enterprises

Examines the effects of coal mining on the miners. Presents interviews with miners in West

Virginia to emphasize the dangerous working conditions and resulting diseases. Poignantly notes that coal is the basis of the West Virginia economy, which makes the viewer wonder how mining can be made a decent occupation.

Venice Be Damned! 52 min.; color. Purchase $500; rental $25. 1971. NBC Educational Enterprises

Explores how air and water pollution are currently consuming both the art of Venice and the city itself. Considers attempts being made to keep the city from being inundated by the Adriatic.

NATURAL RESOURCES

Arizona and Its Natural Resources. 28 min.; color. Free loan. 1966. U.S. Dept. of the Interior, Bureau of Mines

Explains how water development in particular has spurred growth in Arizona. Stresses the need for sound planning and management of development.

California and Its Natural Resources. 30 min.; color. Free loan. 1960. U.S. Dept. of the Interior, Bureau of Mines

Surveys the natural resources of California, and examines the way these resources have been developed in the state. Concentrates on water resources, petroleum, and natural gas.

Challenge of the Arctic. 26 ½ min.; color. Free loan. 1969. Atlantic Richfield Co.

Presents information on the potential value of Alaskan oil, and describes how Atlantic Richfield Company, sponsor of the film, intends to transport the oil to the "lower forty-eight." Includes brief description of how the company plans to avoid environmental damage while exploiting its Alaskan oil claims.

Coal: A Source of Energy. 15 min.; color. Purchase $205; rental $15. 1967. Contemporary/McGraw Hill Films

Explains the value of coal as an energy resource. Describes the way in which coal is formed, and illustrates many techniques of coal mining—both for underground and surface mining.

Conquering the Sea. 25 min.; color. Purchase $325; rental $18. 1967. Contemporary/McGraw Hill Films

Explores a variety of ways man can use the oceans as a resource. Includes discussions of fish farming, harvesting kelp for protein, use of icebergs for fresh water, power generation by the sea, and mining of underwater minerals.

Conserving Our Mineral Resources Today. 11 min.; color and b&w. Purchase c $130, b&w $65. Coronet Instructional Films

Examines the consequences of the increasing dependency of nonrenewable resources in an industrial society. Explains that these resources must be conserved through more efficient mining methods; through development of alternative energy sources, such as solar and nuclear power; and through more intensive development of conventional sources, such as hydroelectric power.

Downstream. 27 ½ min.; color. Free loan. Association-Sterling Films

Tells how oil from many parts of the world is piped and shipped to Europe's refineries for processing into usable fuel. Discusses techniques the refineries use in processing.

The Earth: Resources in Its Crust. 11 min.; color and b&w. Purchase c $130, b&w $65. Coronet Instructional Films

Surveys the variety of resources in the earth's crust, and examines the methods by which some of these resources are extracted. Also discusses the need to conserve resources.

Fire on Ice. 18 min.; color. Free loan. Modern Talking Picture Service, Inc.

Sponsored by Standard Oil of New Jersey. Shows how natural gas from Libya is liquefied and shipped to Italy and Spain for use as an energy source.

It Might Have Happened. 26 min.; color. Purchase $80; free loan. 1967. American Petroleum Institute

Sponsored by the petroleum industry. Explores modern oil industry techniques for conserving fuel. Explains why the United States must conserve oil to avoid becoming dependent on foreign sources.

The Minerals Challenge. 28 min.; color. Free loan. 1970. U.S. Dept. of the Interior, Bureau of Mines

Describes research into finding new ways to economically mine low-grade mineral ores. Presents examples from the copper and iron mining industries.

More Oil and Gas for Today and Tomorrow. 24 min.; color. Purchase $100; free loan. 1963. Interstate Oil Compact Commission

Discusses the reasons for conserving fossil fuels, and explains what regulatory agencies and the fuel industry are doing to conserve fuel.

Nevada and Its Natural Resources. 28 min.; color. Free loan. 1967. U.S. Dept. of the Interior, Bureau of Mines

Explains how arid Nevada was profitably developed by careful planning and conservation of its resources, particularly water. Gives examples of how resources have been conserved by the mining, ranching, and farming industries.

Norman Borlaug: Revolutionary. 15 min.; color. Free loan. 1970. Association-Sterling Films

Examines the role of Norman Borlaug in the Green Revolution, for which he received the Nobel Peace Prize. Discusses Dr. Borlaug's theory that feeding people takes precedent over everything else. Indicates that many environmentalists have recently been distressed at Borlaug's unwavering acceptance of chemical pesticides as crucial to food production.

Oregon and Its Natural Resources. 26 ½ min.; color. Free loan. 1970. U.S. Dept. of the Interior, Bureau of Mines

Reviews Oregon's historically conservationist ideals, as people in the state strive to preserve their rich natural resources. Shows how conservation has been practiced in the mining, fishing, power, agriculture, timber, and recreation industries.

Problems of Conservation: Minerals. 16 min.; color and b&w. Purchase c $200, b&w $102.50; rental c $9, b&w $5.50. 1969. Encyclopaedia Britannica Educational Corp.

Discusses the need to conserve mineral resources. Emphasizes that such resources are being rapidly depleted.

Riches of the Earth. 16 min.; color. Purchase $190; rental $15. Sterling Educational Films

An animated film illustrating how the earth's crust was formed and with it mineral resources, arable land, and water resources.

River of Power. 21 min.; color. Purchase $230; rental $17. 1968. Journal Films, Inc.

Surveys oil exploration and drilling in the United States, beginning in the nineteenth century, gives a comprehensive overview, but excludes discussion of environmental damage caused by enormous demand for oil.

Seaweeds. 22 min.; color. Purchase $295; rental $15. 1969. Contemporary/McGraw Hill Films

A documentary on farming the resources of the oceans. Concentrates on the introduction of an industry based on seaweed to the Maritime Provinces in Canada. Includes discussion of the role of seaweed in marine ecology.

Who Owns the Bottom of the Ocean? 15 min.; color. Purchase $180. 1968. Doubleday Multimedia

Not primarily an environmental film. Devoted to exploring the international ramifications of the mining of minerals on the oceans' floors.

The Whole Earth's Invisible Colors. 20 min.; color. Purchase $260; rental $26. 1972. Perennial Education, Inc.

Explains the Earth Resources Technology Satellite program—whereby photographs taken from a satellite are used to interpret the state of the earth's natural resources. The satellite program works on the basis of photographs taken at wavelengths other than those in the visible range. The film shows students one practical adaptation of modern technology.

NOISE

Can We Have a Little Quiet, Please? 14 ½ min.; color. Purchase $66; free loan. 1971. Federal Aviation Administration

Indicates that noise suppression devices for aircraft can be effective. The Federal Aviation Administration depicts how sound-deadening material and new aircraft operating procedures can reduce noise.

Death Be Not Loud. 29 min.; color. Purchase $340; rental $28. 1971. Contemporary/McGraw Hill Films

Indicates that millions of Americans have already lost some of their hearing acuity because of exposure to excessive noise. ABC science editor Jules Bergman, who narrates this film, explains that the level of noise in the U.S. increases each year. Notes some biological effects of noise and ways in which to reduce noise in the future.

Meet Mr. Noise. 26 min.; color. Purchase $104; free loan. 1962. Purchase: General Services Administration, National Archives and Records Service. Loan: U.S. Air Force Film Library

Describes the physiological effects of noise in general terms, and explains that working in a noisy environment can be dangerous. Offers suggestions of how the worker can protect himself against the adverse effects of noise.

Noise. 10 min.; color. Purchase $135; rental $8. 1970. BFA Educational Media

Designed for young children. Contrasts noise with pleasant sounds and sounds that are necessary for communication.

The Noise Boom. 26 min.; color. Purchase $330; rental $15. 1969. NBC Educational Enterprises

Surveys standard noise sources and ways to defeat them. Also contrasts the acute hearing of an African tribe with average Western hearing ability, showing not only that noise damages hearing, but also implying that noise can contribute to disease.

Noise: Polluting the Environment. 16 min.; color. Purchase $200; rental $9. 1971. Encyclopaedia Britannica Educational Corp.

Emphasizes that noise can impair hearing and that the risk of loss of hearing increases with exposure to increasingly intense sounds. Cites rock music and other sources of noise. Discusses the problem of convincing the public that quiet machines can be as powerful as noisy ones.

Noise: The New Pollutant. 30 min.; b&w. Purchase $125; rental $6.75. 1967. Indiana Univ. Audio-Visual Center

Examines the standard sources of noise, and interviews noise specialists who emphasize the health hazards of noise in addition to its annoying aspects. Produced by National Educational Television.

The Quiet Racket. 7 min.; color. Purchase $90; rental $12.50. 1966. National Film Board of Canada

Humorously depicts one person's attempt to escape the overwhelming din in the city. Shows that even at a campsite, it is difficult to evade nuisance sounds.

PESTICIDES

DDT—Knowing It Survives Us. 30 min.; color. Purchase $325. 1970. Xerox Films

Shows DDT's fat solubility and chemical stability. Surveys the combination of social, political, and economic issues involved in the solution of the problem of DDT contamination.

Environment in Crisis: Pesticides. 30 min.; b&w. Purchase $90; rental $7. Univ. of Michigan Television Center

Explains how pesticides are used, and examines their effects through the food chain. Includes interviews with ecologists and scientists.

The Epidemiology of Pesticide Poisoning. 19 min.; color. Purchase $74.25; free loan. 1969. General Services Administration, National Archives and Records Service

Part One describes epidemiological methodology used to locate pesticide poisoning. Part Two deals with the use of this methodology in two cases: a boy who eats soil contaminated with parathion and use of antimildew additive on diapers causing illnesses and death in a hospital nursery.

Health Hazards of Pesticides. 14 min.; color. Purchase $48.50; free loan. General Services Administration, National Archives and Records Service

Describes how pesticides can be a danger to human health. Includes discussion of studies at the Communicable Disease Center's Toxicology Laboratories to quantify the hazards of various pesticides. Also recommends how to use pesticides safely.

Insect Enemies and Their Control. 11 min.; color and b&w. Purchase c $130, b&w $65. Coronet Instructional Films

For junior and senior high school students. Describes how learning about the habits of insects helps the scientist to devise ways of controlling insect pests. Includes descriptions of such pests as the corn borer, the codling moth, the termite, and the mosquito.

Insect Parasitism. 18 min.; color and b&w. Purchase c $232.50, b&w $119; rental c $9, b&w $6.50. Encyclopaedia Britannica Educational Corp.

Explains one of the concepts behind biological control of insect pests—a nonchemical means of control. Focuses on four types of adult parasites that invade the nests of woodwasps and prohibit many of the wasps' eggs from maturing.

The Insect War. 40 min.; color. Purchase $400; rental $40. 1971. Time-Life Films
Indicates that insects fight back against technology. Emphasizes the aphid and man's attempt to destroy it with parasites and silver foil.

Insects. 14 min.; color. Rental $5. 1954. Cornell Univ. Films
Surveys the principal characteristics of many insect groups, and discusses the differences between true insects and closely related organisms. Examines insect life cycles and feeding habits, and discusses how knowledge of these cycles and habits can assist man in encouraging beneficial insects and combating insect pests.

Of Broccoli and Pelicans and Celery and Seals. 30 min.; color. Purchase $315; rental $11.50. 1970. Indiana Univ. Audio-Visual Center
Shows how spraying DDD and DDT on vegetables in the Ventura Valley affects behavior of seals and pelicans toward their young.

Our Poisoned World: The Human Race is Losing. 30 min.; color. Purchase $300; rental $30. 1971. Time-Life Films
Gives statistics on DDT content in fatty tissues, oceans containing contaminants, and strontium 90 in human bone marrow.

Paradise Lost. 4 min.; color. Purchase $85; rental $15. 1970. Benchmark Films, Inc.
Illustrates the life of a group of birds, butterflies, and plants in ecological balance. Shows that when pesticides are introduced, the group dies out.

Pest Control is Not Simple. 13 ½ min.; color. Rental $5. 1970. Cornell Univ. Films
Gives a brief introduction to insect pest control. Details the kind and extent of destruction wrought by insects, and explains the complexity of controlling the destruction.

Pesticides. 30 min.; color. Purchase $300; rental $30. 1971. Time-Life Films
Deals with dangers of DDT and other chlorinated hydrocarbons. Shows other methods of controlling pests, such as resistant crop strains and natural predators.

Pesticides in Focus. 25 min.; color. Free loan. 1971. Shell Film Library
Indicates that insects demolish plants, and screwworms infest cattle. Calls for the use of pesticides to eliminate these problems.

A Plague on Your Children. 72 min.; b&w. Purchase $400; rental $40. 1969. Time-Life Films
Examines the effects of chemical and biological weapons on animals and men. Shows research in England on nerve gas, and gives comments of people opposed to this research.

The Poisoned Planet. 19 min.; color. Purchase $260; rental $24. 1970. Contemporary/McGraw Hill Films
Considers the use of DDT from both sides of the question. Discusses the advantages of pest control, the side effects damaging to other species, and the economic problems.

Poisons, Pests, and People. 58 min.; b&w. Purchase $350; rental $25. 1960. Contemporary/McGraw Hill Films
Surveys research into alternatives to chemical pesticides for tree spraying. Shows use of natural predators and sterilization.

The Rival World. 27 min.; color. Free loan. Shell Film Library
Describes the insect world in conflict with the designs of men. Presents insects, which outnumber humans by fifty million to one, as rivals for man's food supplies. Shows that technology (primarily in the form of chemical pesticides) can control insects that in many cases have become so numerous because of man's interference with the balance of nature. A Shell Chemical Company film.

The Safe Use of Pesticides. 21 min.; color. U.S. Department of Agriculture gives information on purchase price; free loan to some. 1963. U.S. Dept. of Agriculture
Recommends reading labels on pesticides and following its instructions, thus guaranteeing no ill effects. Shows that the user of pesticides, rather than the manufacturer, must be responsible for safe results.

The Silent Spring of Rachel Carson. 54 min.; b&w. Purchase $275; rental $25. 1963. Contemporary/McGraw Hill Films
Gives an objective approach to Rachel Carson's controversial book, *The Silent Spring.*

Two for Fox, Two for Crow. 16 min.; color. Free loan. 1972. Association-Sterling Films Elanco Products Company of Eli Lilly, discusses the use of pesticides. Tells how pesticides increase yield of livestock and crops and prevent losses. Shows research, government inspection, and testing procedures.

Vegetable Insects. 22 min.; color. Purchase $250; rental $15. International Film Bureau, Inc.
Depicts insects that enjoy feeding off vegetable gardens. Explains how scientists study life cycles and feeding habits of insect pests in order to control them—both by simulating or encouraging natural controls and by using chemical pesticides.

Virus Control of Insect Pests. 8 ½ min.; color. Purchase $46. 1971. Deere & Co.
Reviews research into the use of viral insecticides as a substitute for chemical insecticides. Shows how the viral method can only be directed against a target pest, apparently without danger to man.

Who Shall Reap? 28 min.; color. USDA gives information on price or free loan. U.S. Dept. of Agriculture
Tells about the use of chemicals, genetic control, and pesticides to control pests, weeds, and insects. Reviews the techniques and the threats posed by lack of controls.

POPULATION

Abortion: London's Dilemma. 22 min.; color. Purchase $275; rental $13. 1969. NBC Educational Enterprises
Explores the use of sanctioned abortions in London. Indicates that the English have accepted their fairly recent liberalized abortion laws with little trauma. Describes the simplicity with which abortions can be performed: from admittance to a clinic to the operating table may take only one hour.

Abortion: Public Issue, Private Matter. 25 min.; color. Purchase $275; rental $13. 1971. NBC Educational Enterprises
Raises a number of questions concerning abortion, but gives no answers to an exceedingly difficult problem. Helps to clarify issues through interviews with women who have had abortions, doctors who have performed them, and theologians who argue for the sanctity of life. Also mentions the problem of defining "life."

Challenge to Mankind. 28 min.; b&w. Purchase $200; rental $14. 1961. Contemporary/McGraw Hill Films
Presents a distinguished panel of population experts who discuss the causes of overpopulation, and suggest solutions to the problem.

Competition among Species. 15 min.; color. Purchase $215; rental $12.50. 1968. Contemporary/McGraw Hill Films
Explains population dynamics. Clearly describes how the combination of many species living together helps to control populations. Shows that control derives primarily from food scarcity and predation.

Control or Density. 12 min.; b&w. Purchase $135; rental $10. NBC Educational Enterprises
Concerns the balance between population and food supply. Points out that without birth control measures, the population will rapidly outgrow the earth's ability to provide food for all its inhabitants.

The Day before Tomorrow. 28 min.; color. Purchase $300. Association-Sterling Films
Appropriate for any age. Documents the pressures a growing population places on a nation's environment as well as its economy. Encourages people to practice voluntary birth control. A Planned Parenthood Association film.

Each Child Loved. 40 min.; color. Purchase $225; rental $14. 1971. Planned Parenthood-World Population
A pro-legal abortion film. Contrasts the physical and psychological traumas that can result from illegal abortions with the sanitary conditions and psychological counselling of hospital abortions. Avoids moralizing.

Family Planning. 10 min.; color. Purchase $80; rental $8. Purchase: Buena Vista Productions. Rental: Planned Parenthood-World Population
Presents Donald Duck explaining population problems in developing countries, and advising that family planning can solve these problems. Produced by the Walt Disney Studio for the Population Council.

Five Million Women. 10 min.; b&w. Purchase $40; rental $7.50. 1967. Planned Parenthood-World Population

Deals with the number of women who need but can not receive birth control services, primarily because of lack of money. Points out that most women who want but can not get birth control are white and married—contradicting some common views. Perhaps outdated in some urban areas.

The House of Man, Part II—Our Crowded Environment. 11 min.; color and b&w. Purchase c $135, b&w $70; rental c $8, b&w $5.50. 1969. Encyclopaedia Britannica Educational Corp.

Presents an introduction to the problem of overcrowding. Deals with "the demographic transition," the change from primarily rural societies to urban ones. Reveals that although cities in America seem overpopulated—with attendant crowding and pollution—rural areas of the nation are actually experiencing a decrease in population.

India: Urban Conditions. 19 min.; color. Purchase $255; rental $12.50. 1968. Contemporary/McGraw Hill Films

Follows one family's lives in Calcutta to prove that India's population problem is overwhelming. Shows that food is scarce and life is cheap. Depicts people streaming in to India's cities because the countryside can no longer support the rural people; however, the cities cannot support them either. Presents a poignant, understated appeal for population control.

Japan—Answer in the Orient. 60 min.; color and b&w. Purchase c $350, b&w $200; rental $16.50, b&w $12. 1965. Indiana Univ. Audio-Visual Center

Presents an excellent study of how Japan curbed a rapidly increasing population during a time of increasing industrialization and demographic change. Reveals that Japan is the only country in Asia that has attained a zero percent growth rate, although the actual number of births per year will continue to increase until the current population has completed its reproductive years. Shows absorbing contrasts of modern Japan and Japan of the seventh through the nineteenth centuries.

Once There Was a World. 10 min.; color. Purchase $135; rental $12. 1971. Association-Sterling Films

A short, simple cartoon very loosely based on the story of Adam and Eve. The original character, the only person in the world, gets lonely; a wife appears, and soon they overpopulate the world.

People by the Billions. 28 min.; b&w. Purchase $200; rental $14. 1961. Contemporary/McGraw Hill Films

Visually describes parts of our planet that are already overcrowded. Explains how population increases in a geometric progression, including examples of exactly what would happen if population should grow unchecked.

Population and Pollution. 17 min.; color. Purchase $225. 1971. International Film Bureau, Inc.

Focuses primarily on the fact that increasing populations put extra stresses on the environment. Also enumerates how the U.S. population, though it is not large compared to its land mass, uses enormous quantities of resources in leading an affluent life.

Population Ecology. 19 min.; color and b&w. Purchase c $232.50, b&w $119; rental c $9, b&w $6.50. 1964. Encyclopaedia Britannica Educational Corp.

Presents an introduction to population dynamics. Explains how nature limits populations in the animal world, with the sole exception of man. Explains that if man does not control his own population, nature may again take over, with consequences of famines, diseases, or wars over resources.

Population Explosion. 15 min.; color. Purchase $205; rental $15. 1968. Contemporary/McGraw Hill Films

An animated film that shows graphically what happens when populations are allowed to grow unchecked. Offers suggestions of ways in which human populations can be controlled—primarily through increased affluence, education, and availability of birth control programs.

Populations. 15½ min.; color. Purchase $210; rental $21. 1972. Centron Educational Films

An educational film, complete with study guide. Describes how populations increase, and how environmental conditions control that increase in plants and animals.

The Problem Is Life. 29 min.; color. Purchase $260; rental $11. 1969. Contemporary/McGraw Hill Films

Examines a United Nations birth control program in India. Concentrates on one village where the inhabitants are given free birth control counseling. Also includes a vasectomy—the operation which sterilizes men and has proven to be the most successful form of birth control in India. A United Nations film.

A Single Step. 28 min.; color. Purchase $200; rental $12.50. 1971. Planned Parenthood-World Population

Presents a series of interviews with college students who are frank about their sexuality and use of birth control. Discusses various attempts to institute birth control clinics at universities—some are successful, but others meet opposition from university administrations and local communities.

The Squeeze. 10 min.; b&w. Purchase $115; rental $10. 1964. Perennial Education, Inc.

Eloquently examines many overcrowded conditions, particularly in urban areas. Clearly implies that birth control is necessary. No narration.

Tomorrow's Children. 17 min.; color. Purchase $225; rental $22. 1971. Perennial Education, Inc.

Emphasizes the connection between population growth and resource depletion. Explains that places like India desperately need population control right now in order to feed the citizens. Also points out that the United States, with a far less dense population, uses many more resources than India. Clearly implies that the U.S. population should also be controlled.

Tragedy of the Commons. 23 min.; color. Purchase $295. 1971. Holt, Rinehart and Winston, Inc.

An educational film, complete with study guide. Gives an exegesis of an essay by Garrett Hardin in which he explains that if a natural resource is freely available, an expanding population will quickly consume the entire resource with disastrous consequences for all. Hardin is well known for his theories which advocate enforced population controls. The film does not, however, examine what form those controls might take.

Whose Life? 30 min.; b&w. Purchase $145; rental $15. CCM Films, Inc.

An antiabortion film depicting the desolation of a woman who has had an abortion.

RADIATION

The Atom Underground. 20 min.; color. Free loan. 1969. U.S. Atomic Energy Commission

Examines the Atomic Energy Commission's Plowshare Program, which is designed to develop peaceful uses of atomic energy. Explores how atomic explosives can be used in various types of mining. Discusses the comparative economics of conventional and atomic mining.

Atoms for Peace, Part 1—Introducing the Atom. 20 min.; b&w. Purchase $42.50; rental $7.50. 1955. General Services Administration, National Archives and Records Service

Presents a useful explanation of atomic energy, including animated illustrations of atomic structure and function. Briefly discusses controlled nuclear reactions. Somewhat dated.

Atoms on the Move: Transportation of Radioactive Materials. 24 min.; color. Free loan. 1966. U.S. Atomic Energy Commission

Sponsored by the Atomic Energy Commission. Describes the various types of radioactive materials that must be transported, and discusses how those materials are actually moved. Indicates that increasing transport of radioactive substances (particularly wastes from nuclear power plants) has caused growing concern among environmentalists that the radioactive material will be lost or damaged in transport, potentially contributing to dangerous emissions of radioactivity.

Footnotes on the Atomic Age. 46 min.; color. Purchase $470; rental $23. 1970. NBC Educational Enterprises

An Emmy award-winning production. Discusses the effects of atomic energy on individuals who have been exposed to radiation. Also explains that radioactivity from atomic tests in the United States has crossed international boundaries. Provides excellent background for discussing how and why even peaceful uses of atomic energy can be exceedingly dangerous.

Handle with Care: Safe Handling of Radioisotopes. 21½ min.; b&w. Purchase $130; rental $12. Purchase: National Film Board of Canada. Rental: Contemporary/McGraw Hill Films

Enacts an accident which results in radioactive contamination. Shows that despite routine precautions, some radioactivity is carried outside the accident site. Stresses the need for extreme care in areas where radioactive materials are being handled. Produced for the International Atomic Energy Agency.

Hot to Handle. 60 min.; b&w. Purchase $250; rental $25. 1968. Time-Life Films

Discusses the whole range of effects of atomic radiation, including disease, mutation, ecological damage, and also beneficial effects such as treatment of cancer. Also mentions the problem of radioactive waste disposal.

The International Atom. 26 min.; color. Purchase $220; rental $11. 1961. Contemporary/McGraw Hill Films

Produced for the International Atomic Energy Agency. Surveys research and application of peaceful uses of atomic energy in a number of countries around the world. Focuses on the use of atomic energy in medicine, agriculture, and industry.

The Medical Effects of Nuclear Radiation. 21 min.; color. Purchase $85.75. Originial release: 1951; later updated. General Services Administration, National Archives and Records Service

Presents a general introduction to the effects of nuclear radiation on the human body. Illustrates defense against nuclear weapons, and explains the difference in type and effect of gamma, alpha, and beta particles.

Nuclear Radiation Fallout. 15 min.; b&w. Rental $6.50. Indiana Univ. Audio-Visual Center

Examines the effects of radiation from atomic bomb blasts, including explanations of the various types of radiation released and the effects of each. Particularly correlates radiation with genetic mutations. Concludes with a warning of caution about proceeding with nuclear weapons testing.

The Petrified River—The Story of Uranium. 28 min.; color. Free loan. 1956. U.S. Dept. of the Interior, Bureau of Mines

Examines the geological creation of uranium, and surveys the peaceful uses of this naturally radioactive element.

Plowshare. 28 min.; color. Free loan. 1965. U.S. Atomic Energy Commission

An Atomic Energy Commission film. Surveys the variety of ways atomic energy can be used for peaceful, constructive purposes. Includes discussion of mining and excavation projects and use of atomic energy in scientific research. Although this film is somewhat dated, the AEC is still committed to its Plowshare program.

Principles of Nuclear Fission. 10 min.; color. Purchase $125; rental $10. 1959. Contemporary/McGraw Hill Films

Explains nuclear fission. Begins with a simple description of atomic structure, and ends with the way chain reactions are induced and controlled in nuclear power reactors.

Project Gasbuggy: The Resourceful Atom. 14¼ min.; color. Free loan. 1968. U.S. Atomic Energy Commission

Gives a detailed explanation of the Atomic Energy Commission's joint project with El Paso Natural Gas Company's Project Gasbuggy. Describes this project's use of an atomic explosive to free natural gas trapped in rock that is not profitable to mine by conventional means. Discusses all aspects of the project, from initial drilling to sampling the freed gas for radioactivity.

Project Salt Vault. 11 min.; color. Free loan. 1969. U.S. Atomic Energy Commission

Concerns a two-year study by the Oak Ridge National Laboratory on the feasibility of permanent disposal in salt mines of high-level radioactive wastes from nuclear reactors. Focuses on salt mines in Kansas (a site the Atomic Energy Commission has since found unuseable). A timely film, however, since the AEC continues to regard salt mine disposal as the ultimate fate of this nation's most radioactive wastes.

Radiation Effects on Farm Animals. 13 min.; color. Free loan to selected groups; inquiry should be made to U.S. Department of Agriculture. 1964. General Services Administration, National Archives and Records Service

Examines the effects of varying doses of radiation on farm animals. Includes explicit photographs of the damage that can be caused, explains that some level of radiation exposure can be tolerated by the animals, but fails to discuss the effect of the radiation on the animals' progeny.

Safety in Salt: The Transportation, Handling, and Disposal of Radioactive Waste. 28½ min.; color. Purchase $113.50; free loan.

1971. General Services Administration, National Archives and Records Service

An Atomic Energy Commission film made when the AEC was committed to using salt formations in Lyons, Kansas, as the national radioactive waste depository. Subsequently, the AEC found that the Lyons site was unsuitable for the waste storage. However, the film is still valuable because the AEC is still seriously considering burying this country's most dangerous wastes in salt caverns in New Mexico.

Truman and the Atomic Bomb. 15 min.; b&w. Rental $8.50. New York Univ. Film Library

Analyzes President Truman's decision to drop the only atomic bombs that have ever been used against humanity. Discusses the difficulty in making the decision, and explains the reasoning behind the ultimate choice.

Waste Disposal by Hydraulic Fracturing. 11 min.; color. Purchase $39.50; free loan. 1966. General Services Administration, National Archives and Records Service

Most useful for audiences with some technical knowledge. Explains how medium-level radioactive wastes mixed with cement can be injected into shale formations. Discusses how this method is one alternative in safely disposing of a kind of waste that will remain dangerous for centuries. An Atomic Energy Commission film.

SOLID WASTE

The Abandoned. 10 min.; color. Purchase $130; rental $10. 1970. NBC Educational Enterprises

A well-made film contrasting scrapped cars being disposed of with shiny new cars passing by. Contains an implicit indictment of American consumerism.

Burn, Bury or What? 19 min.; color. Purchase $225; rental $22.50. 1970. Stuart Finley Inc.

Discusses plans to change Washington, D.C.'s solid waste disposal schemes from open dumping to newer techniques. Briefly describes alternatives to dumping.

Cycles. 13 ½ min.; color. Free loan. 1972. Association-Sterling Films

Explains that man is the only organism that has broken the natural cycle of eventually returning to the soil what is removed from it. Examines recycling techniques.

Ecology Lady. 11 min.; color. Purchase $150; rental $15. 1971. Stuart Finley Inc.

Documents the efforts of one woman in Virginia to establish and maintain a recycling center. Includes discussion of the difficulties in running the center.

5,000 Dumps. 21 min.; color. Purchase $200; rental $20. 1971. Stuart Finley Inc.

Describes the federal Environmental Protection Agency's program to get rid of 5,000 dumps within two years. Gives specific examples of areas that have scrapped open dumps and begun to use alternative disposal plans. Also discusses legislation designed to eliminate dumps in a number of states.

Forest Murmurs. 8 ½ min.; color. Purchase $100; rental $10. 1963. Perennial Education, Inc.

Gives a simple, effective, and visual indictment of litter. Depicts a forest filling up with the scraps, cans, and other refuse that man drops in the forest.

A Funny Thing Happened on the Way to the Garbage Dump. 50 min.; b&w. Purchase $300; rental $30. 1970. Time-Life Films

Explains that garbage contains important resources which can be used in a wide variety of ways if the resources are recycled. Explores both experimental techniques of disposing of garbage and the products that can be manufactured out of reuseable resources. A BBC production.

Garbage. 10 ½ min.; color. Purchase $135; rental $15. 1970. Holt, Rinehart and Winston, Inc.

Pictorially describes the ugliness of solid waste, and implicitly states that we will soon be buried in trash if we do not soon do something about it. A catchy film that is a good introduction to a fuller discussion of the solid waste problem.

The Great All-American Trash Can. 13 min.; color. Free loan. 1971. Commonwealth Film Distributors

Explains that costs of solid waste disposal can be severely reduced by recycling materials in the trash. Focuses on glass recycling, and relates the ways in which recycled glass can be made into useful products. Sponsored by the Glass Container Corporation.

The Green Box. 17 min.; color. Purchase $200; rental $20. 1971. Stuart Finley Inc.

Explores the way in which rural Chilton County, Alabama, solved its problem of ugly, unsanitary dumps by installing large containers to which people could haul their garbage. Reveals a practical solution that has worked well with the backing of local planners and citizens.

Junkdump. 15 min.; color. Purchase $200. 1972. ACI Films, Inc.

Presents a sarcastic view of how Americans live. Depicts a family constantly surrounded by junk, including everything from garbage to a "junkmobile." An amusing film, but the message is clear.

Litter Bug. 8 min.; color. Purchase $115; rental $4. 1961. Walt Disney Educational Materials Co.

An amusing film, starring Donald Duck, which clearly demonstrates the unsightly result of littering. Donald manages, in very few minutes, to drop just about every kind of litter imaginable.

The Litter Monster. 16 ½ min.; color. Purchase $110. 1971. Alfred Higgins Productions

Attempts to show children the harmful aesthetic and medical effects of litter. Not particularly designed for urban dwellers. Sponsored by Keep America Beautiful, Inc.

My Garbage. 10 min.; color. Purchase $150; rental $25. 1967. Grove Press Film Div.

Presents a brief introduction to the problems of solid waste collection. Shows that garbage production never ends; as soon as some garbage is collected, more is generated.

Pollution in Perspective: Solid Wastes. 17 min.; color. Purchase $180. 1971. General Electric Educational Films

Presents a panel discussion of the American solid waste problem. A fairly technical discussion which raises a number of interesting questions concerning the difficulties in altering our concepts of what to do with solid waste.

The Realities of Recycling. 38 min.; color. Purchase $300; rental $30. 1971. Stuart Finley Inc.

Takes a sober, informative look at the benefits of recycling, including the economic and political costs of undertaking new solid waste management programs. Offers examples of areas which have successfully instituted recycling projects, as a result of combined governmental and citizen cooperation.

Recycling. 21 min.; color. Purchase $200; rental $20. 1971. Stuart Finley Inc.

Describes various recycling projects that are being carried out across the country, and explains how the recycled material can be made into useful products.

Recycling Atlanta. 3 min.; color. Free loan. 1971. Ruder and Finn, Inc.

A very brief but informative film. Explains how Atlanta's recycling program for ferrous metals constitutes a break from man's historical treatment of garbage—either dumping or incineration. Also mentions the development of new all-inclusive recycling technologies.

Recycling San Francisco. 3 min.; color. Free loan. 1971. Ruder and Finn, Inc.

A brief film which explains that most of San Francisco's garbage is being disposed of in sanitary landfills. Describes a program to begin recycling much of the city's wastes.

Recycling Waste. 12 min.; color. Purchase $145; rental $11. 1971. Journal Films, Inc.

Calls for manufacturers to adopt large-scale recycling efforts to avoid depletion of natural resources, reduce the environmental impact of manufacturing from raw materials, and undermine the spirit of consumerism. Strongly advocates industrial recycling programs.

Steel—The Recycled Material. 10 min.; color. Free loan. 1972. Association-Sterling Films

Discusses how steel is recycled, and explains how the quantities now being recycled could increase in the future. Sponsored by the Committee of Tin Mill Products Producers and the American Iron and Steel Institute.

The Stuff We Throw Away. 22 min.; color. Purchase $200; rental $20. 1970. Stuart Finley Inc.

Describes how solid waste disposal can be well managed by use of new techniques. Examines the new methods, but does not discuss what is necessary financially and politically to implement them.

The Third Pollution. 23 min.; color. Purchase $225; rental $22.50. 1966. Stuart Finley Inc.

Presents a general introduction to the problems of solid waste with some suggestions of what can be done about it. Discusses specific techniques for managing increasing solid wastes.

The Trouble with Trash. 28 min.; color. Free loan. Modern Talking Picture Service, Inc.
Examines new ways of handling a growing solid waste problem, and concludes that sanitary landfills offer the most rational solution. This conclusion is probably biased by the film's sponsor, Caterpillar Tractor Company, manufacturer of tractors used at landfill sites.

Up to Our Necks. 26 min.; color. Purchase $330; rental $15. 1969. NBC Educational Enterprises
Describes the problem of solid waste disposal in large cities. Uses New York City to relate new and potentially feasible methods of solid waste disposal. Somewhat dated, but useful.

Urban Ecology: Garbage Disposal. 7 min.; color. Purchase $110; rental $8. 1971. BFA Educational Media
Explains for children that the solid waste problem cannot be solved by good garbage collection and sufficient landfills. Points out that excess packaging and overconsumption are the roots of the solid waste dilemma.

Waste Away. 22 min.; color. Purchase $74.45; free loan. 1969. General Services Administration, National Archives and Records Service
Uses a Washington State area to depict the benefits of sanitary landfills for solid waste disposal. Gives a good description of how a landfill site is selected and how the landfill is designed. Some of the discussion is moderately technical.

Wealth of the Wasteland. 27 min.; color. Free loan. 1968. U.S. Dept. of the Interior, Bureau of Reclamation
Presents facts and figures on the resources that Americans annually throw out in their garbage. Discusses programs sponsored by the U.S. Bureau of Mines that are aimed at recovering some of these disposed resources. Somewhat dated.

What's New in Solid Waste Management? 37 min.; color. Purchase $300; rental $30. 1970. Stuart Finley Inc.
Discusses new and better ways to handle solid waste. Points out that few of these new techniques are being used, and examines the reasons.

THE URBAN ENVIRONMENT

Bump City. 5 min.; color. Purchase $100. 1968. Creative Film Society
Gives a quick run-through on Los Angeles showing its myriad cars, neon lights, and restaurants—all in a rapid succession of images. Presents a possible moral in its final shot—trash being thrown into the city dump.

The Cities: A City Is to Live In. 54 min.; color and b&w. Purchase c $575, b&w $275; rental $40. 1968. BFA Educational Media
Walter Cronkite looks at what inadequate urban planning has led to—decay, pollution, poor transportation, unemployment, etc. Emphasizes the need for good, coherent planning, and outlines what planners are now doing to solve the crisis of the cities.

The Cities: To Build the Future. 54 min.; color and b&w. Purchase c $575, b&w $275; rental c $40, b&w $40. 1968. BFA Educational Media
Presents an interesting conflict between urban planning theories—individuals who would build within a city, increasing the population density versus those who advocate new towns as alternatives to already existing cities. Implies that people who opt for new towns are abandoning hope of saving existing metropolises.

Cities Have No Limits. 53 min.; color. Purchase $500; rental $25. 1969. NBC Educational Enterprises
In the first part of this fast-moving film, NBC correspondent Frank McGee interviews a number of urbanologists who convey the impression that Americans don't like cities; they earn their money there but they return gratefully to the suburbs. Leaves the impression that Americans are alienated, without a sense of community. In the last part of the film, expert Daniel P. Moynihan puts the blame for America's problems on big business and on the young people who have lost America's moral principles and have become lazy and violent.

A City is People. 22 min.; color. Purchase $225; rental $22.50. 1970. Stuart Finley Inc.
Focuses principally on Washington's tourist attractions, highways, rapid-transit systems, and new buildings. Gives slight attention to the blacks who make up 70 percent of Wash-

ington's population. The title does not accurately describe the film. Sponsored by the National Capital Downtown Committee.

A City Is to Live In. 54 min.; color and b&w. Purchase c $575, b&w $275; rental c $40, b&w $40. 1968. BFA Educational Media

Begins with rather hasty judgments by a number of well-known urbanologists, and then makes a careful analysis of the problems confronting Cleveland, a typical city. Shows that as usual, the central city's wealth is being milked dry by the suburbs. Cleveland has more than 200 local governments. Some 325,000 suburbanites earn their money in the city and spend it nearer home. After the mayor of Parma, a suburb of 100,000 people, says that Parma doesn't need Cleveland, Mayor John Lindsay replies that if the city falls, the suburbs will surely follow. Narrated by CBS commentator Walter Cronkite.

Cosmopolis. 52 min.; color. Purchase $600; rental $35. 1969. Contemporary/McGraw Hill Films

Examines the dilemmas now facing most U.S. cities, particularly the increasing migration to urban areas. Suggests that the solution is to control migration by offering the alternative of planned "new towns," which can reduce congestion by limiting the distance residents must travel during their daily routines.

Don't Crowd Me! 15 min.; color. Purchase $180. 1969. Doubleday Multimedia

Explores what often happens when people migrate to cities—they are met with deteriorating housing and overly crowded conditions. Briefly discusses the physiological and mental effects of crowding, and offers suggestions about planning new urban communities and rehabilitating old ones.

Downtowns for People. 25 min.; color. Purchase $275; rental $35. 1971. Enterprise Productions, Inc.

Advocates pedestrian malls in place of avenues crowded with cars, trucks, and buses, as well as people. Shows some excellent contrasts between U.S. city streets and European malls.

Fur-Lined Fox Hole. 30 min.; b&w. Purchase $125; rental $6.75. 1964. Indiana Univ. Audio-Visual Center

Begins by taking a dim view of suburban living, but ends by praising it. At first, shows suburbs as fear-shrouded, fur-lined fox holes (as some might be considered today). Indicates that encroaching urbanization, increasing taxes, and poor resale values all threaten the suburbanites. Then focuses on Wheeling, Illinois, a suburb of Chicago. Reveals through interviews with Wheeling residents that the suburb offers a release for the "pioneer spirit," as well as refuge from monotonous jobs and an opportunity to build a community. A documentary of primarily historical interest.

How Things Get Done. 30 min.; b&w. Purchase $125; rental $6.75. 1964. Indiana Univ. Audio-Visual Center

Presents a documentary about the South Houston area of New York City, which is still undergoing change. Before 1964, the district had been strictly commercial. A group of New Yorkers decided to redevelop it for middle-class housing. They were particularly attracted to the vacant loft space. But they found that despite its rundown appearance the area was commercially busy and supported many employees. Gives a good picture of the tentative plans of the would-be developers and the realities presented by the commercial interests.

John Kenneth Galbraith: The Idea of the City. 28 min.; color. Purchase $350; rental $50. 1968. Association-Sterling Films

Examines Galbraith's theories on cities—how they were originally formed, what has become of them, and in what direction they should move. Basically, Galbraith calls for more federal input to cities, primarily through regulation and increased revenues. While many may disagree with Galbraith, he poses an interesting argument of how cities in decline may be rescued.

Like Rings on Water. 16 min.; b&w. Purchase $160; rental $10. 1968. Pyramid Films

A Swedish film that uses some innovative cinemagraphic techniques. Uses some symbolic sequences, and offers possible solutions to some urban problems, such as traffic congestion. Advocates carefully planned new towns.

Overspill. 28 min.; b&w. Purchase $150; rental $17. Purchase: National Film Board of Canada. Rental: Contemporary/McGraw Hill Films

Concerns people who have lived in an area in the northernmost part of Sweden. Reveals that changes in industry and agriculture have taken these people's jobs away, and they are being relocated to industrial cities and often placed on welfare. Questions the propriety of severly jolting people by moving them far from their homes, but also asks how else to solve the problem of increasing rural unemployment.

Pandora's Easy Open Pop Top Box. 16 min.; color. Purchase $44; free loan. 1967. General Services Administration, National Archives and Records Service

Sponsored by the U.S. Public Health Service. Does a good job of pointing out various urban ills, and explains that the PHS is optimistic about restoring health to decaying cities. Unfortunately, does not detail how PHS intends to do that. Lacks concrete solutions, but does have merit in contrasting urban and rural areas and their respective effects on health.

The Pedestrian Strikes Back. 25 min.; color. Rental $5. 1967. Portland Cement Assn.

Presents a study of the success of pedestrian malls in southern California. Reveals that the number of people now walking on former streets has increased enormously, and despite shopkeepers' original fears of business losses, sales have risen.

Three Cures for a Sick City. 30 min.; b&w. Purchase $125; rental $6.75. 1964. Indiana Univ. Audio-Visual Center

Presents a study of Washington, D.C., depicting three approaches that have been made toward improving the city—one successful, the others failures. The "Georgetown approach" reclaimed the Georgetown section from the squalor into which it had fallen by the 1930s. Southwest Washington, on the other hand, was torn down—not reclaimed. In its place, townhouses and apartment houses were erected for high- or moderate-income families. In both these rehabilitations, the poor and the blacks were dispossessed. In the Adams Morgan section, these minorities hoped to carry out their own urban renewal, but funds were denied because the inhabitants were judged not poor enough. They certainly would have qualified in either of the previous renewals.

Town Planning. 15 min.; b&w. Purchase $95; rental $8. International Film Bureau, Inc.

Examines how town planning can be used to redirect the growth of a city, as well as to plan new cities. Contrasts unplanned growth with regulated, carefully managed urban expansion.

A Townscape Rediscovered. 29 ½ min.; color. Purchase $350; rental $32.50. 1967. CCM Films, Inc.

Tells how Victoria, British Columbia, revitalized its downtown area through urban renovation. Shows how the renovation was made a priority project by the Victoria Town Council, and funds were made available. The success of Victoria's planned redevelopment does not necessarily directly apply to all other development schemes.

Urbanissimo. 6 min.; color. Purchase $90; rental $12.50. 1970. Contemporary/McGraw Hill Films

A sophisticated cartoon that symbolically depicts the encroachment of urbanization on farmers, primitive peoples, and wildlife.

Visit to a Small Village. 12 min.; color. Purchase $144; rental $10. Association-Sterling Films

Relates the attempt of the government of Ghana to stem the flow of people from countryside to cities. Shows how students go to a village to discuss with the inhabitants what kinds of things the villagers need, and then depicts how cooperative efforts help to make those necessities realities. Reveals that when village life is improved, people are less inclined to move, which lessens pressures on already jammed cities and hardly disrupts villagers' lives.

Vivre Sa Ville. 18 min.; color. Purchase $200; rental $15. 1968. National Film Board of Canada

Presents an introduction to planning concepts, and concentrates on current problems facing Quebec and Montreal. Discusses specific planning problems which can easily be expanded to include other cities. Suggests ways to improve both Quebec and Montreal, including preservation of older sections of the cities, but does not discuss political and financial realities of implementing those improvements.

WATER RESOURCES AND POLLUTION

The Aging of Lakes. 14 min.; color. Purchase $167; rental $8. 1971. Encyclopaedia Britannica Educational Corp.

Describes what man has done to cause eutrophication of lakes. Examines programs to restore lakes, and distinguishes between effects of pollution and causes, which can be alleviated by preventive programs.

Ah Man, See What You've Done. 26 min.; color. Purchase $250. 1971. North American Films, Inc.
Explains that microscopic plankton that live in the oceans are the world's prime source of oxygen, and that pollution of the oceans can kill the plankton, with obvious unfortunate results. Presents a forthright plea for man to stop polluting his world in general and the oceans in particular.

Around a Big Lake. 17 min.; color. Purchase $195; rental $15. International Film Bureau, Inc.
Traces the effects of the weather on the conditions of a typical large lake. Includes discussion of the spring and fall overturns of the water in the lake, and how these overturns greatly affect the distributions of pollutants in lakes. Also shows food chains, involving both plants and animals, that exist around the lake.

Beautiful River. 26 min.; color. Purchase $330; rental $15. 1969. NBC Educational Enterprises
Tells about the fouling of the Connecticut River. Mostly shot from a helicopter, and narrated by a professor from University of Connecticut.

Brush Creek Bounces Back. 22 min.; color. Purchase $225; rental $22.50. 1970. Stuart Finley Inc.
Presents an example of water management that resulted in an improved economic situation for a town in West Virginia. Concerns a $9 million project to halt flooding and increase water resources in the area.

Buttercup. 11 min.; color. Purchase $150. 1971. Churchill Films
Depicts a buttercup floating downstream, first in an unspoiled setting, and then in an industrialized environment. The buttercup becomes stained with wastes, symbolically making a case against pollution. No narration.

The Case against Chicken Little. 15 min.; color. Free loan. 1971. Modern Talking Picture Service, Inc.
Produced by the Weyerhauser Corporation to defend their paper-manufacturing operations and industry in general against charges of creating water pollution. Contends that many such charges are made by uninformed alarmists.

The Changing River. 16 min.; color. Purchase $195; rental $12.50. International Film Bureau, Inc.
Describes a river from its beginnings in raindrops to its mouth where it is a large body of flowing water. Concerns the natural communities that grow up at different points of the river. Shows how some of the communities are better suited to rushing water than others. Stresses the relationships between organisms and their environment.

Clear Water on the Colorado. 13 ½ min.; color. Free loan. 1963. U.S. Dept. of the Interior, Bureau of Reclamation
Examines how dam construction on the Colorado River has cleared the water in the river. Does not mention any adverse farming effects due to the deprivation of silt in downstream agricultural areas.

Colorado River: Water and Power for the Southwest. 16 min.; color. Purchase $190; rental $10. 1967. BFA Educational Media
Shows how man's harnessing the Colorado River through a system of dams has allowed the Southwest to become a productive agricultural area. Does not discuss environmental damage caused by the dams.

Columbia River: Economic Lifeline of the Northwest. 18 min.; color. Purchase $220; rental $10. BFA Educational Media
Presents an examination of the Columbia River. Explores the dams that have been built on the Columbia, and discusses historical and economic aspects of the river. Does not include commentary on environmentalists who are opposed to further development of the Columbia River.

Conserving Our Water Resources Today. 11 min.; color and b&w. Purchase c $130, b&w $65. Coronet Instructional Films
Examines the pressures that a growing population and expanding industrialization place on water resources. Surveys how water is used in the United States today, and explains how both surface and ground water can be conserved.

Ecology of Fresh Water. 16 min.; color. Purchase $215; rental $12.50. 1967. Contemporary/McGraw Hill Films

Presents an introduction to the study of water. Explains the ecology of fresh water systems. Describes the different kinds of organisms found in water.

Element 3. 46 min.; color. Purchase $450; rental $25. 1966. International Film Bureau, Inc.

Stresses the need to conserve water. Shows how beautiful and precious water can be, and explains that water is still often wasted. An award-winning film, made in conjunction with UNESCO's International Hydrological Program.

Estuarine Heritage. 28 min.; color. Free loan. 1969. National Oceanic and Atmospheric Administration, U.S. Dept. of Commerce

Describes the effects of man's pollution of rivers on estuaries (areas where fresh water rivers meet the oceans). Also examines the rich sea life that inhabits estuaries.

The First Fifteen Years. 25 min.; color. Purchase $200; rental $20. 1963. Stuart Finley Films, Inc.

Shows how the Ohio River Compact, created fifteen years ago, makes an attempt to purify the water of the Ohio River. Reveals that almost the entire population of the Ohio Valley has its liquid refuse treated and detoxified.

The First Pollution. 26 min.; color. Purchase $300; rental $30. 1972. Stuart Finley Films, Inc.

Shows classic and new waste water treatment methods for removing oil, acid, and organic chemicals so water can be reused for cooling, irrigation, and in other ways.

The Flooding River. 34 min.; color. Purchase $395; rental $25. 1972. John Wiley & Sons, Inc.

Explains how regular flooding benefits a river's ecosystem. Describes how flooding affects organisms that depend on rivers, and points out that some areas, such as marshlands, could not exist without floods. Also emphasizes that man's tampering with river systems, through dams, etc., may soon have catastrophic results on entire ecosystems.

Ground Water—The Hidden Reservoir. 19 min.; color. Purchase $195. 1971. John Wiley & Sons, Inc.

Presents an introduction to water cycles. Examines the way in which water tables are formed, and explains how the water stored there can be made available, either through natural or man-made means. Discusses the problem of salt water invasion of ground water in coastal areas where man is pumping water out of natural aquifers faster than the water can naturally be replaced.

Hoover Dam. 33 min,; b&w. Purchase $68.25; rental $12.50. 1949. General Services Administration, National Archives and Records Service

Explains why Hoover Dam was built—to control the Colorado River and produce electricity for the area. Examines how the dam was built and the values that have accrued to the area through irrigation and power production made possible by the dam.

A Horseshoe Nail. 18 min.; color. Purchase $200; rental $20. 1966. Stuart Finley Films, Inc.

Considers causes and effects of water pollution and methods of flood and drought control. Describes the efforts of the Interstate Advisory Committee on the Susquehanna Valley to manage the Susquehanna River.

How to Make a Dirty River. 27 min.; color. Purchase $330; rental $15. 1970. NBC Educational Enterprises

Shows how the Passaic River became polluted from industrial and municipal wastes. Reveals that industry avoids abatement as it is nonprofitable. Discusses jurisdictional and political problems encountered in the effort to save the river.

How Water Helps Us. 11 min.; color and b&w. Purchase c $130; b&w $65. Coronet Instructional Films

Explains for young children some of the many reasons why we need water. Includes discussion of the importance of water in cooking, washing, transportation, for maintaining bodily balances, etc. Does not mention pollution directly, but can act as an impetus to discussion of how water pollution interferes with use of water.

Invasion by Oil. 22 min.; color. Purchase $89.75. 1969. General Services Administration, National Archives and Records Service

Relates the story of an accident in which an oil tanker broke in half in the San Juan, Puerto Rico, harbor. Describes the immediate effects of the resulting oil spill, and explains how the U.S. Army Corps of Engineers worked to remove the remains of the tanker.

Irrigation Farming in Australia. 20 min.; color. Purchase $225; rental $10. International Film Bureau, Inc.
Discusses how irrigation has permitted crops to be grown in the Riverina district of Australia. Indicates the vast quantities of water needed for irrigation. Does not include discussion of possible environmental harm to other areas through consumption of the water for farming.

It's Your Decision—Clean Water. 14 min.; color. Free loan. Association-Sterling Films
Reports on the causes of shortages of water supplies—people, prosperity, and products. Explains and evaluates various kinds of sewage treatment plants, and points out that treatment means that the water can be reused, augmenting an area's supply of water. Stresses that water treatment facilities depend on the will of the community. Winner of a number of awards.

Lakes. 9 min.; color. Purhcase $160; rental $5.25. 1970. Indiana Univ. Audio-Visual Center
Geared to young children. Describes the characteristics of both natural and man-made lakes. Explains the values of lake water. Briefly mentions pollution.

Lakes—Aging and Pollution. 15 min.; color. Purchase $195; rental $19.50. 1971. Centron Educational Films
Explains the aging process of lakes in a question-and-answer format suitable for classroom viewing. Points out how sewage, fertilizers, and wastes can bring about the rapid death of lakes.

Load on Top. 14 min.; color. Free loan. 1967. BP North America, Inc.
Illustrates a method by which oil tankers keep ballast water from becoming contaminated with oil and sludge, which eliminates water pollution from discharged ballast.

Man's Natural Environment—The Creek. 26 min.; color. Purchase $175; rental $10. 1971. Film Co.
Presents a case history of a successful effort by citizens to lobby for antipollution laws. Demonstrates how lobbying brought about the enactment of legislation and the construction of pollution-treatment facilities for Minnesota's Nine Mile Creek.

Municipal Sewage Treatment Processes. 13 min.; b&w. Purchase $23.75; Free loan. General Services Administration, National Archives and Records Service
Examines the techniques used by U.S. cities to treat sewage. Explains that sewage treatment both protects public health and conserves water resources.

Nature's Plan: Living Water Series. 15 min.; color. Purchase $167.50; rental $8. 1953. Encyclopaedia Britannica Educational Corp.
Designed for students through high school age. Examines natural water cycles, including the concepts of watersheds, evaporation and condensation, and natural water storage.

New Water for a Thirsty World. 22 ½ min.; color. Free loan. 1965; revised in 1971. U.S. Dept. of the Interior, Bureau of Reclamation
Geared primarily for technically competent viewers. Describes various projects sponsored by the U.S. Department of the Interior to produce potable water from brackish or salt water. Discusses possible future uses of new technology in treating presently unusable water.

Oil Spoil! 17 min.; color. Free loan. 1972. Association-Sterling Films
Illustrates the effects on the ocean and beaches of the 1969 oil spill off Santa Barbara, California. No narration.

Our Poisoned World: Water. 30 min.; color. Purchase $300; rental $30. 1971. Time-Life Films
Describes the effects of industrial pollution on Lake Michigan and other Michigan waterways. Points out the reluctance of industry and government to take prompt abatement actions.

The Problem with Water is People. 30 min.; color. Purchase $350; rental $18. 1964. Contemporary/McGraw Hill Films
Follows the flow of the Colorado River, pointing out where stretches are clean and where man has polluted the river. Reveals striking contrasts.

Problems of Conservation: Water. 16 min.; color and b&w. Purchase c $200, b&w $102.50; rental c $9, b&w $5.50. 1969. Encyclopaedia Britannica Educational Corp.

Explores the problem of water shortages, particularly in the Southwest, and discusses in general terms the ways technology can be used to help conserve water. Examines problems of water pollution, with suggestions of how such problems can be alleviated.

Rain. 10 min.; color. Purchase $120; rental $8. International Film Bureau, Inc.
Describes for young children the need for rain and rain's role in the water cycle. Uses simple illustrations to make the concepts easily understandable.

The River: A First Film. 9 ½ min.; color. Purchase $125; rental $6.50. 1964. BFA Educational Media
Presents an introduction for young children to river systems, including how rivers get their water and what happens to it afterwards. Describes man's diverse uses of rivers, but does not mention how rivers are polluted.

The River Must Live. 21 min.; color. Free loan. 1966. Shell Film Library
Details how water pollution affects aquatic communities. Shows more concern with describing the problem than with recommending abatement methods.

Save Our Sea. 23 min.; color. Purchase $225; rental $15. 1970. Pyramid Films
Originally produced for television by some Monterey Bay area students. Presents a plea for cleaning up the bay. Now somewhat outdated, since Bay area residents in 1970 approved a bond issue to finance treatment of water entering the bay. Could be useful for citizens in other areas of the country who are interested in protecting their environment.

Should Oceans Meet? 30 min.; color. Purchase $300; rental $30. 1970. Time-Life Films
Explains possible damage that could occur if a sea-level Panama Canal is built. Focuses on research at the Smithsonian Tropical Research Institute in Panama where tests have discovered what happens when marine species from the Atlantic and Pacific Oceans meet. Shows some facinating results, but some have disturbing portent.

The Slow Death of Desert Water. 30 min.; color. Purchase $315; rental $11.50. 1969. Indiana Univ. Audio-Visual Center
Explores the ecological effects of man's tampering with natural water systems. Uses the Derby Dam on the Truckee River in Nevada to show that although dams have beneficial effects, unforeseen consequences of such structures may result in environmental damage and economic hardship.

Spirit of 76. 20 min.; color. Purchase $225; rental $40. 1969. American Documentary Films, Inc.
Presents an examination of the blowout of an oil rig in the Santa Barbara Channel in 1969,— a classic story of environmental damage. Also discusses the conflict between environmentalists and oil interests, particularly pertinent during the present energy crisis.

Tennessee River: Conservation and Power. 14 min.; color. Purchase $195; rental $10. 1971. BFA Educational Media
Gives a laudatory presentation of the benefits of the Tennessee Valley Authority. Depicts how dams and the electricity they produce have contributed to the economic viability of the Tennessee Valley.

Water. 14 ½ min.; color. Purchase $174; rental $17.40. 1961. Center for Mass Communication of Columbia Univ. Press
An animated film which depicts natural water cycles, and explains the ramifications of abundant or scarce water resources. Discusses the economic consequences of nations' water resources. Sponsored by the United Nations.

The Water Famine. 54 min.; b&w. Purchase $250. 1961. Carousel Films, Inc.
Presents a documentary of the haphazard way in which water in the United States is tapped and consumed. Although fairly old, the film is still useful in pointing out historical effects of water shortages and for contrasting American water use with that of other nations.

Water for the Valley. 28 min.; color. Price on request. 1961. Byron Motion Pictures, Inc.
Describes the benefits to the Central Valley in California from dams the bureau built to reduce flooding and lessen drought effects. Does not discuss how providing water for one area may adversely affect a downstream area. Sponsored by the Bureau of Reclamation.

Water—Old Problems, New Approaches. 30 min.; color. Purchase $350; rental $18. 1969. Contemporary/McGraw Hill Films
Discusses in general terms what is being done by a number of UNESCO projects to conserve water and reduce pollution.

The Water Plan. 37 min.; color. Purchase $350; reduced price for environmental groups. 1971. Summit Films, Inc.

Surveys the water resource situation in Colorado. Raises the point that expanded water resources are necessary for growing cities, but questions why cities must continue to grow. Implicitly advocates both decreased growth and preservation of wilderness areas.

Water Pollution: A First Film. 8 min.; color. Purchase $120; rental $8. BFA Educational Media

Traces for young children a single stream, revealing what adds to pollution of the stream's water. Shows discovery of a number of polluters near the stream's end. Calls on the viewers to help clean up waterways.

Water Pollution: Can We Keep Our Water Clean? 12 ½ min.; color. Purchase $145; rental $11. 1971. Journal Films, Inc.

Shows six sources and effects of pollution on a mountain stream, including trash and garbage sewage, thermal pollution from power plants, dumping of oil and garbage from boats, and pesticide and fertilizer run-off in agricultural areas. Gives suggestions to reduce this damage.

Water, Water, Everywhere. 5 min.; color. Inquire about purchase price. 1971. National Film Board of Canada

Shows the death of a trout from water pollution.

A Whole New World. 20 min.; color. Rental $15. 1972. Petroleum Equipment Suppliers Assn.

Explains that within hours after offshore oil rigs are in place, marine life comes to inhabit the underwater portions of the rig. Relates that the presence of the oil rigs has encouraged species of fish, which were not previously found in the Gulf of Mexico, to live in that area. Sponsored by the Petroleum Equipment Suppliers Association.

The Wonder of Water. 27 min.; color. Free loan. Association-Sterling Films

Presents a documentary concerning development of our water resources. Includes descriptions of how the U.S. Corps of Engineers works to improve waterways (although many environmentalists claim that the corps does more environmental harm than enhancement). Examines the economic consequences of maintaining the health of the nation's waterways.

The Year of the Disaster. 28 min.; color. Free loan. 1971. Modern Talking Picture Service, Inc.

Examines how five diverse cities have barely avoided either flooding or drought. Suggests that these near disasters could be prevented by judicious water management planning.

Your Friend the Water (Clean or Dirty). 6 min.; color. Purchase $65; rental $6.50. 1954. Encyclopaedia Britannica Educational Corp.

A cartoon for young children, which contrasts clear streams with polluted waterways. Also includes a very brief discussion of water cycles.

WEATHER MODIFICATION

Can We Control the Weather? 25 min.; color. Purchase $350; rental $18. 1969. Contemporary/McGraw Hill Films

Presents a balanced survey of modern weather prediction technology and weather modification techniques. Also explains the hazards of weather modification.

It's an Ill Wind. 17 min.; color. Purchase $220; rental $9. 1970. Universal Education and Visual Arts

An animated film in which visitors from another planet take a close look at the earth's atmosphere, and find that air pollution from man-made sources affects the weather. The strangers discuss how weather modification occurs, and predict that man's activities have the potential for destroying life.

Mountain Skywater. 27 min.; color. Free loan. 1971. U.S. Depart. of the Interior, Bureau of Reclamation

Examines the Bureau of Reclamation's Project Skywater—a weather modification program to increase the water supply in the Colorado River Basin. Does not cover the potential dangers of weather modification as thoroughly as some environmentalists would like.

Rivers in the Sky. 28 min.; color. Free loan. 1967. U.S. Depart. of the Interior, Bureau of Reclamation

Offers technically competent viewers a survey of weather modification programs that have operated under the auspices of the U.S. Department of the Interior. Describes a variety of cloud-seeding techniques, including the technology used in each.

Urban Impact on Weather and Climate. 16 min.; color. Purchase $225; rental $20. 1972. Learning Corp. of America

Examines how cities affect the weather. Shows that heat and air pollution from densely packed buildings and cars can change precipitation and wind patterns. Explains that the ultimate effects of these weather alterations are unknown.

The Weather Watchers. 30 min.; color. Purchase $350; rental $18. 1969. Contemporary/McGraw Hill Films

Primarily concerned with weather prediction. Also explains the ways in which we can already alter some weather, and examines potential weather modification techniques.

WILDLIFE

Adaptations for Survival: Birds. 14 min.; color. Purchase $165; rental $10. 1969. International Film Bureau, Inc.

Describes how various birds have physiologically adapted to their environments. Includes adaptations, such as long bills, stiltlike legs, webbed feet, and protective coloration.

After the Whale. 30 min.; color. Purchase $300; rental $30. 1970. Time-Life Films

Shows modern methods of whaling, and contrasts them with traditional Eskimo hunts. Explains that all the products made from whales can be manufactured from vegetable oils, but the hunt still goes on despite a dangerous decrease in a number of whale species.

Alligator! 10 min.; color. Purchase $145; rental $14.50. 1970. Contemporary/McGraw Hill Films

Stars the alligator, and describes its role in the ecology of the Everglades. Reveals much to many people's surprise, that the alligator is an exceedingly, useful member of its environment. Warns that the alligator's existence is being threatened by man.

The American Bald Eagle. 16 min.; color and b&w. Purchase c $195, b&w $97.50. 1971. Coronet Instructional Films

Follows an ornithologist's field studies of the bald eagle. Reveals that man's interference has caused the near extinction of this American symbol. Presents an underlying message that the bald eagle should be preserved.

Animal Predators and the Balance of Nature. 10 ½ min.; color. Purchase $125; rental $9. 1965. Journal Films, Inc.

Designed for young children. Introduces the concept of the balance of nature, showing how predators and prey actually depend upon one another.

Animals of Africa. 14 min.; color. Purchase $210; rental $15. 1968. Contemporary/McGraw Hill Films

Shows how wildlife experts are protecting endangered species in Africa's largest game park, which is located on Tanzania's Serengeti plain.

Atonement. 52 min.; color. Purchase $500; rental $25. 1969. Films Inc.

Deals with the capture and care of wildlife and the plight of vanishing species.

Birds and Migration. 18 min.; color. Purchase $225; rental. $15. International Film Bureau, Inc.

Explains that migration routes for birds change with alterations in surface features, climate, and food supply. Warns that urbanization is a danger to migrating bird species. Describes a number of species of birds and their migration patterns.

Birds in the City: A First Film. 10 min.; color. Purchase $135; rental $8. 1970. BFA Educational Media

Explains what kinds of birds live in urban areas, and discusses how these species adapt to manufactured environments. Presents an introduction to nature to which urban children can relate.

Birds of the Sandy Beach: An Introduction to Ecology. 10 min.; color. Purchase $120; rental $6.50. 1965. BFA Educational Media

Explains the many different kinds of birds that can live comfortably together in beach areas because each species is specially adapted to his environment—some birds are tall, some are short, and some have oddly shaped bills. Shows how the differences cause the birds to hunt in different ways, so that they do not ordinarily vie with each other for the same food source.

The Buffalo—Majestic Symbol of the Plains. 12 min.; color. Purchase: $135. 1954. Walt Disney Educational Materials Co.

Presents a brief documentary on the buffalo. Tells how huge buffalo herds were decimated by white men. Also shows a number of events in buffalo routine—from the birth of a calf to a fight between two mature animals. Includes some humorous touches which make the film even more enjoyable.

The Catch. 17 ½ min.; color. Purchase $200; rental $15. Purchase: National Film Board of Canada. Rental: Contemporary/McGraw Hill Films
Depicts how some caribou in the subarctic area of Quebec province are rounded up and tranquilized for transport to Cape Breton Highlands National Park as part of a restocking project.

Death of a Legend. 50 min.; color. Purchase $550; rental $30. 1971. National Film Board of Canada
Tells how wolves have been often maligned in the past, and how, in spite of research into wolf behavior, many people have unfounded hatred of the species. Reveals that wolves continue to be the target of bounty hunters, and they are close to becoming extinct in North America.

The Empty Nest. 20 min.; color. Purchase $210. 1972. Jonathan Kress
Deals with the threat posed by DDT and other insecticides to the osprey, a species of bird whose reproductive capacity has been impaired by chemicals.

Endless Chain. 28 min,; color. Purchase $75; free loan. 1971. U.S. Atomic Energy Commission
Surprisingly, this film about wildlife conservation is sponsored by the Atomic Energy Commission. The first part is devoted to the links between predators and prey. The second half presents work being done on animal behavior at the AEC's wildlife preserve called Arid Lands Ecology.

The Farm. 28 min.; color. Free loan. Modern Talking Picture Service, Inc.
Depicts Remington Farm in Maryland—a working farm that is also devoted to preservation of wildlife. Reveals that the farm is owned by the Remington Arms Company, and is carefully managed to protect all its natural inhabitants.

Follow the Wind to Cousin. 19 ½ min.; color. Purchase $285; free loan. 1969. Association-Sterling Films
Depicts Cousin, an island in the Indian Ocean, which as a bird sanctuary, is host to a number of bird species that are either rare or now unknown in other parts of the world.

The Grizzly Bear—A Case Study in Field Research. 22 min.; color. Purchase $265; rental $14. 1967. Films Inc.
Depicts attempts to save grizzly bears from extinction. Emphasizes research on the behavior and needs of grizzlies, so that wildlife experts can develop effective programs to encourage proliferation of this native North American species.

Insect Eaters. 10 min.; color. Purchase $135; rental $8. International Film Bureau, Inc.
Compares and contrasts three insect eaters: the hedgehog, the mole, and the shrew. Illustrates these animals effects on man—some are harmful, such as crop destruction, and some are beneficial, such as consuming insect pests.

Is the Fox Really Sly? 21 min.; color. Purchase $285; rental $25. 1970. Contemporary/McGraw Hill Films
Describes the ecosystem and the interaction within it of various species.

The Losers. 30 min.; color. Purchase $300; rental $30. Time-Life Films
Deals with the relationship between man and horse. Speculates on what the future role of the horse will be, since it is no longer essential as a means of transportation.

Man's Thumb on Nature's Balance. 51 min.; color. Purchase $500; rental $25. 1971. NBC Educational Enterprises
Offers an unpleasant but apparently true thesis—that the slaughter of some animals is necessary to control animal populations. Reveals that if man had never interfered with nature, such limited killing would probably not be necessary, but man has not left nature as he found it. Produced for NBC News.

Nature's Engineer, The Beaver. 10 min.; color. Purchase $135; rental $8. International Film Bureau, Inc.
Examines how well-adapted the beaver is to his task of dam building. Also discusses the advantages the beaver's dams offer to other wildlife: the water stored by the dams is a resource for fish and game, and the dams additionally act to inhibit soil erosion.

Prairie Killers. 30 min.; color. Purchase $315; rental $11.50. 1970. Indiana Univ. Audio-Visual Center

Explores the ways in which man has contributed to the decline of the native inhabitants of the prairie: buffalo, prairie dogs, coyotes, and mountain lions.

The Return of the Nene. 9 min.; color. Purchase $135. 1967. Sterling Educational Films

Describes the successful repopulation of the nene, a Hawaiian wild goose. In 1950, there were only thirty-six nenes in existence. Captive nenes from Britain were returned to their natural habitat in Hawaii, where they have slowly increased in number, assuring the continuation of the species.

S.O.S. Galapagos. 20 min.; color. Purchase $200; rental $8.50. 1965. Contemporary/McGraw Hill Films

Tells how a number of species of animals that naturally inhabit the Galapagos Islands have been endangered by man, who has killed many of the animals for their meat and skins. Discusses how The Charles Darwin Foundation is now trying to save the remaining animals.

Say Goodbye. 52 min.; color. Purchase $500; rental $25. 1970. Films Inc.

Takes a straightforward look at how man has contributed to the extinction of more than 150 species in the last fifty years. Discusses the difference between man killing animals for profit, and animals killing one another in the natural struggle for survival. Also relates the dangers of chemicals in the environment to wildlife with similar dangers for man.

So Little Time. 29 min.; color. Free loan. U.S. Dept. of the Interior, Bureau of Sport Fisheries and Wildlife

Focuses primarily on birds. Also how man's alterations in the natural environment have threatened the survival of many species. Presents interviews with naturalist Roger Torrey Peterson to communicate the need to preserve wildlife.

Survival of the Kit Fox: A Conservation Case Study. 13 ½ min.; color. Purchase $155; rental $12. 1968. Journal Films, Inc.

Explores the demise of the kit fox, an animal that lives on the American prairie. Reveals that the kit fox is being killed off by pesticides sprayed on crops. Ironically, the fox is instrumental in controlling other animals that feed on the crops.

Vanishing Birds. 11 min.; color. Purchase $100; rental $10. 1968. Pictura Films Distribution Corp.

Describes the condor of California, preserved in an obscure valley in California.

Waterfowl: A Resource in Danger. 17 min.; color and b&w. Purchase c $200, b&w $102.50; rental c $9, b&w $5.50. 1966. Encyclopaedia Britannica Educational Corp.

Examines the conflict between farmers of the Canadian prairie and waterfowl that live there. Shows how the farmers are altering the fowl's habitats to increase arable land, and the fowl feed on crops ready for harvest. Indicates that the Canadian Wildlife Service, meanwhile, is studying the problem, hoping to solve it to the mutual satisfaction of all parties involved.

The Whale. 6 min.; color. Purchase $80; rental $10. 1971. Ron Finne

Basically tells about dynamiting a dead, beached whale. Includes statistics on the number of remaining whales in each species.

White Splendor. 11 min.; color. Purchase $100; rental $10. 1968. Pictura Film Distribution Corp.

Considers the factors that threaten the continued existence of the American egret, including such diverse activities as real estate development and the manufacture of women's hats.

Wild Wings. 35 min.; color. Purchase $325; rental $17.50. 1967. International Film Bureau, Inc.

Tells about the Wildfowl Trust at Slimbridge, England, where 122 species of wildfowl have been identified. Examines methods used by researchers at the trust to study the birds. The 1967 Academy Award winner for best live action short.

Wolves and the Wolf Men. 52 min.; color. Purchase $500; rental $25. 1970. Films Inc.

Covers many aspects of wolves, including myths surrounding the species, behavior, and problems of wolf eradication programs. Also discusses studies of wolf-pack behavior.

A Wonderful Bird Was the Pelican. 26 min.; color. Purchase $250. 1970. United Productions of America

Tells how pesticides in the environment have contributed to the near extinction of the brown pelican. Explains that DDT accumulates in the food chain, eventually reaching high enough concentrations in the pelican to affect its reproduction.

FILM DISTRIBUTORS

ABC Media Concepts
1330 Ave. of the Americas, New York, N.Y. 10019

ACI Films, Inc.
35 W. 45 St., New York, N.Y. 10036

Aetna Life and Casualty, Audio Visual Services
151 Farmington Ave., Hartford, Conn. 06115

American Documentary Films, Inc.
336 W. 84 St., New York, N.Y. 10024

American Educational Films
331 N. Maple Dr., Beverly Hills, Calif. 90210

American Iron and Steel Institute
1000 16 St. N.W., Washington, D.C. 20036

American Petroleum Institute
1801 K St. N.W., Washington, D.C. 20006

Association-Sterling Films
866 3 Ave., New York, N.Y. 10022

Atlantic Richfield Co., Public Relations
717 5 Ave., New York, N.Y. 10022

BP North America, Inc.
620 5 Ave., New York, N.Y. 10020

BFA Educational Media
2211 Michigan Ave., Santa Monica, Calif. 90404

BNA Communications, Inc., The Bureau of National Affairs
5615 Fishers La., Rockville, Md. 20852

Benchmark Films, Inc.
145 Scarborough Rd., Briarcliff Manor, N.Y. 10510

Bitterroot Films, Inc.
511 River St., Missoula, Mont. 59801

Byron Motion Pictures, Inc.
65 K St. N.E., Washington, D.C. 20002

CCM Films, Inc.
32 MacQuestern Pkwy. S., Mt. Vernon, N.Y. 10550

Carousel Films, Inc.
1501 Broadway, New York, N.Y. 10036

Center for Mass Communication of Columbia Univ. Press
562 W. 113 St., New York, N.Y. 10025

Centron Educational Films
1821 W. 9 St., Lawrence, Kans. 66044

Churchill Films
662 N. Robertson Blvd., Los Angeles, Calif. 90069

Cinema Associate Productions, Inc.
Box 621, East Lansing, Mich. 48823

Commonwealth Film Distributors
Bldg. 6-K, 1440 S. State College Blvd., Anaheim, Calif. 92806

Conservation Foundation
1717 Massachusetts Ave. N.W., Washington, D.C. 20036

Contemporary/McGraw Hill Films
1221 Ave. of the Americas, New York, N.Y. 10020

Cornell Univ. Films, Film Library
New York State Col. of Agriculture and Human Ecology, Cornell Univ. Ithaca, N.Y. 14850

Coronet Instructional Films
65 E. S. Water St., Chicago, Ill. 60601

Creative Film Society
7237 Canby Ave., Reseda, Calif. 91335

Deere & Co., Audio-Visual Section
John Deere Rd., Moline, Ill. 61265

Walt Disney Educational Materials Co.
800 Sonora Ave., Glendale, Calif. 91201

Doubleday Multimedia
1371 Reynolds Ave., Box 11607, Santa Ana, Calif. 92705

Encyclopaedia Britannica Educational Corp.
425 N. Michigan Ave., Chicago, Ill. 60611

Enterprise Productions, Inc.
1019 Belmont Pl. E., Seattle, Wash. 98102

Environmental Educators, Inc.
732 7 St. N.W., Washington, D.C. 20006

Ethyl Corp., Corporate Public Relations Dept.
330 S. 4 St., Richmond, Va. 23219

Federal Aviation Administration, Film Library AC-44.5
Box 25082, Oklahoma City, Okla. 73125

Film Co.
224 W. Franklin Ave., Minneapolis, Minn. 55404

Films for Social Change
6244 Delmar Blvd., St. Louis, Mo. 63130

Films Inc.
1144 Wilmette Ave., Wilmette, Ill. 60091

Stuart Finley Inc.
3428 Mansfield Rd., Falls Church, Va. 22041

Ron Finne
Rte. 1, Box 43, Springfield, Oreg. 97477

General Electric Educational Films
Bldg. 705, Corporations Pk., Scotia, N.Y. 12302

General Services Administration, National Archives and Records Service
National Audiovisual Center, Washington, D.C. 20409

Grove Press Film Div.
53 E. 11 St., New York, N.Y. 10003

Handel Film Corp.
8730 Sunset Blvd., West Hollywood, Calif. 90069

Alfred Higgins Productions
9100 Sunset Blvd., Los Angeles, Calif. 90069

Holt, Rinehart and Winston, Inc., Media Dept.
383 Madison Ave., New York, N.Y. 10017

Indiana Univ. Audio-Visual Center
Bloomington, Ind. 47401

International Film Bureau, Inc.
332 S. Michigan Ave., Chicago, Ill. 60604

Interstate Oil Compact Commission
Box 53127, Oklahoma City, Okla. 73105

Journal Films, Inc.
909 W. Diversey Pkwy., Chicago, Ill. 60614

Jonathan Kress Kerulos Films, Inc.
1020 5 Ave., New York, N.Y. 10028

Learning Corp. of America
711 5 Ave., New York, N.Y. 10022

Marathon Oil Co.
539 S. Main St., Findlay, Ohio 45840

Mass Media Associates
2116 N. Charles St., Baltimore, Md. 21218

Media for Urban Environment
75 Frost St., Brooklyn, N.Y. 11211

Modern Talking Picture Service, Inc.
2323 New Hyde Park Rd., New Hyde Park, N.Y. 11040

Motor Vehicle Manufacturers Assn., Inc.
320 New Center Bldg., Detroit, Mich. 48202

NBC Educational Enterprises
30 Rockefeller Plaza, New York, N.Y. 10020

National Audubon Society
950 3 Ave., New York, N.Y. 10022

National Council of Churches, Broadcasting and Film Commission
475 Riverside Dr., New York, N.Y. 10027

National Film Board of Canada
1251 Ave. of the Americas, New York, N.Y. 10020

National Oceanic and Atmospheric Administration, U.S. Dept. of Commerce
12231 Wilkins Ave., Rockville, Md. 20852

National Park Service Bookstore, Harpers Ferry Historical Assn.
Box 147, Harpers Ferry, W. Va. 25425

National Tuberculosis and Respiratory Assn.
1740 Broadway, New York, N.Y. 10019

New York Univ. Film Library
26 Washington Pl., New York, N.Y. 10003

North American Films, Inc.
Box 919, Tarzana, Calif. 91356

Northern Illinois Univ. Film Library
Dekalb, Ill. 60115

Perennial Education, Inc.
1825 Willow Rd., Box 236, Northfield, Ill. 60093

Petroleum Equipment Suppliers Assn.
1703 First National Bank Bldg., Houston, Tex. 77002

Pictura Films Distribution Corp.
43 W. 16 St., New York, N.Y. 10011

Planned Parenthood-World Population, Film Library
267 W. 25 St., New York, N.Y. 10001

Portland Cement Assn.
Old Orchard Rd., Skokie, Ill. 60076

Pyramid Films
Box 1048, Santa Monica, Calif. 90406

Jon Royer
10900 S. Airport Rd., DeWitt, Mich. 48820

Ruder and Finn, Inc.
110 E. 59 St., New York, N.Y. 10022

Shell Film Library
450 N. Meridian St., Indianapolis, Ind. 46204

Bill Snyder Films, Inc.
Box 2784, Fargo, N. Dak. 58102

Sterling Educational Films
241 E. 34 St., New York, N.Y. 10016

Summit Films, Inc.
538 E. Alameda Ave., Denver, Colo. 80209

Tennessee Valley Authority, Film Services
Knoxville, Tenn. 37902

Texture Films, Inc.
1600 Broadway, New York, N.Y. 10019

Time-Life Films
43 W. 16 St., New York, N.Y. 10011

Trans-World Films, Inc.
332 S. Michigan Ave., Chicago, Ill. 60604

United Productions of America
488 Madison Ave., New York, N.Y. 10022

U.S. Air Force Film Library
Norton Air Force Base, Calif. 92409

U.S. Atomic Energy Commission, Film Library-TIC
Box 62, Oak Ridge, Tenn. 37830

U.S. Dept. of Agriculture, Office of Information, Motion Picture Service
Washington, D.C. 20250

U.S. Dept. of the Interior, Bureau of Mines
4800 Forbes Ave., Pittsburgh, Pa. 15213

U.S. Dept. of the Interior, Bureau of Reclamation, Film Management Center
Bldg. 67, Denver Federal Center, Denver, Colo. 80225

U.S. Dept. of the Interior, Bureau of Sport Fisheries and Wildlife
Washington, D.C. 20240

U.S. Environmental Protection Agency, Office of Public Affairs
Washington, D.C. 20460

Universal Education and Visual Arts
221 Park Ave. S., New York, N.Y. 10003

Univ. of Michigan Television Center
310 Maynard St., Ann Arbor, Mich. 48108

Univ. of Southern California, Div. of Cinema
University Park, Los Angeles, Calif. 90007

Univ. of Wisconsin Films, Bureau of Audio-Visual Instruction
University Extension, Box 2093, Madison, Wisc. 53701

John Wiley & Sons, Inc.
605 3 Ave., New York, N.Y. 10016

Swain Wolf Southern Baptist Convention, Radio and TV Committee
511 River St., Missoula, Mont. 54801

Xerox Films
Stamford, Conn. 06904

13 Newspapers, Television, and Radio

The three sections in this chapter are intended primarily for individuals or groups interested in disseminating environmental information. The listings include the name or names of persons it would be most helpful to contact at each media outlet. Wherever possible, the names of environmental reporters or editors are included. An alternative is to list the names of science writers or editors. If no such position exists, the names of the city editor, general manager, program manager or director, and/or the news director are supplied.

A word of caution: most news people are swamped by the number of press releases they receive daily. A person or group that wants its important news to be reported should not bother the media by reporting unimportant events. The best way to get acceptance of stories is to get to know the local reporter, find out what kinds of information he or she is interested in and what form is preferred: i.e., written, audiotape, or in-person reports.

In this chapter, the entries include the following information: the name of the outlet; the network affiliation, if any; address and telephone number; the circulation of the newspapers; and whom to contact. Very few environmental or science writers are listed for the radio and television stations because the media do not ordinarily assign a particular individual to cover environmental topics. Media were selected for inclusion because they serve large populations geographically distributed across the country. The listings include for each state approximately two newspapers, one television station, and one radio station.

In most cases, the television and radio stations chosen serve several metropolitan areas, and in some cases these regions are in more than one state. For this reason, the listings are organized on a regional rather than a state-by-state basis. All newspapers and television and radio stations are listed alphabetically within the geographical regions. The following seven regional divisions are used:

New England States: Connecticut, Maine, Massachusetts, New Hampshire, Rhode Island, Vermont.

Middle Atlantic States: Delaware, District of Columbia, Maryland, New Jersey, New York, Pennsylvania.

Southeastern States: Alabama, Florida, Georgia, Kentucky, Mississippi, North Carolina, South Carolina, Tennessee, Virginia, West Virginia.

Midwestern States: Illinois, Indiana, Iowa, Kansas, Michigan, Minnesota, Missouri, Nebraska, North Dakota, Ohio, South Dakota, Wisconsin.

South Central States: Arkansas, Louisiana, Oklahoma, Texas.

Rocky Mountain States: Arizona, Colorado, Idaho, Montana, Nevada, New Mexico, Utah, Wyoming.

Pacific States: Alaska, California, Hawaii, Oregon, Washington.

NEWSPAPERS

New England States

The Bangor News
491 Main St., Bangor, Maine 04402
207-942-4881
Circulation: 77,625
City Editor: Kalil Ayoob

The Boston Globe
135 Morrissey Blvd., Boston, Mass. 02107
617-288-8000
Circulation: 417,318
Science Editor: Victor McElheny

Burlington Free Press
187 College St., Burlington, Vt. 05401
802-863-3441
Circulation: 45,842
Editor: Gordon T. Mills

The Christian Science Monitor
1 Norway St., Boston, Mass. 02115
617-262-2300
Circulation: 213,970
Science writers: Robert Cowen, David F. Salisbury

The Hartford Courant
285 Broad St., Hartford, Conn. 06101
203-249-6411
Circulation: 170,119
Science Reporter: David Rhinelander

The Manchester Union Leader and News
35 Amherst St., Manchester, N.H. 03105
603-668-4321
Circulation: 63,047
City Editor: Walter Healy

The New Haven Register
367 Orange St., New Haven, Conn. 06503
203-562-1121
Circulation: 107,267
City Editor: Francis Whalen

Portland Press Herald and Maine Sunday Telegram
390 Congress St., Portland, Maine 04104
207-775-5811
Circulation: 167,848 combined
Environmental Reporter: Robert C. Cummings

The Providence Bulletin
75 Fountain St., Providence, R.I. 02902
401-277-7000
Circulation: 145,480
City Editor: James V. Wyman

The Springfield News
1860 Maine St., Springfield, Mass. 01101
413-787-2411
Circulation: 91,519
City Editor: James R. Powers

The Worcester Gazette
20 Franklin St., Worcester, Mass. 01613
617-755-4321
Circulation: 91,429
Science Editor: Francis E. Tobin
Environmental Reporter: Everett M. Skenan

Middle Atlantic States

Asbury Park Press
Press Plaza, Asbury Park, N.J. 07712
201-741-5400
Circulation: 64,530
Environment Columnist: Jacqueline Alban

Associated Press (News Service)
50 Rockefeller Plaza, New York, N.Y. 10020
212-262-4000
Circulation: International News Service
Science Editor: Alton Blakeslee

The Baltimore News American
Lombard and South Sts., Baltimore, Md. 21202
301-752-1212
Circulation: 204,702
Science Editor: Joann Rodgers

The Buffalo Courier-Express
787 Main St., Buffalo, N.Y. 14240
716-847-5377
Circulation: 135,215
City Editor: Scott Hayden

The Delaware State News
Box 737, Dover, Del. 19901
302-674-3600
Circulation: 20,630
Editor: Joel D. Smith

Enterprise Science Service
230 Park Ave., New York, N.Y. 10017
212-679-3600
Circulation: International News Service
Science Editor: David Hendin

The Evening Star
225 Virginia Ave. S.E., Washington, D.C. 20003
202-484-5000
Circulation: 301,508
Ecology Reporter: Roberta Hornig

New York Daily News
220 E. 42 St., New York, N.Y. 10017
212-682-1234
Circulation: 2,103,363
Environmental Editor: Robert Carroll

New York Post
210 South St., New York, N.Y. 10002
212-349-5000
Circulation: 702,640
Science Writer: Barbara Yuncker
Environmental Reporter: Steve Lawrence

New York Times
229 W. 43 St., New York, N.Y. 10036
212-556-1234
Circulation: 814,290
National Environmental Correspondent: Gladwin Hill
Local Environmental Reporter: David Bird

The Newark Star-Ledger
Court and Plane Sts., Newark, N.J. 07101
201-877-4040
Circulation: 293,907
City Editor: Walter Healy
Environment Editor: Gordon Bishop

The Philadelphia Bulletin
30 and Market Sts., Philadelphia, Pa. 19101
215-662-7219
Circulation: 640,780
Science Writer: Karl Abraham

The Pittsburgh Press
34 Boulevard of the Allies, Pittsburgh, Pa. 15230
412-263-1100
Circulation: 341,118
Conservation Editor: Fred Jones

The Rochester Times-Union
55 Exchange St., Rochester, N.Y. 14614
716-232-7100
Circulation: 140,248
Ecology Reporter: Graham Cox

Scranton Times
Penn Ave. at Spruce St., Scranton, Pa. 18501
717-342-9151
Circulation: 53,540

Managing Editor: Ed Donohoe
Environment Reporter: Car Kearney

United Press International
220 E. 42 St., New York, N.Y. 10017
212-MU 2-0400
Circulation: International News Service
Science Editor: Al Rossiter, Jr.

The Washington Post
1150 15 St. N.W., Washington, D.C. 20005
202-223-6000
Circulation: 486,420
Science Editor: Victor Cohn
Assistant Managing Editor for Metropolitan News: Harry M. Rosenfeld

SOUTHEASTERN STATES

The Atlanta Constitution
72 Marietta St., Atlanta, Ga. 30302
404-522-5050
Circulation: 211,202
Science Editor: Jeff Nesmith

The Birmingham Post-Herald
2200 4 Ave. N., Birmingham, Ala. 35202
205-325-2222
Science Editor: Leonard Chamblee

The Charleston News and Courier
134 Columbus St., Charleston, S.C. 29402
803-722-5522
Circulation: 65,582
Science Editor: Walter Cruz

The Charlotte Observer
600 S. Tryon St., Charlotte, N.C. 28201
704-374-7391
Circulation: 174,870
Metropolitan Editor: Matt Taylor

The Clarion-Ledger
Jackson, Miss. 39205
601-353-2421
Circulation: 58,585
City Editor: Charles G. Smith, Jr.
Environment Reporter: Miriam May

The Commercial Appeal
495 Union Ave., Memphis, Tenn. 38101
901-526-8811
Circulation: 217,496
Managing Editor: William Sorrels
Science Editor: Ida Clemens

Fort Lauderdale News
101 N. New River Dr. E., Fort Lauderdale, Fla. 33302
305-527-4311
Circulation: 88,200
Environment Writer: Patricia A. Toner

The Huntington-Advertiser
Huntington, W. Va. 25720
304-696-5678
Circulation: 16,557
City Editor: Charles H. Tucker

Huntsville Times
2317 S. Memorial Pkwy., Huntsville, Ala. 35807
205-534-2411
Circulation 54,570
Science Reporter: Barry Casebat

The Knoxville Journal
208 W. Church Ave., Knoxville, Tenn. 37901
615-522-4141
Circulation: 65,020
City Editor: Tom Sweeten

The Lexington Herald and *The Herald-Leader*
237 W. Short St., Lexington, Ky. 40507
606-254-6666
Circulation: 132,368
City Editor: Andrew Eckdahl

Louisville Courier-Journal and Times
525 W. Broadway, Louisville, Ky. 40202
502-582-4011
Circulation: 402,020
Environment Writers: David Ross Stevens, James A. Schwartz

The Miami Herald
1 Herald Plaza, Miami, Fla. 33101
305-350-2667
Circulation: 400,000
Environment writer: Michael F. Toner

The Mobile Press and *Press Register*
304 Government St., Box 2488, Mobile, Ala. 36602
Circulation: 151,565 combined
City Editor: Maurice Castle

The Norfolk Ledger-Star
150 W. Brambleton Ave., Norfolk, Va. 23501
703-625-1431
Circulation: 103,574
Science Editor: Richard B. Bayor

The Raleigh News and Observer
215 S. McDowell St., Raleigh, N.C. 27601
919-832-4411
Circulation: 130,763
Science Editor: Leslie Wayne

The Richmond News Leader
333 E. Grace St., Richmond, Va. 23219
703-649-6000
Circulation: 118,410
Science Editor: Alberta Cliborne

The St. Petersburg Times
Box 1121, St. Petersburg, Fla. 33731
813-894-1111
Circulation: 148,110
City Editor: Laurence Jolidon
Environment Reporter: Christopher Cubbison

Winston-Salem Journal
416-420 N. Marshall St., Winston-Salem, N.C. 27102
919-725-2311
Circulation: 78,400
Staff Reporter: Thomas M. Dillon

MIDWESTERN STATES

The Argus Leader
200 S. Minnesota Ave., Sioux Fall, S. Dak. 57102
605-336-1130
Circulation: 49,608
City Editor: Lloyd Noteboom

Capital Times
115 S. Carroll St., Madison, Wis. 53701
608-255-1611
Circulation: 45,445
Editor: Lawrence Fitzpatrick
Environmental Reporter: Whitney Gould

Chicago Sun-Times
401 N. Wabash Ave., Chicago, Ill. 60611
312-321-2525
Circulation: 531,086
Science Editor: William Hines
Environment Editor: Bruce Ingersoll

Chicago Tribune
Tribune Square, Chicago, Ill. 60611
312-222-3531
Circulation: 728,760
Ecology Editor: Casey Bukro

Cincinnati Post and Times-Star
800 Broadway, Cincinnati, Ohio 45202
513-721-1111
Circulation: 236,670
Environment Writer: Richard F. Gibeau

The Des Moines Tribune
715 Locust St., Des Moines, Iowa 50304
515-284-8000
Circulation: 106,435
City Editor: James B. Cooney

The Detroit Free Press
321 Lafayette Blvd. W., Detroit, Mich. 48231
313-222-6583
Circulation: 574,431
Environment Writer: Gary Blonston

The Detroit News
615 Lafayette Blvd., Detroit, Mich. 48231
313-222-2000
Circulation: 650,180
Environmental Writer: James Kerwin

The Duluth News-Tribune
424 W. 1 St., Duluth, Minn. 55801
218-722-8333
Circulation: 55,735
Ecology Reporter: Les Ormandy

The Evansville Courier
201 N.W. 2 St., Evansville, Ind. 47701
812-424-7711
Circulation: 65,786
City Editor: Phil Jeffries

The Fargo Forum-Moorehead News
101 5 St. N., Box 2020, Fargo, N. Dak. 58102
701-235-7311
Circulation: 60,755
City Editor: Cal Olson

The Flint Journal
200 E. 1 St., Flint, Mich. 48502
313-234-7611
Circulation: 113,303
Outdoor Editor: Kenneth L. Peterson
Science Editor: Christine O. Divelbiss

The Indianapolis Star
307 N. Pennsylvania St., Indianapolis, Ind. 46206
317-633-1240
Circulation: 233,979
Environment Editor: Billy N. Scifres

The Kalamazoo Gazette
401 S. Burdick St., Kalamazoo, Mich. 49003
616-345-3511
Circulation: 60,000
Environment Writer: Thomas C. Stersic

The Kansas City Star
1729 Grand Ave., Kansas City, Mo. 64108
816-421-1200
Circulation: 314,706
City Editor: Tom Eblen

The Lincoln Journal and *Journal-Star*
926 P St., Lincoln, Nebr. 68501
402-432-3331
Circulation: 107,471 combined
City Editor: Bill Kreifel
Environment Reporter: Harold Simmons

The Milwaukee Sentinel
918 N. 4 St., Milwaukee, Wis. 53201
414-224-2151
Circulation: 169,050
Medical-Science Reporter: Dan Patrines

Minneapolis Tribune
427 Portland Ave. S., Minneapolis, Minn. 55415
612-372-4141
Circulation: 240,467
Environmental Reporter: Dean Rebuffoni

The Morning Star
97 E. State St., Rockford, Ill. 61105
815-962-4433
Circulation: 85,410
Environment Writer: Ben Rubendall

The Omaha World-Herald
14 and Dodge Sts., Omaha, Nebr. 68102
402-341-0300
Circulation: 128,613
Ecology Editor: Fred Thomas

The Peoria Evening Journal Star
War Memorial Dr., 1 News Plaza, Peoria, Ill. 61601
309-688-2411
Circulation: 60,830
Environment Editor: Tom Edwards

The Plain Dealer
1801 Superior Ave., Cleveland, Ohio 44114
216-523-4500
Circulation: 409,935
Ecology Editor: William D. McCann, Jr.

Rapid City Daily Journal
507 Main St., Rapid City, S. Dak. 57701
605-342-0280

Circulation: 32,148
City Editor: Jack Weaver
Natural Resources Writer: Dick Rebbeck

The St. Louis Post-Dispatch
1133 Franklin Ave., St. Louis, Mo. 63101
314-621-1111
Circulation: 320,611
Environment Editor: Bob Posen

St. Paul Dispatch
55 E. 4 St., St. Paul, Minn. 55101
612-222-5011
Circulation: 130,340
Environment and Science Reporter: Don Boxmeyer

The Sioux City Journal
5 and Douglas Sts., Sioux City, Iowa 51102
712-255-8991
Circulation: 68,513
Managing Editor: Kenneth Sanders

Toledo Blade
541 Superior St., Toledo, Ohio 43604
419-259-6000
Circulation: 174,610
Science Editor: Michael Woods

The Topeka Capital and *The Capital Journal*
6 and Jefferson Sts., Topeka, Kans. 66607
913-357-4421
Circulation: 132,389 combined
Science Editor: C. J. Petterson

The Wichita Eagle and Beacon
825 E. Douglas St., Wichita, Kans. 67201
316-268-6000
Circulation: 140,940
Business Writer: Marvin Barnes

SOUTH CENTRAL STATES

Arkansas Democrat
Capitol Ave. and Scott St., Little Rock, Ark. 72201
501-374-0321
Circulation: 75,960
Environment Writer: R. O'Neal

The Daily Oklahoman
Box 25125, Oklahoma City, Okla. 73125
405-232-3311
Circulation: 178,303
City Editor: Edward F. Montgomery
Environment Editor: Bryce Patterson

The Dallas News
Communications Center, Dallas, Tex. 75222
214-747-4611
Circulation: 255,491
Science Editor: Douglas Domeier
Ecology Reporter: Dorothy Erwin

Enterprise Science News/Universal Science News (Services)
314 W. Commerce, Tomball, Tex. 77375
713-351-5448
Circulation: International News Service
Contributing Editor: William J. Cromie

Fort Worth Star-Telegram
400 W. 7 St., Fort Worth, Tex. 76101
817-336-9271
Circulation: 100,260
Assistant City Editor: Louis W. Hudson
General Assignment Reporter: Glenn Dromgoole

Lubbock Avalanche-Journal
8 St. and Ave. J, Lubbock, Tex. 79408
806-763-4343
Circulation: 62,423
Science Writer: Lewis Ray Westbrook

The New Orleans Times-Picayune
3800 Howard Ave., New Orleans, La. 70140
504-521-7325
Circulation: 202,061
Science Editor: Podine Schoenberger

The Shreveport Times
222 Lake St., Shreveport, La. 71102
318-423-4113
Circulation: 90,370
Managing Editor: Allan Lazarus

The Tulsa World
315 S. Boulder Ave., Tulsa, Okla. 74102
918-583-2161
Circulation: 112,539
Science Editor: Chuck Wheat

ROCKY MOUNTAIN STATES

The Albuquerque Journal
Box J-T, Albuquerque, N. Mex. 87103
505-842-2300
Circulation: 66,299
City Editor: Bern Ganther

The Arizona Republic
120 E. Van Buren St., Phoenix, Ariz. 85004

602-271-8000
Circulation: 177,855
Science Editor: Clarence Bailey
Ecology Editor: Walter W. Meek

The Billings Gazette
401 N. Broadway, Billings, Mont. 59103
406-245-3071
Circulation: 54,618
City Editor: Charles Rightmire

The Denver Post
650 15 St., Denver, Colo. 80201
303-297-1010
Circulation: 250,990
Science Editor: Gene Lindberg
Environment Editor: Dick Prouty

The Deseret News
34 E. 1 St. S., Salt Lake City, Utah 84111
801-524-4400
Circulation: 82,190
Environment Editor: Joseph M. Bauman

The Idaho Statesman
300 N. 6 St., Boise, Idaho 83702
208-376-2121
Circulation: 54,307
City Editor: Steve Ahrens

The Las Vegas Review-Journal
Box 70, Las Vegas, Nev. 89101
702-385-4241
Circulation: 55,538
City Editor: Roy Vanett

The Rocky Mountain News
400 W. Colfax Ave., Denver, Colo. 80204
303-892-5000
Circulation: 205,415
City Editor: Richard L. Thomas

Salt Lake Tribune
143 S. Main St., Salt Lake City, Utah 84101
801-524-4545
Circulation: 106,470
Medical-Science Editor: Barbara Springer

The Tucson Daily Citizen
208 N. Stone St., Box 5027, Tucson, Ariz. 85703
602-622-5855
Circulation: 55,238
Science Editor: Jay Hall

Wyoming State Tribune
Cheyenne, Wyo. 82001
307-634-3361
Circulation: 9,630
Editor: Warren W. Hoefer

PACIFIC STATES

The Anchorage Times
820 4 Ave., Anchorage, Alaska 99501
907-279-5622
Circulation: 37,601
Managing Editor: William J. Tobin

The Honolulu Star Bulletin
605 Kapiolani Blvd., Honolulu, Hawaii 96813
808-536-7222
Circulation: 124,601
Editor: A. A. Smyser

The Los Angeles Times
Times-Mirror Sq., Los Angeles, Calif. 90053
213-625-2345
Circulation: 981,661
Science Editor: George Getze

Oregon Journal
1320 S.W. Broadway, Portland, Oreg. 97201
503-222-5511
Circulation: 137,960
Environment Writer: Dean Smith

San Francisco Chronicle
905 Mission St., San Francisco, Calif. 94103
415-421-1111
Circulation: 457,275
Science Editor: David Perlman

Seattle Post-Intelligencer
6 and Wall Sts., Seattle, Wash. 98121
206-622-2000
Circulation: 203,060
Environmental Writer: Dick Young

Seattle Times
Fairview Ave. N. and John, Seattle, Wash. 98111
206-622-0300
Circulation: 252,330
Science Editor: Hill Williams

South Bay Daily Breeze
5215 Torrance Blvd., Torrance, Calif. 90509
213-370-5511
Circulation: 63,089
Environmental Writer: Jon F. Thompson

The Spokesman-Review
927 Riverside Ave., Spokane, Wash. 99210

509-624-3321
Circulation: 83,640
Environment Reporter: Kent Swigard

Tacoma News Tribune
711 Saint Helens Ave., Tacoma, Wash. 98401
206-597-8511
Circulation: 102,547
Manager: Charles O. Ellsworth

TELEVISION STATIONS

NEW ENGLAND STATES

WABI-TV, ch. 5 (CBS)
35 Hildreth St., Bangor, Maine 04401
207-947-8321
News Director: Ralph Lowe

WCAX-TV, ch. 3 (CBS)
Box 608, Burlington, Vt. 05401
802-862-5761
General Manager: Stuart T. Martin
News Director: Richard Gallagher

WGBH-TV, ch. 2 (PBS)
125 Weston Ave., Allston, Mass.
617-868-3800
Executive Producer, Science Program Group: Mike Ambrosino

WRLH, ch. 31 (NBC)
The Mall, Lebanon, N.H. 03755
603-448-4550
General Manager: Theodore E. Nixon
News Director: Fred Burnham

WTEV, ch. 6 (ABC)
TV Center, New Bedford, Mass. 02741
617-993-2651
Program Manager: Peter L. Mandell
News Director: Truman Taylor

WTIC, ch. 3 (CBS)
Broadcast House, 3 Constitution Plaza, Hartford, Conn. 06115
203-525-0801
General Manager: Robert S. Tyrol
Environmental Director: Bill Clede

WWLP, ch. 22 (NBC)
Box 2210, Springfield, Mass. 01101
413-786-2200

General Manager: William L. Putnam
Program Manager: Robert F. Donahue

MIDDLE ATLANTIC STATES

ABC Network
1130 Ave. of the Americas, New York, N.Y. 10019
212-581-7777
Science Editor: Jules Bergman

CBS Network
51 W. 52 St., New York, N.Y. 10019
212-765-4321
National Editor: Peter Sturtevent

KYW-TV, ch. 3 (NBC)
1619 Walnut St., Philadelphia, Pa. 19103
215-564-3700
General Manager: Alan J. Bell
Program Manager: Jim Sieger

NBC Network
30 Rockefeller Plaza, New York, N.Y. 10020
212-247-8300
Science Editor: Earl Ubell

Public Broadcasting System
955 L'Enfant Plaza S.W., Washington, D.C. 20024
202-484-1500
Program Director: Chick Cherkazian

WBEN-TV, ch. 4 (CBS)
2077 Elmwood Ave., Buffalo, N.Y. 14207
716-876-0930
General Manager: Leslie G. Arries, Jr.
News Director: Bernard Rotman

WJZ-TV, ch. 13 (ABC)
TV Hill, Baltimore, Md. 21211
301-466-0013
General Manager: Steve Seymour
Program Manager: William W. Hillier

WMAL-TV, ch. 7 (ABC)
4461 Connecticut Ave. N.W., Washington, D.C. 20008
202-686-3000
General Manager: Richard S. Stakes
Public Affairs Director: Len Deibert

WNET-TV, ch. 13 (PBS)
304 W. 58 St., New York, N.Y. 10019
212-262-4200
Science Editor: David Prowitt

334 Newspapers, Television, and Radio

SOUTHEASTERN STATES

WALA-TV, ch. 10 (NBC)
Box 1548, Mobile, Ala. 36601
205-433-3754
General Manager: H. Ray McGuire
Environment Reporter: Gary Mitchell

WDEF-TV, ch. 12 (CBS)
3300 Broad St., Chattanooga, Tenn. 37408
615-267-3392
News Director: Dave Carlock
Environmental Reporter: Vic Gramount

WFMY-TV, ch. 2 (CBS)
Drawer 22047, Greensboro, N.C. 27420
919-274-0113
General Manager: William A. Gietz
Public Affairs Director: Dave Wright

WJXT-TV, ch. 4 (CBS)
Box 5270, Jacksonville, Fla. 32207
904-398-0501
General Manager: Robert W. Schellenberg
Director of Public Affairs: Jan Fisher

WLOX-TV, ch. 13 (ABC)
Box 4596, Biloxi, Miss. 39531
601-896-1313
General Manager: Ray Butterfield
Program Director: Steve Saucier

WPSD-TV, ch. 6 (NBC)
Box 1037, Paducah, Ky. 42001
502-442-8214
General Manger: Sam Livingston
Program Director: James E. English III

WSLS-TV, ch. 10 (NBC)
Box 2161, Roanoke, Va. 24009
703-344-9226
General Manager: Robert H. Teter
News Director: Rich Buddine

WSPA-TV, ch. 7 (CBS)
Box 1717, Spartanburg, S.C. 29301
803-585-7777
General Manager: Charles R. Sanders
News Director: Dave Handy

WTOC-TV, ch. 11 (CBS)
Box 8086, Savannah, Ga. 31402
912-232-0127
General Manager: F. Schley Knight
Program Director: Dwight J. Bruce

WTRF-TV, ch. 7 (NBC)
96 16 St., Wheeling, W. Va. 26003
304-232-7777
General Manager: Robert W. Ferguson
Program Manager: Mary Neal

MIDWESTERN STATES

KCMO-TV, ch. 5 (CBS)
125 E. 31 St., Kansas City, Mo. 64108
816-531-6789
General Manager: Charles M. McAbee
Program Director: Gene Cless

KFYR-TV, ch. 5 (NBC)
Box 1738, Bismark, N. Dak. 58501
701-223-0900
General Manager: Wes Haugen
Program Director: Merton Johnstrud

KOLN-TV, ch. 10 (CBS)
40 and W Sts., Lincoln, Nebr. 68503
402-434-8251
General Manager: A. James Ebel
Program Director: Paul Jensen

KOTA-TV, ch. 3 (NBC)
Box 1752, Rapid City, S. Dak. 57701
605-342-2000
General Manager: Helen S. Duhamel
Program Director: Dan Lesmeister

KTSB, ch. 27 (NBC)
Box 2700, Topeka, Kans. 66601
913-582-4000
General Manager: Alan B. Bennett
News Director: Harry L. Strader

KWWL-TV, ch. 7 (NBC)
500 E. 4 St., Waterloo, Iowa 50703
319-234-4401
General Manager: James Bradley
Program Director: Tim Noonan

WDIO-TV, ch. 10 (ABC)
10 Observation Rd., Duluth, Minn. 55811
218-727-6864
General Manager: Frank Befera
Program Manager: Erwin Parthe

WHIO-TV, ch. 7 (CBS)
1414 Wilmington Ave., Dayton, Ohio 45401
513-CL4-5311
General Manager: Stanley Mouse
Assignment Editor: Gil Whitney

WLUK-TV, ch. 11 (ABC)
Box 7711, Green Bay, Wis. 54303

414-494-8711
General Manager: Thomas A. Hutchinson
Program Director: Monty Stock

WMBD-TV, ch. 31 (CBS)
212 S.W. Jefferson Ave., Peoria, Ill. 61602
309-676-0711
General Manager: William L. Brown
Environmental Editor: Ron Thomas

WOTV, ch. 8 (NBC)
120 College Ave. S.E., Grand Rapids, Mich. 49502
616-459-4125
Program Director: Marv Chauvin
Environment Reporter: Jim Cummins

WPTA, ch. 21 (ABC)
3333 Butler Rd., Fort Wayne, Ind. 46808
219-483-0584
General Manager: Don Dillon
Program Manager: Kathi Nadolny

SOUTH CENTRAL STATES

KGTO-TV, ch. 36 (NBC)
Box 4097, Fayetteville, Ark. 72701
501-521-4111
General Manager and Program Director: Paul W. Milam, Jr.

KPRC-TV, ch. 2 (NBC)
Box 2222, Houston, Tex. 77001
713-622-2950
General Manager: Jack Harris
Consumer Reporter: Susan Wright

KTUL-TV, ch. 8 (ABC)
Box 8, Tulsa, Okla. 74101
918-446-3351
General Manager: Tom Goodgame
Program Director: Bob Hower

WAFB-TV, ch. 9 (CBS)
929 Government St., Baton Rouge, La. 70821
504-348-4921
General Manager: Tom E. Gibbens
Program Director: Ed Lamy

ROCKY MOUNTAIN STATES

KCRL-TV, ch. 4 (NBC)
1790 Vassar St., Reno, Nev. 89502
702-322-9145
General Manager: Charles E. Cord
News Director: Dick DeWitt

KIKI-TV, ch. 8 (NBC)
Box 2148, Idaho Falls, Idaho 83401
208-523-1171
General Manager: James M. Brady
Program Manager: Herman G. Haefle

KKTV (CBS)
Box 2110, 3100 N. Nevada Ave., Colorado Springs, Colo. 80901
303-634-2844
General Manager: George W. Jeffrey
News Director: Hal Kennedy

KOAT-TV, ch. 7 (ABC)
1377 University Blvd. N.E., Albuquerque, N. Mex. 87106
505-247-0101
General Manager: Max A. Sklower
Program Manager: Dan Ricker

KSL-TV, ch. 5 (CBS)
145 Social Hall Ave., Salt Lake City, Utah 84111
801-524-2500
General Manager: L. H. Curtis
Program Director: Scott R. Clawson

KTVM, ch. 6 (NBC)
Drawer M, 340 W. Main, Missoula, Mont. 59801
406-543-8313
General Manager: Lynn H. Koch
Program Director: Richard A. Reid

KVOA-TV, ch. 4 (NBC)
Box 5188, Tucson, Ariz. 85703
602-623-2555
General Manager: G. E. (Doc) Hamilton
Environmental Reporter: Jim Roberts

KYCU-TV, ch. 5 (CBS)
2923 E. Lincoln Way, Cheyenne, Wyo. 82001
307-634-4461
General Manager: William C. Grove

PACIFIC STATES

KFAR-TV, ch. 2 (ABC)
516 2 Ave., Fairbanks, Alaska 99701
907-452-2125
General Manager: Alvin O. Bramstedt
Program Director: Don Andon

KOMO-TV, ch. 4 (ABC)
100 4 Ave. N., Seattle, Wash. 98109
206-MA4-6000
General Manager: W. W. Warren
Director of Special Projects: Art McDonald

KPUA-TV, ch. 9 (CBS)
Box 937, Hilo, Hawaii 96720
808-935-5461
Manager: Hal Boudreau

KVAL-TV, ch. 13 (NBC)
Box 1313, Eugene Oreg. 97401
503-342-4961
General Manager: S. W. McCready
Program Director: John Doyle

XETV, ch. 6 (ABC)
7 and Ash, TV Heights, San Diego, Calif. 92101
714-234-8431
General Manager: Julian M. Kaufman
Public Service Director: Raff Ahlgren

RADIO STATIONS

New England States

WBZ
1170 Soldiers Field Rd., Boston, Mass. 02134
617-254-5670
General Manager: Sy Yanoff
Program Director: Bill Shupert

WFEA (ABC/C)
Box 149, Manchester, N.H. 03105
603-625-5491
General Manager: H. D. Neuwirth
Program Director: Vic Pryles

WGAN
390 Congress St., Portland, Maine 04111
207-772-4661
General Manager: Charles R. Sanford
Program Manager: Wayne Bearor

WJAR (NBC)
176 Weybosset St., Providence, R.I. 02903
401-861-9200
General Manager: Alan H. Andrews
Program Director: Richard Pace

WJOY (CBS)
N. Joy Dr., Burlington, Vt. 05401
802-658-1230
General Manager: Frank A. Balch
Program Manager: Vincent J. D'Acuti

WTIC
Broadcast House, 3 Constitution Plaza, Hartford, Conn. 06115
203-525-0801
General Manager: J. Donald MacGovern
Program Director: Ross Miller

Middle Atlantic States

WBAL (NBC)
3800 Hooper Ave., Baltimore, Md. 21211
301-467-3000
General Manager: Alfred E. Burk
Program Director: Jack Lacy

WCBS (CBS)
51 W. 52 St., New York, N.Y. 10019
212-765-4321
General Manager: Neil E. Derrough
News Director: Lou Adler

WDEL
2727 Shipley Rd., Wilmington, Del. 19899
302-478-2700
General Manager: Clair R. McCollough
Program Director: Michael Connor

WJAS (NBC)
100 Forbes Ave., Pittsburgh, Pa. 15222
412-391-9800
General Manager: Earl Buncher
Program Director: Bill Ross

WTTM
333 W. State St., Trenton, N.J. 08618
609-695-8515
General Manager: James A. Ort
Program Director: Phil Allen

WWDC (ABC)
8800 Brookville Rd., Silver Spring, Md. 20910
202-589-7100
General Manager: William Sanders
Program Director: Gloria Gibson

Southeastern States

WAPI (NBC)
Box 10502, Birmingham, Ala. 35202
205-933-2720
General Manager: Donald D. Wear
News Director: Bob Jones

WCOS
Box 738, Columbia, S.C. 29202
803-252-2177
General Manager: Jess E. Plummer
Program Director: Woody Windham

WGBS (ABC)
710 Brickell Ave., Miami, Fla. 33131
305-377-8811
General Manager: Reggie Martin
Program Manager: Robert Vanderheyden

WGNT (NBC)
824 5 Ave., Box 1187, Huntington, W. Va. 25714
304-523-8401
General Manager: John B. Frankhouser, Jr.
Program Director: Jim Schneider

WINN (ABC)
3 and Broadway, Louisville, Ky. 40202
502-585-5148
General Manager: Art Grunewald
Program Director: Moon Mullins

WMAK
Box 2628, Uptown Sta., Nashville, Tenn. 37219
615-255-3536
General Manager: Jerry A. Adams
Program Director: Scott Shannon

WQXI
2970 Peachtree Rd. N.W., Atlanta, Ga. 30305
404-261-2970
General Manager: Gerald S. Blum
Program Director: Gary Corry

WRBC (ABC)
Box 9801, Jackson, Miss. 39206
601-956-4151
General Manager: Dudley Evans
Program Director: Grady Brock

WRVA
Box 1516, Richmond, Va. 23212
703-643-6633
General Manager: John B. Tansey
Program Director: Walt Williams

WSOC (NBC)
Box 2536, Charlotte, N.C. 28201
704-372-0903
General Manager: Freeman Jones
Program Director: Phil Whitelaw

Midwestern States

KFGO (CBS)
Box 2966, Fargo, N. Dak. 58102
701-237-5245
General Manager: Joel D. Melarvie
Program Manager: Van Vander Ark

KFH (CBS)
Vickers-KSB&T Bldg., 125 N. Market, Wichita, Kans. 67202
316-AM2-4491
General Manager: Thomas P. Bashaw
Program Director: Ken Softley

KIOA
Suite 312, 215 Keo Way, Des Moines, Iowa 50309
515-282-9191
General Manager: Paul Jay Jacobson
Program Director: Peter McLane

KISD (ABC)
130 N. Main, Sioux Falls, S. Dak. 57102
605-336-1230
General Manager: Bruce R. Long
Program Director: Robert W. Walker

KLNG (CBS)
511 S. 17 St., Omaha, Nebr. 68102
402-342-8282
General Manager: Frank Scott
Program Manager: Jerry Misner

KMOX (CBS)
1 S. Memorial Dr., St. Louis, Mo. 63102
314-621-2345
General Manager: Robert Hyland
Program Director: Jim Butler

WCCO (CBS)
625 2 Ave. S., Minneapolis, Minn. 55402
612-332-1202
General Manager: Phil Lewis
Program Director: Val Linder

WIRE (ABC)
4560 Knollton Rd., Indianapolis, Ind. 46208
317-925-9201
General Manager: Don N. Nelson
Program Director: Bill Robinson

WJR
2100 Fisher Bldg., Detroit, Mich. 48202
313-875-4440
General Manager: William R. James
Program Director: J. P. McCarthy

WMAQ (NBC)
Merchandise Mart, Chicago, Ill. 60654
312-644-8300
General Manager: Harry D. Jacobs, Jr.
Program Manager: Lee Davis

WOKY
3500 N. Sherman Blvd., Milwaukee, Wis. 53216

414-442-0150
General Manager: Ralph Barnes
Program Director: Gary Price

WTVN (ABC)
42 E. Gay St., Columbus, Ohio 43215
614-224-1271
General Manager: Carl Wagner
Program Director: Jim Lohse

South Central States

KAAY
1425 W. 7 St., Little Rock, Ark. 72203
501-375-5311
General Manager: Pat Walsh, Jr.
Program Director: Wayne Moss

KNOW
1907 N. Lamar, Box 2197, Austin, Tex. 78767
512-477-9841
General Manager: Harry L. Smith, Jr.
Program Director: Mike Lucas

KTOK (ABC)
Box 1000, Oklahoma City, Okla. 73101
405-235-1671
General Manager: C. Hewel Jones
Program Director: Bob Riggins

WNPS (ABC)
916 Navarre Ave., New Orleans, La. 70124
504-488-2681
General Manager: Edward C. Carlson
Program Director: Bob Castle

Rocky Mountain States

KALL (ABC)
312 E. South Temple, Salt Lake City, Utah 84111
801-364-3561
Station Manager: Bennie L. Williams
Program Manager: Will Lucas

KATI (CBS)
Box 2006, Casper, Wyo. 82601
307-234-4545
General Manager: Larry Wakefield
News Director: Pete Williams

KFXD
Box 107, Boise, Idaho 83701
208-342-8812
General Manager: Wayne C. Cornils
Program Director: Fred Novak

KGGM (CBS)
Broadcast Center, 14 and Coal S.W., Box 1742, Albuquerque, N. Mex. 87103
505-243-2285
General Manager: Andy Sandersier
Program Director: Bruce A. Hebenstreit

KLAV (CBS; ABC/C)
2634 State St., Las Vegas, Nev. 89109
702-735-6633
General Manager: Alex Gold
Program Director: Roy Hill

KMON (ABC)
Box 2285, Great Falls, Mont. 59401
406-453-0336
General Manager: Al Donohue
Program Director: Rhys Morgan

KOA (NBC)
1044 Lincoln, Denver, Colo. 80217
303-244-4141
General Manager: Richard Belkin
Program Director: Dan Tucker

KOOL (CBS)
511 W. Adams, Phoenix, Ariz. 85003
602-271-2345
General Manager: Homer Lane
Program Director: John Johnson

Pacific States

KCBS (CBS)
1 Embarcadero Center, San Francisco, Calif. 94111
415-982-7000
General Manager: Neil Derrough
News Director: Jim Simon

KENI (NBC, ABC)
Theater Bldg., 4 Ave., Box 1160, Anchorage, Alaska 99501
907-272-7461
General Manager: Alvin O. Bramstedt
Program Director: Bob Mikell

KEX
2130 S.W. 5 Ave., Portland, Oreg. 97201
503-222-1881
General Manager: Fulton Wilkins
Program Director: Vic Ives

KFI (NBC)
141 N. Vermont Ave., Los Angeles, Calif. 90004
213-382-2121
General Manager: Edmund Bunker
Program Director: Ned Skaff

KHVH (CBS)
1290 Ala Moano, Honolulu, Hawaii 96814
808-537-3991
General Manager: Lawrence S. Berger
Program Director: Dick Cook

KTAC
2000 Tacoma Mall Office Bldg., Tacoma, Wash. 98411
206-473-0085
General Manager: Jim Nelly
Program Director: Darek Shannon

14 Bibliography

WENDY and MYRON C. MENEWITCH

In selecting books, articles, and reports for inclusion in this bibliography, the editors have sought primarily to provide sources that will serve as introductions to the principal areas of environmental concern. It is hoped that sources cited will prove useful to both lay and professional readers. Many of the sources are reviews that provide essential background information and at the same time, through their bibliographies and source citations, lead the reader to more specialized sources. A large proportion of the listings are annotated, and in a majority of those without annotations the subject matter is clearly indicated by the title. Highly technical literature has been avoided, as have sources devoted to highly specialized aspects of environmental problems and those which, though otherwise useful, are not available from publishers or in libraries.

The bibliographic entries are classified under the following headings: Air; Children's Books; Conservation and Wildlife; Economics and Environment; Energy; Environmental Law and Politics; Food Production; General; International; Land Use and Urban Planning; Noise; Population; Radiation; Reference Works; Solid Wastes; Thermal Pollution; Toxic and Hazardous Substances; Water; Weather Modification; Periodicals.

AIR

Air Conservation Commission. *Air Conservation*. Washington: American Association for the Advancement of Science, 1965.

"Air Pollution Over the States." *Environmental Science and Technology*, February 1972, pp. 111–117. (Examines each state and its prospects for an improvement in air quality.)

American Conference of Governmental Industrial Hygienists. *Air Sampling Instruments*. 4th ed. Cincinnati, Ohio: American Conference of Governmental Industrial Hygienists, 1972.

———. *Documentation of the Threshold Limit Values for Substances in Workroom Air*. 3rd ed. Cincinnati, Ohio: American Conference of Governmental Industrial Hygienists, 1971.

American Institute of Chemical Engineers. *Sulfur and SO_2 Developments*. New York: American Institute of Chemical Engineers, 1971. (Discusses manufacture and supply of these materials, and problems of emissions and wastes.)

American Society for Testing and Materials. *Effect of Automotive Emission Requirements on Gasoline Characteristics*. Philadelphia: American Society for Testing and Materials, 1971.

Argenbright, L. P., et al. "SO_2 from Smelters." *Environmental Science and Technology*, June 1970, pp. 554–568.

Atkisson, Arthur, and Gaines, Richard S., eds. *Development of Air Quality Standards*. Columbus, Ohio: Merrill, 1970.

Atomic Energy Commission. *Precipitation Scavenging*. Washington: Government Printing Office, 1970. (Distributed by National Technical Information Service. Discusses role of precipitation in the environment.)

Ayres, Robert U., and McKenna, Richard P. *Alternatives to the Internal Combustion Engine: Impacts on Environmental Quality*. Baltimore: Johns Hopkins, 1972.

Battan, Louis J. *Unclean Sky: A Meteorologist Looks at Air Pollution.* Garden City, N.Y.: Doubleday, 1966.

Bertrand, Rene R. *A Study of Markets for Air Pollution Measurement Instrumentation, 1971-1980.* Washington: Government Printing Office, 1971. (Distributed by National Technical Information Service.)

Bowen, D. H. Michael, ed. *Air Pollution.* Washington: American Chemical Society, 1973. (Highlights legislation and controls, standards of various pollutants, and monitoring.)

Brodine, Virginia. "Running in Place." *Environment*, January-February 1972, pp. 2-11, 52. (Analyzes possibilities for improving air quality.)

―――. "A Special Burden." *Environment*, March 1971, pp. 22-33. (Discusses greater dangers of air pollution among nonwhites and in low socioeconomic groups.)

Butcher, Samuel S., and Charlson, Robert J. *An Introduction to Air Chemistry.* New York: Academic Press, 1972. (Nontechnical; includes discussion of aerosols.)

"A Clean Air Device that May Pollute." *Business Week*, June 23, 1973, p. 32. (Discusses catalytic converters for cars.)

"Cleaning Up the Atmosphere." *Battelle Research Outlook*, vol. 2, no. 3 (1970). (Entire issue devoted to this subject.)

Commerce Department. *Automobile and Air Pollution.* Washington: Government Printing Office, 1967.

―――. *Scrubber Handbook.* Washington: Government Printing Office, 1972. (Distributed by National Technical Information Service.)

Congress. House Reports. *Clean Air Amendments of 1970.* Washington: Government Printing Office, 1971. (Conference report to accompany H.R. 17255, provides text of the amendments approved Dec. 31, 1970.)

Congress. Senate. Committee on Commerce. *The Search for a Low-Emission Vehicle.* Washington: Government Printing Office, 1969. (Staff report.)

Congress. Senate. Committee on Public Works. *Air Pollution, 1970.* Washington: Government Printing Office, 1970. (Hearings before the Subcommittee on Air and Water Pollution, in five parts.)

Connolly, Charles H. *Air Pollution and Public Health.* New York: Holt, Rinehart and Winston, 1972.

Conservation Foundation. *Your Right to Clean Air.* Washington: Conservation Foundation, 1970. (Guide to citizen activities.)

Croke, E. J., and Roberts, J. J. "Air Resource Management and Regional Planning." *Bulletin of the Atomic Scientists*, February 1971, pp. 8-12. (Advocates air pollution control based on emission rights for segments of land.)

Crouse, William H. *Automotive Emission Control.* New York: McGraw-Hill, 1971. (For the layman.)

Defense Documentation Center, Alexandria, Va. *Air Pollution: Particulate Matters, Vol. 1: Report Bibliography.* Washington: Government Printing Office, 1971. (Distributed by National Technical Information Service.)

Downing, Paul B., ed. *Air Pollution and the Social Sciences: Formulating and Implementing Control Programs.* New York: Praeger, 1971.

Ehrlich, Shelton. "Air Pollution Control Through New Combustion Processes." *Environmental Science and Technology*, May 1970, pp. 396-400.

Environmental Protection Agency. *Air Pollution Aspects of Emission Sources: Cement Manufacturing, A Bibliography With Abstracts.* Washington: Government Printing Office, 1971.

―――. *Air Pollution Aspects of Emission Sources: Electric Power Production, A Bibliography With Abstracts.* Washington: Government Printing Office, 1971.

―――. *Air Pollution Aspects of Emission Sources: Municipal Incineration, A Bibliography With Abstracts.* Washington: Government Printing Office, 1971.

———. *Air Pollution Aspects of Emission Sources: Nitric Acid Manufacturing, A Bibliography With Abstracts.* Washington: Government Printing Office, 1971.

———. *Air Pollution Aspects of Emission Sources: Sulfuric Acid Manufacturing, A Bibliography With Abstracts.* Washington: Government Printing Office, 1971.

———. *Air Quality Criteria for Nitrogen Oxides.* Washington: Government Printing Office, 1971.

———. *Asbestos and Air Pollution, An Annotated Bibliography.* Washington: Government Printing Office, 1971.

———. *Atmospheric Emissions from Chlor-Alkali Manufacture.* Washington: Government Printing Office, 1971.

———. *The Automobile Cycle: An Environmental and Resource Reclamation Problem.* Washington: Government Printing Office, 1972.

———. *Automobile Emission Control—The State of the Art as of December 1972.* Washington: Government Printing Office, 1973.

———. *Beryllium and Air Pollution, An Annotated Bibliography.* Washington: Government Printing Office, 1971.

———. *Chlorine and Air Pollution, An Annotated Bibliography.* Washington: Government Printing Office, 1971.

———. *A Citizen's Guide to Clean Air.* Washington: Government Printing Office, 1972. (Guide for individuals or groups working for clean air, prepared by The Conservation Foundation.)

———. *Clean Air—It's Up to You, Too.* Washington: Government Printing Office, 1973. (Describes how citizens can use the 1970 Clean Air Act.)

———. *Economics of Clean Air.* Washington: Government Printing Office, 1971. (Report of the EPA Administrator to the Congress.)

———. *Effects of Fuel Additives on Air Pollutant Emissions from Distillate-Oil-Fired Furnaces.* Washington: Government Printing Office, 1971.

———. *Fuel Economy and Emission Control.* Washington: Government Printing Office, 1972.

———. *Guide for Air Pollution Episode Avoidance.* Washington: Government Printing Office, 1971.

———. *Guide for Control of Air Pollution Episodes in Medium Sized Urban Areas.* Washington: Government Printing Office, 1971.

———. *Guide for Control of Air Pollution Episodes in Small Sized Urban Areas.* Washington: Government Printing Office, 1971.

———. *Guide to Research in Air Pollution Projects Active in Calendar Year 1972.* Washington: Government Printing Office, 1972.

———. *Guidelines: Air Quality Surveillance Networks.* Washington: Government Printing Office, 1971.

———. *Hydrochloric Acid and Air Pollution, An Annotated Bibliography.* Washington: Government Printing Office, 1971.

———. *Nationwide Inventory of Air Pollutant Emission, 1968.* Washington: Government Printing Office, 1970.

———. *Photochemical Oxidants and Air Pollution, An Annotated Bibliography.* 2 vols. Washington: Government Printing Office, 1971.

———. *Proceedings of Symposium on Multiple-Source Urban Diffusion Models.* Washington: Government Printing Office, 1970.

———. *Progress in the Prevention and Control of Air Pollution.* Washington: Government Printing Office, 1971. (Annual Report of the EPA Administrator to the Congress.)

———. *Workbook of Atmospheric Dispersion Estimates.* Rev. ed. Washington: Government Printing Office, 1970.

Esposito, John C. *Vanishing Air.* New York: Grossman, 1970. (View of air pollution as a form of domestic chemical and biological warfare; the Ralph Nader Study Group Report on Air Pollution.)

First European Congress on the Influence of Air Pollution on Plants and Animals. *Air Pollution.* Wageningen, The Netherlands: Center for Agricultural Publishing, 1968.

Glasser, Marvin, Greenburg, Leonard, and Field, Franklyn. "Mortality and Morbidity during a Period of High Levels of Air Pollution." *Archives of Environmental Health,* December 1967, pp. 684-694.

Goldsmith, J. R., and Landaw, S. A. "Carbon Monoxide and Human Health." *Science,* December 20, 1968, pp. 1352-1359.

Gordian Associates, Inc. *Guide to Technical and Financial Assistance for Air Pollution Control.* Washington: Government Printing Office, 1971. (Distributed by National Technical Information Service. Descriptions of federal, state, and other financial assistance sources.)

Hagevik, George. *Decision-Making in Air Pollution: A Review of Theory and Practice, with Emphasis on Selected Los Angeles and New York City Management Experiences.* New York: Praeger, 1970.

Hagevik, George, ed. *The Relationship of Land Use and Transportation Planning to Air Quality Management.* New Brunswick, N.J.: Rutgers University Press, 1972.

Health, Education, and Welfare Department. *Air Pollution Aspects of Brass and Bronze Smelting and Refining Industry.* Washington: Government Printing Office, 1969.

―――. *Air Pollution in the Coffee Roasting Industry.* Washington: Government Printing Office, 1970.

―――. *Air Pollution Injury to Vegetation.* Washington: Government Printing Office, 1970.

―――. *Air Quality Criteria for Carbon Monoxide.* Washington: Government Printing Office, 1970.

―――. *Air Quality Criteria for Hydrocarbons.* Washington: Government Printing Office, 1970.

―――. *Air Quality Criteria for Particulate Matter.* Washington: Government Printing Office, 1969.

―――. *Air Quality Criteria for Photochemical Oxidants.* Washington: Government Printing Office, 1970.

―――. *Air Quality Criteria for Sulfur Oxides.* Washington: Government Printing Office, 1969.

―――. *Atmospheric Emissions from Sulfuric Acid Manufacturing Processes.* Washington: Government Printing Office, 1965.

―――. *Calculating Future Carbon Monoxide Emissions and Concentrations from Urban Traffic Data.* Washington: Government Printing Office, 1970.

―――. *Characteristics of Particulate Patterns, 1957-66.* Washington: Government Printing Office, 1970.

―――. *Clean Air for Your Community.* Washington: Government Printing Office, 1969.

―――. *Compilation of Air Pollutant Emission Factors, 1968.* Washington: Government Printing Office, 1969.

―――. *Control Techniques for Carbon Monoxide Emission from Stationary Sources.* Washington: Government Printing Office, 1970.

―――. *Control Techniques for Carbon Monoxide, Nitrogen Oxide, and Hydrocarbon Emissions from Mobile Sources.* Washington: Government Printing Office, 1970.

―――. *Control Techniques for Hydrocarbon and Organic Solvent Emissions from Stationary Sources.* Washington: Government Printing Office, 1970.

―――. *Control Techniques for Nitrogen Oxide Emissions from Stationary Sources.* Washington: Government Printing Office, 1970.

―――. *Control Techniques for Particulate Air Pollutants.* Washington: Government Printing Office, 1969.

―――. *Control Techniques for Sulfur Oxide Air Pollutants.* Washington: Government Printing Office, 1969.

―――. *The Cost of Clean Air.* Washington: Government Printing Office, 1970. (Second report of the Secretary of HEW to the Congress.)

———. *Economic Impact of Air Pollution Controls on Gray Iron Foundry Industry.* Washington: Government Printing Office, 1970.

———. *Economic Impact of Air Pollution Controls on Secondary Nonferrous Metals Industry.* Washington: Government Printing Office, 1969.

———. *Emissions from Coal-Fired Power Plants, A Comprehensive Summary.* Washington: Government Printing Office, 1969.

———. *Hydrocarbons and Air Pollution, An Annotated Bibliography.* 2 vols. Washington: Government Printing Office, 1970.

———. *Manpower and Training Needs for Air Pollution Control.* Washington: Government Printing Office, 1970. (Report of the Secretary of HEW to the Congress.)

———. *Nitrogen Oxides, An Annotated Bibliography.* Washington: Government Printing Office, 1970.

———. *Sources of Air Pollution and Their Control.* Washington: Government Printing Office, 1969.

———. *Thanksgiving 1966, Air Pollution Episode in the Eastern United States.* Washington: Government Printing Office, 1970.

Heck, Walter, et al. *Tobacco, A Sensitive Monitor for Photochemical Air Pollution.* Washington: Government Printing Office, 1969. (A publication of the National Air Pollution Control Administration.)

Hesketh, Howard E. *Understanding and Controlling Air Pollution.* Ann Arbor, Mich.: Ann Arbor Science, 1972. (Reference text.)

Hilst, Glenn R. "What Can We Do to Clear the Air?" *American Meteorological Society Bulletin*, September 1967, pp. 710–713.

Hochheiser, Seymour, Burmann, Franz J., and Morgan, George B. "Atmospheric Surveillance: The Current State of Air Monitoring Technology." *Environmental Science and Technology*, August 1971, pp. 678–684.

Holland, W. W., ed. *Air Pollution and Respiratory Diseases.* Westport, Conn.: Technomic, 1972.

Jacobsen, Willis E. *A Technology Assessment Methodology, Vol. 2: Automotive Emissions.* Washington: Government Printing Office, 1971. (Distributed by National Technical Information Service. Analyzes the automobile's role in air pollution.)

Jacobson, Jay S., and Hill, A. Clyde, eds. *Recognition of Air Pollution Injury to Vegetation: A Pictorial Atlas.* Pittsburgh: Air Pollution Control Association, 1970.

Jamison, Andrew. *The Steam Powered Automobile: An Answer to Air Pollution.* Bloomington, Ind.: Indiana University Press, 1970.

Kennedy, Robert F. "Air Pollution and the Death of Our Cities." *Social Action*, May 1968, pp. 38–46.

Lave, Lester B., and Seskin, Eugene P. "Air Pollution and Human Health." *Science*, August 21, 1970, pp. 723–733.

Leinwand, Gerald, ed. *Air and Water Pollution.* New York: Washington Square Press, 1969.

Likens, Gene E. "Acid Rain." *Environment*, March 1972, pp. 33–40. (Discusses effects of nitrogen and sulfur oxides present in rain.)

Lillie, Robert J. *Air Pollution Affecting the Performance of Domestic Animals, A Literature Review.* Washington: Government Printing Office, 1970. (An Agriculture Department handbook.)

Manufacturing Chemists' Association, and Public Health Service. *Atmospheric Emissions from Hydrochloric Acid Manufacturing Processes.* Washington: Government Printing Office, 1969.

Morgan, George B., et al. "Air Pollution Surveillance Systems." *Science*, October 16, 1970, pp. 289–296.

National Academy of Sciences. *Effects of Chronic Exposure to Low Levels of Carbon Monoxide on Human Health, Behavior, and Performance.* Washington: Government Printing Office, 1969.

———. *Particulate Polycyclic Organic Matter.* Washington: Government Printing Office, 1972. (Part of the NAS series on the Biological Effect of Atmospheric Pollutants.)

National Industrial Pollution Control Council. *Air Pollution by Sulfur Oxides: Staff Report.* Washington: Government Printing Office, 1971.

———. *Maintaining Vehicular Emission Control System Integrity.* Washington: Government Printing Office, 1971.

———. *Mathematical Models for Air Pollution Control Policy Decision-Making.* Washington: Government Printing Office, 1971.

Neiburger, Morris. "The Role of Meteorology in the Study and Control of Air Pollution." *American Meteorological Society Bulletin,* December 1969, pp. 957–965.

"New Blueprint Emerges for Air Pollution Controls." *Environmental Science and Technology,* February 1971, pp. 106–108. (Clean Air Amendments of 1970.)

"Next Federal Cleanup Target: Aircraft Noise and Emissions." *Environmental Science and Technology,* March 1972, pp. 220–222.

O'Sullivan, Dermot A. "Air Pollution." *Chemical and Engineering News,* June 8, 1970, p. 38ff. (Includes identification of major sources of air pollution and hazards.)

Panel on Automotive Fuels and Air Pollution. *Automotive Fuels and Air Pollution.* Washington: Government Printing Office, 1971.

Panofsky, Hans A. "Air Pollution Meteorology." *American Scientist,* Summer 1969, pp. 269–285.

Patterson, D. J., and Henein, N. A. *Emissions from Internal Combustion Engines and Their Control.* Ann Arbor, Mich.: Ann Arbor Science, 1972. (Discusses chemical and mechanical engineering aspects.)

President's Task Force on Air Pollution. *Cleaner Air for the Nation.* Washington: Government Printing Office, 1970.

Prival, Michael J., and Fisher, Farley. "Fluorides In the Air." *Environment,* April 1973, pp. 25–32. (Discusses effects on plants and animals and the need for establishing controls.)

Redmond, John C., Cook, John C., and Hoffman, A. A. J., eds. *Clearing the Air: The Impact of the Clean Air Act on Technology.* New York: Wiley, 1971.

Ridker, Ronald G. *Economic Costs of Air Pollution: Studies in Measurement.* New York: Praeger, 1967.

Ross, R. D., ed. *Air Pollution and Industry.* New York: Van Nostrand Reinhold, 1972. (Guide for persons involved in plant operations.)

Rossano, A. T., ed. *Air Pollution Control.* Stamford, Conn.: Environmental Sciences Services Corp., 1970. (Provides basic information and glossary.)

Sargent, Frederick, II. "Adaptive Strategy for Air Pollution." *BioScience,* October 1967, pp. 691–697.

Scorer, R. S. *Air Pollution.* Oxford, England: Pergamon, 1968.

Sheehy, James P., et al. *Handbook of Air Pollution: Training Program.* Washington: Government Printing Office, 1968. (Handbook of the National Center for Air Pollution, Durham, N.C.)

Shepard, Stephen B. "A Corporate Polluter Learns the Hard Way." *Business Week,* February 6, 1971, pp. 52–56. (Describes how Union Carbide Corp. was forced to heed a town's plea for clean air.)

Springer, George S., and Patterson, Donald J., eds. *Engine Emissions: Pollutant Formation and Measurement.* New York: Plenum, 1973.

Starkman, Ernest, S., ed. *Combustion-Generated Air Pollution.* New York: Plenum, 1971.

Stern, Arthur Cecil. *Air Pollution.* 3 vols. New York: Academic Press, 1968. (Authoritative text.)

Stoker, Stephen H., and Seager, Spencer L. *Environmental Chemistry: Air and Water Pollution.* Oakland, N.J.: Scott, Foresman, 1972.

Strauss, Werner, ed. *Air Pollution Control.* Part 1. New York: Wiley, 1971. (Seven articles discussing different areas of air pollution control.)

Teller, Azriel. "Air Pollution Abatement: Economic Rationality and Reality." *Daedalus,* Fall 1967, pp. 1082–1098.

Tennessee Valley Authority. *Sulfur Oxide Removal from Power Plant Stack Gas, Ammonia Scrubbing: Production of Ammonium Sulfate and Use as an Intermediate in Phosphate Fertilizer Manufacture.* Washington: Government Printing Office, 1970. (Distributed by National Technical Information Service. Discusses potential of this method of SO_2 removal.)

Tuesday, Charles S., ed. *Chemical Reactions in Urban Atmospheres.* New York: American Elsevier, 1971.

Waggoner, Paul E. "Plants and Polluted Air." *BioScience,* May 15, 1971, pp. 455–459. (Discusses the role of plants in alleviating air pollution.)

"Will the New Gasolines Lick Auto Pollution?" *Consumer Reports,* March 1971, pp. 156–159. (Use of low- and no-lead gasolines is seen as only a small step in search for clean air.)

Wise, William. *Killer Smog: The World's Worst Air Pollution Disaster.* Chicago: Rand McNally, 1968.

Wolman, A. "Air Pollution: Time for Appraisal." *Science,* March 29, 1968, pp. 1437–1440.

CHILDREN'S BOOKS

Abisch, Roz. *Around the House that Jack Built.* Illus. by Boche Kaplan. New York: Parent's Magazine Press, 1972. (Attractive picture book, written in rhyme, that tells of the interdependence of all living things. Kindergarten through second grade.)

Asimov, Isaac. *ABC's of Ecology.* Photos. New York: Walker, 1972. (Each letter used to define two ecological terms.)

Aylesworth, Thomas G. *This Vital Air, This Vital Water: Man's Environmental Crisis.* Chicago: Rand McNally, 1968. (Includes discussions of noise and oil pollution and contains section on career opportunities in the field of environmental control. Seventh grade and up.)

Behnke, Frances L. *The Changing World of Living Things.* New York: Holt, Rinehart, and Winston, 1972. (Discusses the importance of each member of an ecosystem and the effects of pollution on the plant and animal kingdoms. Sixth grade and up.)

Bixby, William. *A World You can Live In.* New York: McKay, 1971. (Emphasizes need to become aware of our relationship with the environment. Sixth through eighth grades.)

Bloome, Enid. *The Air We Breathe.* Photos. Garden City, N.Y.: Doubleday, 1971. (Introduction to subject of air pollution, covering causes, effects, and possible solutions. Kindergarten through second grade.)

———. *The Water We Drink.* Photos. Garden City, N.Y.: Doubleday, 1971. (An introduction to water pollution. Kindergarten through second grade.)

Brodtkorb, Reidar. *Flying Free.* Photos. Chicago: Rand McNally, 1964. (Story of the author's deep love for eagles and dedication of his life to them. Fourth through sixth grades.)

Chen, Tony. *Run, Zebra, Run.* Illus. by author. New York: Lothrop, 1972. (Author warns that the jungle will one day be a highway and that the animals will be gone. First through third grades.)

Chester, Michael. *Let's Go to Stop Air Pollution.* Illus. by Albert Micale. New York: G. P. Putnam's Sons, 1968. (Introduction to air pollution and agencies studying its effects. Third and fourth grades.)

———. *Let's Go to Stop Water Pollution.* Illus. by Albert Micale. New York: G. P. Putnam's Sons, 1969. (Discusses ways of controlling and cleaning polluted waterways. Third and fourth grades.)

Dwiggins, Don. *Spaceship Earth: A Space Look at Our Troubled Planet.* San Carlos, Calif.: Golden Gate Junior Books, 1970. (Fifth grade and up.)

Elliott, Sarah M. *Our Dirty Air*. Photos. New York: Julian Messner, 1971. (Attempts to motivate children to work for clean air. Includes chapter on the effects of pollution on weather. Third and fourth grades.)

Gates, Richard. *The True Book of Conservation*. Illus. by author. Chicago: Children's Press, 1959. (Story of the decline of the natural forests and wildlife. First and second grades.)

Geisel, Theodore [Dr. Seuss]. *The Lorax*. New York: Random House, 1971. (Story of a greedy man who starts a factory and haphazardly destroys the environment. Kindergarten through second grade.)

George, Jean Craighead. *Who Really Killed Cock Robin?* New York: Dutton, 1971. (An ecological mystery probing the possible causes of the death of Cock Robin. Discusses dangers of pesticides, factory wastes, and water pollution. Sixth grade and up.)

Goetz, Delia. *Rivers*. New York: Morrow, 1969. (Discusses life that exists by the Potomac River and explains how pollution occurs. Second and third grades.)

Green, Ivah. *Wildlife in Danger*. New York: Coward, McCann, 1960. (Discusses various endangered species, and explores motives for and methods of killing animals. Fifth and sixth grades.)

Haley, Gail E. *Noah's Ark*. Illus. New York: Atheneum, 1971. (Up-dated Noah sails off with his family and the animals, vowing to return only when all is clear and beautiful again. Kindergarten through second grade.)

Harrison, C. William. *Conservation—The Challenge of Reclaiming Our Plundered Land*. Photos. New York: Julian Messner, 1963. (Story of how U.S. land has been mistreated. Fifth and sixth grades.)

Henson, Collins M. *Your Environment: Air, Air Pollution and Weather*. Danville, Ill.: Interstate, 1971. (Fifth grade and up.)

Hey, Nigel, and the editors of Science Book Associates. *How Will We Feed the Hungry Billions: Food for Tomorrow's World*. Tomorrow's World series. New York: Julian Messner, 1971. (Discusses new methods of food production and pest control. Younger readers.)

Hilton, Suzanne. *How Do They Cope with It*. Photos. Philadelphia: Westminster Press, 1970. (Explores natural world and how its inhabitants survive in an often harsh climate. Stresses that man's efforts to "improve" on nature require careful prior consideration. Sixth grade and up.)

Hoke, John. *Ecology—Man's Effects on His Environment and Its Mechanisms*. Illus. by Richard Cuffari. New York: Franklin Watts, 1971. (Part One deals with nature and its complex ways. Part Two explores the changes man has made in his environment. Sixth grade and up.)

Hungerford, Harold R. *Ecology: The Circle of Life*. Chicago: Childrens, 1971. (Discusses ways in which man has affected and is affecting the natural environment. Fifth grade and up.)

Hutchins, Ross E. *The Last Trumpeters*. Illus. by Jerome P. Connolly. New York: Rand McNally, 1967. (Examines the trumpeter swan, threatened with extinction. Third and fourth grades.)

Hyde, Margaret O. *For Pollution Fighters Only*. Illus. by Don Lynch. New York: McGraw-Hill, 1971. (Discusses various pollutants and makes numerous suggestions for those interested in actively fighting for a better environment. Sixth grade and up.)

Jennings, Gary. *The Shrinking Outdoors*. New York: Lippincott, 1972. (An angry, extremely informative book that explores the history of man and his treatment of the environment. Seventh grade and up.)

Jones, Claire, Gadler, Steve J., and Engstrom, Paul H. *Pollution: The Air We Breathe*. A Real World book. Minneapolis: Lerner Public, 1971. (Analysis of pollution and polluters with up-to-date information. Fifth grade and up.)

———. *Pollution: The Dangerous Atom*. A Real World book. Photos. Minneapolis: Lerner Public, 1972. (Informative book dealing with all aspects of the complex topic of nuclear energy. Seventh grade and up.)

———. *Pollution: The Noise We Hear*. A Real World book. Minneapolis: Lerner Public, 1972. (Discusses many aspects of manmade noise, including analysis of sound and its effects on nonliving matter. Sixth grade and up.)

Kavaler, Lucy. *Dangerous Air: Will We End Pollution Before It Kills Us?* Illus. by Carl Smith. New York: John Day, 1967. (Discusses pollution, its effects, and what has been done to correct the conditions it has caused. View of the future is optimistic. Fifth and sixth grades.)

Laycock, George. *America's Endangered Wildlife.* Photos. New York: Norton, 1969. (Explains what must be done to save wildlife. Sixth grade and up.)

———. *Water Pollution.* New York: Grosset and Dunlap, 1972. (Discusses the composition and characteristics of water, history of its use, and ways in which it has been polluted. Fifth and sixth grades.)

Leaf, Munro. *Who Cares? I Do.* Photos. New York: Lippincott, 1971. (Poses simple questions about the environment, primarily the problem of garbage, and then answers them. Kindergarten and first grade.)

Lewis, Alfred. *Clean the Air: Fighting Smoke, Smog, and Smaze Across the Country.* Photographs. New York: McGraw-Hill, 1965. (Discusses various aspects of air pollution, including possible methods of obtaining power without burning fuels. Sixth grade and up.)

McClung, Robert M. *Lost Wild America.* New York: Morrow, 1969. (Discusses extinct and threatened wildlife. Seventh grade and up.)

———. *Scoop: Last of the Brown Pelicans.* Illus. by author and Lloyd Sanford. New York: Morrow, 1972. (Story of the natural and manmade hazards faced by pelicans. Fourth and fifth grades.)

———. *Thor, Last of the Sperm Whales.* Illus. by Bob Hines. New York: Morrow, 1971. (Story of another animal theatened with extinction. Outlook is grim as the killing goes on and no international regulations have been set up. Fourth and fifth grades.)

McCoy, J. J. *Saving Our Wildlife.* New York: Macmillan, 1970. (Past and future of man's relationship with other living things. Seventh grade and up.)

———. *Shadows Over the Land.* New York: Seabury Press, 1970. (Detailed account of pollution problems, with emphasis on need for protest, action, and research. Sixth grade and up.)

Marshall, James. *The Air We Live In—Air Pollution: What We Must Do About It.* The New Conservation series. Photos. New York: Coward McCann, 1968. (Concise treatment of air pollution and its dangers. Includes suggestions for action. Sixth grade and up.)

———. *Going to Waste: Where Will All the Garbage Go?* The New Conservation series. Photos. New York: Coward, McCann and Geoghegan, 1972. (Comprehensive book devoted entirely to the problem of solid waste disposal. Sixth grade and up.)

May, Julian. *Blue River.* Illus. by Robert Quackenbush. New York: Holiday House, 1971. (Explains how civilization mistreated this river and why it is dying. First through third grades.)

Miles, Miska. *Wharf Rats.* Illus. by John Schoenherr. Boston: Little, Brown, 1972. (Unusual story about a rat and his fight to escape his enemy—man. Kindergarten through third grade.)

Milgrom, Harry. *ABC of Ecology.* Photos and designs by Donald Crews. New York: Macmillan, 1972. (Each environmentally significant word is followed by a simple explanation and suggestions of things to see or do. Kindergarten and first grade.)

Millard, Reed, and the editors of Science Book Association. *Clean Air, Clean Water for Tomorrow's World.* Tomorrow's World series. Photos. New York: Julian Messner, 1971. (Good source book, containing information on all aspects of water and air pollution. Sixth grade and up.)

Moore, Lilian. *Just Right.* New York: Parents Magazine Press, 1968. (Farmer must sell his farm but wants a person who will not cut down the trees and ruin the land. Kindergarten through third grade.)

Navarra, John Gabriel. *Our Noisy World.* Garden City, N.Y.: Doubleday, 1969. (Sixth grade and up.)

———. *The World You Inherit—A Story of Pollution.* Photos. Garden City, N.Y.: The Natural History Press, 1970. (Covers or touches upon all aspects of pollution and suggests possible solutions. Sixth grade and up.)

Nelson, Gaylord. *What Are Me and You Gonna Do?* New York: Ballantine Books, 1971. (Letters from children to Senator Nelson on the subject of the environment. All ages.)

Olsen, Ib Spang. *Smoke.* Trans. by Virginia Allen Jensen. Illus. by author. New York: Coward, McCann and Geoghegan, 1972. (Delightful story of family setting out for picnic and the smoke they encounter and must clear up. Solutions are simple and clever. Kindergarten through second grade.)

Orlowsky, Wallace, and Perara, Thomas Biddle. *Who Will Wash the River?* A Science Is What and Why book. Illus. by Richard Cuffari. New York: Coward, McCann, 1970. (Simple story of two young children and their discovery of a polluted river. Second and third grades.)

Peet, Bill. *Farewell to Shady Glade.* Boston: Houghton Mifflin, 1966. (Story of some animals who, left homeless by a bulldozer, search for a new home and encounter various types of pollution along the way. Kindergarten through third grade.)

Pringle, Laurence. *One Earth, Many People: The Challenge of Human Population Growth.* New York: Macmillan, 1971. (Presents both sides of the issue and demonstrates that the reader must search out the facts. Fifth and sixth grades.)

——— *The Only Earth We Have.* Photos. London: Macmillan and Collier-Macmillan, Ltd., 1969. (Views the earth from a spaceship and stresses need to care for the land and its limited resources. Fourth through sixth grades.)

Roth, Charles E. *The Most Dangerous Animal in the World.* Reading, Mass.: Addison-Wesley, 1971. (History of man and his relation to the earth's resources. Sixth grade and up.)

Sand, George X. *The Everglades Today: Endangered Wilderness.* New York: Four Winds, 1971. (Fifth through ninth grades.)

Schlechting, Harold E., Jr., and Schlechting, Mary. *An Introduction to Pollution.* Wings to Science and Social Studies book. Illus. by Frank O'Leary. Austin, Tex.: Steck-Vaughn, 1972. (Basic information stressing prevention of water pollution. Fifth and sixth grades.)

Selden, George. *Tucker's Countryside.* New York: Farrar, Straus and Giroux, 1969. (Tucker Mouse and his friends fight to save a meadow home from a bulldozer. Third through seventh grades.)

———. *Tucker's Countryside.* Rev. ed. New York: Avon Books, 1972. (Fourth through sixth grades.)

Shuttlesworth, Dorothy E. *Clean Air, Sparkling Water—The Fight Against Pollution.* Garden City, N.Y.: Doubleday, 1968. (Devoted mainly to air pollution. Outlook is hopeful. Third and fourth grades.)

Smith, Frances C. *The First Book of Conservation.* Illus. by Mary DeBall Kwitz. New York: Franklin Watts, 1972. (Offers suggestions for conserving natural resources. Fifth and sixth grades.)

Soil Conservation Society of America. *The Earth, Our Home in Space.* Ankeny, Iowa: Soil Conservation Society of America, 1972. (Describes the importance of interaction of man and his environment. Younger readers.)

Soil Conservation Society of America. *Plants, How They Improve Our Environment.* Illus. Ankeny, Iowa: Soil Conservation Society of America, 1971. (Educational cartoons explore ways in which plant life improves the environment.)

Stevens, Leonard A. *How a Law Is Made—The Story of a Bill Against Air Pollution.* Illus. by Robert Galster. New York: Crowell, 1970. (Discusses processes necessary to pass a law and the difficulties that are encountered. Sixth grade and up.)

———. *The Town that Launders Its Water.* New York: Coward, McCann and Geoghegan, 1971. (How one man's dream motivated a town in California to deal with the problem of sewage water. Fifth and sixth grades.)

Stone, A. Harris. *The Last Free Bird.* Illus. by Sheila Heins. Englewood Cliffs, N.J.: Prentice-Hall, 1967. (Moving, beautiful narrative—the last bird tells what man did to the environment and the life that once existed in it. All ages.)

CONSERVATION AND WILDLIFE

Adams, Alexander B. *Eleventh Hour: A Hard Look at Conservation and the Future.* New York: Putnam, 1970. (Discusses difficulties of conservation and role of the government.)

Agriculture Department. *Basic Statistics, National Inventory of Soil and Water Conservation Needs, 1967.* Washington: Government Printing Office, 1971.

———. *Controlling Erosion on Construction Sites.* Washington: Government Printing Office, 1970.

———. *Forestry Activities, A Guide for Youth Group Leaders.* Washington: Government Printing Office, 1970. (Includes projects and a list of materials to help teach forest conservation.)

———. *Guide to Natural Beauty.* Washington: Government Printing Office, 1967. (Discusses uses of Agriculture Department programs and services and gives hints for maintaining and achieving natural beauty.)

———. *Restoring Surface-Mined Land.* Washington: Government Printing Office, 1968.

———. *Science and America's Beauty.* Washington: Government Printing Office, 1968.

———. *Search for Solitude, Our Wilderness Heritage.* Washington: Government Printing Office, 1970.

———. *Wildlife, A Measure of Our Environment, How Extension Serves.* Washington: Government Printing Office, 1970. (Contains brief descriptions of the Agriculture Department's cooperative extension service wildlife programs.)

Anderson, Wallace L., and Compton, Laurence V. *More Wildlife Through Soil and Water Conservation.* Rev. ed. Washington: Government Printing Office, 1971. (An Agriculture Department information bulletin.)

Arbib, Robert. *The Lord's Woods.* New York: Norton, 1971 (Obituary for a woodland on Long Island.)

Baron, W. M. M. *Nature Conservation: A Practical Handbook.* New York: Harper, 1971.

Bengtsson, Arvid. *Environmental Planning for Children's Play.* New York: Praeger, 1970.

Benson, N. G., ed. *A Century of Fisheries in North America.* Lawrence, Kans.: American Fisheries Society, 1970.

Borland, Hal. *Our Natural World: The Land and Wildlife of America as Seen and Described by Writers Since the Country's Discovery.* New York: Doubleday, 1965.

Boulding, Kenneth E. "The Dodo Didn't Make It: Survival and Betterment." *Bulletin of the Atomic Scientists*, May 1971, pp. 19-22.

Brooks, Paul. *The Pursuit of Wilderness.* Boston: Houghton Mifflin, 1971. (Discusses the ways in which man misuses the land.)

Burton, Ian, and Kates, Robert W. *Readings in Resource Management and Conservation.* Chicago: University of Chicago Press, 1965.

Carter, Luther J. "Conservation: Keeping Watch on the Road Builders." *Science*, August 4, 1967, pp. 527-529.

"Clear Cutting and Conservation." *Science News*, December 5, 1970, p. 430. (Discusses dangers of clear cutting or commercial cutting of trees.)

Congress. House. Committee on Interior and Insular Affairs. *Designation of Wilderness Areas: Hearings before the Subcommittee on Public Lands and National Parks and Recreation.* Washington: Government Printing Office, 1971.

Congress. Senate. Committee on Commerce. *Endangered Species Conservation Act of 1972: Hearings.* Washington: Government Printing Office, 1972.

Cox, George W. *Readings in Conservation Ecology.* New York: Appleton-Century-Crofts, 1969. (Variety of ecological concerns discussed.)

Cruickshank, J. C. *Soil Geography.* New York: Halsted Press, 1972. (Basic text includes analysis of relationship between man and the soil.)

Crutchfield, James A., and Pontecorvo, Giulio. *Pacific Salmon Fisheries: A Study of Irrational Conservation.* Baltimore: Johns Hopkins, 1969.

Darling, F. Fraser, and Eichorn, Noel. *Man and Nature in the National Parks.* 2nd ed. Washington: Conservation Foundation, 1969.

Dasmann, Raymond F. *Environmental Conservation.* New York: Wiley, 1968.

Dorst, Jean. *Before Nature Dies.* Boston: Houghton Mifflin, 1970. (Impact of man on wildlife.)

Ehrenfeld, David W. *Biological Conservation*: New York: Holt, Rinehart and Winston, 1970. (General introductory text.)

Fish and Wildlife Service. *Birds in Our Lives.* Washington: Government Printing Office, 1966. (Collection of articles designed to give wider appreciation of the impact of birds on civilization.)

Fisher, James. *Wildlife Crisis.* Prepared with His Royal Highness, Prince Philip. New York: Cowles, 1970. (Discusses many animals threatened by extinction.)

Fisher, James, Simon, Noel, and Vincent, Jack. *Wildlife in Danger.* New York: Viking, 1969. (Information from the files of the International Union for the Conservation of Nature.)

Forest Service. *National Forest Wildernesses and Primitive Areas, the National Forests.* Rev. ed. Washington: Government Printing Office, 1971.

Friedberg, M. Paul, and Berkeley, Ellen Perry. *Play and Interplay: A Manifesto for New Design in Urban Recreation Environment.* New York: Twayne, 1969.

Goff, F. Glenn. "Forest as an Ecosystem." *American Forests,* December 1969, pp. 16–18, 53–55.

Gomez-Pompa, A., et al. "The Tropical Rain Forest: A Nonrenewable Resource." *Science,* September 1, 1972, pp. 762–765.

Goor, A. Y., and Barney, C. W. *Forest Tree Planting in Arid Zones.* New York: Ronald Press, 1968.

Graham, Frank, Jr. *Man's Dominion: The Story of Conservation in America.* New York: Evans, 1971.

Grossman, Mary Louise, Grossman, S., and Hamlet, J. H. *Our Vanishing Wilderness.* New York: Grosset and Dunlap, 1969.

Guggenheimer, Elinor. *Planning for Parks and Recreation Needs in Urban Areas.* New York: Twayne, 1969.

Guggisberg, C. A. W. *Men and Wildlife.* New York: Arco, 1970. (History of man's impact upon wildlife and a survey of national parks and nature reserves throughout the world.)

Hamm, R. L., and Nason, L. *Ecological Approach to Conservation.* Minneapolis: Burgess, 1964.

Harrison, C. William. *Wildlife.* New York: Julian Messner, 1970. (Historical view, including list of various parks and wildlife refuges.)

Held, R. Burnell, and Clawson, Marion. *Soil Conservation in Perspective.* Baltimore: Johns Hopkins, 1965.

Hills, T. L., and Randall, R. E., eds. *Ecology of the Forest.* Montreal: McGill University Press, 1968.

Hilton, Richard. "The Birds of Prey." *Environmental Quality,* November 1972, pp.16–18, 41.

Housing and Urban Development Department. *Preserving Historic America.* Washington: Government Printing Office, 1966.

Hunt, Charles B. *Geology of Soils: Their Evolution, Classification, and Uses.* San Francisco: Freeman, 1972. (Introductory text.)

Hutchings, Monica M., and Caver, Mavis. *Man's Dominion: Our Violation of the Animal World*. New York: Humanities, 1971.

Interior Department. *It's Your World . . . The Grassroots Conservation Story*. Washington: Government Printing Office, 1969. (Describes how various agencies in the Department are seeking to improve the environment.)

———. *Surface Mining and Our Environment*. Washington: Government Printing Office, 1967.

———. *Third Wave . . . America's New Conservation*. Washington: Government Printing Office, 1966.

Isaacson, Larry, and Peterson, Barry L. *Parks and Recreational Facilities, Their Consideration as an Environmental Factor Influencing Location and Design of a Highway*. Washington: Government Printing Office, 1971. (A publication of the Federal Highway Administration.)

Jaffee, Joyce. *Conservation: Maintaining the Natural Balance*. Garden City, N.Y.: Doubleday, 1970.

Janssen, W. A., and Meyers, C. D. "Fish: Serologic Evidence of Infection with Human Pathogens." *Science*, February 2, 1968, pp. 547–548.

Jarrett, Henry, ed. *Perspectives on Conservation: Essays on America's Natural Resources*. Baltimore: Johns Hopkins, 1969.

Kesteven, G. L. "A Policy for Conservationists." *Science*, May 24, 1968, pp. 857–860.

Krieger, Martin H. "What's Wrong with Plastic Trees?" *Science*, February 2, 1973, pp. 446–455. (Provides social, political, and economic reasons for preserving the environment.)

Krutilla, John V., ed. *Natural Environments: Studies in Theoretical and Applied Analysis*. Baltimore: Johns Hopkins, 1973. (Attempts to prove that man can maintain some wild environment and still fulfill economic and material needs.)

McCloskey, Maxine, and Gilligan, James P. *Wilderness and the Quality of Life*. New York: Sierra Club, 1969.

McCormick, Jack. *Life of the Forest*. New York: McGraw-Hill, 1966.

McMillan, Ian. *Man and the California Condor: The Embattled History and Uncertain Future of North America's Largest Free-Living Bird*. New York: Dutton, 1968.

McPhee, John. *Encounters With the Archdruid*. New York: Farrar, Straus, Giroux, 1971. (Interplay between David Brower's philosophy that wilderness must be preserved inviolate, and the proposition that conservation and regulated technological exploitation need not be incompatible.)

Marshall, Eliot. "Lumber Lobby: Clearcutting the National Forests." *New Republic*, February 5, 1972, pp. 11–13. (Describes what is happening to one of the nation's resources.)

Metboy, Anthony. *The Atlantic Salmon: A Vanishing Species*. Boston: Houghton Mifflin, 1968.

Methods of Study in Soil Ecology. New York: Unipub, 1970. (Proceedings of a UNESCO conference.)

Milne, Lorus J., and Milne, Margery. *The Cougar Doesn't Live Here Any More*. Englewood Cliffs, N.J.: Prentice-Hall, 1971.

Morison, R. S. "Education for the Changing Field of Conservation." *Daedalus*, Winter 1967, pp. 1210–1223.

Murphy, Robert. *Wild Sanctuaries: Our National Wildlife Refuges: A Heritage Restored*. New York: Dutton, 1968.

Nash, Roderick. *The American Environment: Readings in the History of Conservation*. Reading, Mass.: Addison-Wesley, 1968.

Newman, Marian, and Regenstein, Lewis. "Extinction of the Kangaroo." *Environmental Quality*, April 1973, pp. 32ff.

Olsen, Jack. *Slaughter the Animals, Poison the Earth*. New York: Simon and Schuster, 1971.

Outdoor Recreational Bureau. *Outdoor Recreation Research, a Reference Catalog, 1970.* Washington: Government Printing Office, 1971.

Parson, Ruben L. *Conserving American Resources.* Englewood Cliffs, N.J.: Prentice-Hall, 1964.

Penick, James L. *Progressive Politics and Conservation.* Chicago: University of Chicago Press, 1968.

Pinchot, Gifford. *Fight for Conservation.* Seattle, Wash.: University of Washington Press, 1967.

Porter, Eliot, ed. *In Wilderness Is the Preservation....* New York: Sierra Club/Ballantine Books, 1967.

Regenstein, Lewis. "The Mountain Lion." *Environmental Quality,* March 1973, pp. 28-30.

Ripley, S. Dillon. "Conservation Comes of Age." *American Scientist,* September-October 1971, pp. 529-531.

Roosevelt, Nicholas. *Conservation: Now or Never.* New York: Dodd, Mead, 1970.

Schwartz, William, ed. *Voices for the Wilderness.* New York: Ballantine Books, 1969. (Prepared from Sierra Club Wilderness Conferences.)

Smith, Frank E. *Conservation in the United States: A Documentary History.* 5 vols. New York: Van Nostrand Reinhold, 1971. (Comprehensive.)

Snyder, A. P. "Wilderness Management: A Growing Challenge." *Journal of Forestry,* July 1966, pp. 441-446.

Soil Conservation Service. *Urban Soil Erosion and Sediment Control.* Washington: Government Printing Office, 1970.

Sports Fisheries and Wildlife Bureau. *Bald Eagle.* Washington: Government Printing Office, 1969. (History of bald eagle in America, how it has come to be threatened with extinction, and details on physical characteristics and life habits.)

―――. *Birds Protected by Federal Law: A List.* Washington: Government Printing Office, 1971.

―――. *The National Wildlife Refuge System.* Washington: Government Printing Office, 1971.

―――. *The Right to Exist, A Report on Our Endangered Wildlife.* Washington: Government Printing Office, 1969.

―――. *Wildlife Research Problems, Programs, Progress, 1967.* Washington: Government Printing Office, 1969. (Activities in the Bureau's Division of Wildlife Research.)

Stegner, Wallace. "Conservation Equals Survival." *American Heritage,* December 1969, pp. 12-15.

Stultifer, Morton. *The Case for Extinction: An Answer to Conservationists.* New York: Dial Press, 1970. (Satire of arguments against conservation.)

Teal, John, and Teal, Mildred. *Life and Death of the Salt Marsh.* Boston: Little, Brown, 1969. (Describes the East Coast wetlands.)

Thurber, Scott. "Conservation Comes of Age." *Nation,* February 27, 1967, pp. 272-275.

United Nations Economic and Social Council. *Conservation and the Rational Use of the Environment.* New York: Unipub, 1968.

Welch, Bruce L. "SST: Coming Threat to Wilderness." *Ekistics,* November 1968, pp. 436-437.

Whyte, William H. *The Last Landscape.* New York: Doubleday, 1968. (Advocates creation of small recreational and park areas in the cities.)

Wood, Frances, and Wood, Dorothy. *Animals in Danger: The Story of Vanishing American Wildlife.* New York: Dodd, Mead, 1968.

Zurhorst, Charles. *The Conservation Fraud.* New York: Cowles, 1970. (Indicts special-interest groups that block conservation efforts.)

ECONOMICS AND ENVIRONMENT

Barkley, Paul W. *Economic Growth and Environmental Decay: The Solution Becomes the Problem.* New York: Harcourt, 1972.

Boulding, Kenneth, et al. *Environmental Quality in a Growing Economy: Essays from the Sixth Resources for the Future Forum.* Baltimore: Johns Hopkins, 1966.

Crocker, Thomas D., and Rogers, A. J., III. *Environmental Economics.* Aurora, Ill.: Gallery Direct, 1971.

Dale, Edwin L., Jr. "The Economics of Pollution." *New York Times Magazine,* April 19, 1970, pp. 27ff. (Argues that economic forces will continue to lead men to degrade the environment.)

Dorfman, Robert, and Dorfman, Nancy, eds. *Economics of the Environment: Selected Readings.* New York: Norton, 1972. (A collection of general papers for all readers.)

Galbraith, John K. *The New Industrial State.* Boston: Houghton Mifflin, 1969. (A general economics text.)

Georgescu-Roegen, Nicholas. *The Entropy Law and the Economic Process.* Cambridge, Mass.: Harvard University Press, 1971.

Goldman, Marshall I., ed. *Controlling Pollution: The Economics of a Cleaner America.* Englewood Cliffs, N.J.: Prentice-Hall, 1967.

Goldman, Marshall I. *Ecology and Economics: Controlling Pollution in the 70's.* Englewood Cliffs, N.J.: Prentice-Hall, 1972.

Grosse, Robert N. "Some Problems in Economic Analysis of Environmental Policy Choices." *Ekistics,* March 1969, pp. 198–202.

Herfindahl, Orris C. *Natural Resource Information for Economic Development.* Baltimore: Johns Hopkins, 1969.

Herfindahl, Orris C., and Kneese, Allen V. *The Quality of the Environment, An Economic Approach to Some Problems in Using Land, Water, and Air.* Baltimore: Johns Hopkins, 1965.

Isard, Walter. *Ecologic-Economic Analysis for Regional Development: Some Initial Explorations with Particular Reference to Recreational Resource Use and Environmental Planning.* New York: Free Press, 1972. (Interesting use of quantitative techniques to analyze environmental impacts.)

Jarrett, Henry, ed. *Environmental Quality in a Growing Economy.* Baltimore: Johns Hopkins, 1966.

Kneese, Allen V., Ayres, Robert U., and d'Arge, Ralph C. *Economics and the Environment.* Washington: Resources for the Future, 1970. (Emphasizes relationship between the environment, consumption habits, and production methods.)

Krutilla, John V. "Some Environmental Effects of Economic Development." *Daedalus,* Fall 1967, pp. 1058–1070.

Rose, Sanford. "The Economics of Environmental Quality." *Fortune,* February 1970, pp. 120–123, 184–186.

Simon, Julian L., and Gardner, David M. "World Food Needs and 'New Proteins.'" *Economic Development and Cultural Change,* July 1969, pp. 520–526.

Smith, Dan Throop. "Improvement in the Quality of the Environment: Costs and Benefits." *Tax Policy,* March–April 1970, pp. 3–11.

Solow, Robert M. "The Economist's Approach to Pollution and Its Control." *Science,* August 6, 1971, pp. 498–503.

Wilson, Douglas B. "Tax Assistance and Environmental Pollution." *Tax Policy,* July–August 1970, pp. 3–11.

Wollman, Nathaniel. *Water Resources of Chile: An Economic Method for Analyzing Key Resources in a Nation's Development.* Baltimore, Johns Hopkins, 1968.

ENERGY

Aaronson, Terri. "The Black Box." *Environment,* December 1971, pp. 10–18. (Discusses the energy possibilities of fuel cells.)

Altman, Manfred. *Conservation and Better Utilization of Electric Power by Means of Thermal Energy Storage and Solar Heating.* Washington: Government Printing Office, 1971. (Distributed by National Technical Information Service.)

Artsimovich, L. A. "Controlled Nuclear Fusion: Energy for the Distant Future." *Bulletin of the Atomic Scientists,* June 1970, pp. 47–55.

Atomic Energy Commission. *Atomic Bonus: Non-Nuclear Benefits from Nuclear Development.* Washington: Government Printing Office, 1966.

———. *Civilian Nuclear Power: An Evaluation of Advanced Converter Reactors.* Washington: Government Printing Office, 1969.

———. *Civilian Nuclear Power: An Evaluation of a Heavy-Water Moderated-Boiling Light-Water-Cooled Reactor.* Washington: Government Printing Office, 1969.

———. *Civilian Nuclear Power: An Evaluation of Gas-Cooled Fast Reactors.* Washington: Government Printing Office, 1969.

———. *Civilian Nuclear Power: An Evaluation of Heavy-Water-Moderated Organic-Cooled Reactors.* Washington: Government Printing Office, 1968.

———. *Civilian Nuclear Power: An Evaluation of High-Temperature Gas-Cooled Reactors.* Washington: Government Printing Office, 1969.

———. *Civilian Nuclear Power: An Evaluation of Steam-Cooled Fast Breeder Reactors.* Washington: Government Printing Office, 1969.

———. *Competition in Nuclear Power Supply Industry.* Washington: Government Printing Office, 1969. (A report to the AEC and the Justice Department.)

———. *Cost-Benefit Analysis of the U.S. Breeder Reactor Program.* Washington: Government Printing Office, 1970.

———. *Forecast of Growth of Nuclear Power, January 1971.* Washington: Government Printing Office, 1971.

———. *Fuel for the Nuclear Age.* Washington: Government Printing Office, 1967.

———. *Nuclear Power and the Environment, Understanding the Atom Series.* Washington: Government Printing Office, 1969.

———. *Potential Applications for Nuclear Explosives in a Shale-Oil Industry.* Washington: Government Printing Office, 1969.

———. *Potential Nuclear Power Growth Patterns.* Washington: Government Printing Office, 1970.

———. *Research and Development for Safeguards.* Washington: Government Printing Office, 1968. (Discussion of nuclear power safeguards.)

———. *Soviet Power Reactors, 1970.* Washington: Government Printing Office, 1971. (Report of U.S. Nuclear Power Reactors Delegation visit to the USSR, June 15–July 1, 1970.)

———. *Why Fusion? Controlled Thermonuclear Research Program.* Washington: Government Printing Office, 1970.

Barfield, Claude E. "Energy Report: Broad Campaign against Nuclear Power Begins with Nader Suit on Reactor Safety." *National Journal,* June 9, 1973, pp. 850–851.

———. "Science Report: Nuclear Breeder Reactor Program Delayed by Court Decision, Contract Disputes." *National Journal,* June 30, 1973, pp. 954–962.

Barnes, Joseph. "Geothermal Power." *Scientific American,* January 1972, pp. 70–77.

Berg, George G. "Hot Wastes from Nuclear Power." *Environment,* May 1973, pp. 36–44. (Describes treatment of radioactive wastes at nuclear plant in West Valley, N.Y.)

Berkowitz, David A., and Squires, Arthur M., eds. *Power Generation and Environmental Change.* Cambridge, Mass.: MIT Press, 1971. (Symposium of the Committee on Environmental Alteration, AAAS.)

Bockris, John O'M., ed. *Electrochemistry of Cleaner Environments.* New York: Plenum, 1972. (Discusses advantages of using electrochemical power.)

Bohn, Heinrich L. "A Clean New Gas." *Environment*, December 1971, pp. 4–9. (Discusses the potentials of methane as a fuel.)

Brooks, David B., and Krutilla, John V. *Peaceful Use of Nuclear Explosives: Some Economic Aspects*. Baltimore: Johns Hopkins, 1969.

Brown, Theodore L. *Energy and the Environment*. Columbus, Ohio: Merrill, 1971. (General text.)

Bureau of Mines. *Energy Potential from Organic Wastes: A Review of the Quantities and Sources*. Washington: Government Printing Office, 1972.

Congress. House. *Atomic Energy Act of 1946 and Amendments, August 1, 1946–December 24, 1970*. Compiled by Gilman G. Udell. Washington: Government Printing Office, 1971.

Congress. House. Committee on Interior and Insular Affairs. *Fuel and Energy Resources: Hearings of the Committee*. Washington: Government Printing Office, 1972.

Congress. Joint Committee on Atomic Energy. *AEC Authorizing Legislation Fiscal Year 1972: Hearings before the Joint Committee*. 4 vols. Washington: Government Printing Office, 1971. (Covers a wide variety of topics pertinent to atomic energy.)

———. *Environmental Effects of Producing Electric Power: Hearings before the Joint Committee*. Washington: Government Printing Office, 1969–1970. (In two parts, with part 2 divided into two volumes.)

———. *Nuclear Power and Related Energy Problems, 1968 through 1970*. Washington: Government Printing Office, 1971.

———. *Prelicensing Antitrust Review of Nuclear Powerplants: Hearings before the Joint Committee*. Washington: Government Printing Office, 1970. (In two parts.)

Congress. Senate. Committee on Public Works. *Some Environmental Implications of National Fuels Policies*. Washington: Government Printing Office, 1970. (Report prepared by the staff of the Joint Committee.)

———. *Underground Uses of Nuclear Energy: Hearings before the Subcommittee on Air and Water Pollution*. Washington: Government Printing Office, 1970. (In two parts.)

Cootner, Paul H., and Löf, George O. G. *Water Demand for Steam Electric Generation: An Economic Projection Model*. Baltimore: Johns Hopkins, 1966.

Cottrell, Fred. *Energy and Society: The Relation Between Energy, Social Change and Economic Development*. New York: McGraw-Hill, 1955.

Curtis, Richard, and Hogan, Elizabeth. *Perils of the Peaceful Atom: The Myth of Safe Nuclear Power Plants*. Garden City, N.Y.: Doubleday, 1970.

Daniels, Farrington. *Direct Use of the Sun's Energy*. New Haven: Yale University Press, 1964.

Energy and Power: A Scientific American Book. San Francisco: Freeman, 1971.

"The Energy Crisis." *Bulletin of the Atomic Scientists*, September, October, November 1971. (Issues consist of 26 articles dealing with aspects of the environment and alternative sources of energy.)

"Energy for the World's Technology." *New Scientist*, November 13, 1969, pp. 1–24.

Environmental Aspects of Nuclear Power Stations. New York: Unipub, 1971.

Environmental Protection Agency. *Potential Environmental Effects of an Offshore Submerged Nuclear Power Plant*. 2 vols. Washington: Government Printing Office, 1971.

———. *Thermoelectric Generators Powered by Thermal Waste from Electric Power Plants*. Washington: Government Printing Office, 1970.

Executive Office of the President. Office of Science and Technology. *Electric Power and Environments*. Washington: Government Printing Office, 1970. (Proposes program for resolving conflict between power needs and environmental protection.)

———. *Patterns of Energy Consumption in the United States.* Washington: Government Printing Office, 1972.

Fabricant, Neil, and Hallman, Robert M. *Toward a Rational Power Policy: Energy, Politics, and Pollution.* New York: George Braziller, 1971.(Prompted by Con Edison's proposal to build new plant in Astoria, Queens, but transcends the local issue.)

Fenner, David, and Klarmann, Joseph. "Power from the Earth." *Environment*, December 1971, pp. 19-26. (Discusses the potentials of geothermal power.)

Forbes, Ian A., Ford, Daniel F., Kendall, Henry W., and MacKenzie, James J. "Cooling Water." *Environment*, January–February 1972, pp. 40-47. (Questions the reliability of using water as coolant, in face of the dangers of a nuclear power plant emergency.)

Ford, Daniel F., and Kendall, Henry W. "Nuclear Safety." *Environment*, September 1972, pp. 2-9. (Studies safety of nuclear power plants.)

Foreman, Harry, ed. *Nuclear Power and the Public.* Minneapolis: University of Minnesota Press, 1970.

"From the H-Bomb: Power Without Pollution." *Business Week*, September 12, 1970, pp. 80ff.

Garton, Ronald R., and Christianson, Alden G. *Beneficial Uses of Waste Heat—An Evaluation.* Washington: Government Printing Office, 1970.

Gerber, Abraham. "Environment and the Energy Industries." *Business Economics*, January 1971, pp. 68-72.

Gofman, John W., and Tamplin, Arthur R. *Poisoned Power: The Case Against Nuclear Power Plants.* New York: Rodale Press, 1971.

Gough, William C., and Eastlund, Bernard J. "The Prospects of Fusion Power." *Scientific American*, February 1971, pp. 50-64.

Green, L., "Energy Needs vs. Environmental Pollution: A Reconciliation?" *Science*, June 16, 1967, pp. 1448-1450.

Grimmer, D. P., and Luszczynski, K. "Lost Power." *Environment*, April 1972, pp. 14-22. (Discusses ways in which efficient transportation can decrease energy loss that results from the processing of petroleum.)

Guyol, N. B. *World Electric Power Industry.* Berkeley, Calif.: University of California Press, 1968.

Halacy, Dan S. *The Coming Age of Solar Energy.* New York: Harper, 1963.

Hammond, Allen L. "Breeder Reactors: Power for the Future." *Science*, November 19, 1971, pp. 807-810.

Hirst, Eric, and Moyers, John C. "Efficiency of Energy Use in the United States." *Science*, March 30, 1973, pp. 1299-1304. (Discusses possibilities of more efficient use of energy resources.)

Holden, C. "Energy: Shortages Loom, but Conservation Lags." *Science*, June 15, 1973, pp. 1155-1158.

Holdren, John. *Energy: A Crisis in Power.* New York: Sierra Club, 1971.

Hottel, H. C., and Howard, J. B. *New Energy Technology: Some Facts and Assessments.* Cambridge, Mass.: MIT Press, 1972.

Interior Department. *Environmental Criteria for Electric Transmission Systems.* Washington: Government Printing Office, 1970.

Jones, Lawrence W. "Liquid Hydrogen as a Fuel for the Future." *Science*, October 22, 1971, pp. 367-370.

Landsberg, Hans H., and Schurr, Sam H. *Energy in the United States: Sources, Uses and Policy Issues.* New York: Random House, 1968.

Lapp, Ralph E. "The Four Big Fears about Nuclear Power." *New York Times Magazine*, February 7, 1971, pp. 16ff.

Lincoln, G. A. "Energy Conservation." *Science*, April 13, 1973, pp. 155-161.

Lovejoy, Wallace F., and Homan, Paul T. *Methods of Estimating Reserves of Crude Oil, Natural Gas, and Natural Gas Liquids.* Baltimore: Johns Hopkins, 1967.

Lubin, Moshe J., and Fraas, Arthur P. "Fusion by Laser." *Scientific American*, June 1971, pp. 21–33.

MacAvoy, Paul W., and Petersen, Dean F. *Developing Nuclear Breeder Reactors*. Cambridge, Mass.: MIT Press, 1969.

Metz, William D. "Ocean Temperature Gradients: Solar Power from the Sea." *Science*, June 12, 1973, pp. 1266–1267.

———. "Power Gas and Combined Cycles: Clean Power from Fossil Fuels." *Science*, January 5, 1973, pp. 54–56.

Mills, G. Alex. "Gas from Coal: Fuel of the Future." *Environmental Science and Technology*, December 1971, pp. 1178–1183. (Describes processes for obtaining gas from coal.)

Mitre Corporation. *Energy Resources and the Environment*. Washington: Government Printing Office, 1972. (Distributed by the National Technical Information Service.)

National Academy of Engineering. Committee on Power Plant Siting. *Engineering for the Resolution of the Energy-Environmental Dilemma*. Washington: National Academy of Engineering, 1971.

Novick, Sheldon. *The Careless Atom*. New York: Dell, 1970. (Asks whether nuclear power is really needed.)

———. "Toward a Nuclear Power Precipice." *Environment*, March 1973, pp. 32–40. (Examines problems in the nuclear power industry.)

Rocks, Lawrence. *The Energy Crisis*. New York: Crown, 1972.

Rose, David J. "Controlled Nuclear Fusion: Status and Outlook." *Science*, May 21, 1971, pp. 797–808.

Schurr, Sam H. *Energy Research Needs*. Washington: Government Printing Office, 1971. Distributed by National Technical Information Service. Identifies research needed to understand long-term energy problems.)

Seaborg, Glenn T., and Corliss, William R. *Man and Atom: Building a New World through Nuclear Technology*. New York: Dutton, 1971. (Author was chairman of the Atomic Energy Commission for ten years.)

Soucie, Gary. "Oil Shale: Pandora's New Box." *Audubon*, January 1972, pp. 106–112.

Squires, Arthur M. "Clean Power from Coal." *Science*, August 28, 1970, pp. 821–828.

Tamplin, Arthur R. "Solar Energy." *Environment*, June 1973, pp. 16–20, 32–34.

Vita, Susan H. *Pipeline Constructions in Cold Regions Excluding the Russian Literature: A Bibliography*. Washington: Government Printing Office, 1971. (Distributed by National Technical Information Service. Lists literature on such constructions, including environmental and engineering problems.)

Weinburg, Alvin M. "Nuclear Energy and the Environment." *Bulletin of the Atomic Scientists*, June 1970, pp. 69–74.

Weinburg, Alvin M., and Hammond, R. Philip. "Limits to the Use of Energy." *American Scientist*, July 1970, pp. 412–418.

Weingart, Jerome. "Sun Power: Everything You've Always Wanted to Know about Solar Energy, but Were Never Charged Up Enough to Ask." *Environmental Technology*, December 1972, pp. 38–42.

"Why Utilities Can't Meet Demand." *Business Week*, November 29, 1969, pp. 48–62.

ENVIRONMENTAL LAW AND POLITICS

Baldwin, Malcolm F., and Page, James K., Jr., eds. *Law and the Environment*. New York: Walker, 1970. (Prompted by Santa Barbara oil spill in 1969. Includes extensive bibliography.)

Congress. House. *Laws Relating to Forestry, Game Conservation, Flood Control, and Related Subjects, March 1, 1911–December 19, 1970*. Washington: Government Printing Office, 1971.

Congress. House. Committee on Public Works. *Laws of the United States Relating to Water Pollution Control and Environmental Quality*. Washington: Government Printing Office, 1970.

Cooley, Richard A., and Wandesforde-Smith, Geoffrey. *Congress and the Environment.* Seattle, Wash.: University of Washington Press, 1970.

Davies, J. Clarence. *The Politics of Pollution.* New York: Pegasus, 1970.

Ewald, William R., Jr. *Environment and Policy: The Next Fifty Years.* Bloomington, Ind.: Indiana University Press, 1968.

Fontana, Joseph, ed. *Pollution and the Law.* Washington: Federal Bar Association, 1971.

Grad, Frank P., Rathjens, G. W., and Rosenthal, A. J. *Environmental Control: Priorities, Policies, and the Law.* New York: Columbia University Press, 1971.

Hurley, William D. *Environmental Legislation.* Springfield, Ill.: Charles C Thomas, 1971.

Lewin, Stuart F., et al. *Law and the Municipal Ecology: Air, Water, Noise, Over-population.* Washington: National Institute of Municipal Law Officers, 1970.

Lieber, Harvey. "Public Administration and Environmental Quality." *Public Administration Review*, May–June 1970, pp. 277–286. (Discusses public policy and institutional reaction to environmental crisis.)

Mosher, Charles A. "Needs and Trends in Congressional Decision-Making." *Science*, October 13, 1972, pp. 134–138.

Murphy, Earl F. *Man and His Environment: Law.* Man and His Environment series. New York: Harper, 1970.

Political Economy of Environment. The Hague, Netherlands: Co-Libri, 1972. (Discusses relationships between social systems and disruptions of the environment.)

Reitze, Arnold W., Jr. *Environmental Law.* 2nd ed. Washington: North American International, 1972. (Discusses laws passed through June 1972.)

Ridgeway, James. *The Politics of Ecology.* New York: Dutton, 1970. (Charges that corporate power has taken over the ecology movement to gain control of natural resources and make money with ineffective antipollution devices.)

Smith, Frank E. *Politics of Conservation.* New York: Random House, 1966.

FOOD PRODUCTION

Agriculture Department. *Managing Our Environment, A Report on Ways Agricultural Research Fights Pollution.* Washington: Government Printing Office, 1971. (Articles prepared by Agricultural Research Service.)

"Agriculture Poses Waste Problems: Today's High-Intensity Farming Methods Are Producing More and More Pollutants." *Environmental Science and Technology*, December 1970, pp. 1098–1100.

American Assembly. *Overcoming World Hunger.* Englewood Cliffs, N.J.: Prentice-Hall, 1969.

Borgstrom, Georg. *Hungry Planet.* New York: Macmillan, 1965.

Boyko, Hugo. "Farming the Desert." *Ekistics*, November 1968, pp. 464–468.

Brady, Nyle C., ed. *Agriculture and the Quality of Our Environment.* Washngton: American Association for the Advancement of Science, 1967. (Examines unwanted effects of certain agricultural practices.)

Carter, Luther J. "World Food Supply: Problems and Prospects." *Science*, January 6, 1967, pp. 56–58.

Cochrane, Willard W. *World Food Problem: A Guardedly Optimistic View.* New York: Crowell, 1969.

Congress. Joint Committee on Atomic Energy. *Review of the Food Irradiation Program: Hearing before the Subcommittee on Research, Development, and Radiation.* Washington: Government Printing Office, 1967.

Congress. Senate. Select Committee on Nutrition and Human Needs. *Nutrition and Human Needs, 1970: Part 5: Environmental Health Problems.* Washington: Government Printing Office, 1970.

Dairy and Food Industries Supply Association. *Food Engineering Forum: Environment and the Food Processor.* Washington: Dairy and Food Industries Supply Association, 1971.

Duckham, A. N., and Masefield, G. B. *Farming Systems of the World.* New York: Praeger, 1970.

Dumont, Rene, and Roser, Bernard. *The Hungry Future.* New York: Praeger, 1969. (Presents view that only immediate, massive steps on a global level can alleviate annihilation of life by protein deficiency.)

Evenari, Michael. "Land (II): Ecological Farming." *Impact of Science on Society,* vol. 19, no. 2, 1969, pp. 209–216.

Freeman, Orville L. *World Without Hunger.* New York: Praeger, 1968.

Gray, William David. *The Use of Fungi as Food and in Food Processing.* Cleveland, Ohio: Chemical Rubber Company, 1970.

Hayes, Jack, ed. *Outdoors USA, The Yearbook of Agriculture, 1967.* Washington: Government Printing Office, 1967. (Agriculture Department handbook of conservation, outdoor recreation, and beautification.)

Holt, S. J. "Food Resources of the Ocean." *Scientific American,* September 1969, pp. 178–194.

Hunter, Beatrice T. *Consumer Beware: Your Food and What's Been Done to It.* New York: Simon and Schuster, 1971.

———. *Gardening Without Poisons.* Boston: Houghton Mifflin, 1964.

Idyll, C. P. "Agriculture: Its Promise and Limitations." *Ekistics,* November 1968, pp. 460–463.

Langer, Richard W. *Grow It! The Beginner's Complete In-Harmony-with-Nature Small Farm Guide—From Vegetable and Grain Growing to Livestock Care.* New York: Saturday Review, 1972.

Lowenberg, Miriam, et al. *Food and Man.* New York: Wiley, 1968.

MacBride, G. "New Foods for the Lean Years." *Contemporary Review,* January 1969, pp. 24–29.

McGovern, George, ed. *Agricultural Thoughts in the 20th Century.* Indianapolis, Ind.: Bobbs-Merrill, 1967.

National Industrial Pollution Control Council. *Animal Slaughtering and Processing.* Washington: Government Printing Office, 1971.

———. *Pollution Problems in Selected Food Industries, Excludes Meat, Poultry and Grain-Based Foods.* Washington: Government Printing Office, 1971.

Patton, S., et al. "Food Value of Red Tide (Gonyaulax Polyedra)." *Science,* November 10, 1967, pp. 789–790.

Pinchot, Gifford B. "Marine Farming." *Scientific American,* December 1970, pp. 14–21.

Pirie, N. W. *Food Resources, Conventional and Novel.* Baltimore: Johns Hopkins, 1969.

Public Health Service. *Hot Tips on Food Protection.* Washington: Government Printing Office, 1966.

Scott, John. *Hunger.* New York: Parents Magazine Press, 1969.

Shelton, Robert L., Jr. *Changing Concept of Food Sanitation.* Washington: Government Printing Office, 1968.

Socolofsky, Homer E. "World Food Crisis and Progress in Wheat Breeding." *Agricultural History,* October 1969, pp. 423–438.

Water Quality Office. *Proceedings, First National Symposium on Food Processing Wastes.* Washington: Government Printing Office, 1971.

GENERAL

Ackerman, Edward A. "Population, Natural Resources and Technology." *American Academy of Political and Social Sciences Annals,* January 1967, pp. 84–97.

Adams, R. M. et al. *Fitness of Man's Environment.* New York: Random House, 1967.

Agriculture Department. *Community Improvement through Beautification.* Washington: Government Printing Office, 1965.

———. *Environmental Thrust, Citizen Projects for a Better America.* Washington: Government Printing Office, 1971.

———. *Science and Improving Our Environment*. Rev. ed. Washington: Government Printing Office, 1968.

Allan, J. David, and Hanson, Arthur J., eds. *Recycle This Book!* Belmont, Calif.: Wadsworth, 1972. (Varied opinions on problems and solutions to environmental problems.)

Allen, Shirley Walter, and Leonard, Justing Wilkinson. *Conserving Natural Resources: Principles and Practice in a Democracy*. 3rd ed. New York: McGraw-Hill, 1966.

American Chemical Society. *Cleaning Our Environment: The Chemical Basis for Action*. Washington: American Chemical Society, 1969.

———. *Supplement*. Washington: American Chemical Society, 1971.

Ames, Edward A. *Schools and the Environment*. New York: Ford Foundation, 1970.

Andrew, R. N. L. "The Council on Environmental Quality: An Evaluation." *Journal of Soil Water Conservation*, January–February 1972, pp. 8–11. (Discusses problems and accomplishments of the Council.)

"Anthropics: Man in Relation to His Settlements." *Ekistics*, June 1968. (Whole issue devoted to man in his environment.)

Arthur, Don R. *Man and His Environment*. New York: American Elsevier, 1969.

Arvill, Robert. *Man and Environment*. Baltimore: Penguin, 1967.

Bardach, John E. *Harvest of the Sea*. New York: Harper, 1968.

Bateson, Mary Catherine. *Our Own Metaphor*. New York: Knopf, 1972. (Asks whether man is competent enough to solve the problems he has created.)

Behan, R. W., and Weddle, Richard M., ed. *Ecology, Economics, Environment*. Missoula, Mont.: University of Montana Press, 1971. (Concerns issues dealing with environmental quality.)

Belknap, Raymond K., and Furtado, John G. *Three Approaches to Environmental Resource Analysis*. Washington: Conservation Foundation, 1967.

Bell, Daniel, ed. *Toward the Year 2000: Work in Progress*. Boston: Houghton Mifflin, 1968. (Discusses present social policy and how it may influence the future.)

Beranek, William, Jr., ed. *Science, Scientists and Society*. Tarrytown-on-Hudson, N.Y.: Bogden and Quigley, 1972. (Comments included on various environmental matters.)

Bernarde, Melvin A. *Our Precarious Habitat*. New York: Norton, 1970. (Discusses effects of environmental health hazards on man.)

Black, John D. *Management and Conservation of Biological Resources*. Philadelphia: Davis, 1968.

Blake, Peter. *God's Own Junkyard: The Planned Deterioration of America's Landscape*. New York: Holt, Rinehart and Winston, 1964. (Numerous photographs contrasting the beauty of the land with the unsightliness that is engulfing it.)

Bormann, F. Herbert, and Likens, Gene E. "The Nutrient Cycles of an Ecosystem." *Scientific American*, October 1970, pp. 92–101.

Bramer, Henry C. "Pollution Control in the Steel Industry." *Environmental Science and Technology*, October 1971, pp. 1004–1016.

Brown, Harrison. "Human Materials Production as a Process in the Biosphere." *Scientific American*, September 1970, pp. 194–208.

Brubaker, Sterling. *To Live on Earth*. Baltimore: Johns Hopkins, 1972. (Discusses man's response to environmental threats.)

Bundy, McGeorge. *Managing Knowledge to Save the Environment*. New York: Ford Foundation, 1970.

Bureau of Naval Personnel, U.S. Navy. *Disaster Control (Ashore and Afloat)*. Washington: Government Printing Office, 1968. (Manmade disasters—nuclear, biological, or chemical warfare attack—their characteristics, results, and prevention.)

Calder, Nigel. *Eden Was No Garden: An Inquiry Into the Environment of Man*. New York: Holt, Rinehart and Winston, 1967.

Caldwell, Lynton Keith. *Environment: A Challenger to Modern Society*. Garden City,

N.Y.: Doubleday, 1970. (Urges governmental assumption of responsibility for correction of environmental problems.)

Carpenter, Richard A. "Information for Decisions in Environmental Policy." *Science*, June 12, 1970, pp. 1316–1322. (Describes information services developed by the Congress dealing with ecological issues.)

Charter, S. P. R. *Man on Earth: A Preliminary Evaluation of the Ecology of Man.* New York: Grove Press, 1970.

Ciriacy-Wanthrop, S. V., and Parsons, James J., eds. *Natural Resources: Quality and Quantity.* Berkeley, Calif.: University of California Press, 1967.

Citizens Advisory Committee on Environmental Quality. *Community Action for Environmental Quality.* Washington: Government Printing Office, 1970.

———. *Community Action for Natural Beauty.* Washington: Government Printing Office, 1968.

Coale, Ansley J. "Man and His Environment." *Science*, October 9, 1970, pp. 132–136.

Cohn, Victor. "Protecting Our Environment; Where Are We Now?" *Current*, January 1971, pp. 15–19.

Cole, Lamont C. "Man's Ecosystem." *BioScience*, April 1966, pp. 243–248.

Collins, Donald J. "Environmental Pollution: U.S. and Canada." *SAIS Review*, Summer 1970, pp. 19–31.

Commission on Population Growth and the American Future. *Population, Resources, and the Environment*, ed. by Ronald G. Ridker. Washington: Government Printing Office, 1972. (A collection of articles.)

Commoner, Barry. *The Closing Circle: Man, Nature and Technology.* New York: Knopf, 1971. (Sees environmental crisis as a result of man's social mismanagement of resources.)

———. *Science and Survival.* New York: Viking Press, 1966. (Opposes the unbridled application of science and technology to the manipulation of government and man.)

———. "Technology and the Natural Environment." *Architectural Forum*, June 1969, pp. 68–73.

Commoner, Barry, Corr, Michael, and Stamler, Paul J. "The Cause of Pollution." *Environment*, April 1971, pp. 2–19. (Cites technology as a major cause.)

Congress. House. Committee on Government Operations. *Environmental Decade (Action Proposals for the 1970's): Hearings before a Subcommittee.* Washington: Government Printing Office, 1970. (See also a Report by the Committee, *H. rp. 1082*, 1970.)

Congress. House Documents. *Message on Environment.* Washington: Government Printing Office, 1970. (Message from the president, outlining legislative proposals and administrative actions taken to improve environmental quality.)

Congress. Joint Economic Committee. *The Economy, Energy, and the Environment, A Background Study.* Washington: Government Printing Office, 1970. (Prepared for the use of the Committee.)

Congress. Laws. *Environmental Education Act, Approved October 30, 1970.* Washington: Government Printing Office, 1970.

Council on Environmental Quality. *Environmental Quality. First Annual Report.* Washington: Government Printing Office, 1970. (Systematic assessment of quality of our surroundings.)

———. *The President's 1971 Environmental Program.* Washington: Government Printing Office, 1971.

———. *Environmental Quality. Second Annual Report.* Washington: Government Printing Office, 1971. (Progress in implementing recommendations of the CEQ's First Annual Report.)

———. *Environmental Quality. Third Annual Report.* Washington: Government Printing Office, 1972.

Crawford, G. M. "A Guide for Environmental Health Planning." *Journal of Environmental Health*, January–February 1972, pp. 413–416. (Outlines health concerns arising from the polluted environment.)

Dansereau, Pierre, ed. *Challenge for Survival: Land, Air and Water for Man in Megalopolis.* New York: Columbia University Press, 1970.

Darling, Frank Fraser. *Wilderness and Plenty: The Reith Lectures, 1969.* Boston: Houghton Mifflin, 1970. (Discusses natural resources, population, and pollution.)

Day, John A., Fost, Frederic F., and Rose, Peter. *Dimensions of the Environmental Crisis.* New York: Wiley, 1971. (States that interdisciplinary approach is necessary to find total solution to pollution problems.)

Dayton Museum of Natural History. *The Do-It-Yourself Environmental Handbook.* Rev. ed. Boston: Little, Brown, 1972. (Practical guide for survival.)

DeBell, Garett, ed. *The Environmental Handbook.* New York: Ballantine Books, 1970. (Prepared for the First National Environmental Teach-In. Deals with various aspects of the environment and offers suggestions for improvements.)

Detwyler, Thomas R. *Man's Impact on the Environment.* New York: McGraw-Hill, 1971. (Useful anthology.)

Dickinson, Robert E. *Regional Ecology: The Study of Man's Environment.* New York: Wiley, 1970.

Disch, Robert, ed. *The Ecological Conscience: Values for Survival.* Englewood Cliffs, N.J.: Prentice-Hall, 1970. (Essays discussing the philosphical consequences of the environmental crisis.)

Douglas, William O. *The Three Hundred Year War: A Chronicle of Ecological Disaster.* New York: Random House, 1972. (Supreme Court Justice Douglas calls for government action.)

Dubos, René "Crisis of Man in His Environment." *Ekistics*, March 1969, pp. 151–154.

———. "Humanizing the Earth." *Science*, February 23, 1973, pp. 769–772. (Argues that favorable environment can be produced through ecological concern and scientific knowledge.)

———. *So Human an Animal.* New York: Scribner, 1968. (The Pulitzer Prize-winning classic.)

Dunbar, Max J. *Environment and Good Sense.* New York: University Press, 1971. (Suggests methods of controlling pollution and discusses the damage already in existence.)

Dwiggins, Don. *SST: Here It Comes, Ready or Not.* Garden City, N.Y.: Doubleday, 1968.

Eco-Catastrophe. San Francisco: Canfield Press, 1970. (Articles, originally published in *Ramparts*, expressing radical point of view on ecological crisis.)

"Ecology: The New Great Chain of Being." *Natural History*, December 1968, pp. 8–16.

Egler, Frank E. *The Way of Science: A Philosophy of Ecology for the Layman.* New York: Hafner, 1971.

Ehrenfeld, David W. *Conserving Life on Earth.* New York: Oxford University Press, 1972.

Ehrlich, Paul R., and Ehrlich, Anne H. *Population, Resources, Environment.* San Francisco: Freeman, 1972. (Text on study of the environment.)

Ehrlich, Paul R., and Harriman, Richard L. *How to Be a Survivor: A Plan to Save Spaceship Earth.* Friends of the Earth publication. New York: Ballantine Books, 1971. (Argues that the economy must be altered to fit in with the earth's limited resources.)

Eipper, Alfred W. "Pollution Problems, Resource Policy, and the Scientist." *Science*, July 3, 1970, pp. 11–15.

Eiseley, Loren. *The Invisible Pyramid.* New York: Scribner, 1970. (Plea to curb our technology before it is too late.)

Eisenbud, Merril. "Environmental Protection in the City of New York." *Science*, November 13, 1970, pp. 706–712. (Discusses complexities of dealing with pollution in an urban environment.)

"Environmental Pollution and Its Control." *Ekistics*, August 1968, pp. 196–199.

Environmental Protection Agency. *Action for Environmental Quality: Standards and En-*

forcement for Air and Water Pollution Control. Washington: Government Printing Office, 1973.

———. *Health Effects of Environmental Pollution.* Washington: Government Printing Office, 1973.

———. *Toward a New Environmental Ethic.* Washington: Government Printing Office, 1971. (Discusses work of EPA's divisions, research centers, and laboratories.)

Environmental Workbooks. New York: Institute for Public Information, 1970–1971. (Series of books, each dealing with a different environmental concern.)

Ewald, William R., Jr., ed. *Environment for Man,* Bloomington, Ind.: Indiana University Press, 1971. (Examination of environments of the future, up to the year 2017.)

Fabun, Don. *Dimensions of Change.* Beverly Hills, Calif.: Glencoe, 1971. (Analyzes technological responses to changes in human behavior occurring within the next 30 years.)

Falk, Richard A. *This Endangered Planet: Prospects and Proposals for Human Survival.* New York: Random House, 1971. (Discusses overpopulation, dwindling of natural resources, environmental deterioration, and the war system.)

Fanning, Odom. *Opportunities in Environmental Careers.* New York: Universal Publishing and Distributing, 1971.

Farvar, M. Taghi, et al. "The Pollution of Asia." *Environment,* October 1971, pp. 10–17.

Flawn, Peter T. *Environmental Geology: Conservation, Land-Use Planning, and Resource Management.* New York: Harper, 1970.

Forest Service. *Teaching Conservation through Outdoor Education Areas.* Rev. ed. Washington: Government Printing Office, 1970.

Fortune Magazine, ed. *The Environment: A National Mission for the Seventies.* New York: Harper, 1970.

Foster, Phillips W. *Introduction to Environmental Science.* Homewood, Ill.: Learning Systems Co., 1972. (Presents a programmed learning format.)

Fuller, R. Buckminster. *Operating Manual for Spaceship Earth.* New York: Simon and Schuster, 1969. (Optimistic view of man's potential future.)

Gamow, George. *A Planet Called Earth.* New York: Bantam Books, 1965.

Goldman, Marshall I. "The Costs of Fighting Pollution." *Current History,* August 1970, pp. 73–81.

Grosvenor, Gilbert M., ed. *As We Live and Breathe: The Challenge of Our Environment.* Washington: National Geographic Society, 1971.

Hamblin, Lynette Kaye. *Pollution: The World Crisis.* New York: Barnes and Noble, 1970.

Handler, Philip, ed. *Biology and the Future of Man.* New York: Oxford University Press, 1970. (Good source book that discusses population and food problems as well as medicine, resources, and the environment.)

Hardin, Garrett. *Exploring New Ethics for Survival: The Voyage of the Spaceship "Beagle."* New York: Viking Press, 1972. (Science fiction work that contains controversial remedies for the overpopulated world.)

Hare, R. K. "How Should We Treat Environment?" *Science,* January 23, 1970, pp. 352–355.

Harrison, Gordon A. *Earthkeeping: The War with Nature and a Proposal for Peace.* Boston: Houghton Mifflin, 1971. (Argues that goals of technology must be redirected.)

Harrison, Gordon A., Gates, David, and Holling, C. S. "Ecology: The Great Chain of Being." *Ekistics,* March 1969, 161–164.

Harte, John, and Socolow, Robert, eds. *Patient Earth.* New York: Holt, Rinehart, and Winston, 1971. (Compilation of articles.)

Haskell, Elizabeth H. "State Governments Tackle Pollution." *Environmental Science and Technology,* November 1971, pp. 1092–1097.

Hawkins, Mary E. *Vital View of the Environment.* Washington: National Science Teachers Association, 1971. (For building educational programs.)

Hay, John. *In Defense of Nature.* New York: Viking Press, 1970. (Discusses man's role in the natural environment.)

Health, Education, and Welfare Department. *Environmental Education.* Washington: Government Printing Office, 1970.

———. *Environmental Education Cannot Wait.* Washington: Government Printing Office, 1971. (Reprinted from *American Education,* May 1971.)

———. *Environmental Health Planning.* Washington: Government Printing Office, 1971.

———. *A Strategy for a Liveable Environment.* Washington: Government Printing Office, 1967. (Prepared by HEW's Task Force on Environmental Health and Related Problems.)

Helfrich, Harold W., Jr., ed. *Agenda for Survival.* New Haven, Conn.: Yale University Press, 1971. (Lectures on important issues by scholars from various fields.)

———. *The Environmental Crisis: Man's Struggle to Live with Himself.* New Haven, Conn.: Yale University Press, 1970. (Topics include weather modification, damage to coastal wetlands, and contamination of food.)

Hill, Wilhelmina. "Environmental Education: The State of the Art." *Childhood Education,* October 1970, pp. 14–18. (Progress report on Office of Education activities supporting environmental and ecological education programs.)

Hodges, Laurent. *Environmental Pollution: A Survey Emphasizing Physical and Chemical Principles.* New York: Holt, Rinehart, and Winston, 1973.

Hoelscher, H. E. "Technology and Social Change." *Science,* October 3, 1969, pp. 68–72.

Holdren, John P., and Ehrlich, Paul R., eds. *Global Ecology: Readings Toward a Rational Strategy for Man.* New York: Harcourt, 1971.

"How to Stop Pollution." *U.S. News and World Report,* November 23, 1970, pp. 54–58. (Interview with Russell Train, White House environmental advisor.)

Jackson, Barbara (Ward), and Dubos, René. *Earth: The Care and Maintenance of a Small Planet.* New York: Norton, 1972.

Jarrett, Henry, ed. *Environmental Quality in a Growing Economy.* Baltimore: Johns Hopkins, 1966. (Assesses public attitudes.)

Jennings, Burgess H., and Murphy, John E., eds. *Interactions of Man and His Environment.* New York: Plenum Press, 1966.

Johnson, Cecil E., ed. *EcoCrisis.* New York: Wiley, 1970. (Essays on environmental problems by famous individuals, including Rachel Carson, Paul Ehrlich, and Aldous Huxley.)

Kepes, Gyorgy, ed. *Arts of the Environment.* New York: George Braziller, 1972. (Discusses artist's role in involving man in his environment.)

Kline, A. Burt, Jr. *The Environmental and Ecological Forum, 1970–1971.* Washington: Government Printing Office, 1972. (A Department of Commerce publication on notable economic, social, and environmental features of generating electrical power. Stresses use of nuclear power and its advantages and disadvantages.)

Kneese, Allen V., and Bower, Blair T., eds. *Environmental Quality Analysis.* Baltimore: Johns Hopkins, 1972. Discusses economics, management, politics, and legal institutions.)

Kormondy, Edward J. *Concepts of Ecology.* Englewood Cliffs, N.J.: Prentice-Hall, 1969.

Lambert, J. M. *Teaching of Ecology.* Oxford, England: Blackwell Scientific, 1967.

Landsberg, Hans H. *Natural Resources for U.S. Growth: A Look Ahead to the Year 2000.* Baltimore: Johns Hopkins, 1964.

Laycock, George. *The Diligent Destroyers.* New York: Audubon/Ballantine Books, 1970. (Criticizes Army Corps of Engineers and others whose flood control projects actually cause greater damage. Also discusses strip miners and highway builders.)

Lee, Douglas H. K., ed. *Metallic Contaminants and Human Health.* New York: Academic Press, 1972. (One in series of four books on environmental health.)

Lee, Douglas H. K., and Minard, David, eds. *Physiology, Environment, and Man.* New York: Academic Press, 1970. (Discusses man's physiological adaptation to the environment.)

Linton, Ron M. *Terracide: America's Destruction of Her Living Environment.* Boston: Little, Brown, 1970. (Discusses human reactions to noise, stench, and overcrowding, and suggests answers to these problems.)

Love, Rhoda M., and Love, Glen A., eds. *Ecological Crisis: Readings for Survival.* New York: Harcourt, 1970. (Presents informative papers.)

Love, Sam, ed. *Earth Tool Kit: A Field Manual for Environmental Action.* New York: Pocket Books, 1971.

McCaull, Julian. "The Politics of Technology." *Environment*, March 1972, pp. 2–10.

McClain, Thomas, and Zarefsky, David. *A Complete Handbook on Environmental Control.* Skokie, Ill.: National Textbook, 1970. (For reference.)

McClellan, Grant, ed. *Protecting Our Environment.* New York: Wilson, 1970. (Selected readings on many topics.)

McGovern, George S. "The Federal Government and the Environment." *Current History*, August 1970, pp. 82–83. (Holds that the government must establish penalties for those who fail to do their share in protecting the environment.)

McHale, John. *The Ecological Context.* New York: George Braziller, 1970. (Views problems of ecology as world-encompassing.)

———. *The Future of the Future.* New York: George Braziller, 1969. (Philosophical and technological ideas for the future.)

———. *World Facts and Trends.* New York: Macmillan, 1972. (Discusses man's existing and potential abilities to disrupt his native environment.)

McHarg, Ian L. *Design with Nature.* Garden City, N.Y.: Natural History Press, 1969. (Presents a method for using the environment.)

———. "Is Man a Planetary Disease?" *RIBA Journal*, July 1970, pp. 303–308. (Discusses possibility of extinction and questions whether man is able to understand how the world works.)

McKelvey, V. E. "Mineral Resources Estimates and Public Policy." *American Scientist*, January–February 1972, pp. 32–40.

McNall, P. E., and Kircher, Harry B. *Our Natural Resources.* 3rd ed. Danville, Ill.: Interstate, 1970. (Examines resource use and ecological principles.)

Malin, H. Martin, Jr. "Pollution Detection by Remote Sensing." *Environmental Science and Technology*, August 1971, pp. 676–677. (Describes pollution detection by artificial satellites or aircraft.)

Man's Control of the Environment. Washington: Congressional Quarterly, Inc., 1970. (General survey of major fields of pollution, with particular emphasis on legislation.)

Marine, Gene. *America the Raped.* New York: Simon and Schuster, 1969.

Marsh, G. P. *Man and Nature.* Cambridge, Mass.: Harvard University Press, 1965.

Marx, Wesley, *Man and His Environment: Waste.* New York: Harper, 1971.

Meadows, Dennis L., Meadows, Donnella H., and Behrens, William W., III. *The Limits to Growth.* New York: Universe Books, 1972. (Argues that social control of production and population is necesssary.)

Mesthene, Emmanuel G. *Technological Change: Its Impact on Man and Society.* Cambridge, Mass.: Harvard University Press, 1970.

Michelson, Max. *Environmental Revolution.* New York: McGraw-Hill, 1970.

Mines, Samuel. *The Last Days of Mankind.* New York: Simon and Schuster, 1971. (Discusses important ecological problems.)

Mitchell, John, and Stallings, Constance L., eds. *Ecotactics: The Sierra Club Handbook for Environmental Activists.* New York: Pocket Books, 1970.

Mumford, Lewis. *The Myth of the Machine: The Pentagon of Power.* New York: Harcourt, 1970. (Argues that man can direct the environment and shape technological change to his and society's advantage.)

Murdoch, William W., ed. *Environment: Resources, Pollution, and Society.* Stamford, Conn.: Sinauer Associates, 1971. (Useful for college students studying the relationship between man and the environment.)

National Clearinghouse for Mental Health Information and National Institute of Mental Health. *Pollution: Its Impact on Mental Health: A Literature Survey and Review of Research.* Washington: Government Printing Office, 1972.

National Goals Research Staff. *Toward Balanced Growth, Quantity with Quality: Report.* Washington: Government Printing Office, 1970.

National Industrial Pollution Control Council. *Chemical Industry and Pollution Control.* Washington: Government Printing Office, 1971.

———. *Report, February 1971.* Washington: Government Printing Office, 1971.

———. *Self-Analysis of Pollution Problems.* Washington: Government Printing Office, 1971.

National Institutes of Health. *Environmental Health Sciences.* Washington: Government Printing Office, 1969.

National Science Foundation. *Environmental Science, Challenge for the 70's.* Washington: Government Printing Office, 1971.

Nicholson, Max. *The Environmental Revolution: A Guide for the New Masters of the World.* New York: McGraw-Hill, 1970. (Provides a humanistic and scientific approach.)

Nobile, Philip, and Deedy, John, eds. *The Complete Ecology Fact Book.* New York: Doubleday, 1972. (Includes hard-to-find material.)

Novick, Sheldon. "Looking Forward." *Environment,* May 1973, pp. 4–15. (Presents ideas for cleaning up the environment. Stresses alternative sources of energy.)

Odum, Eugene P. *Fundamentals of Ecology.* 3rd ed. Philadelphia: Saunders, 1971. (Basic text for college courses.)

Odum, Howard T. *Environment, Power, and Society.* New York: Wiley, 1971. (Examination of power as a segment of ecological systems.)

Orions, Gordon H., and Pfeiffer, E. W. "Ecological Effects of the War in Vietnam." *Science,* May 1, 1970, pp. 544–554.

Osborn, Robert. *Mankind May Never Make It.* New York: New York Graphic Society, 1968.

Outdoor Recreation Bureau. *Miniature Environments, An Environmental Education Guidebook.* Washington: Government Printing Office, 1971.

Owen, Oliver S. *Natural Resource Conservation: An Ecological Approach.* New York: Macmillan, 1971.

Pitts, James N., Jr., and Metcalf, Robert L., eds. *Advances in Environmental Science and Technology.* Vol. 2. New York: Wiley, 1971. (Describes causes of and solutions to environmental problems produced through technology.)

Polunin, Nicholas, ed. *The Environmental Future. Proceedings of the First International Conference on Environmental Future.* New York: Barnes and Noble, 1972.

The Progressive. *The Crisis of Survival.* New York: Morrow, 1970. (Consists of articles from *The Progressive,* dealing with aspects environmental hazards, such as pollution, lack of resources, nuclear war, and overpopulation.)

Public Health Service. *Environmental Health Planning Guide.* Rev. ed. Washington: Government Printing Office, 1968.

Ramo, Simon. *Century of Mismatch.* New York: McKay, 1970. (Relationship of present and future technology to society.)

"The Rational Use of Natural Resources for Human Settlements." *Ekistics*, November 1968. (Entire issue devoted to discussion of environmental damage and suggestions for positive action.)

Reid, Keith. *Nature's Network*. Garden City, N.Y.: Natural History Press, 1970.

Revelle, Roger, and Landsberg, Hans H., eds. *America's Changing Environment*. Boston: Houghton Mifflin, 1970. (Discusses decision-making in environmental problems.)

Rienow, Robert, and Rienow, Leona T. *Man Against His Environment*. New York: Sierra Club/Ballantine Books, 1970.

———. *Moment in the Sun: A Report on the Deteriorating Quality of the American Environment*. New York: Dial Press, 1967.

Robertson, John C. "Man's Place in the Ecological Pattern." *Geographical Magazine*, January 1970, pp. 254–265.

Rose, John, ed. *Technological Injury: The Effect of Technological Advances on Environment, Life and Society*. London: Gordon and Breach Science, 1969. (Describes physical and psychological stresses.)

Saltonstall, Richard, Jr. *Your Environment and What You Can Do about It*. New York: Walker, 1970. (Discusses methods of discovering and battling pollution.)

Salvato, Joseph A., Jr. *Environmental Engineering and Sanitation*. New York: Wiley, 1972.

San Clemente, Charles L., ed. *Environmental Quality: Now or Never*. East Lansing, Mich.: Michigan State University Press, 1972.

Sanders, Howard, and Josephs, Melvin. *Chemistry and the Environment*. Washington: American Chemical Society, 1967. (Chemistry's contribution to understanding the solid earth, the oceans, and the atmosphere.)

Sax, Joseph L. *Defending the Environment*. New York: Knopf, 1971. (Argues that concerned citizens must take environmental controversies into court. Introduction is by Senator George McGovern.)

Schurr, Sam H., ed. *Energy, Economic Growth and the Environment*. Baltimore: Johns Hopkins, 1972. (Includes discussion of society's demand for social as well as biological survival.)

Science, Conflict and Society: Readings from the Scientific American. San Francisco: Freeman, 1969. (Introduction by Garret Hardin.)

Scientific American. *The Biosphere*. San Francisco: Freeman, 1970.

———. *Man and the Ecosphere*. San Francisco: Freeman, 1971. (Describes man's potential for self-destruction.)

Segerberg, Osborn. *Where Have All the Flowers, Fishes, Birds, Trees, Water and Air Gone? What Ecology Is All About*. New York: McKay, 1971.

Shephard, Paul, ed. *The Subversive Science: Essays Toward an Ecology of Man*. Boston: Houghton Mifflin, 1969.

Smith, Guy-Harold. *Conservation of Natural Resources*. 4th ed. New York: Wiley, 1971. (Includes works of authorities in various areas.)

Soil Conservation Service and Graduate School, Agriculture Department. *The American Land, Its History, Soil, and Water Wildlife, Agricultural Land Planning and Land Problems of Today and Tomorrow*. Washington: Government Printing Office, 1968. (Television series prepared in cooperation with WETA-TV, Washington.)

State Department. *U.S. National Report on the Human Environment*. Washington: Government Printing Office, 1971. (Prepared for UN Conference of Human Environment, June 1972, Stockholm.)

Steinhart, John S., and Cherniack, Stacie. *Universities and Environmental Quality, Commitment to Problem-Focused Education*. Washington: Government Printing Office, 1969. (Report to President's Environmental Quality Council.)

Stewart, Leland, and Clarke, Wentworth. *Pollution*. New York: Day, 1971. (Describes pollution dangers and possible solutions.)

Strobbe, Maurice A. *Environmental Science Laboratory Manual.* St. Louis: C. V. Mosby, 1972. (Describes fundamental processes of analysis.)

Strobbe, Maurice A., ed. *Understanding Environmental Pollution.* St. Louis: C. V. Mosby, 1971. (Information source for courses in botany, zoology, and biology.)

Taylor, Gordon Rattray. *The Doomsday Book.* New York: World, 1970. (Exhaustive summary of the world's urgent environmental concerns.)

Thomas, William A., ed., *Indicators of Environmental Quality.* New York: Plenum, 1972.

Thoreau, Henry D. *Walden.* New York: Penguin, 1943.

Thoreau, Amos, Turk, Jonathan, and Wittes, Janet T. *Ecology, Pollution, Environment.* Philadelphia; Saunders, 1972. (Basic text discusses economic and scientific factors that must be considered before making decisions affecting the environment.)

Udall, Stewart L. *1976: Agenda for Tomorrow.* New York: Harcourt, 1968. (Explores policies needed to correct environmental problems.)

Underwater Storage, Inc., and Silver Schwartz, Ltd. *Control of Pollution by Underwater Storage, 1969.* Washington: Government Printing Office, 1970. (Discusses feasibility of providing temporary underwater storage of storm overflow from combined sewer system.)

United Nations Conference on the Human Environment. *Documents for the U.N. Conference on the Human Environment.* 3 vols. Washington: Government Printing Office, 1972. (Documents from the Stockholm conference, June 1972. Distributed by National Technical Information Service.)

Use and Conservation of the Biosphere. Vol. 10 of Natural Resources Research series. New York: Unipub, 1970. (Proceedings of 1968 conference, including discussions of coastal zones and inland waters.)

Van Tassel, Alfred J. *Environmental Side Effects of Rising Industrial Output.* Lexington, Mass.: Heath Lexington, 1970.

Vayda, Andrew. *Environment and Cultural Behavior.* Garden City, N.Y.: Natural History, 1969.

"Vested Interests Disagree on How to Fight Pollution." *Congressional Quarterly Weekly Report,* June 1970, pp. 1645–1648.

Wadsworth, R. M. *Measurement of Environmental Factors in Terrestrial Ecology.* Oxford, England: Blackwell Scientific, 1968.

Wagar, J. Alan. "The Challenge of Environmental Education." *Today's Education,* December 1970, pp. 14–18.

Wagner, Richard H. *Environment and Man.* New York: Norton, 1971. (Examines changes in the environment.)

Walia, C. S., ed. *Toward Century 21: Technology, Society, and Human Values.* New York: Basic Books, 1970.

Wall Street Journal. *Our Mistreated World: Case Histories of Man's Pillaging of Nature.* Princeton, N.J.: Dow Jones Books, 1970.

Ward, Barbara. *Spaceship Earth.* New York: Columbia University Press, 1966.

Ward, Barbara, et al. *Who Speaks for Earth?* New York: Norton, 1973. (Contributors to this volume of lectures include Barbara Ward, Thor Heyerdahl, René Dubos, and Lord Zuckerman, each discussing different environmental issues.)

Watson, Richard A., and Watson, Patty Jo. *Man and Nature.* New York: Harcourt, 1969.

Watt, Kenneth E. F. *Ecology and Resources Management. A Quantitative Approach.* New York: McGraw-Hill, 1968.

Where Have All the Flowers Gone? Englewood, Colo.: Arrow, 1970. (Guide to ecological literature.)

White, Lynn, Jr. "Historical Roots of Our Ecological Crisis." *Science,* March 10, 1967, pp. 1203–1207.

Widener, Don. *Timetable for Disaster.* Los Angeles: Nash, 1970. (A portrait of mankind in the process of self-destruction.)

Wilson, Billy Ray, ed. *Environmental Problems: Pesticides, Thermal Pollution, and Environmental Synergisms.* Philadelphia: Lippincott, 1968.

Wilson, Carrol L. *Man's Impact on the Global Environment: Assessment and Recommendation for Action.* Cambridge, Mass.: MIT Press, 1971.

Winn, Ira J., ed. *Basic Issues in Environment: Studies in Quiet Desperation.* Columbus, Ohio: Merrill, 1972. (Selections of about 100 writers, stressing conflicts in values.)

World Health Organization. *Health Hazards of the Human Environment.* New York: Unipub, 1972. (General overview prepared by a multinational committee of experts.

INTERNATIONAL

Amuzegar, Jahangir. "The Oil Story: Facts, Fiction and Fair Play." *Foreign Affairs*, July 1973, pp. 676-689.

Atomic Energy Commission. *International Negotiations on the Treaty on the Nonproliferation of Nuclear Weapons.* Washington: Government Printing Office, 1969.

Baker, Mike. "Plans for Global Atmospheric Research." *New Scientist*, July 30, 1970, pp. 226-228.

Dasmann, Raymond F. *Planet in Peril.* New York: World, 1972. (Discusses how man has altered the biosphere and suggests an international program.)

de Almeida, M. O., Beckerman, W., Sachs, I., and Corea, G. *Environment and Development.* New York: Carnegie Endowment for International Peace, 1972. (Discusses whether persons in underdeveloped countries should be concerned with environmental issues.)

Development and Environment. The Hague, Netherlands: Co-Libri, 1972. (Aims to persuade persons of poorer nations that problems occurring in the environment of wealthy nations are affecting them also.)

Goldman, Marshall I. *The Spoils of Progress: Environmental Pollution in the Soviet Union.* Cambridge, Mass.: MIT Press, 1972.

International Conference on the Peaceful Uses of Atomic Energy. *Proceedings of the Fourth International Conference.* Geneva: United Nations, 1971.

Kay, David A., and Skolnikoff, Eugene B., eds. *World Eco-Crisis, International Organizations in Response.* Madison, Wisc.: University of Wisconsin Press, 1972.

Knapp, Carol E. "Pollution: The Whole World's Problem." *Environmental Science and Technology*, September 1971, pp. 750-751.

Kneese, Allen V., Rolfe, Sidney E., and Harned, Joseph W., eds. *Managing the Environment—International and Economic Cooperation for Pollution Control.* New York: Praeger, 1971.

Krutilla, John V. *Columbia River Treaty: The Economics of an International River Basin Development.* Baltimore: John Hopkins, 1967.

National Academy of Science. *Institutional Arrangements for International Environmental Cooperation.* Washington: National Academy of Sciences, 1972.

———. *International Aspects of Man's Effect Upon the Environment.* Washington: National Academy of Sciences, 1970. (Prepared by the Ad Hoc Committee of the NAS; discusses effects of western technology on environments of underdeveloped countries.)

Newell, Reginald E. "The Global Circulation of Atmospheric Pollutants." *Scientific American*, January 1971, pp. 32-42.

Pescod, M. B., and Okun, D. A., eds. *Water Supply and Wastewater Disposal in Developing Countries.* Bangkok, Thailand: Asian Institute of Technology, 1971. (Consists of papers from a seminar.)

Russell, Clifford, S., and Landsberg, Hans H. "International Environmental Problems—a Taxonomy." *Science*, June 25, 1971, pp. 1307-1314.

Serwer, Daniel. *International Coopertion for Pollution Control.* New York: Unipub, 1972. (Prepared by United Nations Institute for Training and Research.)

State Department. *Treaties and Other International Agreements on Oceanographic Resources, Fisheries, and Wildlife to Which the United States is Party.* Washington: Government Printing Office, 1970.

Strong, Maurice F. "One Year After Stockholm: An Ecological approach to Management." *Foreign Affairs,* July 1973, pp. 690–707.

Wilson, Carroll L. "A Plan for Energy Independence." *Foreign Affairs,* July 1973, pp. 657–675.

Wilson, Thomas W., Jr. *International Environmental Action: A Global Survey.* New York: Dunellen, 1972. (Presents social, political, legal, and economic viewpoints. Extensive annotated bibliography included.)

Wolman, Abel. "Pollution as an International Issue." *Foreign Affairs,* October 1968, pp. 165–175.

LAND USE AND URBAN PLANNING

Agriculture Department. *Our American Land, Use the Land, Save the Soil.* Rev. ed. Washington: Government Printing Office, 1968.

———. *Restoring Surface-Minded Land.* Washington: Government Printing Office, 1968.

American Society of Planning Officials. *Problems of Zoning and Land Use Regulations.* Washington: Government Printing Office, 1968. (Written for the National Commission on Urban Problems.)

Anderson, Wallace L. *Making Land Produce Useful Wildlife.* Rev. ed. Washington: Government Printing Office, 1969. (Bulletin of the Agriculture Department.)

Berkman, Richard L., and Viscusi, W. Kip. *Damming the West.* New York: Grossman, 1973. (A Ralph Nader Study Group Report on the Bureau of Reclamation. Exposes wrongdoings of the bureau and the government in general.)

Brahtz, J. F. Peel, ed. *Coastal Zone Management: Multiple Use with Conservation.* New York: Wiley, 1972.

Clawson, Marion. *America's Land and Its Uses.* Baltimore: John Hopkins, 1972. (A concise account suitable for the layman.)

Delafons, John. *Land-Use Controls in the United States.* 2nd ed. Cambridge, Mass.: MIT Press, 1969.

Detwyler, Thomas R., and Marcus, Melvin G. *Urbanization and Environment.* Belmont, Calif.: Wadsworth, 1972.

Edwards, Gordon. *Land, People and Policy: The Problems and Techniques of Assembling Land for the Urbanization of 100 Million New Americans.* West Trenton, N.J.: Chandler-Davis, 1969.

Elrick, David E. "Land (I): Its Future—Endangering Pollutants." *Impact of Science on Society* vol. 19, no. 2, 1969, pp. 195–208.

Fairbrother, Nan. *New Lives, New Landscapes: Planning for the 21st Century.* New York: Knopf, 1970.

Faltermayer, Edmund K. *Redoing America: A Nationwide Report on How to Make Our Cities and Suburbs Livable.* New York: Harper, 1968. (Describes damage to the social and physical environment and what can be done to control it.)

Frawley, Margaret I. *Surface Mined Areas: Control and Reclamation of Environmental Damage.* Washington: Government Printing Office, 1971. (Distributed by National Technical Information Service. Bibliography of English-language information on United States, 1960–July 1970.)

Herber, Lewis. *Crisis in Our Cities.* Englewood Cliffs, N.J.: Prentice-Hall, 1965. (Discusses effects of air and water pollution on physical and mental health.)

Hite, James C., and Stepp, James M., eds. *Coastal Zone Resource Management.* New York: Praeger, 1971. (Papers by experts from various fields.)

Interior Department. *Our Living Land.* Washington: Government Printing Office, 1971.

Kellog, Charles E., and Enderlin, H. C. "What Urban Building Does to Soil and Water." *Soil Conservation*, November 1969, pp. 83–85.

Ketchum, Bostwock H., ed. *The Water's Edge: Critical Problems of the Coastal Zone.* Cambridge, Mass.: MIT Press, 1972.

Little, Charles E. *Challenge of the Land: Open Space Preservation at the Local Level.* London: Pergamon, 1969.

Little, Silas, and Noyes, John H., eds. *Trees and Forests in an Urbanizing Environment.* Amherst, Mass.: Cooperative Extension Service, University of Massachusetts, 1971.

McCloskey, Paul N., Jr. "Preservation of America's Open Space: Proposal for a National Land Use Commission." *Michigan Law Review*, May 1970, pp. 1167–1174. (Discusses legal aspects of retaining open space.)

Meadows, Paul, and Mizruchi, Ephraim H., eds. *Urbanism, Urbanization, and Change: Comparative Perspectives.* Reading, Mass.: Addison-Wesley, 1969. (Useful for college courses in urban studies. Covers ecological and demographic aspects.)

Michener, James A. *The Quality of Life.* Philadelphia: Lippincott, 1970. (Makes suggestions for saving the city, improving education, preserving the environment, and limiting population.)

National Academy of Sciences. *Waste Management Concepts for the Coastal Zone: Requirements for Research and Investigation.* Washington: National Academy of Sciences, 1970.

National Research Council. *Land Use and Wildlife Resources.* Washington: National Academy of Sciences, 1970. (Report of Committee on Agricultural Land Use and Wildlife Resources.)

Perloff, Harvey S., ed. *Quality of the Urban Environment. Essays on "New Resources" in an Urban Age.* Baltimore: Johns Hopkins, 1969.

Pickard, Jerome P. "Problems of the Cities." *HUD Challenge*, May–June, 1970, pp. 4–10. (Considers present and future environment and lists HUD programs aiding environmental control.)

Prindle, Richard A. "The Health Aspects of the Urban Environment." *Ekistics*, June 1968, pp. 428–431.

Public Roads Bureau. *Highways to Beauty.* Washington: Government Printing Office, 1966. (Discusses Highway Beautification Act of 1965.)

Robinson, John. *Highways and Our Environment.* New York: McGraw-Hill, 1971.

Schmid, A. Allan. *Converting Land from Rural to Urban Uses.* Baltimore: Johns Hopkins, 1968.

Sports Fisheries and Wildlife. *Nature Downtown.* Washington: Government Printing Office, 1970. (One technique by which attractive elements of a natural environment can be brought into the heart of a city.)

Stamp, L. Dudley. *Land for Tomorrow: Our Developing World.* Bloomington, Ind.: Indiana University Press, 1969.

Sturman, Gerald M. "Effects of Highways on Urban Environments." *Journal of Environmental Systems*, March 1972, pp. 61ff.

van Cleeff, Eugene. *Cities in Action.* New York: Pergamon, 1970. (Includes section on pollution and plans for control.)

Washington State University. *A Study of the Social, Economic and Environmental Impact of Highway Transportation Facilities on Urban Communities.* Washington: Government Printing Office, 1968. (Distributed by National Technical Information Service.)

NOISE

American Association for the Advancement of Science. *International Symposium on Extra-Auditory Physiological Effects of Audible Sound.* Boston: Plenum, 1969.

American Speech and Hearing Association. *Noise as a Public Health Hazard.* Washington: American Speech and Hearing Association, 1968. (Conference Proceedings.)

Anthrop, Donald F. "Environmental Noise Pollution: A New Threat to Sanity." *Bulletin of the Atomic Scientists*, May 1969, pp. 11–16.

Athey, Skipworth W. *Acoustics Technology, a Survey.* Washington: Government Printing Office, 1970.

Bailey, Anthony. "Noise Is a Slow Agent of Death." *New York Times Magazine*, November 23, 1969, pp. 46ff.

Baron, Robert A. "The Assault of Sound." *Washington Monthly*, November 1970, pp. 35–43.

———. "Let Quiet Be Public Policy." *Saturday Review*, Nov. 7, 1970, pp. 66–67.

———. *The Tyranny of Noise.* New York: St. Martin's Press, 1970. (Maintains that noisy equipment is a sign of imperfect design and that changes would cost little.)

Beranek, Leo. L. "Noise." *Scientific American*, December 1966, pp. 66–76. (Introductory article on potential solutions.)

Beranek, Lee L., ed. *Noise and Vibration Control.* New York: McGraw-Hill, 1971.

Berland, Theodore. *The fight for Quiet.* Philadelphia; University of Pennsylvania Press, 1972.

Bragdon, Clifford R. *Noise Pollution: The Unquiet Crisis.* Philadelphia: University of Pennsylvania press, 1971.

Burns, William. *Noise and Man.* Philadelphia: Lippincott, 1969.

Cohen, Alexander. "Sociocusis." *Sound and Vibration*, November 1970, pp. 12–20. (Title refers to hearing loss from nonoccupational noise exposure.)

Commerce Technical Advisory Board. *The Noise Around Us: Including Technical Backup.* Washington: Government Printing Office, 1970. (Report of Panel on Noise Abatement. Discusses technological, legal, and economic aspects of noise control. Distributed by National Technicl Information Service.)

Environmental Protection Agency. *Community Noise.* Washington: Government Printing Office, 1971. (Prepared by Office of Noise Abatement and Control.)

———. *The Effect of Sonic Boom and Similar Impulsive Noise on Structures.* Washington: Government Printing Office, 1971. (Prepared by Office of Noise Abatement and Control.)

———. *Effects of Noise on People.* Washington: Government Printing Office, 1971. (Prepared by Office of Noise Abatement and Control.)

———. *Fundamentals of Noise: Measurement, Rating Schemes, and Standards.* Washington: Government Printing Office, 1971. (Prepared by Office of Noise Abatement and Control.)

———. *The Harmful Intruder—Noise in the Home.* Washington: Government Printing Office, 1970.

———. *Highlights—The Federal Noise Control Act of 1972.* Washington: Government Printing Office, 1972.

———. *Laws and Regulatory Schemes for Noise Abatement.* Washington: Government Printing Office, 1971. (Prepared by Office of Noise Abatement and Control.)

———. *Noise from Construction Equipment and Operations, Building Equipment, and Home Appliances.* Washington: Government Printing Office, 1971. (Prepared by Office of Noise Abatement and Control.)

———. *Noise Pollution.* Washington: Government Printing Office, 1972.

———. *Report to the President and Congress on Noise.* Washington: Government Printing Office, 1971. (Prepared by Office of Noise Abatement and Control.)

———. *State and Municipal Non-occupational Noise Programs.* Washington: Government Printing Office, 1971. (Prepared by Office of Noise Abatement and Control.)

———. *Transportation Noise and Noise from Equipment Powered by Internal Combustion Engines.* Washington: Government Printing Office, 1971. (Prepared by Office of Noise Abatement Control.)

———. *Working Paper for the Noise Legislation Workshop.* Washington: Government Printing Office, 1972. (Prepared by Office of Noise Abatement and Control. Material based on National Symposium on State Environmental Legislation.)

Committee on Environmental Quality. *Noise: Sound Without Value.* Washington: Government Printing Office, 1968. (Publication of Federal Council for Science and Technology.)

Franken, Peter A., and Page, Daniel G. "Noise in the Environment." *Environmental Science and Technology*, February 1972, pp. 124–129. (Discusses effects of noise and the control technology available.)

Hildebrand, James L. "Noise Pollution: An Introduction to the Problem and an Outline for Future Legal Research." *Columbia Law Review*, April 1970, pp. 652–692.

Hildebrand, James L., ed. *Noise Pollution and the Law.* Buffalo, N.Y.: William S. Hein, 1970.

Institution of Mechanical Engineers. *Vibration and Noise in Motor Vehicles.* London: Institution of Mechanical Engineers, 1972.

Kryter, Karl. *Effects of Noise on Man.* New York: Academic Press, 1970.

———. "Psychological Reactions to Airport Noise." *Ekistics*, November 1966, pp. 345–352.

———. "Sonic Booms from Supersonic Transport." *Science*, January 24, 1969, pp. 359–367. (Discusses effects of sonic booms on people.)

Lyon, Richard H. *Lectures in Transportation Noise.* Harvard, Mass: Grozier, 1973. (Employs basic principles of acoustics as foundation for noise control technology.)

National Industrial Pollution Control Council. *Lesiure Time Product Noise: Sub-Council Report.* Washington: Government Printing Office, 1971.

National Research Council of Noise. *A Brief Study of a Rational Approach to Legislative Control of Noise.* Washington: National Research Council of Noise, 1968.

Nixon, C. W., et al. *Sonic Booms Resulting from Extremely Low-Altitude Supersonic Flight: Mesurements and Observations on Houses, Livestock and People.* Wright-Patterson Air Force Base: Aerospace Medical Research Laboratories, 1968.

"Noise in the Environment." *Environmental Science and Technology*, February 1972, pp. 124–129. (General overview of noise problem.)

"Non-Auditory Effects of Environmental Noise." *American Journal of Public Health*, March 1972, pp. 389–398.

Organization for Economic Cooperation and Development. *Urban Traffic Noise: Strategy for an Improved Environment.* Paris: Organization for Economic Cooperation and Development, 1969. (Report of the Consultative Group on Transportation Research to governments who are members of the OECD.)

Shih, H. H. *A Literature Survey of Noise Pollution.* Washington: Government Printing Office, 1971. (Distributed by National Technical Information Service. Identifies urgent research needs, lists terminology, and provides bibliography.)

Shurcliff, William A. *SST and Sonic Boom Handbook.* New York: Ballantine Books, 1970. (Calls for halt in the development of supersonic jets.)

Southworth, Michael. "Sonic Environment of Cities." *Environment and Behavior*, June 1969, pp 49–70.

Still, Henry. *In Quest of Quiet.* Harrisburg, Pa.: Stackpole Books, 1970. Transportation Department. *Second Federal Aircraft Noise Abatement Plan.* Washington: Government Printing Office, 1971.

Welch, Bruce L., and Welch, Annemarie S., eds. *Physiological Effects of Noise.* New York: Plenum, 1970.

POPULATION

Appleman, Philip. *Silent Explosion.* Boston: Beacon Press, 1965.

Back, K. W., and Winsborough, H. H. "Population Policy: Opinions and Actions of Governments." *Public Opinion Quarterly,* Winter 1968–1969, pp. 634–645.

Bahr, Howard M., et al. *Population, Resources, and the Future: Non-Malthusian Perspectives.* Provo, Utah: Brigham Young University Press, 1972.

Berelson, B. "Beyond Family Planning." *Science,* February 7, 1969, pp. 533–543.

Blake, Judith. "Abortion and Public Opinion: The 1960–1970 Decade." *Science,* February 12, 1971, pp. 540–549.

———. "Population Policy for Americans: Is the Government Being Misled?" *Science,* May 2, 1969, pp. 522–529.

Bonar, James. *Theories of Population from Raleigh to Arthur Young.* New York: Kelley, 1966.

Borgstrom, Georg. *Too Many.* New York: Macmillan, 1969. (Discusses biological limitations of the earth.)

Bumpass, L., and Westoff, C. F. "The 'Perfect Contraceptive' Population." *Science,* September 18, 1970, pp. 1177–1182.

Carter, Luther J. "Population Crisis: Rising Concern at Home." *Science,* November 7, 1969, 722–726.

Clark, Colin. *Population Growth and Land Use.* New York: St Martin's Press, 1967. (Argues that menace of world hunger from overpopulation is exaggerated.)

Cook, Robert C., and Lecht, J. *People: An Introduction to the Study of Population.* Washington: Columbia Books, 1968.

Djerassi, Carl. "Prognosis for the Development of New Chemical Birth-Control Agents." *Science,* October 24, 1969, pp. 468–473.

Ehrlich, Paul R. *The Population Bomb.* New York: Sierra Club/Ballantine Books, 1968.

Ehrlich, Paul R., and Holdren, J. P. "Impact of Population Growth." *Science,* March 26, 1971, pp. 1212–1217.

Enke, S. "Birth Control for Economic Development." *Science,* May 16, 1969, pp. 798–806.

Fisher, Tadd. *Our Overcrowded World.* New York: Parents Magazine Press, 1969.

Hardin, G., ed. *Population, Evolution and Birth Control.* San Francisco: Freeman, 1969.

Hauser, Philip M. *The Population Dilemma.* 2nd ed. Englewood Cliffs, N.J.: Prentice-Hall, 1969. (Emphasizes need for long-range policies.)

Hawley, Amos N. "Ecology and Population." *Science,* March 23, 1973, pp. 1196–1200.

Hazen, William Eugene. *Readings in Population and Community Ecology.* 2nd ed. Philadelphia: Saunders, 1970.

Heer, David M., ed. *Readings on Population.* Englewood Cliffs, N.J.: Prentice-Hall, 1968.

———. *Society and Population.* Englewood Cliffs, N.J.: Prentice-Hall, 1968.

Hulett, H. R. "Optimum World Population." *BioScience,* February 1, 1970, pp. 160–161.

Hutchinson, C. P. *Population Debate.* Boston: Houghton Mifflin, 1967.

Hutchinson, Sir Joseph, ed. *Population and Food Supply: Essays on Human Needs and Agricultural Prospects.* Cambridge, England: Cambridge University Press, 1969.

Kammeyer, Kenneth C., ed. *Population Studies: Selected Essays and Research.* Chicago: Rand McNally, 1969.

Keyfitz, Nathan, and Flieger, Wilhelm. *World Population: An Analysis of Vital Data.* Chicago: University of Chicago Press, 1968.

Laffin, John. *The Hunger to Come.* New York: Abelard-Schuman, 1972.

Nam, Charles B., ed. *Population and Society: A Textbook of Selected Readings.* Boston: Houghton Mifflin, 1968.

"Next 100,000,000—Where Will They Live." *American Institute of Architects Journal*, January 1969, pp. 30-37.

O'Brien, Fr. John. *Family Planning in an Exploding Population.* New York: Hawthorne, 1968.

Peterson, William. *Population.* 2nd ed. New York: Macmillan, 1969.

Population Reference Bureau. "Food—Population Dilemma." *Population Bulletin*, December 1968, pp. 1-20.

Price, Daniel O., ed. *The 99th Hour: The Population Crisis in the United States.* Chapel Hill, N.C.: University of North Carolina Press, 1967.

Stockwell, Edward G. *Population and People.* Chicago: Quadrangle Books, 1968. (Analyzes population problems by means of demographic yardsticks.)

Tydings, Joseph D. *Born to Starve.* New York: Morrow, 1970. (Senator Tydings' plea for control of population growth.)

Wolfers, D. "Problems of Expanding Populations." *Nature*, February 14, 1970, pp 593-597.

RADIATION

Aaronson, Terri. "Mystery: Microwave Radiation." *Environment*, May 1970, pp. 2-10.

Army Department. *Nuclear Weapons and NATO, Analytical Survey of Literature.* Washington: Government Printing office, 1970.

Atomic Energy Commission. *Benefit-Cost Analysis of Low-Dose Radiation Processed Foods.* Washington: Government Printing Office, 1969.

———. *Compaction of Radioactive Solid Waste.* Washington: Government Printing Office, 1971. (Report to the General Manager's Task Force, AEC Operational Radioactive Waste Management.)

———. *Effects of Nuclear Weapons.* Washington: Government Printing Office, 1964.

———. *Guidance for Control of Radiation Hazards in Uranium Mining.* Washington: Government Printing Office, 1967.

———. *Incineration of Radioactive Solid Wastes.* Washington: Government Printing Office, 1971. (Report to the General Manager's Task Force, AEC Operational Radioactive Waste Management, 1970.)

———. *Manual of Radioactivity Procedures.* Washington Government Printing Office, 1961.

———. *Maximum Permissible Body Burdens and Maximum Permissible Concentrations of Radionuclides in Air and in Water for Occupational Exposure.* Washington: Government Printing Office, 1959.

———. *Nuclear Testing. Review of International Negotiations on Cessation of Nuclear Weapon Tests, September 1961-September 1965.* Washington: Government Printing Office, 1966.

———. *Radiation Shielding, Analysis and Design Principles as Applied to Nuclear Defense Planning.* Washington: Government Printing Office, 1967.

———. *Radiation Surveillance Networks.* Washington: Government Printing Office, 1969.

———. *Radioisotopes, Production and Development of Large-Scale Uses.* Washington: Government Printing Office, 1968.

———. *Radiological Emergency Procedures for the Non-Specialist.* Washington: Government Printing Office, 1969.

———. *Safe Handling of Radioactive Materials.* Washington: Government Printing Office, 1964.

———. *Safety of Underground Nuclear Testing.* Washington: Government Printing Office, 1969. (Summary report on activities for assuring safety of underground nuclear testing.)

———. *Space Radiation Biology.* Washington: Government Printing Office, 1967.

———. *Summary Information on Accidental Releases of Radioactivity to the Atmosphere* from *Underground Nuclear Detonations Designed for Containment. August 5, 1963–June 30, 1971.* Washington: Government Printing Office, 1971.

Ayres, J. A., ed. *Decontamination of Nuclear Reactors and Equipment.* New York: Ronald Press, 1970. (Provides fundamental information on the basis of both successful and unsuccessful experiences.)

Clopton, John C., ed. *Environmental Radioactivity Symposium.* Baltimore: John Hopkins, 1970.

Eisenbud, Berril. *Environmental Radioactivity.* New York: McGraw-Hill, 1963.

Food and Drug Administration. *State Radiation Control Legisltion.* Washington: Government Printing Office, 1971.

Gofman, John W., and Tamplin, Arthur R. "Radiation: The Invisible Casualties." *Environment,* April 1970, pp. 12–19, 49.

Hambleton, William W. "The Unsolved Problem of Nuclear Wastes." *Technology Review,* March–April 1972, pp. 15–19.

Health, Education, and Welfare Department. *Radiological Health Handbook.* Washington: Government Printing Office, 1970.

———. *State and Federal Control of Health Hazards from Radioactive Materials Other than Materials Regulated under the Atomic Energy Act of 1954 (as of Oct. 1, 1969).* Washington: Government Printing Office, 1971.

———. *Summary of Federal Regulations for Packaging and Transportation of Radioactive Materials.* Washington: Government Printing Office, 1971.

Holcomb, Robert W. "Radiation Risk: A Scientific Problem?" *Science,* February 6, 1970, pp. 853–855.

Kondrat'ev, Kirill. *Radiation in the Atmosphere.* New York: Academic Press, 1969.

Menzel, R. G., and James P. E. *Treatments for Farmland Contaminated with Radioactive Material.* Washington: Government Printing Office, 1971. (Prepared by Agriculture Department.)

"Microwave Ovens: Not Recommended." *Consumer Reports,* April 1973, pp. 221–230. (Report indicates oven radiation leakage at levels that may be harmful.)

Morgan, Karl Z. "Never Do Harm." *Environment,* January–February 1971, pp. 28–38. (Describes exposure to X-rays in medicine.)

National Academy of Sciences. *Radioactivity in the Marine Environment.* Washington: National Academy of Sciences, 1971 (Report of National Research Council. Also includes numerous concepts applicable to other wastes released into water.)

National Industrial Pollution Control Council. *Evaluation of the Appliance X-Ray Pollution Problem.* Washington: Government Printing Office, 1971.

Novick, Sheldon. "Seventeen Million Years." *Environment,* November 1971, pp. 42–47. (Discusses Iodine–129, a radioactive waste.)

State Department. *The United States Draft Treaty to Prevent the Spread of Nuclear Weapons.* Washington: Government Printing Office, 1965.

Sternglass, Ernest J. "Infant Mortality and Nuclear Tests." *Bulletin of the Atomic Scientists,* April 1969, pp. 18–20.

Straub, C. P. *Public Health Implications of Radioactive Waste Releases.* Washington: American Public Health Association, 1970.

Tamplin, Arthur R., and Gofman, John W. *"Population Control" through Nuclear Pollution.* Chicago: Nelson-Hall, 1970. (Emphasizes the dangers of radioactive contamination.)

Taylor, Lauriston S. *Radiation Protection Standards.* Cleveland, Ohio: Chemical Rubber Company, 1971.

United Nations Scientific Committee on the Effects of Atomic Radiation. *Ionizing Radiation: Levels and Effects: A Report.* New York; United Nations, 1972.

Woodwell, George M. "Radiation and the Patterns of Nature." *Science,* April 28, 1967, pp. 461–470. (Concerns plant populations.)

REFERENCE WORKS

American Association for the Advancement of Science. *Science for Society.* Washington: American Association for the Advancement of Science, 1972. (Prepared by the AAAS Commission on Science Education. Bibliography on the application of science and technology to human problems.)

Atomic Energy Commission. *Safeguards Dictionary.* Washington: Government Printing Office, 1971. (Deals with nuclear power.)

———. *Selected Bibliography on Radioactive Occurrences in the United States.* Washington: Government Printing Office, 1970.

Bate, Bill. *Directory of Environmental Consultants.* St. Louis: Directory Press, 1972.

Environmental Information Center. *The Environment Film Review.* New York: Environmental Information Center, 1972. (Reviews and ratings of more than 600 films.)

———. *Environment Index.* New York: Environmental Information Center, 1971. (Lists 42,000 entries representing important works for 1971.)

Housing and Urban Development Department. *Environment and the Community, An Annotated Bibliography.* Washington: Government Printing Office, 1971. Jackson, Nora, and Penn, Philip. *Dictionary of Natural Resources and Their Principal Uses.* New York: Pergamon, 1966.

Kiraldi, Louis, and Burke, Janet L. *Pollution: A Selected Bibliography of U.S. Government Publications on Air, Water, and Land Pollution, 1965-1970.* Kalamazoo, Mich.: Institute of Public Affairs, Western Michigan University, 1971.

Knobbe, Mary L. *Air Pollution: A Non-Technical Bibliography.* Washington: Metropolitan Washington Council of Governments, 1969.

Lund, Herbert F., ed. *Industrial Pollution Control Handbook.* New York: McGraw-Hill, 1971. (Examines industries in which pollution has caused major difficulties.)

National Foundation for Environmental Control. *Directory of Environmental Information Sources.* 2nd ed. Boston: National Foundation for Environmental Control, 1972.

National Wildlife Federation. *Conservation Directory.* Washington: National Wildlife Federation, 1971.

Pollution Control Companies, U.S.A. Park Ridge, N.J.: Noyes Data, 1972. (Directory of newly developed industries in area of environmental control.)

Schildhauer, Carole. *Environmental Information Sources: A Selected Bibliography.* New York: Special Libraries Association, 1972.

Siehl, George H. "Our World—and Welcome to It." *Library Journal,* April 15, 1970, pp. 1443–1447. (Bibliographic essay on literature of environmental crisis and related problems.)

Thibeau, Charles E., ed. *Directory of Environmental Information Sources.* 2nd ed. Boston: Cahners Books, 1972. (Includes books, periodicals, conferences, and public and private organizations.)

Thomas, William A., Goldstein, Gerald, and Wilcox, William H. *Biological Indicators of Environmental Quality.* Ann Arbor, Mich.: Ann Arbor Science, 1973. (Bibliography of abstracts.)

Todd, David Keith, ed. *The Water Encyclopedia.* Port Washington, N.Y.: Water Information Center, 1970. (Reference text for basic information on various aspects of water.)

Winton, Harry N. M., ed. *Man and the Environment.* New York: Bowker, 1972. (Bibliography of United Nations publications, 1946–1971.)

SOLID WASTES

Aluminum Association. *Aluminum Statistical Review, 1970.* New York: Aluminum Association, 1970. (Includes statistics on recovery of aluminum from scrap.)

American Paper Institute. *Background Information on Recycling Waste Paper.* New York: American Paper Institute, 1971.

American Public Works Association. *Municipal Refuse Disposal.* Danville, Ill.: Interstate, 1970. (Comprehensive text.)

———. *Refuse Collection Practice.* Danville, Ill.: Interstate, 1966. (Comprehensive text.)

American Society of Mechanical Engineers. *ASME Industry Survey on Disposal of Industrial Wastes.* New York: American Society of Mechanical Engineers, n.d.

Appell, Herbert R. *Conversion of Urban Refuse to Oil.* Washington: Government Printing Office, 1970. (Bureau of Mines report.)

Banks, M. E., et al. *New Chemical Concepts for Utilization of Waste Plastics.* Washington: Government Printing Office, 1971. (Publication of the Environmental Protection Agency.)

Bates, T. M. *Summary Report on the Impact of Railroad Freight Rates on the Recycling of Ferrous Scrap.* Washington: Institute of Scrap Iron and Steel, 1972.

Black, R. J., et al. *1968 National Solid Waste Survey—An Interim Report.* Washington: Government Printing Office, 1969. (Report of the Department of Health, Education, and Welfare.)

Boettcher, R. A. "Air Classification for Reclamation of Solid Wastes." *Compost Science,* November–December 1970, pp. 22–29.

Bouwer, Herman. "Returning Waste to the Land: A New Role for Agriculture?" *Journal of Soil and Water Conservation,* Sept.–Oct. 1968, pp. 164–168.

Bower, B. T., Larson, G. P., Michaels, A., and Phillips, W. M. "Waste Management." *Ekistics,* November 1968, pp. 438–450.

Breidenback, A. W. *Composting of Municipal Solid Waste in the United States.* Washington: Government Printing Office, 1971. (Publication of the Environmental Protection Agency.)

Brunner, D. R., and Keller D. J. *Sanitary Landfill—Design and Operation.* Washington: Government Printing Office, 1971. (Publication of the Environmental Protection Agency.)

Bureau of Mines. *Automobile Disposal, A National Problem, Case Studies of Factors that Influence the Accumulation of Automobile Scrap.* Washington: Government Printing Office, 1967.

Cannon, Howard S. "Can We Recycle Cans?" *Technology Review,* May 1972, pp. 40–44.

Caswell, Charles A. "Underground Waste Disposal: Concepts and Misconceptions." *Environmental Science and Technology,* July 1970, pp. 642–647.

Church, Fred L. "Mission Impossible? Can Recycling Debate Heats Up." *Modern Metals,* April 1972, pp. 29–39. (Discusses tin vs. aluminum in recycling.)

Clark, Thomas D. *Economic Realities of Reclaiming Natural Resources in Solid Waste.* Washington: Government Printing Office, 1971. (Report of the Environmental Protection Agency.)

Collins, C. "Regional Systems Approach and Market Development Seen as Key to Waste Recycling." *Waste Age,* April 1970, pp. 20–22.

Congress. House. Committee on Government Operations. *Effects of Population Growth on Natural Resources and the Environment: Hearings before a Subcommittee.* Washington: Government Printing Office, 1969.

Congress. House. Committee on Interstate and Foreign Commerce. *Air Pollution Control and Solid Wastes: Hearings before the Subcommittee on Public Health and Welfare.* Washington: Government Printing Office, 1970.

Congress. Joint Committee on Defense Production. *Progress Report 50, on Potential Shortages of Ores, Metals and Minerals . . . Recycling of Metals . . . and Related Matters.* Washington: Government Printing Office, 1971.

Congress. Joint Economic Committee. *The Economics of Recycling Waste Materials: Hearings before the Subcommittee on Fiscal Policy.* Washington: Government Printing Office, 1971.

Congress. Public Laws. *Resource Recovery Act of 1970, H.R. 11833, Approved Oct. 26,*

1970. Washington: Government Printing Office, 1970.

Congress. Senate. Subcommittee on Air and Water Pollution. *Resource Recovery Act of 1969: Hearings.* 4 vols. Washington: Government Printing Office, 1970.

"Converting Solid Wastes to Electricity." *Environmental Science and Technology,* August 1970, pp. 631–633.

Council on Environmental Quality. *Ocean Dumping, A National Policy.* Washington: Government Printing Office, 1970. (Report to the president.)

Cross, Frank L., Jr. *Handbook on Incineration: Guide to Theory, Design, Operation, and Maintenance.* Westport, Conn.: Technomic, 1972.

Crysler, F. "The Demand for Recycled Fibers." *TAPPI,* June 1971, pp. 904ff.

Cutter, H. "Role of Transportation in Disposal of Obsolete Metallic Waste—One Year Later." *Waste Age,* July–August 1971.

Darnay, A., and Franklin, W. E. *The Role of Packaging in Solid Waste Management 1966–1976.* Washington: Government Printing Office, 1969. (Report of the Department of Health, Education, and Welfare.)

———. *Salvage Markets for Materials in Solid Wastes.* Washington: Government Printing Office, 1972. (Report of the Environmental Protection Agency. Emphasis on paper, ferrous and nonferrous metals, and textiles.)

Dean, K. C. *Preliminary Separation of Metals and Nonmetals from Urban Refuse.* Washington: Government Printing Office, 1971. (Report of Bureau of Mines.)

"De-inked Newspapers Could De-work Solid Waste Routines." *APWA Reporter,* June 1970, p. 8.

Derrickson, Gardner F. *Motor Vehicle Abandonment in United States Urban Areas, Nature and Extent of the Problem, and Adequacy of Present Methods of Handling It.* Washington: Government Printing Office, 1967. (Report of the Business and Defense Services Administration.)

Dickson, Edward M. "Taking It Apart." *Environment,* July–August 1972, pp. 36–41. (Describes recycling of automobiles.)

Dindall, Daniel L. *Ecology of Compost: A Public Involvement Project.* Syracuse, N.Y.: State University College of Forestry, 1971. (Report of the University's Office of Public Service and Continuing Education.)

Drobny, N. L., et al. *Recovery and Utilization of Municipal Solid Waste, A Summary of Available Cost and Performance Characteristics of Unit Processes and Systems.* Washington: Government Printing Office, 1971. (Report of the Environmental Protection Agency.)

Engdahl, Richard B. *Solid Waste Processing, A State-of-the-Art Report on Unit Operations and Processes.* Washington: Government Printing Office, 1970. (Report of the Bureau of Solid Waste Management, Public Health Service, 1969.)

Engineering Foundation Research Conference on National Materials Policy. *Problems and Issues of a National Materials Policy.* Washington: Government Printing Office, 1970. (Papers delivered at the Conference.)

Environmental Protection Agency. *Accounting System for Transfer Station Operations.* Washington: Government Printing Office, 1971.

———. *American Composting Concepts.* Washington: Government Printing Office, 1971.

———. *Comprehensive Studies of Solid Waste Management: Third Annual Report.* Washington: Government Printing Office, 1971.

———. *Feasibility Study of the Disposal of Polyethylene Plastic Waste.* Washington: Government Printing Office, 1971.

———. *Financing Solid Waste Management in Small Communities.* Washington: Government Printing Office, 1971.

———. *Fluid Bed Incineration of Petroleum Refinery Wastes.* Washington: Government Printing Office, 1971.

———. *Intergovernmental Approaches to Solid Waste Management: Action Plan.* Washington Government Office, 1971.

———. *Make Mission 5000 Your Project to Protect and Improve the Quality of Our Environment, Eliminate Open Dumps.* Washington: Government Printing Office, 1971.

———. *Planning for Solid Waste Management.* Washington: Government Printing Office, 1971. (Symposium of State and Interstate Solid Waste Planning Agencies.)

———. *Proceedings, First National Conference on Packaging Wastes.* Washington: Government Printing Office, 1969.

———. *Role of Nonpackaging Paper in Solid Waste Management, 1966–1976.* Washington: Government Printing Office, 1971.

———. *Rubber Reuse and Solid Waste Management.* Washington: Government Printing Office, 1971.

———. *Safe and Sanitary Home Refuse Storage.* Washington: Government Printing Office, 1971.

———. *Sanitary Landfill Design, Construction, and Evaluation.* Washington: Government Printing Office, 1971.

———. *Solid Waste Disposal Act.* Washington: Government Printing Office, 1971.

———. *Solid Waste Management: Available Information Materials.* Washington: Government Printing Office, 1973.

———. *Solid Waste Management in Recreational Forest Areas.* Washington: Government Printing Office, 1971.

———. *State Solid Waste Planning Grants, Agencies, and Progress—1970.* Washington: Government Printing Office, 1971. (Report of activities through June 30, 1970.)

———. *Summaries of Solid Waste Intramural Research and Development Projects.* Washington: Government Printing Office, 1971.

Executive Office of the President. Office of Science and Technology. *Protecting the World Environment in the Light of Population Increase.* Washington: Government Printing Office, 1970.

———. *Solid Waste Management, A Comprehensive Assessment of Solid Waste Problems, Practices, and Needs.* Washington: Government Printing Office, 1969.

"Glass Recycling Makes Strides." *Environmental Science and Technology.* November 1972, pp. 988–990. (Describes recycling process and uses of recycled glass.)

Goodman, Brian L. *Manual for Activated Sludge Sewage Treatment.* Westport, Conn.: Technomic, 1971.

Grinstead, Robert R. "Bottlenecks." *Environment*, April 1972, pp. 2–13. (Discusses shortcoming of present technology for handling municipal wastes.)

———. "Machinery for Trash Mining." *Environment*, May 1972, pp. 34–42. (Discusses technology being developed in area of recycling.)

———. "The New Resource." *Environment*, December 1970, pp. 2–17. (Concerns solid waste recycling.)

———. "No Deposit, No Return." *Environment*, November 1969, pp. 17–23. (Deals with nonreturnable packaging, including soda bottles, plastic bags, and so forth.)

Hanks, Thrift G. *Solid Waste/Disease Relationships, A Literature Survey.* Washington: Government Printing Office, 1968. (A Public Health Service report.)

Hannon, B. M. "Bottles, Cans, Energy." *Environment*, March 1972, pp. 11–21. (Compares economic aspects of returnable and recycled bottles.)

"Hard Road Ahead for City Incinerators." *Environmental Science and Technology*, November 1972, pp. 992–993. (Describes disadvantages of burning urban trash in incinerators.)

Hart, Samuel A. *Solid Waste Management, Composting, European Activity and American Potential.* Washington: Government Printing Office, 1968. (Report of Public Health Service.)

Health, Education, and Welfare Department. *Accounting System for Incinerator Operations.* Washington: Government Printing Office, 1970.

———. *Accounting System for Sanitary Landfill Operations, 1969.* Washington: Government Printing Office, 1970.

———. *Accounting System for Solid Waste Collection.* Washington: Government Printing Office, 1970.

———. *Comprehensive Studies of Solid Waste Management: First and Second Annual Reports.* Washington: Government Printing Office, 1970.

———. *Developing a State Solid Waste Management Plan.* Washington: Government Printing Office, 1970.

———. *Sanitary Landfill, an Answer to a Community Problem, a Route to a Community Asset.* Rev. ed. Washington: Government Printing Office, 1970.

———. *Systems Analysis of Regional Solid Waste Handling.* Washington: Government Printing Office, 1970.

Hershaft, A. "Solid Waste Treatment Technology." *Environmental Science and Technology,* May 1972, pp. 412–421.

Holman, J. L., et al. *Processing the Plastics from Urban Refuse.* Washington: Government Printing Office, 1972. (Report of the Bureau of Mines.)

Hutchison, S. Blair. "Bringing Resource Utilization into the Main Stream of American Thought." *Natural Resources Journal.* October 1969, pp. 518–536.

Interior Department. *Population Challenge, What It Means to America.* Washington: Government Printing Office, 1966. (A Conservation Yearbook.)

Jensen, Michael E. *Observations of Continental European Solid Waste Management Practices.* Washington: Government Printing Office, 1969. (Report of the Public Health Service.)

Johnson, Huey D., ed. *No Deposit—No Return: Man and His Environment, a View toward Survival.* Reading, Mass.: Addison-Wesley, 1970.

Josephson, H. "Recycling of Waste Paper in Relation to Forest Products." *TAPPI,* June 1971, p. 896. (Supply and demand considerations.)

Kelly, Katie. *Garbage: The History and Future of Garbage in America.* New York: Saturday Review, 1973.

Kenahan, Charles B. "Solid Waste—Resources out of Place." *Environmental Science and Technology,* July 1971, pp. 594–600.

Kenahan, Charles B., et al. *Composition and Characteristics of Municipal Incinerator Residues.* Washington: Government Printing Office, 1968. (Report of Bureau of Mines.)

Kirov, N. Y., ed. *Solid Waste Treatment and Disposal.* Ann Arbor, Mich.: Ann Arbor Science, 1972.

Kudrna, Frank. "Putting Sewage Solids Back to Work." *Compost Science,* January–February 1972, pp. 12–14.

Lefke, Louis W. *Resource Recovery in Solid Waste Management.* Washington: Government Printing Office, 1971. (Report of the Environmental Protection Agency.)

Locke, Edwin A., Jr. "Recycling of Secondary Fibers." *Secondary Raw Materials,* March 1970, pp. 80–85. (Discusses paper and paperboard.)

Meller, F. H. *Conversion of Organic Solid Wastes into Yeasts: An Economic Evaluation.* Washington: Government Printing Office, 1970. (Report of the Public Health Service.)

Meyer, J. G. "Renewing the Soil." *Environment,* May 1972, pp. 22–32. (Discusses composting.)

National Academy of Engineering/National Academy of Sciences. *Policies of Solid Waste Management.* Washington: Government Printing Office, 1970. (Report of the Department of Health, Education, and Welfare.)

National Association of Secondary Materials Industries. *Effective Technology for Recycling Metals.* New York: National Association of Secondary Materials Industries, 1971. (Also considers control of air pollution.)

———. *National Priorities for Recycling: Proposals for a Legislative Action Program.* New

York: National Association of Secondary Materials Industries, 1971.

———. *Study of the Secondary Lead Market in the United States.* New York: National Association of Secondary Materials Industries, 1969. (Prepared in conjunction with the Lead Industries Association.)

National Commission on Materials Policy. *Towards a National Material Policy—Basic Data and Issues—An Interim Report.* Washington: Government Printing Office, 1972.

National Incinerator Conference, 1972. *Proceedings.* New York: American Society of Mechanical Engineers, 1972. (Discusses technological aspects of treatment and disposal of solid wastes.)

National Industrial Pollution Control Council. *Animal Wastes.* Washington: Government Printing Office, 1971.

———. *Deep Ocean Dumping of Baled Refuse: Subcouncil Report.* Washington: Government Printing Office, 1971.

———. *Disposal of Major Appliances.* Washington: Government Printing Office, 1971.

———. *Glass Containers: Subcouncil Report.* Washington: Government Printing Office, 1971.

———. *Junk Car Disposal: Subcouncil Report.* Washington: Government Printing Office, 1970.

———. *Paper: Subcouncil Report.* Washington: Government Printing Office, 1971.

———. *Plastics in Solid Waste: Subcouncil Report.* Washington: Government Printing Office, 1971.

———. *Waste Disposal in Deep Wells.* Washington: Government Printing Office, 1971.

———. *Wood Products.* Washington: Government Printing Office, 1971.

Neal, A. W. *Industrial Waste: Its Handling, Disposal, and Re-Use.* Boston: Cahners Books, 1972.

Noone, J. A. "Environment Report: Federal Role in Solid Waste Programs to Undergo Scrutiny in 93rd Congress." *National Journal,* November 18, 1972, pp. 1773–1782.

Palumbo, F. J., et al. *Electronic Color Sorting of Glass from Urban Waste.* Washington: Government Printing Office, 1971. (Report of the Bureau of Mines.)

Paper Recycling, A Report on Its Economic and Ecological Implications. New York: Bank of America, 1971.

Pearl, Irwin A. "Waste Product Use Helps Paper Industry Control Pollution." *Environmental Science and Technology,* September 1968, pp. 677–681.

"Plastics and Ecology: Special Report." *Plastics World,* June 1971, pp. 41–82.

Public Administration Service. *Municipal Refuse Disposal.* Chicago: Public Administration Service, 1970.

Public Health Service. *Study of Solid Waste Collection Systems Comparing One-Man with Multi-Man Crews.* Washington: Government Printing Office, 1969.

Public Works Association. *Rail Transport of Solid Waste.* Chicago: Public Works Association, 1971. (Preliminary study of the use of railroads.)

Randers, Jørgen, and Meadows, Dennis L. "The Dynamics of Solid Waste." *Technology Review,* March–April 1972, pp. 20–32. (A computer-modeling approach to solid waste management.)

Rasher, Howard William, and Suisman, Michael. *Nonferrous Scrap Metal Guidebook.* New York: National Association of Secondary Materials Industries, n.d.

"Recycling as an Industry." *Environmental Science and Technology,* August 1972, pp. 700–704.

"Reground Materials Are Great, But...." *Plastics World,* April 1972, pp. 46–47. (Guidelines for use of scrap and reground plastics.)

Resource Recovery from Incinerator Residue: Analysis of Factors that Affect Economic Recycling of Ferrous Metals and Other Inorganic Material Contained in Municipal In-

cinerator Residue. Chicago: American Public Works Administration, 1970.

Reuse and Recycle of Wastes. Stamford, Conn.: Technomic, 1971. (Provides information on present research and techniques and outlook for the future.)

Rose, David J., Gibbons, John H., and Fukerson, William. "Physics Looks at Waste Management." *Physics Today*, February 1972, pp. 32-41. (Reviews sorting, recycling, and disposal problems.)

"Sanitary Landfill: Alternative to the Open Dump." *Environmental Science and Technology*, May 1972, pp. 408-410.

Senner, W. S., et al. *Conversion of Municipal and Industrial Refuse into Useful Materials by Pyrolysis.* Washington: Government Printing Office, 1970. (Report of the Bureau of Mines.)

Sheffer, H. W., Baker, E. C., and Evans, G. C. *Case Studies of Municipal Waste Disposal Systems.* Washington: Government Printing Office, 1971. (Report of the Bureau of Mines.)

Siebert, Donald L. *Impact of Technology on the Commercial Secondary Aluminum Industry.* Washington: Government Printing Office, 1970. (Report of the Bureau of Mines.)

Singleton, Eben I., et al. *Recovery of Aluminum from Aluminum-Silicon Alloys.* Washington: Government Printing Office, 1972. (Report of Bureau of Mines.)

Skitt, John. *Disposal of Refuse and Other Waste.* New York: Halsted, 1973. (Introductory text.)

Small, William E. *Third Pollution: The National Problem of Solid Waste Disposal.* New York: Praeger, 1971. (Discusses high costs of reducing wastes and possible developments for the future.)

Smith, D. C., and Brown, R. P. *Ocean Disposal of Barge-Delivered Liquid and Solid Wastes from U.S. Coastal Cities.* Washington: Government Printing Office, 1971. (Report of the Environmental Protection Agency.)

"A Solid Waste Recovery System for All Municipalities." *Environmental Science and Technology*, February 1971, pp. 109-111.

"Solid Waste Treatment Technology." *Environmental Science and Technology*, May 1972, pp. 412-421.

Solid Wastes: An Environmental Science and Technology Reprint Book. Washington: American Chemical Society, 1971. (Articles discuss various aspects of solid waste control.)

"Solid Wastes: An Environmental Science and Technology Special Report." *Environmental Science and Technology*, May 1970, pp. 384-391.

Sorg, T. J., and Hickman, H. L. *Sanitary Landfill Facts.* Washington: Government Printing Office, 1970. (Report of the Department of Health, Education, and Welfare.)

Southern Research Institute. *Selected Bibliography of Electrostatic Precipitator Literature: A Manual of Electrostatic Precipitator Technology*, 3 vols. Washington: Government Printing Office, 1970. (Distributed by the National Technical Information Service.)

Spofford, Walter O., Jr. "Closing the Gap in Waste Management." *Environmental Science and Technology*, December 1970, pp. 1108-1114.

Stear, J. R. *Municipal Incineration: A Review of the Literature.* Washington: Government Printing Office, 1971. (Report of the Environmental Protection Agency.)

Strenge, R. A. "Recycling May Mean Trash for Sale." *Public Works*, November 1970, pp. 81-82. (Considers paper, lumber, and other wood-fiber materials.)

Sullivan, P. M., and Stanczyk, M. H. *Economics of Recycling Metals and Materials from Urban Refuse.* Washington: Government Printing Office, 1971. (Report of the Bureau of Mines.)

Sullivan, T. A., et al. *Recovery of Aluminum, Base and Precious Metals from Electronic Scrap.* Washington: Government Printing Office, 1972. (Report of the Bureau of Mines.)

Thermo-Systems, Inc. *The State of the Art 1971: Instrumentation of Particulate Emissions from Combustion Sources.* 2 vols. Washington: Government Printing Office, 1971. (Distributed by the National Technical Information Service.)

Tonge, Peter. "Series on Recycling." *The Christian Science Monitor*, May 15-20, 1972.

"Turning Junk and Trash into a Resource." *Business Week*. October 10, 1970, pp. 66-75.

Tyrell, Miles, et al. *Fabrication and Cost Evaluation of Experimental Building Brick from Waste Glass*. Washington: Government Printing Office, 1972. (Report of the Bureau of Mines.)

Vaughan, R. D. "Recycling and Reuse of Waste Materials." *Waste Age*, September 1969, pp. 6-7.

Wadleigh, Cecil H. *Wastes in Relation to Agriculture and Forestry*. Washington: Government Printing Office, 1968. (Report of the Department of Agriculture. Ten major categories of entities that contaminate the environment; brief discussion of economic considerations.)

Warner, Arthur J., et al. *Solid Waste Management of Plastics*. Washington: Manufacturing Chemists Association, 1970.

Wilson, David Gordon, ed. *Treatment and Management of Urban Solid Waste*. Westport, Conn.: Technomic, 1972.

Wilson, David Gordon, and Smith, Ora E. "How to Reclaim Goods from Wastes." *Technology Review*, May 1972, pp. 31-39.

THERMAL POLLUTION

Atomic Energy Commission. *Thermal Effects and U.S. Nuclear Power Stations*. Washington: Goverment Printing Office, 1971.

Clark John R. "Heat Pollution." *National Parks Magazine*, December 1969, pp. 4-8.

———. "Thermal Pollution and Marine Life." *Scientific American*, March 1969, pp. 18-27.

Eisenbud, Merril, and Gleason, George, eds. *Electric Power and Thermal Discharges*. New York: Gordon and Breach, 1969. (Papers from the symposium "Thermal Considerations in the Production of Electric Power.")

Environmental Protection Agency. *Guidelines, Biological Surveys at Proposed Heat Discharge Sites*. Washington: Government Printing Office, 1970.

———. *Research on the Physical Aspects of Thermal Pollution*. Washington: Government Printing Office, 1971.

Krenkel, Peter A., and Parker, Frank L., eds. *Biological Aspects of Thermal Pollution*. Portland, Ore.: Vanderbilt University Press, 1969.

Levin, Arthur A., et al. "Thermal Discharges: Ecological Effects." *Environmental Science and Technology*, March 1972, pp. 224-230.

Parker, Frank L., and Krenkel, Peter A. *Physical and Engineering Aspects of Thermal Pollution*. Cleveland, Ohio: Chemical Rubber Co., 1970.

Rossie, John P. *Research on Dry-Type Cooling Towers for Thermal Electric Generation*. Washington: Government Printing Office, 1970.

Yee, William C. "Thermal Aquaculture: Engineering and Economics." *Environmental Science and Technology*, March 1972, pp. 232-237. (Argues that thermal polluted water can be used to increase numbers of fish and seafood.)

TOXIC AND HAZARDOUS SUBSTANCES

Aaronson, Terri. "Gamble." *Environment*, September 1971, pp. 20-24, 29. (Discusses scientific decisions related to 2,4,5-T, an herbicide.)

———. "Mercury in the Environment." *Environment*, May 1971, pp. 16-23.

Ahmed, A. Karim; MacLeod, Donald F.; and Carmody, James "Control for Asbestos." *Environment*, December 1972, pp. 16-22. (Discusses hazards of asbestos and the first protection standards that have been created.)

Albone, Eric, and McCaull, Julian. "Freighted with Hazard." *Environment*, December 1970, pp. 18-27. (States that 500 million tons of dangerous materials are transported annually in the United States.)

Aldrich, John D. *Review of the Problem of Birds Contaminated by Oil and Their Rehabilitation.* Washington: Government Printing Office, 1970. (Report of the Sport Fisheries and Wildlife Bureau.)

American Petroleum Institute. *Air Quality and Lead.* Washington: American Petroleum Institute, 1970. (Describes the existence of lead in air, soil, animals, and plants.)

———. *Prevention and Control of Oil Spills.* Washington: American Petroleum Institute, 1971.

Atomic Energy Commission. *Studies in Workmen's Compensation and Radiation Injury.* Vol. 5. Washington: Government Printing Office, 1970. (Includes discussion of asbestos, beryllium, and ionizing radiation.)

———. *Toxicity of Power Plant Chemicals to Aquatic Life.* Washington: Government Printing Office, 1973. (Detailed literature review.)

Bloom, Sandra C., and Degler, Stanley E. *Pesticides and Pollution.* Washington: Government Printing Office, 1969. (Report of the Bureau of National Affairs.)

Blumer, Max, et al. "An Ocean of Oil: A Small Oil Spill." *Environment,* March 1971, pp. 2–12. (Argues that the smaller, day-to-day spills are probably even more detrimental than the larger ones.)

Brodeur, Paul. *Asbestos and Enzymes.* New York: Ballantine Books, 1972. (Discusses health effects of these materials.)

Button, D. K., and Dunker, S. S. *Biological Effects of Copper and Arsenic Pollution.* Washington: Government Printing Office, 1971. (Distributed by the National Technical Information Service. Studies inhibitory effects of copper toward marine microorganisms.)

Carson, Rachel. *Silent Spring.* Boston: Houghton Mifflin, 1962. (Describes the damage done by the massive use of chemical to control pests.)

Carter, Luther J. "Nerve Gas Disposal: How the AEC Refused to Take Army Off the Hook." *Science,* Sept. 25, 1970, pp. 1296–1298.

Chesters, G., and Konrad, J. G. "Effects of Pesticide Usage on Water Quality." *BioScience,* June 15, 1971, pp. 565–569.

Chisolm, J. Julian, Jr. "Lead Poisoning." *Scientific American,* February, 1971, pp. 15–23.

Chow, Tsaihwa J., and Earl, John L. "Lead Aerosols in the Atmosphere: Increasing Concentrations." *Science,* August 7, 1970, pp. 577–580.

Congress. House. Committee on Agriculture. *Federal Pesticide Control Act of 1971: Hearings.* Washington: Government Printing Office, 1971.

Congress. House. Committee on Government Operations. *Environmental Dangers of Open-Air Testing of Lethal Chemicals: Hearings before a Subcommittee.* Washington: Government Printing Office, 1969.

Congress. House Documents. *Control of Hazardous Polluting Substances: Message from the President of the United States.* Washington: Government Printing Office, 1971.

Congress. House Reports. *Federal Environmental Pesticide Control Act of 1971.* Washington: Government Printing Office, 1971. (H.R. 10729, September 25, 1971.)

Congress. Senate. Committee on Commerce. *Effects of Mercury on Man and the Environment: Hearings before the Subcommittee on Energy, Natural Resources, and the Environment.* Washington: Government Printing Office, 1970.

Congress. Senate. Committee on Commerce. *Effects of 2,4,5-T on Man and the Environment: Hearings before the Subcommittee on Energy, Natural Resources, and the Environment.* Washington: Government Printing Office, 1970.

Congress. Senate. Committee on Interior and Insular Affairs. *Santa Barbara Oil Spill: Hearings before the Subcommittee on Minerals, Materials, and Fuels.* Washington: Government Printing Office, 1970.

Congress. Senate. Committee on Labor and Public Welfare. *Lead-Based Paint Poisoning: Hearings before the Subcommittee on Health.* Washington: Government Printing Office, 1970.

Conway, Gordon R. "A Consequence of Insecticides." *Natural History*, February 1969, pp. 46–54. (Holds that they have led to an increase in insect population.)

Council on Environmental Quality. *Toxic Substances*. Washington: Government Printing Office, 1971.

Craig, Paul P., and Berlin, Edward. "The Air of Poverty." *Environment*, June 1971, pp. 2–9. (Discusses led in the atmosphere.)

Dawson, G. W., Shuckrow, A. J., and Swift, W. H. *Control of Spillage of Hazardous Polluting Substances*. Washington: Government Printing Office, 1971. (Report of the Water Quality Office, EPA.)

D'Itri, Frank M. *The Environmental Mercury Problem*. Cleveland, Ohio: Chemical Rubber Co., 1972.

Environmental Protection Agency. *Conversion of Crankcase Waste Oil into Useful Products*. Washington: Government Printing Office, 1971.

———. *Ecological Effects of Pesticides on Non-Target Species*. Washington: Government Printing Office, 1971.

———. *Effects of Oil Pollution on Waterfowl, A Study of Salvage Methods*. Washington: Government Printing Office, 1970.

———. *Environmental Lead and Public Health*. Washington: Government Printing Office, 1971. (Basic discussion of lead and its effects on the general population.)

———. *Feasibility Analysis of Incinerator Systems for Restoration of Oil-Contaminated Beaches*. Washington: Government Printing Office, 1970

———. *Highlights: The Federal Environmental Pesticide Control Act of 1972*. Washington: Government Printing Office, 1972.

——— *Investigation of Means for Controlled Self-Destruction of Pesticides*. Washington: Government Printing Office, 1970.

———. *Pesticides, What Are Pesticides?* Rev. ed. Washington: Government Printing Office, 1971.

———. *Spill Prevention Techniques for Hazardous Polluting Substances: Inventory and Survey of Hazardous Chemical Facilities*. Washington: Government Printing Office, 1971.

———. *Testing and Evaluation of Oil Spill Recovery Equipment*. Washington: Government Printing Office, 1971.

———. *Toxic Action of Water Soluble Pollutants on Freshwater Fish*. Washington: Government Printing Office, 1970.

Epstein, Samuel S., and Legator, Marvin S. *The Mutagenicity of Pesticides: Concepts and Evaluation*. Cambridge, Mass.: MIT Press, 1971. (Discusses approximately 400 substances.)

Executive Office of the President. Office of Science and Technology. *Oil Pollution, A Report to the President*. Washington: Government Printing Office, 1968.

Faust, Samuel J. *Fate of Organic Pesticides in the Aquatic Environment*, ed. by Robert F. Gould. Washington: American Chemical Society, 1972.

Ferguson, Denzel E. "The New Evolution." *Environment*, July–August 1972, pp. 30–35. (Discusses role of pesticides in changing or destroying various species.)

Fish and Wildlife Service. *Fish, Wildlife, and Pesticides*. Washington: Government Printing Office, 1966.

Foote, R. S. "Mercury Vapor Concentrations inside Buildings." *Science*, August 11, 1972, pp. 513–514.

Friberg, Lars, and Vostal, Jaroslav, eds. *Mercury in the Environment: An Epidemiological and Toxicological Appraisal*. Cleveland, Ohio: Chemical Rubber Co., 1972.

Geological Survey. *Mercury in the Environment*. Washington: Government Printing Office, 1970. (Papers on the abundance, distribution, and testing of mercury in rocks, soilds, water, plants, and atmosphere.)

Gillett, James W. *The Biological Impact of Pesticides in the Environment*. Corvallis, Oreg.: Oregon State University Press, 1970.

Goldwater, Leonard J. *Mercury: A History of Quicksilver.* Baltimore: Johns Hopkins, 1972. (A medical history.)

———. "Mercury in the Environment." *Scientific American*, May 1971, pp. 15–21.

Graham, Frank, Jr. *Since Silent Spring.* Boston: Houghton Mifflin, 1970. (Case history of the pesticide problem.)

Grant, Neville. "Mercury in Man." *Environment*, May 1971, pp. 2–15.

Hall, Stephen K. "Lead Pollution and Poisoning." *Environmental Science and Technology*, January 1972, pp. 30–35.

Harrison, H. L., et al. "Systems Studies of DDT Transport." *Science*, October 30, 1970, pp. 503–508.

Hartung, Rolf, and Dinman, Bertram D., eds. *Environmental Mercury Contamination.* Ann Arbor, Mich.: Ann Arbor Science, 1972. (Comprehensive analysis.)

Headley, J. C., and Lewis, J. N. *Pesticide Problem: An Economic Approach to Public Policy.* Baltimore: Johns Hopkins, 1967.

Health, Education, and Welfare Department. *Report of the Secretary's Commission on Pesticides and Their Relationship to Environmental Health.* Parts 1 and 2. Washington: Government Printing Office, 1969.

"Horizon to Horizon: An *Environment* Staff Report." *Environment*, March 1971, pp. 13–21. (Summary of oil accidents around the world for about one year.)

Hunter, Beatrice T. *Consumer Beware: Your Food and What's Been Done to It.* New York: Simon and Schuster, 1971. (A look at the actual contents of foods offered to the buyer in the marketplace.)

Hyman, M. H. "Timetable for Lead." *Environment*, June 1971, pp. 14–23. (States that the removal of lead from gasoline could have been completed by 1973.)

Interdepartmental Task Force on PCB's, Washington, D. C. *PCB's and the Environment.* Washington: Government Printing Office, 1972. (Distributed by the National Technical Information Service. Details available current knowledge about polychlorinated biphenyls.)

Irving, George W. "Agricultural Pest Control and the Environment." *Science*, June 19, 1970, pp. 1419–1424.

Jacobson, Michael F. *Eater's Digest: The Consumer's Fact Book of Additives.* New York: Doubleday, 1972. (Discusses more than 100 additives and their effects on health.)

Karolinska Institutet, Stockholm. *Cadmium in the Environment, A Toxicological and Epidemiological Appraisal.* Washington: Government Printing Office, 1971. (Distributed by the National Technical Information Service. Discusses toxic effects on humans and animals.)

Kellogg, W. W., et al. "The Sulfur Cycle." *Science*, February 11, 1972, pp. 587–596. (Compares natural and manmade quantities of sulfur.)

Kilgore, Wendell W. *Pest Control: Biological, Physical, and Selected Chemical Methods.* New York: Academic Press, 1967.

Lawrence, R. D. *The Poison Makers.* Toronto: Thomas Nelson, 1969. (Shows that Canadian cities suffer from the same noxious pollutants as U.S. cities.)

Long, K. R. "Pesticides: An Occupational Hazard on Farms." *American Journal of Nursing*, April 1971, pp. 740–743.

McCaull, Julian. "Building a Shorter Life." *Environment*, September 1971, pp. 2–15, 38–41. (Discusses cadmium and its dangers.)

Mather, William G., III, et al. *Man, His Job, and the Environment, A Review and Annotated Bibliography of Selected Recent Research on Human Performance.* Washington: Government Printing Office, 1970. (A special publication of the National Bureau of Standards.)

Melnikov, N. N. *Chemistry of Pesticides.* New York: Springer-Verlag, 1971. (Basic text translated from the Russian.)

"Mercury in the Air." *Environment*, May 1971, pp. 24, 29–33. (Report by the staff of the magazine.)

Miller, Morton W., and Berg, George G., eds. *Chemical Fallout: Current Research on Persistent Pesticides*. Springfield, Ill.: Charles C Thomas, 1969. (Collection of papers exploring various aspects of the problem.)

National Academy of Sciences. *Biologic Effects of Atmospheric Pollution: Lead: Airborne Lead in Perspective*. Washington: Government Printing Office, 1972.

———. *Degradation of Synthetic Organic Molecules in the Biosphere—Natural, Pesticidal and Various Other Man-Made Compounds*. Washington: Government Printing Office, 1972. (Proceedings of conference held under the aegis of the National Research Council.)

National Industrial Pollution Control Council. *Mercury*. Washington: Government Printing Office, 1970.

Newell, I. Laird. "Mercury and Other Heavy Metals in Water Supplies." *Journal of New England Water Works Association*, September 1971, pp. 289-295.

Newell, R. C. "The Effect of Chemical Waste on Marine Organisms." *Effluent Water Treatment Journal*, June 1972, pp. 307-312.

Novick, Sheldon. "The Burden of Proof." *Environment*, October 1970, pp. 25-29. (Studies the degree of safety of Shell's No-Pest Strip.)

Palmer, J. S., and Radeleff, R. D. *Toxicity of Some Organic Herbicides to Cattle, Sheep, and Chickens*. Washington: Government Printing Office, 1969. (Research report of the Department of Agriculture.)

Peakall, David B. "Pesticides and the Reproduction of Birds." *Scientific American*, April 1970, pp. 72-78.

Peterson, James T., and Bryson, Reid A. "Atmospheric Aerosols: Increased Concentrations During the Last Decade." *Science*, October 4, 1969, pp. 120-121.

Pramer, David. "The Soil Transforms." *Environment*, May 1971, pp. 42-46. (Describes the danger of herbicides in the soil.)

Pratt, Christopher J. "Sulfur." *Scientific American*, May 1970, pp. 62-72.

President's Panel on Oil Spills. *Oil Spill Problem: First Report*. Washington: Government Printing Office, 1971.

Pryde, Philip N. "Soviet Pesticides." *Environment*, November 1971, pp. 16-28.

"Red Food Coloring: How Safe Is It?" *Consumer Reports*, February 1973, pp. 130-133. (Discusses possible hazards of use of amaranth, or "Red 2.")

Schroeder, Henry A. "Metals in the Air." *Environment*, October 1971, pp. 18-24.

Selikoff, I. J. "Asbestos." *Environment*, March 1969, pp. 2-7. (Discusses effects of asbestos particulates.)

Shea, Kevin P. "Captan and Folpet." *Environment*, January-February 1972, pp. 22-24, 29-32. (Shows that these two pesticides, though dangerous, are still in use.)

———. "Plastics in the Air." *Environment*, November 1972, pp. 10-11. (Discusses plastics as possible cause of birth defects.)

Sittig, Marshall. *Agricultural Chemicals Manufacture*. Park Ridge, N.J.: Noyes Data, 1971. (Detailed information on insecticides, herbicides, and so forth.)

Smith, Ralph G. *Chlorine: An Annotated Bibliography*. New York: The Chlorine Institute, 1972. (Entries 1824-1971.)

Sutton, H. Eldon, and Harris, Maureen I., eds. *Mutagenic Effects of Environmental Contaminants*. New York: Academic Press, 1972.

Tucker, Anthony. *The Toxic Metals*. New York: Ballantine Books, 1972.

Turner, James S. *The Chemical Feast*. New York: Grossman, 1970. (Report by Ralph Nader Study Group on Food Protection and the FDA.)

van den Vosch, Robert. "The Cost of Poisons." *Environment*, September 1972, pp. 18-22. (Presents alternative methods of pest control.)

Water Quality Office. *Evaluation of Selected Earthmoving Equipment for the Restoration of Oil-Contaminated Beaches, 1970*. Washington: Government Printing Office, 1971.

Wellford, Harrison. *Sowing the Wind.* New York: Grossman, 1972. (Examines the chemicals used in our food supply.)

White, William C., and Collins, Donald N., eds. *The Fertilizer Handbook.* Washington: The Fertilizer Institute, 1972. (Includes section on effects of fertilizers on the environment.)

White-Stevens, Robert, ed. *Pesticides in the Environment.* Vol. 1. New York: Marcel Dekker, 1971. (Presents ideas of experts from many fields.)

Winter, Ruth. *Poisons in Your Food.* New York: Crown, 1969.

Wood, John M. "A Progress Report on Mercury." *Environment,* February 1972, pp. 33–39. (Argues that discharges of mercury by industry have decreased but that mercury already in air is doing damage.)

Woodwell, George M. "Toxic Substances and Ecological Cycles." *Scientific American,* March 1967, pp. 24–31.

Woodwell, George M., Craig, Paul P., and Johnston, H. A. "DDT in the Biosphere: Where Does It Go?" *Science,* December 10, 1971, pp. 1101–1107.

Working Group on Pesticides, Washington, D.C. *Ground Disposal of Pesticides: The Problem and Criteria for Guidelines.* Washington: Government Printing Office, 1970. (Distributed by National Technical Information Service. Examines contamination in wells and groundwater.)

World Health Organization. *Control of Pesticides: A Survey of Existing Legislation.* Geneva: World Health Organization, 1970.

Wurster, Charles F. "Aldrin and Dieldrin." *Environment,* October 1971, pp. 33–41. (Provides more than 140 references on these two pesticides.)

———. "DDT Reduces Photosynthesis by Marine Phytoplankton." *Science,* March 29, 1968, pp. 1471–1475.

WATER

Agriculture Department. *Let's Grow! Community Benefits from Watershed Projects.* Washington: Government Printing Office, 1970.

———. *Sediment: It's Filling Harbors, Lakes, and Roadside Ditches.* Washington: Government Printing Office, 1967.

Alexander, Martin. *Microbial Ecology.* New York: Wiley, 1971. (Describes role of microorganisms in polluted environments.)

Allen, Herbert E., and Kramer, James R., eds. *Nutrients in Natural Waters.* New York: Wiley, 1972.

Allen, Jonathan. "Sewage Farming." *Environment,* April 1973, pp. 36–41. (Describes advantages and disadvantages.)

American Institute of Chemical Engineers. *Water—1970.* New York: American Institute of Chemical Engineers, 1971. (Comprehensive coverage of technological advances.)

Ballinger, Dwight G. "Instruments for Water Quality Monitoring." *Environmental Science and Technology,* February 1972, pp. 130–133. (Explains testing methods.)

Barry, James P. *The Fate of the Lakes: A Portrait of the Great Lakes.* Grand Rapids, Mich.: Baker Book House, 1972. (Emphasizes ecological problems.)

Beasley, R. P. *Erosion and Sediment Pollution Control.* Ames, Iowa: Iowa State University Press, 1972.

Behrman, A. A. *Water Is Everybody's Business.* New York: Doubleday, 1968. (Basic text on water pollution.)

Besselievre, Edmund Bulkley. *The Treatment of Industrial Wastes.* New York: McGraw-Hill, 1969.

Billings, C. H., and Smallhorst, D. F., eds. *Manual of Wastewater Operations.* Austin, Tex.: Texas State Department of Health, 1971.

Blumer, M. "Oil Pollution of the Ocean." *Oceanus,* October 1969, pp. 2–7.

Bolton, R. L., and Klein, Louis. *Sewage Treatment: Basic Principles and Trends.* Rev. ed. Ann Arbor, Mich.: Ann Arbor Science, 1973. (Text appropriate for sanitary engineers.)

Briggs, Peter. *Water, the Vital Essence.* New York: Harper, 1967.

Burke, W. T. *Towards a Better Use of the Ocean.* New York: Humanities Press, 1969.

Campbell, Thomas, and Sylvester, Robert O. *Water Resources Management and Public Policy.* Seattle: University of Washington Press, 1968.

Canale, Raymond P., ed. *Biological Waste Treatment.* New York: Wiley, 1971.

Carson, Rachel. *The Sea Around Us.* New York: Oxford University Press, 1961.

Clark, John W., Viessman, Warren, Jr., and Hammer, Mark J. *Water Supply and Pollution Control.* 2nd ed. Scranton, Pa.: International Textbook, 1971. (Designed for college-level course.)

Commission on Marine Science, Engineering and Resources. *Our Nation and the Sea.* Washington: Government Printing Office, 1969. (Discusses the development, utilization, and preservation of the marine environment.)

Commoner, Barry. "Lake Erie, Aging or Ill?" *Scientist and Citizen,* December 1968, pp. 254ff.

Congress. House. Committee on Government Operations. *Establishment of a National Industrial Wastes Inventory: Hearings before a Subcommittee.* Washington: Government Printing Office, 1970. (See also Report by the Committee, H. rp. 1717, 1970.)

Congress. House. Committee on Government Operations. *Phosphates in Detergents and the Eutrophication of American Waters: Hearings before a Subcommittee.* Washington: Government Printing Office, 1970. (See also Report by the Committee, H. rp. 1004, 1970.)

Congress. House. Committee on Government Operations. *Protecting America's Estuaries, the Potomac: Hearings before a Subcommittee.* Washington: Government Printing Office, 1970. (See also Report by the Committee, H. rp. 1761, 1970.)

Congress. House Reports. *Our Waters and Wetlands, How the Corps of Engineers Can Help Prevent Their Destruction and Pollution.* Washington: Government Printing Office, 1970. (H. rp. 917.)

Congress. Laws. *Water Bank Act: Approved Dec. 19, 1970.* Washington: Government Printing Office, 1970. (Act to provide for conserving surface waters; to preserve and improve habitats for migrating waterfowl and other wildlife resources; to reduce runoff, soil, and wind erosion, and contribute to flood control; and for other purposes.)

Congress. Laws. *Water Quality Improvement Act: Approved Apr. 3, 1970.* Washington: Government Printing Office, 1970.

Congress. Senate. Committee on Public Works. *Water Pollution Control Legislation: Hearings before the Subcommittee on Air and Water Pollution.* Washington: Government Printing Office, 1971. (First four parts deal with general water pollution problems; part 5 deals with ocean dumping; part 6 with agricultural runoff.)

Congress. Senate. Committee on Public Works. *Water Pollution, 1970: Hearings before the Subcommittee on Air and Water Pollution.* Washington: Government Printing Office, 1970. (In five parts.)

Cousteau, Jacques-Yves, and Diole, Philippe. *Life and Death in a Coral Sea: The Undersea Discoveries of Jacques-Yves Cousteau.* Garden City, N.Y.: Doubleday, 1971.

Cowden, R. W. "Municipal Problems in Financing Water Pollution Control." *Water Pollution Control Federation Journal,* November 1970, pp. 1998–2003.

Craine, Lyle E. *Water Management Innovations in England.* Baltimore: Johns Hopkins, 1970.

Crossland, Janice, and Brodine, Virginia. "Drinking Water." *Environment,* April 1973, pp. 11–19. (Discusses many of the chemicals found in our water supply.)

Crossland, Janice, and McCaull, Julian. "Overfed." *Environment,* November 1972, pp. 30–37. (Examines the eutrophication of U.S. waters.)

Culp, Russell L., and Culp, Gordon L. *Advanced Wastewater Treatment.* New York: Van Nostrand Reinhold, 1971.

Cunningham, F. F. *1001 Question Answered about Water Resources.* New York: Dodd, Mead, 1967.

Downing, Paul B. *The Economics of Urban Sewage Disposal*. New York: Praeger, 1969.

Dugan, Patrick R. *Biochemical Ecology of Water Pollution*. New York: Plenum, 1972.

Environmental Protection Agency. *Agricultural Pollution of the Great Lakes Basin*. Washington: Government Printing Office, 1971. (Combined report by Canada and the United States.)

———. *Benefits of Water Quality Enhancement*. Washington: Government Printing Office, 1970.

———. *Combined Treatment of Domestic and Industrial Wastes by Activated Sludge*. Washington: Government Printing Office, 1971.

———. *Control of Infiltration and Inflow into Sewer Systems*. Washington: Government Printing Office, 1970.

———. *Corrosion Potential of NTA in Detergent Formulations*. Washington: Government Printing Office, 1971.

———. *Cost of Clean Water*. 2 vols. Washington: Government Printing Office, 1971. (Volume 1 covers municipal investment needs; volume 2, cost effectiveness and clean water.)

———. *Development of Phosphate-Free Home Laundry Detergents*. Washington: Government Printing Office, 1970.

———. *Disposal of Brine Produced in Renovation of Municipal Wastewater*. Washington: Government Printing Office, 1970.

———. *Development of Phosphate Removal Processes*. Washington: Government Printing Office, 1970.

———. *Economic and Social Importance of Estuaries*. Washington: Government Printing Office, 1971.

———. *Economics of Water Supply and Quality*. Washington: Government Printing Office, 1971.

———. *Electrochemical Method for Removal of Phosphates from Waste Waters*. Washington: Government Printing Office, 1970.

———. *Environmental Impact of Highway De-Icing*. Washington: Government Printing Office, 1971.

———. *Evaluation of New Acid Mine Drainage Treatment Process*. Washington: Government Printing Office, 1971.

———. *Feasibility of Computer Control of Wastewater Treatment*. Washington: Government Printing Office, 1970.

———. *Highlights: The Federal Water Pollution Control Act of 1972*. Washington: Government Printing Office, 1972.

———. *Highlights: The Marine Protection, Research, and Sanctuaries Act of 1972*. Washington: Government Printing Office, 1972. (Discusses ocean dumping.)

———. *Induced Air Mixing of Large Bodies of Polluted Water*. Washington: Government Printing Office, 1970.

———. *Investigation of a New Phosphate Removal Process*. Washington: Government Printing Office, 1970.

———. *Methods for Chemical Analysis of Water and Wastes, 1971*. Washington: Government Printing Office, 1971.

———. *New Technology for Treatment of Wastewater by Reverse Osmosis*. Washington: Government Printing Office, 1970.

———. *Nitrate Removal from Wastewaters by Ion Exchange*. Washington: Government Printing Office, 1971.

———. *Optimum Mechanical Aeration Systems for Rivers and Ponds*. Washington: Government Printing Office, 1970.

———. *Pilot Scale Study of Acid Mine Drainage*. Washington: Government Printing Office, 1971.

———. *Preliminary Investigational Requirement, Petrochemical and Refinery Waste Treatment Facilities*. Washington: Government Printing Office, 1971.

———. *Prevention and Correction of Excessive Infiltration and Inflow into Sewer Systems. Manual of Practice*. Washington: Government Printing Office, 1971.

———. *Primer on Waste Water Treatment.* Rev. ed. Washington: Government Printing Office, 1971.

———. *Purification of Mine Water by Freezing.* Washington: Government Printing Office, 1971.

———. *Reduction of Salt Content of Food Processing Liquid Waste Effluent.* Washington: Government Printing Office, 1971.

———. *Renovation of Municipal Wastewater by Reverse Osmosis.* Washington: Government Printing Office, 1970.

———. *Treatment Techniques for Removing Phosphorus from Municipal Wastewaters.* Washington: Government Printing Office, 1970.

———. *Underground Coal Mining Methods to Abate Water Pollution, A State-of-the-Art Literature Review.* Washington: Government Printing Office, 1970.

———. *Utilization of Phosphate Slimes.* Washington: Government Printing Office, 1971.

———. *Water Quality Control through Flow Augmentation.* Washington: Government Printing Office, 1971.

Evans, Robert H. "Operation of Sea Water Distillation Plants." *American Water Works Association Journal*, October 1969, pp. 663–666.

Executive Office of the President. Office of Science and Technology. *Assessment of Large Nuclear Powered Sea Water Distillation Plants.* Washington: Government Printing Office, 1964. (Report of interagency task group.)

Fair, Gordon Maskew, Geyer, John Charles, and Okum, Daniel Alexander. *Elements of Water Supply and Wastewater Disposal.* 2nd ed. New York: Wiley, 1971. (Basic text for college students.)

Federal Water Pollution Control Administration. *Federal Water Pollution Control Act, as Amended: Approved Nov. 3, 1966.* Washington: Government Printing Office, 1967.

———. *Problems of Combined Sewer Facilities and Overflows, 1967.* Washington: Government Printing Office, 1967. (Prepared by the American Public Works Administration.)

———. *Showdown for Water.* Washington: Government Printing Office, 1968. (Discusses ways in which citizens can help prevent or control water pollution.)

Federal Water Quality Administration. *Clean Water for the 1970's, A Status Report.* Washington: Government Printing Office, 1970.

———. *Collected Papers Regarding Nitrates in Agricultural Waste Water, 1969.* Washington: Government Printing Office, 1970.

———. *Combined Sewer Regulator Overflow Facilities.* Washington: Government Printing Office, 1970.

———. *Combined Sewer Regulation and Management, A Manual of Practice.* Washington: Government Printing Office, 1970. (Prepared by the American Public Works Administration.)

———. *Investigation of a High-Pressure Foam Wastewater Treatment Process.* Washington: Government Printing Office, 1970.

———. *New Mine Sealing Techniques for Water Pollution Abatement.* Washington: Government Printing Office, 1970.

———. *Practical Guide to Water Quality Studies of Streams, 1969.* Washington: Government Printing Office, 1970.

———. *Storm Water Pollution from Urban Land Activity.* Washington: Government Printing Office, 1970. (Procedures for predicting pollution by use of selected urban characteristics.)

———. *Study of Flow Reduction and Treatment of Waste Water from Households, 1969.* Washington: Government Printing Office, 1970.

———. *Treatment of Acid Mine Drainage by Reverse Osmosis.* Washington: Government Printing Office, 1970.

———. *Treatment of Waste Water–Waste Oil Mixtures.* Washington: Government Printing Office, 1970.

Fox, Irving K. "The Nation's Water Resources." *Land Economics*, November 1969, pp. 474–476.

Fox, Irving K., ed. *Water Resource Law and Policy in the Soviet Union*. Madison, Wisc.: University of Wisconsin, 1971.

Franks, Felix, ed. *Water: A Comprehensive Treatise. Vol. 1: The Physics and Physical Chemistry of Water*. New York: Plenum, 1972. (Four-volume set.)

Friedman, Wolfgang. *The Future of the Oceans*. New York: George Braziller, 1971. (Stresses need for international controls.)

Gavis, Jerome. *Wastewater Reuse*. Washington: Government Printing Office, 1971. (Distributed by the National Technical Information Service. Predicts increasing reuse of water, both direct and indirect.)

Graham, Frank, Jr. *Disaster by Default: Politics and Water Pollution*. Philadelphia: Lippincott, 1966.

Grava, Sigurd. *Urban Planning Aspects of Water Pollution Control*. New York: Columbia University Press, 1969. (Guide for urban planners and community decision makers.)

"Groundwater Pollution and Conservation." *Environmental Science and Technology*, March 1972, pp. 213–215.

Gruchow, Nancy. "Detergents: Side Effects of the Washday Miracles." *Science*, January 9, 1970, pp. 151–152.

Hall, Warren A., and Dracup, John A. *Water Resources Systems Engineering*. New York: McGraw-Hill, 1970.

Hamilton, H. R., et al. *Systems Simulation for Regional Analysis: An Application to River-Basin Planning*. Cambridge, Mass.: MIT Press, 1968.

Hartman, L. M., and Seastone, Don. *Water Transfers: Economic Efficiency and Alternative Institutions*. Baltimore: Johns Hopkins, 1970.

Health, Education, and Welfare Department. *Manual of Septic-Tank Practice*. Washington: Government Printing Office, 1969.

Hedgpeth, Joel. "The Oceans: World Sump." *Environment*, April 1970, pp. 40–47.

Helfman, Elizabeth S. *Rivers and Watersheds in America's Future*. New York: McKay, 1965.

Hewings, John M. *Water Quality and the Hazard to Health: Placarding Public Beaches*. Natural Hazard Research, Working Paper 8, Department of Geography. Toronto: University of Toronto Press, 1969.

Hoch, Irving, and Zusman, Pinhas. "Efficient Program of Water Resource Development in a Framework of Growth and Trade." *American Journal of Agriculture Economics*, December 1968, pp. 1635–1640.

Hood, Donald W., ed. *Impingement of Man on the Oceans*. New York: Wiley, 1971.

Hopkins, C. B., Weber, W. J., Jr., and Bloom, R., Jr. *Granular Carbon Treatment of Raw Sewage*. Washington: Government Printing Office, 1970. (Prepared for the Environmental Protection Agency.)

Howe, Charles W., and Easter, K. William. *Interbasin Transfers of Water: Economic Issues and Impacts*. Baltimore: Johns Hopkins, 1971. (Emphasizes western portion of the United States.)

Howe, Charles W., Russell, Clifford S., Young, Robert A., and Vaughan, William J. *Future Water Demands*. Washington: Government Printing Office, 1971. (Distributed by the National Technical Information Service. Summarizes urban, industrial, and agricultural water demands, including effects on water pollution.)

Hynes, H. B. N. *The Ecology of Running Waters*. Buffalo, N.Y.: University of Toronto Press, 1970. (Survey containing bibliography.)

Imhoff, Karl, Muller, W. J., and Thistlethwayte, D. K. E. *Disposal of Sewage and Other Waterborne Wastes*. Ann Arbor, Mich.: Ann Arbor Science, 1971. (Detailed reference source.)

"Injection Wells Pose a Potential Threat." *Environmental Science and Technology*, February 1972, pp. 120–122. (Explains how storage of wastes underground may trigger its own form of pollution.)

"Instruments for Water Quality Monitoring." *Environmental Science and Technology*, February 1972, pp. 130–133.

Interior Department. *Economics of Clean Water.* 4 vols. Washington: Government Printing Office, 1970. (Includes animal wastes and inorganic chemicals industry profiles; fourth volume is a summary report.)

———. *National Conference on Urban Water Research Sponsored by Office of Water Resources Research.* Washington: Government Printing Office, 1971.

———. *River of Life: Water, the Environmental Challenge.* Washington: Government Printing Office, 1970. (Report on progress of the Department in the cleansing of water.)

International Joint Commission, Canada and the United States. *Pollution of Lake Erie, Lake Ontario and the International Section of the St. Lawrence River, 1970.* Washington: Government Printing Office, 1971.

Ives, Joseph S., Jr., ed. *Pollution Control and the Marine Industry.* Washington: International Association for Pollution Control, 1971.

Johnson, James F. *Renovated Waste Water.* Chicago: University of Chicago, 1971.

Kardos, Louis T. "A New Prospect." *Environment*, March 1970, pp. 10–21, 27. (Discusses utilization of sewage as fertilizer.)

Kazmann, Raphael G. *Modern Hydrology.* New York: Harper, 1972. (Reference text for nonprofessionals as well as professionals.)

Kneese, Allen V., and Bower, Blair T. *Managing Water Quality: Economics, Technology, Institutions.* Baltimore: Johns Hopkins, 1968.

Lager, Karl F. *Man-Made Lakes—Planning and Development.* Rome: FAO, 1969.

Landis, Robert C. *A Technology Assessment Methodology. Vol. 5: Sea Farming (Mariculture).* Washington: Government Printing Office, 1971. (Distributed by the National Technical Information Service. Discusses mariculture in coastal and brackish waters, including water pollution problems.)

Legal Aspects of Water Storage for Flow Augmentation. Blackburg, Va.: Virginia Polytechnic Institute, 1970.

Lewicke, Carol K. "Groundwater, Pollution, and Conservation." *Environmental Science and Technology*, March 1972, pp. 213–215. (Argues that a nationwide groundwater policy is needed.)

Loftas, Tony. *The Last Resource: Man's Exploitation of the Ocean.* Chicago: Regnery, 1970. (Discusses using the sea to provide food, minerals, fresh water, and energy.)

McCaull, Julian. "The Tide of Industrial Waste." *Environment*, December 1972, pp. 30–39. (Discusses relationship between type of technology and quantity of wastes.)

———. "Who Owns the Water?" *Environment*, October 1970, pp. 30–39. (Points out that water cannot be considered in limited terms of state or local boundaries.)

McConnell, H. Hugh, and Lewis, Jennifer. ". . . Add Salt to Taste." *Environment*, November 1972, pp. 38–45. (Shows that the salt spread to clear highways in winter is polluting our environment.)

Mancy, Khalil H. *Instrumental Analysis for Water Pollution Control.* Ann Arbor, Mich.: Ann Arbor Science, 1973. (For professionals and students concerned with water pollution.)

Mancy, Khalil H., and Weber, W. J., Jr. *Analysis of Industrial Wastewaters.* New York: Wiley, 1972.

Marx, Wesley. *The Frail Ocean.* New York: Ballantine Books, 1969.

Metcalf & Eddy, Inc. *Wastewater Engineering: Collection, Treatment, Disposal.* New York: McGraw-Hill, 1972. (Appropriate as text.)

Miller, Stanton. "Water Pollution in the States." *Environmental Science and Technology*, February 1971, pp. 120–125.

Moorcraft, Colin. *Must the Seas Die?* Boston: Gambit, 1973.

Morris, Henry M., and Wiggert, James M. *Applied Hydraulics in Engineering.* New York: Ronald, 1972.

National Industrial Pollution Control Council. *Acid Mine Drainage: Subcouncil Report.* Washington: Government Printing Office, 1971.

———. *Detergents: Subcouncil Report.* Washington: Government Printing Office, 1970.

———. *Regionally Consolidated Industrial Wastewater Treatment: Subcouncil Report.* Washington: Government Printing Office, 1971.

———. *Wastewater Reclamation.* Washington: Government Printing Office, 1971.

Nikitopoulos, V. "Influence of Water on Population Distribution." *Ekistics,* July 1968, pp. 14-20.

Oglesby, Ray T., Carlson, Clarence A., and McCann, James A., eds. *River Ecology and Man.* New York: Academic Press, 1972.

Overman, Michael. *Water: Solutions to a Problem of Supply and Demand.* Garden City, N.Y.: Doubleday, 1969.

Patterson, J. W., and Mineam, R. A. *Wastewater Treatment Technology.* Washington: Government Printing Office, 1971. (Distributed by the National Technical Information Service. Surveys industrial waste treatment literature, covering 22 materials found in such wastes.)

President's Council on Recreation and Natural Beauty. *From Sea to Shining Sea: A Report on the American Environment—Our National Heritage.* Washington: Government Printing Office, 1968.

Rathlesberger, James. "Detergents and the Nation's Water." *National Parks,* February 1972, pp. 24-28. (Discusses possible corrective methods.)

Raven-Hansen, Peter. *Water and the Cities: Contemporary Water Resource and Related Land Planning.* Cambridge, Mass.: Abt Associates, 1969. (Prepared for the Office of Water Resources Research, Department of the Interior.)

"Recycling Sludge and Sewage Effluent by Land Disposal." *Environmental Science and Technology,* October 1972, pp. 871-873.

Rey, George, Lacy, William J., and Cywin, Allen. "Industrial Water Reuse: Future Pollution Solution." *Environmental Science and Technology,* September 1971, pp. 760-765.

Shuval, Hillel I. *Developments in Water Quality Research.* Ann Arbor, Mich.: Ann Arbor Science, 1973. (Discusses treatment and management of wastewater.)

———. "Water Pollution Control in Semi-Arid Zones." *Water Research,* April 1967, pp. 297-308.

Smith, F. G. Walton. "What the Ocean Means to Man." *American Scientist,* January-February 1972, pp. 16-19.

Soil Conservation Service. *Soil and Water Conservation around the World.* Washington: Government Printing Office, 1969. (Also available in French and Spanish.)

Sport Fisheries and Wildlife Bureau. *National Estuary Study.* 7 vols. Washington: Government Printing Office, 1970. (Study of the nation's estuaries as well as similar areas of the Great Lakes. Volume 1 is the main report.)

Sullivan, Thomas F. P., ed. *Pollution Control in the Marine Industries.* Washington: International Association for Pollution Control, 1972.

Texas Water Development Board. *DOSAG-1 Simulation of Water Quality in Streams and Canals: Program Documentation and Users' Manual.* Washington: Government Printing Office, 1970. (Distributed by the National Technical Information Service. Describes mathematical model to predict the steady-state dissolved oxygen concentrations in streams and canals.)

———. *Simulation of Water Quality in Streams and Canals: Theory and Description of the QUAL-1 Mathematical Modeling System.* Washington: Government Printing Office, 1971. (Distributed by the National Technical Information Service.)

Thomann, Robert V. *Systems Analysis and Water Quality Management.* New York: Environmental Research and Applications, 1972.

Velz, Clarence J. *Applied Stream Sanitation.* New York: Wiley, 1970. (Examines use of streams for waste disposal, through a discussion of stream self-purification.)

Viets, Frank G. "Water Quality in Relation to Farm Use of Fertilizers." *BioScience*, May 15, 1971, pp. 460–467.

Warren, Charles E. *Biology and Water Pollution Control*. Philadelphia: Saunders, 1971. (Provides biological information needed to control water pollution.)

Water Pollution Control Engineering. New York: British Information Services, 1970. (Covers effluent disposal.)

Water Quality Office. *Cannery Waste Treatment, Kehr Activated Sludge, 1970*. Washington: Government Printing Office, 1971.

Weber, Walter J., Jr. *Physiochemical Processes for Water Quality Control*. New York: Wiley, 1972. (Text and reference book.)

Wenk, Victor D. *A Technology Assessment Methodology. Vol. 6: Water Pollution: Domestic Wastes*. Washington: Government Printing Office, 1971. (Distributed by the National Technical Information Service. Studies U.S. domestic waste disposal for populations not served by a centralized sewer system.)

White, George Clifford. *Handbook of Chlorination*. New York: Van Nostrand Reinhold, 1972.

White, Gilbert F. *Strategies of American Water Management*. Ann Arbor, Mich.: University of Michigan Press, 1969.

———. *Water, Health and Society*. Bloomington, Ind.: Indiana University Press, 1969.

Willrich, Ted L., and Hines, William N., eds. *Water Pollution Control and Abatement*. Ames, Iowa: Iowa State University Press, 1967.

Willrich, Ted L., and Smith, George E., eds. *Agricultural Practices and Water Quality*. Ames, Iowa: Iowa State University Press, 1970. (Examines water pollutants such as pesticides and fertilizers.)

Wollman, Nathaniel, and Bonem, Gilbert W. *The Outlook for Water: Quality, Quantity, and National Growth*. Baltimore; Johns Hopkins, 1971. (Presents economic model for studying national policies for water resources.)

Zajic, J. E. *Water Pollution, Disposal, and Reuse*. Vols. 1 and 2. New York: Marcel Dekker, 1971. (Nontechnical text.)

Zwick, David, and Benstock, Marcy. *Water Wasteland*. New York: Grossman, 1971. (Indictment of federal and state agencies. A Nader Task Force Report on Water Pollution.)

WEATHER MODIFICATION

American Meteorological Society. *First National Conference on Weather Modification*. Boston: American Meteorological Society, 1968.

———. *Second National Conference on Weather Modification*. Boston: American Meteorological Society, 1970.

Atkinson, Bruce W. *Weather Business*. New York: Doubleday, 1969.

Aynsley, Eric. "How Air Pollution Alters Weather." *New Scientist*, October 9, 1969, pp. 66–67.

Battan, Louis J. *Harvesting the Clouds: Advances in Weather Modification*. Garden City, N.Y.: Doubleday, 1969.

Braham, Roscoe R. "One Finger on the Throttle of Nature's Weather Machine." *Weatherwise*, June 1968, pp. 106–109.

Cooper, Charles F., and Jolly, William C. *Ecological Effects of Weather Modification: A Problem Analysis*. Ann Arbor, Mich.: University of Michigan, 1969. (Report of the University's Department of Resource Planning and Conservation.)

Decker, Fred W. "Cloud Seeding Comes of Age." *Weatherwise*, April 1968, pp. 76–77.

Fleagle, Robert G., ed. *Weather Modification: Science and Public Policy*. Seattle: University of Washington Press, 1969.

Fletcher, J. O. "Controlling the Planet's Climate." *Impact of Science on Society*, vol. 19, no. 2, 1969, pp. 151–168.

Halacy, Dan S. *Weather Changers.* New York: Harper, 1968.

Hosler, C. L. "Of Wizardry, Witches and Weather Modification." *Weatherwise*, June 1968, pp. 110–113.

Kahan, Archie M., Stinson, J. Robert, and Eddy, Richard L. "Progress in Precipitation Modification." *American Meteorological Society Bulletin*, April 1969, pp. 208–215.

Landsberg, Helmut E. *Weather and Health: An Introduction to Biometeorology.* Garden City, N.Y.: Doubleday, 1969.

Lowry, William P. *Weather and Life: An Introduction to Biometeorology.* New York: Academic Press, 1969.

Matthews, William H., Kellogg, William W., and Robinson, G. D., eds. *Man's Impact on Climate.* Cambridge, Mass.: MIT Press, 1971.

Peterson, James T. *Climate of Cities, A Survey of Recent Literature.* Washington: Government Printing Office, 1969. (Publication of the National Air Pollution Control Administration.)

Reiter, E. R. *Jet Streams: How Do They Affect Our Weather?* Garden City, N.Y.: Doubleday, 1967.

Schaefer, Vincent J. "Inadvertent Modification of the Atmosphere by Air Pollution." *American Meteorological Society Bulletin*, April 1969, pp. 199–206.

Taubenfeld, Howard J. *Controlling the Weather: A Study of Law and Regulatory Procedures.* New York: Dunellen, 1970.

Taubenfeld, Rita F., and Taubenfeld, Howard J. "Some International Implications of Weather Modification Activities." *International Organization,* August 1969, pp. 808–833.

Tribus, Myron. "Physical View of Cloud Seeding." *Science*, April 10, 1970, pp. 201–211.

Woodley, William L. "Rainfall Enhancement by Dynamic Cloud Modification." *Science*, October 9, 1970, pp. 127–132.

PERIODICALS

AAAS Bulletin. Quarterly. American Association for the Advancement of Science, 1515 Massachusetts Ave. N.W., Washington, D.C. 20005.

AIA Journal. Monthly. American Institute of Architects, The Octagon, 1735 New York Ave. N.W., Washington, D.C. 20006.

Air and Water Pollution Report. Weekly. Business Publishers, Inc., Box 1067, Blair Sta., Silver Spring, Md. 20910.

Air Currents. Quarterly. Citizens for Clean Air, Inc., 502 Park Ave., New York, N.Y. 10022.

Air Pollution Abstracts. Monthly. Air Pollution Control Office, Box 12055, Research Triangle Park, N.C. 27709. (Obtain from the Superintendent of Documents, Government Printing Office, Washington, D.C. 20402.)

Air Pollution Control Association Journal. Monthly. Air Pollution Control Association, 4400 Fifth Ave., Pittsburgh, Pa. 15213.

Air Pollution Notes. Bimonthly. College of Agriculture and Environmental Science, Rutgers University, New Brunswick, N.J. 08903.

Air Quality Control Digest. Monthly. Wayne State University, Scientific and Technical Information Center, Detroit, Mich. 48202.

Air/Water Pollution Report. Weekly. Business Publishers, Inc., Box 1067, Blair Sta., Silver Spring, Md. 20910.

Alternatives: Perspectives on Society and Environment. Quarterly. Trent University, Peterborough, Ontario, Canada.

Ambio. Bimonthly. Royal Swedish Academy of Science, Universitetsforlaget, Box 307, Blindern, Oslo 3, Norway.

American Forests. Monthly. American Forestry Association, 919 Seventeenth St. N.W., Washington, D.C. 20006.

American Gas Association Monthly. American Gas Association, 605 Third Ave., New York, N.Y. 10016.

American Journal of Public Health and the Nation's Health. Monthly. American Public Health Association, 1749 Broadway, New York, N.Y. 10019.

American Naturalist. Bimonthly. Published for the American Society of Naturalists by the University of Chicago Press, 5801 Ellis Ave., Chicago, Ill. 60637.

American Water Resources Association Bulletin. Monthly. American Water Resources Association, 905 West Fairview Ave., Urbana, Ill. 61801.

Archives of Environmental Health. Monthly. American Medical Association, 535 Dearborn St., Chicago, Ill. 60610.

Atmospheric Environment: An International Journal. Bimonthly. Pergamon Press, Ltd., 44-01 21 St., Long Island City, N.Y. 11101.

Audubon. Six per year. National Audubon Society, 1130 Fifth Ave., New York, N.Y. 10028.

Audubon Leader. Monthly National Audubon Society, 1130 Fifth Ave., New York, N.Y. 10028.

Aware. Monthly. Community Performance Publications, Inc., 615 North Sherman Ave., Madison, Wisc. 53704.

BEE/Bulletin of Environmental Education. Monthly. Town and Country Planning Association, 17 Carlton House Terrace, London SW1, England.

The Balance Wheel. Bimonthly. American Association for Conservation Information, Dept. of Natural Resources, Lansing, Mich. 48926.

Biological Conservation. Quarterly. Elsevier Publishing Co., Ltd., Ripple Rd., Barking Essex, England.

BioScience. Bimonthly. American Institute of Biological Science, 3900 Wisconsin Ave. N.W., Washington, D.C. 20016.

Bulletin of Environmental Contamination and Toxicology. Bimonthly. 175 Fifth Ave., New York, N.Y. 10010. Or, Springer-Verlag, Heidelberger Platz 3, 1000 Berlin 3, West Germany.

Bulletin of the Atomic Scientists. Monthly (except July and August). Published by Educational Foundation for Nuclear Science. Inquiries to Bulletin of the Atomic Scientists, 935 E. 60 St., Chicago, Ill. 60637.

Bulletin of the Ecological Society of America. Quarterly. Ecological Society of America, 24 Wildwood Dr., Oak Ridge, Tenn. 37830.

Bulletin of Human Ecology. Quarterly. Human Ecological Society, Box 146, Elsah, Ill. 62028.

Business & Society. Biweekly. Box 132, Lenox Hill Station, New York, N.Y. 10021.

CF Letter. Monthly. Conservation Foundation, 1717 Massachusetts Ave. N.W., Washington, D.C. 20036.

California University, Davis, Institute of Governmental Affairs. Environmental Quality Series. Irregular. Institute of Governmental Affairs, University of California, Davis, Calif. 95616.

Canadian Audubon. Bimonthly (except July and August). Canadian Audubon Society, 46 St. Clair Ave., East Toronto 7, Canada.

Catalyst for Environmental Quality. Quarterly. 274 Madison Ave., New York, N.Y. 10016.

City, The Magazine of Urban Life and Environment. Bimonthly. National Urban Coalition, 2100 M St. N.W., Washington, D.C. 20037.

Clean Air and Water News. Weekly. Commerce Clearing House Inc., 4025 West Peterson Ave., Chicago, Ill. 60646.

Clean Water Report. Monthly. Business Publishers, Inc., Box 1067, Silver Spring, Md. 20910.

Coal Research. Quarterly. Bituminous Coal Research, Inc., 350 Hochberge Rd., Monroeville, Pa. 15146.

Coastal Zone Management. Monthly. Nautilus Press, 1056 National Press Bg., Washington, D.C. 20004.

Conservation Directory. Annually. National Wildlife Federation, 1412 Sixteenth St. N.W., Washington, D.C. 20036.

Conservation Education Association Newsletter. Quarterly. Conservation Education Association, 1144 E. Third South St., Salt Lake City, Utah 84102.

Conservation News. Semimonthly. National Wildlife Federation, 1412 Sixteenth St. N.W., Washington, D.C. 20036.

Conservation Notes. Irregularly. Bureau of Sport Fisheries and Wildlife, Department of the Interior, Washington, D.C. 20240.

Conservation Report. Weekly. National Wildlife Federation, 1412 Sixteenth St. N.W., Washington, D.C. 20036.

Conservation Vistas. Monthly. U.S. Department of Agriculture, Forest Service, Eastern Region 633, W. Wisconsin Ave., Milwaukee, Wis. 53203.

Conservationist. Bimonthly. New York State Environmental Conservation Department, Wolf Road, Albany, N.Y. 12201.

Contamination Control. Bimonthly. Blackwent Publishing Co., Inc., 1605 Cahuenga Blvd., Los Angeles, Calif. 90028.

Contamination Newsletter. Monthly. Contamination Control Laboratories, Inc., 13324 Farmington Rd., Livonia, Mich. 48150.

Council for Planning & Conservation Newsletter. Quarterly. Council for Planning & Conservation, Box 228, Beverly Hills, Calif. 90213.

Crops and Soils Magazine. Nine per year. Soil Science Society of America, 677 S. Segoe Rd., Madison, Wisc. 53711.

Current Publications in Population/Family Planning. Quarterly. Population Council, 245 Park Ave., New York, N.Y. 10017.

Currents. Bimonthly. Manufacturing Chemists Association, 1825 Connecticut Ave. N.W., Washington, D.C. 20009.

Defenders of Wildlife News. Quarterly. Defenders of Wildlife, 2000 North St. N.W., Washington, D.C. 20036.

Demography. Semiannually. Population Association of America, Box 14182, Benjamin Franklin Station, Washington, D.C. 20044.

Design and Environment. Quarterly. RD Publication, 6400 Goldsboro Rd. N.W., Washington, D.C. 20034.

EDF Newsletter. Six per year. Environmental Defense Fund, Drawer 740, Stonybrook, N.Y. 11790.

Ecologist. Monthly. Darby House, Bletchingley Road, Merstham, Redhill, Surrey, England.

Ecology. Bimonthly. Duke University Press, Box 6697, College Sta., Durham, N. Car. 27708.

Ecology (U.S.). Quarterly. Ecology Action Educational Institute, Box 3895, Modesto, Calif. 95352.

Ecology Law Quarterly. University of California, School of Law, Boalt Hall, Berkeley, Calif. 94720.

Ecology Today. Bimonthly. Ecological Dimensions, Inc., Box 180, West Mystic, Conn. 06388.

Ecosphere. Ten per year. International Ecology University, 300 Eshleman Hall, University of California, Berkeley, Calif. 94720.

Effluent and Water Treatment Journal. Monthly. Thunderbird Enterprises Ltd., 102 College Rd., Harrow, Middlesex, England.

Ekistics. Monthly. Athens Center of Ekistics, 24 Strat Syndesmou St., Athens 136, Greece.

Environment (U.S.). Ten per year. Committee for Environmental Information, 438 North Skinker Blvd., St. Louis, Missouri 63130. (Subscriptions to: Box 755, Bridgeton, Missouri 63044.)

Environment and Behavior. Three per year. Sage Publications, Inc., 275 South Beverly Dr., Beverly Hills, Calif. 90212.

Environment Information ACCESS. Biweekly. Ecology Forum, Inc., 200 Park Ave., Suite 303 East, New York, N.Y. 10017.

The Environment Monthly. The Environment Monthly, 420 Lexington Ave., New York, N.Y. 10017.

The Environment Report. Monthly. Capital Sources and Consulting Co., 1606 Union Street, Box 1312, Brunswick, Georgia 31520.

Environment Report. Semimonthly. Trends Publishing Inc., National Press Building, Washington, D.C. 20004.

Environment Reporter. Weekly. Bureau of National Affairs Inc., 1231 25 St. N.W., Washington, D.C. 20037.

Environmental Action. Semimonthly. Environmental Action Inc., Rm. 741, 1346 Connecticut Ave., Washington, D.C. 20036.

Environmental Affairs. Quarterly. Environmental Law Center, Boston College Law School, Brighton, Mass. 02135.

Environmental Control and Safety Management. Monthly. A. M. Best Co., Park Ave., Morristown, N.J. 07960.

Environmental Education. Quarterly. Dembar Educational Research Services, Inc., Box 1605, Madison, Wisc. 53701.

Environmental Health Letter. Semimonthly. Gershon W. Fishbein, publisher, 1097 National Press Building, Washington, D.C. 20004.

Environmental Law. Semiannually. Northwestern School of Law, Lewis and Clark College, Portland, Oreg. 97219.

Environmental Law Reporter. Monthly. Environmental Law Institute, 1346 Connecticut Ave. N.W., Washington, D.C. 20036.

Environmental Law Review. Annually. Sage Hill Publishers, Inc., 435 Hudson St., New York, N.Y. 10014.

Environmental Legislation. University of Pittsburgh, Graduate School of Public Health, 228 Parran Hall, Pittsburgh, Pa. 15213.

Environmental Letters. Eight per year. Marcell Dekker, Inc., 95 Madison Ave., New York, N.Y. 10016.

Environmental Pollution. Quarterly. Elsevier Publishing Co., Ltd., Ripple Road, Barking, Essex, England.

Environmental Quality. Quarterly. Environmental Awareness Associates, 6355 Topanga Canyon Blvd., Suites 327 and 524, Woodland Hills, Calif. 91364.

Environmental Research. Six per year. Environmental Sciences Laboratory, Mount Sinai School of Medicine, New York, N.Y. 10029.

Environmental Science and Technology. Monthly. ACS Publications, 1155 Sixteenth St. N.W., Washington, D.C. 20036.

Environmental Technology and Economics. Biweekly. Technomic Publishing Co., Inc., 750 Summer St., Stamford, Conn. 06902.

Family Planning Perspectives. Bimonthly. Planned Parenthood-World Population, Editorial Offices, 666 Fifth Ave., New York, N.Y. 10019.

From the State Capitals. Sewage and Waste Disposal. Approximately 14 per year. Bethune Johnes, 321 Sunset Ave., Asbury Park, N.J. 07712.

The Futurist. Bimonthly. World Future Society, Box 19285, Twentieth St. Sta., Washington, D.C. 20036.

Ground Water. Bimonthly. Technical Division, National Water Well Association, Water Well Journal Publishing Co., 811 N. Lincoln Ave., Box 222, Urbana, Ill. 61801.

Human Ecology Forum. Quarterly. New York State College of Human Ecology, Cornell University, Ithaca, N.Y. 14850.

Impact of Science on Society. Quarterly. UNESCO, 317 E. 34 St., New York, N.Y. 10016.

Industrial Ecology. Quarterly. Magazines for Industry, Inc., 777 Third Ave., New York, N.Y. 10017.

Industrial Recovery. Monthly. National Industrial Materials Recovery Association, Carolyn House, Dingwall Road, Croydon CR9WYU, Surrey, England.

Industrial Wastes. Bimonthly. Box 21013, El Paso, Tex. 79990.

Institute for Research on Land and Water Resources. Newsletter. Bimonthly. Institute for Research on Land and Water Resources, Pennsylvania State University, University Park, Pa. 16802.

International Journal of Environmental Studies. Quarterly. Gordon and Breach Science

Publishers, 12 Bloomsbury Way, London WC1, England.

International Union for Conservation of Nature and Natural Resources. Bulletin. Quarterly. IUCN, 1110 Morges, Switzerland.

International Wildlife. Bimonthly. National Wildlife Federation, Inc., 1412 Sixteenth St. N.W., Washington, D.C. 20036.

Journal of Environmental Health. National Association of Sanitarians, 1550 Lincoln St., Denver, Colo. 80203.

Journal of Environmental Quality. Quarterly. American Society of Agronomy, Crop Science Society of America, and Soil Science Society of America, 677 S. Sego Rd., Madison, Wisc. 53711.

Journal of Environmental Sciences. Bimonthly. Institute of Environmental Sciences, 940 E. Northwest Highway, Mt. Prospect, Ill. 60056.

Journal of Environmental Systems. Quarterly. Baywood Publishing Co., Inc., 1 Northwest Drive, Farmingdale, N.Y. 11735.

Journal of Human Ecology. Quarterly. Human Ecological Society, Box 146, Elsah, Ill. 62028.

Journal of Soil and Water Conservation. Bimonthly. Soil Conservation Soceity of America, 7515 N.E. Ankeny Rd., Ankeny, Iowa 50021.

Journal of the Air Pollution Control Association. Monthly. Air Pollution Control Association, 4450 Fifth Ave., Pittsburgh, Pa. 15213.

Journal of the Water Pollution Control Federation. Monthly. Water Pollution Control Federation, 3900 Wisconsin Ave. N.W., Washington, D.C. 20016.

Journal of Water Resources. American Water Resources Association, Box 434, Urbana, Ill. 61801.

Journal of Wildlife Management. Quarterly. Wildlife Society, 3900 Wisconsin Ave. N.W., Suite S-176, Washington, D.C. 20016.

Land and Water Development. Monthly. A. B. Morse Co., Box 481, Barrington, Ill. 60010.

Land Economics. Quarterly. University of Wisconsin Press, Box 1379, Madison, Wisc. 53701.

Land, Forest, Wildlife. Three per year. Alberta Department of Lands and Forests, Natural Resources Bldg., Edmonton, Alberta, Canada.

Land Pollution Reporter. Bimonthly. Freed Publishing Co., Box 1144, FDR Sta., New York, N.Y. 10022.

Living Wilderness. Quarterly. Wilderness Society, 729 Fifteenth St. N.W., Washington, D.C. 20005.

Man-Environment Systems. Bimonthly. S-126 Human Development, University Park, Pa. 16802.

Man on Earth. SPR Charter, Olema, Calif. 94950.

Marine Pollution Bulletin. Monthly. Macmillan Journals Ltd., 4 Little Essex St., London WC2R 3LF, England.

The Mother Earth News. Six per year. Underground Press Syndicate, Box 26, Village P.O., New York, N.Y. 10014.

NOAA Week. U.S. Department of Commerce, National Oceanic and Atmospheric Administration, Office of Public Information, Building 5, Rm. 804, Rockville, Md. 20852.

National Association of Soil and Water Conservation Districts. Tuesday Letter. Weekly. National Association of Soil and Water Conservation Districts, Box 855, League City, Tex. 77573.

National Journal. Weekly. Center for Political Research, 1730 M St. N.W., Washington, D.C. 20036.

National Parks and Conservation Magazine. Monthly. National Park Association, 1701 Eighteenth St. N.W., Washington, D.C. 20009.

National Wildlife. Bimonthly. National Wildlife Federation, Inc., 1412 Sixteenth St. N.W., Washington, D.C. 20036.

Nation's Cities. Monthly. National League of Cities, 1612 K St. N.W., Washington, D.C. 20006.

Natural History. Ten per year. American Museum of Natural History, Central Park West at 79 St., New York, N.Y. 10024.

Natural Resources Journal. Quarterly. University of the New Mexico School of Law, 1915 Roma N.E., Albuquerque, N.M. 87106.

Natural Resources Law Newsletter. Irregular. Section of Natural Resources Law, American Bar Association, 1155 E. 60 St., Chicago, Ill. 60637.

Nature. Weekly. Macmillan Journals, Ltd., Brunel Road, Basingsloke, Hampshire, England.

Nature and Resources. Monthly. UNESCO Publications Center, Box 433, New York, N.Y. 10016.

Nature Conservancy News. Quarterly. Nature Conservancy, 1800 N. Kent St., Suite 800, Arlington, Va. 22209.

Nature Study. Quarterly. American Nature Study Society, 1144 E. Third St., Salt Lake City, Utah 84102.

New Pollution Technology. Semimonthly. O. Q. di Maria, Box 191, La Jolla, Calif. 92037.

New York State Action for Clean Air Committee. Newsletter. Bimonthly. N.Y. State Action for Clean Air Committee, 105 E. 22 St., New York, N.Y. 10010.

New York's Waters. Quarterly. New York State Department of Health, Albany, N.Y. 12208.

Not Man Apart. Monthly. Friends of the Earth, 8016G Zuni Rd. S.E., Albuquerque, N. Mex. 87108.

Notes on Water Pollution. Quarterly. Water Polution Research Laboratory, Elder Way, Stevenage, Herts, England.

Our Daily Planet. Monthly. Mayor's Council on the Environment, 51 Chambers St., Rm. 228, New York, N.Y. 10007.

Outdoor America. Monthly. John Bunker, 719 Thirteenth St. N.W., Washington, D.C. 20005.

Outdoor New Bulletin. Semimonthly. Wildlife Conservation, 1801 N. Lincoln, Oklahoma City, Okla. 73105.

Outdoors Unlimited. Monthly. Outdoor Writers Association of America, Outdoors Bldg., Columbia, Mo. 65201.

Pesticides Monitoring Journal. Quarterly. Government Printing Office, Washington, D.C. 20402.

Pollution. Monthly. Microinfo Ltd., 4 High St., Alton, Hampshire, England.

Pollution Abstracts. Bimonthly. Oceanic Library and Information Center, Box 2369, La Jolla, Calif. 92037.

Pollution Engineering (U.S.). Bimonthly. Technical Publishing Co., Thompson Division, 35 Mason St., Greenwich, Conn. 06830.

Population and Vital Statistics Report. Quarterly. United Nations Publications Sales Section, New York, N.Y. 10017.

Population Bulletin. Six per year. Population Reference Bureau, 1755 Massachusetts Ave. N.W., Washington, D.C. 20036.

Population Crisis. Periodically. The Population Crisis Committee, 1730 K St. N.W., Washington, D.C. 20006.

Population Index. Quarterly. Princeton University Office of Population Research, 5 Ivy Lane, Princeton, N.J. 08540.

Population Trends and Environmental Policy: A Natural Resources Information Service. Monthly. Library, U.S. Department of the Interior. (Available from National Technical Information Service, Springfield, Va. 22151.)

Public Health Reports. Monthly. Public Health Service. (Available from Government Printing Office, Washington, D.C. 20402.)

Public Power. Monthly. American Public Power Association, 2600 Virginia Ave. N.W., Suite 212, Washington, D.C. 20037.

Quiet. A Newsletter. Citizens for a Quieter City, Inc., Box 777, FDR Sta., New York, N.Y. 10021.

Reclamation Era. Quarterly. Bureau of Reclamation, U.S. Department of the Interior. (Available from Government Printing Office, Washington, D.C. 20402.)

Reclamation News. Monthly. National Reclamation Association, 897 National Press Bldg., Washington, D.C. 20004.

Re:Search. Quarterly. New Jersey Agricultural Experiment Station, New Brunswick, N.J. 08903.

Response: A Report on Environmental Action. Irregular. U.S. Department of Agriculture, Office of Information, Washington, D.C. 20250.

Resources. Three per year. Resources for the Future, Inc., 1755 Massachusetts Ave. N.W., Washington, D.C. 20036.

Resources Review. Quarterly. Norfold Conservation District, 460 Main St., Walpole, Mass. 02081.

Reuse/Recycle. Monthly. Technomic Publishing Co., Inc., 750 Summer St., Stamford, Conn. 06901.

Rodale's Environment Action Bulletin. Weekly. Rodale Press, Inc., 33 E. Minor St., Emmaus, Pa. 18049.

Roots. Semiannually. Ecology Action East. (Write: Box 344, Cooper Sta., New York, N.Y. 10003.)

SFI Bulletin. Monthly. Sport Fishing Institute, 719 Thirteenth St. N.W., Washington, D.C. 20005.

SIPI Report. Quarterly. Scientists' Institute for Public Information, 30 E. 68 St., New York, N.Y. 10021.

Sanitary Engineering Research Laboratory News Quarterly. University of California, College of Engineering, Sanitary Engineering Research Laboratory, Richmond Field Station, 1301 S. 46 St., Richmond, Calif. 94804.

Science. Weekly. American Association for the Advancement of Science, 1515 Massachusetts Ave. N.W., Washington, D.C. 20036.

Science News. Weekly. Science Service, Inc., 1719 N St. N.W., Washington, D.C. 20036.

Science of the Total Environment. Quarterly. Elsevier Publishing Co., Box 211, Amsterdam, Netherlands.

Selected References on Environmental Quality as It Relates to Health. Monthly. Government Printing Office, Washington, D.C. 20402.

Sewage and Waste Disposal. Fourteen per year. Bethune Jones, 321 Sunset Ave., Asbury Park, N.J. 07712.

Sierra Club Bulletin. Monthly. Sierra Club, 1050 Mills Tower, San Francisco, Calif. 94104.

Sierra Club. National News Report. Weekly. Sierra Club, 1050 Mills Tower, San Francisco, Calif. 94104.

Smokeless Air. Quarterly. National Society for Clean Air, 134-137 North St., Brighton BN1 1RG, England.

Soil and Water Conservation Journal. Monthly. Soil Conservation Society of America, 7515 North East Ankeny Rd., Ankeny, Iowa 50021.

Soil Conservation. Monthly. Soil Conservation Service, Government Printing Office, Washington, D.C. 20402.

Solid Wastes Management/Refuse Removal Journal. Monthly. R.R.J. Publishing Co., 150 E. 52 St., New York, N.Y. 10022.

Special Report: Ecology. Weekly. 280 Madison Ave., New York, N.Y. 10016.

Survival Magazine. Quarterly. 2247 Prince St., Berkeley, Calif. 94705.

Taste and Odor Control Journal. Monthly. Westvaco, Chemical Division, 299 Park Ave., New York, N.Y. 10017.

Technology Review. Nine per year. Massachusetts Institute of Technology, Rm. E219-430, Cambridge, Mass. 02139.

Trail and Landscape. Five per year. Ottawa Field Naturalists' Club, Box 3264, Postal Sta., Ottawa 3, Ontario, Canada.

Underwater Naturalist. American Littoral Society, Sandy Hook, Highlands, N.J. 07732.

UNESCO Courier. Monthly. United Nations Educational, Scientific and Cultural Organization in Paris, France. (Available from UNESCO Publications Center, 317 E. 34 St., New York, N.Y. 10016.)

Washington Environmental Protection Report. Semimonthly. Callahan Publications, Box 3751, Washington, D.C. 20007.

Waste Age. Monthly. Three Sons Publishing Co., 6311 Gross Point Rd., Niles, Ill. 60648.

Water, Air, and Soil Pollution. Quarterly. D. Reidel Publishing Co., 419 Singel, Dordrecht, Netherlands.

Water and Air Pollution Newsletter. Monthly. International Executive Newsletters Co., 52 Rue du Progres, 1000 Brussels, Belgium. Also, 35 West Elm St., Littleton, N.H. 03561.

Water and Pollution Control. Monthly. Southam Business Publications, 1450 Don Mills Road, Don Mills, Ontario, Canada.

Water Control News. Weekly. Commerce Clearing House, Inc., 4025 W. Peterson Ave., Chicago, Ill. 60646.

Water, Land and Life. Quarterly. Western Pennsylvania Conservancy, 204 Fifth Ave., Pittsburgh, Pa. 15222.

Water Newsletter. Bimonthly. Water Information Center, Inc., 44 Sitsink Drive E., Port Washington, N.Y. 11050. (With subscription, 12 issues of *Research and Development.*)

Water Pollution Control. Bimonthly. Institute of Water Pollution Control, 49-55 Victoria St., London SW1, England.

Water Pollution Control Federation. Journal. Monthly. Water Pollution Control Federation, 3900 Wisconsin Ave. N.W., Washington, D.C., 20016. (In English, French, German, Portuguese, and Spanish.)

Water Research. Monthly. Pergamon Press Inc., Journals Dept., Maxwell House, Fairview Park, Elmsford, N.Y. 10523. Also, Headington Hill Hall, Oxford OX3 OBW, England.

Water Resources Bulletin. Bimonthly. American Water Resources Association, Box 434, Urbana, Ill. 61801.

Water Resources Research. Bimonthly. American Geophysical Union, 2100 Pennsylvania Ave. N.W., Washington, D.C. 20037.

Water Resources Review. Monthly. Inland Waters Branch, Canada, and U.S. Geological Survey. Geological Survey, Washington, D.C. 20242.

Weatherwise. Bimonthly. American Meteorological Society, 45 Beacon St., Boston, Mass. 02138.

Wildlife News/Nouvelles de la Faune. Quarterly. Canadian Wildlife Federation, 1419 Carling Ave., Ottawa 3, Canada.

The Wildlife Society News. Bimonthly. The Wildlife Society, 3900 Wisconsin Ave. N.W., Washington, D.C. 20016.

Wildlife Views. Bimonthly. Arizona Game and Fish Department, 1688 W. Adams, Phoenix, Ariz. 85007.

Your Environment. Quarterly. 10 Roderick Road, London NW3, England.

Zero Population Growth Newsletter. Monthly. ZPG, Inc., 367 State St., Los Altos, Calif. 94022.

Glossary

The terms included in this glossary are drawn from the areas presently of greatest environmental concern, most notably air quality, water quality and water supply, solid-waste disposal, and radiation hazards. In selecting terms for definition, the editors have concentrated on terms that are encountered at least occasionally in popular and semi-popular environmental literature. Highly technical terms found principally in specialized scientific and technological sources are largely excluded. For a term having more than one meaning, only the meaning or meanings most relevant to environmental matters are given.

absorbed dose. When ionizing radiation passes through matter, some of its energy is absorbed by the matter. The amount of radiation absorbed per unit mass of matter is called the "absorbed dose." It is measured in rems and rads.

accelerated depreciation. A pollution-abatement incentive allowing a company to deduct from its taxable income the cost of pollution abatement equipment over a shorter period of time than is allowed for other types of capital investment.

acre-foot. A quantity of water that would cover one acre to a depth of one foot. It equals 43,560 cubic feet, or 325,850 gallons.

actinomycetes. A large group of moldlike microorganisms that give off an odor characteristic of rich earth and are the chief organisms involved in the stabilization of solid wastes by composting.

activated-carbon filter. A filter used to remove dissolved organic matter from water.

activated sludge. In wastewater treatment, a sludge containing living organisms that multiply and, in doing so, reduce impurities in the wastewater. Oxygen is restored, and the odor and taste of destroyed bacteria in the wastewater are removed.

adsorption. A taking up of gases or liquids by the surfaces of solids or liquids with which they are in contact.

aeration. In waste treatment, a process in which liquid from the primary clarifier is mixed with compressed air and biologically active sludge.

aerobic. Able to live and grow only if free oxygen is present.

aerosol. Tiny liquid or solid particles suspended in a gas, such as air. Liquid-particle aerosols are "fogs," and solid-particle aerosols are "smokes" or "dusts."

air basin. See *airshed*.

air sampling. The collection and analysis of samples of air usually to measure its content of toxic gases or to measure its radioactivity or detect the presence of radioactive substances.

airshed, or **air basin.** An arbitrarily defined region whose parts often share a common air supply.

algae. Largely aquatic nonvascular plants that grow in either seawater or fresh water. Seaweeds and pond scum are algae.

algal bloom. A visible growth of algae on the surface of a body of water. It is often caused by the presence of excessive plant nutrients derived from sewage or from agricultural runoff enriched by chemical fertilizers and animal wastes.

algicide. A chemical such as copper sulfate used to kill or inhibit the growth of algae.

alkyl benzene sulfonate (ABS). A chemical surface-active agent used in synthetic detergents. It causes foaming, and its compounds do not readily decompose biologically through bacterial action.

alpha particle. A positively charged particle emitted by certain radioactive materials. It is made up of two neutrons and two protons bound together, and, therefore, is identical with the nucleus of a helium atom. It is the least penetrating of the three common types of radiation (alpha, beta, and gamma) emitted by radioactive material, and can be stopped by a sheet of paper. It is not dangerous to plants, animals, or humans unless the alpha-emitting substance has entered the body.

alum. A chemical substance (usually potassium aluminum sulfate) that is gelatinous when wet and is used in water-treatment plants for settling out small particles of foreign matter.

ambient. Surrounding or enclosing. The term "ambient air", for example, refers to the air in the vicinity of a particular place or installation.

anadromous fish. Fish that go up-river to spawn. Salmon and shad are anadromous.

anaerobic. Able to live and grow in the absence of free oxygen.

anaerobic contact process. A waste-treatment process similar to the activated sludge process. Anaerobic organisms digest the organic matter in the absence of free oxygen in sewage sludge.

aquifer. A porous layer of rock that carries a usable supply of water. Gravel, sand, sandstone, and limestone are the best aquifers.

asbestos. An air pollutant of possibly major importance. The most widespread source of the pollutant is the automotive brake lining, which releases asbestos dust into the atmosphere whenever a brake is applied.

asbestosis. Chronic inflammation of the lungs resulting from prolonged inhalation of particles of asbestos; a particularly serious hazard for asbestos miners and for construction workers exposed to loose asbestos insulation.

atomic bomb. A bomb whose energy comes from the fission of heavy elements, such as uranium or plutonium. Compare *hydrogen bomb*.

atomic cloud. The cloud of hot gases, smoke, dust, and other matter that is carried aloft after the explosion of a nuclear weapon in the air or near the surface. The cloud frequently has a mushroom shape.

atomic number. The number of protons in the nucleus of an atom. Each chemical element has its characteristic atomic number.

atomic reactor. A nuclear reactor.

atomic weapon. An explosive weapon in which the energy is produced by nuclear fission or fusion.

atomic weight. The average weight of the isotopes of an element as they occur in nature.

background radiation. The radiation in man's natural environment, including cosmic rays and radiation from naturally radioactive elements, both outside and inside the bodies of humans and animals. It is also called "natural radiation" or "natural radioactivity."

Beccari process. A composting process developed by Giovanni Beccari in 1922. Anaerobic fermentation is followed by a final stage in which decomposition proceeds under partially aerobic conditions. The process was later modified by Verdier and Bordas.

bedrock. The solid rock beneath the loose material, chiefly soil and subsoil, with which most of the land surface of the earth is covered. It is sometimes several hundred feet beneath the surface, but is usually found at a much shallower depth.

benthic. Relating to the bottom underlying a body of water. Mud-dwelling mollusks are examples of benthic organisms.

beta burn. A radiation burn of the skin caused by exposure to beta particles. Compare *flash burn*.

beta particle. An elementary particle emitted from a nucleus during radioactive decay, with a single electrical charge and a mass equal to 1/1837 that of a proton. A negatively charged beta particle is an electron, and a positively charged beta particle is a positron. Beta radiation may cause skin burns, and beta-emitters are harmful if they enter the body. Beta particles are easily stopped by a thin sheet of metal.

bgd. Billion gallons per day.

biochemical oxygen demand (BOD). The amount of oxygen required for aerobic bacteria to oxidize completely the decomposable organic matter in water within a specified time and at a given temperature. BOD is an index of the degree of organic pollution in water.

biodegradable. Capable of being broken down into simpler compounds or molecules by microorganisms.

biodegradable substance. An organic substance that can be broken down, usually quickly, by biological agents such as bacteria and fungi.

biological community. The total interacting animal and plant populations of a given area.

biological dose. The radiation dose absorbed in biological material. It is measured in rems. See *absorbed dose*.

biological half-life. The time required for a biological system, such as a man or an animal, to eliminate by natural processes half the amount of a substance (such as a radioactive material) that has entered it.

biological pest control. The use of predators and parasites to control animal pests, especially insects. The term is sometimes loosely applied to various other control methods that do not rely primarily on chemical poisons.

biological shield. Absorbing material placed around a reactor or radioactive source to reduce the radiation to a level which is safe for human beings.

biome. A complex of biological communities defined by a characteristic climate and habitat. Some examples are grassland biome, forest biome, and desert biome.

biosphere. The life-supporting part of the earth, including all bodies of water, the soil and surface rocks, and the lower atmosphere.

biota. The plant and animal life of a region.

blast wave. A pulse of air, propagated from an explosion, in which the pressure increases sharply at the front of a moving air mass. A blast wave is accompanied by strong, transient winds.

bloom. The excessive growth of algae in a body of water due to an oversupply of dissolved nutrients. It may impart a disagreeable odor to the water, cause fish to die, and impair the use of the water for drinking or recreation.

BOD. See *biochemical oxygen demand*.

body burden. The amount of radioactive material present in the body of a man or an animal.

bog. An area of soft, wet, spongy ground consisting chiefly of decayed or decaying moss and other vegetable matter. A bog oftens forms in shallow, stagnant lakes or ponds, and is largely produced by sphagnum moss, from which eventually peat is evolved. Bogs may also be formed on cold, damp mountain surfaces.

bone seeker. A radioisotope that tends to accumulate in the bones when it is introduced into the body. An example is strontium-90, which behaves chemically like calcium.

brackish water. Water containing more than 1,000 parts per million of dissolved solids.

breeder reactor. A reactor that produces fissile fuel during the course of its operation, especially one that produces more fuel than it consumes.

bremsstrahlung. Radiation emitted when a fast-moving charged particle loses energy upon being accelerated and deflected by the electric field surrounding a positively charged atomic nucleus. X-rays produced in ordinary X-ray machines are bremsstrahlung. In German, the term means "braking radiation."

cadmium. A heavy metal comparable to mercury in toxicity.

carbon dioxide (CO_2). A colorless, odorless, nonpoisonous gas that forms carbonic acid when dissolved in water. It is produced during the thermal degradation and microbial decomposition of solid wastes.

carbon monoxide (CO). A colorless, poisonous gas that has a faint metallic odor and taste. It is produced during the thermal degradation and microbial decomposition of solid wastes when the oxygen supply is limited.

carcinogen. A cancer-causing agent.

catalytic combustion system. A process in which a substance is introduced into an exhaust gas stream to burn or oxidize vaporized hydrocarbons or odorous contaminants. The substance itself remains intact.

catch basin, or **gravity separator.** A cistern, situated at a point where wastewater discharges into a sewer, to catch and retain matter that would not pass readily through the sewer. The term "catch basin" is also applied to a reservoir or well into which surface water may drain.

catchment basin. A watershed.

cesspool. An underground structure designed to hold sewage from a residence; the wastewater is permitted to percolate from the cesspool into the surrounding soil.

cfs. Cubic feet per second, a measure of the rate at which water passes a given point in a stream or pipe.

chain reaction. A reaction that stimulates its own repetition. In a fission chain reaction a fissionable nucleus absorbs a neutron and fissions, releasing additional neutrons. These in turn can be absorbed by other fissionable nuclei, releasing still more neutrons. A fission chain reaction is self-sustaining when the number of neutrons released in a given time equals or exceeds the number of neutrons lost by absorption in nonfissioning material or by escape from the system.

channelization. Straightening and deepening a meandering stream to increase the amount of water it can carry without flooding.

chemical dosimeter. An instrument that indirectly measures radiation by indicating the extent to which the radiation causes a definite chemical change to take place.

chemical oxygen demand (COD). The amount of oxygen needed to oxidize completely the oxidizable inorganic compounds present in a water sample.

chimney plume. See *plume.*

chlorinated hydrocarbons. A class of very long-lasting insecticides, including DDT, DDD, lindane (BHC), aldrin, dieldrin, endrin, heptachlor, and toxaphene. Because of their persistence in the environment they accumulate in the food chain and kill or injure fish, birds, and other nontarget organisms.

chlorination. The application of chlorine or a hypochlorite to water, usually to disinfect it.

clarifier. In a water-treatment plant, a basin or tank in which solids float to the surface or settle to the bottom by gravity.

clean bomb. A nuclear bomb that produces relatively little radioactive fallout; a fusion bomb. Compare *dirty bomb.*

climax community. The biological community that culminates ecological succession in a particular geographical region.

coagulation. In water treatment, the introduction of sulfate of alumina into polluted water, which causes organic matter to form a mass that entangles or entraps particulate matter in the water, thereby increasing the rate of sedimentation.

cobalt bomb. If a nuclear weapon were encased in cobalt, large amounts of radioactive cobalt-60 could be produced when it was detonated. Such a weapon could add to the explosive force of the bomb the danger of the highly penetrating and long-lasting gamma radiation emitted by cobalt-60.

COD. See *chemical oxygen demand.*

coffin. A heavily shielded shipping cask for spent (used) nuclear-power fuel elements. Some coffins weigh as much as 75 tons.

coliform bacteria. Bacteria (*Escherichia coli*) normally present in the intestines of man and other animals. A coliform count serves as a measure of the suitability of water for drinking.

coliform index or **coli index.** An index of the purity of water, based on a count of its coliform bacteria.

collecting sewer. A sewer that collects wastewater from lateral sewers and connects to a trunk sewer.

collodial matter. In wastewater, fine suspended particles that settle out very slowly and hence require special treatment, such as sedimentation with coagulants or dialysis.

combined sewer. A sewer that carries both wastewater and storm water. During dry weather, the combined sewer carries all wastewater to a treatment plant. During a storm, only part of the flow is intercepted, and the remainder goes directly into the receiving stream untreated.

combustion products. The gases, vapors, and solids that result from the combustion of a fuel.

comminutor. In a wastewater treatment plant, a device that grinds solids into small particles to make them easier to treat.

compost. Relatively stable decomposed organic materials, such as food wastes, that have been decomposed by microorganisms. Compost is an excellent soil conditioner.

comprehensive development. The basin-wide development of water and land resources for optimum use of a river system and its watershed.

consumptive use of water. Water use resulting in a large proportion of loss to the atmosphere by evapotranspiration (as in irrigation) or by combination with a manufactured product.

containment vessel. A gas-tight shell or other enclosure around a nuclear reactor. Compare *pressure vessel*.

controlled thermonuclear reaction. Controlled fusion, that is, fusion produced under research conditions or for production of useful power. See *Sherwood*.

control rod. A rod, plate, or tube containing a material such as hafnium or boron that readily absorbs neutrons, used to control the power of a nuclear reactor. By absorbing neutrons, a control rod prevents the neutrons from causing further fission.

conventional wastewater treatment. Wastewater treatment including screening, sedimentation, coagulation, rapid sand filtration, and disinfection with chlorine.

converter reactor. A reactor that produces some fissionable material, but less than it consumes. In some cases, a reactor that produces a fissionable material different from the fuel burned, regardless of the ratio. Compare *breeder reactor*.

cooling tower. A tower in which the waste heat of a power plant is disposed of through the evaporation of water.

cooling water. Water used for cooling in an industrial or manufacturing process. Since its temperature after use is normally higher than that of the lake or stream into which it is discharged, it may constitute a source of thermal pollution.

core. The central portion of a nuclear reactor containing the fuel elements and usually the moderator, but not the reflector.

counter. A general designation applied to radiation detection instruments or survey meters that detect and measure radiation. See *Geiger-Müller counter*.

critical. Capable of sustaining a chain reaction.

critical mass. The smallest mass of fissionable material that will support a self-sustaining chain reaction under stated conditions.

curie. The basic unit to describe the intensity of radioactivity in a sample of material. The curie is equal to 37 billion disintegrations per second, which is approximately the rate of decay of one gram of radium. A curie is also a quantity of any nuclide having one curie of radioactivity. Named for Marie and Pierre Curie, who discovered radium in 1898. See *rem, roentgen*.

cutie pie. A common radiation survey meter used to determine exposure levels or to locate possible radiation hazards.

Dano biostabilizer system. An aerobic, thermophilic composting process in which optimum conditions of moisture, air, and temperature are maintained in a single, slowly revolving cylinder that retains the compostable solid waste for one to five days. The material is later windrowed.

daughter. A nuclide formed by the radioactive decay of another nuclide, which in this context is called the "parent".

decibel (db). A unit for measuring sound intensity, or loudness. The slightest sound audible to humans is 0 on the decibel scale. Normal conversation is about 60 db, a person operating a food blender is exposed to about 80 db, and a person standing near a large jet at takeoff may be exposed to about 150 db.

decontamination. The removal of radioactive contaminants from surfaces or equipment, by cleaning and washing with chemicals. See *radioactive contamination*.

desalination. Total or partial removal of salt from salt water.

destructive distillation. The airless heating of organic matter that results in the evolution of volatile substances and produces a solid char consisting of fixed carbon and ash. See *Lantz process*.

detergent. Any of a large number of synthetic water-soluble or liquid surface-active agents for use in washing. Like soaps, they emulsify oils and hold dirt in suspension. If the detergents are not biodegradable, they create long-term pollution problems, and the phosphate content of many detergents contributes to eutrophication of lakes.

deuterium. An isotope of hydrogen whose nucleus contains one neutron and one proton, and is, therefore, about twice as heavy as the nucleus of normal hydrogen, which is only a single proton. Deuterium is often referred to as heavy hydrogen. It occurs in nature as 1 atom to 6500 atoms of normal hydrogen. It is nonradioactive.

digester. In a waste-treatment plant, a closed tank that uses bacterial action to decrease the volume of solids and stabilize raw sludge into a material that can be disposed of safely.

dirty bomb. A fission bomb or any other weapon which would distribute relatively large amounts of radioactivity upon explosion, as distinguished from a fusion weapon. Compare *clean bomb*.

dissolved oxygen (DO). The oxygen freely available in water. In unpolluted water, oxygen is usually present in amounts of 10 ppm or less. Adequate dissolved oxygen is necessary for the life of fish and other aquatic organisms. About 3–5 ppm is the lowest limit for support of fish life over a long period of time.

dissolved solids (DS). The total amount of dissolved organic and inorganic material contained in water or wastes. Excessive dissolved solids can make water unsuitable for industrial uses, unpalatable for drinking, and even cathartic. Potable water supplies may have dissolved solid content from 20 to 1000 mg/l, but sources which have more than 500 mg/l are not recommended by the U.S. Public Health Service.

distribution factor. A term used to express the modification of the effect of radiation in a biological system attributable to the nonuniform distribution of an internally deposited isotope. Radium, for example, is concentrated in the body's bones. See *dose equivalent*.

DO. See *dissolved oxygen*.

dose. See *absorbed dose, biological dose, maximum permissible dose, threshold dose*.

dose equivalent. A term used to express the amount of effective radiation when modifying factors have been considered. It is the product of absorbed dose multiplied by a quality factor multiplied by a distribution factor. The dose equivalent is expressed numerically in rems.

dose rate. The radiation delivered per unit time and measured, for instance, in rems per hour.

dosimeter. A device such as a film badge or ionization chamber that measures radiation doses.

dosimetry. See *radiation dosimetry*.

dry farming. A method of farming without irrigation in an area of limited rainfall. The land is treated to conserve the moisture it contains.

DS. See *dissolved solids*.

dystrophic. Dystrophic lakes have brownish water with much dissolved humus matter, a small bottom fauna, and a high oxygen consumption.

ecology. The science that deals with the interrelationships of organisms and their living and nonliving surroundings.

ecosystem. A biological community and its environment that is sufficiently self-contained to be studied as a world unto itself. An ecosystem may range from a rotting log (or even smaller) to the entire earth, depending on the purpose of the study.

effective half-life. The time required for a radionuclide contained in a biological system, such as a man or an animal, to reduce its activity by half as a combined result of radioactive decay and biological elimination. Compare *biological half-life*.

effluent. The substances that flow out of a designated source.

effluent charge. A water fee set to compensate downstream water users for damages caused by an upstream user's polluting discharge.

effluent seepage. Diffuse discharge onto the ground of liquids that have percolated through solid waste or another medium. Effluent seepage generally contains dissolved or suspended materials.

electrodialysis. A process in which mineral salts are removed from water by passing the water through an electrically-charged stack of ion-permeable membranes. The mineral salts separate into positive and negative ions that migrate through the membranes, leaving the water behind.

electrostatic precipitator. A device that collects particulates by placing an electrical charge on them and attracting them electrostatically onto a collecting electrode.

element. One of the 104 known chemical substances that cannot be divided into simpler substances by chemical means; a substance whose atoms all have the same atomic number. Some examples are hydrogen, lead, oxygen, nitrogen, and uranium.

elutriation. Separation of solid waste into heavy and light fractions by washing.

emergent (emersed) aquatic plants. Rooted plants, such as the bulrush and cattail, that grow in shallow water with a portion of their stems and leaves above the water surface.

emission. Material released into the air either by a discrete source (primary emission) or as the result of a photochemical reaction or chain of reactions (secondary emission).

emphysema, or **pulmonary emphysema.** A condition in which lung tissues lose their elasticity, and breathing capacity is reduced.

enteric virus. Any virus known to be excreted in quantity in feces; for example, the infectious hepatitis virus.

estuary. Shallow coastal waters, usually associated with the mouth of a river, including adjoining bays, lagoons, shallow sounds, and marshes. Estuaries produce much marine life and are important nurseries for many species of deep-sea fish.

eutrophication. The normally slow aging process by which a lake evolves into a marsh and ultimately becomes completely filled with detritus and disappears. In the course of this process, the lake becomes overly rich in dissolved nutrients (chiefly nitrogen and phosphorus), resulting in an excessive development of algae. First the water becomes murky, then noxious odors and unsightly scums appear. In the lower layers, dissolved oxygen levels become depressed, and bottom-dwelling fauna change from clean-water forms to pollution-tolerant forms. Eutrophication is sometimes greatly accelerated by the nutrients in sewage, chemical fertilizers, etc.

evaporation. The process by which a substance changes from the liquid to the gas or vapor state.

evapotranspiration. Water loss through evaporation (from soil and surface water bodies) and transpiration (from plants).

exclusion area. An area immediately surrounding a nuclear reactor where human habitation is prohibited to assure safety in the event of accident. Compare *low-population zone*.

excursion. A sudden, very rapid rise in the power level of a reactor which results when a reactor becomes supercritical. Excursions are usually quickly suppressed by the negative temperature coefficient of the reactor and/or by automatic control rods. See *scram*.

fallout. Air-borne particles containing radioactive material which fall to the ground following a nuclear explosion. "Local fallout" from nuclear detonations falls to the earth's surface within twenty-four hours after the detonation. "Tropospheric fallout" consists of material injected into the troposphere but not into the higher altitudes of the stratosphere. It does not fall out locally, but usually is deposited in relatively narrow bands around the earth at about the latitude of injection. "Stratospheric fallout" or "worldwide fallout" is injected into the stratosphere and then falls out relatively slowly over much of the earth's surface.

fast breeder reactor. A reactor that operates with fast neutrons and produces more fissionable material than it consumes. See *breeder reactor*.

fast neutron. A neutron with energy greater than approximately 100,000 electron volts.

fill. See *sanitary landfill*.

film-badge dosimeter. A light-tight package of photographic film worn like a badge by workers in nuclear industry or research, used to measure possible exposure to ionizing radiation. The absorbed dose can be calculated by the degree of film darkening caused by irradiation.

fireball. The luminous ball of hot gases that forms a few millionths of a second after a nuclear explosion.

fissile fuel. A material that can be fissioned, especially a fuel such as uranium-235 or plutonium-239 that is fissionable by slow as well as fast neutrons.

fission. The splitting of a heavy nucleus into two approximately equal parts (which are nuclei of lighter elements), accompanied by the release of a relatively large amount of energy and generally one or more neutrons. Fission can occur spontaneously but usually is caused by nuclear absorption of gamma rays, neutrons, or other particles.

fissionable material. A fuel such as uranium-238 that can be fissioned by fast neutrons only. The term is sometimes used as a synonym for fissile fuel.

fission fragments. The two nuclei that are formed by the fission of a nucleus; also referred to as "primary fission products." They are of medium atomic weight and are radioactive.

fission products. The nuclei (fission fragments) formed by the fission of heavy elements plus the nuclides formed by the fission fragments' radioactive decay.

fission weapon. An atomic bomb.

flash burn. A skin burn caused by a flash of thermal radiation. It can be distinguished from a flame burn by the fact that it occurs on unshielded parts of the body in direct line with the source of the thermal radiation. Compare *beta burn*.

flocculation. In wastewater treatment, a process that causes aggregation or coalescence of solid matter into small lumps or loose clusters.

flood plain. The lowland that borders a river, usually dry but subject to flooding when the stream overflows its banks.

flood stage. That elevation of the water surface above which a stream is considered to be in flood. Commonly, it is that stage at which damage begins.

flotation. In waste treatment, the collection of substances immersed in wastewater by taking advantage of differences in specific gravities, or else by entrapping solid particles with air causing them to rise to the surface for subsequent disposal.

flue dust. Solid particles smaller than 100 microns carried in the products of combustion.

flue gas. Waste gas from a combustion process.

fluoride. A chemical concentration of approximately one milligram per liter that helps prevent tooth decay. Fluoride may occur naturally in water or may be added in controlled amounts. Waters that contain excessive fluoride require defluoridation for use as drinking water.

flux. In nuclear physics, a synonym for neutron flux.

fly ash. All solids, including ash, charred paper, cinders, dust, soot, or other partially incinerated matter, that are carried in a gas stream.

food chain. The pathways by which any material (such as radioactive material from fallout) passes from the first absorbing organism through plants and animals to man.

fossil fuel. A fuel such as oil, natural gas, or coal formed from the remains of ancient plant and animal life.

free groundwater. Groundwater in aquifers that are not confined by impervious layers of rocks.

fuel element. A rod, tube, plate, or other mechanical shape or form into which nuclear fuel is fabricated for use in a reactor.

fuel reprocessing. The processing of spent reactor fuel to recover the unused fissionable material.

fungi. Simple plants that lack a photosynthetic pigment. The individual cells have a nucleus surrounded by a membrane, and they may be linked together in long filaments called hyphae, which may grow together to form a visible body. Simple fungi are involved in the stabilization of solid waste and sewage.

fusion. The formation of a heavy atomic nucleus from two lighter ones (such as hydrogen isotopes), with the attendant release of energy (as in a hydrogen bomb). See *thermonuclear reaction*.

fusion weapon. An atomic weapon (such as a hydrogen bomb) which uses the energy of nuclear *fusion*.

gamma rays. High-energy, short-wavelength radiation. Gamma radiation frequently accompanies alpha and beta emissions, and always accompanies fission. Gamma rays are very penetrating, and are best stopped by a shield of dense materials, such as lead or depleted uranium. Gamma rays are essentially similar to X-rays, but are usually more energetic. They are nuclear in origin.

Geiger-Müller counter, or **Geiger counter.** A radiation detection and measuring instrument. It consists of a gas-filled (Geiger-Müller) tube containing electrodes, between which is an electrical voltage but no flowing current. When ionizing radiation passes through the tube, a short, intense pulse of current passes from the negative electrode to the positive electrode, and is measured or counted. The number of pulses per second measures the intensity of radiation.

genetic effects of radiation. Radiation effects that can be transferred from parent to offspring; any radiation-caused changes in the genetic material of sex cells. Compare *radiomutation, somatic effects of radiation*.

greenhouse effect. The trapping of solar energy, in the form of heat, within the earth's atmosphere by ozone, water vapor, and carbon dioxide—much as heat is trapped by glass in a greenhouse. The burning of fossil fuels possibly may increase the greenhouse effect, and thereby warm up the earth, by increasing the amount of carbon dioxide in the atmosphere.

groundwater. Water present in the saturated zone of an aquifer. See *water table*.

half-life. The time in which half the atoms of a particular radioactive substance disintegrate to another nuclear form. Measured half-lives vary from millionths of a second to billions of years. Compare *biological half life, effective half life*.

half-time. See *residence time*.

hand and foot counter. A monitoring device arranged to detect radioactive contamination of hands and feet of persons working with radioactive materials.

hardness of water. A measure of the calcium and magnesium salts present in water. "Soft" water has less than 60 parts per million (ppm) of salts. "Temporary" water has 60 to 120 ppm of salts. "Permanent" water has salts in excess of 120 ppm. Other salts that may occur in water include those of iron, aluminum, manganese, strontium, and zinc.

hardpan. A hardened, compacted, or cemented soil layer.

H-bomb. A hydrogen bomb.

health physics. The science concerned with recognition, evaluation, and control of health hazards from ionizing radiation.

herbicide. An agent (usually a chemical) used to injure or destroy plant life.

hexane solubles. Fats, oils, and greases.

hot. Highly radioactive.

humus. Organic matter in or on a soil, composed of partly or fully decomposed bits of plant or animal matter.

hydrogen. The lightest element, no. 1 in the atomic series. Hydrogen has two natural isotopes—mass numbers 1 and 2. The first is ordinary hydrogen, or light hydrogen; the second is deuterium, or heavy hydrogen. A third isotope, tritium-3, is a radioactive form produced in reactors by bombarding lithium-6 with neutrons.

hydrogen bomb. A nuclear weapon that derives its energy largely from fusion. See *thermonuclear reaction*.

hydrogen-ion concentration. See *pH*.

hydrogen sulfide (H_2S). A poisonous gas with the odor of rotten eggs that is produced from the putrefaction of sulfur-containing organic material.

hydrologic cycle. The continual exchange of moisture between the earth and the atmosphere, consisting of evaporation, condensation, precipitation (rain or snow), stream runoff, absorption into the soil, evaporation, condensation, precipitation, etc.

hydrology. The science of the behavior of water in the atmosphere, on the earth's surface, and underground.

hypertrophic water. Water of high nutrient content.

incineration. The controlled burning of solid, liquid, or gaseous combustible wastes.

Indore process. An anaerobic composting method that originated in India. Organic wastes are placed in alternate layers with human or animal excreta in a pit or pile. Compost is produced in six months. During this period, the pile is turned twice and kept moist.

induced radioactivity. Radioactivity created when substances are bombarded with neutrons, as from a nuclear explosion or in a reactor, or with charged particles produced by accelerators.

industrial waste pollution. A broad category of wastes from manufacturing operations or processes. They include floating matter, settleable solids, colloidal matter, dissolved solids, toxic substances, and sludge.

initial nuclear radiation. Radiation emitted from the fireball of a nuclear explosive during the first minute (an arbitrarily chosen time interval) after detonation. Compare *residual nuclear radiation*.

intensity. The energy of the number of photons or particles of any radiation incident upon a unit area or flowing through a unit of solid material per unit of time. In connection with radioactivity, intensity is defined as the number of atoms disintegrating per unit of time.

intercepting sewer. A sewer that catches wastewater before it empties into a waterway, and transports it to a treatment plant.

intermediate wastewater treatment. Wastewater treatment, such as aeration or chemical treatment, which is supplementary to primary treatment. Such treatment removes substantial percentages of very finely divided particulate matter, in addition to the suspended solids removed by primary treatment. The supplementary processing improves the efficiency of primary treatment so that about 60 percent of both BOD and suspended solids are removed.

inversion. An atmospheric condition in which a layer of cool air lies over a layer of warm air and keeps the warmer air from rising as it normally would. In a persistent inversion, the low-lying warm air may become dangerously polluted.

investment tax credit. In pollution abatement, a reduction in a company's tax by a given percent of the sum invested in pollution abatement equipment and facilities.

ion. An atom or molecule that has lost or gained one or more electrons. By this "ionization" it becomes electrically charged. Some examples are an alpha particle, which is a helium atom minus two electrons; and a proton, which is a hydrogen atom minus its electron.

ionization chamber. An instrument that detects and measures ionizing radiation by measuring the electrical current that flows when radiation ionizes gas in a chamber, making the gas a conductor of electricity.

ionizing radiation. Any radiation displacing electrons from atoms or molecules, thereby producing ions. Some examples are alpha, beta, and gamma radiation and short-wave ultraviolet light. Ionizing radiation may produce severe skin or tissue damage. See *radiation, radiation burn, radiation illness.*

irradiation. Exposure to radiation, as in a nuclear reactor.

isotope. One of two or more atoms with the same atomic number (and thus classified as the same chemical element), but with different mass numbers. An equivalent statement is that the nuclei of isotopes have the same number of protons, but different numbers of neutrons. Thus, $^{12}_{6}C$, $^{13}_{6}C$, and $^{14}_{6}C$ are isotopes of the element carbon, the subscripts denoting their common atomic numbers and the superscripts denoting the differing mass numbers or approximate atomic weights. Isotopes usually have very nearly the same chemical properties, but somewhat different physical properties.

junk. Discarded materials suitable for reuse or recycling.

kiloton energy. The energy of a nuclear explosion equivalent to that of an explosion of 1000 tons of TNT.

Lantz process. A destructive distillation technique in which the combustible components of solid waste are converted into combustible gases, charcoal, and a variety of distillates.

lateral sewer. A street sewer that serves a limited number of properties. Lateral sewers usually discharge into a collecting (submain or main) sewer or into a trunk sewer.

leachate. Liquid that has percolated through solid waste or other matter and has extracted dissolved or suspended materials from it.

leaching. The process by which a soluble material, such as mineral salts, is washed out of a layer of soil into a lower layer by percolating rain water.

lead poisoning. Poisoning caused by lead absorbed through the intestinal tract, through the skin, or through the lungs. Most acute cases involve children who nibble on flakes of lead-based paint.

lethal dose. A dose of ionizing radiation sufficient to cause death. Median lethal dose (MLD or LD-50) is the amount required to kill within a specified period of time (usually thirty days) half of the individuals in a large group of organisms similarly exposed. The LD-50/30 for man is about 400-450 roentgens.

lignin. A substance in woody plants that is often discharged as waste during the manufacture of paper pulp.

limnology. The study of the physical, chemical, meteorological, and biological conditions in fresh waters (especially ponds and lakes).

linear alkylate sulfonate (LAS). A surface-active compound in synthetic detergents that decomposes readily by bacterial action where oxygen is present.

low-population zone. An area of low population density sometimes required around a nuclear installation to reasonably provide that effective protection measures can be taken if a serious accident should occur. See *exclusion area.*

manure. Primarily the excreta of animals which may contain some spilled feed or bedding.

marsh. A tract of soft, wet land, usually low-lying and partly or completely under water. Compare *swamp.*

mass number. The sum of the neutrons and protons in the nucleus of an atom. The mass number of an isotope is sometimes designated by a numerical suffix, as in "uranium-235." For another type of designation, see *isotope.*

maximum credible accident. The most serious reactor accident that can reasonably be imagined from any adverse combination of equipment malfunction, operating errors, and other foreseeable causes.

maximum permissible concentration. The amount of radioactive material in air, water, or food which might be expected to result in a maximum permissible dose to a person consuming them at a standard rate of intake. An obsolescent term. See *radioactivity concentration guide*.

maximum permissible dose, or **maximum permissible exposure.** That dose of ionizing radiation established by authorities as an amount below which there is no reasonable expectation of risk to human health, and which at the same time is somewhat below the lowest level at which a definite hazard is believed to exist. An obsolescent term. See *radiation protection guide*.

mean life. The average time during which an atom, an excited nucleus, a radionuclide, or a particle exists in a particular form.

median lethal dose. See *lethal dose*.

megaton energy. The energy of a nuclear explosion that is equivalent to that of an explosion of one million tons (1000 kilotons) of TNT.

mercury. A highly toxic heavy metal.

methane (CH_4). An odorless, colorless, and asphyxiating gas that can explode under certain circumstances. It can be produced by solid waste undergoing anaerobic decomposition.

mgd. Million gallons per day.

mg/l. Milligrams per liter.

microcurie. A unit of radioactive intensity equal to one millionth of a curie, or 37,000 disintegrations per second.

micron. A measure of dust-particle diameter equal to 1/1,000 of a millimeter (1/25,400 of an inch).

mining. The depletion of a resource without making any provision for replenishment.

moderator. A material, such as ordinary water, heavy water, or graphite, used in a reactor to slow down high-velocity neutrons, thus increasing the likelihood of further fission.

multiple-purpose development. In water projects, a development that takes into account the use and control of water in all possible aspects, including irrigation, power, flood control, domestic and industrial water supply, pollution control, navigation, recreation, and fish and wildlife.

multiplication factor, or **multiplication constant.** The ratio of the number of neutrons present in a reactor in any one neutron generation to that in the immediately preceding generation. Criticality is achieved when this ratio is equal to one. The "infinite" multiplication factor is the ratio in a theoretical system from which there is no leakage; that is, a reactor of infinite size. For an actual reactor (from which leakage does occur) the term "effective multiplication factor," which is the ratio based on neutrons available after leakage, is commonly used.

mutation. A permanent transmissible change in the characteristics of an offspring from those of its parents. Compare *radiomutation*.

natural pollution. Soil, mineral, or bacterial impurities picked up by water from the earth's surface, apart from any human activity.

natural radiation, or **natural radioactivity.** See *background radiation*.

neuston. The community of minute organisms living in the surface film of water.

neutron. An uncharged elementary particle with a mass slightly greater than that of the proton and found in the nucleus of every atom heavier than hydrogen. A free neutron is unstable and decays with a half-life of about 13 minutes into an electron, proton, and neutrino. Neutrons sustain the fission chain reaction in a nuclear reactor.

neutron flux. A measure of the intensity of neutron radiation. It is the number of neutrons passing through one square centimeter of a given target in one second.

nitrates. Nitrogen compounds present in sewage and in the runoff from chemically fertilized farmlands. Nitrates speed up the eutrophication of lakes and ponds, and nitrates in drinking water are toxic to infants.

nitrogenous wastes. Wastes of animal or plant origin that contain a significant concentration of nitrogen.

nonrenewable resources. Resources, such as oil or coal, that cannot renew themselves after they have been used.

nuclear device. A nuclear explosive used for peaceful purposes, tests, or experiments. The term is used to distinguish these explosives from nuclear weapons, which are packaged units ready for transportation or use by military forces.

nuclear energy. The energy liberated by a nuclear reaction (fission or fusion) or by radioactive decay.

nuclear explosive. An explosive based on fission or fusion of atomic nuclei.

nuclear fission. See *fission*.

nuclear fusion. See *fusion*.

nuclear power plant. Any device, machine, or assembly that converts nuclear energy into some form of useful power, such as mechanical or electrical power. In a nuclear electric power plant, heat produced by a nuclear reactor is generally used to make steam to drive a turbine that in turn drives an electric generator.

nuclear reaction. A reaction involving a change in an atomic nucleus, such as fission, fusion, or radioactive decay, as distinct from a chemical reaction, which is limited to changes in the electron structure surrounding the nucleus.

nuclear reactor. A device in which a fission chain reaction can be initiated, maintained, and controlled. Its essential component is a core with fissionable fuel. It usually has a moderator, a reflector, and shielding, coolant, and control mechanisms. It is the basic machine of nuclear energy.

nuclear rocket. A rocket powered by an engine that obtains energy for heating a propellant fluid (such as hydrogen) from a nuclear reactor, rather than from chemical combustion. See *Rover*.

nuclear weapons. A collective term for atomic bombs and hydrogen bombs. Compare *nuclear device*.

nucleus. The small, positively charged core of an atom. It is only about 1/10,000 the diameter of the atom, but contains nearly all the atom's mass. All nuclei contain both protons and neutrons, except the nucleus of ordinary hydrogen, which consists of a single proton.

nuclide. A general term applicable to all atomic forms of the elements. The term is often erroneously used as a synonym for "isotope", which properly has a more limited definition. Whereas isotopes are the various forms of a single element (and, hence, are a family of nuclides), nuclides comprise all the isotopic forms of all the elements. Nuclides are distinguished by their atomic number, atomic mass, and energy state. Compare *element, isotope*.

nutrient. A chemical substance that can be absorbed by a green plant and used in organic synthesis. Plant nutrients are either chemical elements, such as nitrogen, or inorganic compounds, such as nitrates.

oligotrophic. An oligotrophic lake or pond produces little plant life and is typically very clean and clear.

opacity rating. The apparent obscuration of an observer's vision that equals the apparent obscuration caused by smoke of a given rating on the Ringelmann chart.

open burning. Uncontrolled burning of wastes in the open or in an open dump.

organic phosphorous compounds. A class of highly toxic insecticides, including chlorthion, parathion, malathion, and phosdrin.

organophosphates. See *organic phosphorus compounds*.

outfall sewer. A sewer that carries wastewater to a point of final discharge.

PANs. See *peroxyacetyl nitrates*.

particle. A minute constituent of matter, generally one with a measurable mass. The primary particles involved in radioactivity are alpha particles, beta particles, neutrons, and protons.

particulates. Soot, dust, and other tiny particles in the air.

PCBs. See *polychlorinated biphenyls.*

perched water table. A water table of limited area maintained above the normal water table by the presence of an intervening layer of relatively impervious rock. Compare *water table.*

percolation. The downward movement of water through soil, solid waste, or other porous material.

permissible dose. See *maximum permissible dose, radiation protection guide.*

peroxyacetyl nitrates (PANs). Air pollutants created by the action of sunlight on atmospheric hydrocarbons and nitrogen oxides, most of which originate from automotive engines.

personnel monitoring. Determination by either physical or biological measurement of the amount of ionizing radiation to which an individual has been exposed. Measuring the darkening of a film badge or performing a radon breath analysis are common methods. Compare *radiation monitoring, hand and foot counter.*

pesticide. An agent (usually a chemical) used to destroy insects and other pests. Pesticides present in ground and surface waters as a result of direct application, runoff, percolation, or manufacturing discharge may have grave adverse effects on water quality. Careless use of pesticides may result in fish kills.

pH. A measure of hydrogen ion concentration, which reflects the balance between acids and alkalies. The extreme readings are 0 and 14. The pH of most natural waters falls within the range 4 to 9. A pH of 7.0 indicates neutral water; a 6.5 reading is slightly acid; an 8.5 reading is alkaline. A slight decrease in pH may greatly increase the toxicity of pollutants such as ammonia. Alkaline water tends to form a scale; acid water is corrosive; and good water should be nearly neutral.

phenol. Carbolic acid, a powerful caustic poison.

phosphates. Phosphorus-containing derivatives of phosphoric acid. Phosphates in detergents, fertilizers, and pesticides are serious water pollutants.

photic zone. The upper zone of a body of water in which sufficient light is available for photosynthesis. Compare *profundal zone.*

picocurie. A unit of radioactive intensity equal to one trillionth of a curie, or 2.22 disintegrations per minute.

pig. A heavily shielded container (usually lead) used to ship or store radioactive materials.

plankton. The floating or weakly swimming plant and animal life of a body of water, consisting mostly of minute forms but including also some larger forms (such as jellyfish) with weak powers of locomotion.

Plowshare. The Atomic Energy Commission program of research and development on peaceful uses of nuclear explosives. The possible uses include large-scale excavation, crushing ore bodies, and producing heavy transuranic isotopes. The term is based on a biblical reference, *Isaiah* 2:4.

plume. The visible smoke emitted from a chimney.

plutonium. A heavy, radioactive, man-made, metallic element with atomic number 94. Its most important isotope is fissionable plutonium-239, produced by neutron irradiation of uranium-238. It is used for reactor fuel and in weapons.

pollution indicator organism. A plant or animal form, such as the rat-tailed maggot or blue-green algae, that thrives in polluted water.

polychlorinated biphenyls. Highly persistent toxic chemicals used as electrical insulators, plasticizers, and flame retardants.

population equivalent (PE). A measure of the relative strength of a waste (usually industrial) in terms of its equivalent in domestic waste, expressed as the population that would produce the equivalent domestic waste. A population equivalent of 160 million persons means the pollutional effect equivalent to raw sewage from 160 million persons. 1 PE = 0.17 pounds BOD.

ppm. Parts per million. In water analysis, ppm implies a weight/weight (not a volume/volume) ratio.

precipitation. Any form of water, whether liquid or solid, that falls to the ground from the atmosphere; it includes drizzle, rain, snow pellets, snow grains, ice crystals, ice pellets, and hail. The amount of precipitation is usually expressed in inches of equivalent liquid water depth at a given point over a specified period of time.

pressure suppression. See *vapor suppression*.

pressure vessel. A strong-walled container housing the core of most types of power reactors. It usually also contains moderator, reflector, thermal shield, and control rods. Compare *containment vessel*.

primary fission products. See *fission fragments*.

primary wastewater treatment. The first and sometimes the only major treatment in a wastewater treatment plant. It screens out some sticks, rags, and other solids, and floats and settles out others in settling basins. At best, primary treatment removes about 35 percent of the organic waste. A primary wastewater treatment plant may consist of the following units: screens; grit removal chambers; comminutors, clarifiers, or sedimentation tanks; digesters, or sludge digestion tanks; sludge drying beds; or chlorinators, or chlorine contact chambers. Compare *intermediate wastewater treatment, secondary wastewater treatment*.

process water. All water (liquid or vapor) that comes in contact with a product being manufactured.

profundal zone. The deep region of a body of water, lying below the light-controlled limit of plant growth. Compare *photic zone*.

protective action guide (PAG). The absorbed dose of ionizing radiation to individuals in the general population, which would warrant protective action following a contaminating event, such as a nuclear explosion. See *radiation protection guide*.

proton. An elementary particle with a single positive electrical charge and a mass approximately 1837 times that of the electron; the nucleus of an ordinary or light hydrogen atom. Protons are constituents of all nuclei.

pumped storage. Water pumped up into a storage reservoir during periods of low electric-power demand to be used to generate power during peak demand periods.

quality factor. The factor by which absorbed dose is to be multiplied to obtain a quantity that expresses on a common scale, for all ionizing radiations, the irradiation incurred by exposed persons. See *dose equivalent*.

rad. Acronym for "radiation absorbed dose;" the basic unit of absorbed dose of ionizing radiation. A dose of one rad means the absorption of 100 ergs of radiation energy per gram of absorbing material. Compare *rem, roentgen*.

radiation. The emission and propagation of energy through matter or space by means of electromagnetic disturbances which display wavelike, particlelike behavior. Also, the energy so propagated. The term has been extended to include streams of fast-moving particles (alpha and beta particles, free neutrons, cosmic radiation, etc.). Nuclear radiation is that emitted from atomic nuclei in various nuclear reactions, including alpha, beta, and gamma radiation and neutrons. Compare *ionizing radiation*.

radiation accident. An accident resulting in the spread of radioactive material or in the exposure of individuals to radiation.

radiation area. An area in which the level of radiation is such that a major portion of an individual's body could receive in any one hour a dose in excess of five millirem, or in any five consecutive days a dose in excess of 150 millirem. See *absorbed dose, rem*.

radiation burn. Radiation damage to the skin. "Beta burns" result from skin contact with or exposure to emitters of beta particles. "Flash burns" result from sudden thermal radiation.

radiation chemistry. The branch of chemistry that is concerned with the chemical effects, including decomposition, of energetic radiation or particles on matter. Compare *radiochemistry*.

radiation damage. A general term for the harmful effects of radiation on matter.

radiation detection instruments. Devices that detect and record the characteristics of ionizing radiation. See *counter, dosimeter.*

radiation dosimetry. The measurement of the amount of radiation delivered to a specific place or the amount of radiation that was absorbed there. See *dosimeter.*

radiation illness. An acute organic disorder that follows exposure to relatively severe doses of ionizing radiation. It is characterized by nausea, vomiting, diarrhea, blood cell changes, and in later stages by hemorrhage and loss of hair.

Radiation Protection Guide. The officially determined doses of radiation that should not be exceeded without careful consideration. These standards, established by the Federal Radiation Council, are equivalent to what was formerly called the maximum permissible dose or maximum permissible exposure. Compare *radioactivity concentration guide.*

radiation shielding. Reduction of radiation by interposing a shield of absorbing material between any radioactive source and a person, laboratory area, or radiation-sensitive device. See *shield.*

radiation source. Usually a manmade, sealed source of radioactivity used in teletherapy, radiography, as a power source for batteries, or in various types of industrial gauges. Machines such as accelerators, and radioisotopic generators and natural radionuclides may also be considered as sources.

radiation standards. Exposure standards, permissible concentrations, rules for safe handling, regulations for transportation, regulations for industrial control of radiation, and control of radiation exposure by legislative means.

radiation sterilization. Use of radiation to cause a plant or animal to become sterile, that is, incapable of reproduction. Also the use of radiation to kill all forms of life (especially bacteria) in food, surgical sutures, etc. Compare *radiation illness, radiomutation.*

radiation therapy. Treatment of disease with any type of radiation; often called radiotherapy.

radiation warning symbol. An officially prescribed symbol (a magenta trefoil on a yellow background), which should always be displayed when a radiation hazard exists.

radioactive. Exhibiting radioactivity or pertaining to radioactivity.

radioactive cloud. A mass of air and vapor in the atmosphere carrying radioactive debris from a nuclear explosion. See *atomic cloud.*

radioactive contamination. Deposition of radioactive material in any place where it may harm persons, spoil experiments, or make products or equipment unsuitable or unsafe for some specific use; the presence of unwanted radioactive matter. Also, radioactive material found on the walls of vessels in used-fuel processing plants, or radioactive material that has leaked into a reactor coolant. Often referred to only as contamination. See *decontamination.*

radioactive decay. The spontaneous transformation of one nuclide into a different nuclide or into a different energy state of the same nuclide. The process results in a decrease, with time, of the number of the original radioactive atoms in a sample. It involves the emission of alpha particles, beta particles, or gamma rays from the atomic nucleus; or the nuclear capture or ejection of orbital electrons; or fission. Also called radioactive disintegration.

radioactive disintegration. See *radioactive decay.*

radioactive fallout. See *fallout.*

radioactive half-life. See *half-life.*

radioactive series. A succession of nuclides, each of which transforms into the next by radioactive disintegration, except the last nuclide in the series, which is stable. The first member is called the "parent," the intermediate members are called "daughters," and the final stable member is called the "end product." See *radioactive decay.*

radioactive waste. Equipment and materials (from nuclear operations) that are radioactive and for which there is no further use. Wastes are generally classified as high-level (having radioactivity concentrations of hundreds to thousands of curies per gallon or cubic foot), low-level (in the range of one microcurie per gallon or cubin foot), or intermediate (between these extremes).

radioactivity. The spontaneous radioactive decay or disintegration of an unstable atomic nucleus, usually accompanied by the emission of ionizing radiation.

radioactivity concentration guide. The concentration of radioactive material in an environment that would result in doses equal, over a period of time, to those in the Radiation Protection Guide. This Federal Radiation Council term replaces the previously used term maximum permissible concentration.

radiobiology. The body of knowledge and the study of the principles, mechanisms, and effects of ionizing radiation on living matter.

radiochemistry. The body of knowledge and the study of the chemical properties and reactions of radioactive materials. Compare *radiation chemistry*.

radioecology. The science of the effects of radiation on species of plants and animals in natural communities.

radioelement. An element containing one or more radioactive isotopes; a radioactive element.

radiogenic. Of radioactive origin; produced by radioactive transformation. See *radioactive decay transmutation*.

radiography. The use of ionizing radiation for the production of images on a photographic emulsion.

radioisotope. A radioactive isotope; an unstable isotope of an element that decays or disintegrates spontaneously, emitting radiation. More than 1300 natural and artificial radioisotopes have been identified. See *radioactive decay isotope*.

radiology. The science which deals with the use of all forms of ionizing radiation in the diagnosis and the treatment of disease.

radiomutation. A permanent, inheritable change in any characteristic of an organism, due to radiation exposure. See *genetic effects of radiation, mutation*.

radionuclide. A radioactive nuclide.

radiotherapy. See *radiation therapy*.

radon. A radioactive element; one of the heaviest gases known. Its atomic number is 86, and its mass number is 222. It is a daughter of radium in the uranium radioactive series.

radon breath analysis. Examination of exhaled air for the presence of radon to determine the presence and quantity of radium in the human body.

RBE. See *relative biological effectiveness*.

reactor. See *nuclear reactor*.

receiving waters. The bodies of water that receive effluent wastewater from treatment plants.

recharge area. An area in which an aquifer receives water by force of gravity, usually where a permeable layer lies close to the surface.

recirculating cooling system. In a manufacturing or processing plant, a system that reduces the temperature of used water in a cooling tower by evaporating a small percent of the recirculating stream. Although the evaporated water is permanently removed from the supply, overall water withdrawal is reduced to a small percent of what it would otherwise be.

recoverable resources. Materials that still have useful physical or chemical properties after serving a specific purpose and can, therefore, be reused or recyled for the same or other purposes. Compare *renewable resources*.

recycling. In nuclear engineering, the reuse of fissionable material, after it has been recovered by chemical processing from spent or depleted reactor fuel, reenriched, and then refabricated into new fuel elements. See *fuel reprocessing*.

recycling. In solid-waste handling, the transformation of waste materials into new products in such a way that the identity of the original product is lost. For example, newspapers are recycled into rolls of blank paper. Compare *reuse*.

reflector. A layer of material immediately surrounding a reactor core that scatters back or reflects into the core many neutrons that would otherwise escape. The returned neutrons can then cause more fissions and improve the efficiency of the reactor. Common reflector materials are graphite, beryllium, and natural uranium.

refuse. See *solid waste*.

relative biological effectiveness (RBE). A factor used to compare the biological effectiveness of different types of ionizing radiation. It is the inverse ratio of the amount of absorbed radiation required to produce a given effect, to a standard (or reference) radiation required to produce the same effect.

rem. The unit or dose of any ionizing radiation that produces the same biological effect as a unit of absorbed dose of ordinary X-rays. It is an acronym for "roentgen equivalent man." The dose in rems equals the absorbed dose in rads times the relative biological effectiveness. Compare *roentgen*.

renewable resources. Biological resources such as forests that can renew themselves with or without human intervention.

residence time. The time during which radioactive material remains in the atmosphere following the detonation of a nuclear explosive. It is usually expressed as a half-time, since the time for all material to leave the atmosphere is not well known.

residual nuclear radiation. Lingering radiation, or radiation emitted by radioactive material remaining after a nuclear explosion. Residual radiation is arbitrarily designated as that emitted more than one minute after the explosion. Compare *fallout, initial nuclear radiation*.

reuse. The reintroduction of a commodity, such as a soft drink bottle, into the economic stream without any change. Compare *recycling*.

reverse incentive. In pollution control, a penalty connected with use, such as a user charge based on the amount of water withdrawn from the municipal supply or an effluent charge based on the quantity and quality of wastes discharged into a watercourse to cover damages caused by a user's pollutants.

reverse osmosis. A process in which salt-laden water is purified by forcing it through a semipermeable membrane. The membrane holds back salt ions while allowing water molecules to pass.

Ringelmann chart. A printed or photographically reproduced illustration of four shades of gray that can be used to estimate the density of smoke emitted from an incinerator. A clear stack is recorded as 0, and 100 percent black smoke as 5. Number 1 has a 20 percent density, and 2 through 4 are progressively 20 percent more dense.

roentgen. A unit of exposure to ionizing radiation. A roentgen is the amount of gamma rays or X-rays required to produce ions carrying one electrostatic unit of electrical charge (either positive or negative) in one cubic centimeter of dry air under standard conditions.

roentgen equivalent man. See *rem*.

roentgen therapy. Radiation therapy with X-rays.

roentgenography. Radiography by means of X-rays.

Rover. A joint program of the Atomic Energy Commission and the National Aeronautics and Space Administration to develop a nuclear rocket for space flight. See *nuclear rocket*.

runoff. The portion of rainfall or melted snow that ultimately reaches surface streams. The portion that flows off the surface, without sinking into the ground, is called the "immediate" runoff. The part that sinks into the ground but eventually returns to the surface by seepage and from springs is called "delayed" runoff. Runoff is faster and greater during heavy rain than during protracted drizzle, on clay soils than on sandy soils, on frozen soils than on frostless soils, and in treeless areas than in forests.

safety rod. A standby control rod used to shut down a nuclear reactor rapidly in emergencies. See *scram*.

sanitary landfilling. Any of several methods of disposing of solid waste by spreading it in thin layers, compacting it, and covering it with soil by the end of each working day.

sanitary sewer. See *separate sewer*.

scavenger. One who participates in the uncontrolled removal of materials at any point in the solid waste stream.

scintillation counter. An instrument that detects and measures ionizing radiation by counting the light flashes (scintillations) caused by radiation impinging on phosphors.

scouring. The removal of earth or rock by the action of running water or of a glacier; in wool manufacture, the removal of foreign matter from wool by propelling it through a series of bowls and squeeze-rolls by means of reciprocating arms. Scouring wastes are the strongest polluting materials in the textile industry.

scram. The sudden shutdown of a nuclear reactor, usually by rapid insertion of the safety rods. Emergencies or deviations from normal reactor operation cause the reactor operator or automatic control equipment to scram the reactor.

secondary wastewater treatment. Wastewater treatment using biological methods (bacterial action) in addition to primary treatment by screening, sedimentation, and flotation. In secondary treatment, bacteria are used to destroy organic wastes as the water trickles over coarse stones. The process removes up to 90 percent of the dissolved pollutants, but leaves many other pollutants untouched. A secondary waste treatment plant may consist of the following units, in addition to those of the primary treatment plant: trickling filter, aeration or activated sludge, secondary clarifier, secondary settling tank, final settling tank, and final settling basin. Compare *tertiary wastewater treatment*.

sedimentation tank. See *clarifier*.

senescent lake. A lake nearing extinction, especially through the accumulation of the remains of aquatic vegetation.

separate sewer. A sewer that carries waste water but excludes storm and surface waters; also called a "sanitary sewer."

septic tank. A tank in which the organic solid matter of continuously flowing wastewater is deposited and retained until it has been disintegrated by anaerobic bacteria. The liquid effluent flows to a disposal field where it is allowed to seep into the soil.

settleable solids. In water or wastes, bits of debris and fine matter heavy enough to settle out.

settling tank, or **settling basin.** A tank or basin in which settleable solids are removed by gravity.

sewage. See *wastewater*.

sewage lagoon. A shallow pond, three to five feet deep, where natural biological processes purify wastewater to a degree comparable to that accomplished in a secondary treatment plant. The organic matter is broken down into simple compounds by bacterial action. These decomposed products are utilized by algae, which produces oxygen in the course of photosynthesis. The oxygen constitutes the supply needed for aerobic bacterial decomposition.

sewage sludge. See *sludge*.

sewage treatment plant. See *wastewater treatment plant*.

sewage treatment residues. Coarse screenings, grit, or sludge from wastewater treatment plants.

sewage works. Wastewater installations, including both the sewer systems and the wastewater treatment plant.

sewer. A conduit to carry off water and waste matter. See *lateral sewer, collecting sewer, trunk sewer, intercepting sewer, storm sewer*.

sewer system. The system of sewers and related facilities for collection, transportation, and pumping of wastewater.

sewerage. See *sewage works*.

Sherwood. The Atomic Energy Commission program for research in controlled thermonuclear reactions.

shield or **shielding.** A body of material used to reduce the passage of radiation.

shredder. A machine that reduces discarded automobiles and other low-grade sheet and coated metal into fist-size pieces.

silt. Unconsolidated sedimentary rock consisting of particles finer than sand and coarser than clay.

slops. See *swill*.

sludge. The solid matter removed from wastewater; a concentration of solids thick enough to give its fluid carrier a pastelike consistency. Sludge includes both organic matter, which can be burned or composted, and other matter, which cannot. Municipal sewage, food processing, and chemical plants, refineries, and pulp and paper mills produce organic sludge. The noncombustibles are usually water-softener sludge, chemical precipitates, pigments, sand and silt, and miscellaneous debris.

sludge-digestion tank. See *digester*.

sludge-drying bed. A bed on which the humuslike sludge residue from the digester is dried. The dried sludge is usually burned or dumped.

smog. As originally defined, smog = smoke + fog. The term is now applied to any atmosphere in which visibility is seriously reduced by air pollution.

smoke. An aerosol consisting of combustion gases together with the dispersible particles produced by the incomplete combustion of carbonaceous materials.

smoke density. The amount of solid matter contained in smoke. It is often measured by systems that relate the grayness of the smoke to an established standard.

solid waste. Useless, unwanted, or discarded material with insufficient liquid content to be free-flowing.

somatic effects of radiation. Effects of radiation limited to the exposed individual, as distinguished from genetic effects, which also affect subsequent, unexposed generations. See *radiation illness*. Compare *genetic effects of radiation*.

soot. Agglomerations of tar-impregnated carbon particles that form when carbonaceous material undergoes incomplete combustion.

spent fuel, or **depleted fuel.** Nuclear reactor fuel that can no longer effectively sustain a chain reaction.

spontaneous fission. Fission that occurs without an external stimulus. Several heavy isotopes decay mainly in this manner. Some examples are californium-252 and californium-254. The process occurs occasionally in all fissionable materials, including uranium-235.

SST. See *supersonic transport*.

stabilization pond. See *sewage lagoon*.

stack sampling. The collecting of representative samples of gaseous and particulate matter that flows through a duct or stack.

storm sewer, or **storm drain.** A sewer or drain that carries storm and surface waters and drainage, but excludes domestic and industrial wastewater other than nonpolluting cooling water.

strip-cropping, or **strip farming.** The growing of separate crops in successive narrow strips that follow an approximate contour on slopes. Such planting retards erosion.

strip-mining. Mining near the earth's surface by stripping the overlying strata from the ore bed; applied especially to coal mining near the surface.

subcritical reactor. A reactor consisting of a mass of fissionable material and moderator whose effective multiplication factor is less than one, and that hence cannot sustain a chain reaction. Used primarily for educational purposes.

subsoil. That part of the soil beneath the topsoil. Subsoil usually does not have an appreciable organic matter content.

succession. In ecology, the natural replacement of one community by another.

sulfur oxides (SO). Compounds of sulfur and oxygen. They are major air pollutants.

supercritical mass. A mass of fuel whose effective multiplication factor is greater than one. Compare *critical mass*.

supercritical reactor. A reactor in which the effective multiplication factor is greater than one; consequently a reactor that is increasing its power level. If uncontrolled, a supercritical reactor would undergo an excursion.

supersonic transport (SST). Supersonic airplanes designed for regular commercial passenger service. Environmentalists oppose the SST both because of pyschological and physical damage resulting from sonic booms caused by supersonic flight and because of a possible disastrous effect on the atmosphere's ozone ultraviolet screen.

surfactant, or **surface-active agent.** A substance useful for its cleansing, wetting, dispersing, or similar powers. Synthetic detergents contain surfactants.

survey meter. Any portable radiation detection instrument especially adapted for surveying or inspecting an area to establish the existence and amount of radioactive material present.

survival curve. A curve obtained by plotting the number or percentage of organisms surviving at a given time against the dose of radiation, or the number surviving at different intervals after a particular dose of radiation.

suspended solids (SS). Solids suspended in wastewater. The amount of suspended solids is a measure of the polluting effect of sewage.

sustained-yield harvesting. The harvesting of a renewable resource, such as timber, on a basis that permits resource regeneration for undiminished use in the future.

swamp. A tract of low-lying land that is saturated with moisture and usually overgrown with vegetation. A swamp is distinguished from a marsh, which is ordinarily covered with water, and a bog, which consists largely of decaying vegetation. The dampness of a swamp is due to some obstruction to normal drainage—the flatness of the land, the presence of impermeable rocks, or the growth of vegetation.

swill. Semiliquid waste material consisting of food scraps and free liquids.

synergistic. When two or more agents, such as air pollutants, act together so that their total effect is greater than the sum of their separate effects, the combination is synergistic.

tailing ponds. Enclosures or basins constructed for the disposal of mine tailings, the fine rock waste in washings from mills after the grinding and processing of ores. They serve as settling basins and reduce the contamination of streams and other water bodies by such waste.

tertiary wastewater treatment. Wastewater treatment beyond primary and secondary treatment. It may consist of extensions or modifications of secondary treatment, additional forms of chemical treatment, electrochemical processing, carbon filtration, and other more complex procedures.

thermal breeder reactor. A breeder reactor in which the fission chain reaction is sustained by thermal neutrons.

thermal burn. A burn of the skin or other organic material due to radiant heat, such as that produced by the detonation of a nuclear explosive. Compare *beta burn*.

thermal neutron, or **slow neutron.** A neutron in thermal equilibrium with its surrounding medium. Thermal neutrons are those that have been slowed down by a moderator to an average speed of about 2200 meters per second (at room temperature) from the much higher initial speeds they had when expelled by fission. The velocity is similar to that of gas molecules at ordinary temperatures. Compare *fast neutron*.

thermal pollution. The warming of the environment, especially streams and other bodies of water, by waste heat from power plants and factories. Drastic thermal pollution endangers many species of aquatic life.

thermal radiation. Electromagnetic radiation emitted from the fireball produced by a nuclear explosion. Thirty-five percent of the total energy of a nuclear explosion is emitted in the form of thermal radiation, including light, ultraviolet, and infrared radiation.

thermal shield. A layer or layers of high-density material located within a reactor pressure vessel or between the vessel and the biological shield to reduce radiation heating in the vessel and the biological shield.

thermonuclear bomb, or **thermonuclear device.** A hydrogen bomb.

thermonuclear reaction. A reaction in which very high temperatures bring about the fusion of two light nuclei to form the nucleus of a heavier atom, releasing a large amount of energy. In a hydrogen bomb, the high temperature to initiate the thermonuclear reaction is produced by a preliminary fission reaction. See *fusion, Sherwood.*

thorium. A naturally radioactive element with atomic number 90 and, as found in nature, an atomic weight of approximately 232. The fertile thorium-232 isotope is abundant and can be transmuted to fissionable uranium-233 by neutron irradiation.

threshold dose. The minimum dose of radiation that will produce a detectable biological effect.

tidal marsh. Low flat marshlands traversed by interlaced channels and tidal sloughs and subject to tidal inundation. Normally, the only vegetation present is salt-tolerant bushes and grasses.

TNT equivalent. A measure of the energy released in the detonation of a nuclear explosive expressed in terms of the weight of TNT which would release the same amount of energy when exploded. It is usually expressed in kilotons or megatons. The TNT equivalence relationship is based on the fact that one ton of TNT releases one billion (10^9) calories of energy. See *kiloton energy, megaton energy, yield.*

topographic map. A map indicating surface elevation and slopes.

topsoil. The topmost layer of soil. It contains humus and is capable of supporting good plant growth.

transpiration. The process by which water vapor escapes from living plants and enters the atmosphere.

triage. In radiation diasters, the process of determining which casualties (from a large number of persons exposed to heavy radiation) need urgent treatment, which ones are well enough to go untreated, and which ones are beyond hope of benefit from treatment.

trickling-filter process. In wastewater treatment, a process in which the liquid from a primary clarifier is distributed on a bed of stones. As the wastewater trickles through the bed, its organic material is oxidized, and its impurities are reduced by slime organisms on the stones.

tritium. A radioactive isotope of hydrogen with two neutrons and one proton in the nucleus. It is man-made and is heavier than deuterium or heavy hydrogen. Tritium is used in industrial thickness gauges, and as a label in experiments in chemistry and biology. Its nucleus is a "triton."

trunk sewer. A sewer that transports wastewater from collecting sewers to the treatment plant.

turbidity. An empirical measure of the degree to which particles suspended in water interfere with light transmission, causing the light to be scattered and absorbed rather than transmitted through the water in straight lines. The particles usually consist of mud, clay, silt, finely divided organic matter, or microscopic organisms.

uranium. A radioactive element with the atomic number 92 and, as found in natural ores, an atomic weight of approximately 238. The two principal natural isotopes are uranium-235 (0.7% of natural uranium), which is fissionable, and uranium-238 (99.3% of natural uranium), which can be partially converted into fissionable isotopes by irradiation in a reactor. Natural uranium also includes a minute amount of uranium-234. Uranium is at present the basic raw material of nuclear energy.

user charge. In water supply systems, a charge for water based on the amount withdrawn from the public supply.

vadose water. Water clinging to rocks and soil between the water table and the surface of the earth.

vapor plume. Flue gas that is visible when it emerges from a stack because it contains condensed water droplets or mist.

vapor suppression, or **pressure suppression.** A safety system that can be incorporated in the design of structures housing water reactors. In the system, the space surrounding the reactor is vented into pools of water open to the outside air. If surges of hot vapors were released from the reactor in an accident, their energy (pressure) should be dissipated in the pools of water. Gases not condensed should be scrubbed clean of radioactive particles by the bubbling. Another system uses a suppression pool in a separate pressure vessel that can be vented through a stack.

wastewater, or sewage. Water carrying waste from homes, businesses, and industries. It is a liquid mixture of water and dissolved and suspended solids.

wastewater treatment. See *conventional wastewater treatment, primary wastewater treatment, intermediate wastewater treatment, secondary wastewater treatment, tertiary wastewater treatment*.

water cycle. See *hydrologic cycle*.

water table. The top of the zone in which all rocks are saturated with water. The subsurface water that lies below the water table is called "groundwater." Water lying between the water table and the earth's surface is called "vadose water."

watershed. The boundary of an area from which water drains to a single point. In a natural basin, the area contributing flow to a given place or a given point on a stream.

wet digestion. A solid-waste stabilization process in which mixed solid organic wastes are placed in an open digestion pond to decompose anaerobically.

wet scrubber. In a steel plant, a giant cylindrical shower that removes the stubborn particles or raw material (mostly oxides) remaining behind when the heated air that reduces ore, coke, and limestone to molten iron in the blast furnace swirls up the stack. The dust-laden liquid is pumped to a giant settling basin in which the particles drop to the bottom in a thick sludge, permitting the cleared water to overflow the top of the basin and return to the stream.

X-rays. A penetrating form of radiation emitted either when the inner orbital electrons of an excited atom return to their normal state (these are characteristic X-rays), or when a metal target is bombarded with high speed electrons (these are bremsstrahlung). X-rays are always nonnuclear in origin.

yield. The total energy released in a nuclear explosion. It is usually expressed in TNT equivalent. Low yield is generally considered to be a TNT equivalent of less than 20 kilotons; low intermediate yield from 20 to 200 kilotons; intermediate yield from 200 kilotons to 1 megaton. There is no standardized term to cover yields from 1 megaton upward.

Classified Index to Federal Agencies

This index lists federal agencies grouped alphabetically by subject category. The index also includes a number of subdivisions or individual units of the agencies; these listings, while not exhaustive, are intended to call attention to material that might otherwise be overlooked by the reader.

Air Resources and Pollution
    Air and Water Pollution Subcommittee, Public Works Committee, Senate, 40
    Air and Water Programs, EPA, 4
    Air Pollution Control Division, Research and Development, EPA, 5
    Committee on Biologic Effects of Atmospheric Pollutants, National Research Council, 38
    Committee on Motor Vehicle Emissions, National Research Council, 38
    Environmental Protection Agency, 2
    Land and Natural Resources Division, Justice Department, 26
    National Environmental Research Centers and Associated Laboratories, EPA, 5
    National Highway Traffic Safety Administration, 28
    National Oceanographic and Atmospheric Administration, 12
    Oceans and Atmosphere Subcommittee, Commerce Committee, Senate, 40

Energy
    Atomic Energy Commission, 29
    Bureau of Mines, 23
    Bureau of Reclamation, 25
    Communications and Power Subcommittee, Interstate and Foreign Commerce Committee, House, 42
    Delaware River Basin Commission, 32
    Energy Subcommittee, Public Works Committee, House, 42
    Energy Subcommittee, Science and Astronautics Committee, House, 43
    Federal Energy Office, 2
    Federal Maritime Commission, 32
    Federal Power Commission, 32
    Geological Survey, 21
    Minerals, Materials, and Fuels Subcommittee, Interior and Insular Affairs Committee, Senate, 40
    National Transportation Safety Board, 28
    Office of Coal Research, Interior Department, 18
    Office of Oil and Gas, Interior Department, 18
    Public Works, AEC Subcommittee, Appropriations Committee, Senate, 39
    Safety and Consumer Affairs Office, Transportation Department, 27
    Tennessee Valley Authority, 36
    Water and Power Resources Subcommittee, Interior and Insular Affairs Committee, House, 41
    Water and Power Resources Subcommittee, Interior and Insular Affairs Committee, Senate, 40

Environmental Education and Information
    Agricultural Research Service, 8
    Bureau of Mines, 23
    Bureau of Sport Fisheries and Wildlife, 20
    Director, Information Services, AEC, 29
    Environmental Data Service, National Oceanic and Atmospheric Administration, 12
    Environmental Protection Agency, 2
    Geological Survey, 21
    National Agricultural Library, 10
    National Institutes of Health, 17
    National Park Service, 21
    National Science Foundation, 33
    National Technical Information Service, 13
    Public Health Service, 15
    Smithsonian Institution, 34
    Smithsonian Science Information Exchange, 35

430 Classified Index to Federal Agencies

Youth Conservation Program, Bureau of Reclamation, 25
Environmental Health and Safety
Air and Water Programs, EPA, 4
Animal and Plant Health Inspection Service, USDA, 9
Appalachian Regional Commission, 29
Assistant Secretary for Health and Environment, Defense Department, 13
Atomic Energy Commission, 29
Bureau of Mines, 23
Environmental Protection Agency, 2
Food and Drug Administration, 15
Geological Survey, 21
Health Effects Division, Research and Development, EPA, 5
Health Services and Mental Health Administration, 16
National Institute of Occupational Safety and Health, 16
National Institutes of Health, 17
National Library of Medicine, 17
National Museum of Natural History, 35
Occupational Safety and Health Administration, 26
Occupational Safety and Health Review Commission, 34
Public Health and Environment Subcommittee, Interstate and Foreign Commerce Committee, House, 42
Public Health Service, 15
Safety and Consumer Affairs Office, Transportation Department, 27
Soil Conservation Service, 11
Systems Development and Technology Office, Transportation Department, 27
Environmental Quality
Agriculture, Environmental, and Consumer Protection Subcommittee, Appropriations Committee, House, 41
Agriculture, Environmental, and Consumer Protection Subcommittee, Appropriations Committee, Senate, 39
Army Corps of Engineers, 13
Assistant Secretary for Science and Technology, Commerce Department, 11
Citizens' Advisory Committee on Environmental Quality, 2
Committee on Pollution Abatement and Control, National Research Council, 38
Council on Environmental Quality, 2
Division of Biomedical and Environmental Research, AEC, 30
Ecological Processes and Effects Division, Research and Development, EPA, 5
Environment and Urban Systems Office, Transportation Department, 27

Environment Subcommittee, Commerce Committee, Senate, 40
Environment Subcommittee, Interior and Insular Affairs Committee, House, 41
Environmental Protection Agency, 2
Environmental Studies Board, National Research Council, 38
Geological Survey, 21
National Environmental Research Centers and Associated Laboratories, EPA, 5
National Museum of Natural History, 35
Research and Research Applications Divisions, National Science Foundation, 33
Soil Conservation Service, 11
Fish and Wildlife
Animal Science and Technology, National Institute of Environmental Health Sciences, 18
Army Corps of Engineers, 13
Bureau of Reclamation, 25
Bureau of Sport Fisheries and Wildlife, 20
Delaware River Basin Commission, 32
Fish and Wildlife Service, 20
Fisheries and Wildlife Conservation and the Environment Subcommittee, Merchant Marine and Fisheries Committee, House, 42
Forestry, Fisheries, and Wildlife Development Division, TVA, 36
Migratory Bird Conservation Commission, 36
National Marine Fisheries Service, 13
National Zoological Park, 35
Office of Environmental Sciences, Smithsonian Institution, 35
Shellfish Sanitation Division, Bureau of Foods, FDA, 15
Smithsonian Tropical Research Institute, 35
Western Fish Toxicology Laboratory, EPA, 6
Forestry
Agriculture and Forestry Committee, Senate, 39
Appalachian Regional Commission, 29
Delaware River Basin Commission, 32
Forest Service, 10
Forestry Division, Bureau of Land Management, 23
Forestry, Fisheries, and Wildlife Development Division, TVA, 36
Forests Subcommittee, Agriculture Committee, House, 41
National Forest Reservation Commission, 36
Land Use
Appalachian Regional Commission, 29
Army Corps of Engineers, 13
Bureau of Land Management, 23

Classified Index to Federal Agencies 431

Bureau of Mines, 23
Bureau of Outdoor Recreation, 24
Bureau of Sport Fisheries and Wildlife, 20
Delaware River Basin Commission, 32
Department of the Interior, 18
Economic Research Service, 9
Federal Power Commission, 32
Forest Service, 10
Geological Survey, 21
Land and Natural Resources Division, Justice Department, 26
Migratory Bird Conservation Commission, 36
National Park Service, 21
Public Lands Subcommittee, Interior and Insular Affairs Committee, House, 42
Public Lands Subcommittee, Interior and Insular Affairs Committee, Senate, 40
Tennessee Valley Authority, 36
Water Resources Council, 37

Law
Army Corps of Engineers, 13
Federal Maritime Commission, 32
Federal Power Commission, 32
Land and Natural Resources Division, Justice Department, 26
Occupational Safety and Health Administration, 26
Office of Hearings and Appeals, Interior Department, 19
Office of Legislation, EPA, 3

Natural Resources and Conservation
Agricultural Research Service, 8
Appalachian Regional Commission, 29
Army Corps of Engineers, 13
Bureau of Land Management, 23
Bureau of Mines, 23
Bureau of Outdoor Recreation, 24
Committee on Mineral Resources and the Environment, The National Research Council, 38
Delaware River Basin Commission, 32
Department of the Interior, 18
Earth Resources Observation Systems Program, Geological Survey, 22
Environment, Soil Conservation, and Forestry Subcommittee, Agriculture and Forestry Committee, Senate, 39
Federal Power Commission, 32
Forest Service, 10
Geological Survey, 21
Land and Natural Resources Division, Justice Department, 26
Minerals, Materials, and Fuels Subcommittee, Interior and Insular Affairs Committee, Senate, 40
National Museum of Natural History, 35

National Oceanographic and Atmospheric Administration, 12
Soil Conservation Service, 11
Tennessee Valley Authority, 36

Noise
Environmental Protection Agency, 2
Hazardous Materials Control, EPA, 4
Systems Development and Technology Office, Transportation Department, 27

Parks
Bureau of Outdoor Recreation, 24
Bureau of Sport Fisheries and Wildlife, 20
National Forest Reservation Commission, 36
National Park Foundation, 37
National Park Service, 21
National Parks and Recreation Subcommittee, Interior and Insular Affairs Committee, House, 41
Parks and Recreation Subcommittee, Interior and Insular Affairs Committee, Senate, 40

Pesticides
Committee on Effects of Herbicides, National Research Council, 38
Environmental Protection Agency, 2
Forest Pest Control Division, Forest Service, 10
Hazardous Materials Control, EPA, 4
Pesticides Enforcement Division, Enforcement and General Counsel, EPA, 3
Primate and Pesticide Effects Laboratory, EPA, 6

Population
Social and Economic Statistics Administration, 13

Radiation
Atomic Energy Commission, 29
Bureau of Radiological Health, FDA, 16
Center for Radiation Research, 12
Committee on Radioactive Waste Management, National Research Council, 38
Environmental Protection Agency, 2
Hazardous Materials Control, EPA, 4
Nuclear Test Ban Treaty Safeguards Subcommittee, Armed Services Committee, Senate, 39
Radiation Biology Laboratory, Smithsonian Institution, 35

Solid Waste
Appalachian Regional Commission, 29
Hazardous Materials Control, EPA, 4
Solid Wastes Division, Bureau of Mines, 24

Transportation
Advanced Automotive Power Systems Development Division, Air and Water Programs, EPA, 4
Appalachian Regional Commission, 29

432 Classified Index to Federal Agencies

Aviation Subcommittee, Commerce Committee, Senate, 40
Bureau of Outdoor Recreation, 24
Committee on Transportation, National Research Council, 39
Department of Transportation, 26
Federal Aviation Administration, 28
Federal Maritime Commission, 32
Highway Research Board, National Research Council, 38
Mississippi River Commission, 36
National Highway Traffic Safety Administration, 28
Roads Subcommittee, Public Works Committee, Senate, 41
Surface Transportation Subcommittee, Commerce Committee, Senate, 40
Transportation and Aeronautics Subcommittee, Interstate and Foreign Commerce Committee, House, 42
Transportation Subcommittee, Appropriations Committee, House, 41
Transportation Subcommittee, Appropriations Committee, Senate, 39
Transportation Subcommittee, Public Works Committee, House, 42
Urban Mass Transit Subcommittee, Banking and Currency Committee, House, 41

Water Resources and Pollution

Air and Water Pollution Subcommittee, Public Works Committee, Senate, 40
Air and Water Programs, EPA, 4
Appalachian Regional Commission, 29
Army Corps of Engineers, 13
Bureau of Reclamation, 25
Bureau of Sport Fisheries and Wildlife, 20
Delaware River Basin Commission, 32
Department of the Interior, 18
Economic Development Administration, 11
Economic Research Service, 9
Edison Water Quality Research Laboratory, EPA, 7
Engineering Committee on Oceanic Resources, National Resource Council, 39
Environmental Protection Agency, 2
Federal Maritime Commission, 32
Geological Survey, 21
Land and Natural Resources Division, Justice Department, 26
The Maritime Administration, 11
Mississippi River Commission, 36
National and International Programs, NSF, 33
National Marine Water Quality Laboratory, 6
National Oceanographic and Atmospheric Administration, 12
National Water Commission, 37
National Water Quality Laboratory, EPA, 6
Oceans and Atmosphere Subcommittee, Commerce Committee, Senate, 40
Office of Environmental Sciences, Smithsonian Institution, 35
Office of Saline Water, Interior Department, 18
Office of Water Resources Research, Interior Department, 19
Robert S. Kerr Water Research Center, EPA, 6
Soil Conservation Service, 11
Tennessee Valley Authority, 36
Water and Power Resources Subcommittee, Interior and Insular Affairs Committee, House, 41
Water and Power Resources Subcommittee, Interior and Insular Affairs Committee, Senate, 40
Water Resources Council, 37
Water Resources Subcommittee, Public Works Committee, House, 42
Water Resources Subcommittee, Public Works Committee, Senate, 40
Watershed Division, Bureau of Land Management, 23

Alphabetical Index

Indexed herein are the listings of government organizations, private organizations, individual consultants, and consulting firms.

AIR, Inc. (Aerostatics Instrumentation and Research, Inc.), 181
AMSCO Industrial Co., 173
Accu-Labs Research, Inc., 143
Acoustical and Insulating Materials Association, 129
Acoustical Society of America, 129
Acres, Inc., 99
Action for Clean Air, Inc., 100
Acurex Corp., 138
Adirondack Trail Improvement Society, 115
Advanced Acoustical Research Corp., 164
Advanced Waste Treatment Research Laboratory (U.S.), 6
Advisory Center on Toxicology (NRC), 38
Aeronautical and Space Sciences Committee, U.S. Senate, 39
Aeronautics and Space Technology Subcommittee, Science and Astronautics Committee, U.S. House, 42
Aeronca, Inc., Environmental Control Group, 169
African Wildlife Leadership Foundation, Inc., 75
Agri Development Co., 138
Agricultural Environmental Quality Institute (U.S.), 8
Agricultural Research Center (U.S.), 8
Agricultural Research Institute (NRC), 38
Agricultural Research Service (U.S.), 8
Agriculture and Forestry Committee, U.S. Senate, 39
Agriculture Committee, U.S. House, 41
Agriculture Department, U.S., 8
Agriculture, Environmental, and Consumer Protection Subcommittee, Appropriations Committee, U.S. House, 41
Agriculture, Environmental and Consumer Protection Subcommittee, Appropriations Committee, U.S. Senate, 39

Air and Water Pollution Subcommittee, Public Works Committee, U.S. Senate, 40
Air Pollution Committee, Essex County Medical Society, 111
Air Pollution Control Agency Committee, 110
Air Pollution Control Association, 76
Air Pollution Industries, Inc., 163
Aircon Corp., 169
Alabama, State of: government agencies, 43
Alabama Conservancy, 86
Alabama Environmental Quality Control, 86
Alabama Wildlife Federation, 86
Alaska, State of: government agencies, 43
Alaska Conservation Society, 87
Albertson Sharp & Associates, 144
Albuquerque Wildlife Federation, 114
Alken-Murray Corp., 165
Allen, Rhesa M., Jr., 154
Allen & Hoshall, Consulting Engineers, 177
Alliston, Charles W., 150
Alpert, Leo, 181
Alpha Laboratories, Inc., 173
Alvord, Burdick & Howson, 147
Ambient Purification Technology, Inc., 138
Ambient Systems, Inc., 165
Ambionic Designs, Inc., 165
American Academy of Environmental Engineers, 129
American Association for Conservation Information, 92
American Association for Health, Physical Education and Recreation, 129
American Association for the Advancement of Science, 76
American Association of State Highway Officials, 76
American Association of University Women, 76
American Camping Association, Inc., 130
American Cetacean Society, 76
American Chemical and Refining Co., Inc., 144

American Chemical Society, 130
American Committee for International Wild Life Protection, Inc., 76
American Environmental Systems Co., 165
American Fisheries Society, 130
American Forest Institute, 76
American Forestry Association, 76
American Gas Association, 130
American Health Foundation, 77
American Humane Association, 77
American Industrial Hygiene Association, 130
American Institute of Planners, 130
American Iron and Steel Institute, 130
American Littoral Society, 111
American Lung Association, 77
American Lung Association of Boston, 102
American Lung Association of New Jersey, 111
American Lung Association of Santa Clara-San Benito Counties, 88
American Mining Congress, 130
American Museum of Natural History, 77
American National Cattlemen's Association, 131
American Ornithologists Union, Inc., 77
American Paper Institute, 131
American Petroleum Institute, 131
American Pipe Services, Inc., 159
American Public Gas Association, 131
American Shore and Beach Preservation Association, 77
American Society of Limnology and Oceanography, 131
American Society of Planning Officials, 77
American Sportsman Club, Inc., 142
American Standards Testing Bureau, Inc., 165
American Trucking Association, 131
American Water Resources Association, 131
Analytical Quality Research Laboratory (U.S.), 6
Andco Environmental Processes, Inc., 165
Anderson, Gery F., 138
Anderson, Jay E., 143
Anderson and Angevine, Inc., 165
Andrews, Ted F., 148
Animal and Plant Health Inspection Service (U.S.), 9
Animal Parasitology Institute (U.S.), 8
Animal Physiology and Genetics Institute (U.S.), 8
Anti-Pollution League, 111
Appalachian Laboratory for Occupational Respiratory Diseases (U.S.), 17
Appalachian Mountain Club, 102
Appalachian Regional Commission (U.S.), 29
Appalachian Trail Conference, 127
Applied Naturalist Guild, 101
Applied Technology Corp., 173
Appropriations Committee, U.S. House, 41
Appropriations Committee, U.S. Senate, 39
Apt, Bramer, Conrad & Associates, Inc., 173
Aqualogic, Inc., 144
Aquarium Systems, Inc., 169
Aquatic Control, Inc., 150
Aquatic Sciences, Inc., 145
Arctic Environmental Research Laboratory (U.S.), 6
Arctic Health Research Center (U.S.), 17
Arizona, State of: government agencies, 44
Arkansas, State of: government agencies, 44
Arkansas Ecology Center, 87
Arkansas Federation of Water and Air Users, 87
Arkansas Waterways Commission, 88
Armed Services Committee, U.S. Senate, 39
Armstrong, Frank Harris, 181
Army Corps of Engineers, U.S., 13
  Field Offices, 14
Arnold, Frank D., 155
ArRo Labs, Inc., 148
Asbestos Cement Products Association, 136
Asbestos Textile Institute, 131
Association for Preservation of Cape Cod, 102
Association for Voluntary Sterilization, Inc., 77
Association of American Pesticide Control Officials, 131
Association of Conservation Engineers, 131
Association of Interpretive Naturalists, 132
Association of Midwest Fish and Game Commissioners, 107, 119
Association of New Jersey Environmental Commissions, 111
Atlantic County Citizens Council on Environment, Inc., 111
Atomic Energy Commission, U.S., 29
Audubon Council of Kentucky, 100
Audubon Society, National, 82
Audubon Society of Birmingham, 87
Audubon Society of Florida, 94
Audubon Society of Greater Knoxville, 123
Audubon Society of Hawaii, 96
Audubon Society of Illinois, 97
Audubon Society of Jackson, Miss., 108
Audubon Society of Massachusetts, 104
Audubon Society of Michigan, 106
Audubon Society of Missouri, 108
Audubon Society of Mobile Bay, 87
Audubon Society of New Hampshire, 110
Audubon Society of New Jersey, 113
Audubon Society of Penobscot Valley, Maine, 101
Audubon Society of Portland, Maine, 101
Audubon Society of Rhode Island, 122
Audubon Society Western Regional Office, 90
Ault, Curtis H., 150
Austin, George S., 150
Austin Co., Process Div., 148

Austin, Smith & Associates, Inc., 147
Automated Environmental Systems, Inc., 165
Aviation Subcommittee, Commerce Committee, U.S. Senate, 40

BC Laboratories, 138
Badger Co., Inc., 156
Bagby, John R., Jr., 143
Bagley, Walter T., 162
Baker, Michael, Jr., Inc., 173
Balarat Center for Environmental Studies, 92
Baldauf, Richard J., 160
Baldwin & Cornelius Co., 165
Banister, A.W., Co., Inc., 156
Banking and Currency Committee, U.S. House, 41
Banking, Housing, and Urban Affairs Committee, U.S. Senate, 39
Banner, J.T., & Associates, Inc., 176
Barefoot, B.B., and Associates, Inc., 173
Barer, Seymour, 163
Barnebey-Cheney Co., 169
Barnstead Co., 156
Barrow-Agee Lab., Inc., 177
Bartlett-Snow, 170
Bayou Preservation Association, Inc., 124
Beadles, John Kenneth, 138
Beaufort Environmental Protection Association, 122
Bechtel Corp., 138
Beck, R.W., and Associates, 182
Becker, Leroy E., 150
Beco Engineering Co., 173
Bell, Bruce, 165
Bell, Howard K., Consulting Engineers, Inc., 153
Beltran Associates, Inc., 165
Bendixen, Leo E., 170
Bendy Engineering Co., 160
Benham-Blair & Affiliates, Inc., 172
Benjamin, Daniel M., 183
Berger, Louis, Inc., 163
Berkshire Natural Resources Council, Inc., 103
Bernalillo County Planned Parenthood Association, 114
Betz Environmental Engineers, Inc., 174
Bickel, Victor R., 164
Bicycle Ecology, 96
Bigelow-Liptak Corp., 158
Biggs, Maurice E., 150
Bilbyrne Corp., 165
Billings & Gussman, Inc., 156
Biomedical and Environmental Research and Safety Programs (U.S.), 30
Biometric Testing, Inc., 163
Biospheric, Inc., 155

Bird and Mammal Laboratories (U.S.), 20
Bituminous Coal Research, Inc., 132
Black & Veatch, 160
Black, Crow, & Eidsness, Inc., 145
Bleuer, Ned K., 151
Bloodgood, Don E., 151
Blue Plains Pilot Plant (U.S.), 7
Bogert, Clinton, Associates, 163
Boley, Hal D., 138
Bonham, Grant & Brundage Ltd., 170
Booy, Emmy, 158
Boston Environment, Inc., 103
Boston Industrial Mission, 103
Bostrack, Jack M., 183
Bough, Wayne A., 147
Bounty Information Service, 78
Boush, George Mallory, 183
Boutwell, Richard A., 160
Bovay Engineers, Inc., 154, 178, 182
Boy Scouts of America, 78
Braids, Olin C., 165
Brandt Associates, Inc., 145
Brandywine Valley Sales Co., 174
Briley, Wild & Associates, 145
Brinkerhoff, Fred, 152
Brockway, Owen & Anderson Engineers, Inc., 145
Bronstein, Daniel A., 158
Brooklin Center Conservation Commission, 107
Brown, Bahngrell Walter, 160
Brown, Dayton T., Inc., 165
Brown, Henry S., 169
Brown, Kirk W., 178
Brown, Richard D., 151
Brown, Sanford M., 177
Brown & Root, Inc., 178
Brown Engineering Co., 152
Bucher & Willis, 153
Buck, Seifert and Jost, 163
Buffalo Testing Laboratories, Inc., 165
Bureau of Drugs (U.S.), 16
Bureau of Foods (U.S.), 15
Bureau of Land Management (U.S.), 23
Bureau of Mines (U.S.), 23
Bureau of Outdoor Recreation (U.S.), 24
Bureau of Radiological Health (U.S.), 16
Bureau of Reclamation (U.S.), 25
    Regional Offices, 25
Bureau of Sport Fisheries and Wildlife, 20
    Regional Directors, 21
Bureau of Surface Transportation Safety (U.S.), 28
Burnett, Thomas E., 155
Burns, Paul Y., 154
Burns & McDonnell Engineering Co., 160
Burns and Roe, Inc., 163
Buscemi, Philip A., 164
Busser, Robert A., 170

Byers, Horace R., 178
Byron Instruments, Inc., 169

CH₂M/Hill, 181
CWC Industries, Inc., 170
Calcinator Corp., 158
Cale, Richard E., 138
Calgon Corp., 174
California, State of: government agencies, 45
California Academy of Sciences, 88
California Anti-Litter League, 88
California Roadside Council, Inc., 88
Calvert, Willard R., 155
Cambridge Acoustical Associates, Inc., 156
Camp Dresser & McKee, Inc., 138, 156
Camp Fire Girls, Inc., 78
Campbell, David C., 147
Campbell, George S., & Associates, Inc., 177
Canandaigua Lake Pure Waters, Ltd., 115
Carborundum Co., Pollution Control Div., 177
Cardenas, Raul, Jr., 165
Caribbean Conservation Association, 126
Carney, J.H., 137
Carolina Bird Club, Inc., 119
Carpart Corp., 158
Carpenter, Alden B., 160
Carpenter, Jot D., 170
Carr, Donald D., 151
Carroll, Maurice, 178
Carus Chemical Co., Inc., 148
Caskey, Albert L., 148
Catalytic, Inc., 174
Cate, William, 160
Cavanaugh and Copley, 156
Center for Environmental Communication and Education Studies, 127
Center for Environmental Studies, 103
Center for Law and Social Policy, 78
Center for Radiation Research (U.S.), 12
Center for Short-Lived Phenomena (U.S.), 35
Central Atlantic Environment Center, 94
Centri-Spray Corp., 158
Chafetz, Henry, 178
Chamblee Toxicology Laboratory (U.S.), 6
Chartock, Michael A., 172
Chase, Craig C., 174
Chastain, Homer L., & Associates, 148
Chem Systems, Inc., 165
Chemec Process Systems, Inc., 165
Chemed Corp., Dearborn Chemical Div., 148
Chemical Separations Corp., 177
Chemical Specialties Manufacturers Association, 132
Chemico, 165
Chemitrol Co., 148

Chesapeake Bay Center for Environmental Studies (U.S.), 35
Chesapeake Bay Foundation, Inc., 101
Chester Engineers, Inc., 174
Chicago Aerial Survey, 148
Chu, Ju Chin, 139
Ciaccio, Leonard L., 163
Cincinnati Field Investigation Center (U.S.), 6
Circle K Club, 111
Citizen Action Against Pollution, 94
Citizens' Advisory Committee on Environmental Quality (U.S.), 2
Citizens Against Noise, 97
Citizens Against Water Pollution, 111
Citizens Committee for Environmental Protection, 111
Citizens Ecology Committee, 115
Citizens Environmental Coalition, 124
Citizens for a Better Environment (Illinois), 97
Citizens for a Better Environment (New York), 115
Citizens for a Better Environment (Texas), 124
Citizens for a Clean Environment, 115
Citizens for Better Environment Research Department, 97
Citizens for Clean Air (Georgia), 95
Citizens for Clean Air, Inc. (New York), 115
Citizens for Clean Air and Water, Inc. (Ohio), 120
Citizens for Clean Air and Water (N. Mex.), 136
Citizens for Conservation, 112
Citizens for Environmental Action, 112
Citizens for Hike and Bike, 124
Citizens League Against the Sonic Boom, 78
Citizens Natural Resources Association of Wisconsin, Inc., 127
City Planners Association of Texas, 124
Clark, Dayle M., 178
Clark & Groff Engineers, Inc., 173
Clark, Dietz & Associates-Engineers, Inc., 148
Clausen, Judith H., 156
Clayton, George D., & Associates, 158
Clean Air, 120
Clean Air Coordinating Committee, 97
Clean Air Council, 112
Clear Air, Clear Water Unlimited, 107
Coalition for Environmental Quality, 103
Coast Guard and Navigation Subcommittee, Merchant Marine and Fisheries Committee, U.S. House, 42
Coastal Ecosystems Management, Inc., 178
Coffin & Richardson, Inc., 156
Cohasset Environmental Action, 103
Cole, Chas. W., & Son, Inc., 151
Coleman, Richard W., 152
Colorado, State of: government agencies, 45
Colorado Citizens for Clean Air, 92

Colorado Institute on Population Problems, 92
Colorado Open Space Council, Inc., 92
Colorado River Wildlife Council, 110
Colorado Water Congress, 92
Colorado Wildlife Federation, Inc., 92
Columbus Water and Air Association, 99
Columbus Water and Chemical Testing Lab., 170
Combustion Power Co., Inc., 139
Combustion Unlimited, Inc., 174
Commerce Committee, U.S. Senate, 39
Commerce Department, U.S., 11
Commercial Testing & Engineering Co., 148
Committee for National Arbor Day, 78
Committee for the Preservation of the Tule Elk, 88
Committee on Environmental Quality, 100
Committee on Lake Michigan Pollution, 97
Committee on Urban Environment, 107
Commonwealth Associates, Inc., 158
Commonwealth Laboratory, Inc., 181
Communications and Power Subcommittee, Interstate and Foreign Commerce Committee, U.S. House, 42
Communications Subcommittee, Commerce Committee, U.S. Senate, 40
Community Pride Recycling Center, 136
Compact Air Samplers, 170
Concerned Citizens for Conservation, 94
Connecticut, State of: government agencies, 46
Connecticut Association of Soil and Water Conservation Districts, Inc., 93
Connecticut Conservation Association, 93
Connecticut Forest and Park Association, 93
Connecticut River Watershed Council, Inc., 103
Connecticut Wildlife Federation, 93
Conner, David Allen, 177
Conner, John V., 154
Conservation and Environmental Studies Center, Inc., 78
Conservation and Research Foundation, Inc., 93
Conservation Associates, 136
Conservation Council of North Carolina, 119
Conservation Education Council of Maryland, 102
Conservation Federation of Missouri, 109
Conservation Foundation, 78
Conservation Foundation of Missouri Charitable Trust, 109
Conservation Law Foundation of New England, Inc., 103
Conservation Services, Inc., 104
Conservation Society of Southern Vermont, 125
Consolidated Technology, Inc., 166
Consumer Affairs Subcommittee, Banking and Currency Committee, U.S. House, 41
Consumer Alliance, Inc., 89

Consumer Federation of America, 79
Consumer Subcommittee, Commerce Committee, U.S. Senate, 40
Consumers' Research, 79
Contamination Control Labs., Inc., 158
Controlled Thermonuclear Research Division, AEC (U.S.), 30
Controls for Environmental Pollution, Inc., 164
Cook, John B., 146
Cook Research Labs., Inc., 139
Cooling Tower Institute, 132
Cooper Ornithological Society, 89
Copley International Corp., 139
Corbin, H. Dan, 151
Core Laboratories, Inc., 178
Corning Labs, Inc., 152
Cotter, James F., 139
Council for Planning and Conservation, 89
Council on Environmental Quality (U.S.), 2
Council on Population and Environment, 79
Cox, Edwin, Associates, 181
Craig Chemical Consulting Services, Inc., 174
Crain, Clark N., 143
Crawford & Russell, Inc., 144
Crobaugh Laboratories, 170
Crown Pilot Plant (U.S.), 7
Crusade for a Cleaner Environment, 79
Cullinan, Terrence, 139
Cutright, Noel J., 166

Dairy Research, Inc., 132
Daly, Leo A., Co., 162
Dames & Moore, 166
Daniel, Ronald S., 139
Danto, Joseph, 166
Daughters of the American Revolution National Society, 79
Davidoff, Charles, 166
Davidson, John H., Jr., 176
Deady Chemical Co., 152
DeBell & Richardson, Inc., 144
Defenders of Wildlife, 79
Defense Department, U.S., 13
DeLaureal Engineers, Inc., 154
Delaware, State of: government agencies, 46
Delaware River Basin Commission (U.S.), 32
Delaware Wildlife Federation, 93
Demopulos & Ferguson, Inc., 154
Dempster Brothers, Inc., 177
Denio, Allen A., 183
Denney, Richard N., 143
Department of Agriculture, U.S., 8
Department of Commerce, U.S., 11
Department of Defense, U.S., 13
Department of Health, Education, and Welfare, U.S., 15

Department of Justice, U.S., 26
Department of Labor, U.S., 26
Department of the Interior, U.S., 18
Department of Transportation, U.S., 26
Desert Protective Council, Inc., 89
Detailed Engineered Equipment Corp., 178
Detroit Area Coalition for the Environment, 106
Detroit Testing Laboratory, 158
Deutsch, Stuart L., 139
Dewers, Robert S., 178
DeWild Grant Reckert and Associates Co., 152
Dickinson, William A., Jr., 139
Dillingham Environmental Co., 139
Disaster Relief Subcommittee, Public Works Committee, U.S. Senate, 41
District of Columbia: local government agencies, 47
Doepke, Philip A., 158
Domingue, Szabo and Associates, Inc., 154
Donaldson Co., Inc., 159
Dornblatt, B.M., & Associates, Inc., 154
Drew Chemical Corp., 163
Driscoll, Arthur Edward, 156
Ducks Unlimited, 79
Dumas, Philip C., 182
Duncan, Donald P., 161
Du Pont de Neymours, E.I., and Co., Inc., 145
Dusart, Etienne R., 176
Dutterer, Dennis A., 145
Dykeman, Peter A., 166
Dynamic Development, 139

EKONO, 182
EROS Program (U.S.), 22
Eagle Valley Environmentalists, Inc., 97
Earth Action, 127
Earth Awareness Foundation, 124
Earth Resources Observation Systems (U.S.), 32
Earth Science Laboratories, Inc., 170
East Michigan Environmental Action Council, 106
Eastman, Robert M., 161
Eckblad, James W., 152
Eckenfelder, W. Wesley, Jr., 177
Eckrich, Peter, & Sons, Inc.
Eco Center, 112
EcoDynamics, Inc., 181
Ecologic Instruments Corp., 166
Ecological Science Corp., 146
Ecology Action for Rhode Island, 122
Ecology Action of Austin, 124
Ecology Action of Florida, Inc., 136
Ecology & Environment, Inc., 166
Ecology Audits, Inc., 178

Ecology Center, 89, 115
Ecology Center of Louisiana, 101
Ecolotrol, Inc., 166
Economic Development Administration (U.S.), 11
Economic Development Subcommittee, Public Works Committee, U.S. Senate, 40
Economic Research Service (U.S.), 9
Ecotech, 139
Edison Electric Institute, 132
Edison Water Quality Research Laboratory (U.S.), 7
Edminster Hinshaw and Associates, Inc., 178
Edwards, William R., 148
Egan, M. David, 154
Elm Research Institute, 79
Ely Field Station (U.S.), 6
Empire Blower Co., Inc., 166
Endangered Species Committee of Berkeley, 89
Energex, Ltd., 139
Energy and Development Programs, AEC (U.S.), 31
Energy Policy Office (U.S.), 2
Energy Subcommittee, Public Works Committee, U.S. House, 42
Energy Subcommittee, Science and Astronautics Committee, U.S. House, 43
Engelhard Minerals & Chemicals Corp., 163
Engine Manufacturers Association, 132
Engineered Environments, 144
Engineering Chemical Services, Inc., 163
Engineering Dynamics International, 161
Enright, Richard, 156
Envirodyne, Inc., 139
Enviro-Engineers, Inc., 139
Environics, Inc., 139
Environistics, Division of Instrument Systems Corp., 166
Environment Council of Rhode Island, 122
Environment, Soil Conservation and Forestry Subcommittee, Agriculture and Forestry Committee, U.S. Senate, 39
Environment Subcommittee, Commerce Committee, U.S. Senate, 40
Environment Subcommittee, Interior and Insular Affairs Committee, U.S. House, 41
Environment Wisconsin, 127
Environmental Action Coalition, Inc., 115
Environmental Action Committee, 93
Environmental Action Foundation, 80
Environmental Advisory Board, 94
Environmental Awareness Committee, 127
Environmental Clearing House Organization, Inc., 115
Environmental Commission of the Incorporated Village of Roslyn, 116
Environmental Conservation Advisory Board Incorporated Village of Port Jefferson, 116

Environmental Consultants, Inc., 151
Environmental Consumers' Education Council, 124
Environmental Data Service (U.S.), 12
Environmental Defense Fund, Inc., 80, 89
Environmental Engineering, Inc., 146
Environmental Engineering Lab., Inc., 139
Environmental Engineers, Inc., 158
Environmental Forum, Inc., 97
Environmental Information Center, 136
Environmental Information Center of the Florida Conservation Foundation, Inc., 94
Environmental Law Council of N.H., 110
Environmental Law Institute, 80
Environmental Law Society of Boston University, 104
Environmental Management, Inc., 156
Environmental Measurements, Inc., 139
Environmental Parameters Research Organization, 97
Environmental Planning and Information Center, 121
Environmental Planning Lobby, 116
Environmental Policy Center, 80
Environmental Political Action, 112
Environmental Protection Agency (U.S.), 2
  Air and Water Programs, 4
  National Environmental Research Centers and Associated Laboratories, 4
  Regional Offices, 7
  Research and Development, 5
Environmental Quality Analysts, Inc., 140
Environmental Quality Engineering, Inc., 140
Environmental Research & Applications, Inc., 166
Environmental Research Corp., 159
Environmental Science and Engineering Corp., 177
Environmental Sciences, Inc., 174
Environmental Service Center, Inc., 166
Environmental Tectonics Corp., 174
Environmental Toxicology Research Laboratory (U.S.), 6
Erdman, Howard E., 178
Erickson, E.T., Water Technology Consultants, 148
Essex Citizens Conservation Organization, 112
Experimental Biology Laboratory (U.S.), 6

F & J Scientific, 144
Faith, W.L., 140
Farm Electrification Council, 132
Federal Aviation Administration, 28
Federal Energy Office, 2
Federal Executive Departments, 8
Federal Maritime Commission, 32

Federal Power Commission, 32
Federation of New York State Bird Clubs, Inc., 116
Ferguson, H.K., Co., 170
Ferro Corp., 170
Ferro-Tech, Inc., 174
Fillmore, C.F. Earney, 158
Filters, Inc., 178
Fink, Rodney J., 148
First Society of Whale Watchers, 96
Fish and Wildlife Service (U.S.), 20
Fisher, W.L., 178
Fisheries and Wildlife Conservation and the Environment Subcommittee, Merchant Marine and Fisheries Committee, U.S. House, 42
Florida, State of: government agencies, 47
Florida Council for Clean Air, 94
Florida Defenders of the Environment, Inc., 94
Florida Forestry Association, 94
FluiDyne Engineering Corp., 159
Fluor Corp., 140
Foerster, E.L., Sr., 174
Food and Drug Administration (U.S.), 15
Food and Drug Law Institute, 132
Food Forum, 136
Forest History Society, Inc., 89
Forest Service (U.S.), 10
Forests Subcommittee, Agriculture Committee, U.S. House, 41
Foth & Van Dyke and Associates, Inc., 183
Four States Wildlife Association, 88
Foxboro Co., 156
Fram Corp., Industrial Div., 172
Framherz Engineers, 154
Frank, Sidney R., Group, 140
Frankfurter and Associates, Inc., 182
Frederiksen Engineering Co., Inc., 140
Freeman Laboratories, Inc., 148
Frerichs, Bernard H., 182
Fribourg, Henry August, 177
Friedmann, Arnold, 156
Friends of Africa in America, 116
Friends of Animals, Inc., 80
Friends of Nature, Inc., 101
Friends of the Earth, 80
Friends of the Hudson, 112
Friends of the Sea Otter, 89
Friends of the Wilderness, 107
Frumerman Associates, Inc., 174
Future Farmers of America, 80

GCA Technology Div., 156
Gamlen Chemical Co., 163
Gannett Fleming Corddry & Carpenter, Inc., 174

Garden Club of Illinois, Inc.—Environmental Improvement, 97
Gardner, Walter A., 169
Garrell, Martin Henry, 166
Garrett, Harold E., 154
Garrett-Callahan Co., 140
Geisman, J.R., 170
General Environments Corp., 182
Genesee Valley Environment Association, 116
Geo-Engineering Labs., Inc., 148
Geological Survey (U.S.), 21
Geomet, Inc., 140
Georgia, State of: government agencies, 48
Georgia Conservancy, Inc., 95
Georgia Environmental Education Council, 95
Georgia Forest Research Council, 95
Georgia Tuberculosis and Respiratory Disease Association, 95
Gerdes, Raymond A., 179
Gilbert, Douglas L., 143
Gilbert Associates, Inc., 174
Gillman, Joseph, Associates, 145
Gilwood, Martin, Associates, 163
Girl Scouts of the United States of America, 80
Glass Container Manufacturers Institute, 132
Gold-Marc Industries, Inc., 166
Gollob Analytical Service, Inc., 163
Good Outdoors Manners Association, 126
Gray, Henry H., 151
Greater Boston Committee on the Transportation Crisis, 104
Green, John I., 166
Greenberg, Robert E., 148
Greengard, Charles W., Associates, Inc., 149
Greichus, Yvonne A., 176
Griffin, Gordon S., 161
Griffith Engineering, 182
Grosse Isle Laboratory (U.S.), 6
Gulf and Caribbean Fisheries Institute, 132
Gulf Breeze Environmental Research Laboratory (U.S.), 6
Gulf States Pollution Control, Inc., 179
Gupta, G.C., 160
Gurney, W.B., Associates, 154
Gurnham and Associates, Inc., 149

Haefeli, Robert J., 163
Hahn Labs., 176
Hale & Kullgren Associates, Inc., 170
Haley and Ward, Inc., 156
Halff, Albert H., Associates, Inc., 179
Haner, Ross & Sporseen, Inc., 173
Hardwood Research Council, 133
Harp, George L., 138
Harper, George L., 140
Harpers Ferry Center (U.S.), 21

Harr, Thomas H. Vonder, 144
Harris, Frederic R., Inc., 166
Harris Laboratories, Inc., 162
Hartke, Edwin J., 151
Harvard Environmental Law Society, 104
Haskins, Sharp & Ordelheide, 161
Hawaii, State of: government agencies, 49
Hawaii Wildlife Federation, 136
Hawk, Virgil B., 138
Hawksley, Ray W., Co., Inc., 140
Hayden, Harding & Buchanan, Inc., 156
Hazleton Labs, Inc., 182
Health, Education, and Welfare Department, U.S., 15
Health Services and Mental Health Administration (U.S.), 16
Health Subcommittee, Labor and Public Welfare Committee, U.S. Senate, 40
Heath Consultants, Inc., 156
Heberlein, Thomas A., 183
Hedrick, Harold G., 154
Heen & Flint Associates, 166
Heidinger, James, 176
Heil Process Equipment Corp., 170
Hemeon Associates, 174
Hendendorf, Charles E., 170
Heneghan, W.F., Associates, 144
Henning, Daniel H., 162
Herke, William H., 154
Herkimer County Board of Cooperative Educational Services, 116
Herron Testing Labs, Inc., 170
Heyward-Robinson Co., Inc., 166
Hickok, E.A., & Associates, 159
Hicks, K.L., 146
Hill, John R., 151
Hill, John W., 183
Hinchman Co., 158
Hirt Combustion Engineers, 140
Hittman Associates, Inc., 155
Hoad Engineers, Inc., 158
Hoffman, George, 176
Holcomb, Larry C., 162
Holley, Kenney, Schott, Inc., 174
Holt, Ben, Co., 140
Holzmacher, McLendon & Murrell, 167
Horn, B. Ray, 158
Horner & Shifrin, Inc., 161
Horvath, D.J., 183
Housewives to End Pollution, 116
Housing and Urban Development, Space, Science, Veterans Subcommittee, Appropriations Committee, U.S. House, 41
Housing and Urban Development, Space, Science, Veterans Subcommittee, Appropriations Committee, U.S. Senate, 39
Housing Subcommittee, Banking and Currency Committee, U.S. House, 41

Housing Subcommittee, Banking, Housing, and Urban Affairs Committee, U.S. Senate, 39
Houston Research Inc., 179
Howard, Needles, Tammen & Bergendoff, 161
Hoydysh, Walter G., 167
Huang, Ju Chang, 161
Hubbell, Roth & Clark, Inc., 158
Hudson, John D., 184
Hugh Moore Fund, 136
Human Environment House, 106
Huth Engineers, Inc., 174
Hydro Combustion Corp., 140
Hydromation Filter Co., 159
Hytek International Corp., 170

IBM, Federal Systems Div., 155
IIT Research Institute, 149
IKOR, Inc., 157
Idaho, State of: government agencies, 49
Idaho Environmental Council, 96
Illinois, State of: government agencies, 50
Illinois Citizens Clean Air League, 98
Illinois Planning and Conservation League, 98
Illinois Prairie Path, 98
Illinois Water Treatment Co., 149
Illinois Wildlife Federation, 98
Illinois Women's Conservation, 136
Incinerator Institute of America, 133
Indiana, State of: government agencies, 51
Indiana Conservation Council, Inc., 99
Industrial Acoustics Co., Inc., 167
Industrial Filter & Pump Mfg. Co., 149
Industrial Health Foundation, Inc., 133
Industrial Noise Services, 140
Industrial Pollution Control, Inc., 144
Industrial Process Engineers, 163
Industrial Services of America, Inc., 153
Ingram, William T., 167
Inland Bird Banding Association, 109
Innis, George S., 143
Insect Identification and Beneficial Insect Introduction Institute (U.S.), 8
Institute for Applied Technology (U.S.), 12
Institute for Basic Standards (U.S.), 12
Institute for Environmental Education, 120
Institute for Materials Research (U.S.), 12
Institute for Research, Inc., 179
Institute for Storm Research, 179
Institute of Environmental Sciences, 98
Institute of Paper Chemistry, 133
Inter Industry Emission Control Program, 133
Interex Corp., 157
Interior and Insular Affairs Committee, U.S. House, 41
Interior and Insular Affairs Committee, U.S. Senate, 40

Interior Department, U.S., 18
Interior Subcommittee, Appropriations Committee, U.S. House, 41
Interior Subcommittee, Appropriations Committee, U.S. Senate, 39
International Acoustical Testing Labs., Inc., 159
International Air Transport Association, 133
International Association for Pollution Control, 81
International Association of Game, Fish and Conservation Commissioners, 81
International Cooperation in Science and Space Subcommittee, Science and Astronautics Committee, U.S. House, 43
International Crocodilian Society, 81
International Defenders of Animals, Inc., 95
International Game Fish Association, 81
International Hydronics Corp., 163
International Institute for Environmental Affairs, 136
International Pacific Salmon Fisheries Commission, 81
International Pollution Control, Inc., 179
Interprofessional Council on Environmental Design, 81
Interstate and Foreign Commerce Committee, U.S. House, 42
InterTechnology Corp., 182
Ion Exchange Products, Inc., 149
Iowa, State of: government agencies, 51
Iowa Wildlife Federation, Inc., 99
Island Resources Foundation, Inc., 126
Izaak Walton League of America, 81
Izaak Walton League, Kentucky Division, 100
Izaak Walton League, Minnesota Division, 107
Izaak Walton League, Nebraska Division, 110
Izaak Walton League, New York Division, 116
Izaak Walton League, Pennsylvania Division, 121
Izaak Walton League, Wisconsin Division, 128

JBF Scientific Corp., 157
Jahoda, John C., 157
James, Wesley P., 179
Janke, Delmar L., 179
Jayne, Benjamin A., 183
Jebens, Harold J., 184
Johns-Manville, 143
Johnson, Bernard, Engineers, Inc., 179
Johnson, Frederick D., 147
Johnson & Anderson, Inc., 159
Johnson, Depp & Quisenberry, 153
Johnston, Guy H., Associates, 154
Jones, Brian M., 170
Jones & Henry Engineers, Ltd., 171

Jordan, Edward C., Co., Inc., 155
Justice Department, U.S., 26

K-N-B Inc., 179
Kaiser Engineers, 140
Kamarasy, Efon K., 149
Kansas, State of: government agencies, 52
Kansas Wildlife Federation, Inc., 100
Katzen, Raphael, Associates, 171
Keep America Beautiful, Inc., 119
Keep Florida Beautiful, Inc., 95
Kelley, Fenton C., 147
Kellogg, M.W., Co., 179
Kelly, Frank J., 179
Kemlon Products and Development Co., 179
Kem-Tech Laboratories, Inc., 154
Kenco Associates, Inc., 153
Kennedy Engineers, Inc., 140
Kenney, Richard A., 145
Kentucky, State of: government agencies, 52
Kentucky Lung Association, 100
Kerr, Gerald C., 154
Kingsbury, P.J., 152
Kinney, A.M., Inc., 171
Kirkham, Michael & Associates, 162
Klages, Murray G., 162
Klehr, Edwin H., 172
Klemas, Vytautas, 145
Klenz-Aire, Inc., 153
Knight, Lester B., & Associates, Inc., 149
Knowles, Morris, Inc., 174
Kodaras, Michael J., Inc., 167
Koebig & Koebig, Inc., 140
Konečny, Jaro A., 155
Kral, Zepf, Freitag & Associates, 171
Kribel, Robert E., 152
Krick, Irving P., Associates, Inc., 140
Kuljian Corp., 174
Kury, Channing R., 164

LFE Corp., 140
Labisky, Ronald F., 149
Labor and Public Welfare Committee, U.S. Senate, 40
Labor Department, U.S., 26
Labor; Health, Education and Welfare Subcommittee, Appropriations Committee, U.S. House, 41
Labor; Health, Education, and Welfare Subcommittee, Appropriations Committee, U.S. Senate, 39
Labor Subcommittee, Labor and Public Welfare Committee, U.S. Senate, 40
Laboratory of Ornithology, 116

Labrum, Miles C., 181
Lace Engineering, 179
Lacz Associates, Inc., 163
Laicon, Inc., 149
Lake Erie Watershed Conservation Foundation, 120
Lake Michigan Federation, 98
Lamb, George M., 137
Lancy Laboratories, 174
Land and Natural Resources Division, U.S. Justice Dept., 26
Land Improvement Contractors of America, 133
Land Use Foundation of New Hampshire, 110
Landstrom, Karl S., 182
Langley, McDonald & Overman, 182
Langston Laboratories, Inc., 153
Laramore, Douglas and Popham, 149
Larsen, Perry A., 143
Lau, Inc., 171
Lavin, Marve H., 152
League for Conservation Legislation, 112
League of Conservation Voters, 81
League of Women Voters of Alabama, 87
League of Women Voters of Florida, 95
League of Women Voters of Kentucky, 100
League of Women Voters of New Jersey, 112
League of Women Voters of New York State, 117
League of Women Voters of North Carolina, 119
League of Women Voters of Texas, 124
League of Women Voters of the United States, 81
League of Women Voters of the Virgin Islands, 126
League of Women Voters of Wisconsin, 128
League to Save Lake Tahoe, 89
Lebanon Pilot Plant (U.S.), 7
Legislative Subcommittee, Appropriations Committee, U.S. House, 41
Leininger, Richard K., 151
Lester Laboratories, Inc., 147
Levi, Robert S., and Associates, 149
Levit, Joseph L., 157
Lewis, C.G., 161
Liberty Industries, Inc., 144
Life of the Land, 96
Limnetics, Inc., 184
Lindberg, James G., 152
Little, Arthur D., Inc., 157
Lockwood, Andrews & Newman, Inc., 179
Lockwood Greene Engineers, Inc., 167
Lombard Corp., 171
Long Island Environmental Council, Inc., 117
Louisiana, State of: government agencies, 53
Louisiana Forestry Association, 101
Ludwig Consulting Engineers, 154

Lyon Associates, Inc., 155
Lyon Chemicals, Inc., 159

McAllister, Decker G., Jr., Consulting Engineers, 140
McCabe, DeSoto B., 146
McCallum Inspection Co., 182
McConnell, Richard U., 141
McCreath, Andrew S., & Son, Inc., 175
McCrone, Walter C., Associates, Inc., 149
McGrath, James J., 149
McKenna, Harold J., 167
McKenzie, Garry D., 171
McLellan, Alden, IV, 184
McLouth, Malcolm E., 146
McMillion, Ovid M., 177
McVickar, Malcolm H., 141
Macias, Edward S., 161
Main, Charles T., Inc., 157
Maine, State of: government agencies, 54
Maine Federation of Women's Clubs, 101
Malcolm Pirnie, Inc., 168
Male, C.T., Associates, 167
Malley, Harry E., 179
Malone, David W., 151
Malone, Marvin H., 141
Maloney, Thomas J., 149
Man, Eugene H., 146
Manaster, Prof. Kenneth A., 141
Manforce, 136
Manufacturing Chemists Association, 133
Marathon Equipment Co., Inc., 137
Marine Advisory and Associated Services, 182
Maritime Administration (U.S.), 11
Markley Laboratories, Inc., 160
Marshall, Harold G., 182
Martin, A.W., Associates, Inc., 175
Martin, David, 157
Maryland, State of: government agencies, 54
Maryland Environmental Trust, 102
Maryland Ornithological Society, Inc., 102
Maryland Wildlife Federation, 102
Mason & Hanger, 146
Massachusetts, State of: government agencies, 55
Massachusetts Association of Conservation Commissions, 104
Massachusetts Forest and Park Association, 104
Massachusetts Roadside Council, 104
Massachusetts Wildlife Federation, Inc., 104
Master Leakfinding Co., 149
Matrix Engineering, Inc., 175
Max McGraw Wildlife Foundation, 98
Mebus, George B., Inc., 175

Mee Industries, Inc., 141
Melvin, Walter W., Jr., 179
Merchant Marine and Fisheries Committee, U.S. House, 42
Merchant Marine Subcommittee, Commerce Committee, U.S. Senate, 40
Merck Forest Foundation, Inc., 126
Metallurgical Engineers, Inc., 173
Metcalf and Eddy, 157
Metro Clean Air Committee, 107
Metronics Associates, Inc., 141
Metropolitan Aircraft Sound Abatement Council, 107
Metropolitan Ecology Workshop, 104
Michigan, State of: government agencies, 55
Michigan Botanical Club, Inc., 106
Michigan Lake and Stream Associations, Inc., 106
Michigan Natural Resources Council, 106
Michigan Student Environmental Confederation, Inc., 106
Michigan Tuberculosis and Respiratory Disease Association, 106
Michigan United Conservation Clubs, 107
Microchemical Research Institute, 167
Micrographics, Inc., 141
Midcontinent Environment Center Association, 120
Midcontinent Environmental Center Associates, 172
Middleton, W.B., & Associates, 163
Midwest Research Institute, 161
Migratory Bird Conservation Commission (U.S.), 36
Migratory Bird Population Station (U.S.), 20
Miles, Donald, 161
Milk Industry Foundation, 133
Miller, John C., 145
Miller, Richard Gordon, 162
Miller, Robert M., 171
Minerals, Materials, and Fuels Subcommittee, Interior and Insular Affairs Committee, U.S. Senate, 40
Mines and Mining Subcommittee, Interior and Insular Affairs Committee, U.S. House, 42
Minnesota, State of: government agencies, 56
Minnesota Association for Conservation Education, 108
Minnesota Conservation Federation, 108
Minnesota Environmental Control Citizens Association, 108
Mississippi, State of: government agencies, 57
Mississippi Forestry Association, 108
Mississippi Lung Association, 108
Mississippi River Commission (U.S.), 36
Mississippi Wildlife Federation, 108
Missouri, State of: government agencies, 57
Missouri Prairie Foundation, 109

Mitchell, J. Murray, Jr., 155
Mitchell & Associates, Inc., 151
Mogul Corp., 171
Monninger, Robert H.G., 149
Monroe County Environmental Management Council, 117
Monsanto Biodize Systems, Inc., 167
Monsanto Enviro-Chem Systems, Inc., 149
Monsanto Research Corp., 161
Montana, State of: government agencies, 58
Montana Conservation Council, Inc., 109
Montana Environmental Quality Council, 109
Montana Wilderness Association, 109
Montana Wildlife Federation, 109
Monterey Area Conservation Coordinating Council, 89
Monterey Bay Committee for Environmental Information, 90
Montgomery, James M., Consulting Engineers, Inc., 141
Moore, Richter H., Jr., 169
Moore, Wallace & Kennedy, Inc., 183
Morisawa, Marie, 167
Morris County for Clean Air and Water, 113
Morse, Erskine V., 151
Morse, Frederick B., 151
Moutrey & Associates, Inc., 172
Mull, Harold R., Bell and Associates, 144
Municipal Engineering Co., 180
Muster, Douglas, 180

NU-AG, Inc., 150
NUS Corp., 155
Nalco Chemical Co., 149
Nalews-Weston, 167
Nalin Labs., 171
National Academy of Engineering, 37
National Academy of Sciences, 37
National Academy of Sciences/National Research Council, 134
National Agricultural Library (U.S.), 10
National Association of Conservation Districts, 134
National Association of Counties Research Foundation, 82
National Association of State Park Directors, 134
National Automotive Muffler Association, 134
National Bureau of Standards (U.S.), 12
National Canners Association, 134
National Council of State Garden Clubs, Inc., 82
National Dairy Council, 134
National Ecological Research Laboratory, 6
National Environmental Health Association, 134
National Environmental Health Sciences Research Center (U.S.), 17
National Environmental Research Centers (U.S.), 5
National Environmental Satellite Service (U.S.), 13
National Fisheries Center and Aquariums (U.S.), 20
National Flexible Packaging Association, 135
National Forest Reservation Commission (U.S.), 36
National Forest System (U.S.), 9
National Highway Traffic Safety Administration (U.S.), 28
National Industrial Zoning Committee, 135
National Institute of Environmental Health Sciences (U.S.), 17
National Institute of Occupational Safety and Health (U.S.), 16
National Institutes of Health (U.S.), 17
National Library of Medicine, 17
National Loss Control Service Corp., 150
National Marine Fisheries Service (U.S.), 13
National Marine Water Quality Laboratory (U.S.), 6
National Museum of Natural History (U.S.), 35
National Mustang Association, Inc., 125
National Ocean Survey (U.S.), 13
National Oceanic and Atmospheric Administration (U.S.), 12
National Park Foundation (U.S.), 37
National Park Service (U.S.), 21
National Parks and Conservation Association, 82
National Parks and Recreation Subcommittee, Interior and Insular Affairs Committee, U.S. House, 41
National Petroleum Refiners Association, 135
National Reclamation Association, 82
National Recreation and Park Association, 82
National Research Corp., 157
National Research Council, 37
National Rifle Association of America, 82
National Sanitation Foundation Testing Lab., Inc., 159
National Science Foundation (U.S.), 33
National Science Foundation Subcommittee, Labor and Public Welfare Committee, U.S. Senate, 40
National Speleological Society, Inc., 87
National Technical Information Service (U.S.), 13
National Transportation Safety Board (U.S.), 28
National Trust for Historic Preservation, 82
National Water Commission (U.S.), 37
National Water Quality Laboratory (U.S.), 6
National Waterfowl Council, 83

National Watershed Congress, 83
National Wildlife Federation, 83
National Wildlife Federation Endowment, Inc., 83
National Wildlife Refuge System (U.S.), 20
National Zoological Park (U.S.), 35
Natural Land Institute, 98
Natural Resources Council of America, 83
Natural Resources Council of Maine, 101
Natural Resources Defense Council, Inc., 83
Natural Resources Management Corp., 171
Natural Science for Youth Foundation, 93
Nature Conservancy, 83
Nature Conservancy Central New York Chapter, 117
Nature Conservancy, Illinois Chapter, 99
Nature Conservancy Western Regional Office, 90
Nebraska, State of: government agencies, 58
Nebraska Testing Laboratories, 162
Nebraska Wildlife Federation, 110
Neighborhood Environmental Evaluation and Decision Systems (U.S.), 17
Neuman, Edward S., 183
Nevada, State of: government agencies, 59
Nevada Wildlife Federation, Inc., 110
New England Consortium on Environmental Protection, 104
New England Forestry Foundation, 105
New England Natural Resources Center, 105
New Hampshire, State of: government agencies, 59
New Hampshire Natural Resources Council, Inc., 110
New Jersey, State of: government agencies, 60
New Jersey Citizens for Clean Air, Inc., 113
New Jersey Educational Association, Environmental Education Commission, 113
New Jersey State Council for Environmental Education, 113
New Mexico, State of: government agencies, 61
New Mexico Citizens for Clean Air and Water, 114
New Mexico Conservation Coordinating Council, 114
New Mexico Wildlife Conservation Association, 114
New Mexico Wildlife Federation, 114
New York, State of: government agencies, 61
New York Scientists' Committee for Public Information, Inc., 117
New York Testing Labs., Inc., 167
New York Zoological Society, 117
Newing Laboratories, Inc., 167
Newman, Stephen E., 146
Newton Field Site, 6
Nichols, Stanley A., 184
Normandeau Associates, Inc., 162

North American Association for the Preservation of Predatory Animals, Inc., 90
North American Family Campers Association, 83
North American Weather Consultants, 141
North American Wildlife Foundation, 84
North Carolina, State of: government agencies, 63
North Carolina Wildlife Federation, 119
North Dakota, State of: government agencies, 63
North Dakota Natural Science Society, 119
North Dakota Wildlife Federation, 120
North Jersey Anti-Pollution League, 136
North Jersey Conservation Foundation, 113
Northeastern Bird-Banding Association, 105
Northern California Committee for Environmental Information, 90
Northern Environmental Council, 108
Northern Testing Laboratories, 162
Northern Virginia Conservation Council, 126
Norwood Engineers, 176
Noyes Data Corp., 163
Nuclear Test Ban Treaty Safeguards Subcommittee, Armed Services Committee, U.S. Senate, 39
Nussbaumer & Clarke, Inc., 167
Nutrition Institute (U.S.), 8
Nuttall Ornithological Club, 105
Nutter, Lawrence A., 184

Oak Ridge Conservation Club, 123
O'Brien & Gere Engineers, Inc., 167
Occupational Safety and Health Administration (U.S.), 26
Occupational Safety and Health Review Commission (U.S.), 34
Ocean County Fish and Game Protective Association, 113
Ocean Nature and Conservation Society, 113
Oceanography International Corp., 180
Oceanography Subcommittee, Merchant Marine and Fisheries Committee, U.S. House, 42
Oceanonics, Inc., 180
Oceans and Atmosphere Subcommittee, Commerce Committee, U.S. Senate, 40
Ode, Arthur H., 184
Office of Coal Research (U.S.), 19
Office of Consumer Affairs (U.S.), 15
Office of Environmental Sciences (U.S.), 35
Office of Oil and Gas (U.S.), 18
Office of Saline Water (U.S.), 18
Office of Water Resources Research (U.S.), 19
Offshore/Sea Development Corp., 167
O'Hare Area Noise Abatement Council, 2

Ohio, State of: government agencies, 64
Ohio Forestry Association, Inc., 120
Oilwell Research, Inc., 141
O'Keefe, Timothy G., 138
Oklahoma, State of: government agencies, 65
Oklahoma Coalition for Clean Air, 120
Oklahoma Environmental Information and Media Center, 121
Oklahoma Ornithological Society, 121
Oklahoma Wildlife Federation, 121
Olin Corp., 144, 153
Olin Water Service Labs., 167
Open Lands Project, 2
Open Space Institute, 136
Optimal Systems, Inc., 147
Oregon, State of: government agencies, 65
Orgonics, Inc., 176
Orlando Laboratories, Inc., 146
Osterberg, Donald, 167
Ostergaard Associates, 164
Othmer, Donald F., 167
Outdoor Circle, 96
Outdoors Writers Association of America, Inc., 135
Ovitron Chemical Process Div., 175
Ozark Society, Inc., 88

P & W Engineers, Inc., 150
Pace Co., 180
Pacific Environmental Lab., 141
Pacific Northwest Environmental Research Laboratory (U.S.), 6
Pacific Science Association (U.S.), 39
Pack, Edward L., Associates, 141
Packaging Institute, U.S.A., 135
Pamispa, Inc., 168
Pan American Laboratories, Inc., 180
Papier, Bruce L., 143
Paragon Electric Co., Inc., 184
Parker, Norman H., Engineers/Constructors, 141
Parks and Recreation Subcommittee, Interior and Insular Affairs Committee, U.S. Senate, 40
Parsons, Ralph M., Co., 141
Parsons, Brinkerhoff, Quade, & Douglas, Inc., 168
Particle Data Laboratories, Ltd., 150
Partington, William M., Jr., 146
Patuxent Wildlife Research Center (U.S.), 20
Paulson, Glenn L., 168
Pavia-Byrne Engineering Corp., 154
Peabody Welles, 150
Pearce, William B., 146
Peckham, George T., 152
PEDCo-Environmental Specialists, 171

Peloquin, Edward J., 161
Peltier, Jerome C., 160
Peninsula Conservation Center, 90
Pennsylvania, State of: government agencies, 66
Pennsylvania Environmental Council, Inc., 121
Pennsylvania Forestry Association, 122
Pennsylvania Roadside Council, Inc., 122
Peoples Environmental Program, 117
Perley, W.F., & Associates, 173
Perolin Co., Inc., 168
Pesticide Task Force, 124
Pesticides Enforcement Division, EPA (U.S.), 4
Peterson, Philip E., 141
Petroleum Industry Research Foundation, 135
Phillips, James W., 157
Pierce, James C., Jr., 164
Pitillo, Dan J., 169
Planned Parenthood Association, 99
Planned Parenthood Association of Santa Clara County, Inc., 90
Planned Parenthood World Population, 84
Planning and Conservation League, 90
Plant Genetics and Germ Plasm Institute (U.S.), 8
Plant Physiology Institute (U.S.), 8
Plant Protection Institute (U.S.), 9
Plastic Container Manufacturers Institute, 135
Pollution Control Engineering, Inc., 146
Pollution Control Industries, Inc., 144
Pollution Curbs, Inc., 160
Pollution Protection Association, 95
Pollution Research & Control Corp., 141
Pollution Solutions, Inc., 141
Pollution Underground, 136
Polyphase Chemical Service, Inc., 168
Polytechnic, Inc., 150
Pomerening, James A., 141
Pomeroy, Johnston, and Bailey, 142
Pomona Pilot Plant (U.S.), 7
Pope, Evans, and Robbins, Inc., 168
Population Council, 84
Population Crisis Committee, 84
Population Reference Bureau, Inc., 84
Potomac Basin Center, 136
Power Applications, Inc., 168
Prairie Chicken Foundation of Illinois, 136
Prenco Manufacturing Co., 159
Preston, E.S., Associates, Inc., 171
Primate and Pesticides Effects Laboratory (U.S.), 6
Princeton Aqua Science, 164
Princeton Chemical Research, Inc., 164
Procon Inc., 150
Prodehl, Victor H., 173
Progress Without Pollution, 117
Project Recycle, 113
Protect Our Environment, 120
Protect Your Environment Club of Albany, 118

Public Advocates, Inc., 90
Public Buildings and Grounds Subcommittee, Public Works Committee, U.S. House, 42
Public Education Research Committee of California, 91
Public Health and Environment Subcommittee, Interstate and Foreign Commerce Committee, U.S. House, 42
Public Health Service (U.S.), 15
Public Lands Subcommittee, Interior and Insular Affairs Committee, U.S. House, 42
Public Lands Subcommittee, Interior and Insular Affairs Committee, U.S. Senate, 40
Public Works, AEC Subcommittee, Appropriations Committee, U.S. Senate, 39
Public Works Committee, U.S. House, 42
Public Works Committee, U.S. Senate, 40
Public Works Subcommittee, Appropriations Committee, U.S. House, 41
Puerto Rico Association of Soil and Water Conservation Districts, 122
Puerto Rico Pollution Control Association, 122
Pulp Chemicals Association, 135
Pulp Manufacturers Research League, 136
Pulsco-AAF, 142
Puricons, 175
Pyburn & Odom, Inc., 155
Pye, Earl, 142

Quality Environment Group, 136
Quarantelli, E.L., 171
Quinn, R.E., 180

RI Corp., 181
Raboy, Sol, 168
Rachel Carson Trust for the Living Environment, Inc., 84
Rackoff Associates, Inc., 171
Radian Corp., 180
Radiation Biology Laboratory (U.S.), 35
Radiation Management Corp., 175
Radiation Research Society, 84
Radio Chemistry and Nuclear Engineering Research Laboratory (U.S.), 6
Rahn, Perry H., 176
Raizen, Eileen C., 175
Reactor Research and Development, AEC (U.S.), 31
Reactor Safety Research Division, AEC (U.S.), 29
Reclamation Systems Inc., 157
Recycling Information, 118
Regenerative Heat Corp., 164
Reiter, Elmar R., 143

Remington Farms, 102
Rempe Sharpe & Associates, Inc., 150
Rents, Rhombic, 142
Research-Cottrell, Inc., 164
Research Ranch, Inc., 87
Resource Control, Inc., 144
Resources for the Future, Inc., 84
Reutter, John G., Associates, 164
Reynolds, Smith & Hills, 146
Rhode Island, State of: government agencies, 67
Rice, Elroy L., 172
Riddle Engineering, Inc., 161
Riley, Paul J., 181
Roads Subcomittee, Public Works Committee, U.S. Senate, 41
Robert & Co. Associates, 147
Robert S. Kerr Water Research Center (U.S.), 6
Rochester Committee for Scientific Information, 118
Rocky Mountain Center on Environment, 93
Rollins-Purle, Inc., 145
Rose, William I., 159
Rosner-Hixson Labs., 150
Ross, H.J., Associates, Inc., 146
Roswell Branch-Citizens for Clean Air and Water, 114
Rubber Reclaimers Association, 135
Ruble & Associates, Earl, Inc., 160
Rupp, M.F., 150
Rural Development Subcommittee, Agriculture and Forestry Committee, U.S. Senate, 39
Rural Electrification Administration (U.S.), 10
Rust Engineering Co., 137
Ryckman, Edgerly, Tomlinson & Associates, 161

S & B Engineers, 180
SERCO Laboratories, 160
Sadtler Research Lab., Inc., 175
Saint Hubert Society of America, Inc., 118
St. Louis Committee for Environmental Information, 109
St. Louis Testing Labs, Inc., 161
Salem Laboratories, 159
Salt Pond Areas Bird Sanctuaries, Inc., 105
San Francisco Planning and Urban Renewal Association (SPUR), 91
San Jacinto Drilling and Disposal Co., 180
Sanders & Thomas, Inc., 175
Sanderson & Porter, Inc., 168
Sandwell International, Inc., 173
Sanitas Technology & Development Corp., 157
Santa Clara County Bar Association Environmental Law Section, 91
Santelmann, Paul W., 172

Save America's Vital Environment, 96
Save Our Shores, Inc., 105
Save Our Valley Action Committee, 91
Save the Dunes Council, 99
Save the Redwoods League, 91
Saxton & Kennedy, Inc., 183
Scenic Hudson Preservation Conference, 118
Schaffer, F.C., & Associates, Inc., 155
Schlesinger, Lawrence E., 182
Schmid, Merle D., 171
Schmulbach, James, 176
Schneider Instrument Co., 171
Schore Automations, Inc., 168
Science and Astronautics Committee, U.S. House, 42
Science, Research, and Development Subcommittee, Science and Astronautics Committee, U.S. House, 42
Science Spectrum, Inc., 142
Scientific and Educational Services, Inc., 180
Scientific Design Co., Inc., 168
Scientific Gas Products, Inc., 164
Scientists' Institute for Public Information, 85
Scott Research Laboratories, Inc., 175
Seba, Douglas B., 143
Seelye, Stevenson, Valve & Knecht, 168
Sewall, James W., Co., 155
Sewell, James A., & Associates, 183
Shaver, Robert H., 152
Sherborn Forest & Trail Association, 105
Shewfelt, A.L., 147
Siddiqi, Toufiq A., 152
Sierra Club, 85
Sierra Club Florida Chapter, 95
Sierra Club, Great Lakes Chapter, 99
Sierra Club, Massachusetts Chapter, 105
Sierra Club Foundation, 85
Sierra Research Corp., 143
Sill, Webster H., Jr., 176
Sinclair, Peter C., 144
Singer Co., GPE Controls Div., 148
Single Service Institute, Inc., 135
Sirrine, J.E., Co., 176
Sittenfield, Marcus, & Associates, 175
Skadron, George, 152
Slickbar, Inc., 144
Smith, Dudley T., 180
Smith, Owens J., 147
Smith, Richard C., 161
Smith, Roger H., 160
Smith, Stephen C., 184
Smith, Miller & Associates, 175
Smith-Davis & Associates, Inc., 146
Smithsonian Institution, 34
Smithsonian Science Information Exchange, 35
Smithsonian Tropical Research Institute, 35
Snyder, George E., Associates, Inc., 159
Soap and Detergent Association, 135
Social and Economic Statistics Administration (U.S.), 13
Society for the Preservation of Birds of Prey, 91
Society for the Protection of New Hampshire Forests, 110
Society of Tympanuchus Cupido Pinnatus, 128
Soil Conservation Service (U.S.), 11
Soil Conservation Service Farm and Home Center, 118
Soil Conservation Society of America, 85
Solid Waste Research Laboratory (U.S.), 6
Solids Conversion Systems, Inc., 160
South Carolina, State of: government agencies, 67
South Carolina Forestry Association, 123
South Carolina TB and Respiratory Disease Association, 123
South Dakota, State of: government agencies, 68
South Dakota Association of Conservation Districts, 123
Southeast Environmental Research Laboratory (U.S.), 6
Southeast Labs., Inc., 147
Southeastern Wisconsin Regional Planning Commission, 128
Southern Fish Culturists, Inc., 146
Southern Forest Institute, 96
Southern Research Institute, 137
Southwest Research Institute, Central Proposal Office, 180
Space Science and Applications Subcommittee, Science and Astronautics Committee, U.S. House, 42
Speller & Associates, Inc., 180
Spooner, Charles M., 159
Sport Fishery Research Foundation, 85
Sport Fishing Institute, 85
Sportsmen's Club of Texas, Inc., 125
Spotts, Stevens and McCoy, Inc., 175
Sprinkle & Associates, 155
Stanford, Geoffrey, 171
Stanley Consultants, Inc., 153
Stanwick Corp., 182
Staten Island Science Information Committee, 118
Stearns-Roger Corp., 144
Steelcraft Corp., 177
Stein, Hall & Co., Inc., 168
Stephenson, Richard A., 169
Sterling Forest Pollution Control, 118
Stevens, Thompson & Runyan, Inc., 173
Stewart Laboratories, Inc., 177
Stivers Organization, T.E., Inc., 147
Stoddard, Charles H., 184
Stombaugh, Dennis P., 171
Stone, Ralph, & Co., Inc., 142
Stouse, Donald C., & Associates, 153

Strategies for Environmental Control, 100
Streeter, Robert L., 184
Strobic Air Corp., 164
Student Conservation Association, Inc., 127
Students for Environmental Action, 114
Summerfelt, Robert C., 172
Sunshine Chemical Corp., 144
Surface Transportation Subcommittee, Commerce Committee, U.S. Senate, 40
Sverdrup, Parcel and Associates, Inc., 161, 177
Swenson, Royal Jay, 180
Swift Laboratories, Inc., 157
Swindell-Dressler Co., 175
Swope, H.G., & Associates, 184
Sydnor Hydrodynamics, Inc., 182
Syracuse University Research Corp., 168
Systems Applications, Inc., 142

TB-Respiratory Disease Association of Central New Jersey, Inc., 113
TBW International, Inc., 172
Tailor & Co., Inc., 153
Technical Association of the Pulp and Paper Industry, 136
Technology Research & Development, Inc., 173
Teck Labs, 175
Tek-Air, Inc., 172
Tenco Hydro-Aero Sciences, Inc., 150
Tennessee, State of: government agencies, 68
Tennessee Beautiful, Inc., 123
Tennessee Citizens for Wilderness Planning, 123
Tennessee Environment Council, 123
Tennessee Forestry Association, 123
Tennessee Scenic Rivers Association, 124
Tennessee Valley Authority (U.S.), 36
Terra-Cology Services, 184
Terra Marine Scoop Co., Inc., 168
Territorial and Insular Affairs Subcommittee, Interior and Insular Affairs Committee, U.S. House, 42
Territories and Insular Affairs Subcommittee, Interior and Insular Affairs Committee, U.S. Senate, 40
Terry, Richard, & Associates, 142
Texas, State of: government agencies, 69
Texas Bar Association, Environmental Law Section, 125
Texas Forestry Association, 125
Thermal Research & Engineering Corp., 175
Thermo-Kinetics, Inc., 176
Thompson, Marvin, 153
Thornton, John, Jr., 145
Thorstensen Lab., 157
Thorup, Jim, 142
Thorup, Richard M., 153

Tiahrt, Kenneth J., 162
Tighe & Bond, 157
Tisdel Associates, 168
Toups Engineering, Inc., 142
Town of Avon Commission for Conservation, 118
Towne, Robin M., & Associates, Inc., 173, 183
Tracor, Inc., 180
TraDet, Inc., 172
Trainer, Daniel O., 184
Transportation and Aeronautics Subcommittee, Interstate and Foreign Affairs Committee, U.S. House, 42
Transportation Department, U.S., 26
Transportation Research Foundation, 136
Transportation Subcommittee, Appropriations Committee, U.S. House, 41
Transportation Subcommittee, Appropriations Committee, U.S. Senate, 39
Transportation Subcommittee, Public Works Committee, U.S. House, 42
Transportation Systems Center (U.S.), 27
Trees for Tomorrow, Inc., 128
Tri-Aid Sciences, Inc., 168
Triggs, J. Fred, & Associates, 175
Trooboff, Mrs. Rebecca C., 147
Trout Unlimited, 85
Trout Unlimited, Alabama Chapter, 87
Trout Unlimited, Rio Grande Chapter, 114
Truesdail Labs., Inc., 142
Trustees for Conservation, 91
Trustees of Reservations, 105
Turner, William M., 164
Turner, Collie & Braden, Inc., 180
Twin City Testing & Engineering Labs., Inc., 160

URS Research Co., 142
Union of Concerned Scientists, 105
United Acoustic Consultants, 144
United New Conservationists, 92
United States-Mexico Border Environmental Control Project (U.S.), 17
United States Pollution Control, Inc., 173
Upper Hudson Environmental Action Committee, 118
Upper Mississippi River Conservation Committee, 100
Ural, Oktay, 162
Urban Land Institute, 85
Urban Mass Transit Subcommittee, Banking and Currency Committee, U.S. House, 41
Urban Mass Transportation Administration (U.S.), 28
Utah, State of: government agencies, 69
Utah Air Conservation Committee, 125

Utah Association of Soil Conservation Districts, 125
Utah Environmental Center, 125

Valentine, Fisher & Tomlinson, 183
Van Artsdalen, Dr. Ervin R., 137
Van Bruggen, Ted, 177
Van Doren-Hazard-Stallings-Schnacke, 153
Van Eck, Willem A., 183
Van Hyning, Dr. Jack M., 138
Vari-Systems, Inc., 172
Varma, Man Mohan, 145
Velzy, Charles R., Associates, Inc., 168
Veracity Corp., 155
Vermont, State of: government agencies, 70
Vermont Environmental Center, 136
Vermont Natural Resources Council, 126
Vesilind, P. Aarne, 169
Virginia, State of: government agencies, 71
Virginia Forests, Inc., 126
Virginia Wildlife Federation, Inc., 126
Von Ehrenfried, Manfred, 155
Vulcan-Cincinnati, Inc., 172
Vulcan Labs., Inc., Hydro Research Labs. Div., 159

Walden Research Corp., 157
Wallace-Fisher Instrument Co., 157
Walther, Eric G., 138
Wapora, Inc., 145
Ward, Victor W., 180
Warner Co., 175
Washington, D.C. See District of Columbia
Washington, State of: government agencies, 71
Washington County Environmental Council, 128
Washington Ecology Center, 86
Washington Environmental Council, Inc., 127
Washington State Sportsmen's Council, Inc., 127
Waste Management and Transportation Division, AEC (U.S.), 30
Water and Power Resources Subcommittee, Interior and Insular Affairs Committee, U.S. House, 41
Water and Power Resources Subcommittee, Interior and Insular Affairs Committee, U.S. Senate, 40
Water Pollution Control Federation, 86
Water Quality Research Council, 99
Water Resources Council (U.S.), 37
Water Resources Scientific Information Center (U.S.), 19
Water Resources Subcommittee, Public Works Committee, U.S. House, 42
Water Resources Subcommittee, Public Works Committee, U.S. Senate, 40
Watkins & Associates, Inc., 153
Wegman, Leonard S., Co., Inc., 168
Wehking, Milan W., 184
Weidensaul, T. Craig, 172
Wellman-Power Gas, Inc., 147
Wells Laboratories, Inc., 164
Welsh, Stanley L., 181
Wenatchee Research Station (U.S.), 6
Wendel Associates, 169
Wenzel & Co., 162
Wepco, Inc., 180
Werner, Sanford L., 142
West, Neil E., 181
West Virginia, State of: government agencies, 72
West Virginia Wildlife Federation, 127
Western Fish Toxicology Laboratory (U.S.), 6
Western Forestry and Conservation Association, 121
Western Montana Scientists' Committee for Public Information, 109
Western New York Nuclear Research Center, Inc., 169
Western Pennsylvania Conservancy, 122
Weston, Roy F., Inc., 176
Weston & Sampson, Consulting Engineers, 158
Whitman, Requardt and Associates, 156
Whitney, William Bernard, Sr., 181
Whittington, Paul E., 145
Wiel, Stephen, 145
Wier, Charles E., 152
Wild Flower Preservation Society, 118
Wilderness Society, 86
Wilderness Watch, 128
Wildlife Disease Association, 86
Wildlife Management Institute, 86, 93
Willett, Lynn B., 172
Williams & Works, 159
Williams Brothers Waste Control, Inc., 173
Wilsey & Ham, 142
Wilson, Joe R., 155
Wilson, Ihrig & Associates, Inc., 142
Winch, Fred E., Jr., 169
Winkler, Theodore E., 159
Wiram, Vance P., 152
Wisconsin, State of: government agencies, 73
Wisconsin Committee for Environmental Information, 128
Wisconsin Ecological Society, 128
Wisconsin Park and Recreation Association, 129
Wiser, Wymer, 177
Wood, Larry, 142
Woods, Frank W., 178
World Ecology Systems, 169
Worley, Ian A., 181

Wuenscher, James E., 169
Wunder, Charles C., 153
Wyoming, State of: government agencies, 74
Wyoming Association of Conservation Districts, 129
Wyoming Wildlife Federation, 129
Wyssmont Co., Inc., 164

Yancey, Robert M., 182
Young, F.R., Co., 181
Youth Conservation Corps Program (U.S.), 20
Youth Conservation Programs (U.S.), 21
Yudelson, Jerry, 142

Zeimet, Edward J., 184
Zero Population Growth, Inc., 86
Zero Population Growth, Bangor Chapter, 101
Zero Population Growth, Brunswick, Maine, 136
Zero Population Growth, Fort Worth, Texas, 136
Zero Population Growth, Inc., California Confederation, 92
Zero Population Growth, Marinette-Menominee Branch, 129
Zero Population Growth, New York State Federation, 119
Zero Population Growth, Santa Fe Chapter, 114
Zero Population Growth, South Jersey Center, 136
Zero Population Growth, Terre Haute, Inc., 136
Zimmey Corp., 142
Zink, John, Co., 173
Zurn Industries, Inc., 176

MAR 29 1977

TD
171
E58
c.2